THE HALDER WAR DIARY
1939–1942

Franz Halder, circa 1942

THE HALDER WAR DIARY
1939–1942

Edited by
Charles Burdick
and
Hans-Adolf Jacobsen

★
PRESIDIO

for James Walsh
who worried, cared, required

Introduction, commentaries, revisions to basic text, and additions thereto copyright © 1988 Charles Burdick and Hans-Adolf Jacobsen.

Published by Presidio Press
31 Pamaron Way, Novato CA 94949

LIBRARY OF CONGRESS
Library of Congress Cataloging-in-Publication Data

Halder, Franz, 1884–1972.
  [Kriegstagebuch. English]
  The Halder war diary, 1939–1942 / edited by Charles Burdick, Hans-Adolf Jacobsen.
     p. cm.
  Abridged ed. of the English translation of: Kriegstagebuch.
1962–1964.
  Includes index.
  ISBN 0–89141–302–2
  1. Halder, Franz, 1884–1972—Diaries. 2. World War, 1939–1945—Germany. 3. World War, 1939–1945—Personal narratives, German.
I. Burdick, Charles Burton, 1927–   . II. Jacobsen, Hans-Adolf.
III. Title.
DD247.H25A2813   1988
940.54'82'43—dc19   88–10177
                                                  CIP

Printed in the United States of America

CONTENTS

Maps

Charts

EDITORIAL NOTE

Any edited material provides a difficult challenge to both editor and reader. The former must seek the latter's trust through the sense and structure of the text without losing the reality and substance of that material. Expecting a reader to accept selections blindly is an uncertain endeavor.

Franz Halder's diary provides an extraordinary insight into the inner structure and thought of the German military leadership of the Second World War. Halder was one of the decision makers in Germany, as well as an astute, analytical person. His remarks provide a historical document of major worth. Since General Halder did not make his notes for official use or for publication, they reflect his personal interests and needs. By the same token they provide his honest view of circumstances and activities, intended for his personal records. As a result, the original includes a potpourri of details—birthdays, family activities, and informal exchanges in the same entries that describe military decisions, speeches, and official meetings.

In editing the diary we have tried to eliminate the personal, insignificant, and unnecessary remarks. The line between the unimportant and the important (especially as fortified by space limitations) is one beyond clarification. As a guide, we have used our own experiences in using the diary, the activities of other scholars, and the needs of our students. This background provides some awareness of the diary's utility for both scholars and lay people. We have sought to maintain the continuity of direction and purpose inherent in Halder's notes. These concepts provide a useful professional base for judgment.

We also have tried to keep the requirements of historical accuracy, editorial needs, and basic interest in focus. Halder wrote something for almost every day of his service as Chief of the General Staff. Some daily entries have been totally eliminated, and some (we hope not too many!) personal words have been included to facilitate unity. Ellipses have been used to indicate omissions within a given entry.

A word about the format of the diary: the reader will find the presentation consistently inconsistent. Halder sometimes used narrative style, sometimes an outline, sometimes a combination of the two forms. Italics in an entry indicate Halder's underlining of material he found important. The editors have chosen key words to be set in bold face where Halder changes subject within an entry; this approach should help the reader to follow the wealth of detail presented in the diary. In an effort to provide a brief, connecting commentary, we have added a few explanatory notes, set in bold type, for historical clarification.

The translation stems from that supervised by Arnold Lissance for the Nuremberg Trials. We have reviewed that collective effort and have made various corrections of terms. At the same time we have added/ translated some original materials that appeared later and that are not found in the Lissance translation.

Any edited translation merits careful review and criticism. We have tried to provide the sense and the reality with accuracy. While we hope to have helped scholars, we know who is responsible for the errors of commission and omission.

The maps reflect the standards and insight of Dr. Duilio Peruzzi, a cartographer and friend beyond description. He makes a difference! Mike Hardy did the research and drawing of the charts.

We are indebted to Karin Hall for help with translation; to Joan Griffin of Presidio Press for patience, advice, and handholding; to Barbara Youngblood for copyediting; and to Linda Garcia for reading incoherent notes and for typing everything.

LIST OF ABBREVIATIONS

BdE   *Befehlshaber des Ersatzheeres,* commander in chief of the replacement army (the domestic and rear area responsibilities of the field army).

Gen Qu   Chief supply and administration officer in the General Staff.

Ia   Operation officer.

Ib   Supply officer.

Ic   Intelligence officer.

ObdH   *Oberfehlshaber des Heeres,* commander in chief of the army (General Walther von Brauchitsch).

OKH   *Oberkommando des Heeres,* Army High Command. It was divided into the army General Staff, the home army, and the personnel divisions.

           The General Staff was divided into five subdivisions (*Oberquartiermeister* I–V):

           OQu I   *Oberquartiermeister* I,   operations
           OQu II   *Oberquartiermeister* II,   training
           OQu III *Oberquartiermeister* III, organization
           OQu IV   *Oberquartiermeister* IV,   intelligence
           OQu V   *Oberquartiermeister* V,   military history

OKL   *Oberkommando der Luftwaffe,* Air Force High Command.

OKW   *Oberkommando der Wehrmacht,* Armed Forces High Command. Under General Wilhelm Keitel (whose brother, Bodewin, directed the army personnel office).

       The OKW Operational Section (General Alfred Jodl) provided the main military advisory body for Hitler.

LIST OF OPERATIONAL CODE NAMES

ATTILA   Occupation of Vichy France, 1942.

BARBAROSSA   Final plan for attack on Soviet Union, June 1941.

BEAR   Operation by Army Group C against Maginot Line, June 1940.

BLUE   Attack plan for Army Group South, June 1942.

BROWN   Projected Italo-German offensive across Upper Rhine, 1940.

FELIX   Seizure of Gibraltar, 1941.

FREDERICK   Various phases of attack on Soviet salient west of Isjum, April 1942.

GREEN   Short-lived operational proposal for Army Group C, March 1940.

HAWK   Short-lived operational proposal by Army Group C, February 1940.

ISABELLA   Occupation of Spain and Portugal, 1941/42.

MARITA   Operation against Greece, 1940/41.

MERCURY   Attack on Crete, May 1941.

OPERATION 25   Assault on Yugoslavia, April 1941.

OTTO   Early designation for BARBAROSSA.

RED   Second phase, Battle of France, June 1940.

SEALION   Operation against England, 1940.

SEYDLITZ   Name for operation against the 39 Russian Army behind the German 9 Army, June 1942.

SHARK   Deception proposal for possible English invasion to tie English troops down 1941/42.

SILVER FOX   Coordinated attack in northern Finland, June 1941.

SOUTHWIND   Preparation for suppressing a possible uprising in occupied France, 1941

SUNFLOWER	Shifting of German troops to Africa, February/March 1941.
TIGER	Planned attack on the Maginot Line between St. Avold and Saar, 1940.
TYPHOON	Attack on Moscow, October 1941.
YELLOW	Operation against France, May 1940.
WESERUEBUNG	Attack against Norway and Denmark, April 1940.

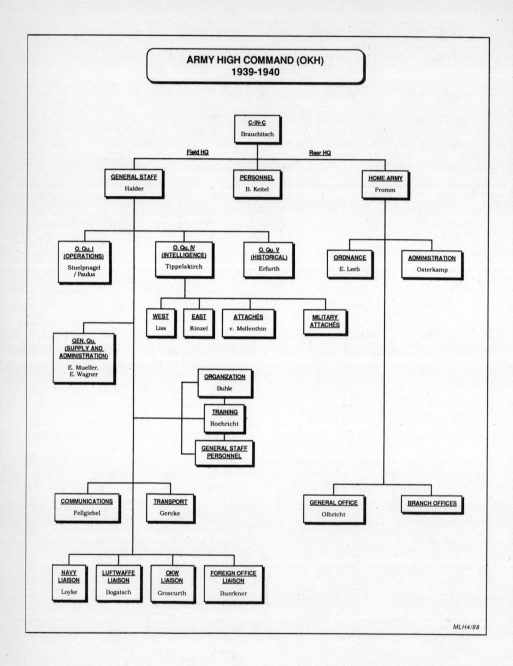

ARMY HIGH COMMAND (OKH)
1939-1940

C-IN-C
Brauchitsch

Field HQ — Rear HQ

GENERAL STAFF
Halder

PERSONNEL
B. Keitel

HOME ARMY
Fromm

O. Qu. I (OPERATIONS)
Stuelpnagel / Paulus

O. Qu. IV (INTELLIGENCE)
Tippelskirch

O. Qu. V (HISTORICAL)
Erfurth

ORDNANCE
E. Leeb

ADMINISTRATION
Osterkamp

WEST
Liss

EAST
Kinzel

ATTACHÉS
v. Mellenthin

MILITARY ATTACHÉS

GEN. Qu. (SUPPLY AND ADMINISTRATION)
E. Mueller,
E. Wagner

ORGANIZATION
Buhle

TRAINING
Roehricht

GENERAL STAFF PERSONNEL

COMMUNICATIONS
Fellgiebel

TRANSPORT
Gercke

GENERAL OFFICE
Olbricht

BRANCH OFFICES

NAVY LIAISON
Loyke

LUFTWAFFE LIAISON
Bogatsch

OKW LIAISON
Groscurth

FOREIGN OFFICE LIAISON
Buerkner

MLH4/88

xii

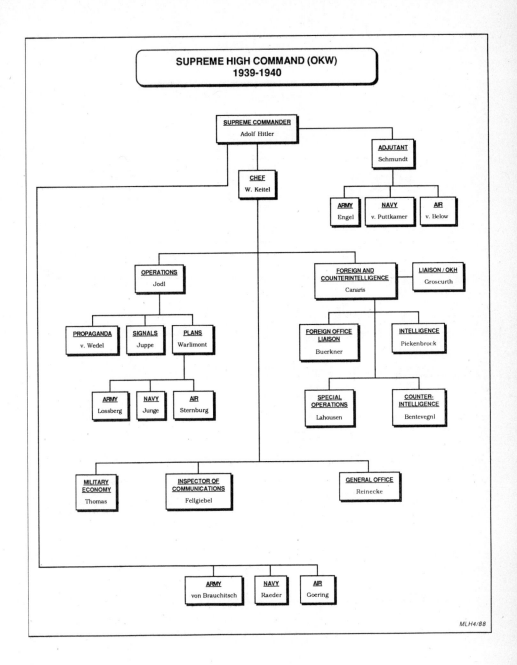

SUPREME HIGH COMMAND (OKW)
1939-1940

SUPREME COMMANDER
Adolf Hitler

ADJUTANT
Schmundt

ARMY
Engel

NAVY
v. Puttkamer

AIR
v. Below

CHEF
W. Keitel

OPERATIONS
Jodl

FOREIGN AND
COUNTERINTELLIGENCE
Canaris

LIAISON / OKH
Groscurth

PROPAGANDA
v. Wedel

SIGNALS
Juppe

PLANS
Warlimont

FOREIGN OFFICE
LIAISON
Buerkner

INTELLIGENCE
Piekenbrock

ARMY
Lossberg

NAVY
Junge

AIR
Sternburg

SPECIAL
OPERATIONS
Lahousen

COUNTER-
INTELLIGENCE
Bentevegnl

MILITARY
ECONOMY
Thomas

INSPECTOR OF
COMMUNICATIONS
Fellgiebel

GENERAL OFFICE
Reinecke

ARMY
von Brauchitsch

NAVY
Raeder

AIR
Goering

MLH4/88

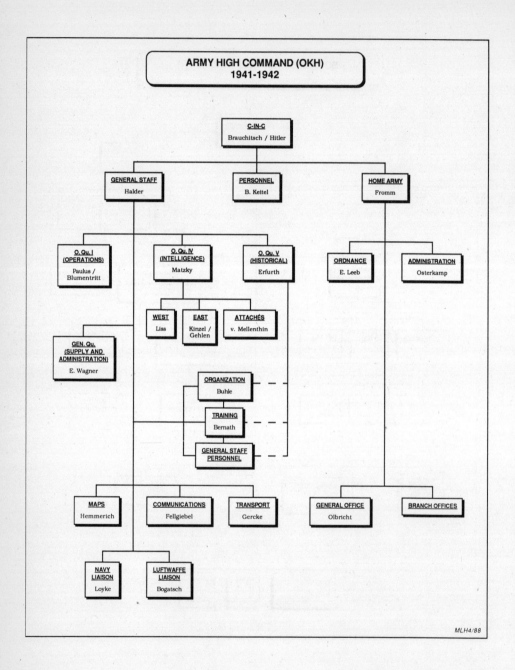

ARMY HIGH COMMAND (OKH)
1941-1942

C-IN-C
Brauchitsch / Hitler

GENERAL STAFF
Halder

PERSONNEL
B. Keitel

HOME ARMY
Fromm

O. Qu. I (OPERATIONS)
Paulus / Blumentritt

O. Qu. IV (INTELLIGENCE)
Matzky

O. Qu. V (HISTORICAL)
Erfurth

ORDNANCE
E. Leeb

ADMINISTRATION
Osterkamp

WEST
Liss

EAST
Kinzel / Gehlen

ATTACHÉS
v. Mellenthin

GEN. Qu. (SUPPLY AND ADMINISTRATION)
E. Wagner

ORGANIZATION
Buhle

TRAINING
Bernath

GENERAL STAFF PERSONNEL

MAPS
Hemmerich

COMMUNICATIONS
Fellgiebel

TRANSPORT
Gercke

GENERAL OFFICE
Olbricht

BRANCH OFFICES

NAVY LIAISON
Loyke

LUFTWAFFE LIAISON
Bogatsch

MLH4/88

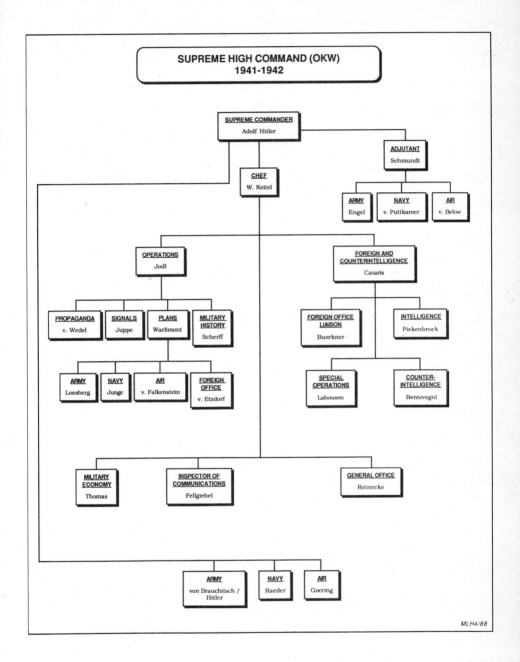

SUPREME HIGH COMMAND (OKW)
1941-1942

SUPREME COMMANDER
Adolf Hitler

ADJUTANT
Schmundt

CHEF
W. Keitel

ARMY — Engel
NAVY — v. Puttkamer
AIR — v. Below

OPERATIONS
Jodl

FOREIGN AND
COUNTERINTELLIGENCE
Canaris

PROPAGANDA — v. Wedel
SIGNALS — Juppe
PLANS — Warlimont
MILITARY HISTORY — Scherff

FOREIGN OFFICE LIAISON — Buerkner
INTELLIGENCE — Piekenbrock

ARMY — Lossberg
NAVY — Junge
AIR — v. Falkenstein
FOREIGN OFFICE — v. Etzdorf

SPECIAL OPERATIONS — Lahousen
COUNTER-INTELLIGENCE — Bentevegnl

MILITARY ECONOMY — Thomas
INSPECTOR OF COMMUNICATIONS — Fellgiebel
GENERAL OFFICE — Reinecke

ARMY — von Brauchitsch / Hitler
NAVY — Raeder
AIR — Goering

MLH4/88

XV

INTRODUCTION:

GENERAL FRANZ HALDER AND HIS "DIARY"

This one-volume, edited edition of General Franz Halder's diary stems from the complete, three-volume edition published (1962–1964) by Hans-Adolf Jacobsen. It remains one of the richest sources of military information of the Second World War from the German point of view. Given the role of the author and the value of his diary, the reader should know some details about both.

Franz Halder was born in Wuerzburg on 30 June 1884. By his own account, the sons of his family had been soldiers for over three hundred years. His grandparents were devout (the Bible was always present) Christians whose beliefs imprinted their lives with a pervasive religiosity. Halder's parents were believing Christians, but, perhaps, more conventional in their values. They went to church, but kept the Bible in the drawer. Despite this evolution of familial attitude, everyone assumed that Halder would continue the family tradition. He became a soldier.

In 1904 he received a promotion to lieutenant in the Bavarian 3 Field Artillery Regiment 9. During the years 1911–1914, he taught at the Bavarian Army Staff College in Munich. In the First World War he was a General Staff officer who served at various command levels. In the Reichswehr Major Halder joined the Training Office (T4). As a department chief, he started keeping a notebook in which he wrote important points, often without date or connection. Once he had completed the action, he drew a line through the note.

Unfortunately the probable five notebooks of the prewar period have disappeared without a trace. The seven notebooks of the wartime period (14 August 1939–24 September 1942), recorded in Halder's handwriting (largely in Gabelsberger shorthand), did survive the conflict.

As he changed positions—Chief of Staff, Military District VI (Muenster), 1931–1934; Commander, 7 Infantry Division (Munich), 1935–1936; and leader of the maneuver staff for the 1937 Wehrmacht maneuver—he maintained the practice. After being assigned to the Army General Staff (OQu II–Training, October 1937, and OQu I–Operations, February 1938), he started a new notebook. After becoming Chief of the General Staff (August 1938)—as successor to General Ludwig Beck—he continued these notebooks to the end of his military service.

Halder's role as Chief of the General Staff was much different from that of his predecessors. His opinions, authority, and conduct of military interests and operations with reference to the head of state were not those of the past chiefs.

1

From the outset of his authority, Adolf Hitler made the decisions and used his subordinates to execute his will. In doing so he paid no attention to the past role or responsibilities of the General Staff.

Within the Army High Command (OKH) Halder was an authority with extensive responsibilities—but always serving the army commander. This relationship was both personal and professional between Halder and General von Brauchitsch. They resolved their differences in a mutually acceptable fashion until Hitler replaced the latter. Thereafter Halder possessed little influence and continually declining authority.

In addition to his role as adviser to the army chief, the Chief of the General Staff was responsible for executing the decisions of the latter. This double activity provided some complexity, especially when added to other official requirements. Halder had charge of the General Staff function (selection, education, assignment, and so on) throughout the army. The tradition, prestige, and role of the membership remained a constant worry, requiring time and attention. Since Hitler disliked the group, with its identifiable red-striped trousers, he made inroads into their authority and independence whenever he could do so. Halder understood this struggle and carried the guild spirit forward with vigor and cunning. He was more a fighter than a survivor.

The office, then, was charged with representing and educating the elite General Staff members and with ensuring their continuance, with organizing and controlling the highest army headquarters, with advising the senior army commander, and with executing the military decisions of that individual and head of state, with supervision of the army's supply and administrative services, with control of the army's communication and transportation needs. Being chief of staff of a massive military establishment in a totalitarian society provided a complicated and challenging assignment. In order to keep control of his multifaceted activities, Halder developed the practice of keeping his summary notes by date as a way of maintaining a personal record of presentations. He kept this system intact until he retired from office (1942).

These diaries have had a strange, adventurous fate. Halder brought the completed volumes to Berlin with him when he had an opportunity and placed them in a safe in his house for safekeeping. When he shifted his permanent residence to Aschau, he took all of the diaries with him and, without reviewing them, stored them, divided into prewar and war bundles, in an attaché case in the family's steel safe. Around the turn of the year 1943/44, Halder received warnings that he might be arrested as part of a show trial. As a result, he entrusted his diaries to a neighbor, Frau Else Schnell, who, without any knowledge of the contents, hid them in her storeroom among a mass of refugees' belongings. As a result, when the Gestapo arrested Halder on 23 July 1944, they found nothing when they searched his house. Subsequent efforts brought them no written materials. Following imprisonment in Dachau and in the cellar jail on Prince-Albrecht Street (Berlin), Halder, with several other prominent prisoners, was freed on 5 May 1945 at Niederdorf (South Tyrol) by American troops.

As other American troops closed in on Aschau in 1945, Frau Schnell, worried about further house searches, buried the attaché case in her garden. Once the Americans had passed through the city, she moved the case back to the storeroom. Apparently someone observed the action, since shortly thereafter a group of Americans appeared and asked to see the storeroom. Without paying the refugees' baskets and boxes in the area the least attention, they moved directly to the attaché case, opened it, and sequestered the contents. A sergeant, Dr. Albert F. Maisel, from Detroit gave Frau Schnell a receipt for the confiscated material.

Eventually the seven volumes arrived in the Document Center of the Nuremberg Trials. A member of the British delegation, Hans Wolfsohn, a former Berliner, accidentally discovered them. Fortuitously Wolfsohn had served earlier in an intelligence assignment where he had had responsibility for collecting information on Halder. The trial prosecutors quickly established a small working group to evaluate the documents' significance. Arnold Lissance, an emigré from Vienna, was in charge of turning Halder's shorthand into sensible German. Lissance, who had mastered Gabelsberger as a youth, visited Halder several times in the prisoner-of-war camp of the U.S. Army Historical Division in Allendorf. They reviewed everything for accuracy before Lissance completed the work in 1947.

In this fashion Halder could see his old notes, albeit without obtaining a complete copy. The chief of the U.S. Historical Division in Europe, Colonel H. E. Potter, mimeographed copies, in English and German, of the Lissance version and distributed them to western command staffs. This text gradually came into general circulation, where it has become a major scholarly source for the period.

Halder received a complete copy of the typescript in 1956 for his critical study of the notes and for clarification of and comment on unclear entries. Halder wrote: "The examination of the Lissance transcription, which is in my hands for the first time, shows a surprisingly good rendering. Only a few points required correction."

The three-volume German version presented by Hans-Adolf Jacobsen was reviewed by General Halder, sentence by sentence. He corrected spelling errors, name and unit mistakes, as well as stylistic variants. There can be no doubts concerning the authenticity, including the smallest details and phrasing, of the text.

Normally Halder made his notes during the exchanges or presentations. When this was not feasible, he put them on pieces of paper and transferred them to his notebook at the earliest opportunity. These later entries normally came after major conferences or trips. When Halder was in his office, the notebook was on his desk. When he left his office, he locked it in his desk. At day's end he put it into a secure cabinet. Halder understood the danger involved if unauthorized people were to try to read his notes. He did not, however, see the danger as very serious since the Gabelsberger shorthand, which he had learned as a youth in Bavaria, had been replaced by other stenographic forms. Among his associates no one knew it. For anyone to decipher his notes would, therefore, have required major exertions. He had no fears of such efforts until after he left his office.

An important point in the construction of the "diary" is the increasingly laconic approach after the winter of 1941. This change was caused by the departure of Field Marshal von Brauchitsch on 19 December 1941. Thereafter the working coordination between the Chief of the General Staff and the Commander in Chief of the army (Hitler) changed abruptly. Until this change Halder's Operations Department had kept von Brauchitsch continuously informed, which allowed him and Halder to discuss major considerations. Hitler wanted reports on details, which created much more work, and which was made more serious since the latter had additionally to contend with air force and SS efforts against the army. After mid-December as well, he spent much time in exchanges with the army groups, seeking to lessen Hitler's influence. Halder suggested that he, after the morning situation conference, listen to the army groups in order to assemble his notes for the presentation to Hitler.

The unlimited breadth of Halder's notes is extraordinary. Among the innumerable remarks, code words, dates, statistics, and details, one can observe clearly the working method, stress, and rhythm of a chief of the General Staff responsible for employing and directing a force of five million (June 1941) officers and men. From his notes one gains some understanding of Halder's thoughts, the problems he confronted daily, and the concurrent decisions required of him. In the immediate notes, which appear here in abridged form, the reader may overlook the totality. Nonetheless, careful consideration of the daily entries shows the multifaceted reality of the event. Among these concerns was the often painful cooperation with other agencies concerning strategic-operational issues (and intelligence, supply, organization, training, equipment, and so on), as well as the challenges of administration, justice, medicine, and the Nazi party. Added to these difficulties were those of coalition warfare, which began with Italy, but increased with the 1941 addition of those countries which joined Germany against Russia. Halder's notes include information on the coordination of the navy and air force and demonstrate the rivalry, the internal tensions, and the constant controversies between the "conservative army," the "Nazi air force," and the "royal navy." Everything considered, these issues posed an inexhaustible program beyond the control of any individual.

The restrained, neutral opinions and the sometimes impersonal reports of military and political details or circumstances are interrupted only occasionally by emotional outbursts, anger, agreement, or rejection. Such views demonstrate the nature of the diary, i.e., the purpose of the notes. Halder was restrained in his views of others—superiors as well as subordinates. In only a few circumstances did he allow his emotions free reign. He was a careful man.

Nonetheless, Halder's notes provide a dramatic and unique source for the political-military development of the period, 1939–1942. From the deployment and victory in Poland, to the "Phony War in the West," through the 1940 Danish, Norwegian, and French operations and the direct battle against England, to the Balkans campaign and the BARBAROSSA undertaking, culminating in the march on Stalingrad (spring 1942) and the war's turning point, these notes mirror the realities of the war in every theater. In this fashion German political decisions led to defeat. The diary provides an incontrovertible source for the unlimited will of Hitler in unleashing the war against Poland, for his personal decision in opening the western offensive, and for the most fateful effort to destroy the Soviet Union in a lightning campaign.

As concerns the insights into the working conditions of the General Staff, the diary provides understanding of the extensive military-operational planning. In order to be prepared for different military eventualities, the General Staff created numerous operational ideas. In April 1940 the Wehrmacht High Command anticipated an Allied landing in the Balkans. The defense of the Romanian oil areas, which was always an important German consideration, required examination for the possible use of army units. Similarly the situation in August 1940, as the Hungarian-Romanian border strife threatened a powerful explosion in southeastern Europe, posed a challenge which Hitler constantly tried to avoid. In the summer of 1940, there was discussion of a continuous West–East African colonial empire, which created the first consideration of a colonial military force. In the late fall of the same year, the Army High Command examined an undertaking through Syria and Turkey (Anatolia) against the Suez Canal, with the help of the Italians coming from Libya. This operation would have rolled up the English positions in the Mediterranean. Both the Supreme Command and the Army High Command pursued the same idea in 1941 and 1942, with the significant variant of using a third assault thrust via the Caucasus. This strategy never could be implemented, but contained the seeds of limitless ambition. In spring 1941 Hitler ordered a careful study of a possible deployment in Afghanistan against India after BARBAROSSA, which did not go too far in Halder's area. On the other hand, the Army High Command did organize the preparations for an occupation of Portugal and Spain in the event of a possible English landing there during the eastern campaign. Finally, in July 1941, in the belief of victory over the Soviet Union, Halder's staff was occupied with an undertaking against the industrial area of the Ural Mountains. This, too, remained an operation on paper alone; the realities of the battlefield prevented implementation.

Halder's notes show clearly the change of German thinking that occurred between 1914 and 1939. At the outbreak of the First World War, the fateful mechanism of the Schlieffen Plan confined the freedom of action of the political leadership (and provided the symptom of a one-sided preponderance of thinking in military categories which coincided with the concurrent failure of the political leadership). In 1939 the political leadership, without any attention to the innumerable assurances to neutral countries, ordered an offensive which ruthlessly destroyed the neutrality of Belgium, Holland, and Luxembourg. The political leadership forced the General Staff to give up the defensive attitude created by the experiences of the First World War and dictated by Germany's military situation. Von Brauchitsch and Halder tried, with the aid of military-technical arguments, to moderate Hitler's expansionistic politics, but their firm efforts against the offense had little impact on the political leadership.

The list of rapid German victories pushed the concerned element of the military into the background. As Hitler, hurrying from one political success to another after 1935, completed three military campaigns victoriously, he reached, in the summer of 1940, the high point of his career. The soldiers and discerning politicians had not been correct; the Fuehrer's personal predictions had proved true. One must understand this particular psychological situation in the fall of 1940 in order to properly evaluate the relative tensions between political and military conduct of the war. Hitler—after Bismarck, the "greatest statesman" was now the "greatest commander" of all time—believed that he could do without the political element. The sharply honed and tested sword of the Wehrmacht should realize his extensive political goals. From this time on, he increased his plans without limitation and encountered no significant criticism or opposition from his closest military associates. It is certain that the Army High Command was highly skeptical of the planned BARBAROSSA undertaking after the summer of 1940. Already, at the end of July 1940, von Brauchitsch and Halder had come to the view that friendship with Russia was better than a two-front war, which frightened them. After the war, Halder collected his personal thoughts on this issue: he had believed that the war with Russia was avoidable. To be sure, he had been convinced that it could come to a test of strength between Germany and the Soviet Union, especially if the Russians continued their distinctive expansionistic efforts in the west. Nonetheless, he represented the view that Germany should not provoke an armed test, especially under the difficult burden of a war against Great Britain. He believed that an alternative to an attack on the Soviet Union was a diversion of Russian expansion toward the Balkans and Turkey. That action would surely lead to a confrontation between Russia and Great Britain, which would alter German-English relations.

Without question the Army High Command chose numerous opportunities to make Hitler conscious of the problems in the campaign. Halder also asked von Brauchitsch (especially 28 January 1941) about the sense of the struggle. He believed at the time that the German offensive would not harm England or improve Germany's economic basis. He warned about the risk in the west which would come from an operation in the east. Moreover, he feared the collapse of Italy after the loss of its colonies and the subsequent construction of a second front by the Allies against Germany through Spain, Italy, and Greece. A meeting of army group commanders in von Brauchitsch's residence on 31 January 1941 reached a comparable concept. In comparison to the efforts by Halder and von Brauchitsch, in the winter of 1939/40, against the western offensive, these endeavors were weak protests. As well, the change revealed the slow emasculation of the Army High Command which began at Dunkirk (May 1940) and reached a conclusion in the battle for Moscow (1941).

Naturally, Halder's notes about his relationship to Hitler, to von Brauchitsch, and, after 19 December 1941, to Hitler as the army Supreme Commander, provide powerful insights. In particular they also give important explanations of Hitler's role as military leader in the years 1939–1942. One can follow the increasing criticism of Hitler's intervention in directing operations in concrete terms. The author expresses himself in the most guarded terms and conceals many observations. For the most part, he noted "Fuehrer," "conference," or "Fuehrer conference." At the same time, one finds designations for Hitler such as "above," "one," "layman's eye," or, as Halder described one activity, "perverse shot from the stratosphere." Occasionally outbreaks of anger were noted—rage or roar—which have no link to the famous "carpet biter."

For many readers of Halder's notes, one of the surprising revelations is his continuing and accurate knowledge, at least to the start of the Russian campaign, of political affairs. In almost regular intervals the Army High Command and the Foreign Office (State Secretary von Weizsaecker) kept each other generally informed of events. Either the OQu IV (Intelligence), von Tippelskirch, subsequently Matzky, who had numerous sources (including the Fuehrer's adjutants), or the liaison official of the Foreign Office, von Etzdorf, made informational presentations. Others provided Halder with material for understanding. Von Brauchitsch, Canaris, Keitel, General von Stuelpnagel, Lieutenant Colonel Groscurth, and many others contributed to Halder's knowledge. With the beginning of the Russian offensive, many of these exchanges stopped—most significantly those between von Weizsaecker and Halder.

These reports and exchanges ranged over reports and intelligence concerning the situation and the mood elsewhere in the world (which included those from Japan and America), but also added information about secret discussion or correspondence of the political leaders with other statesmen (Mussolini, Franco, Pétain, Laval, King Leopold of Belgium, Antonescu, and others); often the notes reveal German and Italian war aims. Occasionally Hitler provided a political situation report, but this was often directed more to his listeners than to providing information.

The continuous flow of details on foreign affairs of the early period fell more and more into the background after the beginning of the eastern offensive. This was, in part, the product of the work load of the campaign imposed on Halder and his staff. In part it was the product of international decisions which left Hitler (in 1942) no useful latitude in foreign affairs. Von Etzdorf made presentations only twice (April and June) in 1942.

A particular characterization of the Second World War was, on both sides, the continuously expanding radical action and idealization of the war leadership. In Germany Hitler ordered, in an approach consistent with realizing his long-term plans for a political "new order" in Europe, measures which, initially, legitimized the actions of the police, SS units, and special units. From early 1941 the army was unavoidably confronted with these issues, especially as the Supreme High Command issued the Commissar Order and other orders contrary to international law. In these areas Halder's notes provide no noteworthy observations, and seldom anything about his thoughts, feelings, or actions. There is information that the Army High Command was knowledgeable of these events and did try to weaken or to go around certain orders.

In the totality the form of revolutionary war leadership, as presented by Hitler and Heinrich Himmler, did not find much support in the army. Numerous sources testify to the contrary. When this negative spirit began infecting the army, slowly but irresistibly, often with devastating consequences, most of the men and officers, mindful of their military traditions, fulfilled their duties. A bitter Hitler acknowledged this fact. As he issued on 18 October 1942 the tradition-breaking Commando Order (liquidation of captured Allied commandos), he surmised the internal rejection the order would find among the troops. In discussion with his adjutants, Hitler suggested that he knew how various orders, as, for example, the Commissar Order (June 1941), were not executed or were delayed. Guilty of this behavior was the Army High Command, which wanted to "make a minister's pulpit out of the soldier's profession." Without his SS, Hitler opined, nothing would have been accomplished.

From historical research of the German resistance, we know in general outline the role played by the Chief of the General Staff in the military opposition and why he delayed at the last moment in overturning the regime by a coup de main. The motives, given his nature and personality, make judgment difficult. An obvious question is whether the notes contain any remarks clarifying Halder's relationship to the government, its practices, or Hitler as an explanation for his inaction. Unfortunately there are very few entries in this regard, and they are concealed, suggestive at best. One must read between the lines. The criticism of Hitler's military leadership is much different: growing out of the difficult atmosphere of the totalitarian system, Halder provides, without mentioning any content, a discussion with someone, who, we know today, was close to the opposition or one of its propelling forces.

Throughout his life Halder, who believed himself obligated to the professional ethics of his position, sought realization of the maxim "Perform well without being conspicuous." In his discussion with the chiefs of staff of the army groups and armies on 13 December 1940, he suggested, "So long as I am the keeper of the grail, I shall not retreat one hair's width from this spirit of the German General Staff. I demand that the German General Staff be trained in this sense. When one's festive uniform and one's assignments mean no more than a star or a pay increase, one lives on another level than the one where the Prussian General Staff was planned and grew to greatness."

His subordinates knew his sincere humanity, his untiring concern for them, and his emotional outbursts. Everyone who had any opportunity to know him admired his military skill and the purity of his character.

That his notes make even more clear Halder's contributions to the military successes of the first war years was not his intent. Nonetheless, they make an important contribution to history. While we would like to know more about his reflections, his thoughts, and aspirations than are recorded in the notes, we can learn more about his role as a strategist and soldierly leader. Many of these details have been concealed behind the field marshals and army commanders. Whether in the Polish campaign, the western deployment, the offensive in Flanders, the battles for France and the Balkans, or, finally, in the campaign against the Soviet Union, Halder continually proved his supreme understanding of organization and leadership. Hitler's increased evil involvement in the operational direction clearly frustrated various available successes.

That is not to suggest that Halder did not make mistakes. An example is a comparison of the entries of 3 July and 11 August 1941, which shows how he underestimated the Soviet Union. Certainly Halder was impressed from the very beginning of the offensive by the combat resoluteness of the Russians. He did not conceal this recognition. An example is his note concerning the Russian General Belov, whom he admired: "The man, after all, forced seven German divisions into motion." Nonetheless, Halder, at the start of the campaign, had envisioned a simpler resolution. Like the majority of German officers and soldiers, he was certain about the command and battle superiority of his forces. During the 1939/40 winter, he had tirelessly tried to dissuade Hitler from the western campaign, but had been wrong. Hitler's prophecy that France would collapse with the lightest "blow against the house of cards" was correct. Subsequent developments after the summer of 1940 apparently convinced Halder, who evaluated the capacity of the German army too highly. By the time he discerned that the boundary of military possibilities had been passed (August 1941), it was too late.

The military experts did not have the power to curb Hitler and lacked the will to do so after the latter had parted from von Brauchitsch and personally taken over command of the army in 1941 with the words: ''Anyone can provide a little operational leadership. The real issue is the training of the army in the spirit of national socialism.'' With justifiable warnings, which did not agree with his view of the situation, he answered cynically. In the fall of 1942, he brushed aside an objection by the Chief of the General Staff (Kurt Zeitzler) with a rapid hand motion: it was his experience that ''the General Staff as a principle overvalued the enemy; Poland and France, in this connection, would have been complete fiascos. . . .''

The diary provides, if viewed in its completeness, a strong current of common sense and a systematic registration of practical factors. Critically analyzed, the innumerable notes and remarks cannot be a diary, certainly not a war diary. Aside from the author's intentions, the absence of many details—personal reflections and considerations, the possible self-enhancement or personal disparagement—are not part of the diary form. The diary shows more the activities of Halder than his thought.

In reality we have a notebook, intended as a help for official requirements, constructed in the form of a diary or a chronicle for the professional duties of a chief of the General Staff. Halder was an active participant, less a passive observer, and a semiofficial registrar in this activity. The notes require an intensive study of the material. If anyone wishes to profit from such study, he must be knowledgeable of the difficult issues of political and military leadership in the Third Reich. With that, one can cautiously interpret the text, follow the author step by step, and set the proper accent for a careful weighing of the circumstances of that epoch.

In their own fashion the comprehensive notebooks provide a source without comparison in recent history. Their extraordinary value lies, in addition to the clarification of many details, in three areas: it reveals the roots of a representative of the German officer class, who remained between tradition and revolution; it makes impressively clear the functions and changing significance of the General Staff; and, finally, it provides insight into the political-military decisions of recent history which have influenced our times so fatefully.

After the war, the American government made General Halder the leader of the Military History Program (Historical Division) in Koenigstein (Taunus) and Karlsruhe (1946–1961). He received the Meritorious Civilian Service Award in recognition of his work.

Franz Halder died on 2 April 1972 in Aschau.

THE ROAD TO WAR

In the early morning hours of September 1, 1939, Germany's Wehrmacht attacked Poland. Adolf Hitler had directed his armed forces and country in using force of arms to seek the territorial demands that he had repeatedly announced since the spring of that year. Hitler, as the Fuehrer, believed that the time was propitious for success. He believed in his success. Given his earlier diplomatic victories, military preparedness, and nonaggression treaty with the Soviet Union (August 23, 1939), Hitler envisaged himself as the first soldier of the German people and had resolved to fight to the last extremity.

Three days after this aggressive act, Great Britain, the British Commonwealth, and France announced a state of war with Germany. Italy and the United States announced their neutrality. While the Western Allies had taken an enviable moral position, they did not seize the initiative and thereby yielded precious time to Hitler.

As a result, the German leadership could accept the risks of the western front and deploy the mass of its forces against Poland. The General Staff could prepare for the operation with professional care and attention to the military options. In particular, the untried and inexperienced Germans could concentrate their armored units, aerial forces, and untried divisions against the valiant but outmanned Poles. The outcome would be determined quickly.

14 August 1939

West: 1. If French feel sure that large German forces are being committed in the east, *they may decide to take the offensive. It must then be assumed* that both frontier mobilizations (France and Germany) would at first run according to prearranged plans because of the technical impossibility of making substantial changes in mobilization plans on short notice.

2. Within this area, the forces lined up on both sides, from the Belgian-Luxembourg border to Switzerland:

11

France	Germany	
14 fortress brigs.	12 divs. first draft	Fifth Army: 7
19 { 7 divs. first draft	7 divs. second draft	First Army: 13
7 divs. second draft	12 divs. third draft	Seventh Army: 6
5 divs. third draft		(AGp.: 5)
5 mot. divs.		
2 cav. divs.		
1 mecz. div.		

41 units of div. strength (possibly 44)	31 units of div. strength

3.   France will surely set in operation its *security mobilization* at the *Italian frontier*. (North Africa would remain unaffected!) That means:

> 7 divs. first draft
> 2 divs. second draft
> 2 divs. third draft
> 1 div. Corsica
> 3 alpine fortress brigs.
> ———————————
> 15 units of div. strength

4.   On this basis, out of a total of 106 divisions on hand, 47 would be immediately available for the offensive. That number could be substantially increased by, perhaps, 20 divisions from the rear area of the defense mobilization, if France feels sure that we are not going to attack her.

5.   Should France decide to launch an attack through Belgium, such an attack could be conducted either as a scheduled plan or as a surprise operation. The latter would be more desirable from a military point of view [for France], but it is more than doubtful that it will occur, because:

   a.   France's decisions, in all likelihood, are contingent on Germany's moves.

   b.   France must at least observe the form of diplomatic discussions with Belgium.

6.   I estimate a timetable as follows:

Luxembourg border: An immediate drive with the objective to secure Luxembourg for French control. Within *forty-eight hours* they could put into the field:

$$4\begin{cases} \text{1 mot. div.} \\ \text{1 mecz. div.} \\ \text{2 inf. divs.} \end{cases} \text{opposite Fifth Army.}$$

Since we have no forces to send out against them, these French forces could reach the German-Luxembourg border on the evening of the third day.

Belgian border: The following forces could be assembled within *forty-eight hours* at the Franco-Belgian border, ready for operations:

$$7\text{–}9\begin{cases} \text{5 mot. divs.} \\ \text{1 or 2 mecz. divs.} \\ \text{1 or 2 cav. divs.} \end{cases} \text{opposite} \begin{cases} \text{Fifth Army, incl.} \\ \text{3 MG bns.} \end{cases}$$

Aachen Regt. [Infantry Regiment 78]

$$\begin{cases} \text{3 divs. first draft} \\ \text{2 divs. second draft} \\ \text{2 divs. third draft} \end{cases}$$

If launched through the area south of the Sambre and Meuse rivers, the French forces could not reach the Belgian-German border before the morning of the fifth day. Accordingly, on the third and fourth days, Fifth Army, which would not yet be fully mobilized, might be faced with a disorganized situation.

Apart from the seizure of Luxembourg, which would be likely in view of basic French security needs, *a French local offensive through the Ardennes corner* is not likely. The reasons are twofold: political, i.e., Belgium must first be made to take clear political sides; and military, i.e., additional forces would not be available before the end of three days and, not being motorized, would arrive slowly, so that an attack across the German border could not be started before approximately the tenth day.

7.   Owing to the fact that the *Belgian army* is able to mobilize within four days—twelve divisions of first and second draft plus two motorized divisions and the Ardennes units (with six divisions of third draft following within two days)—it is *not unlikely that France will march into Belgium only after she has attained sufficient superiority of forces.* This level may be reached on the ninth day of

mobilization when an estimated eighteen divisions and three fortress brigades will become available in addition to the force allocated for Luxembourg. These divisions could reach the German frontier by the twelfth mobilization day, *so that our frontier positions might be subjected to serious pressure on the fifteenth mobilization day.* The necessary regrouping within Army Group 2 could be effected by that time.

8.   For operations *in Holland* with troops of any substantial strength, the French would first have to cross *Belgium.* Considering the time required for mobilization and covering the distance, such a French force need not be expected at the German frontier before the third week after mobilization day. Advance motorized elements, of course, could reach the line much earlier. However, in view of what we know about French operational doctrine and the political difficulties which would first have to be overcome, such a thrust would be unlikely. Discounting the possibility of any serious Dutch military opposition to the French, we would have to be prepared to meet a major attack at the German-Belgian-Dutch border as of the beginning of the third week after mobilization day. In the event that Belgium should permit the use of the Belgian railroads, this date would have to be considerably advanced.

9.   In summing up, I believe:

   a.   France is not very likely to take any steps in anticipation of our own moves, but rather may be expected to react to our measures, move by move. Accordingly, an early French mobilization, which would materially affect the timetable of our preparedness measures, is improbable; nor is there any reason to expect a surprise attack against Belgium.

   b.   France will set in operation its minimal mobilization for defense, since there is no time to make profound changes in her railroad plan based on purely defensive dispositions, and, moreover, the French railroad system is oriented to the northeastern frontier. Hence, of her total strength [106 divisions], 59 are allocated (44 against Germany, 15 against Italy), and 47 divisions still available for employment.

   c.   As regards the employment of the French forces, the following assumptions may be made:

   About six units (two fortress brigades, two infantry divisions, one motorized division, one mechanized division) will promptly move into Luxembourg. Considering the current state of Reich preparedness, movement could start within two days, so that the Luxembourg-German border would be reached in the evening of the third day. Its mission will not be a local offensive against German territory, but merely the securing of Luxembourg territory as a French base of operations.

About seven to nine divisions (five motorized divisions, one to two mechanized divisions, one to two cavalry divisions), at the current state of French preparedness, could cross the Franco-Belgian border within two days and—if unopposed—reach the fortified German border north and south of Aachen in the morning of the fifth day.

Such an advance motorized group (if and when France should organize it, which I believe would be possible only with the early and total assent of Belgium—in itself quite unlikely) would probably have the initial mission to occupy the Belgian-Dutch operations base, and nothing else. An offensive with long-range objectives need not be expected of this group.

Another attacking force to be reckoned with is a concentration of about 22 divisions which might be assembled at the Franco-Belgian border on the ninth mobilization day (3 fortress brigades, 18 divisions with very strong corps and GHq. artillery—400 battery—and 50 to 60 tank units—including about 50 light units. Should passage through Belgium come off without difficulty without using railroads, this group, together with those mentioned before, could launch a major offensive across the Belgian-Dutch-German border about the fifteenth day.

In the follow-up, an additional *fourteen divisions* from reserves could be fed into the drive before the twentieth mobilization day, in addition to a number of units with a total strength of ten to twelve divisions, which would be combed out of the quiet Maginot front and perhaps also the alpine front; however, no approximate date could be set when these forces would be available for commitment on the northern wing.

10. The resulting overall picture appears in the separate tabulation [lost]. The estimate is based on the assumption that neither Belgium nor Holland will oppose the French moves.

Belgium can prepare for commitment:

Border guard	within 6 hours
Marching units of 11 inf. and 3 arty. regts. (about one-half strength)	within 12 hours
2 cav. divs. mot. and Ardennes inf. div.	within 2 days
6 divs. first draft	within 3 days
6 divs. second draft	within 4 days
6 divs. third draft	within 12 days

Holland can prepare for commitment:

8 divs. first draft, plus 1 light div.	within 5 days
4 divs. second draft	later
At present handicapped by reorganization now in progress.	

11.   To oppose possible French action (see 9.c.) by six divisions (two fortress brigades, two infantry divisions, one motorized division, and one mechanized division) at the German-Luxembourg border, we have ready for commitment on third to fourth mobilization day:

Fifth Army sector. . . . . . . two divisions (16th and 26th), which will be sufficient for an emergency.

12.   To oppose possible French action by seven to nine mobile divisions at the Belgian-Dutch-German border, on both sides of Liège, we have ready for commitment on fifth mobilization day, apart from border guard:

Fifth Army sector. . . . . two MG battalions and 1 reinforced infantry regiment which is inadequate.

13.   To meet a Franco-British all-out offensive after the fifteenth day (a force of about thirty divisions), we have:

Army Hq. 5 with 22 to 26 divisions, including

6 divs. foreseen in general mobilization plan
6 divs. allocated for Belgium
up to 10 divs. of fourth draft, whose combat efficiency is not
    very high as yet; possibly exchange for other divs.
plus 2 (4 later 12) divs. to be taken out of army group.

The trouble thus does not lie so much in the manpower as in the deficiencies with respect to artillery and antitank guns. The maximum that could be taken out of the western front (since that is all there is):

> 14 med. arty. bns.
> 4 light arty. bns. mot.
> 3 AT bns.

and out of army reserves:

> 4 med. arty. bns.
> 2 light arty. bns.
> 5 AT bns.
> <u>1 eng. bn.</u>

approximately 300 pieces, not counting divisional artillery. They are confronted with 1,600 pieces on the French side, on top of which we must bear in mind that French divisional artillery is appreciably stronger than the artillery of German divisions.

Accordingly, the defensive battle at the Dutch-Belgian border calls for transfer of medium artillery from the east and shifting of the defense line to a water (i.e., tank) obstacle (i.e., the Meuse River).

14. With a view to forestalling the temporary crises which might develop in the west, the following proposals are made:

a. Extension of the frontier positions to the Dutch border will be initiated immediately by construction of field fortifications (to become second line upon advance to Meuse).

b. [no entry]

c. Of the six divisions tentatively allocated for the event of an active front against "Belgium," under XXX Corps, hidden activation of at least four, but better all six, divisions must be started immediately.

d. Of the ten divisions of the first installment of fourth draft, six must be immediately activated under camouflage, and put to work on the northward extension of the frontier positions.

e. Camouflaged activation of a MT regiment from the civil economy.

> If orders are issued on the fifteenth, the divisions will be able to move as of the twenty-second, and so be on the ground on the twenty-fifth. Details of disposition later!

15. With these preparations completed, we are ready to shift the northern wing to the Wilhelms Canal, if so desired by the political leadership. Since we are weak in bridging equipment, consent of Dutch government would be desirable for this movement. (Six divisions for a 60-km front.)

16. Authorization of statement to Belgian and Dutch military attachés: Germany is in possession of information that the Western powers would not respect Belgian and Dutch neutrality in the event of a European conflict. While Germany believes that the two nations will make use of their military power to defend their neutrality, Germany deems it appropriate to make preparations for protection of her own borders. This is the explanation for the construction of field fortifications by troops. The statement is to be completed with the assurance that these preparations in no way relate to any design on Germany's part to violate her neighbors' neutrality.

17. Reinforcement of AAA from east as soon as enemy air force is eliminated in eastern theater.

Hitler Remarks

First off is recognition of the fact that neither political nor military success is possible without risks: in the political field, because there are resistances to overcome; in the military, because sober assessment of all factors often reveals the possibility of failure.

Clear appraisal of the factual conditions. —Historical facts.

Britain's position must be viewed in terms of internal political conditions. Decision in 1914. Britain would not have stepped in if she had suspected the consequences. No nation wants a long war as such. Britain stands only to lose. The difference between 1914 and now is in the recognition that a wealthy nation has little to gain, but a great deal to lose; that every nation must pay with blood; and that, even with a victorious war to his credit, the victor emerges diminished in strength. This is the key to an understanding of the actions of men of less than heroic cast. —Britain overburdened with commitments in all parts of the world.

Fight Germany? Yes. Fight for Allies? Open question. Fight for others? No.

In view of their experience in World War I, there is little chance that the opposition will deliberately run the risk of a major war. They know that it is a different Germany they would have to tackle today. 1914: Socialists, church.

The factors involved:

Political:

Primary opponents: Poland
Britain (active), France

Russia is not in the least disposed to pull chestnuts out of the fire. Has nothing to gain, but much to fear. War on the periphery is possible, perhaps even welcome. Not so in the center. Losing a war is as much of a threat to the Russian state as a victorious army. Interested in disruption of Western nations, access to Baltic.

Neutrals: Norway, Sweden, Denmark. Will be genuinely neutral, from inner convictions. Britain's overtures to Russia have caused irritation.

Switzerland, Belgium, Holland:

Switzerland surely will remain neutral.

Holland: On principle neutral; danger to Far East possessions.

Belgium will endeavor to remain neutral. Belgium would be battlefield. Could stand only to lose. A section of the population, with French or Jewish family ties, might wish to pull in the opposite direction as long as the cannons do not speak.

Hungary requires no mention.

Friends: Italy is not interested in a major conflict, but would welcome certain adjustments. A victory of the democratic nations would be the end of Italy. —A Man [Mussolini].

Spain will look with disfavor upon any victory of the democratic nations. Democracies would introduce a monarchy dependent on Western powers.

Britain and France alone must take the burden upon themselves. Nor will the Balkan states be of any use to them.

Military:

Status of *British* armaments: Supplementary armament program passed (navy, air, ground forces). So far, the *naval program* has not been put into effect, not even started. There will be no increase in battleship strength before 1941, no increase in cruisers and destroyers before 1940. Additional program, just passed, is still in the misty future.

Ground forces: One class of conscripts called. It will be months before they are shaped into fighting units. Crews primarily needed for AAA. Months will pass before they could be available in any numbers.

Air: Progress has been made in bomber and fighter strength; improvement in ground organizations. No fundamental changes in ratio of bombers/ fighters. No major improvement in AAA (ten to twelve pieces a month). Three years will be needed to build up an adequate AAA force. Armament program is being pushed in too many areas, with resulting mutual interference. On the whole, in the developing stage (similar to our situation in 1934).

France: Resembles a weak man trying to carry machine guns, guns, etc., on his back. Age classes of conscripts are small, and service for a long time has been only one year. Armament, too, is not in the best condition. Potential of army on the whole limited. Colonial troops tied down.

If Fuehrer were in the place of opponents, he would not accept the responsibility for a war.
One hundred twenty-five million lined up against eighty [German].

What are the potentialities of the British and the French?

Offensive: Between Basel and Saarbruecken hopeless. Local successes possible. Do-or-die attack improbable. Eventuality of violation of neutrality of Luxembourg, Belgium, and Holland: A quick success likely to relieve pressure on the east is completely out of question.

British could give support with a few divisions. —Blockade (countermeasures!), moreover, is only a long-range affair. *No immediate relief could be afforded by any Franco-British action. There is nothing to force them into a war. The men of Munich will not take the risk.* Risk of worldwide repercussions. —*Ready cash for armament is not available, and credit is not to be had anymore.* The only clearheaded people left are the British Imperial General Staff and the French General Staff. In the political field some British spokesmen are beginning to back down (Duff-Cooper). The Press!

Extreme measures open: Recall of ambassadors. Embargo on commerce with Germany, promotion of trade with Poland. League of Nations.

Line of retreat possible: Uncertainty about Russia. —Poland has not lived up to her promises. —Neutral states oppose passage through their territories. The pacts have not been ratified. Observe formulation: "To support with all our power." —*All this has touch of bad faith:* were England resolved to help, she would have given money to the Poles. But the British will not put any more money into a bankrupt business. —Politicians take cover behind Ironside Report. Polish mentality: If Britain had made any positive commitments, the Poles would be much more cocky. Tapped telephone conversations! *Fuehrer is concerned lest Britain hamper showdown by last-minute offers.*

Summing up: The last weeks have brought increasing conviction of [Poland's] isolation.

A prerequisite: Clear-cut military decision must be achieved within measurable time. He would expect Poland to collapse within eight to fourteen days. Final disposition might take longer.

Second requirement: Resolution to fight on all sides. Buildup in west must be completed to last detail.

Relations with Russia: Loose contact, starting out from negotiations for trade agreement. Still under advisement whether a negotiator should go to Moscow, and whether or not this should be a prominent figure.

Russia does not feel under any obligation toward the West. Russians are sympathetic to dismemberment of Poland. On subject of Ukraine, promise has been given regarding delimitation of spheres of interest. —Baltic states? The issue is Lithuania (not the Baltic states). Russians want to discuss subject more closely. Distrust. Want no common frontier. —Fuehrer inclined to meet halfway.

Fuehrer has hinted to Britain that he will approach her with a new offer after disposition of the overriding Polish question. Fuehrer's attitude has registered in London. Paris, too, is no longer in any doubt as to his determination. The great drama now is approaching its climax. —The show put on recently by the British came off so well because of some German indiscretion in boasting that the Fuehrer's calculations had always proved correct.

The other nations must be given proof that there will be a shooting war no matter what. (Poland will be polished off in six or eight weeks, even if Britain should step in.)

Afternoon session.

If situation should develop adversely, we may be deprived of chances of gaining victory cheaply. Decision must be withheld until forty-eight hours before 0-hour.

- **a.** Central problem is Poland. Must be carried off at all cost?

- **b.** Situation if western front is under pressure: All-out drive against German fortified zone unlikely. Possibly an attack might be launched by enemy violating Belgian-Dutch neutrality. No need for a change in our attitude before the proper time arrives. Starting a drive to gain a better front line cannot be considered at this time because of lack of manpower. So, what we would have to do is: (a) ensure protection of our frontier with least delay, (b) invest the possibilities for creating new reserves or moving up existing ones, (c) [no entry], (d) occupation of the [Dutch Frisian] islands and the northern corner.

- **c.** *East:* How can we seize the Dirschau Bridge? What about Graudenz? —Fuehrer has ordered study on what could be done about Dirschau Bridge. *Dirschau:* (Himmler) Armored train, coup de main. *Graudenz:* Possibly raiding force in civilian clothes. Dive-bombers practically out of question.

Slovakia has signed protective agreement.

Disposition of forces has been reviewed. Nothing will be taken away from troops earmarked for east.

Danzig will be left to its own resources.

Navy: Fleet of one cruiser and eleven submarines allocated for operation; will put out to sea for exercise on 18 August.

Aerial attack: Gdynia: eight dive-bomber groups with eighty craft. Mixed bombs.

Party Rally [Nuremberg]: Will decide by 15 August if it is to be held.

Date for calling of units for west advanced to 15 August.

SUMMARY

Morning session: Review of political situation.

Success, political or military, cannot be had without taking risks. After reviewing the risks which he had to take in all his undertakings to date, and which, to his mind, grew progressively smaller as he forged ahead, the Fuehrer strikes a balance of the possible international complications arising from a German attack on Poland.

Only *Britain,* apart from Poland, could come on the scene as an antagonist, with *France* pulled in after her.

Britain, unlike in 1914, will not allow herself to blunder into a war drawn out over years. Talk of Britain wanting a long war is discounted. No government would promote a long war. Britain, knowing war, is well aware that she has to lose in a war, and that even a victorious war would not make up for the cost of such a war. That is the fate of rich countries. Britain is overburdened with responsibilities because of the vastness of her empire. She has no leaders of real caliber. ("The men I met in Munich are not the kind that start a new world war.") Moreover, the other side is well aware that it is not the Germany of 1914 they would have to deal with (Socialism, church). (Why should Britain fight? You don't let yourself get killed for an ally.) Not even England has the money today to fight a world war. Nothing can be had on credit.

France is not directly interested in waging a war.

Russia has no intention of pulling Britain's chestnuts out of the fire, and will keep out of war. Stalin has to fear a lost war as much as he would a victorious army. Russian aspirations, at most, extend to the Baltic states.

Norway, Sweden, Denmark are neutral from innermost conviction. Deeply perturbed over Britain's wooing of Russia.

Switzerland, Belgium, Holland: Switzerland surely neutral, Holland the same. Belgium will do her best to preserve her neutrality. As a likely theater of war, she stands only to lose. Possibly certain forces at this time favor participation at the side of France, but they will be silenced once the guns begin to speak.

In sum, Britain and France alone will have to shoulder the burden. Nor can the Balkan states help them.

Appraisal of military potential of opponent:

Britain has not gained in *naval power* over last year. On *land,* it will be months before stepped-up conscription can take effect in the form of efficient fighting units. Progress in the *air:* bombers, fighters, improved ground organization. Air defense has not made any basic improvements. On the whole, everything is still in *the developing stage, similar to ours in 1934.*

France's potential is curtailed by the limitations of her manpower. Colonial troops are tied down. Equipment not at its best. Fuehrer states that if he were in the shoes of the Franco-British statesmen, he would not assume responsibility for a world conflict. One hundred twenty-five million oppose eighty.

What military measures can France and Britain undertake? Drive against West Wall unlikely. A northward swing through Belgium and Holland rules out speedy victory. None of this would help the Poles. Blockade works slowly and provokes undesirable countermeasures.

All these factors argue for the likelihood of Britain and France refraining from entering the war, particularly since they are not under any compulsion.

Pacts are not yet ratified. Formula: "Aid with all our power" lacks good faith. Proof: Britain does not give Poland any money to buy arms in other countries. Politicians are beginning to back out, taking cover behind Ironside Report.

British and French General Staffs take a very sober view of the prospects of an armed conflict and advise against it.

Further evidence that no determined action is expected on the part of Britain may be inferred from Poland's attitude. Poland would be even more insolent if she knew she had the unqualified backing of Britain. Britain has strongly remonstrated with Poland over the latest Polish notes and is a continuously restraining influence. Tapped telephone conversations in Poland! Even now Britain is putting out feelers to find out how the Fuehrer envisages developments after Poland's disposal.

All this supports the conviction that while Britain may talk big, even recall her ambassador and in the end put an embargo on trade with Germany, she will not resort to armed intervention in the conflict.

The requisite conditions are:

1. Successes must be scored in Poland in the very near future. "Within eight to fourteen days the world will have to be convinced that Poland

is at the point of collapse. The operations themselves may well continue past that date.'' (Six to eight weeks.)

2. We must show determination to fight on all fronts.

3. Activation of the western front must be complete.

Separate issue: Russia.

Questions concerning the army:

a. Advance of date for calling up older classes required for western front (asked 250,000, i.e., twelve divisions) still under advisement. Decision will be given on 15 August. Decision on entry into Holland and northward extension of defense line still pending!

b. Cancel Party Rally? Decision on 15 August. (Yes!)

c. Advance notice to railroads? Decision on 15 August. (Yes!) One must consider the course of the timetable.

d. *Dirschau:* Coup de main. Himmler! Armored train? Report and pertinent information to be submitted. *Graudenz:* Paratroops on evening of first day.

e. Gdynia. Shelling with K-5 gun [28-cm railway gun].

f. Mobilization in east as prearranged, also for East Prussia. Consult with von Bock.

[end of Hitler's remarks]

Commander Weser-Uebung.

g. Treaty with Slovakia signed.

Evening: Von Stuelpnagel (through v. Weizsaecker):

Von Ribbentrop-Ciano: Ciano exceedingly surprised. Mussolini would like to have peace for a few more years. Germany's encirclement complete. Italy exhausted; no raw materials; deficiencies in armament; no coastal fortifications. —Nothing could be undertaken out of Libya base.
General Staff estimates fighting strength Italy-France at 1:5.

Albania was a disappointment. Operations on Balkans not feasible in near future.
Von Ribbentrop: We don't need you. —Ciano: The future will show.

15 August 1939

Talk with State Secretary v. Weizsaecker:

He confirms the picture of the situation presented yesterday.
Chamberlain and Halifax in particular wish to avoid bloodshed.
U.S. observes marked reserve.
Concurs in estimate of developments in the next ten days.
Until the evening of 19 August, no changes. Other vehicle changes not before 22 August.

General Keitel: Timetable to be announced today:

1. *Cancellation of Party Rally to be kept secret.* 1430 hours. Word given to Transportation Chief's Office that Fuehrer will go to Nuremberg. ObdH informed.

2. All preparations for state ceremony at Tannenberg are being continued. ObdH informed.

3. *No* decision today on advancing calling-up date of divisions.

4. Study question of shifting defense line into Dutch territory! (Also about islands, advancing the line possibly across Meuse.) (Discussed with OQu I.)

5. Confirmation of conference of 14 August will be sent over. Dirschau! Send officer. (Cleared with OQu I.)

. . .

Conference of commanding generals: Sparing use of ammunition. Jump-off hour, places, and times of "surprise" remain unchanged. —No new orders from ObdH, only 0-hour. —Von Bock: Orders as given. "Orderly progress of [Poland's] mobilization, however, would have to take its course."

Instruction for West: Siting of main line of resistance. —Setting up of ammunition dumps must not be started too early. —Evacuation by Todt Organization.

Latest situation report on Poland: Polish mobilization will be completed on 27 August; that puts us in arrears with our mobilization. In order to keep step with their preparations, we would have to start mobilizing on 21 August; in this manner the divisions of even the third and fourth drafts would be ready on 27 August. With ObdH.

21 August 1939

Canaris:

a. Present version of guarantee pact does not meet Russian wishes. — Program: Von Ribbentrop can go (to Moscow) eight days after signing and publication of trade agreement (20 August); would have to take with him draft of guarantee pact, covering all points of joint interest to Germany and Russia. Russian draft provides for exclusion of use of force against third parties and of support to aggressors, arbitration in event of disagreements, and duration for five years from date of ratification.

b. Attolico [Italian ambassador] at Fuschl was outspoken in expressing misgivings. Italy won't go along. Von Ribbentrop was quite annoyed. Attolico returned to Rome.

c. Belgium: (Buelow-Schwante).

1600. **Von Weizsaecker.**

2400. **OQu IV** brings word of Russian Treaty.

West:

Maximum immediate buildup against Germany: 44 divisions. Additional strength available against Germany: 40 divisions. Together with British troops a total of approximately 90 divisions may be reached, which means 50 divisions on the northern wing.

French timetable (capability): Luxembourg on third day. Belgian border, first wave (motorized) on sixth day. Major offensive at end of two or three weeks.

Artillery: France can put up 1,600 guns over and above division artillery on northern wing, against 300 German pieces; moreover, French divisional artillery superior in firepower to German.

Tanks: France has 50 to 60 battalions (ca. 2,500 tanks), Germany 0.

Intentions OKH.

22 August 1939

1000. **Report to ObdL** (Obersalzberg).

    1. Introduction: Fuehrer's directive:

        a. Open hostilities with heavy surprise blow.

        b. Achieve swift victories.

        { Mobilization starts on jump-off day. Some measures will be taken earlier.

Objective: Destruction of Polish army.

    2. Available forces: 102 divisions.

Defense west	30 divisions (with Belgium staying out)
	6 divisions foreseen for Belgian eventuality
Fourth draft	14 divisions.
Not allocated	52 divisions.

    3. Operational plan: Based on *pincer.* —Importance of Warsaw.

      Left prong: Seventeen divisions, plus one cavalry brigade.

        a. Balance of strength of opposing forces and maneuverability in terrain.

        b. Junction of Pomeranian and East Prussian forces.

        c. Main effort.

      Right prong: Thirty-five divisions.

        a. Terrain, roads, industry.

        b. Reasons for direction of drive, main concentration.

        c. Echelonning (Galicia).

    4. *Poland:* Strength: Thirty-three infantry divisions, plus fifteen cavalry brigades, plus ?. Armor AT? Antiaircraft assembly. —Mobilization 27 August.

    5. In what way does Polish buildup cut across our preparations? — Army Group North. —Opportunities on Vistula, on Narew.

Present status of assembly preparations in Poland.

6.   *Requests to air force:*

    a.   Support to assure *initial success.* At Vistula, at Mława, to facilitate tactical assembly. Warsaw.

    b.   Possibilities of *airborne operations.*

1200.   Conference held by Fuehrer (Obersalzberg). Attended by commanding generals (army groups and armies) of the three services.

Morning:

I.   **Outline of situation and decision:**

1.   *Developments leading up to decision* to settle eastern problem: Theoretically it would have been more desirable to square accounts in the west first, but it has become increasingly plain that Poland would be sure to take advantage of any difficult situation to attack us in the back. It has therefore become necessary to dispose of the eastern problem before tackling the west.

2.   *Germany's position at the moment* is favorable for getting the eastern question settled. A number of factors are in our favor today, which would not exist a few years hence.

    a.   *Personalities on our side:* The Fuehrer. —Mussolini, the sole champion of the empire idea today, has demonstrated his strength in Abyssinian conflict. —Franco, the champion of centralized, progressive leadership and of pro-German policy in Spain. *On the enemy side:* There are no men of the caliber hard and heroic enough to carry through the decisions called for by the situation, and which are especially difficult in the case of Britain. The enemy has much to lose, while we only gain.

    b.   *Political advantages: England* is kept busy in the *Mediterranean* by tension with Italy, in *East Asia* by the tension with Japan, and in the *Near East* by the tension with the Islamic nations. —Britain has not gained anything through last war. Entering a new war would entail changes in the structure of the empire. *France*'s position, too, has deteriorated. Drop in birth rate. On the *Balkans:* The forces have been held in balance ever since Yugoslavia was neutralized by the events in Albania. Romania is vulnerable and at the mercy of conflicts between other powers. Turkey has no leadership.

"A clash, which it would not be safe to put off for four or five years, might as well come off now." "Army must see actual battle before the big final showdown in the west; testing of the tools." "What we want now is not a general showdown, but rather the disposition of specific issues; this is the proper procedure not only politically but also from the military standpoint."

c.   *Poland:* Polish-German relations cannot go on as they are. Proposals on Danzig and railroad through Corridor (currency problems) were turned down at *British* instigation. Settling of the Polish conflict must not be left to arbitration by third parties. The time is favorable for a solution, so the blow must be struck! Political risks cannot be entirely avoided. No whole decision without a risk!

3.   *Reasoning leading up to the decision:*

Only two nations will feel any obligation to come to the aid of Poland: England and France. England primarily, with France pulled in behind.

Britain's rearmament effort has not yet materially changed the situation in Britain's favor. (Strengthening of her navy will not become effective before 1941/42; in the ground forces also the effects will not be visible for some time yet; only air force has made progress.) Britain's vulnerability in the air is still very great today. For that reason, she would like to put off an armed conflict for three to four years.

France's armament is partially outdated, but its quality is not bad. Population is dwindling. France cannot afford a prolonged war.

The Western powers have only two lines of action.

Blockade: Unpromising, because we have the use of the entire Danube basin.

Offensive in the west:

a.   Attack on the West Wall is psychologically impossible and also very difficult militarily.

b.   Violation of neutral states. These countries have the honest desire to stay neutral. Besides, Britain, too, wants these countries to stay neutral. We may therefore expect that Britain and France will respect neutralities. This rules out any military operation as hopeless. A "long war" is an untempting prospect. Germany can be counted on to make a better showing of herself in a long war than she did in 1914.

Russia will never be so out of her mind as to fight for France and Britain. —Developments in Russia: Dismissal of Litvinov marks end of interventionist era. Next the trade agreement. Even before that conversations were initiated by Russia on a nonaggression pact. German intervention in Russo-Japanese conflict, and Baltic states. Russians have informed us that they are ready to sign the pact. Direct contact between Stalin and Fuehrer. "With this I have knocked the weapons out of the hands of this gentry. [English and French.] Poland has been maneuvered into a position where our military victory is assumed." Ultimate effects cannot yet be predicted: New course! Stalin has written that he promises himself much for both sides. Radical changes in European political picture.

II. The Fuehrer's demands on his military chiefs:

1. *Hard determination:* Countermoves by Britain and France must be expected. We must stand fast. Buildup plan for western frontier will be set in operation. "Iron steadfastness of all responsible authorities."

2. *Goal:* Annihilation of Poland, that is, destruction of active power. We are not setting out just to reach a specific line or establish a new frontier, but rather we seek the annihilation of the enemy, which we must pursue in ever new ways.

3. *Means to this end:* It does not matter what they are. *The victor is never called upon to vindicate his actions. The question is not one of the justice of our cause, but exclusively of achieving victory.*

4. *Execution:* Harsh and remorseless. We must all steel ourselves against humanitarian reasoning! —Speed: Have confidence in the German soldier, even if reverses should occur. —Of paramount importance are the wedges that must be driven from the southeast toward the Vistula, and from the north to the Narew and Vistula. —Promptness in meeting new situations; new means must be quickly devised to deal with them.

5. *New frontiers:* Possibly incorporation of some areas into Reich, with a protectorate to the east. Military operations need not be affected by regard for future frontiers.

III. Particulars:

1. *Start probably* on Saturday morning.

2. *Slovakia:* (List) Instruct Barckhausen to strengthen Slovak border guard. Elements of 7th Air Force Division to Zipser-Neudorf. Slovak fliers will be grounded. We assume responsibility that Hungary will not undertake anything against Slovakia.

3. *Dirschau:* Attack with dive-bomber groups on Y-day, at dawn. Targets: Western end of bridge and town (barracks, power plant, etc.). Simultaneously, start of freight train from Marienburg, followed by armored train and remainder of Group Medem.

4. *Gdingen:* Air attack simultaneous with Dirschau; also [naval] blockade of harbor.

5. Operation of *Army Reichenau:* No comments.

6. Review of enemy situation in sector of Army Group North.

.   .   .

24 August 1939

OQu I:

.   .   .

5. Polish concentrations: Infantry and artillery east of Mława. Reinforcements reported south of Danzig (three infantry regiments). Two new divisions in Bydgoszca. One additional division south of Katowice (Auschwitz). (Checked with 11th Sec. [should be 12th Sec.: Foreign Armies East].)

1000. Jeschonnek: Goering concurs with von Brauchitsch on Luxembourg. (ObdH) Fourth Air Fleet reports that Barckhausen has no instructions. (Op. Sec. states they were dispatched last night by OKW courier; yesterday afternoon orders were sent by us directly to Army Group South and Fourteenth Army.) Bratislava garrison has left for northern border. Barckhausen does not know what is to go to Zipser-Neudorf, and when. Air force buildup practically completed. Supply arrangements still being worked on.

6. *France:* Three draft waves called for German border, possibly also against Italians. (Checked with 3d Sec. [Foreign Armies West].) Railroad services alerted: Border crossing points closed; Rhine bridges closed (not everywhere). Border guard not yet mobilized. Evacuations on very minor scale (Saint Avold). Preliminary mobilization Monday. Time lapse until French can be ready for attack, ten days (Friday).

Belgium: Measures on very small scale (military furloughs canceled, field exercises called off, specialists called into service).

Holland: Border and coastal defenses again at full strength (50,000). Light brigade in southern part (Maastricht corner).

Britain: No confirmation of report that British fliers have arrived on French side of Channel coast.

7. *Reports from Budapest:* Poland intends to march into Danzig on 24 August, afternoon, or 25 August, morning. (Report received by OKW.)

.   .   .

25 August 1939

Britain: (estimate) If 23 August is first mobilization day and troops are embarked *immediately,* a buildup of five motorized divisions and two armored divisions could be completed in Saint Quentin area on seventeenth mobilization day, i.e., 8 September.

OQu IV: *France:* As of 25 August: seventeen fortress brigades and ten regular infantry divisions at full war strength in security zone [the Maginot Line]. — Elements of one motorized division at Belgian border. —Border guard in place on 25 August. —Closing of frontier expected today. —No compulsory evacuations (voluntary only: some minor evacuations going on in Forbach area).

Belgium: No mobilization as yet. Vague reports about heavy manning of French border.

Holland: No change on German border. Reports state that general mobilization was proclaimed yesterday (24 August). Transfer of troops from Utrecht to Amsterdam (unconfirmed). Dutch are said to have stated that infraction of neutrality by England would be regarded as treaty violation.

Poland: Military situation. Civil administrations have left Katowice and Poznań. Schools closed. All motor trucks requisitioned. Civilian air-raid protection organized. British and French citizens are leaving Poland.

Britain: Vague reports on a troop transport across Channel (improbable). —Halifax speech.

Canaris: Situation at Berlin police Hq. Concern over role of Deathhead Organization. What will Communists do, any labor trouble to be expected in industry? What are the air force missions? —*Positive evidence that Britain will strike.*

Time factor for British and French military intervention. (Taken up with ObdH.)

OQu I reports: Everything running smoothly.

1200.   Call from OKW. Decision may have to be postponed. What would be last deadline? Reply: 1500.

1330.   Call from OKW. Postponement must go into effect (Henderson).

1545.   ObdH: Fuehrer ruling on Luxembourg. Op. Sec. is notified. Evacuation of Red Zone in XII Corps area [Saarbruecken industrial area] starts tomorrow in accordance with instructions of army group. (Cruewell is already notified.)

Chevallerie: Wartime organization of General Staff. —What about the press? —Printing of new situation map.

1930.   ObdH: [Call from Reich Chancellery]:

    a.   Treaty between Poland and Britain ratified.

    b.   Don't open hostilities. All troop movements must be stopped, even near border; before, if impossible.

    c.   Mobilization continues.

    d.   Buildup west and east continues.

    e.   Evacuation of Red Zone, Corps Command Area XII, canceled.

2035.   Keitel confirms postponement.

Canaris: Telephone restrictions lifted on Britain and France. Confirms development of events.

2100.   Von Bock: Inquires whether preparations should be maintained for tomorrow.

2130.   Von Boeckmann: Stop proclamation on Executive Power. All political as well as military measures scheduled for 26 August must be called off.

2150.   Talk with Wagner on rescinding of proclamation on Executive Power.

26 August 1939

Morning report: No hostilities have occurred. Local shooting in Upper Silesia opposite von Reichenau's sector (K-men) [saboteurs].
0630: Three major demolitions (tunnel) reported from Jablunka Pass.
West quiet. Progressing according to plan. Wire entanglements on Upper Rhine. Assumption of command in Fifth Army Hq., including control of construction [West Wall].

.   .   .

1600.   Siewert: a. Conference at Reich Chancellery has just ended.
b. Situation unchanged. No decision taken as yet on main problem (not before late tonight).
c. Feelers have been extended, but no results so far.

1715.   Engel (through OQu IV): Fuehrer wrote letter to *Il Duce* yesterday. Fuehrer must act. Origin of the Russian Pact. Japan's attitude. Italy must come in. Will benefit Axis. —Attolico transmitted letter to Ciano. Attolico makes statement for Italy; the Italians and their General Staff have doubts. Britain is sure to step in. Italy is not in a position to conduct even a defensive war. — Renewed request to prevail on *Il Duce,* which caused delay from 1400 to 1500 on twenty-fifth. Fuehrer then gave stop-operation order at 1502, without waiting for Mussolini's reply. Italian reply arrived at 1745: Italy must stick to its statement. Participation is out of question without our pledge for and actual delivery of large quantities of war and raw materials.

Fuehrer deeply shaken. Ciano has communicated his Salzburg impressions to British.

Neurath: He can thank the Italians for that. —Roatta. Cancellation of attack order followed at 2230.

Subsequent developments: A faint hope that Britain might still be brought around by negotiation to accept the demands rejected by Poland. Danzig—Corridor. (Henderson has made an offer on solution of Corridor and Danzig questions; is now in London.)

Should we build up Italy's strength? ObdH says no; Goering says no! Italy's idea seems to be to ask such a high price that we cannot accept: fuel, steel, 600 tubes for heavy AAA guns, etc. Fuehrer intends to make another try at urging on the Italians.

Treaty with Russia has secret clause: Ukraine and Baltic states, exclusive of Lithuania, are thrown to the Russians.

. . .

27 August 1939

. . .

OQu IV:

1. Coulandre has been to see Fuehrer. Daladier's urgent appeal to leave the sword in the sheath. (Letter was acknowledged, reply deferred.) In telephone conversation with Daladier, Coulandre has seemingly negative view of situation; does it mean then that the Germans will strike? If so, I put my confidence in strength of the nation.

2. *Navy:* Destroyer sunk in collision.

3. *Henderson* is expected back at 1700.

4. *Japan* deeply displeased. Oshima has sought to lodge protest with von Weizsaecker. "Relations seriously endangered." Von Weizsaecker sees no grounds for accepting this protest and yielding to his insistence. —Cable from Ott: Very bad impression in Japan, especially among army. —Advisability of a testimonial by German army in tribute to Japanese?

France: Frontier assembly transport movements rolling since 2000; only against German border. Corps commanders still in their peacetime garrisons. Confirmation that *fourth draft has been called.* General mobilization not confirmed. No change in disposition of troops on border. —Units stationed in army districts in center of country, slated for frontier assembly, have started moving, but only some elements seem to have been entrained so far.

Britain: Mobilization started 23 August. First contingent: (regular army) two to three divisions and two armored divisions were ready on 25 August, morning. No evidence of transports (embarkation).

Belgium: First phase: Preliminary mobilization. Frontier troops identified only east of Liège. *Belgium will defend integrity of the country under all circumstances.*

Holland: Anything that can fight is already on the border.

. . .

OQu IV: (Inform ObdH.)

> **West:** *Britain has no general mobilization.* First wave: two infantry divisions and one armored division. First wave not yet on move. Territorial army not yet called. AAA defense mobilization in top gear.

> **Belgium:** *First phase of mobilization, i.e., only the regular army:* nine divisions, i.e., six infantry divisions, two motorized divisions, one Ardennes infantry division have been mobilized (begin earliest on 25 August). Movement to border not yet started. Special powers for King have not yet gone beyond first phase of mobilization.

> **France:** No change. Clothing depots in army districts in south shifted to north. *Rumor that alpine troops were moved north from Italian border.* Moves hesitant? General mobilization apparently not yet announced. Units in army districts in central France, earmarked for frontier assembly, are said to have started only partial movement.

> **Poland:** No news of consequence.

28 August 1939

. . .

1215.   Oster: Finance Minister Popitz (citing Hitler): Those who would again try to intrigue behind my back better watch out.

> a.   *Conference at Reich Chancellery at 1730:* Reichstag and several Party notables, Fuehrer accompanied by Himmler, Heydrich, Wolff, Goebbels, and Bormann. Situation is very grave. Determined to have eastern question settled one way or another. Minimum demands: "Return of Danzig, settling of Corridor question." Maximum demands: "Depending on military situation." If minimum demands not satisfied, then war: brutal! He will himself be in the front line. Position taken by Il Duce serves our best interests. The war will be tough, we may even fail, but "as long as I am alive, there will be no talk of capitulation." —Soviet Pact widely misunderstood in Party. A pact with Satan to cast out the Devil. —Economic situation. "Applause on proper cues, but thin." Personal impression of Fuehrer: Worn, haggard, creaking voice, preoccupied. "Keeps himself completely surrounded now by his SS advisers."

> b.   *Talk between Coulandre and Forbes.* Opponents know about target date (26 August) and postponement. Britain and France hold that

yielding would be impossible as long as troops are on borders. Henderson is working to gain time. Chamberlain outraged over personal insults.

c. Von Ribbentrop has received *Chinese* ambassador. —Chiang Kai-shek. —Trade agreement. Conversations held. —Civil faction has won in Japan, urges conclusion of alliance with France and Britain.

d. *Italian press has changed course?* British pressure in Mediterranean will increase with ceasing of pressure by Japanese.

e. British broadcast: Mobilization in Germany. No signs in Italy.

f. *Sequence of events.*

23 August, 1400.   Chamberlain's letter to Fuehrer at Berghof: "We are standing by our commitments."

1800.   Reply: Rejection of meddling.

24 August, 0200.   Russian Pact signed.

1500.   Chamberlain makes statement on Britain's determination to aid Poland.

1900.   Von Ribbentrop returns from Moscow.

25 August, 0100.   Von Ribbentrop–Ciano. Changed situation. "Armed action by Western powers impossible."

1200.   Scheduled telephone conversation postponed.

1330.   Henderson sees Fuehrer. Presents memorandum. Henderson: "No basis for negotiations." Fuehrer would not resist if Britain were to wage a sham war.

1400.   Attolico sees v. Ribbentrop, is informed on letter to Mussolini. Russian Pact has modified situation. Romania powerless. Turkey must change course. Il Duce backs Fuehrer.

1500.   Ciano to Attolico. "Expected improvement is not forthcoming."

1630.   Anglo-Polish Pact announced.

1700.   Coulandre appeals to Daladier not to interfere, "eternal frontiers."

1800.   Il Duce's reply through Attolico: Agrees with Russian Pact. However, if Western powers should attack, Italy

	would not be able to resist without raw materials and war materiel.
2000.	March order canceled.
2115.	Il Duce says that list of demands will arrive tomorrow.
26 August, 0730.	Letter Henderson–von Ribbentrop. Will transmit letter to Cabinet. "Will hurry and not play for time."
1330.	Il Duce's list of demands arrives. Offers his good services as mediator. —One hundred fifty AAA batteries with crews wanted at once.
1600.	Reply to Il Duce, stating capacities for delivery. Question of transport merely touched. "Not afraid to enter conflict alone."
1835.	Il Duce: "Since Germany is unable to furnish needed raw materials, active participation on my part is ruled out." A political settlement still possible on favorable and honorable basis.
1900.	Daladier's reply to Fuehrer's appeal. Offers mediation, but France will have to support Poland.
2300.	Fuehrer's letter to Il Duce. Appreciates that Italy not in position to attack. Impression that Italy would come in, should, however, be maintained until outbreak of hostilities, in order to tie up enemy forces! This would enable me to settle the eastern question and in the winter appear in west with forces equaling those of British and French. Blockade rendered ineffective by German autarchy. Italy could help with industrial manpower.

Von Brauchitsch [citing Hitler]: If I am pushed to it, I shall wage even a two-front war. [Citing Romanian ambassador]: Henderson brought very little with him. War inevitable unless a miracle happens. Romania will be neutral if Hungary does nothing foolish.

Ask von Weizsaecker [for discussion].

1522.   ObdH telephones from Reich Chancellery: Get everything ready for seventh mobilization day.

1615.   Second Armored Division already en route to Sillein. First Mountain Division, half via Sillein, half south of Deutschendorf.

ObdH

1. Attack starts 1 September.

2. Fuehrer will let us know promptly if we are not to strike.

3. Fuehrer will let us know immediately if further postponement is necessary.

4. The plan is to put Poland into an unfavorable position for negotiations and so achieve maximum objective. (Henderson)

Fuehrer was very calm and clear. Appraisal of military situation agrees with ObdH's. —Rumor has it that Britain is disposed to consider a broad proposal. Details on return of Henderson. Another rumor has Britain stressing that decision to go to war turns on her own declaration that a threat exists against Poland's vital interests. In France, representatives urging the government against war are mounting. Italy reportedly has agreed to Fuehrer's proposal (to tie up forces). The bill. —The plan is to ask for Danzig, corridor through Corridor, and plebiscite on the same basis as Saar. Britain perhaps will accept, Poland probably not. *Wedge between them!* Line to be followed: Try to agree with Britain on big solution: Danzig, corridor through Corridor, several corridors.

Selection of date: Political considerations. *Japan* uncertain.

2200.   At v. Weizsaecker's. No news. There is a proposal to get into conversation with Russia.

29 August 1939

. . .

1620.   **OQu IV:**

Contents of letter (*brought by Henderson*): Germany must be aware that Britain has commitments with respect to Poland. On the other hand, there is satisfaction in noting the fact that Germany is desirous of relieving the tension with Britain. The British government concurs in this approach. —There are two distinct problems: the German-Polish and the German-British. The first must be settled before the second may be dealt with. It is imperative to arrive at a peaceful solution of the former. To this end it is necessary for Germany and Poland to consider the issue jointly and to have the settlement backed by international guarantees. Britain has commitments to Poland. Any solution which compromises Poland's interests is unacceptable for Britain. Britain is ready to participate in working out a solution in which, relying on Fuehrer's own statement, Poland's interests would be safeguarded.

Subsequent conversation with Henderson: H. does not deny Fuehrer's assertion that Danzig does not constitute a problem, nor that autobahn is one. Re Corridor: Couched in tortuous language, but yet recognizable, is proposal to resettle minorities in Corridor. (Fuehrer: Not a bad idea at all.) Germany is entirely free in drafting and timing her reply. Britain does not set any deadline for a reply. The present state of affairs cannot endure. It is anticipated that situation will be clearer by 3 or 4 September.

Fuehrer's statement: That is an idea to my liking; from now on I shall act only on an international basis. Send in international troops, including Russians. Fuehrer hopes to drive wedge between British, French, and Poles.

Today: Poland directed by British to go to *Berlin,* as requested by Germans. —Fuehrer wants to have them come tomorrow.

Strategy: Keep up a barrage of demographic and democratic demands. Ask for plebiscite within six months, under international supervision. Anyone opting for Germany must remain German citizens, and conversely the Poles. Poles will not want Germans in their territory. — The Poles will come to Berlin on 30 August. On 31 August the negotiations will blow up. On 1 September start to use force.

Foreign Office: They seem to be under impression that these maneuvers leave military preparations entirely unaffected.

Lithuania: No official feelers from Lithuanian side. Lithuanian government has not responded. We have made affirmation of neutrality. Reference to Vilna.

Holland piqued that no one is paying any attention to her.

Russia: Von Ribbentrop has suggested that something be undertaken on western border.

Britain: Unconfirmed reports that transports to Continent have left port.

Bulgaria: Bruckmann reports that forty cars with ammunition and several cars with machine guns for Bulgaria have been stopped by Yugoslavia.

Polish fliers reported to have landed in sector of Group Wartenberg (Eighth Army).

Buhle: Additional seven heavy batteries will be forthcoming in latter half of September (four replacement batteries). SS unit *"Feldherrnhalle"* has been offered. Do we want to use it?

1800. Jodl (on telephone; ObdH has been informed directly):

Chamberlain's letter was conciliatory. Endeavor to find a modus vivendi. (Opinion of Cabinet divided.) Dignified in tone. Clearcut on point that Britain cannot withdraw from obligation to aid Poland. Defines vital interests. Integrity. All this is elastic. Britain herself is doing the defining. They must save face. Britain gives assurance that Poles will come to conference.

Fuehrer will answer letter still *today:* Danzig no longer an issue, small corridor through Corridor no problem, question of large corridor left open. Fuehrer will pull out all the stops of democratic systems (plebiscite, exchange of populations, international observers to investigate atrocities). Wants England to use her influence to get Polish negotiators with full powers to Berlin tomorrow noon; deadline for reply 31 August, evening.

The impression received is that Britain is "soft" on the issue of a major war.

"Directives" for us will come soon: In the west, the other side will have to shoot first. Neutral borders will be respected.

.   .   .

30 August 1939

.   .   .

Siewert: Make all preparations for attack on 1 September at 0430 hours. Should negotiations in London require postponement, then 2 September. We shall be notified before 1500 tomorrow. *Army Group North has information.* Second September last day on which we would strike. (Goering has objected to 0430.) Get in touch with Jeschonnek, Poland has answered: Notice for conference too short. Going to Berlin would be tantamount to submission. Fuehrer insists on demand for immediate dispatch of a Polish negotiator. Fuehrer drafts letter to Britain, outlining in detail demands on Poland.

.   .   .

ObdH: Fuehrer's proposal to Poland: Danzig, plebiscite; (calls from Goering's office). Poles have not arrived yet; Britain has become party to negotiations. Fuehrer: We strike either on 1 or 2 September; all off after 2 September.

2000. **Von Greiffenberg:** Instruct him as my deputy at OKW conference on 31 August, where time of jump-off will be decided.

31 August 1939

0630. Hauser brings word from Reich Chancellery that jump-off order for 1 September has been given.

0700. Discuss with von Greiffenberg best methods for transmission of Fuehrer order on 1 September attack.

0730. Take-off at Rangsdorf for Frankfurt/Main (arrive 0940).

0945 to 1150. Conference at Army Group C (also present, CGs First, Fifth, and Seventh armies): *General von Leeb* makes formal report that army group is ready for defense. By tonight, all front divisions will be in line, except 211th, which will arrive tomorrow. Reserves are moving in and by and large will be complete by Monday, leaving only three or four divisions yet to come in.

. . .

1130. Take-off Frankfurt.

1350. On arrival, von Stuelpnagel reports that jump-off time has now been set for 0445. Armed intervention by Western powers now said to be unavoidable. In spite of this, Fuehrer has decided to strike. ObdH goes to Berlin. Polish navy [three destroyers] reported to have sailed for British ports. Naval operation against Gdynia therefore canceled.

Von Greiffenberg–OQu I: Orders are prepared. 1600. OKW order for attack. On receiving word from Canaris, that Lipski is seeking to reach Fuehrer, another call is put in to ObdH, to find out whether we strike tomorrow.

Gercke: Reports on progress of railroad movements. In the main satisfactory, but strain is very great.

1620. **ObdH calls: Start sending out the orders.** (Fuehrer refuses to receive Lipski.)

1625. **Gen Qu:** Supply service all set; Communications Zone organizations are arriving. Ammunition trains have in part been canceled. Traffic control in Tenth Army area still in need of improvement.

Wagner: Evacuation? —Heavy Power Generator Company to Wiesbaden. — Executive Power in Danzig. —Protectorate (Neurath will stay). East Prussia has rescinded mail embargo. Ruling: Restore immediately by direct order! (This is not an issue for Executive Power; merely a military order.)

Our field strength: 2.6 million. In the west, we put up 1.07 million (if we must operate against Belgium). (Figures include 155,000 laborers on West Wall fortifications; 0.95 million, if not.)

In the east: 1.5 million. AGp. North: 630,000 (Third Army, 320,000; Fourth Army, 230,000). AGp. South: 886,000, of which 674,000 are in Silesia (Eighth Army, 180,000; Tenth Army, 300,000; Fourteenth Army, 210,000).

1800.   ObdH: Fuehrer calm, has had good sleep. Fuehrer's letter was not transmitted because it was contingent on Poles coming to him. Letter read to Henderson, who reports it to London. Poles were going to use dilatory tactics (tapped telephone conversation). Failure to authorize evacuations allows inference that he expects Britain and France not to strike. Reichstag will meet tomorrow; demands will be submitted (Danzig, Corridor, plebiscite). Enormous impression on the German people and on the world. Italy is putting up a comparatively big show. Hopes that Mussolini's influence will make its contribution to the avoidance of a big conflict. Restraining influence on France.

Some troop movements in Russia (alarm!). By no means impossible that the Russians will move, once we have had our first successes.

Belgium. No agreements on cooperation. No agreement yet.

Lithuania. No news from the north. "I cannot carry on much longer in this situation; a decision is imperative."

Goering: Von Stuelpnagel relieved of his post; Fromm has taken over (appointed acting Chief). Fritsch—Blomberg.

Situation: Is furious about von Ribbentrop.
Impression: England wants to keep out. *We should receive the Poles!*
Attolico: Il Duce has got in touch with London. Pressure on Poland.

OQu IV: General mobilization in Britain? (Makes it possible to call up 5th and 6th divisions.)

Wagner: Danzig only through Reich law.

2100.   Special announcement on radio: Fuehrer's offer to Poland.

2130.   **Bogatsch:** Aerial photographs, reconnaissance, bomber units.

2200.   **OQu I:** Possible sensitive spots in the coming days.

2250.   **ObdH:** Fuehrer has called up: Ratification of German-Russian Treaty. Molotov's speech.

THE POLISH CAMPAIGN

1 September 1939

0630.   Frontier crossed everywhere. Dirschau: Planes have started. Westernplatte; Landing Company. Fuehrer's proclamation to armed forces.

Weather: In List's sector, very good.
Tenth Army: Clearing up. Eighth Army: Fog.

0800.   Dirschau. Apparently did not come off. Air attack had no effect. Ic Koenigsberg: Unsuccessful; bridge blown up.

0840.   **ObdH.** Order of the Day. —Conference with staff (Schaefer). Several possibilities to get to East Prussia by sea and by air. No reports to Fuehrer that are not cleared with ObdH.

0850.   **OQu IV:**

West: Nothing new. No indications of general mobilization. —Time for assembly of troops extended by forty-eight hours. —Frontier not closed.

Intelligence work more difficult (numbers of the units covered); large units have mobilization number. England, Switzerland, Holland: Nothing new.

Belgium: Mobilization of second phase completed (peacetime army mobilized). First September: Three drafts ordered; this means activation of seven to twelve reserve divisions. Will be completed by 3 September. Ardennes border with France occupied by weak forces. West of the Meuse (5th Infantry Division), stronger forces.

Italy: Border guard against France mobilized. Reinforced by alpine battalions; behind them eighteen divisions in reinforced peacetime strength. First to Fourth armies.

Hungary: French pressure on Hungary to join the Yugoslav-Romanian block. Turkey friendly. *Bulgaria* neutral.

Yugoslavia: Talks with Italy —Western powers in London? (Grandi there.) Italy sends another division to East Africa. —Air force increased.

1000.   Fuehrer's Reichstag speech (ObdH in the Reichstag).

1130.   OQu I. *Fortifications in the west:* Eight hundred railroad trains for construction materiel (troop assembly 4,000).
Inspectorate of Fortifications: Construction materiel positioning. Pistorius.

Reserve depots in Cologne, Mannheim, Muelheim (200 km, 10 m obstacle). Request report by Inspectorate of Fortifications.

AGp. North: Overall impression: On the East Prussian and Pomeranian front the enemy has moved back from the frontier.

Dirschau (fighting also from the north).

East Prussia and Pomerania: Fog.

Oder-Warthe area: Group Graudenz has advanced. Group Mława has started off.

Suwałki: Nothing reported. (Brigade Brand: Three regiments.)

AGp. South: Fourteenth Army: Weak enemy. Entire 2nd Armored Division committed. Hauenschild advancing. Roadblocks.

Fourth Light Infantry Division and Second Armored Division 89 km [?] to the east at 0830. Third Mountain Division starts off at 1000.

Seventh Infantry Division, 0820 at Jablunka.

XVII Corps on the commanding heights west of Teschen.

VIII Corps [no entry].

Tenth Army: Only weak enemy. Second Light Infantry Division has crossed the forest area through the IV Corps.

XVI Corps: Panki passed through at 0800. —Opatów.

Eighth Army: All divisions advancing according to plan. Railroad bridges at Oderberg and Olza blown up. (Railroad troops on the spot!) K-organization has occupied several bridges. Polish infantry is counter-attacking.

Air force: No raid on Warsaw. Air force must make good what ground forces cannot handle.

West: French cabinet in session: Chamber of Deputies will meet tomorrow. No closing of the frontier, no evacuation, no military measures. Radio: No reaction. London Cabinet 1130. Evening both Houses of Parliament.

Disposition of the divisions on the northern wing of East Prussia. Check with ObdH.

1615.   At 1800. Cabinet meeting; want report before meeting. Text of report: Our troops have crossed the frontier everywhere and are sweeping on toward their objectives of the day, checked only slightly by the Polish forces thrown against them.

East Prussia: No change. Fighting 8 to 10 km south of the frontier at Neidenburg. At Grudziądz (Graudenz) our troops are but a few kilometers outside the city.

Pomerania: Our troops advancing from Pomerania are approaching the Brake River and have reached the Netze River around Nakel.

Silesia: Good progress of the attack in the direction of Częstochowa.

Industrial district: Our eastward offensive is advancing south of Katowice.

Olza district: Our offensive has crossed the Olza River south of Teschen.

Slovak frontier: Our forces advancing across the mountainous Polish southern frontier are approaching the Sucha-Neumarkt road, 50 km south of Cracow.

.   .   .

2 September 1939

.   .   .

1015.   **OQu IV:** Fuehrer wants to receive the ambassadors of France and England; we must not commit ourselves; links must not be broken off.

Eight Polish submarines in the Baltic.

British want to have their entire merchant fleet in safe ports by 3 September. Protection by naval forces on both sides of the Channel. Strong naval patrols in the northern North Sea. No blockade line yet.

1200.   Fuehrer

a. Review of the situation: Question is examined whether it would be desirable to move troops from the Corridor to East Prussia or perhaps better to cross the Vistula and attack the Mława Group from the south. After OKH presents its views, the idea is dropped. Report on the situation and appraisal of the situation.

b. Westernplatte: Will be done today, with ground forces in charge.

   1. SS *Schleswig-Holstein* moves out so that it may use its artillery to full effect.

   2. Counterbattery fire by navy, army, and AAA, which will be at the disposal of the ground forces for this purpose.

   3. Air attack (50-kg bombs).

   4. Infantry attack. Eberhard.

c. Evacuation authorized. XII Military District Red Zone.

d. (with Keitel) Allocation of raw materials must give due consideration to ground forces' demands.

. . .

OQu IV: Rome-Paris-Berlin: What do we demand for ceasing hostilities? Il Duce mediator.
Fuehrer inquires: Is the note in the nature of an ultimatum?
Reply: No.
British ambassador in Rome: No.
Latest suggestion from Paris via Rome: Conference at the earliest date, meanwhile truce.

1810.   To von Salmuth: (According to the recommendation of army group): Westernplatte 4 September. Has agreed.

1830.   Fuehrer's wish: Wants us to enter Poznań with strong forces soon. Inquiry to ObdL: Support by 7th Air Division.

. . .

Warsaw: Effects of air attacks. On the eastern bank of the Vistula neither traffic nor trench digging. On the Kielce-Warsaw line large number of trains in the district of Warsaw.
Radom-Dęblin line: Much rolling stock on sidings.

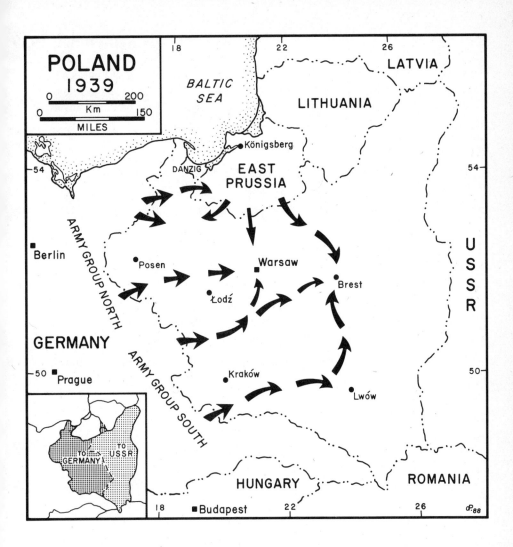

3 September 1939

0800 to 1000. Morning reports. Phone talks with chiefs of staff of Fourteenth, Tenth (Ia), and Eighth armies. Report by Chief Op. Sec. On the whole, good progress. Tenth Army must put its weight west of Pilica, divert nothing to the sides. Reserves must be brought up.

. . .

1015.   Report of Anglo-French ultimatum. ObdH called to Fuehrer.

1140.   Order from the Reich Chancellery: 76th Division must be stopped. —Poznań no longer acute. Westernplatte called off.

. . .

Declaration of war, England 1130. France 1700.

Changeover to war economy ordered.

Keitel OKW: English Admiralty has announced opening of hostilities. Fuehrer: Missions for navy: War against enemy commerce and naval forces. Air force authorized to attack naval forces, not the homeland.

State of war with French since 1700 hours. Do not open hostilities, but return fire.

. . .

5 September 1939

. . .

1000.   Talk von Bock/von Brauchitsch

We now have a different picture of the mobilization of Polish reserve divisions. Only regiments. Enemy practically defeated. AGp. North must not swing to the north, via Różan, but will use only Group Lyck to contain the enemy in the direction of Łomża.

Fourth Army will advance on Warsaw on both sides of the Vistula: III Corps to the south, II Corps to the north (perhaps reinforced by 23d and 228th Divisions). The motorized elements of XIX Corps must be sent to Third Army. The right wing of the army will advance on Warsaw, the left wing on Ostrów Mazowiecka.

. . .

6 September 1939

. . .

Op. Sec.: Report that AGp. South is taking a northeastern instead of a northern direction.

1620.   Stapf. Air reports on movements between Warsaw and Łódź to the southeast, and from Kutno to Warsaw. Also from the northwest toward Sandomierz.

Air force attacks *columns* and Vistula *bridges*.

Polish government leaves Warsaw during the night.

7 September 1939

. . .

ObdH sees the Fuehrer (P.M.). Three possibilities:

1.   Poles enter into negotiations: We are ready to negotiate. Sever ties with France and Britain; Rump-Poland will be recognized by us. Narew + Warsaw = Poland. Industrial district to Germany, Cracow, Poland. Northern border to the Beskid Mountains to Germany; western Ukraine independent.

2.   Russians have filed their claims. Narew-Vistula-San line.

3.   In the event of operations in the west, same line.

Politically we have no interest to enter Romanian territory. We must throttle supplies from Romania. Recognition.

Operation in the west not yet clear. Some indications that there is no real intention of waging a war. Gamelin: He has been requested to submit a report on whether he can promise successes in a very short time. Memorandum not yet delivered.

French Cabinet lacks heroic caliber.

Also from Britain first hints of sobering reflection.

. . .

8 September 1939

. . .

OQu I reports:

Left wing of AGp. South is making good progress.
Armor on the right wing of Fourteenth Army must be pushed ahead
more vigorously.
Vistula bridges Culm-Graudenz. Will!
Army boundaries Fourteenth, Tenth armies?
Long-range reconnaissance.

1030.   Stapf: Railroads Jarosław-Lwów, Jarosław-Sandomierz, Jarosław-
Dębica dead.

1715.   *Fourth Armored Division has penetrated into Warsaw. British troop
shipments Dover-Calais have started at noon.*

. . .

10 September 1939

OQu IV: Exchange of telegrams with Koestring.

ObdH: Study effects on Polish fortresses. West; air reconnaissance.

General von Bock (1015):

Turns Third Army sharply in the direction of road and railroad line
Minsk Mazowiecka–Siedlce.

Guderian's left wing (10th Armored Division, 20th Reconnaissance
Battalion) east of the line Ostrów. —Siedlce is crossing Bug River
wherever possible. Additional forces to Brest Litovsk.

Situation at Lómża: Still holding out (18th Polish Division) Nowogród.
—Wizna: Several lines of pillboxes with steel cupolas. Weakly or very
weakly held (18?); attack is getting under way in this sector. At Nowogród
and Wizna elements have crossed the river. Von Bock expects crossing
for today. Guderian is out front, pistol in hand!

Troops everywhere in good shape. Signs of fatigue in some instances.
One division has bad leadership; report will follow. SS artillery of the
armored corps herded Jews into a church and massacred them. Court-
martial sentenced them to one year's penitentiary. Von Kuechler has

not confirmed the sentence, because *more severe punishment is due.* Unit is offered to OKH.

Performance of troops is marvelous. Roads bad beyond words. Entire armored division ferried over vehicle by vehicle.

Gdynia will be left to burn out slowly.

Requests transport battalion for army group.

. . .

1235. **Fuehrer** has authorized flights across the French-German frontier for close and combat reconnaissance against deployment of French troops. Close liaison with Air Fleet III essential, since unleashing of an air war must be avoided at this time.

1245. **Von Sodenstern.** Reconnaissance. Artillery. SS units and motorized battalions.

Request: 1.   Divisions ready for operations as soon as possible.
2.   Bad impression of Raschick. ObdH.

Evening. San River crossed north of Przemyśl.

Britain: British soldiers at Perl. French troop movements from Lille toward the Luxembourg frontier.

Wagner: a.   Proclamation and public notice that all weapons must be turned in to the occupied territory. Death penalty.
b.   Directive: Uniformity of administrative procedure.

Jeschonnek:

Air Marshal Goering has ordered: Air Fleet 1 remains committed against Prague east of the Vistula. Will continue operations tomorrow morning, extending also to the roads from the northeast. Von Richthofen is given additional mission to prevent passage of troops west of the Vistula by attacking northern elements west of the Vistula, north of Blonie-Wołomin tomorrow morning.

. . .

ObdH: Strict separation between the political (OKW) and military establishment (OKH) has proved a great drawback. OKH ought to have exact knowledge of the political line and of its possible variations. Otherwise no planned action on our own responsibility is possible. The High Command of the army must not be left at the mercy of the vagaries of politics; else the army will lose confidence. (Breakdown of confidence!)

Changeover from East to West.

I.   *Eastern relief.* Staff Bockelberg is *set up.*
Staff Heitz to be set up soon, middle of this week.
Staff Cracow to be set up soon, end of this week. Initially under Fourteenth Army.
Staff Łódź initially under Eighth Army.

Later conversion of army Hq. into Administrative Staffs Cracow, Łódź, West Prussia.
Army Hq. 4, 14 for western front.
The entire setup under High Command East, i.e., Army Group South.
In addition Minister Frank.

Insert in western front

One army Hq. (Fourteenth Army, List) in First Army sector.

One army Hq. to replace Hammerstein (Fourth Army Kluge).

One army group for northern wing (von Bock).

Procedure in exchange of staffs. Organizations. Army Hq. already discussed (army troops will have to remain).

II.   *Forces for West.*

a.   Some Corps Hq. with corps troops. GHq. troops: Artillery, engineers. Divisions of first draft also Mountain Division (Pfaelzer Wald, Eifel).

b.   *Timetable.* Start right now. Order to army group soon. (Op. Sec.)

c.   *Area:* (a) zones for rehabilitation and training for stationary warfare, (b) army formations for exchange, (c) BdE.

III.   *Changeover to position warfare* means demotorization. Question of static corps Hq. versus change of corps Hq. with each set of new divisions motorized reserve group under von Reichenau.

11 September 1939

. . .

OQu IV: Enemy propaganda campaign on German atrocities in Poland. How can we counter it? (Wedel?) Reply:

1. We must get details of the accusations, then dispatch an officer by plane to investigate the facts.

2. Put propaganda companies to work.

Organized Polish units have begun crossing the border into Romania.

OQu IV: Telegram: a.   Molotov cannot keep what he promised. Russia wants to help the Ukrainians.

                          b.   Hungarians will not allow use of their railroads by our troops. *Is being worked on.*

. . .

12 September 1939

. . .

ObdH comes from Fuehrer: Russians probably do not want to start anything.
    Wants to form a Ukrainian state (to keep out the French).
Thinks it likely that Poles want peace.
Il Duce is forming block of neutrals. (ObdH: Work fast!)
Oslo Conference. Romania does not want to offer Polish government asylum; close frontier. He is thinking of limiting his demands to Upper Silesia and Corridor, if the West stays out. Clearing up of war damage.
—Executive Power! Fuehrer will let us know his ideas on the subject.

15 September 1939

0915.   Stapf

1.   Leaflets will be dropped this afternoon between 1400 and 1500. Deadline twelve hours. Civilian population (not eligible for military service, women, and children). Twelve hours after dropping of leaflets. Direction Siedlce and Garbolin. Tomorrow morning massed air attack [on Warsaw].

2.   Enemy radio message: Enemy at Wyzogród must break through to the north. Intercepted.

Enemy movements from Kutno to Płock, this morning. Air observation Air Fleet 4. Enemy movement from Kutno against Płock today: Aerial observation of Air Fleet 4.

. . .

2030.   **Jodl** calls up: We must now come to a decision as to what to do
about the Polish capital. Asks for an appraisal of the ground situation.
Reply: Complete encirclement of Warsaw in the west is progressing. I
am against an attack into the city. Starvation! We are in no hurry and
don't need the forces now outside Warsaw anywhere else.

16 September 1939

. . .

2400.   The Fuehrer has ordered the cancellation of the ground and air attack
on Warsaw scheduled for 17 September.
Planes will attack enemy group at Kutno.

17 September 1939

0200.   Report that Russia has started moving forces across the frontier.

0700.   Our troops must stop on the line Skole–Lwów–Włodzimierz–Brest Litovsk–Białystok.

. . .

Parliamentary from Warsaw.

18 September 1939

. . .

Jodl: 1550. Fuehrer will speak at Danzig tomorrow. Wants statistics on military
successes, prisoners, numbers, officers, generals, guns, tanks, planes,
etc., by 2200. (OQu IV with Gen Qu and Op. Sec.)

Von Ondarza–Haase–Lowiecz.

From Fuehrer's train

1.   Warsaw: Warsaw broadcasts indicate conflicting political parties.
Main reason: Communist government in Warsaw—already reflected
in Polish reports. Fuehrer would not like to negotiate with Russia
on Warsaw. Sacrifice no more lives than absolutely necessary.
Leaflets over Warsaw and over the radio stations. Result of Kutno
battle will make an impression. So would Russian advance. Open
up with artillery fire.

ObdH: Preparation for eastern bank. If there is an opportunity, have infantry make assault on the eastern part of the city. Opportunistic artillery barrage; if possible blast electric power stations and waterworks out of existence. We must find out where we can effect a surprise penetration from the north after the Lozo corner has been decided day after tomorrow: eastern part. (Kinzel, von Brockdorff to Fuehrer.)

No battle for center of city, if avoidable.

2. ObdH wants a few days in the present line; only question of days' marches to demarcation line.

Erfurth: War history OKW.

19 September 1939

Morning reports: No unnecessary movements to the east now! Regrouping toward Warsaw! Free Kinzel for Warsaw!

ObdH: Unauthorized activations ("senior artillery commander," interference with organization of replacements). Change in the top figures.

Heydrich (Wagner)

a. Missions must be known to the army. Liaison officers. Himmler/ObdH.

b. Housecleaning: Jews, intelligentsia, clergy, nobility.

c. Army insists that "housecleaning" be deferred until army has withdrawn and the country has been turned over to civil administration. Early December.

.   .   .

20 September 1939

Frictions with Russia: Lwów.

(Talk with Colonel General von Brauchitsch) Jodl: Jointly with Russians. Joint settlement of questions on the spot! If Russians insist on their territorial claims, we evacuate.

Decision: Russians "Liberators of Lwów." —German troops withdraw from Lwów. —Definitive demarcation line; disputes left for later settlement. No political tension must develop. "San line final."

Von Brauchitsch: Keep distance of 10 kilometers. Russians do not advance (Keitel!). Final evacuation step by step.

Jarosław-Przemyśl to the south-Turka-Four nations corner.

A day of disgrace for German political leadership!

Von Vormann: Upon urgings by Voroshilov, the Fuehrer has decided on the following final demarcation line, which is to be officially announced today: Pisia-Narew-Vistula-San (Przemyśl). Railroad line from Chynów up to the Uzcker Pass—not clear.
Wish to Fuehrer that we must not lose another man east of this line.

Von Weizsaecker: What is now the final line?

Von Bock: Russian leaflets dropped on Białystok. Warsaw counter-thrust to the southeast.

Von Weizsaecker: Procedure: Through military channels. Does not want to break his word. "Not a soldier must be sacrificed."

1710. Krebs: Negotiations concluded on amiable note. ObdH. Russian movements will start this evening. Demarcation line will not be reached before 23 September, morning. It is not known whether this line will be reached at all points. Order to advance cautiously.

Additionally: There will be no fixed special zones of evacuation. Movements must be carried out at 25-km distance. Thirty September has been agreed on as the date when the Russian troops will reach the line. On 3 October, evening, the final demarcation line must be cleared by the German troops. The political negotiations on the exact line are still in progress.

Great emphasis is put on handing over of all important objects directly by the German to the Russian units (airfields, large cities, RR stations, all objects of economic value, to prevent destruction by bandits). Agreement by liaison officers who will settle details depending on the size of the object. Russians have offered armed help against local Polish resistance. Final text now being drafted.

. . .

Text for OKW and OKH!

Von Vormann (from ObdH): After receiving report by ObdH, the Fuehrer has agreed to the following ruling: Purely military reasons compel us to withdraw German troops behind the demarcation line in eight stages. Time needed: Fourteen days, since actions partly still in progress must be broken off or carried through to conclusion.

Russians can move into German forward lines (Black line) including the towns of Białystok, Brest, Chełm (10 km west of Lwów), Drohobycz, Borislav by 22 (*p. 12*), noon.

Further westward movements from this line not until 25 September, 0600 hours, and in stages marked on maps to be transmitted in time by fashion.

Withdrawal of all troops behind the demarcation line will be completed by 4 October. There must always be half day's march between German and Russian troops.

Jodl: What needs to be done? Stipulate 25 September.

ObdH: 1.   Agreement with Russians on withdrawal.

2.   Warsaw. Eight days(!) softening-up attack, then air attacks; (water system, smashing of artillery; AAA out of action).

3.   Executive Power:

I.   a.   Fuehrer will inform ObdH on all decisions.

b.   Reichs Leader SS will do the same.

c.   Chief of the Security Police.

d.   Police commanders have to notify the competent military commanders.

II.   Extensive resettlement. Former German territory will be cleared of those who moved in after 1918.

III.   For every German moving into these territories, two people will be expelled to Poland.

IV.   a.   Ghetto plan exists in broad outline; details are not yet settled; economic needs are prime considerations.

b.   While operations are still in progress, which includes redeployment of troops, there will be no major movements and resettlement of populations.

c.   What could be done at present is a survey and study as to which population groups must be resettled and where.

   d.   Nothing must occur which would afford foreign countries an opportunity to launch any sort of atrocity propaganda based on such incidents. Catholic clergy! Not possible this time.

Action to be taken: Army Hq. must be informed on the special instructions which will be issued to the armies. The instructions will be officially announced. Local commanders will report before anything is done. Summary police courts. Reviewing authority is Reichs Leader SS.

.   .   .

21 September 1939

Krebs, 0800.

1.   Negotiations were resumed, in Russian, on 21 September, 0200 hours.

2.   Russian text of agreement fixed at 0400 hours. Idea of provisional intermediate line has been dropped, since the Russians attach overriding importance to reaching the demarcation line, if in any way possible, at an even earlier date.

3.   Dates fixed for the withdrawal of German troops behind the demarcation line: Pisia, 27 September, evening.
Narew at Ostrołęka, 29 September, evening.
Narew at Pułtusk, 1 October, evening.
Vistula at Warsaw, 3 October, evening.
Vistula at Dęblin, 2 October, evening.
San at Przemyśl, 26 September, evening.
San at Sanck and to the south, 28 September, evening.

(Southern frontier—compensation at Suwałki!)

Russians will reach the cited sectors twenty-four hours later. German text will be announced this afternoon after signing at 1600, Russian time.

Von Weizsaecker: Confirms information on the political situation.
Compensation on the southern wing (Ukraine) and on the northern wing (Suwałki).

ObdH: Will talk to Krebs.

.   .   .

24 September 1939

Morning: von Bock

. . .

3. Had to modify his impression after long conferences with commanders: Infantry is far below 1914 caliber. The impetus given by the
first line of attackers is lacking; all depends on the initiative of
the commanders; hence, high officer casualties. The light machine
guns in the advanced lines are silent for fear of giving themselves
away.

Von Manstein: Masses of refugees streaming westward toward our lines. Order
to shoot has been given for the night. If the refugees are allowed to
leave, it would be impossible to starve out the city. Moreover, the
city's garrison would be enabled to take full advantage of the opportunities for street fighting, with all its incalculable complications. A decision
must be made.

26 September 1939

. . .

Grosscurth: Lithuania and the other Baltic states will be sold to Russia (Finland
not yet clear).

Von Bock, 1840. Parliamentary Warsaw. Letter from Rommel. Twenty-four-
hour truce to spare population turned down. Officer for surrender negotiations promised. Shelling continues; will even be strengthened.

Army Hq. 8, Felber: Leaflets with text agreed on yesterday dropped at 0930
hours. Troops will be discharged. Officers will keep their swords. (Fuehrer agrees.)
Order: Step up fire! Air attack will start tomorrow 0630 hours.

Von Bock, 2015. Complains about alleged discrimination against Third Army.
Settled by telephone to Third and Eight armies and to army group.

27 September 1939

0900.   Surrender of Warsaw. Also of Modlin. *Rommel* (Polish) with Third
Army. Eighth Army turns over operations. Discussions with Felber.

Jeschonnek: Reports on Warsaw.

1700.   Fuehrer conference.

View of the situation:

> With understanding no extension of the war. Reasons for this view. Dangerous to view such hopes as realities. Reaction is not always with understanding; national interests, prestige—difficult to evaluate. Experience suggests that the war will continue.
>
> Consequences: Current situation known; in six months it will be different; agreements are not certain basis for evaluation. National interests are more important than agreements (Bismarck) (examples from the most recent history). The only enduring standard is success, power.
>
> Any opinion concerning the longer view is not possible.
>
> The majority of the neutrals shake before us and see ''our unsatiatedness'' as the major danger. They are used to the harsh handling by England but understand that their existence is not threatened, i.e., Portugal as example. These countries do not worry us. Their admiration corresponds to the bird's admiration of the snake.
>
> Large countries see us as the greatest danger, as the instrument to change Europe's status. The war, to this point, has increased fear and respect. There is no love for Germany. One must accept that responsibility.
>
> No certainty that in seven to eight to ten months the commitment to neutrality remains so strong as currently because of German victories. England will attempt to work against us. Given that effort, there is no certainty in viewing the future. With time the situation must deteriorate.
>
> ''Time'' will, in general, work against us when we do not use it effectively. The economic means of the other side are stronger. The enemy can purchase and transport. Time does not work for us in the military sense either.
>
> The hope is that everything, after a demonstration of power, will run into the sand. Chamberlain has reformed his war aims. The questions of peace discussions are already being assembled (not Poland).
>
> We must keep busy with other circumstances [continuing the war]. The conflict must be controlled by military means. Military measures must be organized for the continuance of the war. Militarily, time, especially in the psychological and material sense, works against us.

Psychologically: The current praiseworthy action is over, Warsaw. Growth of prestige. All historical successes come to nothing when they are not continued. The enemy's propaganda will attempt to undermine our successes. View that German infantry is poor quality increases enemy's chances in West. This view will be widely expected to increase courage and élan. Great victories have little staying power. Enemy acclimatization. By the first encounter with the enemy, even poor troops improve. The French can be better in six months than currently: clearly time does not work against the enemy.

On the French side one observes strong opinions that Britain does not carry a proper share in the bloodbath. That will change as the British arrive. They will contribute in one to two years a number of divisions which, while not necessarily good enough for offensive activities, will suffice for defensive action. This transfer will weaken the French arguments; the English tenacity will carry over and improve the French.

Views of other countries. Propaganda is uncertain.

Materiel: Our armament is not totally complete. The relative strength will not improve in our best interests. The enemy strength will gradually improve:

    a.   The AT capability will improve because of the experiences in Poland.

    b.   AAA is not bad today and will be much better in six months.
The opportunity for movement is possible only through the elimination of defense weapons. The defenses eliminate tanks.

Commitment of extensive motorized units possible only through control of the air. Motorized units will suffer through enemy aerial threat. Significance of AAA: Currently the enemy is very weak in this area. Tanks and air force are the keys to our success. If the Poles had possessed antitank weapons, we would not have enjoyed a victory parade.

The west is not well armed with these weapons today. In six to eight months they will be better. That time may suffice to close the deficiencies.

The most difficult is not the psychological or purely material, but in the possible change in the strategic situation. It is not impossible that one believes in France and Britain in an attack on the West Wall to end the war. Such thoughts will not disappear. The French will not attack.

Should they do so—where occupying space is possible—they will find only their destruction. That could only damage Belgian-Dutch neutrality. For us, such action would be threatening to the Ruhr area.

Long-range artillery fire. Every breakthrough increases the danger. Our air force possesses three or four times more fuel requirements than the enemy's. Consequences for the Ruhr industry and the coal requirements.

The continuing force of the blockade will soften. Belgium and Holland: No breach of neutrality. Gradual shift of the Belgian forces from the French border to our frontier in ten to twelve hours. They can do better with a specific time requirement. We would be too late in a counterattack. If they [the Allies] are on our border, they do not need any more space, but can destroy the Ruhr.

Therefore, no delay until the enemy arrives, but, should peaceful efforts fail, direct assault in the West. The sooner, the better. No delay until the enemy attacks, but our attack at earliest opportunity. The same is true for the navy. Ruthless methods. Lost time cannot be recovered.

Effort to evaluate the possibilities of troop strength and materials:

During the winter create as many units as possible. The British will do the same example as the Kitchener Army, which even the military did not believe possible. As in 1914, we have superiority, experience, aggressiveness. Some highly emotional remarks on the issue of attack weapons against a defensively organized opponent.

No doubt: In the area of armored and aerial defense the enemy is in poor situation; but six to eight weeks will change these circumstances. Mines will play a role which AAA can change; the small-caliber AAA increases quickly.

AAA security in depth impossible. Division has a depth of 30 to 40 kilometers. One can deploy more than that.

In the west every road must be utilized. The needed AAA guns must be moved expeditiously. To secure continuous protection, an AAA battery must be stationed every 10 to 15 kilometers. Must serve as air defense for troops as well. We are currently the only ones able to utilize such motorized movements. Our opponents do not possess this capability.

Where will the French find six hundred AAA batteries? In war seven hundred AAA guns? Why should the French develop such weapons when Germany had no air force? Estimates with genuine sources. English situation worse than French. In terms of AAA defense, our enemy is worse off than we are. If they could have helped the Poles, they would have done so. They could not help because they had nothing.

The weapons which today permit proper resistance against the shift from tactical rigidity to movement are in shorter supply on the other side than by us. Our attack weapons have demonstrated their value in Spain and Poland.

From these considerations comes the conviction that it would be wrong to let the enemy establish the rules concerning our operational conduct. Our ability to wage defensive battles improves.

Should we be forced into a positional warfare, then our only chance for success would be through submarines and aircraft. The best approach to eliminating the enemy's combat willingness remains the land attack. Throughout history we have beaten France when we were united. Population! Doubt the estimated French strength. No preparation for mobile war. A German division is worth more than a French division. French have less value than the Poles. Question of nerves! AT! The English are deciders.

Essential that immediate plans for an attack against France be prepared. Two essential points, even if returns limited: Improvement of the situation for the navy and the air force.

Can we demand further action from the troops? The greatest number did not see action. Others had action which demanded very little of them (in First World War one needed ten days to renew 70 percent losses).

Rainy period will arrive in a few weeks. The Polish campaign was the best practice/maneuver. Within ten days the troops will be totally under control.

Materiel: Insignificant losses. We transport as much munitions as we expend. War of movement consumes less munitions!

Motorized units: Medium tank losses replaced, light tanks short, perhaps, fifty tanks—broken tracks. If a force cannot make these losses good in twenty days, it is a poor force.

Guderian: Fifteen to twenty percent losses which will be made good quickly. Total replacement not possible. Views of the new tanks, thirty to forty tons, type III with 5-cm guns. Type IV are the best.

The pontoon bridge issue is ridiculous. Air force similar: better in spring, but we cannot wait.

France has no people. Here they are vulnerable. *Attack is no more difficult than Poland. When we cannot destroy the enemy,* then new positions with thousands of cement bunkers. *Our goal is the destruction of the French army*. Troop strength: Use what can be used. As many divisions as possible. Quality is less important. Eventually we may need two divisional forms which might permit only four weeks' training. There are always useful purposes for such units, if they can defend themselves.

In 1940 only the weather may be better than the 1918 weather situation by the offensive—comparison to Verdun. With decent weather the first three to four weeks are decisive. It decides operational success.

Fuel use of the air force: Concerning the attack on the industrial heart of the enemy (England?!). Leadership for a long war: Major concern is winning space. That is minimal. Better is the goal of destroying the enemy. Italy will give up its nonparticipatory attitude and participate. That is possible in three weeks! If we can't bring that off, we will deserve to be beaten. AAA as equipment for infantry use. Decision through:

1. Give up everything and settle with Chamberlain. No more a government, but security.

2. When not possible, smash the enemy until he collapses.

    The goal is to bring England to its knees; to destroy France. The best chance is in the north, which also is the most valuable.

Von Weizsaecker: Evening: Role of the neutral powers. —Distrust of Russia. —Fuehrer sidesteps Italian peace efforts.

Von Brauchitsch: Evening: talk regarding our stand on the subject set forth at the Fuehrer conference of 27 September.

29 September 1939

Thomas: Demands of the three services by far exceed our productive capacity. *ObdH must make clear-cut demands in the economic field*. Not only military and political demands, also economic demands. Air force in the east has used up fuel equivalent to production of one-half month.

Major increase of powder production not before 1941.

Germany has monthly steel deficit of 600,000 tons.

Clearly defined priorities within the military demands!

Ordnance offices must make full use of existing factories.

Within the army quotas ammunition production would be difficult to increase, even if we had the steel. If we start an offensive, production for the air force would have to be cut down. Improvement may be expected within six to nine months. —Supply of fuel and iron depends on decision regarding the west.

ObdH: Conference with Keitel on offensive in the west.

Stapf: Conference on offensive in the west, and instructions to inform Jodl on our plans and ideas.

Afternoon. ObdH. Conference on *report for Fuehrer:*

I.   We must explain to him our ideas:

    a.   Protection of the Ruhr.

    b.   Preparations in the event of a French offensive.
Ground forces available.
Air forces to attack enemy road movements.

    c.   French and British will reinforce their defenses against air and tank attacks. Counterargument.

    d.   Techniques of Polish campaign no recipe for the west.
No good against a well-knit army.

    e.   Season of the year. Days in November very short; fog, air support cannot be depended on.

II.   Recommendation on how we can stay. [Garbled—means their view of German intentions] behind Dutch and Belgian fortifications ready to go out to meet the enemy. We must resign ourselves to the existence of the fortifications. Declaration to Belgium! In the meantime joint naval and air action against British naval forces. —India.

Enemy situation: How can the enemy react? Effect on balance of forces and ammunition stocks.

If we want to make a really valuable gain on the political chessboard, we must risk a daring move. Our aim is to make the army an instrument of maximum suppleness.

Keitel (OKW): History three times.

Political pressure on France by means of a demonstration.

"Belgians are facing the wrong way. We shall surprise them." We must start out from having the army stand by against the event of a violation of neutrality, and remain flexible to meet possible political developments: What could possibly happen in the next few weeks? Possible developments resulting from our "readiness position."

7 October 1939

Wagner: Heydrich has seen the Fuehrer. Complaint about Mława. Treatment of Jews. Prueter comes here by air.

Order to von Bock on assumption of command.

1500.   Report to Fuehrer on northwestern operation. Keeps material submitted.

Fuehrer emphasizes:

    a.   The Belgians will call the French to come to their aid. We must not wait for that since France will do that in the period of the autumn fogs.

    b.   We must anticipate all this with an operation designed to gain a decision, even if we fall short of the original objectives and attain only a line which would afford better protection for the Ruhr.

    c.   Deception on fronts where we do not attack.

THE PHONY WAR

From the outset of the Second World War, Hitler had set great value on the Soviet Union's intervention in Poland. Not only was he convinced that the military action would be completed sooner, but also that this would leave the Western powers no alternative to war on Stalin or to a settlement with Germany. He believed that the Soviet intervention would assure a short conflict. This assumption proved false.

With the fourth historical division of Poland, signed by Germany and the Soviet Union on September 28, 1939, Hitler turned away from the east for the moment. He left the area administration to political missions who established a ruthless area exploitation (resettlement, cleansing, etc.) infamous in history.

Having tasted the sweet fruit of victory, Hitler disregarded the advice of his closest military advisers in favor of a peace settlement. He refused all suggestions of peace, except on his terms. With success, he involved himself more in military matters and assumed increasing soldierly authority. His interest was control of the European continent by defeating France. The political developments in Scandinavia (chiefly the Soviet-Finnish Winter War) caused him concern about his strategic northern flank. The escape portal to the Atlantic and assurance of Swedish iron ore supplies forced consideration of an unusual operation.

The real issue, however, was France, Germany's traditional enemy. Hitler never thought otherwise. For the next few months he pursued various operational concepts. Hampered by internal concerns, unruly weather, and political requirements, he found resolution difficult.

10 October 1939

ObdH: Blaskowitz ⎱Looting—general pardon.
Von Rundstedt ⎰

    Brand: Discipline behind the front. Divisional commanders.

Von Bock has inaugurated his "reign."

Experiences by Hoepner and Reinhardt.

1100. Fuehrer conference.

    1. He reads us a memorandum giving the reasons for his decision to strike a swift and shattering blow in the west in case he is compelled to continue hostilities.

    2. The possibility must be preserved to extend the safety zone of the Ruhr to the west, in the event of an enemy movement into Belgium.

    3. "Directive" will be issued later today.

    4. Mobilize everything possible and with the greatest speed! Transfer from the east.

Fortress divisions must be taken out and brought up to full divisional strength. Captured enemy material must be utilized immediately for the forces in the east!

5. Aims of the operation: We must make the French and British give battle and beat them. Only in this way can our superiority in leadership, training, and materiel be applied to full advantage. It is unlikely that the French would stop at their northern frontier. But if they do so, it does not matter; we shall then have an air base against England.

6. He is convinced that Belgium will collapse immediately.

7. Attack on such a wide front that the French and British would not be in a position to build up a solid front.

    We must not form a massive front.
    Split up the enemy front! Concentrate attacks against single sectors by a continuous flow of troops from the rear. This enables us to prove our superiority in generalship.

8. Even if we do not gain a decisive victory, we have still an opportunity to gain ground. In this event there would be little danger that we fritter away our strength in defensive warfare.

9. We must free all units suited for attack, including fortress brigades. The French fortress brigades will be of no use to them if they take the offensive.

10. He is convinced that we can force a decision if we are determined to bring to bear all our strength. (Compares our situation with the much greater difficulties faced by Frederick the Great.)

11. East. No change in the Russian attitude need be anticipated in the near future. Later on perhaps doubtful. In any event, Russia needs Germany's friendship to achieve her aims. Fifteen divisions in the east instead of twenty?

12. No deluge of new activations. Number of divisions must remain limited so that we can keep them replenished.

13. Date of the offensive: Through delays in the transfer of units and in the buildup of the western front, the army may cause the political leadership to miss the best date of the offensive.

14. No offensive with inadequate forces. We cannot be too strong for the offensive. Any unit capable of moving is better than nothing. Fortress divisions must be brought up to full strength!

15. Improvement of frontier must be omitted in case of previous enemy advance.

16. We cannot start the offensive with only sufficient armor and motorized elements, and air force. Our aim must be to advance the date as far as possible.

17. In case the air force cannot strike at all, we shall not launch an offensive. Air force must make preparations for launching coordinated counteroffensive.

18. The operation will have been planned right if from the outset it aims at a wide front.
    In the north we must interrupt as soon as possible the communication between Antwerp and the British Expeditionary Corps. British landing at Antwerp unlikely. Attack on Antwerp from the west makes fall of the city a foregone conclusion.

19. *It makes no difference to us whether a besieged city holds out a month or two.* In the east political reasons compelled us to reduce fortresses swiftly; but such reasons do not apply here. In the west our actions must be guided exclusively by entirely matter-of-fact calculations. Second- and third-rate troops are quite suitable for siege operations. "Every rifleman in an encirclement is a loss."

20. *It is particularly important that our air force should harass the French countermovements and counteroffensive.*

21. *Save ammunition! No medium calibers where light calibers can do the job! Must be thought through and borne in mind in drafting orders.*

22. *Armored units must not be used against cities.* They attain their maximum effect in the open field, in massive surprise attacks. He fears they may be scattered hopelessly in Belgian cities, above all, in the mazes of the industrial areas.

23. *Of paramount importance is the will to smash the enemy.* Enemy forces are limited. The French cannot replace losses after reverses. It is easier for them to replace their losses in materiel, but manpower losses pose a difficult problem for them.

24. He expects manifestations of defeatism in France. Question of blame for new blood sacrifices. Pacifist opposition. The French people cannot be expected to suffer irreparable losses.

25. An offensive is the only way to sweep Italy into action on our side. Italy now no longer interested in peace. Il Duce is eagerly waiting for the suitable moment to take the plunge. That is why he is not now making any offers of mediation. His armaments are increasing; very serious efforts. There is no reason to doubt the sincerity of his statement to von Mackensen. One hundred sixty-five thousand men in Libya; more reinforcements are going there. Fuel situation has improved. Oil consumption controlled. Various measures indicate that war production is getting under way. As long as we are sitting idle behind the West Wall, Italy will not enter the war.

. . .

14 October 1939

Prolonged conference with ObdH on overall situation. ObdH: Three possibilities: attack, wait, change.

None of these three possibilities offers prospects of decisive success, least of all the last, since it is essentially negative and tends to render us vulnerable. Quite apart from all this is our duty to set forth military prospects soberly and to promote every possibility to make peace.

Stapf: Travel report.

Instructions for assembly of troops ready.

16 October 1939

ObdH: Preparation for Fuehrer report.

Canaris-Raeder.

Summary of conference ObdH-Fuehrer: Hopeless. The British will be ready to talk only after defeats. We must get at them as quickly as possible. No use swinging out too far. He does not believe that the French can get there fast enough. French infantry not as hard as ours; use dive-bombers against artillery. Date: Between 15 and 20 November at the earliest; exact date cannot yet be fixed. Preliminary notice seven days before.

18 October 1939

Wagner: Points in conference with Fuehrer on Poland:

We have no intention of rebuilding Poland. Precautions against [sentence not finished]. Assembly area for future German operations. Poland is to have its own administration. Is not to be turned into a model state by German standards. *Polish intelligentsia must be prevented from establishing itself as a new governing class.* Low standard of living must be conserved. Cheap slaves. All undesirable elements must be thrown out of German territory.

The administration in Poland will have complete authority except on military matters.

Only one supreme authority: Governor-General.

Total disorganization must be created! No cooperation of Reich government agencies!

The Reich will give the Governor-General the means to carry out this devilish plan. Military demands roads, railroads. Garrisons as "Ordensburgen" on the security line or forward of it.

West Prussia and province of Poznań are to build up an internal administration under military government.

. . .

22 October 1939

. . .

Keitel, with Jodl:

1. Conference with ObdH.

   Conference with von Bock, von Kluge, von Reichenau Wednesday. It will be left up to him to decide whether he wants it on Wednesday before the general conference, or on Tuesday, and whether he wants it alone or together with the generals, perhaps at the same time. (Decisions: 1200–1400.)

2. Re: Directive for assembly:

   Army Group North: Ijssel inundation area will be first obstacle. Attempt not worthwhile. Trrops will be cut off! (Objections denied.) Group too strong (two divisions).

Second Army: One more division. Antwerp must be cut off from the north. Navy cannot cut off communications to Vlissingen. Second Army is given mission to encircle the fortress from the north, northeast, and east.

Sixth Army:

    a. From which army does OKH expect greater things, Sixth or Fourth? A tangle.

    b. After breakthrough, the ratio of motorized forces must be enlarged. Sixth Army must look after its flanks.

    c. Army Group Reserve.

Twelfth and Sixteenth armies: No comments.

AAA: [omission].

Main effort: In Sixth or Fourth armies. Army Group Reserve within reach.

Could we infer the following development from these intentions?

    a. Infantry divisions are apparently depended on to force the breakthrough. (Five crossings, two siege operations.)

    b. Has it been taken into account that Sixth Army must be divided after the obstacles have been overcome? Independent "GHq. Cavalry Group."

. . .

25 October 1939

. . .

Fuehrer conference 25 October 1200–1800:

    a. Still more from the east.

    b. Ten divisions from AGp.C.

    c. No more movements after start of offensive.

    d. Offensive will be broadened later on.

    e. For attack, move to front AT companies of other divisions, medium and light AAA. No need to tie ourselves rigidly to the order of battle.

    Army North: By what means are inundations produced, by locks or by dams? Would blowing up of locks serve any purpose?

ObdH: Area north of the Meuse not needed? Islands.

Von Kluge on Charleroi. Von Reichenau on Ghent.

In between, a new army which must be able to withstand heavy blows. Covering of southern flank. If possible, List should also participate in the offensive. Groups on both wings very strong. Catastrophe similar to that on the Vistula bend. Plan of operation: Wants main effort south of Liège to the west, but still unwilling to stake all on one card. Mountain artillery for airborne operation.

. . .

26 October 1939

. . .

Jodl: Fuehrer wants reports. Important change from original plans: Attempt to break through everywhere.

Hollidt: Himmler calls up in Warsaw.

Negotiations with Moscow on exchange of Germans in Volhynia (Galicia) for settlement in German territories, against Ukrainians and Jews. Four hundred German officials will go to Russia, 1,000 Russian officials will come to the area of High Command East. Will stay in country for four weeks, will be watched by Himmler's men (espionage). Inquiry whether we have any objections. Reply: None. ObdH.

. . .

3 November 1939

AGp.A: Morning, Twelfth Army (Mayen); afternoon, Sixteenth Army (Bad Bertrich).

The points of discussion are detailed in the prepared program for ObdH and in the protocols of Op. Sec., Org. Sec., Gen Qu. Other participants: Artillery Officer, Engineer Officer, Air Officer, Chief of Transportation.

Salient points:

1. At the moment we cannot launch an offensive with a distant objective.

   a. Personnel replacements have on the whole been received, but they have not yet been integrated into real teams. In some cases we are short of some officers.

    b. Level of training: Among the western divisions, even regular army troops have suffered from the long period of defensive warfare. The eastern divisions must get at least two weeks' intensive training to prepare them for the wholly different situation in the west. We must have these two uninterrupted weeks before the assembling movements are started.

    c. Materiel. Some of the divisions are obliged to pick up their deficiencies directly at the depots in the interior (will take ten days).

    Much of the damage cannot be repaired, e.g., broken axles of AT guns. Trucks of the supply services also show faulty materiel. Spare parts for MG34 and trucks. Horse replacements will not arrive in time. Ammunition, rations, fuel sufficient for current consumption.

    d. Some divisions will be absent from the lineup for the time being. Engineer, 2nd and 3rd Mountain divisions; and 34th and 72d Infantry divisions are still one-third understrength.

2. None of the higher Hq. thinks that the offensive ordered by OKW has any prospect of success. No decisive success can be expected on ground operations.

3. On the whole, appraisal of enemy parallels that of OKH. Naturally, every army group feels it will have to bear the brunt of enemy countermeasures. I do not share AGp.A's anticipation that the enemy will become active outside the Maginot Line soon, staging a strong counteroffensive, with distant objectives (right wing on the Moselle River).

4 November 1939

Notes for ObdH:

    a. Strategic analysis of the Polish Campaign. Interference by Fuehrer.

    b. Transfer of GHq. possible in twenty-four hours. (Signal Center forty-eight hours.)

    c. Fuehrer wants air-landing troops. Two more in addition to 16th Regiment! Details must be settled between Sixth Army and Student.

    d. In the event of an offensive, Gercke will not be able to move any civilian goods for a considerable time.

    e. Todt has been given orders for a new West Wall. Hannecken has to allocate steel for the new West Wall.

    f. Work completed on road movements of motorized units. (Maps of 7 November, time schedule 9/10.)

1100. von Bock:

    1. Von Reichenau again back in Berlin. In the course of today (Savoy Hotel).

    2. Goebbels will inspect the West Wall on 7 and 8 November, then go to the offensive wing.

Talk with ObdH on future measures.

1530. Thomas (Keitel not notified!)

    a. *Effects of a violation of neutrality on sources of supply:* Repercussions in Sweden (iron ore); U.S. wants to get it in Romania. (Fuel, food), Yugoslavia: (copper).

    b. *If we hold the Flanders coast, there will be continuous fighting in that sector.*
Will absorb large proportion of our supply. Cannot be done by air force and navy.

    c. *Belgium:* Needs 50 percent food imports. Will be very short on food next year (sowing).

5 November 1939

(report to the Fuehrer by ObdH)

Op. Sec.: Warlimont outlines the ideas of the Fuehrer!

    1. Armored units in Twelfth Army (Schell's recommendation).

    2. How can tanks be camouflaged in transit? (Change silhouette, cover with tarpaulins!) Time needed for loading!

    3. Radio deception in connection with Operation Student. (Throw enemy command into confusion! But care must be taken that this deception does not cause disorganization of our own operation.)

Long-range reconnaissance authorized over France.

Twenty-second Division, 7 and 8 November, Muenster.

Bork (on Keitel's inquiry): Once transport movements have been stopped, they cannot be restarted before forty-eight hours. If unloading points are changed, resumption of movement would take even seventy-two hours.

ObdH's report to the Fuehrer

Condition of the troops.

Memorandum—Countermemorandum.

Stand taken: Questions can be solved only by military measures.

Impossible in bad weather. (Yes, but also the enemy suffers under bad weather.)

He goes into a rage when told that front shows the same symptoms as in 1917/1918. Wants data: In which units have there been cases of lack of discipline? What happened? Wants to fly there himself tomorrow. As regards the level of training, what is argued now would still hold good four weeks from now.

Weather unfavorable also in spring. —Any other method to protect the Ruhr not debatable.

Any sober discussion of these things is impossible with him. Army did not want to fight, and so buildup of armament was slow and lagging. "Instance of insubordination occurred, such as we knew in 1917/1918." Which troops? What action has been taken? (Death sentence, West, East.) Gen Qu has full data. —Railroads. Refer to Gen Qu, Chief of Transportation, BdE, Personnel Division.

17 November 1939

Guderian: Two worries:

1. "On both sides" of Arlon.

2. Suggests 0-hour at midnight.

Jodl: a. No more hope for capturing the bridges across the Albert Canal in surprise attacks. Attempts to prevent blowing up by destroying cables. Dive-bombers attack (Monday), followed up by parachutists.

Plan to use gliders against bridges dropped, but Eben Emael project remains.

If we fail to get across the Albert Canal, withdraw motorized forces. Chances better on southern wing. (Enemy expects attack on Holland, bulk of his operational forces in the north. Make all necessary preparations!)

b. Utilize.

c. Under no circumstances without air force. An organization should therefore be set up that would enable us to hold off start of operation until receipt of a last-minute code word (2300 at OKH).

Conference: Goering(?), Student, von Richthofen, von Reichenau, Reinhardt, ObdH. Monday (twentieth), 1500.

.   .   .

20 November 1939

Memo for ObdH:

1. AGp.B. Plan of attack Holland, distribution of forces.

2. AGp.A. Plan of attack for Guderian.

3. Reserved roads.

4. Air and AAA map.

5. Deadline for stop: Armies see no difficulties if "checkpoints" are used. Von Rundstedt wants to talk about it on Tuesday. Von Bock on return.

6. Report of Gen Qu.

7. "Broken word."

8. OKW Liaison Officer at High Command East (von Glaise-Horstenau). Foreign Office Liaison Officer at army groups Hq. Bader's letter.

1500–1900. Fuehrer conference (Goering, Jeschonnek, Student, ObdH, myself, von Reichenau, Reinhardt):

Air operations in the sector of Sixth Army, and Sixth Army intentions are discussed in detail.

Notes: 1.   Next issue of orders 27 November.

      2.   Conduct tests with gliders in the units (Op. Sec.).

      3.   Blasting tests on canal emplacements (Engineers).

      4.   Holland and Belgium as one operation.

      5.   Armored units must be moved closer to the front. If possible all stagings should be so arranged that operations could be started on three days' notice (weather report).

. . .

23 November 1939

1200.   Fuehrer's address to commanding generals, Army commanders (including General Staff): Appraisal of the situation, necessity for taking the offensive.

1430.   Fuehrer's address to division commanders on the planned operation. Again the purpose is to arouse enthusiasm for the offensive.

1800.   ObdH and myself "Spirit of Zosen"; (Day of crisis!). Preparations must allow launching of offensive with three days' alert. Operations: Objectives. —Possible enemy reaction. —Further plans (cooperation of Italy). French frontiers of 1540!

24 November 1939

. . .

Von Etzdorf: Italy: Naval blockade. "We fully understand the political implications of the problems." Population exodus from southern Italy. Difficulties! Military reinforcements. Bastianini (London) two weeks ago: Every possibility still open, evacuation of Poland a prerequisite. ObdH.

Gercke reports to Keitel on moving up of armored units to staging and jump-off areas.

. . .

1 January 1940

1000.   Conference with Keitel OKW:

      I.   Reasons for tensions. Annoyance caused by obituary for *von Fritsch*. Top level distrusts everybody, including navy and Four-Year Plan.

II. I point out the difficulties in the conduct of operations. Interference in command a grave danger. Promise that there will be no interference in such matters. Von Bock to come to AAA conference! (*OQu I.* Send for Jodl to discuss with him our objective. Dinant.)

III. What happens if the offensive is postponed for a prolonged period, say six to eight weeks, i.e., middle of March? Directives are prepared for *navy* (stepping up of sinkings) and *air force* (attack on England).

Army: Preparedness must be maintained:

(Moving up of armor.)

Training (Tng. Sec.).

Activations. (Every postponement raises the question of how the loss can be made up.) Replacement army now has fully trained men; losses can already be covered by men now in training. Oldest artillery pieces must be brought into use:

Heavy artillery must be manned by old men. Potential must be increased. (Org. Sec.) (Check all points relating to army with OQu I.)

ObdH:

a. Airborne operations on a large scale. Airborne troops (paratroopers attached to ground forces as assault battalions).

b. Armored division to the outpost area in First Army sector. Divisions of First Army back for training. Motorcycle rifle battalion to the outpost area (Regiment. "Grossdeutschland"). SS units to the outpost area.

Deception movements also with tanks, e.g., practice advance movements, shifting, etc., within army sectors.

Scandinavia: Russia will limit herself to Finland (1914 frontier); agreement von Ribbentrop-Molotov . . . Sweden and Norway strictly neutral. General [sic] Quisling, Norway (one of Rosenberg's acquisitions), has no followers. It is in our interest to keep Norway neutral. In case England threatens Norway's neutrality, our policy will change. Memorandum OKW. Fuehrer has stopped the memorandum (Jodl). OQu I must get it!

c. *Bessarabia.* Dangerous! It is in our interest that the Balkans remain quiet under all circumstances. "Military diversion" would be most embarrassing for us. We are trying to arrange a compromise between Russia and Romania (1914 frontier) (von Ribbentrop himself has been put on the job for this); we have also got in touch with the Italians to reach a common formula. It is our aim to divert the Russians from the Bosporus to Afghanistan and India. Stalin reportedly not averse.

d. Progress of trade negotiations with *Russia* has improved due to our aggressiveness. (Russian demands very far reaching.) *Romania,* satisfactory progress.

e. *Italy:* Mussolini has sent word that he will approach the Fuehrer's proposals by middle of January. Use of *Italians in German operations in the west.* The Fuehrer is thinking of independent missions: Southern France, through Savoy, to the southwest. Even our promise to Switzerland would be no real obstacle. OQu I.

f. Decision based on weather situation possibly will be made as early as 3 January; this would mean start of offensive as early as 11 or 12 January. Op. Sec., Transportation Chief, OQu I.

. . .

8 January 1940

Gen Qu map exercise: Comments

1. Buildup for "Battle of the Meuse." Problems of organization and of road communications. Very difficult. Could be eased by cutting out returning supply traffic. —Advancing of railheads. —Maximum utilization of railroads.

2. Traffic control basically a command function. It does not make any difference who prepares the traffic regulations.

3. Fuel supply and truck situation must be handled by a central agency. Exchange of horses (heavy and light horses).

Op. Sec: **1.** X-hour! Three hours before jump-off.

2. Time needed by motorized troops in AGp. A equals time needed by foot troops (to reach Arlon).

3. How waiting period could best be put to use.

Von Salmuth: Speidel and von Sponeck state that tactical air support will not be available for several days (fourth day).
Elements with great striking power. Effectiveness of action.

Von Etzdorf:

a. *France and England:* Assistance to Finland under their League of Nations obligations. Land route via Narvik. Agreement of Norway and Sweden. Are we going to be informed? Prerequisite would be British promise of aid to Norway and Sweden in the event of a war with Russia.

Iron deposits in northern Lapland.

No indications that the Fuehrer is demanding bases.

b. Csaki-Ciano.

c. Kerchove's telegram (Belgium).

d. Caucasus British objective.

e. Debate in the French Chamber. Gamelin attacked.

f. Trade talks with Russia are not moving *Romania:* Very much in arrears with oil deliveries. —Railroad cars.

g. Bulgarian-Russian Trade Treaty.

h. Peace questions. Dutch Premier Colijn not received by Il Duce. —Roosevelt?

i. Visit to the Pope.

j. [omitted]

k. Today meeting at Fuehrer Hq.

. . .

10 January 1940

. . .

OQu IV (Grosscurth):

1. Il Duce. Warns against Russia. Continuation of present course means separation from us. Asks not to attack. Peace guarantees (Polish buffer state). Italy cannot enter the war now (armed forces not ready!); will join us only at the very last moment. ("Do not believe in my victory.")

2. Instruction to call meeting of the Ic officers in the west (to warn them against representatives of the Foreign Office).

3. SS decree.

OQu IV: British.

1500–1730.   Fuehrer conference:

a. Target date: . . . 0-hour: Fifteen minutes before sunrise at Aachen (0816 hours on 17 January). Basis for selecting this date: A high of rare intensity and permanence. January, then again clear winter weather with 10 to 15 degrees below freezing in Belgium and Holland for twelve to fourteen days. Op. Sec. Get information on thickness of ice. Embargo on flying: Air force specifications. OKW order tomorrow. Should the weather deteriorate in the meantime, date will be put up.

b. Thirteenth January, perhaps even 12 January. Big bombing attack by air force against airfields along the entire northern border. Also air attacks against pilot schools (70 percent of enemy fighter strength in the zone of attack). Then own air force will be withdrawn; dummies on airfields. (Have OQu IV ascertain effectiveness!) Pounce again just before jump-off.

Op. Sec.: Army groups must now establish close contact with their air formations. Air defense against enemy retaliation.

Chief Air Officer calls on ObdH.

c. Dinant—Ghent—Amsterdam. New supplementary instructions of OKW for ground armies are coming.

Op. Sec. Study implications! Make most of opportunities. Notes for report.

d.   Original preparations for Eben Emael stand. Op. Sec., AGp.B.

.   .   .

Keitel (on phone):

a.   Memorandum on Norway. Planning staff at OKW. Through Denmark. Winter? One division. —Op. Sec.

b.   Special directives on civil administration. "Simultaneously Fuehrer decree will order closing of the frontier." New version. —Gen Qu.

c.   Wagner proclamation redrafted; now on Fuehrer's desk. Gen Qu.

d.   Our directives for military government approved by ObdH. *Soon* to OKW.

e.   Conference of Ic officers. Foreign Office representatives. — Propaganda. OQu IV.

f.   Setup for last-minute stoppage of attacking forces must be maintained. Prepare redispersal. Op. Sec.

.   .   .

11 January 1940

.   .   .

OQu IV: Il Duce's letter:

1.   Proposal to seek ways to reach a peace. Restoration of Poland. Question of frontiers left open.

2.   Warns against offensive in the west. Military successes are possible, but all the greater then the danger that the war may spread. U.S.A.

3.   Go slow with pro-Bolshevist policy. As recently as six months ago Public Enemy No. 1. Now a friend.

"As an old revolutionary, I know that it is impossible to change ideologies to suit the exigencies of day-to-day politics."

Asks us to revert to struggle against Bolshevism. Conviction that fight against the Western powers is possible only after Bolshevism has been smashed. Remember common graves! Great sympathies for the Finns, although Finland stood in the enemy camp when sanctions were imposed. Possibilities of military participation are being studied by experts. Similar as in Spain. "If you go one step farther in your present Russian policy, a terrible situation may arise, which would compel Italy to make her position clear."

. . .

12 January 1940

Von Greiffenberg: Case of the flyers landed in Belgium (on 10 January). It must be assumed that at least parts of the documents are in the hands of the Belgians. What material did they get? Fuehrer has reserved decision. Should location of Hq. be changed? What has been divulged: location of Hq., number of armored units, Hq. of 7th Air Division, airfields of Air Group 2?

Report of air force to Fuehrer; ObdL wants to do the air attack on 15. (Offsets danger.) Fuehrer himself will give a signal for attack.

. . .

13 January 1940

. . .

Jodl calls 1345: Stop movement! Postponement probably two days. Chief Op. Sec. and Deputy Transportation Chief to Chancellery not later than 1430 hours.

Von Greiffenberg 1545: Air attack 14 January. Ground offensive, 20 January. Conference at Fuehrer's office.

. . .

14 January 1940

Conference with ObdH, 1130–1315.

    1.   Take up with OKW:

        a.   The repeated postponement of the date for the offensive is undermining confidence.

        b.   Effects of the last cancellation. (Some of the troops were already entrained and en route to front.)

. . .

15 January 1940

. . .

1245–1800.   **Fuehrer conference:**

        a.   Weather uncertain because of penetration of a center of low pressure. Impossible to forecast weather for an eight-to-ten-day period.

        b.   Minimum needed, eight days; battle at the Meuse on the fourth day at the earliest.

        c.   Air-landing inside Fortress Holland. New orders!

17 January 1940

. . .

Von Greiffenberg: (Jodl):

    1.   Decision: Jump-off with troops echelonned in great depth. No surprise (neither operational, nor tactical). Weather uncertain. Troops must be poised to strike instantaneously. No previous notification of 0-hour. At any moment! Complete readiness must be assured at all times (twenty-four hours). Infantry and armor west of the Rhine. During these twenty-four hours, no railroad movements, no return movements, etc.; resumption only after frontier has been crossed. Missions and objectives remain the same. Possible slight variation (main effort south of Liège preferable).

Holland in its entirety.

Not tied to a fixed time schedule: 7th Air Division. Time needed for reorganization. (Easter?)

2. In the future Fuehrer will divulge his plans only to a very few.

3. Deception measures: Old deception plan, tanks, staff exercises, etc. Plan of operations. —Battle only against British!

   a. Closure of frontiers with Holland and Belgium.

   b. GHq.? (1 February)

18 January 1940

. . .

OKW: No surprise. In contrast to 1918. *Changed method:* Keep them on edge. —Abandonment of plan must not be openly stated. Fiction must be preserved that we may start off any day. No massive buildup; a flowing assembly. Start of attack sets flowing assembly in motion. Preceded by air force action. Strategic surprise as in invasion of Czechoslovakia. Air force. Smoothly running on third day. Assembly of units in the rear must be telescoped. Railroads will remain at the disposal of the army until further notice (Fuehrer).

Conference with Chiefs Op., Org., Transp. Secs., and Gen Qu:

1. In view of the fact that the enemy in the past reacted drastically and with promptness to our successive attack alarms, the Fuehrer has come to the conclusion that the original system of assembly no longer affords surprise. Our policy must be changed.

2. The new method will be characterized by the following features:

   a. At the frontier and directly behind it, only the forces necessary to attain the *first objectives*. That is, *infantry divisions* as far as required for initial jump-off; engineers and roadblock *clearing organization* to clear the path for armor. (Air cover and AAA for potential road bottlenecks.) Buildup such that operations could be started at shortest notice (twenty-four hours).

    b. All battle forces and supplies destined for the follow-up must be echelonned in the rear in a manner that enables them to catch up during the inevitable stops due to road jams, border battles, etc., and so have closed up when the initial offensive wave has reached the first objective.

    c. Railroad shipments, large-scale road movements, transfer of Hq. will be initiated only after the frontier has been crossed.

3. Our job now is:

    a. To decide on "first objectives."
To allocate forces needed.   ⎫ Op. Sec.
Specify missions for air force.⎭

    b. It is necessary to think out carefully what effects all this will have on the work of other staff sections.

        Transport: Not affected!
Supply: Trains scheduled to run on the first day must stand by.

        Tomorrow I shall be at the disposal of the section chiefs to talk over their ideas.

4. In working out our plans we must bear in mind:

    a. Holland (difficulties with air-landing).

    b. Deception.

    c. Readiness to strike any time in response to enemy offensive.

5. There will be no "let-up period." Readiness to initiate operations in conformity with the present plan must be maintained until the new plan has entered into force. (Op. Sec.—Reply to von Bock.)

6. Organizational program will go on during regrouping.

7. Training program will go on.

8. Transfer of OKH Hq. Camouflage and security.

Wagner: Reorganization of columns: Three 30-ton MT columns and three horse-drawn columns for every division.

Buhle: Organization orders.

20 January 1940

. . .

Fuehrer conference, 1500 hours:

Situation compels us to adopt new methods. Reasons:

1.   Enemy has a fair idea of our plans.

2.   That plane accident has made everything very clear to the enemy.

Takes the gravest view: Is convinced that we shall win the war, but are bound to lose it unless we learn to maintain secrecy. Carelessness may lose us the war. We must have the fanatical determination to keep operational matters absolutely secret and to act swiftly in the case of an alert. ("Offensive through Sedan," date known.)

Careless talk, faulty organization, or keen observation of many separate facts (unusual occurrences): Means must be found to eliminate all these factors. Number of those initiated into operational plans must be kept to an absolute minimum.

And within this group, each individual must be told only what is essential for his function; no overall picture. Information must be given out at the latest possible moment. In giving instructions purpose must not be revealed. A request need not explain the underlying intention. Execution requires a large number of workers; intentions must be known only to a vey small group (departure dates, typists).

No one must be told that we have abandoned system of four-day alert. Everything will be done out of hand. (Wants report on measures taken to implement new system!) Enemy must not become aware of change in procedure.

Air effort to destroy enemy aviation is of prime importance. Present clear-weather spell is not long enough. Better chances not before March.

1.   Hence: Air force must deliver first blow; orders not until the night before.

2.   Other missions: Enemy command organization must be smashed. *Headquarters.* All must be attacked at the same minute, and with heaviest bombs. Other points of strategic importance.

Maastricht bridges must be captured intact: Occupation of Holland. Offensive must attain maximum penetration of enemy territory: Ju. 88. England thus will not be attacked from the air in the first days. From third day onward, small groups of Ju. 88 can attack England.

Target for the first days: Immediate action on limited number of especially important objectives. More may be expected from an attack with small forces, using maximum surprise, than with larger forces, but against an enemy poised for defense.

Clearing of roadblocks. Fieseler Storch planes to drop assault troops and transport ammunition and men.

Orders will be issued in the afternoon. Movement during night. Attack in the morning. "Leap from positions."

Our change of method must not become known to troops. Enemy must be left in belief that we still follow original method. Essential prerequisite of success. —Wants list of officers who have to be in the know.

Secret must be guarded in issuing orders. Divide orders! Don't say anything about intentions, just pass down the order!
    Total of "immediate" actions. Leap from stand! Desirable to include in "immediate" actions: Holland on full scale. Operation Maastricht. Passage through the Ardennes. Prevent demolitions. Figure out in advance at what points we might have to repair demolition damage. (Study those points enemy will leave.)

Timing: October would have been best. Enemy cannot do much construction work during period of frost. Frozen Holland affords great advantages. Weather always keeps one guessing. Even now we must take advantage of any period of good weather. Making the most of opportunities offered is better than waiting for the "perfect" weather. Accordingly, every opportunity must be seized. Not likely before March. *We must stand by prepared at all hours!*

Transfer of GHq. by airplane.

Idea that we keep alert period must be fostered also on the railroads.

Block telephones! (Fellgiebel). Spread rumors (Marras).

Order to all participants at the conference on observing secrecy.

Order to first attack echelon: Start off with two-thirds; improvisations. Make arrangements for elements left behind.

21 January 1940

1200. **(with ObdH) at Fuehrer conference:** We submit the recommendations of the army. He wants maintenance of instant readiness so as to be able to take advantage of any favorable weather period.

Thoughts of the Fuehrer:

1. In basic agreement with the long-range goals of Plan YELLOW and the effort to conceal the preparations of the main assault; especially on the south flank.

2. Because of the betrayal of the air-landing effort at Namur, the possibilities for the rapid seizure of the Meuse bridges between Namur and Givet—also in view of the freezing (armor)—are much worse.

3. Must consider the overwhelming significance of the surprise seizure of the Meuse in the direction of Sedan and the absolute necessity for protecting this opportunity through security measures.

4. Apart from an opportunistic attack one must, perhaps, wait for a long winter period of good weather, which can be expected, if at all, in the first half of February.

5. Must make the greatest efforts to have the preparations for Plan YELLOW completed in the shortest time.

6. The completion of the previously planned organization, at least for the first and second waves, is possible only in stages. Possible that the final effort must rest on the structure available at the time.

7. These stages needed for the final preparations must be organized to allow the troop formation and time which secure the important (operational and tactical) assault against the enemy and for the following forces (armored units).

8. Given the urgency, the following sequence might be considered:

a.	Holland	1 mot. unit;
b.	Sedan	strong armored strength screening the mission;
c.	Maastricht	1–2 armored units
d.	Ardennes	

Since the obstacles in the Ardennes (Fourth Army) must be overcome, strong armored units have the least possibility of operational impact. That should not hinder the use of small armored units.

9. It is a failure when armored units are committed to action without guarantees of operational impact and, as a result, arrive too late

or are absent at the decisive point, while overloading the approach roads of other troops.

1800.   Fuehrer (with ObdH):

    a. Disposition of troops generally approved. Wants arrival of divisions from the rear planned so that they can be immediately committed.

    b. To be carried out first off: Original plan called for smashing of enemy air force: Ghent, Maastricht. Now, Maastricht and Ghent (and Dinant) have been dropped, leaving only smashing of enemy air force (on which, as a result, all weight can be thrown).

    c. Holland "now in first line; the whole country." Employment of sufficiently strong forces to preclude any setback. He wants a buildup that ensures full success.

    d. *Maastricht* not yet completely ruled out (no air betrayal). Strong forces would be needed to exploit success; tanks on Hasselt and Maastricht. If action impracticable, tanks can be withdrawn from sector.

    Fourth Army: Cooperation of air force to blast obstacles. No tanks in the lead (mines). At the head of column infantry and engineers with assault guns. Tanks will be held up at Meuse (Givet). In this sector, therefore, tanks are not the primary weapon; come in second line.
Gliders for assault detachments against tank obstacles.

    e. *AGp.A.* Things will be much easier because now they will have no enemy opposition in cutting through Luxembourg. Held by comparatively weak forces with large gaps. Cargo gliders to Bastogne, etc. Sowing of mines by planes in southern Luxembourg. Difficulties to be coped with in a battle on the Meuse. Assembly of artillery will take five to six days.

    f. Importance of armor: Holland (including Maastricht corner): Army Hq., one armored division with motorized division (also tanks).

    AGp.A. Maastricht still open. Initially, keep back armor, using only some elements with others standing by. Fourth Army impossible. Blast roadblocks with medium infantry guns, etc., armor, whose strength in the attack must be closely followed by infantry.

g. Start so that armor is available at all critical points from the start.

h. Disposition of battle forces about as originally planned.

i. Air force for Holland.
Air force (on a small scale!) in AGp.A for mine sowing.
Fieseler Storch.

2200. **Conference with von Greiffenberg** on developments of the day.

.   .   .

1 February 1940

.   .   .

Warlimont: 1. Holland. "Armed protection of Dutch neutrality." Kiewitz.

2. Supervision after surrender of arms.

3. Doorn. "Courtesy visit must be paid to the Emperor; he is to be informed that nothing will change."

4. Removal of GHq. to Honnef. ObdH is to inform Fuehrer when he is going to move (Fuehrer wants to conform his own move to that of army's). Perhaps not expedient on first day. ObdH.

.   .   .

7 February 1940

Through the night on train to Koblenz. Arrival 0900.

War game at Hq. AGp.A: Notable points:

Red Army: Northern wing does not advance beyond line Antwerp-Namur. Southern wing proceeding from the area of French First and Second armies, enters Belgium in the Ardennes with mechanized forces and advances to the Semois River with mounted troops; reconnaissance elements from (French) AGp.A enter Luxembourg for reconnaissance (stop at the Alzette River). Plans to attack on A plus 7 (or 8) with about forty divisions on front Diedenhofen-Sedan, striking in direction of Malmédy-Liège.

Blue Army follows out our ideas. Ninth Armored Division not under its command. XIV Corps not yet set in motion.

Guderian insists on 9th Armored Division on the right wing for "tank battle forward of the Meuse River." (ObdH: This is impossible for reasons of camouflage, possibility of transferring of 9th Armored Division to the left wing is being studied by AGp.)

Direction of operation (very good!). Operation is developed so that XIV Corps reaches the bank of the Meuse at Charleville-Sedan on A plus 2; XIV Corps follows closely behind XIX Corps (two divisions).

Guderian wants to force crossing of the Meuse alone with XIX and XIV Corps on fifth attack day.

AGp. Command (Blumentritt) disappears. (Suggests to have XIV Corps strike northward.)

Red wants to launch its armored division on the eastern bank of the Meuse for an attack from the north on fifth attack day.

AGp. Command wants to attack across the Meuse according to plan on ninth attack day. Asks for seven medium artillery battalions with requisite Hq.

Results:

> *Attacking force:* Armor assault echelon must be reinforced by 9th Armored Division, which in any event could not be committed in time anywhere else! Behind it, 2nd Motorized Division and motorized regimental groups, followed by XIV Corps, which must start off on A-day and closely follow behind the motorized formations.

> *Infantry assault* echelon is handicapped by its depth. The follow-up movement, as originally planned, worked better. There is danger that steady flow might be disrupted on approaching the Meuse. Special steps to avert this are necessary, such as having infantry divisions leave behind their trains and moving up the combat troops on side roads.

> *Timing:*

> **a.** XIV Corps must start at once.

> **b.** I think there is no sense in the armored corps attacking alone across the Meuse on fifth attack day. No later than third attack

day, OKH must be able to decide whether it wants to launch a *concerted* attack across the Meuse or let the army groups slug it out on their own.

c. A concerted attack across the Meuse would be impossible before the ninth or tenth day of the offensive.

d. Red may at the same time start a heavy attack against the left flank. It would run into a defensive front nearly sufficient strength (half that of the attack).

e. GHq. Reserves must be brought up in very close succession.

f. Air force thinks it will be able to fly across the frontier not earlier than seventy minutes after the army has started off (state of training). (Von Rundstedt expects that it will take at least ninety minutes for the alarm to get through to the enemy air force.)

Conference at Hq. AGp.B, 1800:

1. *British capabilities.* Can move up four motorized columns against the Hasselt-Tilburg line as a first echelon, with a second echelon following directly behind. Belgian left wing can swing over to Tilburg. OQu IV.

2. Antwerp Tunnel: Are there other bridges or preparations for such?

3. *Timetable:*

The British can move four columns into the area Waal-Belgian frontier on second attack day.

Eighteenth Army can commit eight armored divisions and two-thirds of SS division against this force on third attack day, and 254th Division on fourth attack day.

4. *Regular army divisions for Eighteenth Army* must be moved up via Muenster (208th Division then remains GHq. Reserve). Approved. Op. Sec.

5. Missions for 22d and 7th Air divisions still in need of clarification. Air force.

6. *Follow-up of Army Group Reserves in the present disposition* is very slow (especially Sixth Army).

7. Proclamation for air-landing in Holland. Air force.

8. Air force is reported to have given order to bomb everything not positively identifiable as German forces.

9. *Transfer of officers is believed liable to cause serious complications.*

10. *SS is reported to have started large-scale recruiting drive, including age group 23* (several age groups ahead of us). Party circulates recruiting leaflets promising early registrants exemption from army service and assignments in Poland. (Fromm is said to have had them a week ago.) If this is allowed to go on, age groups 20, 21, 22 would be claimed and their best material eliminated before we had a chance at them. Allegedly no deferment applications for SS. Weitzel boasts of recruiting drive for 100,000 men for the SS. Fromm/Org. Sec.

11. Applications for deferments: Use method adopted in France. Fromm/ Org. Sec.

12. Hesse. Propaganda extolling the ethical ideals of the German soldier. OQu IV.

12 February 1940

. . .

Foreign Office

1. Sumner Welles. Rome, Berlin, Paris, London.

    Mission:

    a. Information.

    b. Groundwork for mediation proposal.

    Restoration of a Polish state. Restoration of Czechoslovakia on the lines of the Munich Agreement. No interference in the internal affairs of Germany. No limitless reparations. American contribution: Gold backing for European currencies, to rehabilitate European economy.

    Reasons:

    a. Surprise and confusion about the course of the war to date.

    b. It is anticipated that the U.S. would not be able to keep out of the conflict. —Collapse of Finland. —Military action on the Balkans and in the Near East. Repercussions on the U.S.

    c.   Domestic politics: Elections! Angel of Peace! Perhaps English initiative to draw in Roosevelt.

2.   Hull: Peace proposals to neutral powers. Formation of a front of neutrals. Peaceful restoration of international trade. Worldwide disarmament. Pope's help is sought!

Our reaction cannot yet be predicted. Welles will arrive in Italy on 1 March.

3.   Italy. Increasing strain between Italy and England. Tightening up of ocean controls. Time of Italy's entry into the war must not be allowed to hinge on any accidental clash over exercise of sea control.

Prince of Hesse: Il Duce wants to enter the war at any time when doing so helps, and adds no burden on Germany. The British are convinced that Il Duce is still following his old line. New phase of British-Italian relations. Any further deterioration of the situation would result in open rupture.

4.   Russo-German Agreement will be signed tonight.

. . .

14 February 1940

0900–1500. War game, Mayen, Hq. Twelfth Army.

    a.   Most vulnerable spots of *Red:* Carignan and on both sides of Sedan (especially to the west). Mézières bridgehead is being held.

    b.   Blue's using of XIX Corps in line at the outset of operations *indicates that they did not have enough infantry divisions up yet.* This employment of large armored units in a coordinated offensive must be organized in different fashion:

       1.   A tactical echelon distributed through the first wave of the assault force without regard to order of assault, and behind it.

       2.   An *operational echelon,* to be formed during the assembly of troops, which has the mission to follow up in exploiting the breakthrough. Details of disposition of units, see map.

XIX Corps strikes for Sedan with 2nd Motorized Division (2nd Armored Division in corps reserve) and for Mouzon, with Regiment. "Grossdeutschland" (10th Armored Division in corps reserve).

c. The ninth attack day is the earliest possible date for the front-wide attack. Technically it will not be possible before the tenth attack day. Transport for ammunition: Two truck battalions!

d. The wheeling movement of Twelfth Army, which is feeling pinned down on its left wing, would cause a splitting of the army when the northern wing continues to advance to the west. On the other hand, if the army keeps contact with the left while swinging the entire army southward, our entire front would be split on the army group boundary line.

e. The gap in our air defense system, in the Luxembourg area, must be closed by moving in AAA from the Home Air Districts.

f. Shortage in bridging equipment.

Conference with List: He is endeavoring to find new patterns for teamwork between armor, air force, and the conventional arms.

Guderian and von Wietersheim plainly show lack of confidence in success. Guderian has lost confidence. —The whole tank operation is planned wrong!
XIV Corps thinks it need not be alerted before the morning of A-day.

Conference with AGp.A. 1500–1600.

a. We review the resources for rapid closing up of infantry divisions from the rear areas.

b. It would be possible to bring 9th Armored Division to the left wing of XIX Corps. Best to commit the division in the second echelon.

Leave for Bad Kreuznach.

Conference with Commander of First Army:

a. Political matters. Attitude toward the SS. His own ideas on the subject. Directions from a central point.

b. Groppe case has gone wrong.

   c.   Von Witzleben thinks that Raschick has not been much good since his accident. Does not want him in First Army.

   d.   Heavy artillery will be kept in readiness for concentration on right wing.

   e.   AGp.A will have to determine the sector for 9th Armored Division.

. . .

18 February 1940

Fuehrer conference, 1200.

Introductory: Original plan was to break through the enemy front between Liège and the Maginot Line. Drawback was construction between "Fortress Belgium" and Maginot Line. Extension of the attack northward of the Liège area was considered to obtain wider frontage. The central feature of that plan was to concentrate the main weight in the south and to use Antwerp instead of Liège as the pivot of the great wheeling movement.

Now we have reverted to the original scheme.

Discussion:

   1.   *Surprise* may now be regarded as assured. It took the enemy ten to fourteen days to learn some of our regrouping movements, which proves that the earlier leaks were in Berlin. The enemy will find means to watch the border area more closely.

   2.   *Enemy offensive:* We have no definite idea as to:

      a.   Whether the enemy will advance automatically in reaction to our crossing of the frontier.

      b.   Whether the French High Command will give the starting signal for the offensive which assuredly has been carefully prepared.

      c.   Whether this signal will be given by the French government. It may be taken for granted that the operational details of the offensive have been formulated and drafted, but that the commanders in the field have no liberty of action. Most likely the French High Command or the Cabinet will make the decision. This means that the French will lose at least twelve hours.

Some people believe that the French plan is for the Germans to expend their strength in Belgium, and then have them run head-on against the strong French northern front.

3. *Our plan,* therefore, must aim at getting behind the fortification line in northern France at the very start. This calls for:

4. *Sixteenth Army* to get to the border in southern Luxembourg with the utmost speed. Advance combat teams! *Motorized eleménts.* Obstacle-removal detachments. Planes sowing land mines, etc. Purpose: To seize the terrain needed for the defense as quickly as possible, and organize it for sustained defensive warfare. The enemy would be able to launch a strong counterattack in this sector after three to four days, covered by his fortress system (Camp of Chalone, etc.). It would thus be five or six days before the main body of Sixteenth Army arrives and takes up positions, and the critical stage is overcome. Sixteenth Army will then be placed under AGp.C. AGp.C must closely watch this operation in the meantime. Question of rear positions. Question of artillery reinforcements. Supply route network (including field railroads) and signal communications network. Op. Sec. with Gen Qu, and Transportation and Signal chiefs. Think through implications.

5. *Twelfth Army* will become an offensive extension of the defensive front.

6. *Fourth Army* is now poised for attack with whole weight in western direction. This will not do, all the more so, as it is still doubtful that Fourth Army will be able to make a frontal breakthrough on the Meuse.

7. We need one more army. The weak link in the entire operation is the moment when List is engaged with the enemy and von Kluge reaches the Meuse. This weakness can be rectified only:

    a. By strengthening the assault wedge, or

    b. By having another army ready when needed.

8. *Allocation of armor* in detail:

    a. We must not adhere too closely to the *order of battle.* Form mixed commands.

b. *Tanks* allocated to any sector must be of the type best adapted for the specific tasks.

c. *Holland* will oppose our armor only with antitank defenses (4.7-cm Boehler), not with tanks; therefore, all we need on that front are about fourteen tanks IV and thirty tanks III, with the rest tanks I and II, for antitank defense at Antwerp. (Eighteenth Army)

d. *In Belgium* we shall have to expect enemy tanks *north of the Meuse-Sambre line;* accordingly there will be no change in original allocations. Self-propelled guns are a good weapon. (Sixth Army)

e. *In Belgium, south of the Meuse-Sambre line,* we need only a few tanks III and IV (7-, 5-cm), but all the more infantry and engineer troops (Fourth Army). Bulk of tanks IV and III, together with some II, should be in the assault group (Twelfth Army). With it go ATR units, motorized heavy-infantry guns, etc.

. . .

21 February 1940

. . .

Heusinger: Operation WESERUEBUNG:

Von Falkenhorst saw the Fuehrer. Fuehrer put him in charge of preparations for the Norway operation. Hq. XXI Corps will be placed under OKW, in order to avert trouble with the air force. Planning group will soon go to Berlin (Corps Hq. to Luebeck?). Reinforce von Falkenhorst's Hq.

Troops: 7th Air Division, 22nd Division.
One regiment of 1st Mountain Division.
Two divisions with assault equipment (seventh draft). Selection of commanders.
11th Rifle Brigade, reinforced with tanks.

Maps!

Denmark. Air force wants Denmark. Troops must be readied. Timing: Shortly *after* substantial conclusion of offensive in the west. Then as quickly as possible!

Not a single word has passed between the Fuehrer and ObdH on this matter; this must be put on record for the history of the war. I shall make a point of noting down the first time the subject is broached, not until 2 March.

24 February 1940

Report to ObdH: ObdH. —Tank ditch. —Jews in territory of High Command East. We must hear Blaskowitz on the subject—Gehlen. —Reply to Himmler. High Command East divisions as of May! Should they be replenished at once or one after the other? (Op. Sec.!) Buhle. Sequence in which they are to be released by High Command East. Industrial guards will be organized by High Command East itself.

1100. **Conference with the army group and army commanders** (simultaneous conference of Ia officers), Tirpitzufer. Points discussed:

New assembly order to meet the changed situation. Regrouping and disposition of forces. Date for the completion of regrouping (7 March). Training programs. Truck position. Subjects relating to Political Liaison Section.

Commander AGp.A is skeptical about the effectiveness of the armored wedge. Is afraid that the second and third echelons would not be able to catch up.

. . .

25 February 1940

. . .

Von Bock: 1230 (at his home). Worries:

1. Von Reichenau's army is too weak to take advantage of its opportunities. In particular it needs more armored divisions to exploit a success at Maastricht or Maeseyck.

   Reply: Cannot be done. Giving R. the armor would break up the concentration of the armored echelon as now planned; armor would then have to be committed teamed up with infantry.

   Training: Combined exercises of infantry and armor.

Available immediately for close support. Twentieth Division (motorized) and those elements for which von Kuechler has no room at his front.

2. Engineers and artillery cannot be released without jeopardizing von Reichenau's mission. (Op. Sec. must check whether and when new forces become available.) (Jacob: More needs to be done for construction of improvised bridges.)

3. Replacements necessary for canceled two divisions. Von Bock now also wants to close up more compactly to the front and so make room in the rear for two additional divisions.

(*Op. Sec.* These two divisions must be brought up. Consult with Tng. Sec. on locations. Divisions may remain GHq. Reserve.)

. . .

26 February 1940

. . .

OQu IV: Welles wants to form a block of neutrals if his peace mission fails.

Von Papen:	France wants to relieve Finland by an attack on Baku(?!). Turks will not agree.
Bruns:	Spanish report on alleged low morale in France. Question of the exchange of codes with Italy.
	Exchange of material on Yugoslavia with Hungary disapproved.
	Bircher-Xylander. German-Swiss doctors on our western front.

Notes:

Gen Qu:	If mission of Sixth Army is altered, could they do without some of their units?
Org. Sec.:	Fifteen corps artillery commanders, eight regimental artillery commanders. At what time intervals?
Tng. Sec.:	Officer candidate schools for three-year NCOs.

> *Org. Sec.:*   XXXVII Corps Hq. (reduced). (Ras-
> chick) will get new CG and will relieve
> IX Corps. Schwandner, Raschick, gen-
> erals on special assignment, for training.
> Get them an adjutant and a clerk each!

8 March 1940

. . .

Conference, von Greiffenberg/Liss about study on movements incidental to Operation YELLOW. Very good and sound job! Envisage attacking tank spearheads appearing on the Meuse on the fourth day, and possibility of enemy attack in force across the Meuse in fourteen days at the earliest.

13 March 1940

Conference at Koblenz.

1000. AGp.A: Outline of the fundamental and special features of Operation YELLOW in line with *von Sodenstern's* memorandum, designed to ensure unified conception and action.

Fourth Army: Presentation of plans. Airfields, especially fighters, are a long way off; must be moved forward quickly; transfer, if possible, by air.

Twelfth Army: Question of XVIII Corps is brought up.

Sixteenth Army: No special problems.

Group Kleist: On the whole all right. Objectives of airborne operation (Storch planes) not yet decided. —Training of armored troops! (Must be so arranged that elements of the armored divisions are ready for operations at any time.)

1400. AGp.B: Development of the plan of operations. Reasons for the present plan.

!!
Bock
{ Fourth Armored Division ready for commitment, but not for attack. No command tanks; company commanders may not be in a position to exercise control over operations.

Ninth Armored Division has unusually high number of tanks not ready for action.

Second AAA Corps will take no responsibility for AAA protection of X and IX Corps; protection on the Meuse.

Trojan Horse [attack on the Nijmegen bridges]?

Radio channel to 7th Air Division must still be clarified.

Eighteenth Army: It would be well to reexamine advisability of moving SS V to the front earlier. (Alert the night before.) Everything apart, it does seem to me that the commitment north of the IJssel is too large a force.

Sixth Army: Possibility must be preserved to make an instant thrust with 3rd Armored Division on Hasselt.

1600. **AGp.C:** Sixtieth Division around Kaiserslautern. Will go into action *x* plus 2 or *x* plus 3. Saarbruecken first, then other subsidiary attacks so that impression is maintained for some days after Saarbruecken that they are the preliminaries to a major offensive.

Army Group: Submit proposals on timing! Five days after announcement.

Material for obstacle and position construction: Order must be issued.

Right wing. Von Witzleben! Nine 10-cm batteries have been prepared. Signal communications after transfer of Sixteenth Army to AGp.C Hq. AGp.C at Wittlich?

Dollman thinks he cannot free the good divisions before the end of four weeks—middle of April.

Von Witzleben is eight hundred men short in each division.

17 March 1940

Fuehrer conference on 16 as well as that on 15 March produced no new viewpoints.

General impression: The Fuehrer now approves the preparations made and is manifestly confident of success.

Interesting points:

1. Decision reserved on further moves after the crossing of the Meuse.

2. He reckons with the possibility that the French and British might adopt a passive attitude in the face of our invasion. This belief,

he feels, is justified by the difficulties of prompt communication between the political and military authorities.

3. He plays with the idea that a mild bleeding of the enemy forces will suffice to break their will to resist.

1100–1330. **Long conference with Dr. Goerdeler,** who, emphasizing the economic problems, stresses the necessity of making peace before outbreak of open hostilities, and points to the possibility of a favorable compromise.

. . .

26 March 1940

. . .

5. Upper Rhine operation.

 a. Forces: Thirty German divisions unlikely and initially probably not more than twelve [Italian divisions].

 b. Time required: Logistical preparations at least three weeks; movement to the front at least three weeks; a total of six weeks. Italian army not mobilized; needs time for mobilization; i.e., at least six weeks. All in all, twelve weeks. Not likely to be ready for operations before July, and it may be even later if more divisions come.

 c. Purpose of the operation—two possibilities:

  (1) If the operation is calculated to play a part in smashing the enemy fighting forces, i.e., to complete or continue on another front the job started in Belgium and Holland, it must be staged in sufficient strength, which requires long preparation. It would be pointless in pursuing this objective to combine the operation with an operation through Savoy.

  (2) If the operation is designed to *contain* enemy forces, it must be launched concurrently with our big offensive. Inasmuch as it would have to be called on short notice, it would, of necessity, be a weaker effort, at least in the initial phase.

> On no account must the operation be allowed to divert our attention from the major operational objective so long as we can see any possibility of attaining it. That objective is the Lower Seine.

d. The suggestion might be made to change over to Operation GREEN in the event that the results of the Belgian offensive are inconclusive, and to launch a strong Upper Rhine offensive within the framework of Operation GREEN. I have no sympathy at all for this scheme which is reminiscent of Ludendorff's policy of unceasing attacks in 1918. It would mean the adoption of the strategy of attrition, a policy that is sterile of success. If we reach that point, I'd rather shift to the defensive.

e. Meanwhile some more intensive work must be put into computation of strength requirements, especially artillery and bridging equipment, and into planning the disposition of troops for battle, the initial attacks, and the individual missions.

> Even now we can be sure that the Italians will make heavy additional demands for AAA, medium artillery, and bridge-construction units.

> Also take along material on preparations for pillbox destruction.

Holland: Von Falkenhausen? Op. Sec.

1700–1900. Conference at ObdH with Generals von Leeb and Felber on YELLOW, GREEN, and BROWN.

1330. Luncheon with the Fuehrer. Present: Generals von Leeb, von Witzleben, Dollmann, Felber, ObdH, and I.

1415–1730. Fuehrer conference:

1. General von Leeb presents reports:

a. General situation, French and German combat tactics.

b. Construction of fortified positions: He emphasizes importance of not stinting in the use of steel on the weak spots north and south of Saarbruecken. Attention is forcefully drawn to weakness of the position north of Saarbruecken. Fuehrer interjects here that his desire to have the main battle line on the dominant heights on the southern bank of the Saar was frustrated by the outbreak of the war.

    c.   Diversionary attack YELLOW. The claim is made that no feinting operations should be initiated on the Rhine front because of a possible later offensive on the Upper Rhine. Closing of the *Swiss* frontier is discussed; will be impracticable until the start of the actual attack, on account of coal shipments to Italy.

        The question of an alternate route for coal shipments to Italy must be studied. (Op. Sec. Gercke.)

    d.   Operation GREEN.

2.   General von Witzleben reviews Operation YELLOW. The report is accepted without comment. In the subsequent discussion on fortifications construction the Fuehrer stresses the importance of artillery emplacements. *Jacob.*

3.   General Dollman speaks briefly on the situation in Seventh Army, stressing its deficiencies. Outlines three assault crossings for Operation YELLOW. Op. Sec.

4.   Afterwards, the Fuehrer discourses on the general situation, without mentioning operation on Upper Rhine (BROWN). He emphatically reiterates his confidence in Mussolini and expresses his understanding for the fact that Italy is too weak to come in before France has been dealt a heavy blow. He observes the eastern situation continuously and with great care. French actions aiming at a rupture with Russia are evidently just what he wants. He is pleased with the recall of the Russian ambassador from Paris. In conclusion he expresses his satisfaction with the good use made by the Wehrmacht of the forced inactivity of the past six months and acknowledges the efficacy of the preparations effected, which inspire him with faith in full success. (Never since 1870 has there been such a favorable balance of political and military strength.)

5.   Afterwards, conference of the Fuehrer with ObdH and Chief of General Staff on continuance of the operation following the first assault, and on an offensive on the Upper Rhine.

Regarding GREEN: At the moment, a decisive major offensive against the Maginot Line is ruled out by a lack of the requisite means. However, as the situation develops and the French forces are inflicted punishing blows, it would be possible to follow up with this attack, even with comparatively weak forces reinforced by Italian troops, within the general scope of Operation GREEN.

Regarding YELLOW: We must gain a better jump-off line in the Saar for a subsequent offensive within scope of Operation GREEN. On the Upper Rhine we must drop the plans for a feint attack.

On continuance of the main offensive: It would be desirable to push the offensive all the way to the Seine, leaving Paris aside. Then, when the enemy attacks the front of Twelfth and Sixteenth armies, we must strike in the direction of the Plateau de Langres and destroy the enemy in northeastern France by an offensive from the sector of AGp.C, also using Italian forces.

Regarding BROWN: For this offensive we may reckon with about twenty Italian divisions. At the outset of the offensive, Italy will be requested to get ready. Italy will need two weeks for mobilization. During those fourteen days it will become clear whether or not we have any prospects of a major success.

If the prospects are good, Italy is sure to march. It will take the Italians twenty days to get their troops over to us; so if everything goes according to plan, we should be able to strike on the Upper Rhine about six weeks after the initial assault in the Upper Rhine.

Road signs, maps must be held in readiness. Prepare ammunition dumps with field railways, quarters, staging areas, etc.

Target dates: Fuehrer tells me that he wants to start Operation WESERUEBUNG on 9 or 10 April. YELLOW will be launched four to five days later (probably Sunday, 14 April). Gercke, Chief Op.

. . .

28 March 1940

Blumentritt (1000–1100). Reports on preparations by AGp.A. Readying of armored divisions.

Mieth, von Greiffenberg, Heusinger: Results of Fuehrer conference. —Target dates.

Assignments: Select planning material that has to be turned over to von Leeb.

Order to von Leeb: Compute necessary strength.

Work schedule for preparations.

1430. *Strength estimates:*

a.   *For offensive operation:* 72 divisions earmarked for offensive.

Added now	16 divs.
By May	14 divs.
Total about	100 divs. for the offensive.

Enemy: About 100. [divs.]
Nothing must be taken away from that force.

b.   *For von Leeb:* Four static divisions, twenty-nine divisions of varying value.

For BROWN we need at least six divisions in addition to the twenty Italian divisions, leaving for GREEN, twenty-three divisions (First Army at present has thirteen divisions), i.e., ten more divisions than originally allotted. With that, one cannot undertake an effective offensive.

The *order to von Leeb* accordingly runs: He can figure on a total of about thirty divisions (not counting the static divisions) and twenty Italian divisions. With that force he is to conduct an operation for the capture of the Burgundian Gap and the western edge of the southern Vosges Mountains, which would permit continuance of the operation in either a western or southwestern direction. We must ascertain whether our forces would be sufficient to support this offensive by a drive from the Saarbruecken area. Thought should also be given to planning for extension of this operation toward Baccarat in the event that substantial forces should become available in consequence of failure of the northern operation to push through.

List of demands for Italy.

.   .   .

1 April 1940

0945.   Arrive at Berlin Gruenewald Station.

OQu IV: Telegram to von Rintelen. Conference with Roatta middle of April. Von Rintelen will come here probably on 8 April.

Weinknecht: Economic measures prepared for prospective occupied territories (digest).

Wagner: Survey of terrain in Black Forest. —Todt Ministry. —Tank spare parts. Depots at Bittburg and Cologne. —Fuel situation: Consumption.

Von Greiffenberg: Von Stuelpnagel. —Operation BROWN. Current matters.

Mieth: Proposal to launch offensive across the Upper Rhine north of Strassburg. Reasons: Easier terrain, better roads, better tactical coordination with Operation HAWK, left flank can lean on the Danube. Forces to be committed in HAWK eighteen divisions, in this offensive twenty divisions.

In my opinion such an offensive is on too narrow a frontage and would produce only tactical results. Moreover, it would not fit into the military-political requirement of the Supreme Command.

Heim: Organization of the section on "special assignment," i.e., guerilla fighting in the east!

8 April 1940

. . .

Winter, Op. Sec.: Operational study on Romania. Result: The enemy coalition, using Saloníki as disembarking point, could start operations at the Romanian border with motorized forces after six days, with infantry after about twenty-eight days, that is, in the wholly unlikely eventuality that Bulgaria stands by without intervening.

Stapf: Reports after recovery from illness. Wants to talk with the Field Marshal [Goering] as to whether in future it would be necessary to assign liaison officers, considering that the Op. Secs. were maintaining very close contact with each other. To me it would seem desirable to retain this institution, (if only) for its extramilitary usefulness.

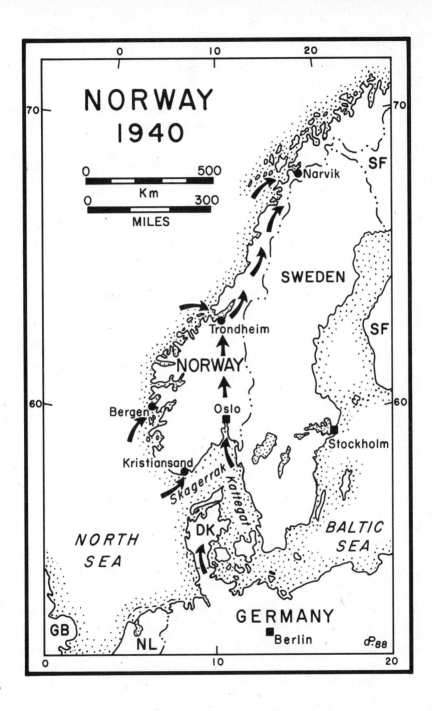

Von Etzdorf:

> a. Orientation on the diplomatic strategy in connection with Operation WESERUEBUNG.
>
> b. Anglo-French note on mine laying in Norwegian waters. Unconfirmed report that Sweden has posted a first preliminary stage of mobilization (von Puttkamer).
>
> c. Radio silence in England; indication that the British fleet is putting to sea.
>
> d. I brief him on target dates in immediate future and on military conversations with the Italians.

. . .

THE NORWEGIAN CAMPAIGN

9 April 1940

Since 0515 hours our troops have been landing in Norway and marching into Denmark.

> a. Trondheim, Bergen, Narvik occupied. There is still action off Kristiansand. Fighting at Oslo. Landing at Moss and Droeback.
>
> b. Denmark, under protest, has accepted the German conditions. Troops have been ordered not to resist. Occupation of Jutland and of the islands entirely according to plan.
>
> c. Air force commenced operation at 0730, as scheduled. Order has been given to attack military targets at Oslo.
>
> d. 0515. *Von Scharnhorst* and *von Gneisenau* in action west of the Lofoten Islands. No new reports up to now, engagement apparently broken off.

1000.   Talk with Colonel Wagner on preparations for taking Denmark under our administration. (Gen Qu)

Gercke: The 198th and 214th divisions, which will be used as reinforcements for Norway, instead of Denmark, must be directed to the Baltic ports between Luebeck and Stettin.

Von Brauchitsch: New man to replace Becker. —Activate new corps Hq. (middle of April), but leave appointment of commanding generals open. I suggest Colonel Buhle (or also Stapf and Geib) to replace Becker. V. Br. has Bockelberg in mind.

Wagner:

    a. Reports on survey in the Black Forest.

    b. Buerckel rather than Sprenger as Civil Administrator, Chief in First Army, or we shall never see the end of that tug-of-war.

    c. Supply base *Vienna* (fuel, ammunition).

    d. Steps to preclude careless destruction of economic assets (collection of booty, propaganda, order through General Staff channels).

General Jacob: Friction with Todt (Orscholz barrier rules).

Kinzel, report on tour:

    1. Hungarian ideas on Romania. Hungary requests early *conference* of experts, to enable her to start preparations. Budapest. Hungary would have to appear as the liberator in *Transylvania*. Horthy insists on role of Commander in Chief. Demands Italy must be informed if such conversations are going to take place. (Not of substance, but of the fact.) We would have to look after our own logistical arrangements. —Hungarians will mass forces against northwest. Reply by ObdH.

    2. Exchange of views of Yugoslavia. Agreement.

    3. Domestic situation: Jews, clergy, nobility.

    4. Disappointment over our failure to deliver arms.

    5. Hungarians are not going to fortify Carpathian border.

1630.   All landing operations completed, except at Oslo. 1800: Oslo in our hands; proclamation asking population to return.

1900. General Jodl:

    a. Occupation completed. Completion of defensive preparations not yet assured, owing to delay in arrival of transports with requisite forces. Air force will help out.

    b. Four air transport squadrons scheduled for cargo lift will be used for shipment of additional forces to Norway instead.

    c. Losses: SS *Bluecher* sunk. One transport vessel sunk with one 10.5 AAA battery, ammunition, horses, and infantry elements of 69th Division. Combat casualties highest at Kristiansand and Oslo; elsewhere light.

    d. British fleet attacked by Ju. 88; serious hits scored on three ships.

    e. Rumor of Swedish mobilization unfounded.

1915. *Buschenhagen:* Denmark landing went smoothly. At the very beginning some MG fire on the border. Casualties light. Air-landing came off smoothly.

Norway: Narvik without losses, only weak resistance. Trondheim taken without losses; weak resistance. Bergen and Stavanger, the same.

Kristiansand: Heavy fighting, losses. Egersund and Arendal: Slight resistance. Oslo was alerted. Opposition of the shore batteries, especially in the Droeback Strait. SS *Luetzow* sunk. She carried the Hq. of 163d Division, parts of Hq. of XXI Corps, and eight hundred men. Bombers silenced shore batteries. With two battalions, we now are in full control of the city. A third battalion will be moved today (of 163d Division, Engelhard). Tomorrow four to six additional battalions!

Norwegian government has fled to Hamar. Paratroops have been sent after it. Losses: SS *Luetzow,* some minesweepers, one transport vessel, nine Junkers, two Heinkels. Coastal fortifications are all in our hands.

Troops: The 196th Division is now in transit in the Belt. The 198th Division will embark in Hamburg tomorrow. Will go through the Kiel Canal to Norway.

. . .

11 April 1940

. . .

ObdH: a. Situation: Many British submarines in the Skagerrak and Kattegat. British report thirteen steamers sunk; we know of only seven, mostly close to the coast. Continuance of troop shipments by the sea route is possible only if the submarine threat is eliminated. SS *Luetzow* was sunk off the Swedish coast. Had put out against Fuehrer's orders. Situation in Norway difficult. Communication link only by air. Supplies dropped from air. The King of Norway has refused any negotiations on formation of a government on the lines of the German proposal; has issued proclamation calling for resistance.

Army signal equipment lost on sunk transports.

Telephone communications via Sweden.

Railroad transit to Norway through Sweden authorized only with sealed cars.

b. Eleventh Rifle Brigade to go to Norway as soon as possible.

c. We must find out what air force took away from forces earmarked for YELLOW. Will be ascertained also by agencies in the field. ObdH.

d. Buschenhagen must keep us continually informed on the distribution of our forces in Denmark. ObdH.

OQu IV, Von Etzdorf:

a. Situation report. Proposal to form a Cabinet headed by Quisling.

b. Request to pass on to the State Secretary my questions concerning Romania. (War not against Romania, but for Romania.)

1700.   Funeral service in Berlin for General Becker, at his home.

1800–1900. Foreign Office, State Secretary von Weizsaecker.

a. Situation in *Scandinavia*. Blunder with Quisling. We have made an official request to Sweden for permission to use the Swedish railroads in connection with our occupation operation. No answer yet.

b. *Romania:* Von Weizsaecker believes the only way to impress Romania is by making her realize that we would act with greater dispatch and vigor than the British. In any event, he is partial to the formulation ''against Romania'' rather than ''for Romania.''

Russia has some unsettled scores with Romania, e.g. Bessarabia. We cannot prevail on Russia to give an official promise to maintain a hands-off policy. Russia will not start anything, but neither will she make any promises which we could exploit in negotiations with Romania. *Bulgaria* will keep quiet of her own accord, and moreover we would always be able to control her. Hungary pursues a policy of doing nothing without our approval.

If we want to induce *Romania* to adopt a negative attitude toward a British landing, this could be most readily accomplished through the military attaché, not through diplomatic channels. As to *Bulgaria,* it is believed that any Anglo-French invasion attempt from the south would meet real opposition.

Italy will come to the support of Romania in the event that Russia should disturb the peace on the Balkans; in case the British break the peace there, Italy will probably consolidate her position in Albania and perhaps occupy Croatia, without declaring war on anyone or taking the side of the one or the other party.

Turkey is positively against war. But she may tolerate a march through her territory, under protest. Commitments arising from her alliance with the Allied powers become operative only if hostilities involving Italy spread to the eastern Mediterranean.

c.   *Situation in the west:* France has offered her protection to Belgium. The King and the Cabinet have declined. Holland is reported to have closed her frontier today.

12 April 1940

OQu IV: Franco-British semiofficial step in Brussels confirmed (offer of protection). In Holland, doubtful. Report of closing of Dutch frontier probably unfounded.

. . .

ObdH (Southeast Study):

a.   Canaris must mobilize his Near East sources to get us advance notice!

b.   Five to six days before they land. A motorized force takes two, infantry three weeks to advance across the Danube. South.
Could have one division at Constanza, Braila, ⎫
Galatz within forty-eight hours.   ⎬ East
Crossing from Bosporus to Constanza   ⎭
forty-eight hours at the most.

c. Preparations for movements normally five days, movements eight to seventeen days (completed). Preparations if Operation YELLOW has not yet started, seven days. Movements then could start at the end of ten days.

d. Shipment by air.

e. For ObdH: Sliding-scale Airborne Forces/Air Combat Forces. Two possibilities: West is already on fire or the west is quiet. Timetable: (a) if there is no agreement with Hungary, (b) if there is an agreement. Same for Russia. Supply base: Vienna.

13 April 1940

. . .

OQu II, OQu I: Planning data for BROWN. Conclusion: We do not have enough artillery to extend the offensive by an attack from the Saarbruecken sector.

a. Such a plan would require additional 360 medium batteries, i.e., the entire GHq. artillery. If we drop Operation TIGER, we would have enough with 60 medium battalions, of which 35 can probably be furnished by the Italians (20 battalions corps artillery, 15 battalions GHq. artillery). This would be feasible. We would then have to take care of the pillboxes while the Italians attend to counterbattery fire.

b. Without TIGER: Bridging equipment—for eleven bridges we need 86 bridge columns, or 68, if we use "Brirago" bridging equipment. (We have on hand a total of 160.) Of these 30 could then be freed to go along with the advance.

Fortunately we will now get about fifty new assault boats each month. Italy would be able to furnish an estimated total of 10 to 15 bridge columns.

c. Without TIGER: *Engineering battalions.* Available thirty-two GHq. battalions; we are running very low!

d. *Signal units:* We must help out from GHq. Reserves. That requires trucks and raw materials.

. . .

14 April 1940

Nolte: Situation at Narvik confused. "Has held so far" (OKW). German destroyers out of action. British have penetrated into the side fjord. Pack battery has arrived; all transport planes cracked up. The 181st Division is coming. Patrol-strength raids beaten off by 257th Division.

Airfield situation the same as yesterday.

British fleet is reported to have left the Mediterranean on 11/12 April.

Gercke: Transport routed through Sweden has left.

Von Greiffenberg: Yesterday's conference: Map. —Plans of navy: Three batteries will be taken to the west coast! MG, armored units, and air battalion to Norway. Utilization of Danish airfields at Aalborg, Esbjerg, and points north by air force. Front facing westward and northward. No protection of Denmark. One division, one light armored division.

Question of police: OKW has no intention to show its hand.

Agent report from Luxembourg. French troops in Deuth Oth south of Esch, alerted yesterday afternoon. French planes over Luxembourg territory.

Luxembourg: All railroads on weekday schedule today. Jews have started running away. (Through army group!)

Yesterday's strategy conference: If things get ugly up north, we won't force the issue, but turn to the west! In eight or ten days.

.   .   .

Talk with General von Brauchitsch. Wants to see the Fuehrer at 1200.

1400.   *General von Brauchitsch* comes back from the Fuehrer. Results:

1.   Hopes have been abandoned to hold Narvik. "We have had bad luck." The British apparently penetrated into the fjord and effected a landing. The destroyers in there must in all probability be written off as lost. The Fuehrer does not intend to throw more troops into the northern operation. It is a question of what Sweden's attitude would be in the event of a British advance on the Swedish iron ore region, which certainly is intended. Goering believes the Swedes would resist; the Fuehrer does not think so.

2.   YELLOW with paratroops and transport planes diverted to the north; it will be several days before the air force can be ready

again for operations. In consequence, we shall have to wait until the twenty-first or twenty-second. Goering pleads for the twenty-second. Von Brauchitsch has put up a strong argument to the *Fuehrer* that long waiting would not improve the situation. (Enemy obstacles increase, level of training of troops cannot be improved, morale mediocre, the high pitch reached cannot be maintained indefinitely.)

. . .

15 April 1940

. . .

ObdH: a. Review of the situation. OQu IV: Whereabouts of the French and British forces, supposed to be en route to Norway.

b. Get in touch with the Foreign Office about the situation in Sweden: Foreign Office must protect our interests in iron ore mines. Pressure can be exerted on Sweden by reminding them that we might destroy the iron ore mines from the air. —Have military attaché get busy.

. . .

ObdH: Is told by Keitel that Narvik will be evacuated. We must not allow that. Talk with Jodl.

Jodl: Town area of Narvik cannot be held. Mountain troops will be moved back to surrounding mountains.

Question of the evacuation of the Narvik area not yet decided.

OQu IV: Sweden's role in the Norwegian conflict. Yugoslavia: Prince Regent has pro-German sympathies. Is distrustful of Italy and Russia. Molotov wants iron ore from our mines.

State Secretary von Weizsaecker (1800):

1. We must insist that the Foreign Office do something to protect our interests in the Swedish ore mines. State Secretary informs me that a note concerning "British stragglers" has been handed to Sweden. I demand stronger pressure, for they may be regular British or French troops. We come to an understanding that, if necessary, we are going to put on pressure through the military attaché route.

2. Southeast. Reports of Russian reinforcements on German and Romanian borders. Request him to stress on top level the essential military importance of having peace in the southeast.

3. So far no confirmation of report that the British fleet has left the Mediterranean. Presence of French naval forces is being felt in eastern Mediterranean.

ObdH (at his home, 1900): Talk on the situation and my conversation with v. Weizsaecker.

16 April 1940

OQu IV-Canaris: Requests authorization for Chief of 12th Branch to fly to Oslo. I inquire about disposition of Swedish forces. —Unconfirmed reports of regrouping of Russian troops? Arrangements are made to ensure warning in ample time on movements in southeast. —Major British attack against Norwegian coast is expected. —Attack against Danish coast possible, but not likely in immediate future.

. . .

17 April 1940

. . .

Von Tippelskirch: Fuehrer does not like the idea of a Resident Representative of Reich Supreme Court; would make German influence too apparent. Admiral Tamm (Sweden) has gone to the Fuehrer. Good! Supply movements through Sweden will probably start today. Three British cruisers are shelling Stavanger.

. . .

Heusinger: Reports about Narvik from a naval staff officer evacuated by plane. Destroyers had fired all their ammunition, and so their artillery was of no use any longer. Have been beached. Crews of destroyers are almost completely on shore. They have taken over operation and protection of the ore railroad line. Railroad bridge on Swedish border blasted. Transshipment possible. Morale of troops good.

. . .

18 April 1940

Lieutenant Colonel Winter reports on plans for southeast.

Colonel von Greiffenberg: Predictions on weather. —Report to OKW on ground conditions.

Heusinger:

a. Jodl: ObdH's views on Narvik must be given a hearing. —Repercussions on army. We will receive a copy of orders.

b. Fuehrer: Narvik cannot be held in the long run (several divisions). Fuehrer wanted to withdraw all troops from Narvik yesterday, but has deferred decision for the moment. —No orders have been issued.

c. Preliminary alert (Jodl-Gercke). —Start of Operation YELLOW not before middle of next week. —Fuehrer does not let himself be hurried. The three-day preliminary alert will be dropped after next Sunday.

. . .

19 April 1940

. . .

OQu IV: a. Sweden determined to defend borders. The best Swedish troops in ore district.

b. Fuehrer's view on negotiations with Hungary. General Staff conversations approved generally, but must be preceded by political talks to obtain clarification of the partner's position.

c. Liss: Report on obstacles on the Belgian border in sector of Fourth Army.

23 April 1940

OQu IV: a. Situation in the north. —Dalmatia not until we have field to ourselves. Also Russia (Bessarabia). —Threat from Dardanelles greater now, but the British have no jump-off base.

b. Hungary, latter part of May.

c. Ciano? Mussolini wants to take over Foreign Ministry himself.

. . .

1300.   General Keitel: Only mountain troops are suited for fighting north of Oslo. Accordingly, the Fuehrer has ordered 2nd Mountain Division to be moved north through Oslo at the earliest. Report requested as to when 2nd Mountain Division would be ready for shipment. Destination (Stettin or Aalborg) will then be decided by the OKW.

In its place, 170th Division is immediately made available; eventual relief through police troops.

. . .

24 April 1940

. . .

1530.   Fuehrer conference:

   a. *Review of political situation:* Teleki has sent Fuehrer a letter: Heretofore Hungary had to make all the sacrifices. That must change. Suggests a three-power conference.

      Fuehrer is afraid Hungary might want to use force against Romania. That certainly would not fit into our policy of maintaining peace on the Balkans, but we are sure Hungary could do nothing of that sort by herself and would get a thrashing. The state is ripe for internal collapse. Last summer he was assured Hungary could not wage war for more than three days, for lack of ammunition, etc. Accordingly, they would immediately place enormous demands on us.

      Il Duce has done his best to keep Hungary quiet, but evidently has not been completely successful. Fuehrer therefore has got in touch with Il Duce through von Mackensen, and will make his decisions dependent on Il Duce's.
He wants to leave the southeast entirely to the Italians.

      It is not unlikely that the Hungarians are being egged on by the British. Press rumors on German troop concentrations on the Hungaro-Slovak frontier are evidently created by Hungary to get the Balkans stirred up. It would serve Britain's interest very well to have the oil fields blazing, and it would not matter who puts the match to them. We vitally need the oil deliveries from the Romanian wells, at least until next spring.

      After that we should be freer.

Fuehrer has advised Il Duce: (a) Hungary has made no sacrifices at all to date, (b) Hungary cannot act alone, if only because of Yugoslavia, (c) precipitate action by Hungary might draw Russia to the Balkans, which would be a most serious business. Initiative is left to Il Duce.

b. *General Staff conversations* with Hungary would not be expedient at this time. We might go as far as very discreet talks (with Werth) on railroad questions. (England and Hungary one heart and one soul. Morosow, the man who played with us, has disappeared.) Italy's attitude on the Balkans questions will determine the character of our conversations with the Hungarian General Staff. General Staff conversations on a broad basis are ruled out. "Only normal exchange of views and no three-power conferences, which might be misconstrued and start rumors." (The Fuehrer has not yet forgiven the Hungarians for not letting him use the Košice railroad in the Polish campaign, which they owe to him.)

c. *Italy:* Il Duce has informed his provincial chieftains that it may be only a matter of a few weeks before Italy enters the war on Germany's side. (Report from U.S.)

d. *Basic military factors of a campaign on the Balkans* are discussed. Fuehrer approves our outline and expresses appreciation that we have been thinking ahead. Suggests that the Dardanelles and the Bosporus might be closed by air action from a base in the Brindisi area. Raises question of surprise attacks on Crete and on British shipping in Gibraltar.

26 April 1940

OQu IV (on phone): Reports resignation of the Belgian Cabinet and arrival of British prisoners from Norway, who are to be shown to the Fuehrer.

. . .

General Keitel: I warn him against doing anything with British PWs that might boomerang on German officer prisoners (interrogation in presence of journalists).

Brand: Report on factors responsible for the shorts in light field howitzers. (Miscalculations in the firing table, damp powder?) Informational handbook for corps and army artillery. Commanders.

Hungarian OQu IV, Viszaszy: Talk on the Balkans.

Von Etzdorf: Attolico-Alfieri. Latest target dates.

Gehlen: Construction workers for the Upper Rhine sector. Construction battalions will carry on with fortifications; forty labor service battalions for preparations for BROWN.

28 April 1940

Von Tippelskirch:

a. Exchange of letters Reynaud/Mussolini. Reynaud proposed a talk. Mussolini's reply negative, cool. Echo in the press.

b. Trade negotiations between Germany and Sweden are running into snags, with Sweden insisting on freedom to carry on her foreign trade within existing treaties also outside the Baltic Sea.

c. OQu IV tour to Bucharest-Sofia-Belgrade. Mission for Sofia.

Weinknecht: Letter from Kaupisch regarding activation of SS "Nordland" in Denmark. Instructions for letter to Keitel, OKW:

1. Acknowledgment.

2. Mission.

3. Regulation of relationship with the political and military representatives.

29 April 1940

Liss: New intelligence on the British army extracted from documents captured in Norway: the five divisions of the second draft which were thought to have been activated do not exist yet. Apart from those in Egypt, there are only two divisions of armor, one at home and one in France. In Norway they have two brigades made up of independent battalions, and the 49th Division (the former at Andalsnes, the latter at Namsos and Narvik). In addition, four French battalions of Chasseurs Alpins have been identified.

Von Greiffenberg: Current matters. (Employment of the elements left behind by the divisions now in Norway.) —Conference with air force.

Von Stuelpnagel: Status of Italian preparations. Have made no progress. — Marras. —Proposal to launch the offensives against Holland and Belgium at different times. (Rejected.)

Waldau: Report on Norway. *Transfer of air units to that theater affects AGp.B* (units remaining have only two-thirds of their striking power). —An alert period of no less than three days will be needed. —Aerial photographs.

Meyer-Ricks: Report on his trip to Italy. On the whole very cheering, general atmosphere favors participation on our side, but slow progress in the preparations for the conferences.

. . .

2 May 1940

Von Puttkamer: Communications between Bergen and Oslo restored: Norwegian general in Andalsnes has initiated surrender negotiations.

Von Etzdorf: *Britain:* Shipping detoured around Mediterranean. "Precautionary measure."

Italy: Ciano speaks to the Yugoslav envoy "shaking his forefinger at him."

Allies: Report through The Hague: Latest War Council meeting discussed the question of removal of British government to Canada. Spanish minister in Bern reports "spreading gloom" in the enemy countries, caused apparently by disappointment after announcement of initial victories in the north.

Sweden: Negotiations on arms transit to Narvik. Authorization of arms transit in exchange for AAA! Foreign Office has given instruction to von Uthmann and German minister. Introduction of the subject of AAA deliveries has restored the interrupted negotiations. Earlier informal inquiries regarding arms transit had not registered in Sweden.

(Von Etzdorf is asked to keep ObdH currently informed on instructions sent to our minister in Sweden.)

3 May 1940

. . .

Von Stuelpnagel: It appears from a remark by Marras that the U.S. is trying to exert pressure on Italy; we may expect a lively diplomatic offensive and an exchange of important notes between Rome and Berlin in the next few days.

4 May 1940

Von Stuelpnagel: Talk with Marras: Italian General Staff is skeptical about success of an offensive on the alpine front or in Libya. On the other hand, they are obviously interested in the Balkans front, for which the deficient equipment of the Italians would suffice. Von Stuelpnagel is instructed to inform Chief OKW. Attention is to be called to Crete.

Von Etzdorf: Exchange of letters Il Duce–Fuehrer

Occasioned by verbal communication of the U.S. government: Extension of war is Germany's fault. Further extension is feared. In that eventuality, the U.S. will not be in a position to keep out any longer. President hopes that Italy is aware of that.

Il Duce:
Allies to blame for extension of the war. Germany is against any extension, as is Italy. "No peace is possible without solution of the basic problems of Italy's freedom. Italy is prepared to cooperate in a better organization of the world, as the situation permits and on condition that the reality of accomplished facts is recognized."

Fuehrer (letter of 3 May): Reviews the developments in Scandinavia.

Operations completed in southern and central Norway. Now northern Norway is being cleaned up. Sorry the British did not send larger forces. Concerning the American statement: "I think the undertone of threat ringing through all of Roosevelt's utterances is sufficient grounds for us to be on our guard and bring the war to a close as quickly as possible."

Sweden: We deliver AAA in return for arms transit to Narvik. In the negotiations with the military attaché, Sweden at first gave an evasive answer pointing out that the problem was one involving the entire complex of neutrality, but conversations will be resumed after examination of the question by the Cabinet. Meeting von Ribbentrop–Guenther?

Italy: The State Secretary believes that Italy is determined to attack Yugoslavia in any case once she enters the war. Attolico has corroborated that interpretation.

5 May 1940

. . .

Fuehrer conference: Review of the *Italian situation:* Il Duce has forwarded three letters to the Fuehrer:

1. Reynaud's letter "a piece of craven whining," to which Il Duce replied in a manner which formerly would have been grounds for war.

2. From the Pope, preaching a peace of justice. Reply: The Allies had a chance to make such a peace, but they chose Versailles and so caused the conflict.

3. On Roosevelt's efforts in Rome (covered by earlier information from the Foreign Office).

Military preparations: Another age group will be called up by 15 May. Additional forces by 24 May. The target set is two million men under arms. OQu IV, OQu I.

Internal situation: Mussolini has on his hands a tough struggle against the crown, the nobility, and the church. Also finance and industry are for the most part against the war. In the army, large sections of the Officers' Corps oppose the war and side with King and Crown Prince, who is the most vicious German hater.

Balkans: Hungary is still causing concern (OQu IV). Mussolini, just as much as the Fuehrer, is against three-power talks; such talks would only attract the attention of the whole world. A new possibility suggested is that Hungary might work together with Russia. If Hungary strikes alone or only with Bulgaria as an ally, defeat is certain. Italy admits that the "laborers" sent to Albania are really soldiers.

North: Norway as far north as Namsos will not be given out of our hands.

There has been no decision yet as to the form by which Denmark is to be incorporated into our national territory.

Allies: Atmosphere is pessimistic. In the event of serious military reverses, we may expect either a complete changeover or extensive alterations. Chamberlain's Cabinet will not be overthrown at the present moment. Only when Britain will have to bear the brunt of the war set off by him, will an antiwar party rise in the country.

Russia: The antagonism between Italy and Russia affords us excellent opportunities in the political field.

6 May 1940

Mieth: *Conference with v. Leeb on BROWN. Results.* Southeast Studies turned over to OQu I. —Course of action opening in the event of peaceful settlement with Holland. —Plans for the event that we must do BROWN alone.

Von Etzdorf: Von Weizsaecker: Italy's entry into the war will set the Balkans ablaze. Italy must secure for herself the Greek position. This would bring Turkey into the conflict. The Balkans will be on fire.

Italy's attitude: Mussolini will come after we have gained one or two spectacular successes in the west. British preventive action against Italy is not feared, because Britain does not want to force an Italian decision.

Moscow: Russo-Italian relations. Molotov has sounded our ambassador as to whether the Italian government has expressed any readiness to exchange envoys. Schulenburg: Yes. —The Russian government evidently is in no hurry. Schulenburg: The tension between Russia and Italy is caused by Italy's objection against the projected understanding between Russia and Bulgaria.

At the moment, economic negotiations are in progress between Russia and Yugoslavia. The press in Rome and Berlin differs in the interpretation of British naval concentrations in the Mediterranean.

. . .

7 May 1940

. . .

Homlok (Hungarian attaché): outline my ideas for orientation of General Werth.

    a. Political foundation still lacking. No three-power talks. (He mentions political visit after 20 May.) We have a vital interest in peace on the Balkans, and so has Italy.

    b. Preliminary planning can be only of theoretical character. It should be done on the following bases:

        1. Each partner works with his own resources.

        2. Hungary furnishes covering force for assembly of troops.

        3. Hungary in the north, we in the south. (Aid to Bulgaria, cover against Yugoslavia on Romanian territory.)

        4. Demarcation line: Bihar Mountains.

        5. Exploration of utilization of railroads, roads, signal communications, and airfield facilities against the event that we should have to move swiftly into the southern assembly area. Will be the subject of special conversations.

        6. No planning data in writing!

Von Greiffenberg: Stopping possible at 1200. Order for the event of postponement of A-day: (automatically 9 May, same X-hour).

Von Stuelpnagel: Preparations for BROWN: Air force reinforcements assured (reconnaissance flights [three airplanes]). Survey battalion (partially mobile) assured for 15 May. Delay in conclusion of German-Italian railroad agreement.

. . .

OQu IV: Balkans unanimously against war. —*Romania:* Much German spoken. —Oil: 130,000 tons a month. Morosow: Not afraid of England and France, but all the more of Russia. —*Bulgaria:* Frightened. Prime Minister sensible, Foreign Minister not military-minded. —Yugoslavia: Masses sympathetic, made so by experiences of the last war; they want no war; afraid of Italy, barrier against Hungary.

Railroad Belgrade—Nish not out of question. Defenses in good shape. They want no British military operations in their country.

Foreign Armies West: Dutch radio at 1700 recalled military personnel from furloughs.

Von Ziehlberg: Current General Staff personnel matters. —"Mountain Corps." —Higher artillery commanders.

Buhle: Activation of a mountain corps. (Only XXI Corps can do it.)

8 May 1940

. . .

ObdH:

1. Fuehrer nervous. Leaks? Complication for political strategy if bad weather delays start.

2. Mountain corps. Will 2nd Mountain Division remain in Norway? Will newly activated 3rd Regiment stay down here? Can be decided only by von Falkenhorst. Narvik? Take over anything that is left. Clear instructions to XXI Corps. Op. Sec.

3. Denmark: Polish artillery and artillery of cavalry division attended to. Op. Sec. Org. Sec.

4. Staff Greiff. Op. Sec.

5. OQu I. Fuehrer has vetoed sending of any arms to Italy (exception: one experimental AAA battalion).

. . .

9 May 1940

Mueller (Gen Qu): Action on von Bock's proposal concerning centralized administration of occupied territory under OKH.

Von Brauchitsch: Teletype v. Bock–Roehricht.

OQu IV: Alarm reports from von Neuhausen (Yugoslavia): Toussaint is burning files. —Atmosphere tense.

Mobilization continues. —French and British tanks may have landed. —Leaflets dropped by planes. —Rumors that three corps are deployed on Albanian border (in reality three divisions). —The facts are that the Serbian army has been brought up to war strength, but reserve divisions probably have not been mobilized.

. . .

Yugoslavia: Foreign Office (von Weizsaecker) expects military action by Italy against Yugoslavia. "Essential" measure of navy to safeguard the Adriatic Sea.

Von Greiffenberg: 10 May. 0535.

. . .

THE CAMPAIGN IN THE WEST

10 May 1940

9 May 1940, 1800. Leaving Zossen by special train for Godesberg. Accompanied by von Greiffenberg, Heusinger, Liss, Thiele, Nolte, and the advance party.

2215. Nordhausen: Telephone signal "Danzig" [execute plan]. No unusual events.

10 May, about 0500. Arrived at Godesberg; about 0600, at Felsennest; overtook marching columns, good marching discipline.

About 0700. First reports:

   a.   "Trojan Horse" did not succeed; Nijmegen bridge destroyed. Gennep bridge undamaged.

   b.   Roermond and Maesijk bridges destroyed. Bridges at Lannaeken and Canne (north and south of Maastricht) destroyed. Status of bridges at Veldwezelt and Vroenhoven still uncertain.

   c.   XXVII Corps reports: Belgians were alerted around 0300, telephone warning net in operation shortly after 0500. Dutch apparently were taken by surprise.

   d.   Sixteenth Army reports: Border bridges were captured by 0535, according to plan. Only slight resistance. Detonations can be heard from farther inland.

About 0800. Moerdijk bridge reported in our hands.

About 1000. Report that Luxembourg railroad station was seized at 0815 (line serviceable on two tracks). Group Kleist apparently continues advance according to plan. Fourth Army advancing according to plan. Roadblocks numerous, but unmanned.

Maastricht, all bridges blown up. Order to Sixth Army to force crossing. Attacks against our paratroops at canal bridges. Airborne landings in Fortress Holland seem to proceed according to plan.

About 1100. Message from Sperrle: Guderian, with advance elements, reported near Bastogne. No troop movements have been observed in Belgium, nor in northern and eastern directions.

1300.   Roehricht instructed to ascertain whereabouts of 1st Mountain Division.

1400.   Good progress of Eighteenth Army, satisfactory progress of Sixth and Fourth armies. Group Kleist seems to be getting on well.

1800.   OQu IV confirms earlier reports. Some Belgian units along Meuse raising white flags. Meuse reported crossed south of Eben Emael.

1830.   ObdH. I ask him to see the Fuehrer to get air force support.

1845.   Talk with Waldau: AGp.B has contacted Kesselring requesting night air interdiction of enemy motorized movements. Not the business of OKW! Night reconnaissance has been provided over roads leading to front.

AGp.A: Sperrle has moved most of his fighters to forward fields, enabling him to operate beyond Meuse. Intention to pound the roads leading from Châlons area westward toward Meuse River tomorrow.

Airborne landing in Holland: center of operation Rotterdam-Moerdijk, two regiments landed. Dijon as well as Lyn purely air force targets.

1900.   Roehricht: First Mountain Division resting near Pruem during afternoon, continues movement in direction of Houffalize at 2000, scheduled to arrive at right wing of III Corps by tomorrow. In continuous contact with corps to ensure uninterrupted flow of movement.

2000.   OQu IV reports (Op. Off. and ObdH present): OQu IV must find out what enemy is moving into Belgium. Have any troop movements started?

Reports of Op. Sec. show that all corps of AGp.A have fairly well closed to von Kleist. Excellent marching! The 269th Division has crossed Meuse and Canal south of Eben Emael. Success of Sixth Army thus gains satisfactory width at decisive point.

Important: Keep pushing left wing of Sixth Army! Enemy retreating from Liège must be cut off. Get on with right wing of Fourth Army. Don't wheel on Liège too soon.

Decisions: Eleventh Motorized Brigade into area west of Dillenburg. The 82d Division to proceed westward after arrival near Frankfurt.

No decision yet: Attacks *Scharnhorst* and *Gneisenau;* probably A plus 2.

Fuehrer (through ObdH): Il Duce reacted very warmly to news of attack. Promises intensified stepup of mobilization and arms production. Navy will move by the end of this month. Everything else to be speeded up.

2100. **Bogatsch:** Digest of air observations: Enemy massing motorized forces between Valenciennes and Hirson on both sides of Sambre River. This may be interpreted as preparation for a drive on both sides of Sambre. Particularly strong concentration near Maubeuge, tanks.

Enemy intelligence: Only Dutch 5th and 6th divisions and Brigade B in reported areas. In the evening, motorized movement of enemy from Douai toward Brussels.

11 May 1940

Evening and morning reports on the whole corroborate satisfactory picture developing yesterday.

Moot points: Eighteenth Army: Why have tanks not been committed? Why has SS "Deathhead" been kept so far in rear? Why is army Hq. way back in Wesel?

Von Kleist: Behavior of left wing of 10th Armored Division probably due to anxieties about left flank.

Gratifying: Forward surge of infantry, in particular, marching and fighting of III Corps. Sixteenth Army moving fast into line; offensive intentions against enemy forward of Maginot Line.

Unclear: Situation of 22d Airborne Division.

Conference with ObdH: Wants to put steam behind *AGp.A.* (Army group report advance very difficult on account of numerous road demolitions.) I am prodding Eighteenth Army. (Army reports that peel line was breached at 0830; 9th Armored Division is heading for Breda after crossing Gennep bridge at 0800; SS division following behind.)

Chief Air Officer again requested to get us clear picture of situation of 22d Division. All we know is that two reinforcement battalions of 22d put down north of Rotterdam are encircled by enemy. Have radio

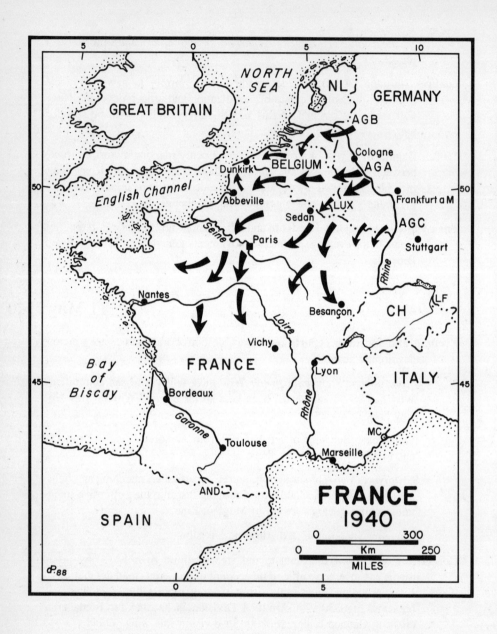

GREAT BRITAIN

NORTH SEA

NL

GERMANY

AGB

BELGIUM

Cologne

AGA

English Channel

Dunkirk

Frankfurt a M

Abbeville

LUX

AGC

Seine

Sedan

Stuttgart

Paris

Rhine

Nantes

Besançon

CH

LF

Loire

FRANCE

Vichy

Bay
of
Biscay

Lyon

ITALY

Bordeaux

Rhône

Garonne

MC

Toulouse

Marseille

AND

SPAIN

**FRANCE
1940**

0   300
0   Km   250
MILES

dP.88

contact. Ammunition and reinforcements are being dropped continuously. No clear picture of situation south of Rotterdam.

Chief Engineer Officer is instructed to relieve tight bridge situation in AGp.B sector at the earliest and to give all possible help.

About 1100. Enemy moving toward line Libramont-Neufchâteau-Tintigny opposite our XIX Corps, also in direction of Ypres-Tournai (apparently second wave).

. . .

Have radio contact. Second Air Fleet assisted by Putzier. ("Dispatching of additional elements is under consideration.") (Condition of landing fields?)

1500.   Sizable British troop movement through Antwerp reported in direction of Breda and Tilburg.

1545.   Von Salmuth talked to ObdH: Enemy columns at Breda and Tilburg, and east of Turnhout, at 1400.

. . .

1630. **a.**   Reports of British movements in direction Fortress Holland have not been confirmed. Positive reports on columns moving toward Rosendaal which were attacked from the air. Bogatsch (through Mieth).

  b.   Concentration north of Moerdijk dispersed by air action. Moerdijk securely in our hands. Situation stabilized with exception of direction Antwerp; protected by canal position.

  c.   Twenty-second Division in dunes west of Leiden, southwest of The Hague, west and southwest of Delft. Area Delft-Rotterdam: Attempt will be made to put down additional troops this afternoon.

1740.   Fuehrer visit at GHq. Review of situation until 2000. Pleased with success, expects attack from south.

2230.   Gen Qu: Reports good development. Losses slight. Supply situation good. Luxembourg and Alzette Valley railroads in operation with eighteen trains. Luxembourg taken over by German administration. Expenditure of ammunition low, fuel consumption normal.

2300.   Gehlen reports on Sixteenth Army.

2330.   Reports of British landings in Schelde estuary and at Helder (at Helder apparently evacuation of refugees).

12 May 1940

Morning reports show further extension of objectives attained.

Picture of enemy movements: Enemy moving troops out of Holland in direction of Breda, apparently on account of damage in Antwerp Tunnel, east of Antwerp. Since Tilburg is already in our hands, these forces will not accomplish a great deal. East of French border we assume presence of between twelve and fifteen British and French divisions, which are probably approaching Dyle and Meuse positions.

No major railroad movements have been observed. Enemy air force shows surprising lack of activity.

1100.   **Talk with Jodl:** Movements of AAA Corps must come under control of army group Hq.

1200.   **Gercke:** Railroad plan discussed. Speeding up of movement "Cigars."

Felber: Which corps Hq. can army group offer for relief? Felber states: XXX Corps.

Wagner: Supply situation in Sixth Army. I release MT Battalion (GHq. Reserve) for Sixth Army.

Von Gyldenfeldt: Reports that 10th Armored Division, contrary to orders by Group Kleist, has swerved northward, possibly shying away from enemy tanks reported to the south. Present location behind 1st and 2nd Armored divisions interferes with their movements.

Group Kleist believes that tanks could have advanced faster if they had not had to wait for infantry to close up. Attacks should have been accompanied by armored infantry brigades.

.   .   .

Von Salmuth (through OQu IV): Reports that contact has been established at Libramont at 1904. Movements from Metz and northwest toward Charleville. Seventh Armored Division reached Dinant; Bioul on west side of Meuse, western bridge in Godinne reported in our hands. Fourth Armored Division reported to have reached Landen.

Von Salmuth, 2130.

    a. No decision yet on direction of new drive of 9th Armored Division. Depends on situation estimate of CG of Eighteenth Army. Von Bock contemplates ordering 9th Armored Division to turn and drive in direction Antwerp, etc., with flank covered by SS division. This would enable three divisions to follow penetration of armored division into Fortress Holland. Three divisions, SS included, could move toward the Schelde estuary and cover flank against Antwerp.

    b. Noordwijk reached at 1825; armored battalion sent as reinforcement.

    c. Unconfirmed reports of landing of naval vessels at Noordwijk.

    d. Von Reichenau has clashed with French tanks (1st Mechanized Division) near Hannut; intends driving on Gembloux tomorrow.

    e. Four thousand prisoners taken.

. . .

Attitude of population varies. Most mayors accept situation. Fifteen May. Military government Luxembourg; Regional Hq., Commandant Guthmann. Secretary General Wehrer (formerly envoy to Berlin) has taken over civil administration.

Von Brauchitsch–v. Bock: Decision has been taken to attack Fortress Holland from the south. Attacking force: 9th Armored Division plus two infantry divisions; flank cover against Antwerp: SS division plus two infantry divisions.

AGp.C has scored gains in attacks near Saarbruecken and southwest of Zweibruecken, but suffered about eight hundred casualties. About six hundred prisoners taken from three different divisions.

13 May 1940

Morning reports: Most important: Elements of the French Seventh Army, identified northeast of Antwerp, are reported to have mission of keeping areas open for slowly arriving bulk of army. It may be assumed that Seventh Army includes also the British elements around Antwerp.

Reports of railroad movements from the direction of Charleroi toward the Wavre-Mons Gap seem to confirm reported advance of French First Army. That would indicate that French Ninth Army has the mission of holding Meuse south of Namur, between First and Second armies.

Our movements are developing as planned. It remains to be clarified how Fourth Army will carry out its mission to reduce Fortress Holland. First, they would have to enter Rotterdam and then follow up with Amsterdam-Utrecht.

There is nothing to worry about from direction Antwerp. Here Eighteenth Army has enough depth against the unlikely contingency of a counteroffensive at this time. Right wing of Sixth Army can be safely stretched a little by extending it southward toward left wing.

Report of crossing at Yvoir, south of Namur, has not been confirmed. On the other hand, Seventh Army has got across near Dinant. Bridge is destroyed. Left wing of Fourth Army still weak (32d Division).

Right flank of Twelfth Army somewhat dangling in the air. Gap to Fourth Army still open, XVIII Corps has not yet moved in. Group Kleist bunched together near Sedan, intends attacking at 1600. Plan of attack rather complicated. Sixteenth Army has made very good advance; right wing is already at Meuse River with sufficient depth.

Of our reserves, 11th Motorized Brigade and 94th Division are being moved more closely behind AGp.A. German flag reported to be flying over Liège citadel.

OQu IV: Allied pressure on Ankara to induce Turkey to break off relations with us. Allied fleet put out from Alexandria on 10 May, with northern course. British government demands cession of Spanish territory in order to be able to close Mediterranean (20 km on Mediterranean, 10 km on Atlantic side).

. . .

1130. Paulus reports: French First Mechanized Division south of Turnhout. In Diest-Tirlemont area several British artillery groups. Heavy flooding. Orders: Concentrate XI Corps at Diest; 31st Division joins drive of IV Corps on Tirlemont; XVI Corps (3rd Armored Division, 4th Armored Division, 35th Infantry Division, and 30th Motorized Division) to the south of IV Corps as directed, and 269th Division to the south of XVI.

Liège: Situation fine. The 223d Division is already fighting within inner defense belt.

Von Greiffenberg: Situation of Eighteenth Army developing according to plan. Parts of army moving to the west, south of Waal River; others, to the north, through Rotterdam.

OQu IV: Air reports received throughout day, some delayed, show:

    a. Prearranged troop and supply movements of the French Seventh Army and at least parts of the British army in the Brussels-Antwerp area started Friday night, continued through Saturday and Sunday. Upon arrival of the bulk of these armies, estimated to have strength of about sixteen motorized divisions, mechanized divisions will be moved forward on the Antwerp-Namur line. Identified: Three French mechanized divisions and one British group, the latter east of Louvain.

    b. French First Division has been moving toward line Namur-Brussels since Saturday–Sunday. This movement for the most part will be completed by today.

    c. Toward line Namur–Sedan Carignan only local closing movements reported; they may represent buildup of some reserves behind Meuse.

    d. In area Dijon-Troyes-Nancy, preparations reported allow various interpretations. Material for two to three divisions.

My estimate of the situation: In the area north of Namur we are now confronted with a completed buildup, comprising approximately twenty-four British and French, and about fifteen Belgian, divisions. Against these forces we can put up fifteen divisions in line and six divisions in reserve, a total of twenty-one (which, if necessary, can be reinforced from the depth of Eighteenth Army). Fourth A-day! We are strong enough to fight off any enemy attack. No need to bring up any more forces. An offensive mounted by us now would not produce anything apart from gaining ground for Hoepner.

South of Namur we are faced with a weaker enemy, about half our strength. Outcome of Meuse drive will decide if, when, and where we would be able to take advantage of this superiority. The enemy has no substantial mobile forces in the rear of this front, no more than three armored divisions at best, but he does have a very well integrated railroad system.

Goth (Liaison Officer, Fourth Army): Reports on Fourth Army's situation. Moving up of III and II Corps to Meuse is the only development to be expected on 14 May; resumption of drive west of Meuse not before 15 May.

Evening situation: Left wing of AGp.A makes only slow headway against partly mechanized French forces north of Namur. VIII Corps of AGp.A has reached Meuse south of Namur; XV Corps has secured lodgement on west bank of river near Yvoir and Give, XXXXI Corps has crossed Meuse near Monthermé; XVI Corps has passed to west bank north and south of Sedan. Later in the evening 2d Armored Division also reports to have pushed across Meuse.

14 May 1940

Computation of enemy strength clearly shows that the area between the Antwerp-Dyle line and Namur contains about twenty-five British and French divisions, mostly motorized or mechanized. Outposts of advance elements were holding Turnhout Canal and Grebbe line until this morning; as a result of gains by 3rd and 4th Armored divisions, they are now falling back to the main line.

French Ninth Army, opposing our breakthrough wedge, which now has gained a small bridgehead across Meuse, is weak.

Nor have French Second and Third armies any real strength. Second Army apparently cannot stand up to our onslaught. This is evident from northward movements from Metz and Verdun, which have been going on since 14 May, morning.

The important thing now is to have AGp.B liquidate Holland speedily. Here, following our capture of Rotterdam, enemy seems to be giving up the Grebbe line and retreating in direction of Fortress Antwerp. It is also imperative that AGp.A should throw to left wing everything not needed elsewhere in order to push on to the south of Brussels and contain enemy strength.

The breakthrough wedge of AGp.A must be aimed in such a way that:

Fourth Army will push on westward along the boundary line Charleroi-Mons-Peruwelz-Tournai on either side of the French Border Defense Line, which it will roll up.

Second Army (newly committed) will advance to the south of line Cambrai-Arras, in general direction of Amiens.

Twelfth Army pushing through Signy le Petit–Signy l'Abbaye will gain line La Fère-Rethel.

Sixteenth Army must turn out right wing into line Montmédy-Rethel.

At the same time, *Group Kleist* in massive formation must drive toward the sea at Saint Omer along the boundary line of Fourth and Second armies. The important point for AGp.B in this is to concentrate strong forces on southern wing soon, which should not be difficult once Holland has been eliminated. The moving up of troops behind AGp.A has already been organized, partly by railroad (one division, with truck transportation regiment), partly by foot marches, through Sixteenth Army sector (coming from First Army sector).

ObdL: Reports dense motorized movements from Verdun and Metz, in northerly direction, since 0700. Air fleet has already been briefed for mission. Probably reserves of AGp.2 (French) moving up behind Second and Third armies.

Fellgiebel: Conference on forward move of GHq. to Phillipeville area.

V. Salmuth (on phone): Discuss advance of Sixth Army with strong left wing. Intentions of army group are in accord with our ideas.

Railroad mobilization of French GHq. Reserves seem to have started. Heavy movements from area around and west of Paris to Belgium, and from direction Soissons and Metz toward Sedan.

1800.   Von Salmuth (AGp.B): Long columns of mixed arms, including tanks reported moving southwest from Brussels, between 1300 and 1400. Withdrawals from area northwest of Charleroi in western and southwestern direction.

Own troops: Advance elements of IV Corps enter Wavre without opposition. Spearhead of XVI Corps reached Sambre River at 1540. First indications of change in enemy's plan of operation. Will they give up Belgium entirely or in part? Regrouping in order to stop us or perhaps counterattack on French soil.

.   .   .

Von Brauchitsch/von Bock:

1.   Fighting in Holland has ceased (except in Zoeland Province).

2.   Pull out motorized forces at earliest.

3.   Eighteenth Army could possibly be reassigned to right wing.

4.   Third Armored Division not yet pushed through. Enemy still holding line Wavre-Namur.

5.   Liège: Three forts in eastern sector holding out and still firing; likewise some forts in southern and northern sectors on western bank. All bridges destroyed. Military admin. Hq. set up at Liège.

Von Salmuth: Takes back his report of this afternoon, on withdrawal of enemy around Brussels and Dyle line. Sharp discussion over order to all ground forces issued this afternoon. Army group has not taken the trouble of trying to understand it.

V. Kahlden: Reports on operations of Eighteenth Army and situation in Holland.

Afternoon. Final orders for continuance of operation by AGps.A and B, dictated by myself, go out on teletype.

15 May 1940

Morning reports bring no confirmation of enemy withdrawal from Dyle-Namur line; instead, they indicate that enemy is still holding this position. Success near Charleville gaining in width and depth. The enemy defense position on the Meuse can now be considered definitely breached. This bears out the premises on which Order No. 234, of 14 May, is based.

AGp.A, contrary to our orders, wants to insert Second Army between Twelfth and Sixteenth armies. Disapproved.

AGp.B offended again, because no special mention of them was made in my order of 14 May.

Gen Qu prepares a base for airborne supply at Charleville.

AGp.C expects withdrawal of enemy lines opposite 93d, 268th, 262d, and 246th divisions.

Enemy apparently pulls out field troops, relying on fortress brigades. Blasting of Kehl bridge would point in same direction. Consequence for us: We can reduce strength of AGp.C.

OQu IV: Tension between England and Italy increasing. British residents leave Italy; Italians leave Egypt. Allied embassies in Switzerland sending families home. British troops in Egypt at Libyan frontier. Ambassadors are called to Rome by Mussolini for meeting. England: Beaverbrook is Minister for Aircraft Production. Tokyo: England will not intervene in Dutch East Indies, where independence movements have developed.

L'Oeuvre: Possibility of defeat must be faced. Concern about Italy.

Vatican: Italy's entry into war imminent. (Twenty-four May, a historic day.)

Von Rundstedt: "Cannot accept responsibility" if Twelfth Army should now be ordered to move south, after initially pointing west. Hopeless chaos would result.

1550.   ObdH: gives his approval to von Rundstedt's recommendation.

Wagner: Supply running smoothly; temporary fuel shortage in Hoepner's group.

Railroads: As far as Bastogne, 15 May; Libramont, 17 May.

Von Kleist: Arrangements for fuel supply:

a.   By air.

b.   By road transport: one transportation battalion (1,800 tons) today at Bastogne.

.   .   .

16 May 1940

Our breakthrough wedge is developing in a positively classic manner. West of the Meuse our advance is sweeping on, smashing tank counterattacks in its path. Superb marching performance of the infantry (5th Division, 1st Mountain Division).

It is now essential to organize a feeder line through Visé or Maastricht so that we can move reinforcements to the right wing of the wedge through Sixth Army sector; to the left wing, through Sixteenth Army sector; and at the same time get reinforcements to the central sector from our prepared unloading points directly behind. Three corps Hq. have been added to breakthrough wedge; one additional army Hq. and three more corps Hq. will stand by.

The French seem to move reinforcements from their reserves in the Dijon and Belfort areas toward the left flank of our wedge. Reinforcements moving up from the Charleroi area toward the right flank have been cut off. The large general reserve has not yet been drawn upon; nor are there any indications that they will be committed now. New reserves are apparently being formed from elements assigned to the fortified front of the French Second Army Group.

If the French accept the decisive battle now, they would be able to move about thirty divisions against our breakthrough wedge.

We can free additional reserves from AGp.C for the left wing of AGp.A. The overall picture of the situation and the balance of strength consequently appears to be quite in our favor.

During the morning, the reports coming in for yesterday and today make it evident that the French are moving up an army of about three corps against the southern flank of our breakthrough wedge, partly from the direction of their fortified front (western edge of the Vosges Mountains), partly from their reserve pool around Dijon. At the same time they are concentrating opposite our breakthrough front with troops moved in through Laon and Saint Quentin, in all probability from GHq. Reserve.

The front facing von Bock is reported softening south of Louvain since this morning.

1540.   Talk with von Bock (on phone):

    a.   Proclamation of the commanding general in Holland;

    b.   Keitel visited von Bock: Communicated Fuehrer's urgent wish that motorized forces be moved to the front.

    "Von Bock accepts personal responsibility that motorized units will be in line at the earliest." Following withdrawal of enemy before Sixth Army, XVI Corps has again been committed on von Bock's direct orders. "XV and XVI Corps form a single operational movement."

    Twentieth Motorized Division will be used only in extreme need.

1700.   Von Waldau/General Stapf: Discussion on air-ground cooperation. I develop my view of the general situation and request blocking of roads on which enemy reinforcements are moving against southern flank, and destruction of that enemy. Particular attention should be given to enemy attempts to build up a defensive front at the breakthrough gap. Blockade of line Laon-La Fère-Chaulnes-Amiens-Abbeville. Watch enemy regrouping from Belgium to northern France.

2200.   Evening report to Fuehrer after phone talk with von Brauchitsch, who is at AGp.A. Enemy is holding out at Antwerp and Louvain, while giving way at Wavre and to the south, toward Brussels. Spearheads of AGp.B have reached Franco-Belgian frontier near Beaumont-Hirson; Rethel, on the Aisne, reached. On southern flank counterattack has been beaten off, and contact has been established with fortified line at Carignan. In sector of this army group, VIII, II, XVIII, and IV Corps are standing with two divisions each on southern and western banks of Meuse. Regrouping for continuance of drive westward offers no difficulties. The follow-up divisions are following closely.

. . .

17 May 1940

The morning picture clearly indicates that enemy has not taken any serious steps to close the breakthrough gap. North of the Sambre River he is bending back his southern wing, giving up Brussels and Charleroi, while holding on to Antwerp.

South of the Sambre, where we have reached Avesnes, Guise, and Rethel, the enemy may at best succeed in holding the canal line Valenciennes–Cambrai–Saint Quentin–Chauny, with an extension to the Aisne along the Aisne-Oise Canal. Sporadic movements, disrupted by our air activities, are pointing in this direction.

On the southern flank of our breakthrough, the enemy has moved up at least six divisions and tries to bolster his front. We have no intention of attacking in this area, and enemy is not strong enough to attack us.

The overall situation has reached a stage where we can now turn our minds to continuing our operation in a southwestern direction. Final reduction of the French Seventh, the British, and the French First armies may be left to army group, which is following up in staggered formation and will pivot toward the coast at Lille. In carrying out this maneuver, AGp.B will have to take over Fourth Army. Since the enemy is not likely to attack from Antwerp, AGp.B will be able to put its weight on the left wing, accepting the risk of having its flank attacked by the enemy from his canal positions. That would be quite desirable.

Continuance of our drive in southwestern direction is based on the condition that AGp.A does not tie up any of its strength on the southern flank, but keeps pushing westward in echelon formation. This involves no risk, as the enemy here is too weak to attack at this time. Later one can build up a defensive front with following troops.

The main effort of the southwestern drive would have to be aimed at Compiègne, with the possibility of subsequently wheeling the right wing in a southeastern direction past Paris left open. A great decision must be taken now!

1130. Talk with AGp.A (von Sodenstern): No halt on Oise. Push ahead in direction Valenciennes–Cambrai–Saint Quentin. Seize canal crossings. Secure southern flank only with echelonned forces.

1150. Talk with AGp.B: Brief reference to plans sketched above. Transfer XVI Corps to Fourth Army through Mons! No change in army group boundary yet; depends on major decision now being contemplated; keep open reserved road for SS "Deathhead" to Fourth Army through Huy.

Noon. Meeting Fuehrer with ObdH: Apparently little mutual understanding. The Fuehrer insists that main threat is from the south. (I see no threat at all at present!) For that reason, infantry divisions should be moved up at the earliest for protecting south flank; the armored divisions by themselves would be sufficient to extend breakthrough in northwestern direction.

ObdH discusses matter with von Rundstedt, whom Fuehrer intends visiting in afternoon, and they agree on turning off XVIII, III, and VII Corps in southwestern direction.

1440. Talk with Sodenstern on same subject. Teletype orders on transfer of XVI Corps (Third Armored Division, Fourth Armored Division, Twentieth Motorized Division) to area west of Charleroi, and of XXXIX Corps together with Waffen SS division, Ninth Armored Division, and SS Adolf Hitler to AGp.A's Fourth Army Sector, through Huy.

1630. Conference with General von Falkenhausen, commander general of German forces in Holland. Others present: Colonel von Bock, Administrative President Reeder, Vice President v. Kraushaar, Legation Councilor Woerkmeister.

    a.   Von Kraushaar details his impressions. Dutch officials cooperative. It would be desirable to put a generally respected Dutchman at the head of the Dutch administration (van Vlissingen). Trust in German army. Emphasizes need to assure permanency of the established military administration.

2005. General von Bock calls up: A telephone conference between General Keitel and von Reichenau has caused some confusion. K. mentioned that the Fuehrer did not want XVI Corps to expend itself. *Von Reichenau* has our orders to shift this corps to Fourth Army, through Mons, which could be accomplished only by an attack. Now he does not know what to do.

2100. *Answer:* Stop XVI Corps and move it to Fourth Army by shortest route, in direction Beaumont.

2200.   Talk ObdH von Rundstedt (*on phone*): Seize Le Cateau–Saint Quentin with strong advance combat teams. Protect left flank.

2120.   Talk ObdH with Keitel: Setup in Holland to be the same as in Norway. No elaborate administrative machinery of our own, as Seyss-Inquart will be put in charge. We are to furnish personnel and equipment. ObdH insists on forthright definition of jurisdictions for military and civilian chiefs.

An unpleasant day. The Fuehrer is terribly nervous. Frightened by his own success, he is afraid to take any chance and so would rather pull the reins on us. Puts forward the excuse that it is all because of his concern for the left flank!

Keitel's telephone calls to army groups on behalf of Fuehrer and Fuehrer's personal visit to AGp.B have caused only bewilderment and doubts.

Action in the question of military administration in Holland has demonstrated once more the utter dishonesty of our top leaders in relation to OKH.

18 May 1940

The morning situation shows the enemy making an orderly withdrawal north of Sambre River while apparently shifting major forces from Belgium to the western front of our breakthrough. At the Aisne River, the enemy is building up strength for a defensive front with troops brought from the Paris area and, for a line between Aisne and Meuse, from his AGp.2. No concentrations foreshadowing a counterdrive can be discerned, nor would one be practicable in the time and with the railroad capacity available. French GHq. Reserves have been committed only on a small scale to date.

The fact that the Allies are evacuating Belgium by degrees (the German flag is flying from the city hall of Antwerp) and that they are frantically trying to improvise a front to block our advance proves that I was correct in yesterday's conclusion that the operation must be continued in a southwestern direction (with the main effort south of the Somme) without the least delay. Every hour is precious.

Fuehrer Hq. sees it differently. The Fuehrer unaccountably keeps worrying about the south flank. He rages and screams that we are on the best way to ruin the whole campaign and that we are leading up to a defeat. He won't have any part of continuing the operation in westward direction, let alone to the southwest, and still clings to the plan of a northwestern drive.

This is the subject of a most unpleasant discussion at Fuehrer Hq. between the Fuehrer on the one side and ObdH and myself on the other (1000).

While there, we are handed a directive soon followed by the written summary of the conference.

ObdH talks with General von Rundstedt, and I with von Salmuth to communicate the Fuehrer's concept: Turn spearhead divisions hard to southwest to protect the south flank, while holding bulk of motorized forces in readiness for a drive to the west.

Teletype order to AGps.A and B regarding grouping, boundaries, and follow-up of reinforcements.

Noon. Antwerp has fallen, Cambrai reached 1130, Saint Quentin 0900. It is becoming increasingly evident that the enemy is taking back the Belgian front, apparently establishing an intermediate line somewhere north of the French border, and trying to cover this movement against the advancing Fourth Army by tenacious opposition in the Maubeuge-Valenciennes area. Apart from this, he is attempting, with elements from Belgium and from the south, to organize a line of resistance facing roughly the line Valenciennes–Cambrai–Saint Quentin–La Fère.

We must punch through this new line before it has a chance to consolidate; additionally, we must keep open the possibility of crossing the Somme at Peronne and Ham later on.

Accordingly, an order is issued at 1530 directing main armored force to advance on line Cambrai–Saint Quentin, while securing the south flank. Advance elements are to take Ham and Peronne. Armored formations still hanging back must be brought up speedily. Minimum of forces against Maubeuge and Valenciennes.

Afternoon. Picture of enemy withdrawing before AGp.B is confirmed. Antwerp and Brussels in our hands. The measures instituted by AGps.A and B pursuant to our orders are showing results; southern front of AGp.A is beginning to consolidate. Our tanks are now in line and ready to attack.

1800.   **Report to Fuehrer:** I outline situation and request permission to start drive, which is granted. So the right thing is being done after all, but in an atmosphere of bad feeling and in a form calculated to give the outside world the impression that it is a plan conceived by OKW. The logistical program is reviewed and approved as adequate.

.   .   .

19 May 1940

The breakthrough wedge is developing in a satisfactory manner. Follow-up proceeds as planned. Bulk of enemy forces lately operating in Belgium probably straddle Belgian border. Our big tank drive in direction Arras (starting 0700) consequently will squarely hit the bulk of the retreating enemy. It will be a big battle, lasting several days, in which we have the advantage of the initiative, while the enemy has that of heavy concentration.

But since all psychological factors work in our favor and we have the benefit of a superior and tremendously effective air force, I am certain of success. Perhaps it will become necessary in the course of the battle to shift the main effort to the south of Arras.

1100.   Talk von Bock/ObdH: Nothing of special importance. Difficulties in passing XVI Corps across Sambre arose partly from failure of Fourth Army to take over the corps immediately, partly in method of command in rerouting it. Problem of a direct supply line to Fourth Army through Sixth Army sector. The reports received at noon bear out the conclusion that we still have before us sizable enemy forces, which supposedly are withdrawing south across the Somme to the shelter of a hastily prepared defense line. Some enemy elements are vigorously attacking the line Mons-Valenciennes, while others, which have been drawn together from Belgium and France, are attempting to organize a holding line Valenciennes-Cambrai-Peronne-Noyon, behind which the withdrawal from Belgium is to be completed.

Opposite the gap in our front near Laon, French forces are cautiously feeling their way from Soissons. Farther east, on the Aisne, all is quiet. It is possible that the enemy may attempt a counterdrive over a narrow front close to the still intact Maginot Line, i.e., between Le Chesne and Montmédy.

The reports of enemy attacks in direction of Mons-Valenciennes are worrying OKW. The air force has been ordered to concentrate its effort against this attack. Fortunately, Jeschonnek first asks our opinion. I tell him that, as a matter of fact, I welcome these attacks, since north of them, the left wing of the Sixth Army is already driving into the rear of the attacking force. I ask him to adhere to our previous arrangement to concentrate air strength against the enemy's north-south movements toward the lower Somme, together with providing cover for the left flank at Laon.

Afternoon. Report by von Stuelpnagel: Preparations for Operation BROWN. His conference with von Leeb, AGp.C, and negotiations with Italy. All goes as anticipated.

Von Etzdorf reports to me on political situation. Of real importance are only Italy and U.S.A. Italy is not expected to enter war at a very early date. "It is not a matter of days" (Ciano), although eventual entry into war is a foregone conclusion; perhaps within a few weeks. It is hoped that Italy will choose a method of warfare on the sea and in the air which will allow the Balkans to remain quiet. Yugoslavia probably is a weighty factor in the shaping of policy. Occupation of Greek islands, including Crete, is a growing possibility.

Attitude of U.S.A. toward Italy is considered mere bluffing, a view that is shared by us. Attitude of President dictated by domestic political considerations.

Fellgiebel reports on observations at Eighteenth and Sixth armies. Holland very friendly toward us, little fighting; fighting in eastern part of Belgium apparently heavy. Enemy severely beaten.

Trunk cables are being extended past Liège and Valenciennes to Amiens and through Saint Vith–Jemelle–Hirson to Saint Quentin. Farther north a line must be put through Brussels to Amiens.

Wagner: Gen Qu reports smooth flow of supplies today and promises same for tomorrow.

Plans to build up a large supply base around Brussels or Valenciennes with long-distance truck hauls from Krefeld; the whole is to be operated by Chief of Armament. Agreed!

20 May 1940

Morning situation shows rapid advance of left wing of von Bock north of the armored wedge in his sector. Between this strong left wing of von

Bock and the right shoulder of Fourth Army, French forces have apparently been pinched in and are attacking desperately in a southwestern direction. In view of the proximity of the two wedges pushing on side by side, we are likely to see similar situations develop from time to time.

The question to be decided now is whether von Kleist, who must move closer to the Somme and may even have to swing out southward across the Somme, will still be able to effect a large envelopment movement from the south on von Bock's flank, or whether von Bock is already driving the game away, as it were, past von Kleist.

In view of von Bock's ambition to dash out in front, such a development seems entirely possible. As a result, our attempt to force the enemy to accept a battle with inverted front north of the Somme is likely to eventuate in a conventional envelopment, in which von Bock would turn up at the extreme wing next to von Rundstedt. With this development taking shape, Armored Corps Kleist is bound to be compelled to turn increasingly in a southwestern direction.

Analysis of the operational drafts of AGp.C for an offensive on the Upper Rhine front plainly shows that von Leeb is unable to free himself from the concepts of position warfare in 1918. Accordingly, *von Stuelpnagel* is given instructions to see to it that von Leeb and the men around him assimilate the lessons of the drive across the Meuse. (Visits to Hq. AGp.B and Sixth Army.)

Instructions to Mieth: Ascertain minimum strength required for First Army front. Make Hq. First Army available for Upper Rhine front. The divisions taken out from rear of First Army must be acquainted with experiences gained at the Meuse; the same should be done for Busse's division, which will be ready 15 June. Discuss with Buhle release of Hq. First Army and replacement by Kaupisch.

Noon. Air force reports that our armored and motorized forces have reached Saint Pol and Amiens.

Afternoon. Final conference with ObdH on continuance of operation after coast has been reached. What I have been preaching for the past three days has finally been adopted. The operation in southwestern direction will be conducted in the following order: *Under AGp.A* (from left to right): *Twelfth Army,* attacking west of the Argonne in direction of Saint Dizier. *Second Army,* closing to the west, striking from area west of Laon, in direction Brienne le Château. *Ninth Army,* to the west of Second, pushing from the area between Ham and Moreuil in direction of Forêt d'Oth, with right wing bypassing Paris to the east. *Under AGp.B:* Bulk of armor, under von Reichenau, followed by Fourth Army, under AGp.B, will operate across the Lower Seine, bypassing Paris to the west. It is unnecessary to decide now whether this force, after crossing the Seine, should provide flank cover for the envelopment maneuver of AGp.A, or else be given special mission to drive along the coast to the Bay of Biscay.

Coordinated with the drive of AGp.A, an offensive with fifteen divisions will be initiated from the Upper Rhine in direction of Langres, with perhaps a concurrent drive of eight divisions from the Saarbruecken area toward Sarrebourg. This would leave us with sufficient reserves to see the operation through.

Following this in the evening, conferences with OQu II and Op. Sec. on execution of this operation and regrouping of armies for the new offensive.

Afternoon. Planning conference with Gen Qu at ObdH, who concurs with my proposals. Establishment of large supply base for our field forces in the area Brussels-Tournai-Charleroi calling for development of a large-scale motor truck hauling system from the Ruhr to this area pending restoration of railroads. This plan requires forming transport groups comprising several thousand civilian trucks mobilized in Belgium and Holland. With this organization to be set up in cooperation with BdE, who will later take over, supply bases must be built up for Twelfth Army in Charleville area, for Second Army around Avesnes-Le Cateau, for Ninth Army in Cambrai-Arras area, and for Armored Group Reichenau and Fourth Army north of line Amiens-Abbeville. Eighteenth Army can be directly supplied from main ground forces base.

Other subjects discussed: Prisoner-of-war problems and drafting of laws needed for administration instituted by Hq. Falkenhausen.

Wuestefeld: Regulation of allocation of construction battalions and construction orders for preparation of positions in sectors of Sixteenth and Twelfth armies as well as in areas of Hq. Lower Rhine and Eifel.

Fellgiebel and Bogatsch are briefed on new plans. Several AAA battalions will be released to ObdL.

Buhle: Current organizational problems, including activation of new mounted division.

Eupen-Malmédy, German again!

21 May 1940

Day begins in a rather tense atmosphere. Incoming reports dictate serious pressure on north flank of Fourth Army. No detailed reports yet on advance of our armored and motorized forces.

1100. **Report to Fuehrer:** Plans worked out yesterday are approved. With regard to timing, it has been decided that drive against Lower Seine will start as soon as possible, independent of progress in buildup of offensive front. Start of southeastern drive, east of Paris, is contingent on outcome of battle which only now is reaching full strength.

Once this drive is rolling, we shall launch the Upper Rhine offensive, which in any case could not come off before mid-June, and with it our offensive from the Saarbruecken area, as the final push against the wall, as it were.

A report is submitted on the logistical preparations for the operation.

After return, conference with OQu II and Chief Op. on execution of planned operation. Preparations for conference tomorrow.

1630. **Von Stuelpnagel** *reports on talks with Keitel* OKW, concerning the conversations with Italy. We are not going to urge them any longer, but let them come to us, especially as it is now certain that we are going to mount the Upper Rhine offensive with our own fifteen divisions alone, without the Italians.

1700. **Kinzel** in from Hq. Sixth Army: Army has come up against solid front. Would like to shift main effort to right wing, which is believed to afford better tactical conditions. I make it very plain to him that the important thing is to keep going on the left wing in order to help along Fourth Army. The decision will fall on the high ground of Arras. That is the place that the infantry of Fourth Army must reach as soon as possible. If left wing of Sixth Army lags behind, Fourth Army will be compelled to tie up forces at Valenciennes.

The same problem was hinted at in an obscurely worded teletype message from army group at noon, without stating it plainly. My reply seems to have failed to clarify the matter.

. . .

1830. **Von Etzdorf:**

   a. Italy: No concrete commitments of military or political character. Recent exchange of letters contained boastful reports of successes by Fuehrer and applause by Il Duce. Last letter of Il Duce hints that state of nonbelligerency will not last much longer. Inquiry regarding military aid expected from Il Duce was answered: We are not going to give any. He has been informed of the view held by us now that no Italian soldier would be needed in German theaters.

Greece may remain passive in face of Italian strong-arm methods. Earlier assumption that Greece would immediately react by entry into war is no longer fully maintained, even if Gulf of Patras and Crete should be affected. Key to Greece's attitude is in Britain's hand.

Turkey has changed her tune. Inclination to remain passive is increasing. It is quite probable that Italy would occupy Adriatic coast. Political structure of Yugoslavia rotten, and Cabinet probably incapable of decision to make war. This is how *Italy* views the situation. It remains to be seen if it proves to be correct.

In the overall picture, some minor differences begin to stand out between Italy and ourselves. Italy's chief enemy now is Britain, whereas Enemy No. 1 for us is France. We are seeking to arrive at an understanding with Britain on the basis of a division of the world.

Internal Italian resistance against war is dwindling. Crown Prince reported to be enthusiastically prewar. Mussolini has a free hand. He is also becoming active against the Vatican.

b.   Hungary: Letter to Teleki. Italy and Germany do not want the peace and harmony on the Balkans disturbed. Russia's interest is the same. Germany desires good relations with all Balkan states. Hungary's interest ought to be the same: peace.

A three-power conference undesirable now. Would excite public. Csaki's visit would be welcome. My talk with Hungarian military attaché has caused unnecessary stir.

1930.   **Heim:** Recognition for units without mentioning of names. Morale boosters for battle-worn troops.

2100.   **Wagner** has called on Todt Organization for reconstruction of roads and bridges on Meuse (Namur-Mézières). Todt has set up field office on Meuse, 20 km north of Mézières. I call attention to necessity for cooperation between Todt and OQu II.

2400. **Telephone call by von Bock** regarding our teletype order indicating ObdH's emphasis on need for pushing on with left wing of Fourth Army. He complains that my liaison officer had talked about "holding back." In the end he gets the idea why left wing of Sixth Army must not get stalled and promises to take action accordingly.

Overall picture of the day, which has been substantiated by visit of ObdH to von Rundstedt and by his talks with von Kleist and List, shows that the big battle is in full swing. Constant pressure will be necessary to keep the infantry moving close behind armor. Only when we have seized the high ground of Arras shall we have won the battle.

0030. **Von Bock calls again:** Situation on von Kluge's right wing cannot be so serious. Only local actions. Von Reichenau has taken prisoners from four different divisions.
Von Bock now adds 269th Division of the GHq. Reserve to his left wing.

22 May 1940

Morning situation indicates that the probably unnecessary delay of VIII and perhaps also XVI Corps around Maubeuge, and the southwestern detouring of rear corps, might jeopardize an early advance of infantry divisions into the Arras area, where our armor, fighting south of Arras, has met a strong enemy who is pushing south. The armor drive on Calais, ordered by us, has been temporarily halted by AGp.A on the line Saint Pol–Étaples, and will not be resumed until the situation at Arras is clear.

This estimate of the situation sets off the following reasoning:

AGp.A:

a. The detouring of I Corps to the south, as well as the delay of VIII and II Corps, is incomprehensible.

b. II Corps must advance on Beaurains-Bapaume. V Corps on Albert, XXXX Corps on Saint Quentin–Ham.

c. Tanks west of Arras must be started off as soon as situation at Arras has been consolidated.

Above all it is important for infantry to get to Arras and westward as quickly as possible.

AGp.B:

Eighteenth Army must secure its north flank and not attack into the water line. Left wing of Sixth Army must push on; transfer 227th Division from Holland.

In order to translate these ideas into action, ObdH flies to Hq. Fourth Army. I talk them over with von Sodenstern (1045).

1100.   Conference OQu I, Chief Artillery Officer (Wandel), Chief Engineer Officer, Operations Section: Orientation on intentions for next phase of operations. Needed data for strength estimate and troop disposition are requested.

1230.   Heusinger:

    a. Today no decision on resumption of halted railroad movements.

    b. Setup of daily reports must be changed. Intentions must be specified.

    c. Jodl's call: Fuehrer is worried about following points:

        1. Main effort of Sixth Army is directed not nearly enough to the south. (We have been plugging this line for the last twenty-four hours!)

        2. Sixteenth Army has too many casualties and is attacking needlessly; also troops may be held back in this area. (Pater noster!)

        3. I Corps has not closed up yet. (That is the fault of the interference from the top.)

1300.   Talk with von Rundstedt: Has moved II Corps toward Bapaume, on its right 8th Division, west of Valenciennes. V Corps moved into Peronne area, since everything farther north is congested with motorized troops. One division of XXXX Corps directed toward Saint Quentin. Nothing can be gotten through. I Corps slated to go to Le Cateau (will take time, as all roads are taken up by Twentieth Motorized Division).

Heusinger: Air force activities: Sperrle was to attack enemy movements near Paris, but could not do so on account of bad weather. Kesselring is attacking Calais and Boulogne; afterwards will give close support to our armor at and west of Arras. It is most important that planes no longer needed over Paris area cooperate with armored corps. Kesselring is to support drive of Sixth Army.

Overall situation around noon indicates a letup of tension: The enemy is giving way at Arras, and west of Arras our tanks face only a comparatively weak enemy; area south of Lower Somme apparently cleared of enemy as far as Bresle River.

AGp.A is vigorously pushing infantry in westward direction.

1345.   **AGp.A** states that AGp.A and Sixteenth Army consider capture of high ground of Stonne an absolute necessity.

1435.   **Von Salmuth** reports on situation in VIII Corps sector. I talk with him about the need to hold down to minimum employment of troops on northern wing. The 225th Division will be moved in, perhaps by water transport.

1530.   **Goth** *(Liaison Officer, Fourth Army)* brings report on situation. Situation is much better than we thought. On right wing, 28th Division is still busy cleaning up around Fortress Maubeuge, where fortress troops reinforced by remnants of field units apparently put up a gallant defense. They must be eliminated before we can use the roads. Eighth Division now moving toward Valenciennes (should close this pocket west of Valenciennes) by passing through Denain. II Corps, with 12th and 32d Divisions, is already east of Arras.

Hoth is attacking with 5th Armored Division east, with 7th Armored Division west of Arras, and is in frontal attack from the south with 11th Rifle Brigade and "Totenkopf" SS Division since 1200.

Also since midday, von Kleist is attacking west of the line Avesnes–le Comte–Houdan–Aire–Saint Omer, pushing with XXXXI Corps on the right and XIX Corps on the left wing northward between Saint Pol and the sea.

At the Lower Somme, 2nd and 13th Motorized divisions are providing cover for the operation and hold open the bridgeheads, which are not seriously threatened. In the event of increasing pressure, only the bridgeheads of Amiens and Abbeville will be defended.

Directly east of 13th Motorized Division is 29th Motorized Division. To relieve them, V Corps is being moved from Peronne, and portions of XXXX Corps from Saint Quentin.

1700.   **Koerner:** *Railroad situation* is developing satisfactorily.

Forty-eight trains will get through to Antwerp via Gennep today. Waterways must be utilized more extensively. From Maastricht, cargoes are transferred to Gembloux. Liège–Namur totally unusable. To Dinant and northward, twenty-four trains are now running daily. Are reloaded on trucks for transfer across Meuse, and then by rail to Hirson. At Bertrix reloading on trucks for Charleville and thence by rail in direction Cambrai. Luxembourg supplies Sixteenth Army.

Translation:

   a.   Letter from Churchill to Il Duce: Having taken over the Office of the Prime Minister I feel strongly impelled to send you, the leader of the Italian nation, a message of goodwill across that gap which seems to be widening so rapidly.

   Is it too late to prevent the shedding of blood between the British and Italian peoples? Of course, we could annihilate each other and redden the Mediterranean with our blood. If this should be your will, then it must be, but I wish to say that I have never been an enemy of the Italian people, nor have I in my heart ever been opposed to the man who rules Italy.

   It is futile to predict the course of the great battles which are now being joined in Europe, yet I am certain that no matter what may happen on the continent, Britain will hold out to the last, even if she should stand alone, as she has done in the past.
   I believe with some degree of assurance that the United States, indeed, the whole of the American continent, will come to our aid on an ever-increasing scale.

   I ask you to believe me that it is not out of a spirit of weakness or fear that I am addressing to you this solemn appeal which will be entered upon the annals of history. It is above all imperative that the heirs of Latin and Christian civilization should not enter into a deadly conflict with each other. In the name of honor I implore you to heed my words before the fearful signal is sounded. Never will it be sounded by us. (17 May 1940)

   b.   Answer of Il Duce to Churchill: I reply to the message which you sent me to say to you that you must certainly be aware of the momentous and grave considerations of historical and compelling nature, which have forced our two countries into opposing camps. Without going back too far, let me remind you of the initiative which was taken by your government in Geneva in 1935 in organizing the sanctions against Italy, when we were about to secure for ourselves a small portion of African soil, without causing the slightest injury to your or any other interests or territories. I furthermore remind you of the actual and virtual state of slavery in which Italy is finding herself in her own sea.

As your government declared war on Germany in order to uphold its word, you will appreciate that the same sense of honor and respect for the obligations undertaken under the terms of the German-Italian Treaty will today and in the future determine the policy of Italy in every development. (18 May 1940)

   c.   Personal message of Il Duce to the President of the United States: In reply to your message which was handed me at midnight of 14 May; I fully understand the motives that have prompted you and I consider them to be honorable and worthy of the highest respect. Yet two basic aspects of the present position of Italy cannot have escaped your sense of political reality, namely, that it is the intention of Italy to remain an ally of Germany and, furthermore, that Italy cannot stand aloof at a moment when the future of Europe is in the balance. I therefore cannot but reaffirm what I have said in my first message. (18 May 1940)

. . .

ObdH: Returns during evening, satisfied with results. According to von Greiffenberg (who went with him) and his own account, Goth's report is substantially correct. At conference in Fuehrer Hq., ObdH raised the question of Russian attitude. Fuehrer believes that Russia, following his advice, will limit claims to Bessarabia. (2300)

Issuance of orders to armies in the field on next intentions (wheeling northward with protection of south flank).

. . .

23 May 1940

Morning situation: The situation continues to develop in a satisfactory manner. The left wing of our armored forces is approaching Calais. In the central sector, west of Arras, strong armored forces are pushing toward Béthune.

The situation at the army group boundary line still is somewhat uncomfortable. The right wing of Fourth Army in the area of Valenciennes is still a little thin. The gap between Valenciennes and Cambrai is being "secured" by 8th Division, which has not even arrived in full strength. Very inconveniently, 28th Division is still engaged in mopping up operations way back at Maubeuge. By directing 1st Division on Bavay instead of Valenciennes, more time has been lost for our westward drive.

In the Conde area Waeger's corps, on the left wing of Sixth Army, is advancing too slowly. Instead of the whole of 217th Division, as was promised, only the artillery of the division has been committed in the sector of 269th Division. On the other hand, von Reichenau is still fighting his private battle in the area of Audenarde, which probably will cause bloody losses without a return of operational advantage. The attacks of XXVI Corps north of Ghent likewise serve no operational purpose. Moving of troops through Second Army sector seems to be well under way, but it will be days before a strong infantry force is assembled in the Arras area.

The southern front is quiet.

The developments of the past few days show that AGp.A is indeed experiencing considerable difficulties in managing this unwieldy mass of seventy-one divisions. I have a good idea its staff has not been energetic and active enough. OKH must take the organization of liaison with the several armies in hand in order to ensure execution of its orders up front. (More liaison officers, aides for them, and establishment of Forward Message Center at Chimay.)

. . .

1230.   Von Salmuth (on phone): Has impression that enemy is giving up or at least decreases resistance on the Escaut River.

Sixth Army reports that XI Corps is making headway in direction of Courtrai and that IV Corps is gaining ground south of Courtrai. (The reports are passed on by radio to Hq. Fourth Army and army group.)

1300.   Resumption of phone talk: The 269th Division, on left wing of XXVII Corps, has reached Escautpont, south of Conde, and is advancing in direction of Saint Amand. At Thulins, a battalion of 269th Division has beaten back a breakout attempt of the enemy and taken many prisoners. —Complaints about slow rate of advance of VIII Corps, their neighbor on the left.

Von Greiffenberg: Aides for our liaison officers. —Liaison officers to Army Hq. 9. —Forward CP Chimay will be operational within two days.

1300. **Von Sodenstern:** OKH thinks it desirable to commit Army Hq. 9 next to Twelfth Army. Its sector will extend only to Peronne, so as not to crowd area needed for movement of armed forces. Army Hq. 9 assigned to army group.

1410. **Von Salmuth** claims that SS "Adolf Hitler" and 1st MG Battalion had to go over to the defensive southeast of Valenciennes, and complains about failure of Fourth Army to attack with its right wing.

AGp.A contends that the unit referred to could not possibly be SS "Adolf Hitler," but perhaps is the advance combat team of 1st Division.

1600. **Major General Brand** *reports* of his visit to Twelfth Army sector. Conditions for initiating a drive would be favorable around Laon and Rethel, less favorable in between these points. For a defensive-offensive operation, conditions also are favorable. Surveying has been well prepared. Method of employment of observation battalions still in need of improvement.

Von Ziehlberg: Organization of improved signal communications for OKH. —Forward Message Center at Chimay. —Current General Staff personnel matters.

1730. **Von Gyldenfeldt** communicates von Kleist's anxieties. He feels he cannot tackle his task as long as the crisis at Arras remains unresolved. Tank losses are as high as 50 percent. —I point out to him that crisis will be over within forty-eight hours. I am aware of the magnitude of his task. He will have to hold on until then. No danger on the Somme.

. . .

Political note: The Fuehrer has become more skeptical about Italy's policy toward Yugoslavia, but believes that he still has the situation under control.

Evening situation: If enemy brings in all available divisions, we may expect arrival of three divisions from North Africa and five divisions from Syria.

Evening. *Upon instruction of ObdH*, orders are issued to AGps.A and B regarding changeover of tactical control of Fourth Army and attached units to AGp.B on 24 May, 2000 hours.

Wagner (Gen Qu) reports that Ammunition Base Mons-Maubeuge has begun to operate; functions also as supply base for motor transport. I direct him to set up a tank-repair base in Arras–Saint Pol area.

Org. Sec.: The recently requested forty regional defense battalions will not be ready before 10 June.

The stated desire of *ObdH* to unify direction of operations under AGp.B for the last phase of the encircling battle will get us into serious trouble owing to the personalities of the commander of AGp.B and his staff, and the difficulties for von Bock to get through to all commanders at a point of the battle when to do so would be difficult even through well-established communications.

ObdH's insistence on unification of command looks to me like a device to sidestep responsibility. He keeps arguing that he has no choice but to coordinate the efforts of the various elements converging on the pocket, under his own command or under that of von Bock. The first alternative, which I should think he would accept as the logical and manly one, he feels unsure about. He seems to be glad to let someone else take the responsibility. But with that he also foregoes the honors of victory.

Operational order 5852/40 goes out without my signature, to signify my disapproval of the order and its timing.

24 May 1940

The situation continues to develop in an entirely satisfactory manner even though it takes quite a while for infantry to get to the Arras area. Since there is no threat south of the Somme at the moment, the delay is not too serious. The enemy's fighting power is no longer significant, other than local resistance. Events will take their due course; all we need is patience to let them come to a head. For the first time now enemy air superiority has been reported by von Kleist.

. . .

1530. **The Fuehrer** *arrived at von Rundstedt's Hq. this morning.*

    a. He orders that new boundary line is not to go into effect today. Wants to talk to ObdH.

    b. ObdH summoned to Fuehrer.

1600. Talk this over on phone with ObdH, who is at Hq. Sixth Army. Orders to comply with Fuehrer's wishes are issued to AGp.A by myself, to AGp.B by ObdH.

1600.   **Von Salmuth** reports on counterattacks by mechanized enemy forces in Abbeville and Amiens area, which are especially vigorous at Corbie and Peronne; thinks it is a British tank corps.

. . .

2000.   **ObdH** returns from OKW: Apparently again a very unpleasant interview with Fuehrer. At 2020 a new order is issued, canceling yesterday's order and directing encirclement to be effected in area Dunkirk-Estaires-Lille-Roubaix-Ostend. The left wing, consisting of armor and motorized forces, which has no enemy before it, will so be stopped dead in its tracks upon direct orders of the Fuehrer! Finishing off the encircled enemy army is to be left to air force!!

25 May 1940

The day starts off with one of those painful wrangles between von Brauchitsch and the Fuehrer on the next moves in the encircling battle. The battle plan I had drafted called for AGp.A, by heavy frontal attacks, merely to hold the enemy, who is making a planned withdrawal, while AGp.B, dealing with an enemy already whipped, cuts into his rear and delivers the decisive blow. This was to be accomplished by our armor. Now political command has formed the fixed idea that the battle of decision must not be fought on Flemish soil, but rather in northern France. To camouflage this political move, the assertion is made that Flanders, crisscrossed by a multitude of waterways, is unsuited for tank warfare. Accordingly, all tanks and motorized troops will have to be brought up short on reaching the line Saint Omer–Bethune.

This is a complete reversal of the elements of the plan. I wanted to make AGp.A the hammer and AGp.B the anvil in this operation. Now B will be the hammer and A the anvil. As AGp.B is confronted with a consolidated front, progress will be slow and casualties high. The air force, on which all hopes are pinned, is dependent on the weather.

This divergence of views results in a tug-of-war which costs more nerves than does the actual conduct of the operations. However, we will win the battle.

For the rest of the morning I am not in for anyone. I see only von Sponeck for a minute to congratulate him on receiving the Knight's Cross, and work on the regrouping of our forces for the next phase of the campaign.

In the afternoon, conference with von Brauchitsch, who approves my recommendations without comment.

1830.   Conference at Fuehrer Hq.: As usual, he receives me in a cool, almost hostile manner. No major changes in my plans for regrouping, in which I stress the objectives of the armored forces and the terrain problems involved. The following points stand out from his, at times agitated, analysis:

a.   The group forming the western wing must be made strong (about twelve to fifteen divisions). Infantry must attack vigorously from the east on the line Peronne–La Fère. A strong tank force will assist this attack by a flank thrust from the direction of Amiens. Immediately following, some portions of this group will drive directly on Le Havre–Rouen and establish a bridgehead across the Lower Seine, while others will join the main drive farther to the east. The objectives selected for this first phase of the operation are approved.

b.   Decision on continuance of drive by the Seine group west of Paris must be deferred. Long-winded recapitulation of all the dangers presented by a city like Paris, from which 400,000 to 500,000 soldiers could burst out at any time. (If the enemy has any left!) Continuance of the drive west of Paris can be considered only after the main drive on both sides of Reims has made substantial ground gains.

c.   Drive east of Paris must be carried through with strong right wing. A strong armored force must be held in readiness for a quick thrust into Paris in the event of internal disorder. Left wing of main attacking force must capture Verdun.

d.   Speed is of the essence. The main thing is to seize the various key positions within the shortest time. This is as important on the right wing as it is on the left.

e.   Preparations for TIGER should be advanced to the point where the operation could start on 24-hours' notice.

f.   Diversion of the drive west of Paris toward Bay of Biscay is left open.

g.   Timetable: Submit as soon as possible!

Evening report: Resistance continues strong in front of AGp.A and in Douai pocket. Transport movements of enemy to Lower Somme seem to continue. Now we have built up such strength that we have nothing to fear. However, in our next moves we must reckon with stiff opposition there.

26 May 1940

No significant change in situation. Von Bock, suffering losses, is pushing slowly ahead between inner wings of Eighteenth and Sixth armies; von Kluge's II Corps gains some ground around La Bassée. Our armored and motorized forces have stopped as if paralyzed on the high ground between Béthune and Saint Omer in compliance with top-level orders, and must not attack. In this way, cleaning out the pocket may take weeks, very much to the detriment of our prestige and our future plans. All through the morning, ObdH is very nervous. I can fully sympathize with him, for these orders from the top just make no sense. In one area they call for a head-on attack against a front retiring in orderly fashion and still possessing its striking power, and elsewhere they freeze the troops to the spot when the enemy rear could be cut into any time you wanted to attack. Von Rundstedt, too, apparently could not stand it any longer and went up front to Hoth and von Kleist, to get the lay of the land for the next moves of his armor.

Around noon, a telephone call notifies us that the Fuehrer has authorized the left wing to be moved within artillery firing range of Dunkirk in order to cut off, from the landside, the continuous flow of transport (evacuations and arrivals).

1330.   ObdH summoned to Fuehrer. Returns beaming at 1430. At least the Fuehrer has given permission to move on Dunkirk in order to prevent further evacuations. Farther south, infantry will advance to a point where the road Bailleul-Cassel-Bergues can be controlled by artillery fire.

Another drive, with two or three armored divisions and the requisite number of motorized divisions aiming at Ypres, is to be put on between Bailleul and Armentières, in order to link up with AGp.B. After effecting junction, this group comes under control of AGp.B and then pushes on to Ostend, to prevent evacuations from that port and encircle the Belgian army wing. Another force of about two armored divisions will attack on the axis Seclin-Tournai in order to pinch off the enemy forces south of Lille and link up with AGp.B. Orders to this effect are issued at 1510.

In afternoon, talk with Heusinger on drafting of regrouping directives.

1700.   Wagner (Gen Qu): Setting up of supply base for drive to the south. —Railroad difficulties in Luxembourg. —Evacuation of prisoners. — Military administration in Belgium and northern France.

Evening. A report on foreign situation. The political developments on Balkans are of particular interest. Hungary begins to get cocky. Our political command is confident it has Russia on a short enough rein to keep her from reaching out beyond Bessarabia. If Hungary does not fall in line, she will be turned into a protectorate. The attitude of the political command toward Holland is also interesting. The policy is to prevent formation of a responsible government, so as to avoid the issue of the Dutch East Indies.

Any revolutionary change in France would be undesirable. It could result only in creation of a Popular Front, and peace offers from such a source would be difficult to reject. A refusal would bring about a fusion of the Popular Front with Nationalist elements.

Transport difficulties in Twelfth Army and apparently also in Sixteenth Army.

Later in the evening, final formulation of the plans for the next phase of the campaign, which is to follow conclusion of fighting in Flanders.

27 May 1940

Early morning reports only confirm start of attack against encircled enemy. On left wing, von Kleist seems to encounter stronger resistance than expected.

By noon, the attack has made very slow progress in the pocket at Douai, done somewhat better in the area of Béthune, while considerably more headway seems to have been made between Bailleul and the coast. Sixth Army, too, seems to be getting ahead in the direction of Ypres. The enemy is beginning to break, but it is a slow process. We must bear in mind that a total of four enemy armies are packed into this pocket and that there is nothing left for them but to fight back as long as there is any ammunition; it must give out eventually.

0930.   *After morning conference with ObdH:* Drive to Euskirchen airfield. From there in our Ju. to Mezières-Charleville for conference at Hq. AGp.A with the Ia and OQu officers regarding continuance of operation (RED). After this conference, which takes about an hour and a quarter, von Greiffenberg speaks on operational details and Wagner discusses redirection of supplies.

. . .

2045.   **Report from AGp.B** that a Belgian general has come to Sixth Army Hq. on behalf of his King to ask for surrender terms for the Belgian army. Inquiry to Fuehrer. Answer: Unconditional surrender. No other agreements! (2055)

More reports are coming in on landings of paratroop detachments in rear area around Charleville during night. Countermeasures are time-consuming and a nuisance but will have to be attended to.

Captain Gaedke reports on his tour to the Somme and the bridgehead at Amiens and Peronne.

Kossmann: Administration of Holland turned over to Seyss-Inquart. Fuehrer orders 28 May. Reason: Mussert.

28 May 1940

The surrender negotiations of the Belgian army initiated last night have been concluded. At 1045, General von Bock informs ObdH that the surrender document has been signed. According to the Belgians, the surrender will affect about half a million men.

0930–1100. Lengthy conference with ObdH, who is rather restless for want of something to keep him busy and can hardly wait until the detailed regrouping orders have been worked out. He wants regrouping of AGp.A planned in such a way that divisions which will be freed in the Saint Amand area could be shifted to the northern wing at the earliest, to relieve the armored divisions, which then could be taken back immediately for refitting.

I bring up the subject of Belgium, which in the impending operations must be treated differently from Holland. The Fuehrer must be advised of this subject.

ObdH sees Fuehrer during morning and returns with the following results at 1300:

a. The proposed change in alignment of armies has been approved. Blaskowitz will be replaced by Strauss, the latter by von Stuelpnagel.

b. Guderian will be given command of an armored group. This can best be accomplished by transferring Hoth to Fourth Army, von Kleist to AGp.B (with XIV Corps going with him), and Guderian to AGp.A.

c. Six regional defense divisions are to remain in the east (in addition to two replacement divisions under Oven and Keiser, plus fourteen regional defense battalions from Fromm).

    d. Liquidation of Belgium:

Step 1: Disarming; feeding; prisoners from pocket to be dispersed in direction Antwerp-Brussels, leaving industrial areas free for time being. Status of King not yet decided.

Step 2: Separate Flemings from Walloons. Release Flemings. Walloons will probably be evacuated to Reich as labor force.

    e. Coast: Demands on navy. They must take charge of coastal defense. Crews for fortress guns will be drawn from AGp.C.

    f. Operations:

      1. At long last my idea has penetrated that for this operation we must concentrate our armor in front of our left wing, with direction on Bar le Duc (AGp.A)–Saint Dizier (AGp.B). With this base, we can establish a strong grouping in front of the more slowly following infantry divisions, which will drive to the eastern bank of the Moselle on the axis Saint Mihiel–Pont-a-Mousson, to form an inner ring, and through the area south of Nancy, to form an outer ring; an inward thrust from the inner ring will aim at Verdun from the rear.

      2. Operation TIGER is deferred until such time when effect of operations from the northwest makes itself felt on eastern bank of Moselle.

      3. Draw a ring around Paris, then go in with infantry, not with armor. Accordingly, von Bock's right wing must have great depth; MG and AT.

    g. Projected peacetime army:

24 armd. divs.,
12 mot. divs.,
30 to 40 other divs.

Problem of greater mobility of tanks may be solved by putting dollies powered by tank engines under them on railroad tracks.

    h. Airborne troops: Marne, Moselle, in front of First Army. Not available at time being.

. . .

29 May 1940

The enemy pocket has again shrunk. It will indeed be interesting to see how much of the enemy did get caught in this pocket, 45 km in length and 30 km in width. Even now, with Lille, Roubaix, Tourcoing in our hands, the enemy is still fighting desperately against our troops pressing on his flanks.

ObdH: Receives Blaskowitz and informs him about the Fuehrer's decision to relieve him of his command.

Conference with ObdH regarding agenda for conference with the CGs in Charleville this afternoon.

Jeschonnek wants return of AAA. Asks for four million liters of aviation gasoline captured by us (Chievre, southeast of Laon).

1400–1600. Conference in Charleville. Present: ObdH, myself accompanying staff officers, commanders of army groups and armies (without AGp.C and First and Seventh armies).

Supplementary to the Ia conference of 27 May, the basic ideas underlying the operation are reviewed and the details of execution discussed. (For particulars see agenda notes on conference.) No queries of any importance, no fundamental disagreements.

Afterwards, Wagner speaks briefly on supply, and Fellgiebel on signal communications.

. . .

30 May 1940

Disintegration of the bottled-up enemy forces is continuing. Some of British units in there are still fighting stubbornly and with determination; others are streaming back to the coast and trying to get across the sea in anything that floats. La Débâcle.

On the southern front, the French are making local attacks to eliminate our bridgehead across the Somme, and so put the river between us and themselves. This would be an indication that they are bent on defense only, which need not surprise us. With the balance of strength being what it is, they could not even dream of staging a coordinated drive calculated to turn the outcome of the campaign, but must do everything possible to stretch their forces.

Among the pinched-off French elements we have captured another commanding general of an army.

Morning conference with ObdH: He is angry, and the reason is that the effects of the blunders forced upon us by OKW (detour in direction Laon and holding back the tanks at Saint Omer) are beginning to be felt now. We lost time, and so the pocket with the French and British in it was sealed later than it could have been. Worse, the pocket would have been closed at the coast if only our armor had not been held back. As it is, the bad weather has grounded our air force and now we must stand by and watch how countless thousands of the enemy are getting away to England right under our noses.

31 May 1940

The morning reports do not give a substantially changed picture of the situation. The ring around Dunkirk has further contracted. However, the British, who are continuing the evacuation under the most difficult conditions, are still fighting desperately. The situation must be attacked with all the resources of a full-scale operation. The Lille pocket seems to contain substantial enemy forces.

On the southern front, the enemy is making forceful attempts to wipe out our bridgeheads, but has made only trifling local gains to date. Meanwhile, our position there has been materially improved by the arrival of infantry divisions.

Regrouping of our forces has started, AHq. 18 has formally taken over command, but apparently has not yet been able to reach all units now under its control.

Later in the morning, drive to AGp.C in Bad Schwalbach. En route I stop for an hour on Reich Motor Highway near Limburg, where Wagner (Gen Qu) submits his order for the reorganization of rear communications in the impending drive. The logistical arrangements will be completed by 3 June, and first issues can be made on 4 June.

Conference at AGp.C: Obdh reviews our plan in broad outline. Commander of army group and CGs of armies state their intentions. ObdH emphasizes that efforts to achieve breakthrough must not be restrained by preoccupation for flanks. The conference produces no new viewpoints, but holding it was necessary to give an extra lift to the commanders of this quiet front.

Return via Bad Ems–Rhine Valley–Ahr Valley. Back at 1900.

The reports received during the day confirm the picture given by the morning reports. Lacking unified leadership (Army Hq. 18 could not get through to all Hq. in time), our attack resolved itself into individual actions against an enemy stubbornly defending himself behind the canals, and so achieved only slight local successes. An intercepted radio signal indicates that the enemy is going to resume evacuation operations during the night. It will be difficult to stop him. We are now paying for our failure, due to interference from above, to cut off the coast.

Effectiveness of our artillery against the enemy is greatly reduced in the sand dunes, where neither ricochets nor impact fuzes produce the desired effect. (Fuehrer suggests use of Aa explosive train fuzes.)

Regrouping is making good strides. Fourth, Sixth, Ninth, and Second armies will take over their sectors by noon tomorrow, next to Twelfth and Sixteenth armies, which were there before. AGp.B will then assume command on 2 June, 1200, completing the buildup of our front. A number of long-distance calls are made during the evening to make sure that our new offensive front is set up as planned and that 5 June will be adhered to as target date for the attack.

Goth: (Liaison Officer, Fourth Army): Gives an account of the situation on the Somme. The enemy tank attacks turn out to have been quite serious. He reports also on the condition of our armored units.

The latest strength reports are cheering. They show that 50 percent of our tanks are ready for immediate commitment. Within a few days (about five), required for minor repairs, fighting strength will be up to 70 percent. The tanks which have been brought up as loss replacements are ready for issue. It is well to remember, however, that the useful life of a tank is limited. We may expect a substantial number to be out of the running after about another 300 km. This would do nicely for our purposes. Besides, we could make use of some of the many tanks captured from the enemy.

1 June 1940

Operations have produced no significant developments. The small coastal strip still held by the enemy has again been narrowed, but our attacks are making only slow progress. The remnants of the enemy are fighting gallantly, but demoralization is beginning to show in some places. We must reckon with another evacuation attempt during the night. Apart from this, the operation started on 10 May is now concluded.

This fact will have its outward expression also by the Fuehrer's visit to Hq. AGp.B today, and AGp.A tomorrow, to express his thanks and appreciation. It will further be marked by the decoration of OKH and General Staff officers.

The efforts of all commands and OKH now are bent on assuring the opening of the new drive on 5 June. Regrouping by AGps.A and B must be effected substantially along the lines of our orders. The army Hq. will take over their sectors on the new front today in the following order: Fourth, Sixth, Ninth, Second; Twelfth and Sixteenth armies will adjoin them in their old sectors.

. . .

ObdH: Has been informed by the Fuehrer that Italy will enter the war within coming weeks. The Fuehrer does not want 5 June so as not to compromise secrecy of our plans.

On 4 June, a large-scale attack will be launched against enemy (French) air force. In other respects, Fuehrer conference with commanders in chief and chiefs of staff of armies did not produce anything of importance.

. . .

2 June 1940

The overall situation is unchanged. It is quite obvious that the enemy is getting a little nervous. He cannot but realize that we have considerable forces available for new operations, but he will not have a clear picture of our new offensive plans. He is probably considering these three possibilities:

    a.   Rolling up of the Maginot Line.

    b.   Thrust on Paris via Reims.

    c.   Drive against the Lower Seine with a strong right wing.

Accordingly, he will group his reserves around Paris and will reinforce the corner buttress, the Maginot Line.

An estimate of enemy losses at the end of the first phase of the campaign indicates that the enemy has lost about 1.5 million men and equipment, equivalent to that of about seventy divisions.

ObdH: Flies to Berlin.

Iron Crosses: After presenting the Iron Cross, First Class, to von Greiffenberg and Thiele yesterday, I shall decorate a considerable number of officers in the three sections with Iron Crosses today. To do this I have to drive to Godesberg and take a plane to Giessen.

During the afternoon valuable intelligence extracted from captured enemy transport orders is received. It appears that we still have to reckon with a strong group south of the Somme, comprising fifteen to eighteen divisions, including several divisions of GHq. Reserve.

The great picture accordingly presents a front between the sea and the Meuse River, for the most part held only by moderately strong forces, and, behind it, a reserve divided into two groups, north and northeast of Paris, respectively. Another reserve group probably is inside the fortress triangle.

Paris in all likelihood is guarded by third draft divisions.

Regrouping and shifting of our forces is making progress. Naturally this result is not brought about without some frictions. I would not be surprised if tomorrow and the day after tomorrow we see some people try to get us to extend the target date 5 June.

3 June 1940

Move to Forges.

No material changes in the situation. Everything is on the move for regrouping.

In working out our plans, special stress must be laid on the need for making the right wing strong and keeping our reserves close up to the line.

As far as numbers are concerned, we have all that would be needed for a strong right wing. The difficulty will be to move our forces up quickly enough to obviate drawing on army troops for covering the flank facing Paris.

We must let today and tomorrow go by without interfering in current movements. Afterwards it may become necessary to revise the grouping of the reserves.

ObdH: Brings nothing of consequence from Berlin. Infantry training regiment is not yet ready.

Canaris tells me about activities and achievements of his organization. I thank him. —Wahle, attaché Bucharest.

1230. Departure for Hangelar, via Godesberg. (Call on Baroness Duecker, thank her for her hospitality.) By plane to new GHq. Arrival 1630.

The layout of the new GHq. is badly arranged. Op. Sec. is twenty minutes away from my office. On the other hand, ObdH is wall-to-wall with Op. Sec. The internal telephone system still functions very spottily. The outside lines seem to be working fairly well. Facilities for directing major operation are not nearly as good as those in our former GHq.

1700. General von Brauchitsch *on phone:*

    a. AGp. Bock has shown him that they cannot move up their reserves, especially 18th and 61st divisions, which are still engaged in heavy fighting at Dunkirk. X Corps also is still tied up in that sector, but IV Corps is now free.

    b. Amiens bridgehead seems to be too narrow for tank jump-off. Accordingly, XVI Corps will start drive via Peronne and link up with XIV Corps in direction of Montdidier.

    c. He says that only parts of the GHq. artillery and engineers have arrived so far, and he is also worried that 9th Armored Division might not come up in time. Nor have replacements reached the divisions. All this adds up to a request for postponement of our offensive.

    Now this is what I think:

    Re **a.**   Switching AGp. Reserves for IKH Reserves is a mere bookkeeping matter. For all we care, the divisions can follow up as OKH Reserves. IV Corps can be substituted for X Corps.

    Re **b.**   Is an operational matter of army groups.

    Re **c.**   A one-day postponement won't do much good, and to get away from improvisations it would be necessary to allow several days.

    . . .

2300. Evening conference with ObdH: Review his findings. The movements of foot troops and motorized elements are crisscrossing pretty badly, and road jams and delays are unavoidable.

Another factor is that the troops are in need of rest. It will be difficult to keep the 5 June dateline. To me, on the contrary, it seems both

4 June 1940   177

necessary and important to stick to that date. Fourth Army has established British units.

4 June 1940

The enemy situation at the front has not changed materially. Still, the continual reports about enemy concentrations around Paris and the appearance in Fourth Army sector of British troops, believed to be newly landed, are something to think about. The strength of the enemy is limited. We can continue operating on our assumption that the Allies have about sixty divisions in France. This would be enough for a weakly held front and some reserve groups. The disposition of those reserve groups will be dictated by our threat to Paris. We may assume that the enemy is expecting our attack to come from the direction of Laon and that he reckons with a strong German right wing, from both the clues furnished by the development of the campaign and our obvious aim to threaten England from the air. For this reason he will keep substantial forces also between Lower Somme and Lower Seine. Behind the concentrations around Villers Cotterêts and Beauvais, we may reckon with a group around Paris. From behind this triangle the enemy could take his dispositions against the grouping of German forces as it is actually developing now.

Such a policy necessarily weakens the French eastern front. The enemy will try to mask this weakness, or mitigate its consequences, by heavily reinforcing the northern wing of the Maginot Line. All this, however, would not affect massing of large forces in the wider Paris area, which, in the course of the developing German attack and perhaps also of an Italian drive, might become the pivotal point of a strategy backing against the sea. Such a solution certainly must be seriously considered by a military command which would have only the Atlantic route left to get to its manpower reserves in North Africa if an Italian drive should cut it off from the Mediterranean; and, an even weightier reason is that it must ultimately look to America for aid.

Another factor in favor of such a solution is that for France, deprived of her industrial North and depending largely on overseas imports to maintain her production, holding her seaports and the lines of communications to them is a matter of life and death.

If these conclusions prove correct, our drive will at first gain ground in the Somme and Aisne sectors (owing to the tactical weakness of the French forces strung out over a sprawling front), but eventually come up against stronger forces north and northeast of Paris.

Accordingly, our organization in depth must enable us to shift the main effort of AGp.A and wheel this group in the Champagne toward the west. Massing of armor on this wing must be prepared now. It still has to be decided whether or not to shift some of the armor to the Moselle in order to assist the jump-off of operation TIGER. In any event, TIGER must not be lacking in punch, for if the contemplated wheeling movement is carried out, the TIGER group, as wing echelon following AGp.A in southwestern direction, may yet play a decisive part.

At the *morning conference,* these schemes of thought are discussed.

ObdH goes out to AGp.A, and Sixteenth, Twelfth, Second, and Ninth armies.

General Mieth flies to Eighteenth Army in order to initiate withdrawal and transfer of the reserves now committed with the Dunkirk group.

Op. Sec. issues orders on regrouping of GHq. Reserves.

Wilke is put on the job of restoring liaison with air force, slackened by removal of GHq.

Gen Qu is prodded to speed movement of regional defense divisions in Belgium to the coast in order to ensure earliest possible release of line units still tied up in the area.

1200. Von Salmuth:

    a. Dunkirk taken. Coast has been reached. French are gone.

    b. Beyer, XVIII Corps, sick. Replaced by Boehme, 32d Division. The 32d Division will be taken over by General Bohnstedt, of the 18th Division.

    c. Attack set for 5 June, 0500 hours.

. . .

1500. Von Salmuth: Two French divisional commanders (25th and 68th) have been captured at Dunkirk. Several other generals are claimed together with forty thousand men and immense quantities of materiel.

1746. Liss: Air reconnaissance of area south of Somme to Seine and Marne shows absence of enemy movements. AAA defense at Routen; especially heavy between Soissons and Fismes. Radio intelligence locates an army Hq. at Beauvais. This means that we have to count on two armies between the Oise River and the sea.

. . .

Reports are received that our air force has apparently made a very successful attack against the enemy fighter base at Paris on 4 June. Defense was weak. A big success. One of the men states: "It was like a Party rally flight over Paris."

5 June 1940

Our offensive has started at 0500. Early reports seem to indicate that the enemy in the open country south of the Somme has made things easy for us on the first forward bound.

The days to come will show if the enemy is really accepting a battle of decision at the Somme and Aisne. It is hard to say what would be the best course of action for him. Withdrawal to his fortifications belt along the Seine north of Paris and Marne would enable him to maintain contact with his frontier fortifications in the east. Yet doing so would overextend his front, and he would no longer be strong in any place. He will be beaten on this line, which will be breached probably east of Reims and perhaps simultaneously also in the direction of the Lower Seine. It remains to be seen whether this will lead to an encirclement of the remaining enemy in the northeastern sector—as envisaged and ordered by us—or to an encirclement in the wider Paris area. It is important for us to dispose our reserves in order to have them available for either contingency.

Morning conference with ObdH is unproductive of any important viewpoints. Steps must be initiated for Blaskowitz's assignment to an administrative post in northern France.

.   .   .

Conference with ObdH about new phase of campaign: We must bear in mind that the enemy, on the one hand, cannot afford to give up his communication lines with the coast, but, on the other, cannot afford to lose contact with his fortified northeastern front, if for no other reason than national morale.

The Maginot Line represents everything that stands for security in the French people's mind. The line cannot be given up without risking the moral collapse of France. These considerations will compel the enemy to group the bulk of his forces in the region protected by the Maginot Line, the fortresses on the one side and the sea on the other, so as to have a defensive front facing the frontal attack of the German army from the north. This means we shall find up to twenty divisions of the GHq. Reserves under AGp.1 generally along the Châlones-Paris line, a smaller group perhaps in the fortress triangle, and a third one as a reserve group south of Saint Dizier.

If these assumptions are correct, it would be against every concept of generalship to direct the striking power of our armies against empty or nearly empty fortifications. It is the living fighting forces of the enemy that we must aim at in the operation.

In executing these assumptions it will be necessary to exploit the ground gains at the inner wings of AGps.A and B so as to effect a large-scale wheeling movement to the right. This maneuver would move the boundary line of the two army groups from the area west of Reims toward the confluence of Yonne and Seine, and carry the left wing of AGp.A, which would give up Sixteenth Army to AGp.C, toward Auxerre. The armored divisions would have to be massed in front of left wing of army groups at the earliest and placed under von Kleist, whose Hq. has been organized for such a task from the first.

As Group Guderian is sweeping forward, it is desirable to detach a reinforced armored division for a surprise attack on Verdun from the south. This division would follow Guderian as soon as it is relieved by arrival of the right wing of Busch.

Accordingly, von Leeb would have to advance the date of start of First Army drive to 9 June, take over Sixteenth Army, already committed, and have Dollman start his drive on 11 June. It would be his mission to reduce the French forces east of the Meuse and, as soon as possible, follow with everything he can spare in echelon formation behind von Rundstedt's left wing in the general direction of Dijon.

OQu IV: I impress upon the Sec. the need for having a clear picture of the disposition of enemy strength by 7 June, noon.

Von Etzdorf will be oriented on our estimate of the situation, the possibilities of a new political reorganization of Holland and Belgium, and on the impending entrance of Italy into the war.

Von Greiffenberg: Outline of operational intentions. Current matters.

Wagner: a.   Employment of Regional Defense Units in Belgium and Holland. I have to bear down a little to get them released for coastal defense.

      b.   Future administration of northern France.

Mieth: Sixteenth Infantry Regiment —Air reconnaissance.

Late into the night at work on plans for wheeling offensive toward southwest.

Liss: Rings up informing us he has reliable information that the army of ten-to twelve-divisions' strength, which had been standing in Dijon area, has been shifted to area of Montmédy-Reims.

6 June 1940

Morning conference: I outline to ObdH my conception of the next moves in the campaign, as well as proposals regarding military administration in northern France and the former Reich territories, which will soon be occupied by us.

.   .   .

Up to *noon,* the developing offensive gives the following picture:

Fourth Army has made relatively good progress. It has apparently broken through the enemy defense zone, reached the lower Bresle, and taken the area north of Poix.

Sixth Army has split into three widely separated offensive wedges.

XIV Corps, south of Amiens. Organized opposition supported by artillery is expected on road Conty-Moreuil, and the intention is to take out XIV Corps and put VIII Corps in its place.

XVI Corps, south of Peronne, where the armored spearhead is approaching Roye. XXXX Corps, to the west, is battleworn; V Corps, to the east, seems to have spread itself too far.

South of the Oise, where one regiment of 263d Division apparently hit upon an unprotected boundary line, 263d Division, together with 98th Division, took advantage of this opening and quickly gained ground; counterattacks were repelled.

Immediately to the east, XXXXIV Corps, which is making slow but steady headway toward the Aisne. Ninth Army is moving slowly but steadily toward the Aisne.

1500.   ObdH at Fuehrer Hq.: The interview, as we may gather from his rather weary account on returning, developed as follows:

The Fuehrer thinks that changing the direction of the offensive, as proposed by me, is still too hazardous at this time. He wants to play absolutely safe. First, he would like to have a sure hold of the Lorraine iron ore basin, so as to deprive France of her armament resources. After that he believes it would be time to consider a drive in westerly direction, probably having in mind a strong wing at the coast (Fourth Army).

There we have the same old story again. On top, there just isn't a spark of the spirit that would dare put high stakes on a single throw. Instead, everything is done in cheap piecemeal fashion, but with the air that we don't have to rush at all. However, we can be pretty sure that before thirty-six or forty-eight hours are over, the ideas proposed by us today will be served right back to us in the form of a top-level directive.

The following points of his argumentation should be noted. The present campaign is calculated to deny the enemy possession of his iron ore resources in Lorraine. With them gone, it's all over with his armament industry. And meanwhile our political command is in no hurry. We can take our time cleaning out the northeast and, when this is done, turn either south or southwest, with a strong western wing (Fourth Army) playing an important part in the operation. For the time being we should watch how the current operation develops and in a day or two decide what we should do after von Kleist has forced the Oise.

Air power is to be concentrated in front of Fourth and Sixth armies.

With regard to Norway, we learn that a new operation has been planned, for which additional forces will have to be furnished by OKH. Detailed directives may be expected soon.

1800.   Von Salmuth: Von Bock wants to take out XIV Corps and combine it with XVI in the latter's offensive sector under von Kleist. Movements to this effect have been initiated, but it is not expected that Group Kleist will be complete before 8 June.

In addition to AGp. Reserves, VIII Corps will be committed between Amiens and XXXX Corps sector. Jump-off 8 June.

The success of XIV Corps, according to army groups, represents a major victory. The enemy fronting XVI Corps has been smashed. Now there is a hole.

We have no objections against taking XIV Corps out of sector where the enemy is putting up strong resistance, and committing it in sector of offensive wedge of XVI Corps. This fits into the situation and promises success.

Evening. Talk with ObdH turns mainly about von Bock's decision to withdraw XIV Corps and transfer it to sector of XVI Corps, instead of concentrating Group Kleist more forward.

2100.   Inquiry at AGp.B shows that situation had developed much more favorably than was expected in the afternoon. In fact, Fourth Army has made good strides and reached the Aumale-Poix-Conty road. Signs of demoralization are reported in this sector. To the right, in XIV Corps sector, the situation has also eased to such a degree that a determined stand of the enemy along the Conty-Moreuil road may well be discounted. The plan to shift XIV Corps has been dropped, and 13th Motorized Division has been brought up as reinforcement.

XVI Corps also has gained ground and is now around Roye.

South of the Oise, 1st Mountain Division has reached the Aisne and has put across advance elements. Similar reports from 25th Division, east of Soissons.

Instructions are issued for the reserves to follow, so that they will be directly behind AGp.B.

7 June 1940

The morning reports round out last night's picture: Several powerful wedges of AGp.B have broken through the enemy defense line just west of the Oise. We are now confronted with two important questions:

1.   When should AGp.A start its drive?

2.   Would it not be advisable already now to gear everything to the southwestern drive? We'll have to make this shift as surely as the amen, even if the Fuehrer has vetoed the plan for the moment just because it was our idea.

As to 1.: Von Kluge's forces must have beaten an enemy of superior strength, or else he could not be dominating the country between the Bresle and the Aumale-Conty road. There are now two alternatives: either the enemy will throw against him the forces which we surmise to be concentrated north of Paris, or von Kluge will keep a free hand. Some signs are pointing to the former alternative. In that case, there will be fighting today in the Breteuil-Montdidier area, which will open the way toward Creil.

On this basis we can expect that von Bock's right wing will have pushed to Creil by 9 June, and that von Kluge will be able to open his drive to the Lower Seine from the Formerie-Marseille area on the same day.

In that way, the front-wide drive would get under way on 10 June; that is, von Rundstedt would join in the offensive on that date. When Ninth Army and left wing of Sixth Army have crossed the Aisne, they will have to be temporarily halted until that time.

As to 2.: Following out the thoughts developed under 1., we need not orient ourselves in accordance with my proposed turning movement toward the southwest before 9 June, and orders to this effect need not be issued before 10 June, i.e., the day von Rundstedt, with Group Guderian, will have gained freedom of movement in the Champagne.

On 10 June Operation TIGER also can be started. This, however, depends on the timely arrival of the eleven medium artillery battalions which are needed as mobile reserves for the jump-off. Right now they are still with AGps.A and B, and it will take three days to shift them. It is all right if SMALL BEAR can be set in operation a few days later. A day more or less won't make any difference here.

These ideas are discussed with ObdH at the morning conference.

1030. **OQu IV** reports that the schools in Paris have been ordered closed and that preparations are being made for defending Paris in case of an attack.

1100. **Report from AGp.C (through Op. Sec.):** TIGER can start as soon as artillery and motorized engineer elements, which were promised for the operation, have arrived. Depending on their arrival, the attack could start even before 10 June.

Twenty-four hours warning requested. If we are hard pressed, receipt of order not later than 1400 would do.

Operation BEAR. Earliest date 13 June. Orders must be issued forty-eight hours in advance.

AGp.A: Orders for jump-off must reach AGp. Hq. by 1600, or, on the outside, 1800 hours.

1230. **Phone talk with Felber, AGp.C:** Our inquiry seems to have made those people nervous. He calms down when I explain that our inquiry regarding earliest possible date for attacks was only by way of general information. Dollmann grumbles again that the division sent to him would have to be trained yet.

Heusinger: Telephone talk with AGp.A. They are worried that Twelfth Army is working too methodically and therefore will be too late in sending off its tanks.

. . .

Jodl: a. Wants to know what we think about jump-off date for AGp.A. Answer: If present operational plans stand, we need not hurry, but if new plans recommended by us are accepted, attack should commence soon. (It's too late now for anything before 8 June.)

There are rumors of an agreement to consider our plan, but with the modification of having AGp.B attack in southwestern and AGp.A in southeastern direction. Very dangerous!

b. There will be no new divisions from interior. Apparently the idea is to leave more manpower for the economy. I inform Jodl of the activation of two replacement divisions and also emphasize the requirements for controlling large areas. We don't want to increase number of divisions.

c. Background stories with the names of higher commanders, to supplement the Wehrmacht Communiqués, are not wanted, but reports on individual feats, which give no clue to the operations involved, are acceptable.

Evening conference with ObdH: He tells me what he found at XVI and XIV Corps. Their attacks make slow progress. At times they seem to be short on ammunition for tanks. In XVI Corps 30 percent of the tanks are reported total losses. Rifle and motorcycle rifle elements of the armored divisions seem to be much weakened by combat losses. All are begging for replacements. (Arrival of replacements seems to have been delayed by regrouping movements and railroad difficulties.) Drinking water is a problem in combat area. Danger of epidemics! (Put prisoners to work!)

Wagner (Gen Qu) reports on difficulties in delivering ammunition and rations owing to railroad accident (derailment) and congestion caused by troop transports (replacements).

2300. An interesting situation. General von Bock calls up to develop the following three points:

a. Hoth has reached Forges les Eaux and Saumont. He has no enemy before him, "is in the rear area." II Corps behind him is still fighting at Bresle and Liège sectors.

It is still a question whether XVI and XIV Corps can quickly effect planned junction through Saint Just and Mory. Possibly the enemy may not make a stand, but we cannot be sure.

As right wing of Sixth Army continues to advance on Creil and Fourth Army, as ordered, drives toward Lower Seine (left wing on Vernon), a gap begins to show up at Beauvais. This is precisely where the enemy is bringing in forces from Paris. The question now arises whether Hoth should not be turned on Gisors.

I express my doubts on the advisability of departing from the basic plan set out in the operational orders and stress the effect that a surprise seizure of Rouen would have, but yet I must admit that ObdH, in our conference earlier this evening, expressed misgivings about a premature turning of Hoth's forces toward the Lower Seine.

Von Bock also refers to disembarkments at Le Havre and possible British movements in northwestern direction. Le Havre is said to be full of enemy warships. That is the first thing I hear about it. But there is no hurry about Le Havre and, besides, we cannot attack before Rouen is securely in our hands.

b. The ridge Luzarches-Dammartin dominates the country to the south, way beyond Paris, as well as to the north. Von Bock must have control of this ridge. For this purpose he wants to move strong reserves behind the right wing of von Reichenau and requests us to get Eighteenth Army Hq. ready for immediate commitment in that area.

c. Everything is being done to effect the linkup of Group Kleist, but completion may still take some time. Junction is planned on line Saint Just–Mery.

Immediately afterwards I consult with *ObdH*. He is worried that Hoth might make raid, away from the main battlefield, that he is not moving up his supplies, and that he does not have sufficient infantry strength. For the present he is mainly interested in seeing right wing of Sixth Army get ahead. The push toward the Lower Seine will have to be shelved until then.

Right after conference I call *von Bock:* He intends to instruct Hoth to seize Rouen with strong forces and organize reconnaissance in strength against the line Beauvais-Gisors. By doing so he thinks he will be in a position to hold Rouen and turn south at the same time.

Second Motorized Division has moved close to armored division. Von Bock will try to move up more motorized forces (SS "Adolf Hitler").

ObdH is being informed of this decision.

8 June 1940

This is another day of nervous tension, which is the usual thing when decisions are in the making in which top level also wants to have its say.

Hoth apparently closed up at the front of Fourth Army and, after getting the necessary fuel, has struck out for Rouen. North of him, the British are still hanging on behind the Bresle River, south of him the French. It is one of those typical breakthrough situations which first look quite critical but after a while turn into a picture of complete success. The precariousness of such a situation dominates the morning conference with ObdH.

1100. **Chief of Staff of von Bock** on phone: Informs us that he has decided to issue the following orders:

Fourth Army will take Rouen, cover its flanks on both sides of Rouen, and drive with strong eastern wing across line Gournay-Crèvecoeur in direction of Lower Oise.

Sixth Army will contain the enemy north of the Oise. Left wing (pivot) will advance to the general line Crepy en Valois–Villers Cotterêts and wooded terrain to the east.

Ninth Army, with weight chiefly on right wing and with left flank covered, will seize ground toward the Ourcq River.

The boundary line between Fourth and Sixth armies is being changed. XIV Corps (without 9th Division) will be transferred to Fourth Army. Fourth Army, moreover, will have at its disposal I Corps with 1st, 11th, and 217th divisions, and Brig. Senger.

These measures are taken on the strength of reports that the enemy west of the Oise has been reinforced and apparently wants to accept the battle there. Frontal attack against a strong enemy is pure waste of armor without any prospect of success.

The question as to when this regrouping will make itself felt cannot be answered with any certainty now.

After that, some rush work to compile material on enemy disposition, etc., for Fuehrer conference.

1430.   Report to Fuehrer:

1.   First, I outline the principles of employment of armor. Tanks are operational assets only where they have open country to maneuver in. In slow-moving battles they only burn themselves out. Such fighting is the department of the infantry, with which we are amply supplied. Armored divisions which have gained a free field of movement must be followed up by motorized divisions (shaft of the spearhead).

2.   Critical review of development of situation in area north of Beauvais. The tanks have been in frontal attacks too long, but since von Bock has just committed them again, nothing can be done about it now. It would have been more desirable to launch the armored forces in the area of Laon east of the Oise.

3.   For the time being, operations will continue in the original direction set out in our operational orders until the Marne has been crossed. The Fuehrer still counts on the possibility of delivering a decisive blow against strong enemy forces in the fortified area of northeastern France. The following moves are considered necessary:

   a.   Group Hoepner (XVI Corps) must be brought to bear east of the Oise in direction Château Thierry, at the earliest.

   b.   Reserves must be introduced so as to sustain the advance of Ninth Army, which has now become the right wing of our offensive front, with a continuous flow of forces. Sixth Army, at variance with our original plan, will thus be echelonned off this new right wing of our attacking front.

   c.   Our efforts to extend and expand bridgehead of Ninth Army south of Aisne must be kept up.

   d.   AGp.A will launch drive on 9 June, morning.

   e.   Grouping of forces in drive of AGp.A will be such that the armored wedge will be driven forward not at the inner wing, but as close as possible in direction of Reims.

   f.   After crossing the Vitry le François–Sainte-Menehould road, an armored division and a motorized division will make a thrust against Verdun from the south and so break into the fortress by surprise.

After return from Fuehrer Hq.: Orders are issued for redisposing Group Hoepner and moving up reserves.

. . .

2000.   **Von Bock** calls up: Hoth has not advanced as far as was expected. Around Beauvais, the enemy is falling back and calls in his outlying troops which had been fighting Hoepner stubbornly.

XIV Corps, which, driving south, reached the Breteuil–Saint Just road, is now standing in the rear of this enemy.

His intention is to launch Fourth Army against original objectives specified in operational orders, but put off Le Havre for time being. Sixth Army will drive in direction Creil, as set forth in our orders. Approved.

. . .

9 June 1940

During the night we received report that *King Haakon* of Norway has left the country, directing one of his generals to enter negotiations with the German army.

The drive of AGp.A has started according to plan. All along the front our troops have crossed the Aisne in the first bound. A superb achievement, in which the exemplary work of the General Staff officers in this group has a substantial share. Naturally, enemy resistance will stiffen after we have reached the southern bank of the Aisne, and we shall especially feel the effect of the enemy's artillery before long. But by then our tanks will be coming.

In AGp.B, developments have moved at great speed. Hoth keeps on pushing westward. At noon a report comes in that he has battered his way into Rouen. All bridges in Rouen are down, as are also some bridges farther west. However, the bridges at Vernon and Les Andelys are still intact. We should be able to secure them.

Von Wietersheim is pressing on behind the rapidly withdrawing enemy and has reached the Clermont-Compiègne road during the morning. In front of center of Sixth Army, where enemy forces from Montdidier area are streaming back in disorder, a major disaster is in the making. It would be good if XV Corps could thrust quickly across the Oise at Verberie and link up with the elements of left wing, Sixth Army, which has advanced as far as Villers-Cotterêts from the north. Then the forest of Compiègne, into which also the famous French 11th Division (Iron Division) has been driven, would become a large pocket where a half dozen French divisions would meet their end.

Morning rather quiet. Talk with Felber, who is not sure he will have First Army ready for 12 June, and is very doubtful that he could be ready on the upper Rhine on 13 June, owing to the difficulties experienced there. He would like a postponement of several days. I make it very clear to him that he will have to be ready on time.

1530.   **Talk with von Witzleben,** to whom I show that a few battalions more or less won't make much of a difference and that in the light of recent experience an attack against fortifications is a matter of surprise and efficient combat engineer work, rather than of massed artillery. Schroth, who has come back again, is not to take over command now from Heinrici.

Talk with Olbricht (General Army Office): He will endeavor to scrape together a few more mobile units from his schools and get them ready for 15 June: Two armored reconnaissance battalions; one motorcycle rifle company; one company light and one company medium tanks; one flamethrower company; one battalion from training regiment (two rifle companies, one MG company, one platoon of infantry guns); one AT company; one battalion of motorized light field howitzers; one signal company; and one engineer company.

I stipulate that nothing more is to be sent to Norway. Sixth Mountain Division must be made ready for Dollmann!

Replacement divisions: Two will be ready by 22 June, two more by 25 June.

General von Rocques, former infantry commander of 6th Division, reports in. Special assignments as CG of OKH Reserves.

In the afternoon I have an hour out for some private letters.

Talk with von Witzleben: Get ready for 12 June. He need not wait for the rest of the artillery. No mass attacks! Von W. claims he needs more engineer troops! Will get them! Schroth is not to take over command now.

Mueller (AGp.C): I give him the gist of my talk with von Witzleben (also as regards Schroth).

Meyer-Ricks comes from Ninth Army and reports on situation. In some places fighting has been very heavy. Now everything is on the move. Performance of 50th Division poor.

OQu IV: Reports on transport movements. About three divisions were moved from the area Épinal-Belfort-Vesoul in direction Paris yesterday and today (destination undetermined; possibly Paris, Lower Seine, or area northeast of Paris).

General Mieth brings reports on situation from Group Kleist and AGp.A. He discussed with them our ideas, namely to avoid any unnecessary buildup of forces on the Oise, near Creil and Verberie, and to concentrate Group Kleist in front of left wing, Sixth Army, at the earliest. These views have penetrated.

AGp.B has intention to put whole left wing of Sixth Army under von Kleist's command and to set it off in such direction as to enable XVI Corps, which seems to have been a little weakened, to cross the Seine in the morning of 11 June, with its western wing via La Ferté Milon, and its eastern wing along the road Soissons–Château Thierry, and get XIV Corps to the Oise at the earliest, without fighting.

Fourth Army Hq. considers leadership of II Corps not very distinguished, but commander of army group did not want to interfere in command of army. Against Le Havre, only reconnaissance activities for the present.

2400.   Gercke reports on railroad situation in area of OQu Belgium which needs a strong hand to get it straightened out.

10 June 1940

The morning picture (situation map) shows some very cheering developments in Fourth Army sector. Under very good leadership, it has established itself firmly in the part of Rouen north of the Seine (bridges were destroyed by the enemy), has seized Les Andelys with forces under von Manstein's command (bridgehead), and is covering its left wing with 1st Cavalry Division. Its right wing, pressing on in direction of Dieppe, is attacking from the rear the British group which is still holding out on the coast. The bulk of its armored forces is pushing on Le Havre.

In Sixth Army sector, the enemy, apparently under efficient leadership, has been extricated from the Montdidier pocket which was developing yesterday. On right wing of Sixth Army, XIV and XXXX Corps are crowded together northwest of the Oise between Creil and Verberie and apparently are still confronted with units covering the enemy's withdrawal across the Oise. IV Corps from the north is pushing toward the western bank of the Oise.

Progress has been made east of the Oise. It is becoming doubtful that the enemy will make a stand in the forest of Compiègne.

Left wing of Sixth Army, east of Villers-Cotterêts, is advancing south, and farther to the east, Ninth Army has already reached the Marne east of Château Thierry.

Second and Twelfth armies are advancing. In Twelfth Army sector, Group Guderian came into line this morning and has already reached the area of Juniville (two armored divisions, 1st and 2nd divisions in front). Sixteenth Army reports that enemy seems to be softening.

At morning conference with ObdH, decision was taken to issue order to have XIV Corps moved ahead of left wing of Sixth Army, through Noyon or possibly Compiègne, since it would be pointless to have them make a frontal assault against the Oise between Creil and Verberie. (ObdH telephones this decision as an order to von Bock.)

The insertion of Army Hq. 18 in the front is also discussed. By doing this we want to make it possible to push left wing of Sixth Army, which will also include Group Kleist, to the Marne without having to worry about the northern front of Paris. It is yet to be decided whether AHq. 18 will take command of the right wing or the left wing of Sixth Army.

Afterwards, conference with Chief Op. Sec.: Send Ia of Eighteenth Army immediately to AGp.B to establish liaison and to make preparations for commitment.

Concentrate reserves behind left wing of Sixth Army and right half of AGp.A!

Wagner (Gen Qu): Study logistical problems arising from transfer of Eighteenth Army and make necessary preparations.

1050.   Von Bock (on phone): Transfer of XIV Corps has been initiated. — Calls attention to difficulties caused by road conditions in V and XXXXIV

Corps areas. Complains that V Corps, now all bunched together, will first have to be disentangled by detouring it through Villers-Cotterêts before it can be put on the move in southern direction. Stresses his endeavors to push left wing of Sixth Army to the Marne. Is unenthusiastic about commitment of Eighteenth Army, claiming he does not need them.

1100.   **Von Brauchitsch** talked to Fuehrer on the phone: Has not yet got approval for commitment of AHq. 18. —Goes to see Fuehrer. I inform von Bock.

The overall picture shows that the entire enemy front is now moving backwards. The fact that the enemy has lost little artillery proves that he is now effecting an orderly and well-planned withdrawal. It is still an open question whether the enemy is merely going behind the Marne or whether he is at the end of his resources. It is also uncertain whether he is giving up contact with the Fortress Zone in the northeast.

I believe the time has come for going back to my plan to push south through the Champagne and continue westward south of Paris. As a result, the Fortress Zone will have to be reduced from the depth of Twelfth Army and by operations TIGER and BEAR.

1200.   **Bogatsch:** Air reconnaissance shows that railroad movements from the Belfort-Vesoul-Langres area to Paris have been going on for the past two days and three nights. (There is also some traffic in the opposite direction, but we can probably dismiss the theory that this represents a movement toward Vesoul.) Detraining areas unknown (Paris? Marne?). Minor transport movements in direction Saarburg are perhaps in reaction to von Witzleben.

1245.   **Von Brauchitsch** returns from Fuehrer. "One could cry if it were not such a farce." What I recommended a few days ago is now being dispensed piecemeal and haltingly as the products of supreme generalship. For results of conference, see the following telephone conversations.

1330.   **Telephone talk with von Salmuth:**

   1.   Eighteenth Army is made available to army groups for commitment; written order follows.

   2.   ObdH thinks of employing Eighteenth Army between Fourth and Sixth armies for the purpose of safeguarding inner wings of the armies (which will be bypassing Paris) and of moving up reinforcements behind Fourth Army, as they are becoming available.

> Drive by Fourth Army across Lower Seine in general direction of Alençon must be prepared. I Corps and cavalry division will be kept ready for this purpose. If possible prepare base for Fourth Army on Lower Seine (Mantes).
>
> 3. Left wing of Sixth Army, east of the Oise, and Ninth Army will continue in direction laid down by operational orders. Group Kleist, whose concentration in front of inner wings of Fourth and Sixth armies is of overriding importance, will have to drive in direction Sézanne and, later, Troyes.

1345. I outline our plans as developed in talk with von Salmuth. Guderian must push into area Vitry le François–Saint Dizier–Bar le Duc.

> A "Battle of Cannae" is in the making. —One armored and one motorized division will move on Verdun, as originally ordered. Bulk of Group Guderian will continue drive in direction of Troyes, his right wing on Arcis sur Aube for junction with von Kleist. AGp.C is set for Operation TIGER on 12 June. Exact time of jump-off still open.

During afternoon order is issued to AGp.B on insertion of AHq. 18, together with order to Supply Service on same subject. Difficulties in maintaining supply of Czech ammunition.

> A lot of friction developed in the railroad organization servicing Supply Base Belgium in the past week. Through intervention of Gercke and the continuous efforts of Gen Qu, things are now beginning to straighten out.

1545. A radio signal from Guderian to air force claims he has reached Mourmelon le Grand. Confirmation has yet to come. (Not confirmed!)

Reports received during the evening indicate that western wing (Fourth Army) has reached Saint Valéry on the Channel coast with 7th Armored Division, and that 5th Armored Division and 2nd Motorized Division are driving into the rear of the British forces, which are still holding out in front of II Corps. Von Manstein's corps is said to have gained ground west of the Lower Seine between Louviers and Bonnières without meeting any strong resistance on the southern bank of the river.

> It is becoming increasingly evident that the successes of the Sixth Army on the Lower Oise constitute a major defeat of the enemy. The enemy is fleeing in disorder toward Paris. Not clear is the situation of IV and V Corps in the forest south of Compiègne. To the east the Marne has been reached at Château Thierry. Farther to the east, around Reims,

the enemy is fighting back desperately. Here we are opposed by good French regular army divisions south of Rethel. Corps Schmidt (Group Guderian) has pushed into the wooded country northeast of Reims; Corps Reinhardt will move through Château Porcien and be committed to the east of Corps Schmidt tomorrow. Sixteenth Army has gained its limited objectives.

The great picture shows that the enemy is fighting uncertainly along the entire front. Nor are there any indications of a voluntary withdrawal by the enemy in front of Twelfth Army. The enemy infantry keeps on fighting after our tanks have broken through their lines. Again and again the enemy launches counterattacks supported by tanks.

Under these circumstances we must, for the time being, at least, dismiss the thought that the enemy might give up his Fortress Zone without a fight. Operation TIGER had better be postponed until Twelfth Army has smashed the enemy fronting it. Operation BEAR could then follow at a few days' interval.

2400.   **Von Bock** (on phone): Gives his picture of the situation as of this evening: Concentration of rolling stock at Le Mans, Tours, Orléans; transport movements from Rennes to the east, and from Tours toward Orléans. New British radio station located at Granville. Airfields at Caen, Tours, Saumur, Oucques; 435 planes confirmed southwest of Paris. Heavy AAA defenses at Paris, Dieux, Evreus.

Yesterday's and today's ship movements to Le Havre and Cherbourg, together with the railroad movements of the past two days from the general direction of Vesoul to Paris, seem to point to the buildup of a major grouping of forces southwest of Paris. We cannot make out yet whether this move is in reaction to von Kluge's drive across the Lower Seine or to our threat to Paris or, finally, whether it represents a last attempt of the enemy to mount an offensive. Under these circumstances we shall have to be careful about pushing von Kluge's drive across the Lower Seine, continuation of which in any case is not in our plans for the time being, and better look after protecting the right wing of the group (V and XXXXIV Corps) advancing east of the Oise. Accordingly, I have reminded Sixth Army to bring up 255th Division and, for myself, I must do some prodding about moving our GHq. Reserves to the front.

11 June 1940

(Italy enters the war.)

The morning situation indicates that the enemy, who previously offered stiff resistance to the west wing of Sixteenth Army, now is falling back. The fact that, to the west, the enemy is still holding out on the left wing front of Twelfth Army has only local significance. Our divisions are advancing on both sides of Reims in the direction ordered. Guderian can start his drive on Vitry le François today at noon. So, toward evening, the question will become acute as to whether final orders should be issued to Guderian to continue his drive in the direction of Troyes.

ObdH has gone to AGp.A and Twelfth Army.

AGp.C stands by to strike on 13 June.

Moving the reserves will be organized in such manner that some divisions could follow Fourth Army across the Somme, while the bulk would be moved along both sides of the army group boundary.

1500.   Meyer-Ricks (Liaison Officer, Twelfth Army) reports successful crossing of Marne east of Château Thierry. Difficulties are encountered in channeling von Wietersheim through Ninth Army area.

1600.   Warlimont comes to talk over some points causing concern at OKW:

    a.   Fourth Army is to establish a bridgehead across Lower Seine of sufficient depth to allow staging of a large assault force south of the river. OKW is afraid that Fourth Army might not be strong enough for their subsequent missions.

    b.   It is essential that the armored divisions of XVI Corps, newly committed on the army group boundary, in cooperation with Group Guderian, should destroy the enemy around Reims on and close to the Marne.

    c.   Target date for offensive in Saarbruecken area: Not before strong forces are standing south of the Argonne.

    d.   GHq. Reserves behind Sixth and Ninth armies still seem to be too far off for prompt commitment in the breakthrough to the south when we wheel on Paris.

1700.   Von Thoma reports on condition of armored troops. At least 60 percent of the tanks are operational in the regiments of Corps Hoepner. Resupply of tools and spare parts is functioning. The repair shops are working fine. Not one of the armored divisions has dropped below 60 percent in tank strength.

1800. **Von Etzdorf:** Political situation. Foreign Office is perturbed by the idea that a situation might arise where France would be without a government in a position to negotiate.

ObdH: Returns from AGp.A, Twelfth, and Second armies. Everything moving smoothly. No supply difficulties. Group Guderian had some delay at the Suippe River. Heavy losses in bridging equipment. In some places enemy is putting up a vigorous defense. In one instance, the enemy launched a counterattack with as many as fifty tanks, half of which were knocked out. I discuss questions put by Warlimont with ObdH, who then settles these matters in a telephone talk with Fuehrer.

2030. **Von Leeb** reports that AGp.C is ready for action. We agree on 1500 hours of day preceding attack as deadline for final attack signal. If possible, Operation BEAR should follow three days later to allow time for transfer of engineer troops and artillery. It would be desirable to leave choice of date to AGp.C.

2200–2300. **Reports by various officers** who were sent to the front:

General Mieth, on sectors of Ninth Army and XXXXIV Corps (Château Thierry area).

Colonel v. Greiffenberg, on Second and Twelfth armies (Reims area).

Lieutenant Colonel Heusinger, Marne, on sector of Ninth Army.

Lieutenant Colonel Stieff, on XIV Corps (withdrawn to area north of Noyon).

All reports agree that the enemy is fighting tenaciously all along the front, but that his strength is already beginning to give out. Some of the troops are conglomerates of the most diverse units. The enemy artillery has lost a great number of its guns and makes itself felt only sporadically. Grateful acknowledgment and recognition of air force support, which the enemy apparently cannot counter with anything even approaching in strength.

Special mention is made of the battle performance of 25th Division, which has been weakened, however, by heavy losses, as well as of the inspiration given his troops by von Speck, CG XXXXIII Corps, who is constantly in the front line.

The terrain is extremely difficult in some places. In the extensive woods, snipers firing from trees (especially colored troops) are a great nuisance. The bridge situation is not always easy, though generally bridging equipment seems to arrive in time. Traffic discipline on the roads appears to be good, except in AAA units, which are pushing themselves into moving columns everywhere.

Reports from XIV Corps state that it now is down to only 35 percent of its tank strength of 10 May. Worst off is 9th Armored Division, which has suffered heavily through mines. The tank situation is better in 10th Armored Division: one hundred tanks, for which there is much praise.

The troops are said to have reached the limits of their physical endurance. They are fit now only for pursuit fighting, but not for heavy attacks (battle fatigue). Striking power of the rifle units of the divisions is down to 50 percent. The losses in 9th Armored Division could be made up by two replacement transfer battalions, which are on hand; those in 10th Armored Division (sixteen hundred) from overstrength of 13th Motorized Division, XIV Corps, will not reach staging area north of Noyen before 12 June.

2300.   **Gehlen** reports on Armored Group Guderian. Difficulties on right wing at the Suippe River. Its left wing (Corps Reinhardt) has been attacked from the Argonne by French 3rd Mechanized and 3rd Armored divisions. During afternoon Group Guderian has apparently resumed advance on free roads.

12 June 1940

The view that the enemy front before Guderian is just about to break is not borne out by developments. A teletype message from Guderian received during the night again stresses that he is up against several enemy divisions (though three of them are divisions which yesterday he reported destroyed), and states that armor is tangled up with infantry and has not yet gained an open road to move ahead. Perhaps the situation of the armored forces will change for the better during the day.

The overall picture, based on reports received during the night, shows that the enemy has not yet consolidated his front on the Lower Seine and so cannot do anything to keep us from expanding our bridgehead. The elements which were thrown back on Paris seem to be badly crowded together in the "Paris defense position"; the right wing around this area has been closed in the north; the left wing of the Sixth Army is closing it on the east, only temporarily slowed by mopping-up operations in the forest of Compiègne. The western sector of Sixth Army has now been taken over by AHq. 18.

The soft spot in the enemy's position is the sector on both sides of Château Thierry. Here we are holding the southern bank as far as Dormans. Farther to the east the enemy is retreating on both sides of Reims under cover of rear-guard action. Frontal resistance in the Champagne has not yet been broken. The enemy still has contact with the forces falling back step by step in the Argonne. As to the continuation of the operation, the situation would indicate that it is still too early to divide the front and swing to the east and the west. First, we must press on southward from the line Château Thierry–Suippes east of Paris until the stretched band of the enemy front snaps. Only then will it be possible to fan out, as planned.

1130.   **Felber** repeats yesterday's agreement between ObdH and von Leeb. Would like to start drive on 13 June, and not before. Enemy fire has decreased since yesterday. Today's weather very bad, improvement expected tomorrow afternoon.

ObdH has talked to AGp.B: Fourth Army is expanding and deepening its sector on left bank of Seine between Rouen and Mantes for the coming drive. Eleventh Rifle Brigade is to take Le Havre (probably 13 June). I Corps will remain AGp. Reserve, but stand by to follow up behind Fourth Army.

VIII Corps is to attack the defense block south of Creil in order to get at the line Luzarches-Dammartin. In sector of IV and V Corps, the enemy is still resisting stubbornly. Apparently it has not yet been possible to effect the linkup south of the forest of Compiègne. The gap between IV and V Corps seems to be closed.

Von Kleist has taken over command and will start out with XVI Corps as soon as the bridges at Château Thierry are completed (two 16-ton bridges). The SS units then follow automatically.

I discuss with him my plans for reserves to AGp.B to be moved in such a way that two divisions will come behind Ninth and Sixth armies, and three divisions behind Fourth Army. This leaves our western reserve group with only three divisions, and so additional forces must be moved from the eastern reserve group toward the army group boundary.

. . .

1230.   Report that Guderian did break through and is now advancing on axis Châlons sur Marne–Vitry le François with 2nd Armored Division, 29th Motorized Division, and 1st Armored Division. XXXXI Corps still held up by fighting in Somme-Py area.

1300.   Châlons sur Marne has been reached.

1330.   Decision that Operation TIGER (offensive of First Army) is to start on 14 June; issue of orders.

1345.   **Stapf** comes with complaints of Air Marshal about a report circulated by Busse to various Hq. in which the undigested experiences of Division Sponeck are presented together with comments on the air force.

1400.   **Warlimont** communicates wishes of the Fuehrer:

1.   Drive on Le Havre (filled warehouses).

2.   Bridgehead desirable west of Rouen.

3.   Is Paris going to be cut off from the west? If the enemy has no substantial forces left behind the Seine, we must look into whether we are strong enough there for that purpose.

4.   It would be a great advantage if we could push the enemy out of his defense positions north of Paris past the wooded areas to the south, in order to have these woods in our back.

5.   Coast between Étaples and Le Havre must be protected.

6.   SS "Adolf Hitler" is to take part in Hoepner's operations.

Reports received during the afternoon show advances in our drive across the Marne in Ninth Army sector and at the extreme left wing of Sixth Army, and progress of Group Guderian in direction Châlons sur Marne. The bridge which we secured intact unfortunately was demolished by a delayed-action charge later on. In the course of the evening, French forces breaking out of the Argonne, apparently in a southwestern direction, have been attacking the left shoulder of List. Guderian, who had already reached Châlons sur Marne with Corps Schmidt, while Reinhardt was still standing echelonned out to Suippes, has now been compelled to turn his front toward the east and southeast!

The infantry divisions are now moving into line between the armor, especially in Reinhardt's sector. The battle has taken an interesting turn, which offers a good chance of success against an enemy who seems to be withdrawing in a southwestern direction from the Fortress Zone. Inasmuch as Sixteenth Army, east of the Argonne, reports finding deserted pillboxes in the Maginot Line, it would appear that the attack from the Argonne is not a coordinated assault on List's left shoulder by troops especially assembled for such an operation, but rather a breakout attempt by these forces from an area which they have been ordered to evacuate. There are signs of slackening of the enemy also in the sector of First Army.

1700.   Report received that IX French Corps, which was cut off on the coast near Saint Valéry, has surrendered after heavy fighting. Together with their troops were captured the CG of IX Corps and the commanders of the French 40th, 31st Mountain, 2nd and 5th Light divisions, as well as a British general. Bloody casualties of the enemy are very high. Twenty thousand prisoners have been counted up to noon; immense booty.

2230.   **Talk with von Bock:** He thinks he has evidence that enemy withdrawing in front of Second, Ninth, and Twelfth armies is trying to escape in southwestern direction. —Army group has ordered Fourth Army to start assault on Le Havre. —Discussion about direction to be given to von Kleist's drive (Sézanne-Troyes).

During evening: Report of von Salmuth on Fourth Army. He thinks that enemy fronting the army is not capable of putting up any serious resistance, and therefore presses for attack (14 June). Wants instructions on direction of drive.

Chevallerie's son killed in action.

13 June 1940

A day of restlessness. The tension that can always be felt when portentous decisions are maturing is beginning to tell.

The morning situation report brings nothing of importance. A satisfying development is that II Corps of Fourth Army has gained a bridgehead west of Rouen, while its bulk has closed up to Rouen. Another pleasant note is the report from VIII Corps that the enemy at Beaumont sur Oise is softening.

1100.   Liaison Officer to Guderian comes to complain about the muddle in Twelfth Army sector where the closely packed infantry divisions have tangled up with armor. Guderian wants the infantry to stay put and let him through, but infantry is pushing ahead on the road.

The whole situation illustrates the sort of tensions which the development of events has long resolved before one comes to hear about them. A subsequent call to Blumentritt brings out that 6th and 8th Armored divisions have meanwhile reached the road Châlons–Sainte-Menehould, and the question of road priority thus has been settled.

ObdH goes to the Fuehrer for a conference on the situation. The result is again pathetic. Gracious consent has been given to start offensive of First Army (Operation TIGER) on 14 June. Seventh Army is to follow up at the earliest date (wish of ObdH, apparently no date fixed with Fuehrer). The rest of the interview seems to have dealt exclusively with details of local situations, such as encirclement of some minor enemy groups. It is impossible to form a broad operational picture from that sort of talk. So I'll have to figure things out for myself and see how I can get on.

Radio intelligence fortunately clarifies the situation. By noon it has become evident that French army Hq. have been taken back toward the south; the farthest now is French Second Army, which has withdrawn toward Chaumont. The command organization of the French army is thus shown to be in frontwide retreat before our troops. It remains to be seen whether the Hq. still can fully control their troops.

In addition, we learn through diplomatic channels, via the American ambassador, that the French government has declared Paris an open city. All troops are being withdrawn from the vicinity of the city, and only the commandant of Paris is left behind with the police and the fire departments.

This now gives us a clear idea of what we have to do: push Fourth Army as quickly as possible between the French army retreating south-southwest and the coast. The remainder of AGp.B must pursue that enemy by passing through and east of Paris. AGp.A, together with AGp.C, will have the mission of liquidating the enemy still in the northeastern Fortress Zone. What is yet to be decided is whether Second Army is needed by AGp.A for this purpose, or may be transferred to von Bock.

Movements from the northeastern Fortress Zone in southwestern direction can now be made out distinctly. They indicate that at least all mobile commands are to be taken out of the Fortress Zone by the withdrawing French army. Blocking their path will be a rewarding mission for Group Guderian.

All through the afternoon there is a great deal of telephoning to have these ideas approved by OKW and accepted by AGp.B. Von Bock, on his own initiative, has ordered Eighteenth Army to send the first available complete division into Paris at the earliest possible moment. By doing so he is accommodating the Fuehrer, who, for political reasons (Turkey's attitude), wants, as soon as possible, concrete tokens to demonstrate to the whole world that France's power of resistance has been broken.

My efforts to have the two SS divisions follow behind von Kluge for quick reinforcement of this now-so-very-important wing have failed. The Fuehrer wants them to follow up behind von Kleist's tanks instead. On the other hand, the Fuehrer did not get 9th and 10th Armored divisions, which he so wanted in Paris, because they are already on the Marne.

Fuehrer Hq. now is slowly seeing the point of the recommendation made by me as early as 5 June, to the effect that the swing to the southwest should be made in the area east of Paris. Now we are going to get a "directive" to this end. One would laugh about all this if that system did not always obstruct efficient work.

Fourth Army is pressing forward and intends to push beyond the Seine tomorrow. After having made sure that this will not be opposed by OKW, I issue instructions for the left wing to move in direction Chartres, and arrange with von Salmuth that the Seine bridgehead will be expanded to such an extent on 14 June that Fourth Army can start a full-scale drive on 15. As a matter of fact, this is the beginning of our offensive, in camouflage. Behind Fourth Army, I move three more GHq. Reserve divisions, together with a corps Hq., from the area of Peronne.

2000. Reception of Marras, Italian attaché. Exchange of generalities. The only interesting point is his frank statement that Italy intends starting operations on the alpine front only if we open it up from the rear.

Evening. Return of ObdH, who went to see the Fuehrer upon my request. He obtained authority for me to start off Fourth Army at last. Paris is to be kept under control by five divisions. South of Paris I am now allowed to move in the direction of the Loire and direct Twelfth and Sixteenth, cooperating with First and Seventh armies, against the enemy withdrawing from the Fortress Zone.

AGp.A: As interim order I give verbal instructions to AGp.A to move up Second Army south of the Upper Marne, with central sector on Brienne.

Army group boundary: From Épernay along a line running midway between Fère Champenoise and Sommesous to the road junction 12 km northwest of Troyes (on western bank of Seine).

Verbal instructions to AGp.B: Order Fourth Army to start offensive tomorrow. Secure Paris with strong forces (five divisions). Left wing of Fourth Army must push through to Chartres in order to prevent escape of enemy to the coast. Eighteenth Army will advance through and on both sides of Paris. Sixth Army will advance with central sector on Montereau. Ninth Army will advance with center on Romilly.

AGp.C receives verbal instructions not to spend too much time on artillery preparations, but rather keep itself ready for immediate pursuit if the enemy should try to withdraw; Seventh Army would also join in the pursuit.

In the evening I draft the formal orders for turning the entire front in southwestern direction and for the simultaneous reduction of the enemy in the northeast.

14 June 1940

A great day in the history of the German army. German troops have been marching into Paris since 0900.

The overall picture of the situation shows that the enemy is falling back along the entire front, apparently with a view to building up another defensive front far to the rear, presumably along the Loire. It remains to be seen if he will succeed. At the moment we are in danger of losing contact with him.

Fourth Army, which was visited by ObdH today, is advancing toward the Avre River against slight opposition, and has ordered Hoth to move up from Le Havre. For the time being, left wing of Fourth Army has been directed by ObdH to strike for Chartres and Tours. A "directive" which has meanwhile been received from OKW states that right wing of army is to push toward the Loire estuary and occupy the harbors in the area. Orders to this effect will later be issued as supplements to our teletype orders of this morning. We shall also have to arrange for the follow-up of reserves.

Eighteenth Army is busy with Paris today. I hope they will not be delayed too long, as the enemy on their front is now on the run. Von Kleist, spearheading Ninth and Second armies, has likewise pushed into empty space. The enemy here is trying to evade him by going southwest. We are capturing only rearguard elements. Von Kleist is now crossing the Seine in direction of Troyes.

In the northeast, the enemy received orders to withdraw apparently three days ago. Also in that area now we are capturing mainly rear-guard elements. It is therefore necessary to order Guderian to make a swing deep to the south from south of Nancy through Joinville and Neufchâteau and to direct von Kleist to strike for Dijon, in order to block the route between the Plateau de Langres and the Swiss border. In doing this, we would dispose of what enemy troops are left in the northeast and then could concentrate on the Loire. Our armor committed in northeastern France would then form a comfortably strong left wing, which could seize the French armament center of Le Creusot and, after crossing the Upper Loire, crack the last French redoubt.

.   .   .

Drive of First Army (Operation TIGER) has started with some delay owing to bad weather; air force apparently has given effective support. Although enemy artillery defense has not been very strong, it will probably take quite some time to overwhelm the resistance in the prepared fortification zone offered by the garrisons, now probably only the rear guards of the fortress brigades. In some places the drive has penetrated to the terrain under direct fire of the fortress guns.

The offensive on the Upper Rhine has been ordered to start on 15 June.

15 June 1940

Another important day in military history. Verdun, scene of the heroic struggle in World War I, is in our hands.

Yesterday's drive against the French northeastern corner pushed by Twelfth Army and Corps Guderian from the west, and by First Army from the east, is completing the collapse of the French northeastern front. Seventh Army, which started its drive across the Upper Rhine this morning, and has thrown three divisions across the river in the first wave, has surprised the enemy, asleep in some bunkers. My effort to get the attack launched without artillery preparation has paid off handsomely.

The situation presents in broad outline the picture of a running fight all along the front, with the enemy offering local resistance on the western wing (Fourth Army), while signs of demoralization are becoming apparent on the front south and east of Paris. Once the fighting forces of the enemy in the northeast will have been disposed of by the drives of Armored Group Guderian on Vesoul, and of Armored Group Kleist on Pontarlier, through Dijon, the enemy will no longer be in a position to build up any systematic defensive front on the Loire.

In the morning a Fuehrer "directive" comes in. It directs immediate initiation of measures to lay the foundations for a reduction of ground forces to 120 divisions, including 20 of armor and 10 of motorized infantry. The directive is based on the assumption that with the now-imminent final collapse of the enemy, the army would have fulfilled its mission and so, while still in enemy country, could comfortably start on work to prepare the projected peacetime organization. Air force and navy alone would be carrying on the war against Britain.

. . .

16 June 1940

The development of the situation prompts the following conclusions:

> For our right wing the important thing will be to reach the Lower Loire rapidly with the bulk of Fourth Army; capture of the coastal towns of Cherbourg, Avranches, Brest, Lorient, Saint Nazaire will then follow automatically. I do not think the British will risk any major fighting once we are approaching the Lower Loire. They will evacuate their precious manpower and make every effort to secure for themselves the French navy and French merchant shipping.

> The symptoms of enemy collapse are most marked in the central sector of our front. Here we shall be able to push to and across the Loire bend at Orléans without much trouble.

> On the left wing, the encirclement of the enemy forces withdrawing from the northeast is proceeding speedily and smoothly. Guderian, who has at least freed and moved up Corps Reinhardt (which had been frontally impacted in the Argonne), is now heading full speed for Besançon, and will get to the Swiss frontier still today. List, driving from Saint Dizier, and Busch, coming from Bar le Duc, are overtaking the pursued enemy, while von Witzleben has punched through the Maginot Line in direction of Lunéville, and Dollmann has crossed the Rhine in direction of Colmar. Developments will have to be watched for the right moment to turn List in a southwestern direction and coordinate Sixteenth, Seventh, and First armies, and Group Guderian under von Leeb in order to liquidate the large enemy pocket in Lorraine and Alsace.

> Von Kleist has departed from his instructions in that he has straightaway pushed some of his forces to the Loire, above Gien, in order to secure

bridgeheads in this area; otherwise, he is striking for Dijon and Chalon sur Saône in order to be ready if he should be needed to drive in southern direction. Once he is no longer required as a second line behind Guderian, he will have to be directed toward the Lyon area for a drive either down the Rhône Valley or across the headwaters of the Loire, in southwestern direction, to match Hoth's drive advancing to the Lower Loire. In either case, von Kleist will have the mission of capturing the French armament center of Le Creusot.

After morning conference with ObdH, at which armistice and demobilization problems also were discussed, General Mieth comes for a conference on the basic conditions of an armistice. Entire coastline must be occupied by us; French army will surrender arms and be concentrated in the hill country between Rhône and Bay of Biscay (excluding Biscay); industrial areas; schedules for movements of disarmed troops; demobilization in "reservation," beginning with farmers, followed by other categories. Inventory and surrender of all arms, stocks, ammunition dumps, and armament factories; roads, railroads, waterways, and transport materiel.

Organize defenses of coast with mobile reserves. Fifteen divisions to the east, 5 infantry divisions to Norway, in addition to the 7 divisions already there, plus 2 or 3 armored divisions (in order to facilitate negotiations with Sweden about Narvik road and railroad). Denmark, 1 division. Of the 120 divisions (including armor) which are to be formed by contraction of 160 divisions, about 85, including 65 of infantry, would be left in France. In addition to the 120 divisions to be stocked available, equipment for additional 45 divisions is to be stocked at troop training centers to assure speedy activation of that number of divisions.

1045.   **Telephone talk with von Bock.** He does not want to direct his armored group (Hoth) against coastal points; he wants it to operate against the Lower Loire in order to settle accounts with the enemy ground army first. Complains about increasing enemy air activity.

. . .

17 June 1940

The picture of the enemy situation is still the same. Apart from apparently slight resistance encountered by right wing of Fourth Army, possibly by British troops covering their retreat rather than new concentrations, the enemy is retreating along the entire front in a state of complete disorganization and under constant bombing by our air force. Enemy AAA defense is almost completely absent, perhaps because of the withdrawal of the French air force, now under way.

Guderian is at the Swiss frontier and von Kleist, south of him, has arrived at the Upper Loire and in the Dijon area.

We are now faced with two major decisions:

    a.   To continue without delay operations against the remnants of the enemy in the Loire area, so as to keep them on the move.

    b.   To bring operations against the enemy forces encircled in northeastern France to the earliest possible conclusion.

As to a: Fourth Army must get a little more active, and take the ports of Cherbourg and Brest, and generally advance at greatest possible speed on Lower Loire. Second and Ninth armies, together with Group Kleist, will have to push on to the Upper Loire in order to envelop the French mountain redoubt west of the Rhône with a strong left wing. Twelfth Army will follow in same direction (toward line Dijon-Besançon) as soon as it has been squeezed out of the tightening ring in the northeast.

           Boundary line between the two army groups must be extended from Gien through Issoudun and Ruffec to the Bay of Biscay.

As to b: Guderian must swing his right wing northward to join Sixteenth, First, and Seventh armies in closing the ring. To this end, he must bring his right wing to Mulhouse and, on securely sealing the ring, immediately make a thrust on Épinal. Sixteenth Army and Group Guderian (the latter only tactically) will for this purpose come under the control of AGp.C. Twelfth Army will follow Group Kleist in southern direction (toward Dijon-Besançon) as soon as it is freed by the linkup between the inner wings of Sixteenth Army and Guderian.

Orders to this effect will be issued in the course of the day. Assumption of control of Sixteenth Army and tactical control of Group Guderian by AGp.C will be effective as of 18 June, 0000 hours.

The major work of the day is concerned with armistice problems, which are taken over by Mieth. Work on this subject matter, which is a little unfamiliar to us soldiers, is going rather slow. I recommend a demarcation line which would include the mountain area of southern France and so would give us the Rhône Valley and the coast all the way to Spain. All French army units still in existence then would have to be transferred to the zone behind the demarcation line for demobilization. OKH puts these proposals before OKW.

During the day I have several talks with von Ziehlberg on current personnel matters and the prospective change of GHq. Reims has been abandoned as a new location, and Fontainebleau is being considered in its place.

Wagner receives instructions regarding evacuation to Saar and Baden of the approximately two hundred thousand PWs which we expect to take in northeastern France.

I discuss with Buhle program for reduction of ground forces to 120 divisions.

Political command announces at noon that the French government, through the good services of the Spanish government, has approached Germany for armistice terms. The Fuehrer is now going to Munich to meet Mussolini. Reply will be held until then. Nothing is known as yet about Britain's reaction.

18 June 1940

The Fuehrer has left for consultation with Mussolini. So for a day and a half we will be our own masters. We are going to make the most of this time and push our drives in the prearranged directions, so as to establish a basis for armistice negotiations. The morning picture shows nothing specifically new, just the gradual evolution of the situation.

1100. **Conference with Fromm and Olbricht** in ObdH's office. The basic features of the shrinking process by which the army will be reduced from 165 to 120 divisions, and distribution in the interior are discussed.

. . .

19 June 1940

The advance continues according to plan. New victories are reported:

The German flag is flying from the cathedral of Strasbourg. Toul is in our hands. Belfort was taken yesterday. On the Channel coast we have reached Cherbourg. Almost everywhere the front of our armies has reached the Loire, and in some places even crossed it.

Notwithstanding this continuous succession of victories following one another with extraordinary speed, ObdH seems to have been called down quite roughly by the Fuehrer on his return from the talks in Munich, and all that just because there are still a few French soldiers left fighting us in the northeast.

Various talks and reports during the day:

With ObdH: Projected peacetime organization of the army and the transitional phases leading to it:

Future Army:

20 armd. divs.		
10 mot. divs.	10 corps Hq.	4 group Hq.
6 mt. divs.		
26 inf. divs.	13 corps Hq.	6 group Hq.
		10 group Hq.

Holland and Belgium as well as Norway: Occupation in rotation. Government-General still undecided.

The Hq. of military districts should control only the infantry corps, not also the other branches of armed forces in their territories. Groupings should be so that motorized divisions would be stationed all over the country behind a ring of infantry divisions along the border.

Colonial troops.

Cavalry will not be abolished. Question of how to utilize the horses.

Buhle: Overall proposal on future strength and geographical distribution of our forces. Schedule for reduction of army from 165 to 120 divisions.

Wagner: Refugee problems. (Order issued.) New boundary line for army group rear areas. (Order issued.)

During the evening we receive an OKW ''directive'' setting forth a boundary line which must not be crossed by us (in the main it follows the Cher River) as well as a line east of the Atlantic coast. It also directs that we push parts of Group Kleist across the Lower Loire in AGp.B sector, to occupy the Atlantic coast, while other parts of the Group are to drive on Lyon to get into the rear of the Italian front.

The latter move has already been prepared and will be effected. The former requires a movement across the entire width of the front and so will not become effective at the desired time. Some days ago I tried desperately hard to get permission to commit the armor and motorized divisions on von Kleist's right wing. At that time the plan was directly vetoed on the top level. Now, after these forces have been racing off in a southeastern direction for several days and not meeting any organized resistance, they have to be reversed and ordered in a northwestern direction.

It is indeed an effort to keep calm in the face of such dilettantish tinkering with the business of directing military operations.

We learn that the Italians are going to start their offensive on the alpine front in two or three days. By that time we are expected to have gotten through the Rhône Valley into the rear of the French front. I believe it probably cannot be done within that time.

The orders necessitated by these ''directives'' are completed at midnight.

.   .   .

20 June 1940

The day starts with a rather sharp-worded telephone conversation with ObdH. Yesterday's meddling by the Great Master has thrown him off balance. ObdH now wants right wing Twelfth Army (XVII Corps, including 86th Division) to be transferred to AGp.C to assist in completing the encirclement. I object to this entirely illogical order, but in the end I yield because it doesn't really matter where these four divisions are. They are no longer needed in Twelfth Army sector, where the enemy has been smashed. In another two days at the latest they will be redundant also in AGp.C and then can be employed as OKH Reserve in the rear area.

The morning reports, in the way of important news, announce the capture of Lyon and of Nantes on the Loire estuary (with bridges intact). I just cannot comprehend what more the political command could want of us, and which of its wishes have remained unfulfilled. But, as an underling, one has to bear with the frayed nerves of those in high positions.

Following the morning conference with ObdH, orders are issued regarding organization of a group for Lyon, under the commander of Twelfth Army, for a special mission in the Chambéry and Grenoble areas. In addition to XVI Corps, it is to comprise combat teams made up of all improvised motorized commands in AGp.A and as large a portion as possible of 1st Mountain Division, on trucks, furnished by AGp.B.

In my estimate, such advance combat teams would be ready to start from the Lyon area on 21 June; if teamed with foot infantry, not before 25 June. Corps Hoepner, of course, could start right away, if required.

By 21 June, evening, likewise, the elements of Group Kleist, which were moved to AGp.B sector, will be ready on the Lower Loire to start the drive on Bordeaux; I would say they could reach that city on 25 June.

1025.   We receive word from Fuehrer Hq. that French armistice emissaries are expected to reach Tours from Poitiers at 1700. I send General von Tippelskirch to meet the French representatives at our front line and accompany them to Tours, where OKW apparently will take over. The armistice terms will be handed them at a formal ceremony at Compiègne tomorrow morning (21 June). Subsequently an armistice commission is to be formed, which will have its seat at Wiesbaden. Specific OKW instructions on this matter will be forthcoming.

. . .

21 June 1940

The French armistice delegation did not cross our lines until late last night. Without stopping for sleep, they could reach Compiègne by 1130; presentation of armistice terms has therefore been postponed to 1500.

The Italians claim they would start their offensive at and south of the Little St. Bernard today. The weather is so bad that the air force cannot take part. It is therefore safe to assume that these attacks will be limited to some patrol activities. Starting our drive from the Lyon area is out of the question before the Italian drive has seriously gotten under way, i.e., not before 22 June. Whether we shall start this drive at all can be decided only after conclusion of the armistice negotiations. From a purely practical viewpoint, 23 June would be the earliest date.

Our troop movements are proceeding according to plan. Wherever the demarcation line has been reached, the troops close up and the armies regroup. Von Kleist's group, ordered to the Lower Loire, is not on its way. The List group assembles around Lyon. Hoth, with his armor now no longer needed at the coast, is moving toward the Lower Loire. In sector of AGp.C, sizable enemy groups, though tightly surrounded, are still putting up a stout fight; there seem to be some aggressive leaders left in these troops, which have suffered less in the recent fighting than those in the Champagne. The fortress troops in the Maginot Line, too, are holding out.

Air reconnaissance and the picture of the enemy situation confirm my views expressed a long time ago. The enemy fronting our right wing, after the battle with Fourth Army between the Somme and the Seine, was never again about to regroup for effective action. Operations in Normandy and Brittany now amount merely to a cleaning-up job. On Eighteenth Army front, south of Paris, too, the enemy has not been able to organize any opposition. Sixth and Ninth armies have only sporadic engagements with rear guards. Second Army has lost contact with the enemy altogether. Group Kleist has no longer any enemy before it near Lyon. This shows that the broken remnants of the beaten French army are streaming back across the Loire bend in a southwestern direction.

East of the line Troyes-Moulins a wide gap is left open. We may assume that it was the intention of the French command to close this gap with forces shifted from the northeast. This plan was frustrated by our armored thrust to the Swiss border. As a result, the right wing of the enemy in the Clermont-Ferrand area now is dangling in the air and has no contact with the alpine front built up against Italy. The French army as a whole has only one front intact, the alpine front, but the road into its rear is already open to us.

. . .

2000.   ObdH returns from Compiègne. He is deeply stirred. The French (the most likable of whom was the army representative) had no warning that they would be handed the terms at the very site of the negotiations in 1918. They were apparently shaken by this arrangement and at first inclined to be sullen. The Fuehrer and ObdH were present only at the reading of the preamble. In the following negotiations, presided over by Keitel, there seems to have been a great deal of wrangling, and ObdH is worried that the French might not accept.

I don't understand his apprehension. The French must accept and, with Pétain at the helm, will do so. Moreover, our terms are so moderate that sheer common sense ought to make them accept.

French attempts to have our terms bracketed with those of the Italians, and to make acceptance of our terms contingent on what the Italians demand have of course been rejected by us. They have been given until tomorrow noon to accept. Aerial assault of Bordeaux has been authorized.

The Italians have asked us to set 22 June as date for the start of our drive in support of their attack across the Little Saint Bernard Pass. We are not going to do this; List's group will not be ready before 23 June. Apart from this, we must first see whether this so-called attack of the Italians will be anything more than a patrol skirmish.

. . .

22 June 1940

The dominant event of the day is the conclusion of the armistice with the French.

The armistice instrument will be signed at Compiègne, at 1850. Throughout the day, exchange of telegrams with Italian General Staff urging us to push from Lyon on Grenoble and Chambéry to open the way through the Alps for them. These requests are given dilatory treatment, since Group List would not be ready to start before 23 June. Moreover, the Fuehrer has made it known that the word for the start of this operation would be given by him. Orders to this effect for List are being drafted.

Noon: Gercke reports on railroad situation. General Directorate of Belgian railroads at last shows willingness to cooperate in restoration and operation of railroads. Some pressure had to be applied. Railroad capacity will be considerably increased by end of this month, so that we can then start with troop movements by rail. The railroad line in Lorraine will thereby be linked with the German railroad network within a relatively short time. We discuss modifications of plans for impending regrouping of troops in the light of the railroad situation.

Afternoon. Conference with Buhle, Wagner, and von Greiffenberg on regrouping program from standpoint of operational requirements (coastal defense, preparations against England), the reduction in number of divisions and the reorganization of the army setup. The difficult question in this connection is how to ensure the unified administration of France without impairing the authority of military command.

A formula must be found for establishing OKH as the central authority also on administrative matters, without burdening us directly with the whole governmental machinery. One way of doing this would be to let army group Hq. continue in their command functions and to set up under OKH supervision a Military Administration which would be exclusively concerned with establishing uniform administration policies, making use to the greatest extent of the existing French civil administration. This is a political matter, and decision must therefore be left to the Fuehrer.

I put the matter before ObdH.

After return from ObdH I find at my office Freiherr von Enzberg, my former aide in the East in 1917, who has come to call. Soon afterwards, Rohowsky drops in.

In the evening, the decision is announced that List will attack on 23 June, but must not advance beyond Grenoble-Chambéry. In the drive along the coast toward the south, AGp.B must not advance beyond the line going through Cognac.

The raids of the British air force at home are becoming bothersome. Now they are extending their attacks to Berlin, and ObdL therefore wants us to transfer army AAA units. Lengthy discussion of the subject over the phone. There is nothing to be said against the principle of the request.

The near future will show whether Britain will do the reasonable thing in the light of our victories, or will try to carry on the war single-handedly. In the latter case, the war will lead to Britain's destruction, and may last a long time.

23 June 1940

Today's operations are confined to further advances of the right wing (Fourth and Eighteenth armies) and the drive of Group List. The latter started on schedule and at noon was reported to have reached the area northeast of Valence, northwest of Grenoble and Chambéry, and northeast of Aix les Bains. They have before them defense positions equipped with AT guns and manned by mountain troops. In reply to an inquiry during the evening, AGp.A is told that any increase in pressure involving major German casualties would not be in line with intentions of OKH.

.   .   .

Afternoon. Fuehrer conference. The following points were dealt with:

a.   *PWs:* Break up PW concentrations. Colored PWs are to be put in special battalions, receive good treatment, and will not be taken to Germany. Separate labor detachments will be formed for farming and industry. PWs of German ancestry to be screened out. — PWs will be shipped to Germany as needed. Darre will be consulted on matters of interest to agriculture.

b.   *Repatriation of refugees:* In addition to the boundary line previously announced, on which returning refugees are to be halted, it would be desirable to throw cordons around Strasbourg and other German towns in order to prevent return of the French elements of the population.

c. *Setting up of Military Administration France* has been recognized as necessary. Similarly, as in Belgium, it should make most extensive use of the existing civil administration. (Proposals to this end should be awaited from French quarters.) Whether French government will be allowed to return to Paris later on is still uncertain; certainly not now.

d. Mission for Twelfth Army: Wants us to think it through. List with Kuebler, Bergmann, Fahrnbacher, Schoerner.

. . .

24 June 1940

Morning reports show a piquant note. The Italians have been stalled by the French fortifications and cannot make any headway. But as they want to present themselves at the armistice negotiations with as large a piece of French territory as they could occupy in a hurry, they have approached us with a scheme to transport Italian battalions behind List's front, partly by air via Munich, partly directly to the Lyon area, so as to get them to make occupation claims. The whole thing is the cheapest kind of a fraud. I have made it plain I will not have my name connected with that sort of trickery.

In the end the whole thing turns out to have been a plan hatched out by Roatta, and disapproved by Marshal Badoglio. The people in OKW will have to swallow it that they allowed themselves to be hooked by a scheme proposed by a subordinate, which the responsible Italian marshal (who seems to be the only respectable soldier in the lot) has rejected as dishonorable.

ObdH flies to Seventh Army. His anxieties move him to make some preparations against the contingency of a failure of the Italian armistice negotiations. In that event it would be necessary to launch a major drive into the rear of the French alpine fortifications, with a thrust to the Mediterranean coast as a secondary effort.

Such an operation requires coordination and employment of motorized mountain troops, and must be properly prepared. It cannot be improvised out of hand with hurriedly introduced mountain battalions.

It is again the same frustrating game that we had in making contact with the Russians in the Polish Campaign. The political command wants the direct connection between Switzerland and France severed, and would like to have this political expediency dressed up as a military necessity. This is sure to have some unpleasant consequences.

1020.   **Talk with von Tresckow (AGp.A):** I sketch out for him the political background and the resulting fluctuations in military requirements. AGp.A should draw up a timetable for preparations of a major operation against the Savoy front and continuance of operations against the French army, with strong left wing.

. . .

Von Greiffenberg: Parade plans.

2100.   Word received that armistice between Italy and France has been concluded. OKW issues cease-fire order, effective 25 June, 0135 hours. Advances and withdrawals are to be stopped. Will be settled by Armistice Commission.

In the evening *ObdH* returns from Seventh Army, much impressed by the effect produced by our great victory. Dollmann, von Witzleben, and von Leeb have received the Knight's Cross.

25 June 1940

0135.   The fighting has ceased; now the bureaucratic activities.

Morning. Disagreement with ObdH: The political command wanted to have railroad connection severed between Switzerland and France. To this end List had been given orders to do a thoroughgoing wrecking job on the railroad line La Roche–Annecy. Owing to the course taken by events, this order was not executed. Now ObdH wants that, with armistice in force, destruction of the line should be carried out by patrol action. I object. Once a truce has been declared, any such military undertaking is ruled out. If at all, this could be done only by Canaris. After consultation with Keitel, I issue instructions to this effect to Canaris. Otherwise, the day is filled with sometimes strenuous conferences about matters that have to be arranged now.

. . .

OQu IV: Russia wants Bessarabia. We are not interested in Bessarabia. The issue of the Bukowina raised by Russia is new and goes beyond our agreements with the Russians. In any event, it is imperative for our interests that there should be no war on the Balkans.

In the evening, ObdH gives a very successful party in his quarters. In warm
words he pays tribute to his staff and to my work.

26 June 1940

Front reports, of course, have lost all importance. Movements for occupation
of the coast will now be carried out with increased speed, while the withdrawal
from places inside the Green Boundary Line will not start until later on; orders
to this effect are issued.

In the foreign field, Russia's attitude stands in the foreground. The opinion
prevails that it will be possible to solve the Bessarabian question without war.

THE BATTLE OF BRITAIN TO BARBAROSSA

. . .

The May 10 offensive achieved rapid success. The German offensive
surprised and confused the Allies, who misread their situation completely.
While the spearhead of Army Group B's assault drew in the Allied units,
the fast units of Army Group A broke through the Ardennes Forest and
reached the Channel. The success was complete.

With the Dunkirk evacuation and uncertain British-French political relationships, the issue was clear. The strongly demoralized French could no
longer resist the triumphant enemy. The Germans pushed them south and
southwest, compressing them against the useless defensive Maginot Line.
Throughout, the operation resulted in an unprecedented military victory.
The English were off the mainland; the French were humiliated. Hitler's
predictions, ambitions, and dreams had reached fruition.

Only the last enemy, Great Britain, stood in his path to becoming the
"greatest conqueror of all times." He had reached the peak of his unexpected
career. His Continental enemies had succumbed within a brief time and
had provided him proof of his prophecies. Without question his intuition
had guided his military and diplomatic policies into the correct channels.
His empire stretched from the North Cape to the Spanish border, secured
by the most effective army in the world. Hitler's prestige was at its apex.

The blitzkrieg had created success. It had the advantage of avoiding
long materiel battles and the burdens for the civilian German population.
It compensated for the natural weakness of the German economy and was
coupled with diplomatic peace overtures; in addition it put the onus for

continued warfare on Great Britain's leader, Winston Churchill. Hitler held the destiny of Europe and, in a realistic sense, the world in his hands.

The war changed complexion as Hitler confronted the realities of strategy, time, resources, geography, will. By whatever means, he had to create victory over his only foe—Great Britain. The world changed as the Fuehrer sought a new system, a new methodology, a new insight. With partial success came uncertainty and difficulty. The nature of the conflict was different. A conqueror must seek new conquests.

30 June 1940

My birthday. Many affecting congratulations. From ObdH, a photo with cordial dedication.

1100. Conference with von Weizsaecker:

    a.   We can preserve the victories of this campaign only with the means with which they were achieved, that is, with military power.

    b.   No concrete basis for any peace treaty yet.

    c.   We shall keep a steady eye on the east.

    d.   Britain probably still needs one more demonstration of our military might before she gives in and leaves us a free hand in the east.

. . .

1 July 1940

Schniewind (Naval Operations Staff): Discussion of basis for warfare against England.

    a.   Prerequisite is air superiority (which might make a landing unnecessary). —Smooth water!

    b.   Fog after middle of October.

    c.   Bases Ostend, Le Havre.

    d.   A large number of small steamers (sixteen hundred) could be assembled. Camouflage, air protection! One hundred thousand men in one wave. Only small coastal craft suitable.

    e. Artillery cover for second half of approach across water and on beaches must be furnished by air force.

    f. Underwater threats can be neutralized by net barrages. Surface threats can be minimized by mines and submarines supplementing land-based artillery and planes.

    g. Cliffs are at Dover, Dungeness, Beachy Head. Rest of coast suitable for beach assault. Firm bottom.

    h. Dr. Feder–type concrete barges are now being developed. Production in sufficient numbers held possible in July. In addition to these we want railroad ferries (Todt's proposal) for transporting tanks.

Von Leeb [Ordnance Office]: He was told all along that invasion of England was not being considered. I tell him that possibilities have to be examined, for, if political command demands a landing, they will want everything done at top speed.

Army Ordnance Office enumerates the following capabilities:

    1. About one hundred tanks III and twenty tanks IV can be fitted for amphibious operations.

    2. As many as forty tanks can be carried by one railroad ferry. Unloading on special landing tracks.

    3. Persistent smoke screens can be produced by new smoke bombs.

    It is necessary to set up special experimental teams soon in order to get tank, engineer, and naval experts together for practical tests on a broad basis. Problem of direction of such teams and part to be played by each branch of armed forces in it must be clarified soon.

. . .

3 July 1940

Von Greiffenberg: Matters discussed:

    a. Operational questions. Britain, which must be dealt with separately, and the east are the primary problems now. The latter must be viewed chiefly with reference to the requirements of a military intervention which will compel Russia to recognize Germany's dominant position in Europe. Special issues, such as the Baltic and Balkan countries, may introduce some variants.

b. Organization of OKH staff. Von Greiffenberg must take over OQu I.

. . .

Von Greiffenberg-Buhle: Operations against England.

1. Paramount factors: Weather, air superiority.

2. Method: Similar to large-scale river crossing, on line Ostend–Le Havre.

3. Potential beachheads: Cliffs at Dover, Dungeness, and Beachy Head. Elsewhere many good landing spots, even if beaches rise at steep angles.

4. *First wave:* Six divisions (picked units reinforced by four armored battalions).

5. *Technical means:* Amphibious tanks, rafts, flamethrowing tanks, assault boats from the Rhine. (Six-barreled rocket projectors not before October.) Use of chemical smoke. —Airborne landings. —Amphibious engineers.

. . .

4 July 1940

The reports of a sea battle between the French and the British at Oran are confirmed. The British tried to prevent the French ships from leaving port. Battleship *Strasbourg* and one submarine did get through. The remainder of the ships were put out of action at their anchorages.

The Fuehrer has ordered that armistice clauses relating to decommissioning of French navy are to be suspended.

Personnel of French Navy Ministry interned near Rochefort will be released.

0930.   Von Kuechler and Marcks: Orientation on mission of AHq. 18 with regard to control of troops, fortifications, and administration in the east. *Kinzel* reviews disposition of Russian forces.

Wuestefeld: Transfer of fortifications in west to control of BdE. Administration of western fortifications. —Dismantling of obstacles.

Stapf:

    a. Air plans. Primary objective: Destruction of enemy air force and of supporting installations and means of production. The two targets cannot be sharply separated from each other. (Secondary objective is damage to enemy fleet.) Every opportunity must be used to attack the enemy in the air and on the ground. But a prime consideration is to preserve own strength for the long-range execution of these tasks.

    Enemy air warning and signal networks seem to be good. Enemy apparently received several successive warnings prior to our attacks. Our planes must vary routes to and from targets. Cover by long-range fighters and fighters.

    Plans for interim period: Hit-and-run attacks similar to those by the British against us. Disruption of production and attacks on airfields.

    Ready to change over to large-scale attacks by end of this week, when air buildup will be completed. Will have four issues of ammunition and four fuel quotas.

    b. Air force now has total strength of:

        45 bomber groups
        12 dive-bomber groups
        10 long-range fighter groups
        19 fighter groups in air fleet
        13 fighter groups in air force districts

    At beginning of war we had 1,200 bombers. Present strength: Crews 1,100 planes; 900 machines. British strength is about one-half ours.

. . .

5 July 1940

. . .

    2. *England:*

        a. Locations for seaborne landings (jump-off also from Cherbourg), for airborne landings?

   b. What is available for airborne landings? (Stapf)

   c. Size of units to be especially equipped for airborne landings will be adapted accordingly. (Buhle's job: May have to shift to air force.)

   d. *Jump-off:* Put across armor (seaborne) initially from both sides of Calais; another echelon later also from Cherbourg. Transport of airborne forces to follow at the earliest to give them mobility.

   e. *Amphibious tanks* available on 1 August 1940:

     90 tanks III with 3.7-cm guns
     10 tanks III with 5-cm guns   ObdH wants 180
     28 tanks IV   amphibious tanks.
     12 med. tank destroyers

     Present depth: Maximum 7-m (we need 15-m); speed between 5- and 7-km, interference of buoyancy.

3. *Colonial troops:* ObdH has given orders in Berlin for activation of colonial regiment, of two battalions, of four companies each. Post: Bergen. Personnel will be drawn from divisions slated for deactivation and from replacement army. Department for colonial questions will be organized at General Army Office. Canvas automotive firms to collect data on types of automobile best adapted to use in colonies (effect of sand?).

4. *ObdH* wants OKH in Berlin.

5. *Guarding of PWs in interior:* Twenty-five battalions will be formed with personnel from deactivated divisions.

6. *Reichstag Session in Berlin:* Outstanding troop/commanders (decorated with Knight's Cross) up to rank of Corps Commander will attend. Corps Commanders retained by urgent business must send deputies (only general officers). Afterwards they can go on leave for several days.

7. Meeting in Berlin must be anticipated after Reichstag Session; prepare for it.

8. *Reorganization of OKH:* Fromm has been instructed to prepare transfer of Inspectorate of Schooling and Education to Inspector of Training, and of Political Liaison Section from General Staff to General Army Office under a new head.

. . .

9 July 1940

Von Wietersheim: Talk on part to be played by XIV Corps. Personal matters.

OQu IV: a. Italian war: Offensive in Libya on 15 July.

  b. Southeast: Delicate situation in Romania. Attitude of Russia obscure. Might have designs on Danube delta. Repercussions on Bulgaria and Hungary.

  Romania is trying to get chummy with us on the military end, with a view to creating the impression on the outside that she is being taken under German protection. Caution!

  Reports on evacuation of southern Dobruja by Romania. Iron Guard has become active again!

  c. Northeast: Development in Baltic countries; Finland's position appears to be reassuring.

  d. Russia—Britain.

. . .

11 July 1940

. . .

Stapf: a. Air force once more requests change in control of army units supporting air force defenses of airfields. I object to changing anything in the established setup; besides, the matter has already been settled, and can be laid down in written orders.

  b. Invasion of England:

  Airborne troops will be ready by 15 August;
  400 transport planes carrying 20 men each, a total of 8,000 men.
  110 cargo gliders in squadrons of 12 each.

Air transport only within limits of above-mentioned numbers.

c. General orientation on line of our policy for invasion of England.

d. Britain has now about six hundred bombers; we also have six hundred.

British operational procedure to move bombers from dispersal areas to take-off areas and back again makes it difficult to bring our air superiority to bear in concentrated attacks. It will take between fourteen to twenty-eight days to smash enemy air force.

Von Greiffenberg brings in maps for report to Fuehrer.
Discussion of operational disposition of forces for assault of England. —Organizational measures for two-thirds of the thirteen divisions of first wave must be prepared (Buhle). —Organization of the artillery fire plan for the coast. —Dispositions regarding coastal defense, safe-guarding of Green Boundary, air defense.

Von Etzdorf: *Internal situation of Britain:* Discord between Churchill and Halifax. Churchill has prevailed: "War to the finish."

Britain and Russia are both seeking a rapprochement. Possibility of an understanding on Iran is not out of question and could provide basis for an overall understanding between the "bear and the whale," as in 1908.

Balkans: Dobruja is apparently being evacuated for the Bulgarians. Hungary has been advised to mind its own business. How long this policy can be maintained remains to be seen.

The danger that Romania, and in her train the whole Balkans, will be convulsed by domestic crisis cannot be discounted. Such a development would serve British interests.

America by and large is held under the spell of coming elections. It appears that Roosevelt's position is no longer undisputed.

East Asia: Japan seems to get busy in French Indochina. Naval demonstration. Commission in Annam. Additional Japanese advances in this area are not particularly desirable for us. Settlement of Chinese question does not make any progress.

. . .

13 July 1940

0730.   Departure from Fontainebleau, 0800 take-off from airfield. Traveling with strong tail wind, we arrive in Salzburg at 1015; drive to Berghof, 1100.

1200.   Report to Fuehrer on invasion of Britain.

Introductory remarks on overall objective of armed forces. Initial mission of army. General basis for their attainment. Prerequisite conditions, time factors, strength.

Execution of attack:

    I.   *Enemy:* Land army, coastal defenses, disposition of forces, and probable defense tactics.

    II.   *Own development:* Configurations of coast, terrain in England, jump-off base; disposition and strength requirements for jump-off; subsequent phases of operations.

    III.   *Our organization* and technical preparations.

    IV.   *Our method:* "River crossing." —Landing. —Next steps in operation. —Strength requirements. —Order of battle.

    V.   *Summing up of proposals* and demands on other services.

    VI.   *Time schedule* and preparations to date.

Recommendations are approved as basis for practical preparations.
Order has been issued for immediate start of invasion preparations.

The following suggestions are made in this connection:

    a.   Separate raids on Isle of Wight and Cornwall in order to impair morale and undermine will of resistance.

    b.   Artillery cover of water lanes under unified command of navy. For this purpose all available guns (also railroad guns) will be concentrated, first on our coast, later on enemy coast in order to protect our water lanes against enemy surface action. Underwater protection will be provided by navy through submarines and mines.

Subsequently, review of political situation from military angle.

    a.   It would be desirable not to deactivate twenty of the thirty-five divisions slated for deactivation in the homeland. Instead, the personnel of these divisions should merely be discharged on a furlough basis, thus maintaining prompt availability of the divisions. Must tell Buhle to study possible effect of this plan and to submit list of divisions to be definitely deactivated.

b.   Political analysis.

1.   The Fuehrer wants to draw *Spain* into the game in order to build up a front against Britain extending from the *North Cap* to *Morocco*. Von Ribbentrop will go to Spain.

2.   *Russia's* interest not to let us grow too big is recognized. Russian aspirations to Bosporus are inconvenient for Italy.

3.   *Romania* will have to foot the bill. *Hungary* has to get a slice; *Bulgaria* is taking the Dobruja anyhow and looks for access to the Mediterranean at the expense of Greece. No difficulty is seen in that direction. The King of Romania has addressed a letter to the Fuehrer, quasi putting himself under his protection. Answer: He can afford to cede some territory to Hungary and Bulgaria.

4.   Italy seems to want some Greek islands in the Ionian Sea. The attempts of the Fuehrer at interesting Italy in Crete and Cyprus have not been successful. Italy's aspirations moreover are directed toward obtaining a corridor from her North African possessions to Abyssinia.

5.   In *Africa* we are claiming the coast (apparently together with Spain); Italy wants the hinterland. We also claim French and Belgian Congo for us.

The Fuehrer is greatly puzzled by Britain's persisting unwillingness to make peace. He sees the answer (as we do) in Britain's hope on Russia, and therefore counts on having to compel her by main force to agree to peace. Actually that is much against his grain. The reason is that a military defeat of Britain will bring about the disintegration of the British Empire. This would not be of any benefit to Germany. German blood would be shed to accomplish something that would benefit only Japan, the United States, and others.

1900.   Return. Left Berghof 1300, took off by plane from Salzburg 1345. Later: Instructions to Org. Sec. regarding reduction of number of divisions slated for deactivation. Discussion with Op. Sec. on results of conference. Preparations for conference with Section Chiefs on Sunday, [14 July] 1100.

19 July 1940

Arrive at office at 1000. *Directive No. 16* has come in. It contains in form of an order the essential points of my recommendations made at Berghof on 13 July.

New in it is the request that OKH should put an army group Hq. in charge of the execution of the operation, and that OKH sections essential for the operation are to arrive in Giessen on 1 August.

We are also to send over information on a great number of points. It will be the basis of more "directives" later on.

Afterwards, conference with ObdH:

    a. Saalwaechter will go to Paris. Will be in charge of the actual crossing and of artillery. Liaison staffs will be assigned to armies.

    b. Shipping space allocated to us will be less than previously estimated (consideration for the economy). Shipping space available in occupied countries must be brought into use by every means. Engineers of the eighteen divisions in interior and of divisions slated for deactivation are placed at disposal of Reinhardt. Conversion of watercraft by navy at Mannheim, Duisburg, Antwerp, Amsterdam, Rotterdam, Ostend.

    c. Sweeping Channel strip, 120 km wide, clear of mines is impracticable. Minesweeping experts must be assigned to our staffs.

    d. Navy cannot assume responsibility for flank cover. Lanes can be cleared through mine fields by expendable craft.

    e. Artillery fire direction: Brigade Hq. in charge of entire ground forces artillery. Will be put under navy command. No assignment of individual units.

    f. Reinhardt and Ordnance Office:

Instructions have been given to assign army experts (Engineer Corps and Ordnance Office) to navy.

Army will have own project for readying of invasion craft, will fit barges for experiments to develop suitable types.

Reinhardt has been instructed to furnish drawings of invasion craft and handling instructions to troops, make proposals for infantry training course, and interchange experiences with Jacob.

The three problems to be solved are: (a) how to unload heavy vehicles from landing barges; (b) to find simple methods for converting barges (to be done by troops); and (c) to ascertain what shipborne weapons could deliver fire during landing operations.

. . .

Order of battle of amphibious tank units has not yet been settled. —Must not be committed in small groups; employ in massed formation (question still open).

g. Divisions slated for deactivation. By deactivating seventeen divisions, the following results could be attained:

Remaining divisions could be brought to normal strength. Activation of eighty plus forty PW guard battalions. Transfer of forty-five hundred parachutists and fifteen thousand AAA personnel (the latter to air force). Discharge of age group ninety-six and older. Half a million older men would have to remain at the front, because we do not have the young men to replace them.

h. Colonial force, ten thousand strong, will be activated (ten battalions, half of them motorized).

. . .

22 July 1940

. . .

1000. **Conference with ObdH**

1. Report to ObdH on progress of invasion preparations.

2. ObdH summarizes his Berlin *conference with the Fuehrer* on 21 July.

   a. Usual setting.

b. Fuehrer: No clear picture on what is happening in Britain. Preparations for a decision by arms must be completed as quickly as possible. The Fuehrer will not let the military-political initiative go out of his hand. As soon as situation becomes clear, political and diplomatic procedures will take its place.

c. Reasons for continuance of war by Britain:

(1) Hope for a change in America (Roosevelt's position uncertain, industry does not want to invest. Britain runs risk of losing her position of first sea power to United States).

(2) Puts hope in Russia.

Britain's position is hopeless. The war is won by us. A reversal in the prospects of success is impossible.

d. Navy has been asked: Within what time can shipping space be made available? In what way can flank be given artillery cover? What can be done to provide protection against attacks from the sea? Admiral Raeder will make binding statements by middle of the week.

e. Crossing of Channel appears very hazardous to the Fuehrer. On that account, invasion is to be undertaken only if no other way is left to bring terms with Britain.

f. Britain perhaps sees the following possibilities:

(1) Create trouble in the Balkans through Russia, to cut us off from our fuel source, and so paralyze our air force.

(2) To gain the same ends by inciting Russia against us.

(3) To bomb our synthetic oil plants.

g. *Romania:* King Carol has opened way for peaceful settlement. Has sent a letter to the Fuehrer.

h. If Britain persists in waging war, efforts will be made to confront her with a solid political front, Spain, Italy, Russia.

i. *Britain must be reduced by the middle of September,* at the time when we make the invasion. Will be done by air assaults and submarine warfare. Air force proposes all-out effort against enemy air force; smash enemy fighter strength by luring them off the ground and then make them fight up in the air. Army likewise stresses this necessity and wants to have the air offensive combined with intensified submarine warfare.

k. Appraisal of the effect of the peace feeler: Press initially violent in its rejection; later turned on a softer tune.

Lloyd George: Letter to King and Parliament.

Duke of Windsor: Letter to King.

Thomsen: Information on Britain: Situation is considered hopeless.

British ambassador to Washington is quoted: Britain has lost the war. Should pay, but do nothing derogatory to her honor. Possibility of a cabinet Lloyd George, Chamberlain, Halifax.

. . .

6. Fuehrer will decide by middle of the week, after Raeder's report, whether invasion will be carried through *this fall*. If not now, not before May next. We shall probably know conclusively by the end of the week. Final decision whether submarine and air warfare will be waged in its sharpest form probably will not be taken before beginning of August. In that case, invasion will take place about 25 August.

7. Stalin is flirting with Britain to keep her in the war and tie us down, with a view to gain time and take what he wants, knowing he could not get it once peace breaks out. He has an interest in not letting Germany become too strong, but there are no indications of any Russian aggressiveness against us.

8. Our attention must be turned to tackling the Russian problem and prepare planning. The Fuehrer has been given the following information:

a. German assembly will take at least four to six weeks.

b. Object: To crush Russian army or at least take as much Russian territory as is necessary to bar enemy air raids on Berlin and Silesian industries. It is desirable to penetrate far enough to enable our air force to smash Russia's strategic areas.

      c. Political aims: Ukrainian state,
                               federation of Baltic states,
                               White Russia—Finland,
                               Baltic states "a thorn in the flesh."

      d. Strength required: Eighty to one hundred divisions. Russia has fifty to seventy-five good divisions. If we attack Russia this fall, pressure of the air war on Britain will be relieved. United States could supply both Britain and Russia.

      e. Operations: What operational objective could be attained? What strength have we available? Timing and area of assembly? Gateways of attack: Baltic states, Finland, Ukraine. Protect Berlin and Silesian industrial area. —Protection of Romanian oil fields. (Check with Op. Sec.)

V. Etzdorf:

Romania: Talks with Hungarians at Munich were aimed at urging peaceful compromise. Exchange of letters between Fuehrer and King Carol along this line. Full concurrence of Il Duce. Carol's answer is agreeable to solution.

Bulgaria demands return of about three hundred thousand nationals.

Hungarian "minimum demand": Arad-Braşov.

Italy: Participation of Italian troops in invasion of Britain has been declined. Ciano is apparently out to get hold of some pawns on the Balkans. Fuehrer wants Italy to defer drive against Suez reported to be planned for near future.

Russia-Britain: The two want to get together. The Russians are afraid of compromising themselves in our eyes; they don't want any war. The official announcements of the Stalin-Cripps talks indicate a very gratifying reserve toward Britain on the part of Stalin. Russia rejects Britain's "balance of power" policy and British terms for trade between the two countries. Russia does not want to claim leadership for coordination of Balkan states, as it would not augment her power. Yet Russia's actual mood shows itself on other occasions (talk between Kalinin and Yugoslav minister). Here a direct appeal is made for struggle against Germany: "Unite in a solid block."

Britain: Official reaction to Fuehrer speech: Rejection, America expects rejection.

Information through Hungarian sources: Britain is fighting shy of concluding peace at this moment. Shift of political power in Britain toward Attlee.

Spain and Portugal: There have been rumors of Spanish intentions to conclude a military alliance with Portugal. We are agreeable. Prerequisite would be that Portugal renounce her alliance with Britain.

German policy: Greater Germanic Reich. There are sympathies for this idea in Denmark, and it is also discussed in Sweden. Germanic sectionalism must be transcended!

.   .   .

26 July 1940

.   .   .

Kinzel (OQu IV): Reviews enemy intelligence relating to an operation against Russia. The best chances of success lie in an operation in direction of Moscow with flank on the Baltic Sea, which, subsequently, by a drive from the north, compels the Russian concentrations in the Ukraine and at the Black Sea to accept battle with inverted front.

Keitel (Chief, Personnel Division): Out-of-turn promotions in General Staff (Chiefs of Staff of AGps., Chief of Op. Sec., Ia officers). Assignments in newly activated armored divisions. —Out-of-turn promotions outside General Staff. —Award of Iron Crosses and War Merit Crosses.

Jacob (with *Captain Loyke—navy—and v. Greiffenberg*): Jacob reports on engineer troops exercise (Reinhardt) at Emden. Results:

    a.   First assault wave must use only self-propelled craft (about one-third of total craft available).

    b.   Assault boats lowered sideways from the transports on slides are very practical.

    c.   It might be possible to drive *péniche* river barges without self-propulsion, propelled by cutters tied alongside, directly onto beach.

    d.   As far as possible, each regiment of the main assault groups would be equipped with about fifty assault boats lashed together in pairs, and seventy-five large pneumatic floats. This would provide a fairly adequate number of craft for disembarking.

    e.   *Péniche* river barges without self-propulsion can be used only in subsequent waves.

f. Taking all self-propelled craft, together with barges propelled by cutters lashed alongside, would give us about one-half of our entire landing fleet for the first assault wave.

g. Beached landing craft could not be refloated before the succeeding high tide, i.e., eight hours later. They could make another trip to the enemy coast within twenty to twenty-four hours. Accordingly, each barge fleet would have to be followed up by a different barge fleet on the succeeding high tide, on the following timetable:

0000:   First high tide:
      Fleet 1 moving out; Fleet 2 loading.

1200:   Second high tide:
      Fleet 1 returns; Fleet 2 arrives at beachhead.

2400:   Third high tide:
      Fleet 1 moving out; Fleet 2 returns, and so on.

h. Proposal: Decrease number of horses. First assault wave still has forty-two hundred, second assault wave fifty-seven thousand horses. Too many. Make maximum use of automotive transportation.

i. Strobel has developed rafts of Herbert and B-bridging equipment (floated on barrels). Gasoline drums, bullet-proof gasoline tanks, and Kapok cushions. Ferries for medium guns (AAA guns) and floating landing bridges will be built with the same materials.

k. Training: First group to take instruction course at Reinhardt's Hq. will be the engineer commanders. Meanwhile rafts and landing craft will be moved to our jump-off beaches, and training courses organized for instructors and troops. With the craft ready, troops can immediately start embarking and disembarking training as they arrive.

27 July 1940

OQu IV with Meyer-Ricks: Italian preparations for offensive against British. The Italians have superiority in numbers (8: five divisions), but the British have greater combat efficiency. Operational possibilities are limited. Success can therefore be expected only from a coordinated effort of the greater Italian strength on land, on the sea, and in the air. Whether such coordination can be achieved is questionable. Difficulties of land supply.

28 July 1940

. . .

Von Greiffenberg: Preliminary work on invasion timetable. Afterwards, discussion of timetable with the individual army chiefs.

In the evening we receive a memorandum from the Naval Operations Staff which upsets all draft plans for the Channel crossing. Apart from asserting that loading for the jump-off would be impossible on open beaches and could be done only in designated ports, it states that navy needs ten days to put the first assault wave across. If that is true, all previous statements of the navy were so much rubbish and we can throw away the whole plan of an invasion.

29 July 1940

Von Greiffenberg: Discussion of problems created by navy memorandum.

Conference with ObdH: We agree that we cannot carry through our part of the operation on the basis of the resources furnished by navy. Important points:

    a. The whole problem of transport must be approached from the landing aspect and not from the point of view of the departure.

    b. We must demand that the first assault wave be brought to the shore on self-propelled (not towed) craft on the widest possible front and in maximum strength.

    c. The stipulation of navy that ten days must be allowed for putting across the first assault wave is unacceptable.

    d. Abandoning our plan for landing north of Folkestone cannot be considered by us.

    Von Greiffenberg is sent to Berlin.

General Marcks (Chief of Staff, Eighteenth Army), on special assignment to OKH, is briefed on particulars of his work. (Stays for luncheon.)

1700. **General Stapf** reports on air situation.

    a. Air force will be ready for large-scale offensive by end of the week.

b. Estimate of monthly losses: 120 to 150, i.e., 10 percent of the 1,350 operational aircraft. Replacement of personnel and machines is assured.

c. Strength of British air force on 15 July:

Fighters: 50 squadrons of 18 each = 900; 75 percent operational = 675.

We have 1,075, including long-range fighters.

Best British type is Spitfire (40 percent of total). Our Me 109 (cannon) superior; Me 110 (2 cm) is match only in formation.

Bombers: British have 55 to 60 squadrons of 20 each 1,150 (first-class); 75 percent operational 860 (400 Hampton).

We have 1,350 bombers, including dive-bombers.

The British are at a disadvantage owing to their inferior aiming devices and more valuable planes.

AAA:

British have:	We have:	
1,194 medium guns	8,730	2 cm
1,114 light	1,434	3.7 cm
	3,040	8.8 cm
	146	10.5 cm

British fire control devices are poor, AAA defenses weak; strong night defenses, 3,200 searchlights.

Great numbers of barrage balloons; limited value, altitude range 1,000 to 2,000 m.

d. *Personnel:* No difficulties on British side. Officer pilots in general have poor tactical, but good technical training; sports! Contrary to our practice, bombers are piloted by NCOs.

e. *Supply* at present still fully covered from British sources, not from the U.S. Undelivered balance of French orders in U.S. will be taken over by the British before the end of fall.

Current deliveries: 180 to 200 fighters and 100 bombers per month.

Our harassing raids are hitting British aircraft production plants (engines) and naval bases. *Fuel situation:* British supply assured.

Supply of bombs is sufficient.

British bombs:	Our bombs:
112 kg	50, 250, 500,
224 kg	1,000, 1,800 kg

f. *Leadership*

Top level, mechanical. Intermediate level directs from ground through airfield Hq. Lower level: Unadaptable to new tactics.

g. *Airfields:*

Many landing fields in southern England and in the Midlands. They do not have the requisite trained ground crews and technical equipment which are available only at peacetime air bases.

Our air force on the whole feels they have the edge on the British in equipment, leadership, skill, and with respect to the geographical factors. Decisive results will be forthcoming before the close of the year.

Allocated for attack against Britain are: 9 bomber groups on Channel coast (northeast), 9 bomber groups in Brest area, that is, 18 out of total strength of 40 groups. Thus, about 50 percent of total strength is available for direct support of the landing assault.

Five groups will remain in Norway (for operations against Scapa Flow).

Long-range and short-range reconnaissance squadrons will be allocated to army, as scheduled. Of AAA, only seventeen mixed battalions (one for each corps). Long-range reconnaissance squadrons for coastal artillery under air force control(?). Film strip on English coast.

2100. Buhle:

a. Should motorized artillery for invasion be taken from the east? (Decision can be made only after it has been ascertained whether or not the four existing battalions have already been broken up for new activations.)

   b.   Comb army for trucks needed by assault divisions.

   c.   One rocket projector regiment of three battalions can be activated before next fall.

30 July 1940

. . .

Von Greiffenberg returns from Berlin conference with OKM:

   a.   Naval Operations Staff cannot under any circumstances be ready before 15 September. Earliest jump-off date 20/26 September (moon, tides). If not then, next May. Air force is not doing anything about landing preparations at present.

   b.   Speedier construction of landing craft impossible. Two thousand river barges are now being converted. Steamer tonnage: 200,000 tons for first assault wave, 400,000 tons for second assault wave.

      Losses due to ice.

      Towing vessel situation bad. River barges unsuited because they cannot handle current; could manage only last stretch along coast. Situation will not be improved next May.

   c.   Operation cannot be protected against British navy. *Scharnhorst, Gneisenau,* and *Scheer* are in dry dock. Available: *Hipper. Prince Eugen* will be commissioned in late fall. In addition, only four destroyers, three torpedo boats (forty-eight submarines).

   d.   Tide mines not yet available in sufficient quantities.

   e.   Mine protection for our invasion fleet cannot be provided, because . . . [sentence unfinished].

   f.   Effectiveness of air force against naval craft said to be exaggerated.

   g.   Embarkation: Navy not disinterested in disembarkation. Considers task fulfilled only after ground forces in sufficient strength for operation have been put on land. Whether Dunkirk can be used is questionable.

   h.   Embarkation on open beaches has been ruled out. River barges cannot be anchored, might grind themselves into the sand if lying there for any length of time, or be holed, as they have no double bottoms.

Readying of craft in river estuaries has been carried out to the fullest extent.

i. Crossing of first wave can be effected on entire assault frontage. Subsequent waves will not be able to cross on such a front owing to the threat to flanks.

k. Monitors only at expense of tugboats. All passenger boats have already been put into service (German Bight). Only four destroyers and three torpedo boats are available as escorts.

l. No small-caliber guns will be issued for protection of ships, as they are needed for protection of docks.

m. It is anticipated that the river barges used in the initial assault would be lost and so could not be counted on for successive crossings.

n. Ramsgate is considered unsuited for landing because of the Downs. Cable water: We would have to travel 15 km parallel to the coast. This is impossible in the face of an enemy disposed for defense; can be done if he is unprepared for our coming.

o. Timing of landing: In the morning, two hours after peak of high tide (advantage of bad visibility). Time required for disembarking: twelve hours, for initial wave. Subsequent waves will take much longer, as ships are larger. Transfer from steamers to river barges will take thirty-six hours.

p. Landing Isle of Wight. —Portsmouth considered unpromising by navy.

q. Very satisfied with results of submarine warfare. Effectiveness greatly increased. Submarine base at Bordeaux for Italians.

One-half of British fleet is at Alexandria, the other half at Scapa Flow.

1900. Von Rintelen:

a. Offensive against Egypt is being actively prepared. Everything will be ready 5/7 August. They seem to be waiting for word of start of our operation against England. "The Fuehrer wants to start off Il Duce."

b. Two new battleships are now only on their trial runs. Italians allow six weeks, our navy estimates six months. Postponement desirable until these big ships are ready to partake in operations.

    c. Overall impression: Nothing big can be achieved with the Italians. The offensive on Egypt will accomplish no decisive results if executed by the Italians alone. Handicapped by their economic straits and their ineffectualness, the Italians are in no position to achieve anything on a decisive scale.

2000–2200. **ObdH** comes in to discuss overall situation created by position taken by navy. We concur on the following points:

    a. The navy in all probability will not provide us this fall with the means for a successful invasion of Britain. If the navy holds that it cannot, before mid-September, give us these ships which it believed to be able to get together, there remain only two possibilities for us:

        Postpone the invasion to the bad-weather period, which might bring us some local advantages for our landings, but on the whole would be detrimental to our effort, or else.

        Wait until spring '41 (May).

    Our position in relation to Britain would not be improved by the delay. The British could strengthen their defenses, augment their armaments, and increase their air strength. America might become effective. On the other hand air and naval warfare may cut down further Britain's resources to keep the country going.

    b. The greatest risk to postponing lies in the fact that it might weaken our hold on the military-political initiative.

    c. If we decide that we cannot conduct a successful operation against the British Isles this fall, the following lines of action are open to us:

      1. Attack on Gibraltar (from the land side, through Spain).

      2. Support Italians with armor in North Africa (Egypt).

      3. Attack British in Haifa.

      4. Attack Suez Canal.

      5. Incite Russians to a drive on Persian Gulf.

    d. The question whether, if a decision cannot be forced against Britain, we should, in the face of a threatening British-Russian alliance and the resulting two-front war, turn first against Russia, must be answered to the effect that we should keep on friendly terms with Russia. A visit to Stalin would be desirable. Russia's aspirations to the Straits and in the direction of the Persian Gulf need not bother us. On the Balkans, which fall within our economic sphere of interest, we could keep out of each other's way. Italy and Russia will not hurt each other in the Mediterranean. This being so, we could deliver the British a decisive blow in the Mediterranean, shoulder them away from Asia, help the Italians in building their Mediterranean empire and, with the aid of Russia, consolidate the Reich which we have created in western and northern Europe. That much accomplished, we could confidently face war with Britain for years.

31 July 1940

1130.   *Berghof.* (Left by plane 0645.)

Grand Admiral Raeder:

By 13 September all preparations will have reached a stage where invasion operations could be initiated, unless extraordinary adverse factors intervene.

Weather: Week of 20 to 28 September as a rule is a bad-weather period in Channel; better weather can be expected for end of September and beginning of October. At that time it would be possible also to replace personnel. Calling up of barge crews has severely affected inland shipping and the entire economy (coal, iron ore, food supply of Berlin and Hamburg). The requisitioning of trawlers needed as towing vessels jeopardizes fresh fish supply. Commerce with Scandinavia will be greatly curtailed, with Baltic states to a lesser extent.

Proposes postponement of invasion to next spring. Army and navy disagree on timing of attack: Dawn is bad for navy.

Darkness hinders reconnaissance. Best time: Two hours after peak of high tide.

Dawn landing requires night crossing of Channel; in that case at least half moon.

Only a few days meet these requirements every month. On 22 to 26 August we shall not be ready yet, and 22 to 26 September falls into the bad-weather period.

Landing in Lyme Bay leads us into area where enemy is strongest; he will come out at least with large destroyer force. Disembarking will take thirty-six hours.

It is impossible to give adequate protection to widely separated landing areas, and concentration of landing on narrowest possible coastal strip must therefore be urged.

Summary: (1) earliest possible date: 15 September; (2) primary consideration of navy is ability to assure safe landing; and (3) most favorable time of year: May–June.

The Fuehrer:

The following factors have to be borne in mind in considering the crossing:

a.   Weather conditions against which human effort is unavailing (recognizes factor of storm tides, etc.).

b.   Enemy action. In land battle, German forces need to reckon only with a poor British army, which has not had time to apply lessons learned in this war. It has not yet been possible to activate new units. New activations within eight to ten months; equipment sufficient for thirty to thirty-five divisions will be available next spring. Concentrated in Britain, this would be a very formidable force. Perhaps industrial plants could be bombed to an extent that would seriously impair activations. Possibilities for our propaganda. Offsetting factor is British hopes on Russia and the United States.

Problematic: Staying power of Italians, especially in East Africa. What could be accomplished in the meantime, apart from air warfare? If impracticable now, invasion of Britain cannot be carried out before May. How can we bridge this interval? Air force, submarine warfare, Gibraltar (bring in Spain).

Proposal by army: Support Italians in North Africa with two armored divisions. Fuehrer: These diversional maneuvers must be studied. — Repercussions on France? Positively decisive result can be achieved only by invasion of Britain.

Grand Admiral Raeder proposes to limit cross-Channel operation to assault by ten regimental groups in area north of Folkestone. *Bismarck* and *Tirpitz* will be ready by May. This would give us four major naval units. Cruisers-destroyers: One a month, beginning next September. Twelve torpedo boats are completed now, number will be eighteen by next spring.

Twenty motor torpedo boats on hand now; more will be added during winter.

No substantial reinforcements from units now on high seas missions.

Fuehrer: What will be the ratio of the two navies by next spring?

Answer: This depends on effectiveness of air warfare. No replacement yet for *Royal Oak* and *Queen Elizabeth*. British have total of thirteen battleships. Possibly we may manage to get *Scharnhorst* and *Gneisenau* to Brest during coming winter.

Fuehrer: Things will become more difficult with passing of time. Air warfare will start now. Its results will determine our ultimate relative strength.

If results of air warfare are unsatisfactory, invasion preparations will be stopped. If we have the impression that the British are crumbling and that effects will soon begin to tell, we shall proceed to the attack.

So, let us bear with economic dislocations for another ten days. In case of a postponement until next year, conversion of river barges could be continued during winter.

Diplomatic front: Spain. North African question is under discussion. Fuehrer weighs effect on enemy ports and navy. Are dive-bombers effective against armored decks?

Order: Preparations must be continued. Decision on whether invasion is to take place within eight to ten days. Army: Gear everything to target date 15 September. On wide frontage.

Fuehrer asks about results of submarine campaign.

Raeder: With Lorient and Brest as bases, submarines will double effectiveness.

Air force is attacking Saint George's Channel; navy, North Channel.

Trondheim will be fully protected against big ships by fall. Antisubmarine defense is being strengthened. Narvik secure. Heavy artillery for Kirkenes is en route. Recommends extension of submarine-building program past fall '41. Needs raw material and manpower for this purpose. (Raeder leaves.)

Fuehrer:

a.   Stresses his skepticism regarding technical feasibility; however, satisfied with results produced by navy.

b.   Emphasizes weather factor.

c.   Discusses enemy resources for counteraction. Our small navy is only 15 percent of enemy's; 8 percent of enemy's destroyers; 10

to 12 percent of his motor torpedo boats. So we have nothing to bring into action against enemy surface attacks. That leaves mines (not 100 percent reliable), coastal artillery (good!), and air force.

In any decision we must bear in mind that if we take risks, the prize, too, is high.

d.　In the event that invasion does not take place, our action must be directed to eliminate all factors that let England hope for a change in the situation. To all intents and purposes, the war is won. France no longer part of the setup protecting British convoys. Italy is pinning down British forces.

Submarine and air warfare may bring about a final decision, but this may be one or two years off.

Britain's hope lies in Russia and the United States. If Russia drops out of the picture, America, too, is lost for Britain, because elimination of Russia would tremendously increase *Japan's power* in the Far East.

Russia is the Far Eastern sword of Britain and the United States pointed at Japan. Here an unpleasant wind is blowing for Britain. Japan, like Russia, has her program which she wants to carry through before the end of the war.

Russia is the factor on which Britain is relying the most. Something must have happened in London!

[Marginal note to above paragraph] The Russian victory film on the Russo-Finnish war!

The British were completely down; now they have perked up again. Intercepted telephone conversations. Russia is painfully shaken by the swift development of the western European situation.

All that Russia has to do is to hint that she does not care to have a strong Germany, and the British will take hope, like one about to go under, that the situation will undergo a radical change within six or eight months.

With Russia smashed, Britain's last hope would be shattered. Germany then will be master of Europe and the Balkans.

Decision: Russia's destruction must therefore be made a part of this struggle. Spring 1941.

The sooner Russia is crushed the better. Attack achieves its purpose only if Russian state can be shattered to its roots with one blow. Holding part of the country alone will not do. Standing still for the following winter would be perilous. So it is better to wait a little longer, but with the resolute determination to eliminate Russia. This is necessary also because of contiguity on the Baltic. It would be awkward to have another major power there. If we start in May 1941, we would have five months to finish the job. Tackling it this year still would have been the best, but unified action would be impossible at this time.

Object is destruction of Russian manpower. Operation will be divided into three actions:

First thrust: Kiev and securing flank protection on Dnieper. Air force will destroy river crossings. Odessa.

Second thrust: Baltic states and drive on Moscow.

Finally: Linkup of northern and southern prongs.

Successively: Limited drive on Baku oil fields.

It will be seen later to what extent Finland and Turkey should be brought in.

Ultimately: Ukraine, White Russia, Baltic states to us. Finland extended to the White Sea.

```
  7 divisions will stay in Norway (must be made self-sufficient!).
     Ammunition.
 50 divisions in France
  3 divisions in Holland and Belgium
 ─────────
 60 divisions
120 divisions for the East
─────────
180 divisions
```

The greater the number of divisions we have at the start the better. We have 120 divisions, plus 20 furlough divisions. Activations of new divisions by withdrawal of three battalions from existing divisions, in three stages, at intervals of several months (in all, one-third of every division).

Spread rumors: Spain, North Africa, Britain. Activations in areas safe from aerial incursions. In eastern area: Forty divisions, with battle-seasoned troops.

Projected Balkans settlement. Proposed arrangement between Hungary and Romania, to be followed by guarantee for Romania.

Left Salzburg by plane 1345. Arrived at Fontainebleau 2000.

1 August 1940

. . .

1200.   **Marcks** presents report on Russian operation:

Objectives of operations; road, railroad, and transport situation. Buildup of two large operational groups, directed against Kiev and Moscow. I point out (a) that Operational Group Kiev, based on Romanian territory, is treading very insecure political ground; and (b) that the extension of the operations of the Moscow group into the Baltic states should be treated as a subsidiary action which must not detract from the main thrust on Moscow.

Role of navy and air force.

Instruction: Draft planning data for operation and submit list of organizational requirements as well as the tasks for other branches of armed forces they entail.

. . .

6 August 1940

. . .

Von Greiffenberg-von Witzleben: Discussion of points which have to be cleared up with navy. Information brought by von Witzleben shows that navy insists on landing to be made on narrowest frontage. Plans of this sort are undebatable because success of landing operations cannot be assured on so narrow a frontage.

Moreover, navy asserts that inasmuch as weather conditions and postponement of large-scale air force operations have delayed start of minesweeping, 15 September date for jump-off has already been jeopardized.

We have here the paradoxical situation where the navy is full of misgivings, the air force is very reluctant to tackle a mission which at the outset is exclusively its own; and OKW, which for once has a real combined forces' operation to direct, just plays dead. The only driving force in the whole situation comes from us, but alone we would not be able to swing it either.

. . .

7 August 1940

. . .

Evening (leaving by special train at 2000): Conference with OKM (Schniewind, Fricke) and Reinhardt.

Conference results merely in confirming the existence of irreconcilable differences between us. Navy maintains that landing is possible only on narrowest frontage, between Folkestone and Beachy Head, and feels confident of being able to assure a continuous shuttle service to the lodgement. However, this front would be too narrow for us, all the more so as it leads into a terrain that offers unacceptable obstacles to any swift advance. A landing between Folkestone and Ramsgate is held practicable by navy only after coastal defenses have been rolled up from the land side. Navy opposes any westward extension of the assault front out of fear of Portsmouth and the British high seas fleet. There could be no adequate air defense against these threats.

In view of the limited transport resources, completion of the cross-Channel operation on a broader frontage would take forty-two days, which is utterly prohibitive for us. Our views are diametrically opposed on that point. The issue must therefore be settled on higher level.

9 August 1940

. . .

Through Canaris: *Spain* will not do anything against Gibraltar on her own accord. German intelligence reports to date. Drawing Spain into war, desired by Fuehrer, will be difficult. Economic problems!

. . .

14 August 1940

OQu IV: a. Italians propose to invade Yugoslavia, and want German help: German transport for the buildup, German supply organization, five thousand trucks, etc. What incredible nerve!

Have requested talks with German General Staff within fortnight, listing staff sections they want to participate. This is a political matter and must be referred to Fuehrer for decision.

b. Agent reports from Paris. Next generation will be the planners of revenge.

c. Russia has revamped political commissars into political indoctrination aides to unit commanders. Everything pertaining to operations is the exclusive responsibility of the commander. The connection between command function and indoctrination, as we see it, thus apparently still has not been understood. Leaving that aside, the revamping of the commissar post makes for a strengthening of the Russian army.

.   .   .

Stapf reports on results of air operations on 8, 11, 12, and 13 August.

Primary objective: Reducing enemy fighter strength in southern England. Results very good. Ratio of own to enemy losses, 1:3.

We have lost 3 percent of our first-class bombers and fighters, the enemy 15 percent.

Fighters: ratio of losses 1:5, in our favor; in percent of first-class machines: 4%:30%.
We have no difficulties in making good our losses. British will probably not be able to replace theirs.

Ground organization: Eight major air bases have been virtually destroyed.

Massed attack by entire air force is not always possible. Individual air fleets must therefore be given greatest possible operational discretion.

Continuation of assault depends on weather conditions, which do not look too good for the immediate future. Remote control by ObdL allows considerable operational freedom.

Next targets: Essential production plants. (Naval bases and units are for time being classified as targets of opportunity.)

.   .   .

18 August 1940

. . .

Von Greiffenberg:

    a. "Directive" from OKW on final plan for preparations for Operation SEA LION. Cherbourg drops out. West of Beachy Head, there will be only one landing, without any follow-up. All capabilities must now be calculated on this basis.

    b. Directive on Norway. Coast as far as Kirkenes must be occupied. To this end von Falkenhorst will be reinforced with small complementary units. This measure cannot but be interpreted as being directed against Russia.

. . .

20 August 1940

Conference with ObdH:

    a. Discussion on latest OKW directive: ObdH wants to keep together Cherbourg group for its original mission. I don't think this will serve any purpose, because we won't have the requisite landing-craft lift.

    b. Projected distribution of armored forces:

        1 armored corps in France
        3 armored corps in southeast
        6 armored corps in northeast

    My idea is, for the present, to have three groups in the east, and one each in the southeast, the northeast, and Germany, ready to be shifted in accordance with the development of our buildup.

. . .

OQu IV: a. Von Rintelen: *Yugoslavia* question not acute. Il Duce does not agree.

        Greece: Our misgivings about Italian pressure on Greece. [Marginal note:] We don't want any new theaters of war.

    b. Greece appeals to Germany for support in her effort to remain neutral.

    c. *Slovakia:* German minister is given status of Cabinet member; also has representatives in government parties.

. . .

23 August 1940

Von Etzdorf: German-Russian relations.

1. Mariampol will be claimed by us (3.86 million dollars).

2. Compensation for Germans in Bessarabia. Legal claim is rejected.

3. Closure of our diplomatic missions in the Baltic states; to be converted into consular agencies.

Balkans: Foreign Office does not want army to undertake anything in Romania. Russo-Italian talks on new order on Balkans. Fuehrer: "Balkans must be kept in state of unsettlement." Wants German-Italian talks without Russia.

Italy has been told to lay off Greece.

Spain is willing to enter war on our side. Wants 700,000 tons of grain in return. Disarmament of French in North Africa. —Postwar claims: Gibraltar, Morocco, Algeria as far as Oran.

Colonies: Our demands are based on the concept of a compact East-West African empire.

Spain wants northwest Africa; Italy northeast Africa.

Japan: A special ambassador is on his way to secure Japan's accession to the Tripartite Pact against the event of America's entry into the war. Success doubtful.

United States: Date for Philippine Treaty to enter into effect has been put off for ten years. —Will take over a number of British naval bases in Atlantic and Pacific in return for fifty to ninety old destroyers. — Negotiations with Portugal about Azores, which are being considered for a base for joint Anglo-American naval forces. —American efforts to acquire bases on Greenland and Island. —America's intention to "bail out" Britain is becoming increasingly obvious.

. . .

26 August 1940

. . .

2000. **Obdh** returns from today's Fuehrer conference. Results:

I. *Operation SEA LION* stands. Interest in this operation seems to have increased.

    a. Draft orders and instructions for assembly of invasion force on basis of elimination of Cherbourg and restriction of Le Havre to jump-off of a small first wave of the Brighton Group, with one first-wave division and the entire second wave of the group starting from Boulogne (Plan B).

    b. Navy has presented memorandum to OKW, specifying transport capacity and timetable for its transport plan; we are directed to make counterproposals.

II. *Romania:* Concern that Russians might make another push if Hungarians start off again. Our policy makers have not made up their minds yet whether: (a) to side with Hungary, or (b) to give Romania a guarantee against Hungary (!)

Finland would get arms and ammunition from us. In the event of a Russian attack against Finland, we shall occupy Petsamo.

In the east, we must have greater strength: Ten divisions will be moved to the east, to reinforce our troops in the Government-General and East Prussia.

Norway: Mountain equipment for 196th Division (Trondheim). Activation of a new division from personnel of the four divisions in southern Norway.

Libya: Armored division or brigade? (Sixth Division?)

III. *New activations* to be prepared as projected. BdE wants to issue pertinent orders on 10 September.

Feyerabend (in place of von Greiffenberg, who is sick) **and Buhle:** Orientation on military-political situation. Discussion of measures to be taken.

Wagner: Current matters in military administration. Creation of a Military Administration Sec. and Army Supply Sec.

27 August 1940

0900. **Conference with ObdH:** It brings out some new points about the last Fuehrer conference. For all appearances it was the usual political potpourri. Pipe dreams: Spain is to be brought into war, but the economic consequences for that country are ignored. North Africa is viewed as a theater of operations against Britain (Egypt, Asia Minor; pushing British away from Cyprus and Haifa?!). Romania is to be drawn into our orbit, but in a way that would not rouse Russia too much at this early date. We are going to be ready in the north (Petsamo) when Russia attacks Finland. The army is supposed to have everything nice and ready without ever getting any straightforward instructions.

1030.   Canaris:

   a.   Gibraltar: Franco's policy from the start was not to come in until Britain was defeated, for he is afraid of her might (ports, food situation, etc.). Now the Fuehrer is working on him to swing him over to our side. Suñer is supposed to come here.

   Spain has a very bad internal situation. They are short on food and have no coal. The generals and the clergy are against Franco. His only support is Suñer, who is more pro-Italian than pro-German.

   Military preparations to date have been confined to scouting out the situation; work on concrete preparations will have to wait for specific orders. Apparently the undertaking is conceived as an OKW operation in the manner of Norway. It would be high time now for OKW to inform us about their intentions. The consequences of having this unpredictable nation as a partner cannot be calculated. We shall get an ally who will cost us dearly.

   b.   Romania: Two hundred men in the oil region to guard production plants. —Stationed outside Romania are 120 men.

   c.   A new wave of liquidation of intellectuals and Jews is on in the east.

. . .

30 August 1940

Stapf: a.   ObdL has ruled that AAA battalions will not be allocated to individual corps. Instead AAA corps will be employed to cover embarkation and disembarkation. Army will not get any AAA units at all.

b.   Progress report on air war against Britain:

Total Operational Planes	Losses from 8 to 26 August (four all-out battles)	Monthly Production
Germany:		
1,464 first-class fighters	169 = 12%	900
1,800 first-class bombers	184 = 10%	Next spring (beginning April) 1,350–1,400
Britain:		
915 first-class fighters	791 = 50%	Including American
600 second-class fighters		production:
1,515 total fighters		620–650; later increasing to maximum of 950
1,100 first-class bombers	80 = 5%	
600 second-class bombers		
1,700 total bombers		
British Orders in America:		
915 twin-engine Martin bombers		Deliveries beginning next September
1,200 twin-engine Douglas bombers		Deliveries beginning next October
300 single-engine Bell fighters		Deliveries beginning next September
1,500 single-engine Curtis fighters		Deliveries already started

This would indicate that British bomber force is still intact. It can be smashed only by direct attacks on its bases.

Von Greiffenberg, Buhle, Feyerabend: Planning data for regrouping of forces. Changeover to the east. Selection of divisions to serve as cadres for new divisions.

. . .

31 August 1940

0700.   Take-off by plane. 1115 arrival at Berlin. 1315 at Fuehrer's office in Reich Chancellery.

Breakfast: Talk with *von Uthmann* on Swedish and Norwegian matters, and with *von Rintelen* on Italian situation.

The Fuehrer: Following luncheon, *the Fuehrer* talks to several of our attachés.

Russia: Three points must be brought home to the Russians.

a.   Germany has a vital interest in Romania and "will stop short of nothing to safeguard it." "Romania is inviolable."

b.   Shipments now being made to Finland are merely the last of arms deliveries held up by the war and now being completed. (In place of large-caliber artillery, which was retained for German needs, medium calibers are being supplied.)

c.   Buildup at Kirkenes, requiring transit through Finland, is directed against Britain.

Finland: Fuehrer wants to supply Finland with liberal quantities of first-rate equipment. Rush! Same line of explanation with respect to Russia.

Italy: Emphasis on North Africa. Fuehrer considers sending aid in form of dive-bomber units.

Hungary: Transit on roads and railroads for our troops.

Turkey: General orientation.

Bulgaria: Fuehrer stresses the significance of Bulgaria's strength, which now seems to find increasing recognition.

.   .   .

3 September 1940

1000.   Conference with ObdH:

a.   Main subject: Regrouping during next winter and activation of new AHq.

b.   ObdH tells of complaints about inefficiency of NCO Corps heard on his tour.

c.   ObdH is very bitter about the obstacles put in his way whenever he wants to reach the public. The Fuehrer obviously is jealous. Now ObdH wants to organize the Langemark celebration without consulting the Fuehrer.

OQu IV: Current matters: Procedure for evacuation of Transylvania. —Canaris's report on Spain. Spanish demands with respect to arms and fuel. Troop requirements for Gibraltar.

Wagner presents draft on reorganization of Gen Qu Sec. Top staff, two departments: (1) supplies, and (2) administration; legal department? Setting up of Military Administration Hq. Bordeaux. —Current Gen Qu matters.

Koestring: Reports on Russian army: Improving, but will take four years to reach its former level. Difficulties in collecting intelligence owing to GPU supervision. —Role of Baku. —Orientation on our intentions. —Review of terrain features and conditions restricting movement in various parts of Russia; stresses restriction on motorized movements. —New intelligence mission.

Toussaint: Conference on Yugoslav situation. Holds that any military action on Italy's part would serve only to impair Yugoslavia's usefulness to us. At present, Yugoslavia is 100 percent at the disposal of our war economy.

.   .   .

11 September 1940

0830. **Conference at Hq. Ninth Army** (north of Rouen) with XXXVIII, VIII, XV (Hoth), and X Corps. Ninth Army presents operational plan. Disposition of jump-off of corps and divisions. Here it is evident again that the system of successive echelons, as specified in our first basic directives, has been applied much too mechanically. It must be left to the operational commands to decide whether it is more important to put across supply elements or the medium artillery on the second trip.

The crossing schedules indicate that actually only advance combat teams, of a strength of six thousand to seven thousand, with armament not heavier than 3.7 cm will cross from Le Havre (Echelon Ia), while heavier armament and artillery will be ferried over later, in Echelon Ib, which is slated to start from Boulogne. This involves very grave risks. Steamers and Herbert Ferries with AAA and 2-cm guns must go across in Echelon Ia, if we want to avoid serious trouble for our left wing.

The conference brings out that present grouping of 8th and 28th divisions in relation to 6th Division should be looked into again.

It also shows that it is necessary to arrive at a better balance between Calais and Boulogne, in favor of Ninth Army. Movements must be coordinated on basis of synchronized timetables. Follow-up organization needs tightening up. Improve ships by increasing the number of disembarking ports on sides. Preparations for overcoming tank obstacles.

. . .

14 September 1940

The Fuehrer:

I. Successful landing followed by occupation would end war in short order. Britain would starve to death.

Although invasion of Britain as such is essential, execution is not tied to any particular date. It cannot be overlooked, however, that prolongation of the war is likely to aggravate the situation, especially in the political field. In world politics one can never count on stability. Upsets may occur at any time.

The enemy will be aware that developments on which he was relying have not materialized. We did not "bleed to death," as Russia anticipated. We have achieved the greatest victories without great cost. This fact compels the enemy to reevaluate the entire situation. Russia's calculations went wrong, and this realization has already had a restraining effect on Russia's actions against Finland and on the Balkans. It is in our interest to maintain the present status quo in the Balkans. In the Baltic area, too, it is to our benefit to keep a situation from developing which might embarrass our strategic position in that region.

The Fuehrer is not alarmed by tensions there. We shall not yield an inch where our interests are concerned. However, there is no guarantee for any long-range stability. Sudden changes may occur (witness Norway).

America's rearmament will not reach its peak before 1945.

A long war is undesirable for us. We have obtained all that could be of any practical value to us. Politically and economically, the bases gained by us satisfy our needs.

II.   The war would be brought to a close most swiftly by the invasion of England. The navy has attained all targets set for it in the preparation for the Channel crossing. (Praise for the navy!)

Armament of the coast is completed.

Accomplishments of air force are beyond praise. Four or five more days of good weather, and a decisive result will be achieved. Maximum strength has been brought to bear over enemy territory, with all the difficulties entailed. We have a good chance to force Britain to her knees. Effects to date are enormous, but total victory must wait for these four or five days of clear weather. Every pause benefits the enemy. In the air effort, exploitation of success is just as important as pursuit is for the army in following up a success on the ground. That, however, is practicable only during prolonged good weather. Bad weather means increased drain on strength of air force. Bulk of British antiaircraft defense has been transferred to London. Expenditure in ammunition for barrage fire is enormous.

Enemy fighter forces have not yet been completely eliminated. Our own air victory reports fail to give an entirely reliable picture. In any event, the enemy has suffered severe losses.

Seen as a whole, however, and notwithstanding all our successes, *the prerequisites for Operation SEA LION have not yet been completely realized.*

III.   The following conclusions can be drawn from this appraisal:

1.   Successful invasion means victory, but it is predicated on complete air domination.

2.   Bad weather has so far kept us from seizing complete mastery of the air.

3.   All other factors have been worked out as desired.

Decision: Operation SEA LION is not going to be called off yet.

Attacks to date have had enormous effects, though perhaps chiefly upon nerves. Part of that psychological effect is the fear of invasion. That anticipation of its imminence must not be removed. Even though victory in the air should not be achieved before another ten or twelve days, Britain might yet be seized by mass hysteria. If, within the coming ten or twelve days, we achieve mastery of the air over a certain area, we could, by a landing operation, compel the enemy to come out with his destroyers against our landing fleet. We could then inflict upon the enemy such losses that he would no longer be able to protect his convoys.

Cancellation of our plans would not remain a secret. It would ease the strain on the enemy's nerves, and consequently must not be ordered now.

Raeder shares the Fuehrer's views. Risk involved is very great. Air position will not change before the next period favorable for the landing assault, between 24 and 27 September, and so that target date must be dropped. Next favorable date would be 8 October. That date should be kept in mind. If air force has achieved complete victory by that time, we might not even need to undertake the invasion.

Fuehrer: For the time being, everything must be set for 27 September. Accordingly, the next alert date would be 17 September. After that, the next target date would be 8 October.

Von Brauchitsch: Agrees. Advances proposal to make army independent of dates set by navy and execute landing under protection of smoke screens. Points out aerial threat to crowded harbors. Suggests counter battery fire against enemy coast.

Jeschonnek: Draws attention to attacks on railroad artillery spurs.

Fuehrer: The decisive factor is the relentless prosecution of our air effort.

Jeschonnek: Physical destruction exceeds our expectations. But there has yet been no mass panic, because residential sections have not been attacked and destroyed so far. Wants free hand in attacking residential areas.

Fuehrer: All right, but attacks on strategic targets must have first priority, because they destroy war potential which cannot be replaced. As long as there is still a strategic target left, we must concentrate on it. Railroad stations, targets in outlying districts, gas and water works. Bombing calculated to create mass panic must be left to the last (possibility of retaliation against German cities). The terrible threat of bombing population concentrations must be our last trump.

In conclusion, the following subjects are discussed between Fuehrer and army:

    a. *Libya:* Fuehrer orders preparations for dispatch of one armored corps.

    b. *Situation in northwest Africa:* Danger of establishment of enemy air base against Italy.

c. *Gibraltar:* No definite orders. Merely expression of intention to promise Spaniards everything they want, regardless of whether the promises can be kept.

. . .

17 September 1940

OQu I: Conference on disposition of forces in buildup in east.

Distribution of troops now:

West	44 inf. divs.	1 mobile div. in addition to two armd. divs. (equipped with captured materiel).
Norway Denmark } Protectorate	10 inf. divs.	—
East	96 inf. divs.	31 armd. and mot. divs., plus 1 cav. div.

(2 armd. divs. off for Libya)

Distribution of forces in the east (tentative estimate):

Infantry Division		Armored and motorized divisions	
Army Hq. 1 } 2	20	3 } 3 } 6	
Army Hq. 3 } 4	30	6 } 6 } 12, plus 1 cav. div.	

Army Hq. 5 }
         6 }
         7
	30	3 }
		3 } 9
		3 }	

Total	80	27, plus 1 cav. div.	
GHq. Reserve	16	4	
	96	31, plus 1 cav. div. (less 2 armd. divs. for Libya)	

. . .

30 September 1940

Reports are increasing that Russia expects an armed conflict with us in 1941. Preparations for this eventuality are quite manifest in the training of Russian troops; particular emphasis is placed on utilization of wooded terrain. This operational and tactical utilization of forest areas confronts us with quite a number of new problems of operational planning, organization, and training.

1130.   Talk with ObdH after his return from Berlin, where he conferred with OKW. The political developments are still completely in suspense. Conclusion of the Tripartite Pact, by its very nature, presses for political decisions. It would also be advisable to come at last to some decision on the policy to be taken with respect to France, but here, too, the political game is still moving, and no one can foresee what the outcome will be.

The Fuehrer notified Stalin of the conclusion of the pact with Japan twenty-four hours before it was signed. Now a letter has gone out designed to get him interested in dividing up the estate of a defunct Britain, and to induce him to join up with us. If the plan succeeds, it is believed we could go all out against Britain.

The question as to whether Germany can pay herself out of the British booty or has to look to France for compensation is the crux of our French policy; right now the trend is toward greater concessions. But our policy toward France again hinges on Italy's attitude. A conference with Il Duce is now planned, with the following agenda:

1.   Prosecution of the war in the Mediterranean.

2.   Italian demands on France. No major difficulties are anticipated on that score, as Italy is keenly interested in an early conclusion of the war.

3.   Settlement of war costs.

In connection with the talks with Italy, it will be necessary also to consult Spain, on account of her interests in Morocco.

Germany's demands on France are not by any means fixed yet: it seems that annexation of Alsace-Lorraine and of portions of Burgundy is a foregone conclusion. On the question of the departments in the north of France, however, there seems to be still some wavering. In any event, the issue of the northeastern line is going to be impressed so emphatically on the minds of the French people that in the end they will deem themselves lucky to get off with their whole skins at least in that corner. In addition, Germany puts forward a claim to the Azores, the Canary Islands, and Dakar (to be obtained by exchange, if necessary), as well as to that often-discussed strip of Africa from the west coast across the continent to the east coast. The questions of Libya and Gibraltar, which are being worked upon by us, are not to be brought up officially as yet.

1230. Heusinger: Letter to OKW regarding status of preparedness for SEA LION. Current minor matters. No positive information on use of German markings by British air force.

Noon luncheon with the lucky pheasant hunters Kinzel and Hansen, and others.

Von Ziehlberg: General Staff personnel matters. —Misconduct of GHq. personnel.

4 October 1940

(Birthday of ObdH)

0945. Keitel (Personnel Division): Various current personnel matters.

1000. Presentation of wishes on ObdH's birthday.

1100. OQu IV:

    a. Reports on effect of our air attacks on London. Immense size of city and specific character of our targets have confined effect of bombing to surprisingly small areas. It is hard to see why the same docks are being attacked over and over again when to all appearances they have been largely evacuated. Nor has the effect on industrial plants been critical.

    b. Reports on Italian operations in Libya. Evidently the Italian command is lacking both ability and the means to achieve any conclusive success. Now the Italians show interest again in getting aid from us. They want one armored division; transfer would take ten weeks, and it would be the New Year before the division could go into action.

c.   Army Hq. 7 has been reconnoitering transport facilities in Spain without our knowledge.

. . .

11 October 1940

. . .

Evening. Conference with ObdH after his return from Berlin:

a.   Political decisions have not yet matured to the stage suggested by von Stuelpnagel's information. It is intended to get in touch with Russia first, and invite Molotov.

Hungary wants to join Tripartite Pact. *Romania* and *Bulgaria* show a similar disposition.

Spain's domestic situation is so rotten as to make her useless as a political partner. We shall have to achieve the objectives essential to us (Gibraltar) without her active participation.

Italy's effectualness as an ally is curtailed by the passivity of her generals and Ciano's inner resistance.

France is to be brought around to collaborate with us against Britain. The Fuehrer wants to get in touch with Pétain (trip to France).

It is hoped to draw the *Scandinavian states* into the orbit of the Tripartite Pact.

b.   Preparations for *Libya*. Third Armored Division with supporting complements.

c.   Preparations for Gibraltar.

15 October 1940

. . .

Von Etzdorf: Brenner conference:

Fuehrer, on military situation: War is won, rest is mere question of time. Aim is to terminate war at earliest date. Review of preparations against Britain since last summer. "Mistake": Excessive crowding of invasion fleet (losses). The decisive factor was poor weather: only five consecutive days of clear skies were needed, but they did not come. Crossing would have taken eight to ten days. New weapons: Marine mine effective from depth of 30 m, with necessary special aircraft. Reasons for Britain's staying in the war lie in the dual hope on:

a.   *America.* Will furnish only war materials. Big bluff (labor question, aluminum, engines). U.S.A. has taken Tripartite Pact as a warning. Fear of a two-front war.

b.   *Russia.* Russia's calculations went wrong. We are now at her border with forty divisions, and will have one hundred divisions later on. Russia would bite on granite; but it is unlikely that she would deliberately pick a quarrel with us: "Russia is ruled by men with horse sense."

Both these hopes, it can be seen, are based on British miscalculations, but still it is imperative to look for means to get at Britain without invasion.

Gibraltar is tied up with the French question. Bringing in of Spain raises the issue of the French colonial possessions and entails collaboration with France in North Africa. But again, any collaboration conducive to a peace treaty is contingent on Italy's receiving satisfaction of all her demands.

Il Duce: Demands 8,000 sq. km: 1,000 sq. km in Nice area, and 7,000 in Corsica, Tunisia, and Djibouti.

Fuehrer: German demands: Alsace-Lorraine with certain corrections to round out territory. Colonial bases on West African coast. Return of old colonies with certain corrections. French central Africa. Trondheim as permanent German naval base.

Might accept one of the Canary Islands instead of Agadir, or some other base on coast of northwest Africa.

Franco has proposed leasing of ports. Fuehrer wants to have outright possession of one port so as to be able to construct military installations in it. Collaboration with Spain is of interest to us because of Gibraltar; we don't want anything else from Spain. Spain's domestic situation is bad. She has asked for delivery of very large quantities of bread grain. We shall do our very best even though we have already been compelled to add potato flour to our own bread. When Fuehrer raised the question of payment of Spain's Civil War debt, Suñer's answer was: "Such mingling of idealism with materialism is incomprehensible for a Spaniard." Fuehrer is said to have felt "like a little Jew."

Spanish demands: Gibraltar, Morocco, Oran. If France hears that she will cease defending her colonies and play them into British hands, that would put the Axis powers in a position in which they would have to secure Morocco by force of arms. Spain wanted a protocol that guaranteed satisfaction of her claims. Fuehrer refused to sign such a commitment.

The question now is to find a suitable compromise between Spain and France. It is essential to organize a European coalition against Britain. Germany's colonial claims will be no obstacle. Germany wants colonies only as sources of lumber, oils, and fats for her immediate needs. It took the Dutch two hundred years to make their colonies yield real wealth. We cannot let ourselves in for such long-term projects.

France will never be a friend. No matter what we do, the thought of revenge will shoot up again at the first opportunity, and turn also against Italy. The French are Gauls, not Latins. The notion of the "Latin sisters" is a fallacy. In the long run, the British and the French will come to terms with each other again. At the moment a European coalition is the best solution. To that end it is essential right now to put out feelers to the French government.

Military possibilities:

a. Gibraltar must be taken. In that operation we shall employ our specially developed weapons, which have already proved successful against the heaviest French fortifications.

b. The Fuehrer is willing to furnish armored troops, dive-bombers, and long-range fighters for operations against Egypt. Special mines with mine-sowing aircraft can also be made available.

Il Duce: Italy is facing up to another winter of war. Feels no anxiety. Russia is no threat. America will confine herself to furnishing war materials; it is too late for America to play a decisive part. Il Duce is in general agreement with the ideas developed by the Fuehrer. Wants to know the size of France's future population.

Fuehrer: Perhaps 38, possibly even 40 million. Germany wants Alsace-Lorraine. Also the iron ore basin of Briey and a border corridor south of Belfort. Claims to northern France are contingent on the development of our relations with Holland and Belgium. The Netherlands, with which we have only loose ties, are to be left independent, mainly on account of their colonial possessions; Belgium, on the other hand, would have to change her ambiguous position and come out squarely for Germany. If she does, she might be allowed to remain a sovereign state; in any event Germany would have to keep bases on the coast.

Il Duce: It is quite essential to arrive at a peace treaty with France. This would be the best means for preventing the rise of a second de Gaulle. Greatest caution is indicated in relation to Spain. She is unreliable and wants too much. The best method with respect to Spain is to "wait and see."

Italy's military position: Launching of the second phase of the drive against Egypt has been ordered for middle of the month. Italian generals consider this unwise, but Il Duce has given positive orders.

There are fifteen Italian divisions in North Africa, twelve of them from the mother country. For the second phase, in which Italy is in a position to commit two hundred tanks, including one hundred heavies, German support would be too late.

For the third phase, in mid-November, he wants one hundred tanks of the heaviest type available, together with dive-bombers. Aviation fuel, as also fuel for the navy, will be sufficient for thirteen months.

Of her navy, Italy has lost to date: ten submarines, five destroyers, and one cruiser.

Fuehrer: Puts German naval losses at twenty-eight submarines, ten destroyers, two light cruisers, and 1 heavy cruiser, the *Graf Spee*. Current monthly submarine production is ten, will later be stepped up to seventeen, and eventually to twenty-five. Eight new destroyers have been commissioned in addition to three heavy cruisers.

Il Duce: Italian air force has lost two hundred planes in action, four hundred in practice flights. Current monthly production five hundred. A new fighter type now coming out will outclass anything that has ever been sent up into the air.

Fuehrer: German losses are also being replaced from current production. Germany, too, is bringing out a new, superior aircraft type. Aerial effort is going to be continued. Main weight based on fields in northern France, which are less liable to the hazard of fog.

Miscellaneous:

a.   Fuehrer will write a letter to *Franco*. Oran out of question. Afterwards he is going to have a meeting with Franco on the French-Spanish frontier.

b. *Il Duce* also wants to meet with *Franco,* but will do it outside of Rome, on account of the Vatican. "Spain's claims cannot be satisfied before conclusion of peace." (Direct quote of Il Duce.)

c. *Abetz* came to see Fuehrer on Saturday, 12 October. The plan to call in François-Poncet has been dropped. *Pétain* will be asked to come to the Fuehrer for a talk; tentative date, between 24 and 27 October. Meeting Fuehrer/Franco will follow. Subsequently, another talk with Pétain, at which it is hoped to arrive at an accord.

d. *Hungary* wants to join the Axis (Tripartite Pact). Japan agreeable. *Romania* and *Bulgaria* want to come in too. Object: Continental front against Britain.

e. *Letter von Ribbentrop to Stalin:*

1. Reassurance on our measures in Romania.
2. Reassurance on our measures in Finland (they are of a purely technical nature).
3. Japan. Nonaggression pact would be desirable. Prospects not bad. Russians perhaps want to await the effects of Tripartite Pact.
4. Mariampol.
5. Compensation for resettled Germans.
6. Invite Molotov to come to Berlin.

f. Romania's relations with Britain have reached a critical stage. Attaché has left; documents were burnt.

g. *East Asia: Thailand:* —Question of Burma Road not very important. Japan will give an emphatic answer. —New Japanese offensive in China. —U.S. aware that she can avoid trouble only if she withdraws from east Asia in time.

.   .   .

16 October 1940

Morning: Current business for Op. Sec., Org. Sec., and OQu V.

1200. Lieutant Colonel Mikosch: Results of Gibraltar scouting mission. M. holds that the task assigned to the infantry, or at least the first phase (northern sector), could be accomplished with 1½ engineer battalions and 1 infantry regiment.

That's not what I think. He underestimates the defense capabilities and forgets that the enemy facing us has no place to withdraw. Nor has he taken into account that British naval forces might also be on the scene. Gibraltar is merely a symbol of prestige. I think it by no means impossible that the British might evacuate Gibraltar of their own accord in the face of preparations for an assault, since a voluntary evacuation would not be as much of a blow to their prestige as would be the loss of the fortress after a struggle. Should the British decide to hold, however, we would find it necessary to secure the entire peninsula right down to its southern tip, or else it might become another Alcázar.

Also in respect to timing, Lieutenant Colonel Mikosch is overoptimistic. In his estimates he takes it for granted that the approaches north of the peninsula (neutral zones, etc.), which certainly have been prepared with every means, could be overrun in ninety minutes.

The command in the field will have to prepare itself for an operation of a much slower pace.

. . .

22 October 1940

(meeting Fuehrer/Laval near Tours)

0930.   (with OQu I): Conference at ObdH. Libya: Entire 3rd Armored Division will be made available for North Africa.

OQu IV (with Staubwasser and List): Report on Staubwasser's trip to Gibraltar. Nothing new of importance. Spanish army agencies cooperate readily and seem to help wherever they can.

(With Kinzel): Frontiers and historical claims of Hungary and Bulgaria against Yugoslavia.

(Alone): Exchange of officers with Hungary. —Possible swing in Greece to join Axis (?) —Good news from Russia (Stalin's reply to letter).

Italo-German Commission will arbitrate Romanian issues (Transylvania). Report from Romania (Antonescu is developing well). —Turkey's attitude obscure.

. . .

24 October 1940

. . .

Conference with ObdH:

1. Orientation on preparation for Gibraltar and Libya. According to conference with Fuehrer, Operation GIBRALTAR will not come off before early 1941. That would leave us plenty of time for special training of Group Kuebler. Training orders will be issued.

2. Hansen's request for mountain battalions, and mountain batteries. I shall try to get them from BdE.

3. Points of the conference with the Fuehrer:

   a. The basic outline of the Spanish operation (Gibraltar) is not yet quite clear. Possibly an airborne operation might first be launched to seize the Canary Islands. Spain is substantially in accord on cooperation, but wants to come out into the open only after military operations have actually started. There has been a verbal promise to join the Axis, but nothing has been signed yet. It is quite evident that Spain is still very much afraid of Britain.

   b. Greece. Italy now has nine divisions in Albania. Ciano is apparently busy again to promote occupation of Corfu and the Greek coast to the southward. Fuehrer thinks that this is nonsense and wants to write Mussolini.

      Fuehrer keeps repeating that possession of Crete would assure quick success in the eastern Mediterranean. Airborne landing.

   c. Britain: All-out air attacks will go on. There is a chance that this might force her to give in. It will be necessary to check as to whether resources of air force are sufficient to carry out seizure of Canary Islands and eventually Crete, and participate in the operations at Gibraltar and in Libya.

   d. Tripartite Pact. Hungary, Bulgaria, Slovakia, and Spain have already joined. Yugoslavia is said to be on the point of doing so; possibly also Greece. Public announcements only after European circle has been closed. Countermeasures in the event of Roosevelt's election.

   e. Russia: Molotov will be in Berlin on 10 November. Stalin's reply to Fuehrer's letter: He concurs with Fuehrer. Molotov will come to Berlin. After that, it is expected, Russia would join the Tripartite Pact.

f. France: Pétain has been told we want a straightforward statement. France will have to cede territory in the Nice area (not the city itself), Corsica, Tunisia down to Lake Chad, and Djibouti.

g. Spain. No definite promises were made with regard to Morocco. If France can be compensated elsewhere, we shall satisfy Spanish wishes. Gibraltar will be turned over to Spain after it has been taken by German troops.

h. Postwar construction program: Motor highways (11 m wide!).

Four east-west, three north-south trunk roads.

i. Poland: No self-sufficient Poland. Germany will furnish raw materials; Poland the manpower.

. . .

General von Thoma. With General Paulus and Colonel Heusinger: Report on conferences in Rome and especially the inspection trip to Libya. Results: The Italians are not particularly keen on our participation. Libya offers very poor conditions for warfare by reason of topography, desert, sand, and climate (water supply). —Italian strategy lacks any spark of imagination. The commands in Rome and in Libya do not seem to be seeing eye to eye. Everyone is scared of the British. The two opponents barely hurt each other. If the Italians know they can expect German assistance, they will hold back, even with the attack on Mersa Matrûh, until our arrival. This would not in any way fit in with our intentions. We want to take over Mersa Matrûh from the Italians. What the Italians are afraid of is that the arrival of German troops might cause the reinforced British to become more active.

The Fuehrer has to be informed of these facts.

25 October 1940

Wagner:

a. (With Colonel Weinknecht.) Logistical preparations for Gibraltar. In accordance with my recent orders, the supply organization has now been geared to correspond with the troop transport groupings in such a way that in two weeks it will be possible to have complete coordination between troop movements and supply organization.

As a result, the entire assembly period could now be reduced to six weeks.

b.   Subordination of Paris military Hq. under Military Commander France.

OQu IV and Meyer-Ricks: Report of Meyer-Ricks on Libya is substantially in agreement with von Thoma's report. We shall have to reckon with the fact that Graziani will not attempt to tackle Mersa Matrûh before December, that is, after completion of a serviceable supply road. The British will avoid a battle by withdrawing and then make a stand on the Nile. This would completely change the character of the campaign for us. The British have meanwhile been considerably reinforced (two hundred thousand men). We would have to operate with the desert at our backs, and that, according to Geyr von Schweppenburg, is just what the British are aiming at. Such a campaign would call for a larger force in both combat and supply elements than envisaged heretofore. The supply question will not be solved satisfactorily until we have Alexandria for a base. That, however, is predicated on mastery of the eastern Mediterranean and possession of Crete, and, in turn, requires a large air force and air-landing on Crete.

.   .   .

26 October 1940

.   .   .

With Heusinger at ObdH: Report on preparations for Libya.

Commitment of only one armored division appears insufficient in face of present British strength of two hundred thousand. In order to accomplish conclusive results, we must strike simultaneously at Crete and Egypt. To this end we would have to induce Bulgaria and Turkey, the latter by force, if need be, to grant passage to Syria, across the Bosporus. Italian military pressure on Greece is likely to fit into that pattern.

.   .   .

27 October 1940

. . .

General Paulus: Has thought over the objectives of the drive in Libya. His conclusion is that there is just no point in starting anything with a single armored division. That is perhaps saying a little too much. Naturally, an armored division is not enough for a campaign with distant objectives beyond the Nile, but it might accomplish throwing the British across the Nile and so, by enabling the German air force to control Suez and Haifa, deny the British their vital bases in the eastern Mediterranean. A landing on Crete might be desirable, but holding the island would be difficult.

Any operation by land forces in the eastern Mediterranean, calculated to produce conclusive results, requires a drive through Anatolia and Syria executed concurrently with the drive in Egypt. That again raises complex questions of high policy which can be answered only by the supreme command. This reasoning agrees entirely with the views I have repeatedly discussed with ObdH.

Talk with Admiral Canaris: He offers his good services for introducing all officers sent to Gibraltar with scouting missions.

By way of political news we hear that the Fuehrer is on his way to Sorrento (Florence?) for a conference with Il Duce. Fuehrer/Pétain meeting evidently has left a deep impression on both. A development in the direction we desire does not appear hopeless. The developments of relations with Spain will not be quite so simple.

28 October 1940

(Italy invades Greece.)

In the morning, excitement over Italy's invasion of Greece. After a while it turns out that von Mackensen was duly informed on 27 October, 2100 hours, but the report which von Rintelen sent us did not reach the Attaché Sec. until quite late this morning on account of coding. There is no clear indication of the objective of the Italian invasion. Some say Saloníki and Athens. British countermeasures against Athens and Crete are expected. In any event, the immediate effect is a completely new picture of the situation in the Eastern Mediterranean and the Balkans, which sooner or later cannot fail to affect also Bulgaria and

Greece, unless Italy succeeds in delivering a very swift, devastating blow followed by a speedy settlement with Greece. Italy's assertion that she is coming as a friend of Greece sounds a little strange when bombs are dropping on Greek airfields.

1100.   Conference with ObdH:

    a. Logistical arrangements for Libya. ObdH is somewhat annoyed at the estimate which allows three months for completion of our buildup in the Mersa Matrûh area, after he told the Fuehrer that it would take only two months. Perhaps it will not be too hard to pare down the estimate, especially if the German navy, instead of the Italian, takes charge of transportation.

    b. Guard units for Military Commander France. The matter is to be given dilatory treatment since changes in the administrative setup are expected in the near future. In any case, the requirements must be cut to a minimum.

Before noon the announcement is made that Greece, after rejection of Italian demands in connection with a border incident, has been in a state of war with Italy since 0600 hours this morning.

. . .

1 November 1940

. . .

Heusinger: Order regarding Gibraltar reconnaissance is being prepared.

OQu IV: Buzzings from the Reich Chancellery (Engel):

    a. Conference with Laval was a success. The Fuehrer wanted the French to state officially that England is the troublemaker. The sooner this power is removed, the quicker will peace be restored in Europe.

    b. Conference with Franco did not satisfy. "Jesuit swine," "misplaced Spanish pride."

Fuehrer's line of argument: Joining the Tripartite Pact is not primarily adhesion to the Anticomintern Pact, but joining a combination to overthrow Britain's preponderance. Germany wants bases on the Canary Islands and the Azores; the latter should be arranged with Portugal by Spain. This demand apparently has severely disillusioned the Spaniards, who are out only to gain their own ends without making any sacrifices. Spanish desire for active participation is very weak. Regaining Gibraltar is one of their national aspirations, but the material chances to do so are slight. They are still carrying on a brisk trade with England, e.g., ore against fuel. If we want Spain to come over to our side, we would have to supply her with all her needs. Navy (Doenitz) demands Spanish ports for submarine warfare. In consideration of Spanish participation in the war, the following stipulation has been made: Gibraltar will be captured by us and turned over to Spain, together with a part of French Morocco "provided France can be compensated elsewhere."

We have not succeeded in inducing France to enter the war right away.

c.   *Pétain.* The personality of the old marshal has made a strong impression on the Fuehrer. Both Pétain and Laval are trusted by him. The Fuehrer has handed Pétain a memorandum defining Germany's claims. It is very moderate as far as colonial and economic demands are concerned. France will retain her Colonial Empire. We need France in the fight against England. Pétain needs time for readjustment. Even the cooperation of the French fleet against England appears possible eventually.

French attitude toward Italian demands: They are prepared to cede Tunis. Corsica still opposed; Nice was not discussed.

d.   Conference with King Leopold on Obersalzberg scheduled for the near future.

e.   *Molotov* has accepted the invitation for conversation in Berlin. (This is still not definite!) Fuehrer hopes he can bring Russia into the anti-British front.

f.   *Il Duce:* After the conference with the French, Il Duce wrote an excited letter to the Fuehrer, in which he expressed alarm over a premature recovery of France (distrusts military measures in her colonies, etc.). The result was the Florence conference, where Il

Duce became fully convinced that the Fuehrer is following the right policy toward France.

Il Duce: Italian monarchy is playing a double game (keeps up its sleeve the possibility of going over to the other side); Italy has no outstanding generals!

g. Fuehrer very much annoyed at Italian maneuvers in Greece. Right now he is in a mood not to send anything to Libya or to Albania. Let the Italians do it by themselves! Diplomatic relations between Italy and Greece have not yet been broken off. A rupture of diplomatic relations between Greece and Germany is out of the question.

Evening to Berlin. (Air raid alarm.)

2 November 1940

Several talks with Admiral Canaris. Apparently he feels hurt that we thought he wanted to meddle in the business of the OKH. At my request he recalled Major Kautschke from Algeciras. I call a joint conference with Op. Sec. Artillery Officer and Abwehr.

1600. **Conference at OKH** (Berlin) with Canaris, Heusinger, Ehlfeldt, and Kautschke. The following arrangements were made:

1. Kautschke turns over to Op. Sec. and Artillery Officer his material on Gibraltar (on Monday) and then goes to Kuebler, where he will receive additional detailed instructions. (Steinbauer)

2. Canaris will be at our disposal to get the necessary intelligence work under way and to make arrangements with Vigón and Franco for the shipment of our troops. His organization will also provide cover for our reconnaissance work against British intelligence. Overall impression on Spain: They are afraid of a conflict with England, and so are very much worried about a possible British landing in Spain or Portugal and an occupation of the Canary Islands by the British. The internal administrative machinery has completely broken down: they are wholly dependent on England for food and fuel and deliver ore in return. Franco's position difficult, as he has nothing left to bolster him up and so cannot afford to take risks. His position is weakened rather than strengthened by Suñer, who is easily the most-hated man in Spain. Mutual understanding

is handicapped by unwarranted hauteur and their morbid sensitive-
ness. To this must be added Franco's shyness. Canaris's conference
with the Air Marshal: He has an impression of absolute lack of
planning in the air operations against England.

Notes for the presentation to Hitler on 2.11.

General:

I. Purpose of the report:

   a. Request decision concerning the basic intentions which the army's
   preparations should support.

   b. Report from the army's perspective concerning time and force for
   these needs.

II. *The purpose of all military activities must be to force England to understand
   that the war is lost.* In addition to continuing the aerial attacks and the
   sea blockade, as well as the army's improvements of SEA LION, there
   are possibilities to combat the English in the Mediterranean, Gibraltar
   and Libya, the western Mediterranean, and northwest Africa.

III. *Gibraltar* not easy, but resolvable. Time requirements: Approximately
   six weeks to starting the attack. Force needs: Two reinforced infantry
   regiments, twenty-six medium artillery battalions for the assault, possibly
   one division, nine medium artillery battalions for coast defense.

   After closing the Mediterranean entry, should close the English lines to
   South America and South Africa. Thereafter seek the occupation of the
   Canary Islands. Will need the 7th Air-landing Division. These forces do
   not signify any lessening of the commitments. Specific points—see special
   notes [not found].

IV. *East Mediterranean*—a very difficult problem. Question: Which goal is
   first?

   a. Should the English, who are superior to the Italians on land and
   water, be pushed back to the point that they must give up Alexandria
   and the territory west of the Nile, permitting our effective aerial
   attack on the Suez Canal and Haifa; a single German armored division
   would be enough, assuming securing sufficient Italian participation.

   b. Should the English be beaten in Egypt and the Suez Canal occupied,
   then German forces of two armored divisions and one motorized

division with a large number of special units (engineers, bridging columns, etc.) are required.

c. The time, issue which must be presented in detail, allows an armored division to be operational in February, unless unexpected improvements in the sea transport situation take place.

An armored corps requires for commitment a very extensive preparation (as a basis 80,000 tons of fuel, munitions, rations; for twenty days a continuing need of 12,000 tons). This can be achieved only:

(a)   If Benghazi is expanded.
(b)   If the roads east of Benghazi are improved.
(c)   If the water supply to Mersa Matrûh is extended.

The rear areas service requirements will be so extensive that they will influence Continental operations.

By the time these preparations are completed and the three mobile divisions brought up, autumn 1941 will be here. Extensive German influence on the Italian leadership is an essential need for rapid success.

For the execution of such an attack, the occupation of Crete would be useful. The army could participate only with the 22d Air-landing Division, if it is not required elsewhere and if the air corps can provide the means for the unit's use of North Africa.

d. A further army possibility to attack England in the eastern Mediterranean would be an *operation through Anatolia and Syria*. It is already studied conceptually and can be presented at any time. (Force requirement, two motorized corps; time needs, six months.) The political requirements will establish the clarification.

Any army measures of extensive significance in the east will take so much time that they would have some effect on the air force and naval efforts against the British Isles. One must assume that intentions are to keep these forces together for this latter operation. The decisive point in this issue concerns the significance of these preparations in shifting the main emphasis of war leadership to the eastern Mediterranean.

. . .

b.   Kuebler informed, training Besançon.
Attack leaders: Infantry Colonel Lanz (1st Mountain Division)
Artillery Colonel Steinbauer (106).

   c. Everything set for order of distribution 15.11.
Assault ready, then on 1.1.1941.

   d. Advance reconnaissance through civil, sudden border crossing.

   e. Arrangements, as organized through the attaché and embassy, can be completed when allowed. Will be requested.

North Africa:

. . .

   b. *Italy will do nothing;* waits until decisions are made elsewhere. Wishes to leave Mersa Matrûh to us. They must do it! We leave Tripoli when Mersa Matrûh is captured.

   c. *Italians do not want us.* They know a thousand difficulties. Since we require their assistance in many areas (ex. harbors), all time estimates are "in the air."

   d. *There is no agreement between the military leadership in Rome and the operational leadership (Graziani).*

   e. Operational leadership has no contact with the troops, no inspiration.

   f. Concern over English sea power and air force. In contrast the English soldier lacks self-confidence.

   g. The military theater forces unusual demands, demands careful preparations (subsequent improvements not possible) and requires, therefore, time and resources.

   h. The military theater is under the influence of English sea and air power, which places high demands on our air force and navy.

   i. There is no experience concerning the time needed for acclimatization. This time factor cannot be put into the calculations.

Anatolia:

Presentation purely military. Political materials require explanation. Orders?

. . .

4 November 1940

1415. **Meet ObdH** at the Reich Chancellery. I outline to him my ideas on Spain. The Rock alone won't do it. The following questions present themselves:

Spain is exposed to a British attack and therefore relies on constant support. Economically she is on the verge of collapse and therefore also needs continuous economic assistance. Internally she is racked by the gravest tensions. We might, as a result, be forced to take sides in internal disputes.

Portugal: Military and economic dependence the same as Spain's.

Northwest Africa: Tangier, Morocco, together with the Canary Islands, may become British objectives (later perhaps in conjunction with U.S.). Northwest Africa, together with equatorial Africa, may become the object of a great struggle between the European and Anglo-Saxon powers.

1420.   Fuehrer (present Keitel, Jodl, Deyhle, Schmundt, Engel, ObdH, and myself):

> **1.**   *Libya:* Fuehrer has formed for himself the following picture:
>
> > **a.**   More time is needed than was thought at first. We can no longer count on the Italians to start their thrust on Mersa Matrûh before the end of December. This will be followed again by a delay for preparing the water supply, road building, etc. (three months). Then comes the hot season. Nothing can be done before fall 1941.
> >
> > **b.**   Italy has informed us that she needs Tripoli herself as a supply base and would like us to take Tunis as our supply base.
> >
> > **c.**   He has little confidence in Italian generals. Italy wants us only "to save the blood of her own soldiers."
> >
> > **d.**   From the operational standpoint it is dangerous to use German troops in operations across seas which we do not control, and with an ally who does not put in his last ounce to keep these seas open.
>
> **2.**   *Spain:* Franco has promised in a letter to the Fuehrer that he would faithfully uphold the verbal agreements, viz., that he would enter the war on our side. Fuehrer now wants to hasten Spain's entry into the war.
>
> Possible British reactions: The British might establish a foothold on the West African coast, or make landings in Morocco or on the Spanish or Portuguese islands.
>
> France has the will and the power to defend her territories unaided.

If necessary, Spain will have to be supported in defending her islands.

3. *Question of the islands:* At present OKW is still weighing the question of which islands are to be occupied and with what forces this should be done. OKH representative must be called in! (Heusinger)

4. *Gibraltar:*

    a. At the same moment that we cross the Spanish frontier, our planes must be attacking the British fleet in Gibraltar. An air base must be prepared in advance.

    b. Troops must be kept standing by to march into Portugal.

    c. Artillery must be shipped over to the southern shore of the strait as soon as feasible.

5. *Greece:*

    a. British attempts to establish air bases at Lemnos and Saloníki. Air defense service has been advanced to the southern border of Bulgaria. Turkey's attitude probably noncommittal. (Attempt to mobilize Russia against Turkey.)

    b. German army must make preparations to support a swift march into Turkish Thrace. Recommendations to OKW (strength, time required).

    c. Air force must make preparations for smashing the bases on Greek islands.

6. *Turkey:* This brings up the problem of Russia. The question cannot be tackled before Russia has been eliminated. With Bulgaria pressing in the south, Turkey can be kept quiet with the help of Russia.

7. *Russia:* Remains the great problem of Europe. We must do our utmost to be prepared when the great showdown comes.

8. *U.S.:* If at all, not before 1942.

9. SEA LION. Not before next spring. Preparedness must be maintained. (We seize this opportunity to stress the "improvements" achieved.)

10. *France:* Will be helped to the extent of her contribution. Details of the new agreements which the Foreign Minister is going to conclude with Laval. First off, the internees in Switzerland will be returned.

. . .

After an uncertain effort to make peace with Britain, Hitler had ordered invasion preparations. The German air force could not deliver the main requirement for crossing the English Channel: aerial superiority. Hitler's misgivings found support among his army and naval leaders. The Fuehrer thought of himself as a specialist for land operations and looked upon sea activities with skepticism. He believed the risk too great to jeopardize his recently acquired calling as the greatest of all field marshals.

With the erosion of interest in any invasion, Hitler had cast about for other areas and decided on a small attack on Gibraltar to close the Mediterranean and a major assault on the Soviet Union. In the waning weeks of 1940, Hitler pushed forward these two operations as the decisive undertakings to conquer the Continent and force Britain into submission.

13 November 1940

. . .

Meyer-Ricks: *Spain:*

> Army: 27 divisions of 9,000, peacetime strength, each.
> War strength of army 500,000; armament on hand.
> Lacking AAA. —Armor consists of a great variety of models, as does aviation.
> Armaments industry: Meets only peacetime requirements; coastal artillery.
> Ammunition stocks very low.
> Officers' corps severely depleted: 50 percent were massacred.
> Morocco: Border has only field fortifications; Ceuta.
>> Obsolete harbor fortifications: Two to three 24-cm batteries.
>> Tangier open roadstead.
> Canary Islands: Twenty-five thousand men. Little is known about artillery defenses. No air defense.
> Rio de Oro: Only weak police force.
>
> Army not free from political tensions. The men to be looked to as leader personalities are: Franco, Varela, Martinos-Campos (deaf), Vega (Under-Secretary of State in the War Ministry), Vigón (Minister of Aviation, former Chief of General Staff), Assentie (Morocco).

Morocco:

Seven divisions (including five crack divisions) with full complement of divisional artillery regiments, plus three corps artillery regiments of six battalions (10, 5, and 15.5 cm).

. . .

14 November 1940

. . .

OQu IV: *Molotov:* No binding agreement. Fuehrer not dissatisfied. Tripartite Pact: Statement of concurrence is not equivalent to joining. Inclusion of *Italy* and *Japan* in the discussions for the present opposed.
Molotov: What is the Greater Asiatic Area?
Molotov: What is Germany's attitude on a Russian guarantee of Bulgaria? (Romania called us in.)
New statute offered for the Straits-Privileges, but no bases. No such offer was made on our part.
Evasive answer to suggestion of a nonaggression pact with Japan.
Heavy Russian demands for machinery. —Can be met.
The Fuehrer apparently has talked the Russians out of Finland.

Program: 18 November, von Ribbentrop with Ciano and Suñer. Sometime around 18 November, Leopold.
12 November, Csaky (Vienna).
22/23, state visit Antonescu to Berlin.
25/26 Boris on Obersalzberg.
    ? Tuka (Tiso).

Accessions to the Tripartite Pact: Romania, Hungary certain; Bulgaria uncertain.

Greece: They are looking for the culprit in Italy and Germany.

. . .

16 November 1940

. . .

Von Etzdorf:

   a. *Molotov.* Fuehrer: Second conversation with the Fuehrer: Finland. No new shipments scheduled. Finland must not, however, become the subject of a conflict. Danger of British air operations, new theater of war. We maintain a hands-off attitude, economic interests only. Remains within the Russian sphere of interest.

Molotov, third phase: Repercussions of German successes in the west on Russia. Germany has given no reply to various questions. Mariampol. (We shall presumably let the Russians have Mariampol for 14 millions.)

Fuehrer: Wants peace in the Baltic area!

"The Baltic Sea is the last area left where we can move freely." We are engaged in a life-and-death struggle and expect Russian understanding for our situation. A war in the Baltic is ruled out. We must come to a decision, whether we want to stand back-to-back or breast-against-breast. Historic decision! Concepts on the big scale!

Molotov: Complains about Finnish provocation and about German-Finnish relations.

Fuehrer: A war to conquer Finland would put a severe strain on German-Russian relations.

Molotov: Russia demands the same freedom in her dealings with Finland as in her dealings with the Baltic states. (Moscow Agreements)

Fuehrer: Britain must be crushed; divide up the leftover pieces. Anything that distracts from the crushing of the British Empire is undesirable. This includes question of Saloníki. —Powers interested in division: Italy, Russia, Japan, Germany.

Molotov: German-Russian relations in the first place; Japan and Italy after that.

Fuehrer: Turko-Russian relations. Greater Asiatic Area—purely Asiatic territory.

Molotov: Russian dissatisfaction about our Romanian guarantee. "It is in fact directed only against us." —Revocation!

Straits: England has twice succeeded in penetrating into the Black Sea. Now the situation is more menacing. Suggests to give the Bulgarians a Russian guarantee.

Fuehrer: Projected revision of the Montreux Agreement concerning the Straits.

Molotov: In giving a guarantee to Bulgaria, we would not alter the internal order of the country by one hair's breadth. "Tangible guarantees for our key position on the Straits." Russia will come to a direct understanding with Turkey. Requests provisional reply: Would you let us put Bulgaria under our protection?

Fuehrer: Fuehrer sidesteps with reference to Il Duce. "If we ever want any frictions, we won't have to bring up the issue of the Straits."

Molotov: Relations between Russia and Japan have improved. Quicker pace possible. Concern about China. Ought to be shared by Germany!

Fuehrer: Settlement of the Sino-Japanese conflict.

Molotov: Not averse. Peace with honor necessary for China. Japan is reaching out for Indonesia, and so might be willing.

Result: Constructive note; Russia has no intention of breaking with us. Impression on the rest of the world.

Finland: Any further Russian action casus belli. Accent on economic interests. The Russians will do the Straits alone. They are pursuing a policy of their own toward Turkey. Readiness to come to an understanding with Japan.

As regards the Tripartite Pact, it is clear that Russia wants to be a partner, not its object. Pact must be reframed!

b. *Straits question:* British efforts to support Russian claims.

c. *Thailand* raises claims on Indochina. Not until after the war.

d. *Spain's entry into the war?*

e. *Laval's talk with the Axis partners postponed.*

f.   *Csaky* will be requested to grant transit for eight to ten divisions (20 November).

. . .

18 November 1940

Heusinger: Report on his talk with OKW (Saturday, 16 November).

1.   Portugal will be included in Operation FELIX only if absolutely necessary.

2. The islands must be taken in hand by the navy. They hope that Raeder would be able to do that, since the air force has declined. We are mainly interested in the Spanish Canaries. But the Fuehrer is also eyeing the Portuguese islands.

3. Shipping for the crossing of the Straits has been set aside.

    Coastal artillery prepared; one battery each of 28-cm and 15-cm guns for the European shore. One battery each of 24-cm and 15-cm guns for the African shore.

4. We have notified OKW of the *time restrictions imposed* on the Spanish and Bulgarian projects by the eastern operation.

5. *Restrictions* reported imposed on General Hansen by a direct Fuehrer order will be clarified.

6. *Innsbruck conference:* Was evidently in an atmosphere of great frankness. Attack on Egypt is ruled out entirely at this time. The plan is to take Mersa Matrûh and later to attack Alexandria and the Suez Canal with the air force. For this purpose they have asked us for Ju. 88s and Ju. 87s. The Italian High Command expects to attack Mersa Matrûh early in December.

7. *Albania:* There had been two opposing conceptions. Badoglio wanted to wait until he had twenty divisions in Albania. The governor of Albania, on the other hand, expected with certainty a political movement favoring Italian aims in the part of Greece inhabited by Albanians. Ciano forced through the latter view, which turned out to be wrong. Badoglio is very incensed. Now they will commit a total of twenty divisions. Beginning of the offensive set for latter half of February.

8. The Italians would like us to attack from Bulgaria. Could the two offensives be synchronized?

9. *Italy was informed of our intentions in Gibraltar;* also of the fact that they will be carried out without Italy's cooperation. Badoglio is not interested in joining.

10. *France:* Badoglio keeps emphasizing that we must be very careful in our dealings with France if we want to avoid serious trouble in North Africa. The Italians are very suspicious of Weygand and Noguès. Italy promised that no demands will be made on France without prior consultation with us. However, they are

interested in a speedy demobilization in Tunisia. Early clear-cut agreements with Laval are necessary. (Cannot be expected before ten days.)

11. *Yugoslavia:* Germany is asked to exert pressure to relieve Italy. (Scared rabbits!) The OKW has not yet considered the question of getting Yugoslavia interested in Saloníki.

12. The Hq. slated for Bulgaria will not yet be briefed. OKW has no objections against transfer of the earmarked divisions to start training.

Von Stuelpnagel (Wiesbaden):

a. Originally the Fuehrer had an idea to negotiate an understanding with England at the expense of France. —Failed!

b. *Italian economic demands on France* without our knowledge. Fifty percent of the raw material shipped from North Africa. A 250-million-Franc credit for Italy.

c. Realization that the situation is not yet ripe for the final defeat of England produced a new European conception. This led up to the conference with Mussolini, which was interpreted very differently on the German and the Italian sides. The report that Mussolini concurred with the Fuehrer's ideas is probably only a subjective impression on our part.

Conference with Spain (Serrano Suñer) did not go well.

d. The Brenner conferences resulted in a welter of confusion in the Foreign Office. Report of the Research-Institute. Italy wants to keep France as weak as possible, especially in North Africa. Italy is annoyed at our measures in Romania. They are looking for ways to demonstrate that they still retain full freedom of decision. Hence, the Greek adventure.

e. Italy's attitude gave a new turn to the Fuehrer's thinking. The result was the order to go slow on France.

f. Eventually, the conviction that Italy is an unreliable partner became the determining factor in the decision to continue in our original policy toward France.

We will continue our efforts to coax Spain into the Axis orbit. Up to now she has been treated rather coolly, but with this objective in mind we shall have to be more friendly. Result is anyone's guess.

g.   *Innsbruck conferences* did not result in any binding agreements. Abyssinian situation apparently less difficult than expected. (Import of rubber from the Dutch East Indies; fuel stocks will last till spring.) —Offensive against Greece will be resumed in three months.

h.   Italy has no interest in preserving *France's economy*. A contraction would not be unwelcome.

i.   Partial military solutions must be worked out with France (base in northwest Africa) before the conference with Laval on the bigger issues can be continued.

Raeder also wants bases. ObdH!

k.   Fuehrer is handicapped in his policy toward France by the attitude of the Party.

l.   The expulsions of Lorrainers by Buerckel had in the end to be swallowed by the French.

m.   Documents on gas warfare will be surrendered to us. ObdH!

. . .

Heusinger: Has talked to Jodl once more. (Instructions from the Berghof.) We are to send another armored division to Romania, which will *not* be used against Macedonia. We have to keep twelve divisions ready for Macedonia. (Apparently the Russian operation has been pushed in the background.) Bulgarians assert that the terrain prohibits any action before the end of February.

Gercke: Railroad situation still tight. Backlog of 547 trains in the east and in Berlin. Coal: Running well in the west. (Lorraine mines damaged during war not yet back in production.) In the east, output is still lagging.

. . .

24 November 1940

Work on the more important papers accumulated during my absence. Interesting points:

1.   Again liaison between OKW and us is deficient, this time relative to the Balkan question. The matter seems to be developing further, i.e., in the direction of a possible German attack on Turkey. This, of course, radically changes the picture. We must not lose sight

of the fact that our chances against Russia diminish if we commit forces against Turkey. At the last conference I was told by the Fuehrer: "We can do the Straits only after Russia has been beaten." This idea necessarily implies another one: We must avoid war against Turkey as long as Russia is not beaten. For this reason we have based all our planning on the assumption that our political leadership is doing its utmost to avoid a conflict with Turkey at this time. If this viewpoint has now been abandoned for another, namely, that we can afford the risks of an attack on Turkey, and that we would throw her out of Europe if she does not keep still while we attack Greece, then we must postpone the Russian project!

2.   An intercepted British radio signal speaks of a transfer of "Headquarters" to Ireland on 22 November. It is doubtful whether this means that the British High Command agencies are pulling out. For my part I do not believe it. It probably refers to a British Expeditionary Corps which will use Ulster as a base for the occupation of the whole of Ireland, in order to open the ports on the west coast of Ireland to the British fleet. In any case the report warrants our attention.

3.   A report by the French General Staff on conduct of the campaign of the French army from the beginning of the war through to the conclusion of our western operation. The absence of any big conception is striking. Total inability to get away from the concepts of position warfare, which on the one hand led them to allocate enormous forces to the fortress front, and on the other hand confined their operational thinking within purely defensive lines after entering Belgium (first, middle course of Scheldt River; later, line Antwerp-Namur).

25 November 1940

. . .

Taken as a whole this day shows again the vast amount of unnecessary work imposed on the General Staff in consequence of the failure of OKW to furnish any positive leadership. No directives have been forthcoming on what they really want in Bulgaria, but there is endless talk about troop strength, even about individual units.

Any way we look at this Bulgarian business, it is nothing that would really hurt Britain. But that after all is the only thing that should count.

In this connection it is heartening to see that the Fuehrer is again taking an interest in SEA LION. That is the surest way to hit England. But then again the Spanish question does not seem to be getting anywhere. Neither Bulgaria nor Spain is to let herself be dragged into the war. They know that they would have to pay the piper even after German victories.

England's plans against Ireland seem to be near realization.

27 November 1940

. . .

Heusinger:

  a. (Gehlen) Result of the map exercise on the Bulgarian operation:

      From the start the weight must be on the western wing. The central group is of no importance. The eastern group is important, but will not be effective operationally.

  b. About six divisions may be used as a defense screen for the march to the south. As against our original plans, the movement will take no more than four days longer. Additional forces for current requirements may follow behind, at a rate of one division every two days.

  c. Effects of possible operations in Spain and on the Balkans on the Russian problem. The diversion of strength to these operations would compel us to give up SEA LION and to confine ourselves to reaching the first objectives in the Russian offensive. They would certainly give us a jump-off base for a pincer operation, but such an operation does not look promising in these immense spaces.

. . .

28 November 1940

. . .

Von Etzdorf:

  a. Conferences of the Reich Foreign Minister with the Yugoslav Foreign Minister (Berghof and Fuschl). Mussolini approves. No results so far. Prince Paul must be called in. Yugoslavia to get Saloníki and a guarantee of her frontiers. Demilitarization of the Adriatic coast.

b.   *Italy:* Anxiety whether Albania can be held. Shift blame on the army.

c.   Codreanu-Day. Anniversary of assassination (Morosow). *Romania.*

d.   Von Papen to the Turkish foreign minister: Axis is willing to respect the territory and the sovereignty of Turkey and to offer guarantees, provided Turkey is willing to cooperate in the New Order of Europe.

"Formation of a British front in the Balkans would be intolerable for Germany."

e.   *Bulgaria* is becoming the center of interest. Russia has asked Bulgaria about her attitude toward a guarantee pact; "If it is accepted, Russia would draw closer to the Tripartite Pact."

f.   *Russia:* Conditions for joining a Quadripartite Pact. Finland: "Russian sphere of interest," but will not be invaded. Guarantee of Bulgaria; interest in the Straits. Bulgaria is evasive.

g.   *Ireland:* Show of will to resist. Our minister will talk with De Valera.

h.   *Spain:* Reported agreement among the leading generals that Suñer must be fired.

i.   *Japan:* New ambassador in Washington, one-time head of a friendship mission. Cutting back of political objectives!

.   .   .

3 December 1940

Morning. OQu I map maneuver (eastern operation). Part II of the operation, bringing us to the line Minsk-Kiev.

OQu IV: *Romania:* Internal situation still very tense:

Antonescu: Illegal movement was armed by Germany (stated in the presence of the generals). Number of political assassinations exceeds two hundred.

Truce with Sima will not last. Further disturbances must be expected. His only hope is the German army.

Romania: Romanian General Staff states in daily situation report: Russians have moved four divisions nearer to the Romanian border near Cernăuţi.

Heusinger: Jodl, Rasp, Baentsch, Bork:

> Report on schedule of movements in FELIX: Our reconnaissance party (fifteen strong) goes to Spain on 6 December. They will be followed by a group of reconnaissance planes, then SS "Deathhead," then artillery, etc. An interval of thirty-two to thirty-eight days will elapse between the crossing of the frontier by the planes and the start of the operation. This is plenty long and anything but a lightning war. But the need for rigorous camouflage necessitates this long delay.

1800.   Conference with ObdH on political situation, FELIX, MARTA, and eastern operations. No new viewpoints.

. . .

Von Etzdorf: Report on recent conferences:

> **a.**   Fuehrer/*Cinkar-Marković*, 28 November: Yugoslavia's existence important for us, for economic reasons. We want a strong Yugoslavia. We have no interest in the Balkans.

> **Fuehrer:** "Nothing has ever changed between us. It is our partner who was wavering. Typical example of how a big state can underrate the power of resistance of a small state. Criminal folly."

> Unique opportunity for Yugoslavia.

> We shall drive England out of Greece with 20 divisions, but willing to use 180 divisions if need be. In connection with this operation, frontier readjustments possible in favor of Bulgaria.

> Hungary: Boa constrictor. Indigestion.

> Russians have offered Assistance Pact to Bulgaria and have promised treaty revisions also with respect to Yugoslavia.

> If Yugoslavia joins the German combination, she would obtain a guarantee for her existence, plus Saloníki. In return she would have only to demilitarize Dalmatia.

> Il Duce, too, would be glad to confront his hotheads with accomplished facts.

> "Events permit us to bring influence to bear in the Italian sphere."

"Three months from now the situation might be less favorable for Yugoslavia." Neither Bulgaria nor Yugoslavia need take part in any military action. Naturally, Germany will use its discretion in distributing what is conquered by German arms.

Stalin wants to do business along the lines of traditional Russian policy. If he finds no field for his activities in the Balkans, he will turn elsewhere. Germany will buy Yugoslavia's production over a long period and at fixed prices.

b. Fuehrer/Ciano, end of November:

A campaign against Greece is a liability. Fuehrer will attack only with sufficient forces.

In pursuing his policies, he will deal also with countries for which he has little sympathy (Yugoslavia). Insists that Italian air force operate over the Mediterranean day and night.

Program for next spring: Gibraltar, Mersa Matrûh, Greece.
Program for fall 1941: Egypt.

c. France more unpredictable than ever. Sets no date for her entry into the war. "Completion of preparations cannot yet be predicted." Wants experts also for economic organization of country. France demands that operation in eastern Mediterranean coincide with the western operation.

d. *Schnurre-Molotov:* Russians want to send us 1 million tons of grain ("from reserve stocks"). They expect bigger counterdeliveries. Balance must be settled!

e. *Turks* very suspicious about "personnel policy in the Kremlin."

f. *Laval, Huntziger, Darlan, Abetz, Warlimont:* Fight de Gaulle through Nigeria; not before November 1941. Requires careful preparations; there must be no reverses. Want fewer restrictions for their navy.

g. *Our proposal to Molotov:* An open and two secret agreements, to run for ten years. Russia would join the Tripartite Pact if five secret protocols are accepted:

1. Concerning Finland, with whom they want to come to terms without force of arms.

2. Concerning Bulgaria, with whom Russia wants to conclude an Assistance Pact. In return, Bulgaria would be allowed to join the Tripartite Pact.

3. Lease of bases on the Bosporus.

4. Turkey must be requested to join the Tripartite Pact, then give a guarantee. In the event of a refusal, "diplomatic and military enforcements by Germany, Italy, and Russia."

Japan must renounce her Sakhalin concession.

5. Russian sphere of interest south of the line Batum-Baku.

.   .   .

5 December 1940

.   .   .

1500–1900. **Fuehrer conference** (ObdH and myself; part of the time, General Brand):

1. He outlines the political situation and his plans. Details: See note on the conference. *Summary:* FELIX as soon as possible. Latest date for F-day, 10 January 1941. He wants shortest possible interval between the first air attack and the start of the artillery bombardment. The decision to do FELIX is final.

   MARITA. Preparations must be carried out to the full in accordance with the recommendation, and in such a manner that we can march into enemy territory early in March. The decision whether MARITA will be done is still left open.

   OTTO. Preparations must get fully under way in accordance with our basic plans. Proposed date: End of May.

   SEA LION. Can be left out of our considerations.

   Libya: No longer contemplated.

2. *Details on FELIX:*

   a. Tactics: Every inch of English territory must be pulverized. To do this we need much siege gun ammunition. Unlimited expenditure of ammunition; twenty to thirty ammunition trains through France, or by sea to Málaga.

Negotiations with French authorities on transit of these shipments not before X-day. Workers through Spain.

b. Ensure installation of coastal artillery in Tarifa and Ceuta through a sales arrangement with Spain. Must be set up in time to prevent escape of British ships.

c. Preparations must be completed for ferrying troops to Morocco.

d. Heaviest tanks; new heaviest type carrying twenty-seven rounds of ammunition.

3. *Details on OTTO:*

a. What matters most is to prevent the enemy from falling back before our onslaught.

b. Maximum objective: Occupation of an area which will render Germany safe from air attacks. After attainment of this objective, combined operations to destroy the sources of enemy war potential (armaments industries, mines, oil fields).

c. Aim of the campaign: Crushing of Russian manpower; no groups capable of recuperation must be allowed to escape.

d. Allies: Finns, Romanians, but not Hungarians.

e. One division will be brought up from Narvik by train through Sweden and will strike on the northern wing together with Dietl's two mountain divisions. Objective: Polar Sea.

f. Make the southern group strong! The Russians must be beaten this side of the Dnieper. Concentrate air force against Dnieper crossings! All Russian forces this side of the Dnieper must be destroyed.

g. Cut off Baltic area! The rest can be done by Landwehr divisions.

h. By striking with strong wings north and south of the Pripet marshes, we must split the Russian front and encircle the enemy in separate pockets. (Similar to

Poland.) These two outer wings must be fast and strong!

    i.   Moscow of no great importance.

After return in the evening, review of the outcome of the conference with Heusinger.

Résumé of the conference put to paper.

Notes of the discussion with the Fuehrer on 5.12.1940 at 1500.

1.   Question Libya: Finished for us.

2.   Current situation in Albania: The outcome remains uncertain. The Italian defense line is in a shambles. When they cannot hold it, the assembly of thirty divisions, as intended, is impossible. There is then a danger that Yugoslavia will seize Albania. The uncertainty of the Albanian situation comes forward since the Yugoslavians have not answered our invitation to join the Three-Power Pact. For the moment one should wait before exercising any pressure.

3.   *Russia* complicates the development of the situation on our terms. The Russians seek to gain influence over Bulgaria and, via a digression through a guarantee agreement, station troops near the Straits. The ensuing difficulties can be resolved when Bulgaria temporarily declines joining the Three-Power Pact. The Bulgarians have asked for experts on coastal defense, air defense, etc. We will provide them.

Every weakness in the position of the Axis brings a push by the Russians. They cannot prescribe the rules for transactions, but they utilize every opportunity to weaken the Axis position.

Should England be forced to ask for an armistice, she would try to persuade Russia to serve as a continental dagger.

4.   Help for Italy:

    a.   Introduced today: Commitment of dive-bombers for an attack on the British fleet. Two Stuka groups to Sicily, two Stuka groups to Apulia, which should use Tobruk as an intermediate landing field. A Condor squadron should mine the Suez Canal.

    b.   Seizure of Gibraltar: The psychological impact of the Italian defeat makes the capture necessary. It is not required that England fall through combat but through a number of blows (air force, submarines), to include a cordon of international combinations. In that context the fall of Gibraltar—a symbol of British power—is a decisive element.

5.   *France* rejects sharply any concessions to Italy. If the Vichy government met the Italians halfway the French colonies would not go along. A centrified colonial effort against Vichy is not impossible. Should French North Africa declare its independence, it would complicate our situation. There is a danger that the Vichy government would declare its inability to do anything. It would be much different if we were in Morocco. By our occupation of Morocco and control of the Gibraltar Straits we resolve the English and French danger simultaneously. If the Straits are in our hands and our troops stand in Morocco, we can speak directly with the Vichy government; they cannot sidestep.

6.   *Balkans:* Our threats against Greece have the success that the English have not yet attacked Romania. The Greeks do not wish a conflict with us through the British. The Turks appear to be working in the same direction, i.e., impeding the construction of a British front in the Balkans. It is to be hoped that these efforts will keep the English from any offensive efforts against the Romanian oil fields for two to three months.

Yugoslavia cooperates with us totally, but not with the Italians. They believe that they are not politically or militarily trustworthy.

7.   The unpleasant situation in *Albania* has some advantage: Italy softens her demands. The failure creates a healthy withdrawal of Italian demands for the natural boundaries of Italian power.

8.   If the Greeks do not evict the British, we will be forced into a Bulgarian action. It is possible that this understanding dawns on the Greeks, especially if the Italians should leave Albania.

Should the Greeks remove the British, there would be no necessity for our attack. In all events it is necessary to prepare the MARITA operation.

9. The decision concerning hegemony in Europe will come in the battle against Russia.

10. *Attack FELIX*. Should be operative at the beginning of February. It will influence Greece to alter its relationship to England. Given this reason, we should maintain our relationship to Greece properly. In relationship to Greece we are a neutral state.

11. The Turks are fearful of being drawn into the conflict. The end would be the loss of Thrace. Turkey will not intervene in a battle between Germany and Greece. If we attack Turkey, Russia will also be on the plan. The preparations for Operation MARITA will not create difficulties for our other plans.

12. *Romania* will join against Russia.

13. If we march through Bulgaria against Greece, the Russians will do nothing beyond watching Turkey. The Finns and Romanians must work with us because their future is tied to a German victory.

14. When the Italians hold in Albania, the Greeks cannot gain any strength before spring. It is possible that, given the altered strength relationship, the Greeks might accept lower Italian demands.

The execution of Operation MARITA is planned for the beginning or end of March. The execution of the operation will require four weeks.

15. *Air situation:* The current air war does not cost us very much. We increase our materiel and personnel resources. The English are not weakened numerically through the air war. They were evidently at a critical point once. Perhaps the shelving of our daylight attacks spared the destruction of their fighter strength. Our attacks could not destroy British industry. The effect of these attacks was similar to a windfall. The losses could not be replaced by the British themselves. American deliveries make up the difference. One dares not overestimate the results. In the previous year England—converted to market

value—purchased materials for only 150 million from America.

The American help will not increase significantly before next summer (new construction will be finished in 1941).

The English will not have a stronger air force in the spring than they have now. They cannot mount a significant offensive against the Ruhr area. Our night fighters will be significantly better in the spring. Our fighter force is much better than the Russian because of the aircraft. In May/June the new series of our new models will appear. They will go to the west. The older types should be employed against the Russians.

The rapid progress of the land operation is a prerequisite for keeping the aerial situation at an acceptable level.

16. *Russia:* The earlier campaigns prove that an attack must begin at the opportune moment. The favorableness of the moment depends not only on the weather, but also on the relative strength of the forces, the equipment, etc. The Russians, like the French, are inferior to us in equipment. They have a few modern artillery batteries, but everything else is rebuilt old material. Our tank III with 5-cm gun (in spring, fifteen hundred of them) has a clear superiority. The majority of the Russian tanks are poorly armored.

The Russian is inferior. The army lacks leadership. It is questionable if the military leadership has exploited the most important recent experiences. The new inner orientation of the Russian army will be no better in the spring.

We will have in the spring a perceptibly better position in leadership, material, troops, while the Russians will be at an unmistakable low point. When the Russian army is battered once, the final disaster is unavoidable.

By any attack against the Russian army, one must avoid the danger of simply pushing the Russians back. We must use attack methods which cut up the Russian army and allow its destruction in pockets. A starting position must be created which allows the use of major envelopment operations. When the Russians are hard hit by these desperate blows, a moment will come when, as in Poland, the travel and communications networks will collapse and create total disorganization.

By spring sixteen hundred heavy German and captured AAA guns will be added. Earlier, twenty-five hundred to three thousand small-caliber AAA. They will eliminate low-level strafing attacks in the summer.

17.   SEA LION: Only possible when the English fighters are totally eliminated. That cannot be expected, even though our air force will be stronger this spring than it was in spring 1940.

18.   *Result:*
FELIX: as soon as possible. Latest F-day, 10 January 1941. There should be the smallest possible time delay between the first air attack and the beginning of the artillery attack.

MARITA: Preparations should progress as proposed and in such fashion that they can be executed at the beginning of March.

OTTO: Preparations should be advanced in full force to include the planning groundwork. The anticipated time for execution is the end of May.

SEA LION: Will not be considered.

Libya: No longer an issue.

6 December 1940

. . .

General Konrad (Liaison Officer in Goering's Hq.).

a.   Strategy of aerial warfare.

b.   Details.

c.   Operations against England: Britain did not sacrifice her fighter strength over London; is sacrificing London instead. Our fighters have only limited range over England, extending not much beyond London. This enabled Britain to conserve and increase her fighter planes. We were forced to change over to night attack. Selection of targets: Emphasis on armaments industry (especially aviation). Next in order, critical port installations. London is under constant day-and-night attack in order to destroy the city. Defense organization is tied down there.

Special missions: Destruction of specified plants of critical industrial importance (also by day, through clouds).

Attack on selected night airdromes (night attacks). Targets (of opportunity): Individual ships and convoys.

At present we do not emphasize attack on supply movements. These operations will be concentrated on only when the main task (destruction of armaments industry) is nearing completion. The attack on supplies will be launched in spring, in conjunction with submarine warfare.

Determining factors in the selection of targets for daylight sorties: Weather, effectiveness of direction beams, taking-off facilities. On dark nights possible to fly only by instruments (direction beams, direction finding). This precludes extension of operations beyond the parallel of Birmingham or, at most, Liverpool. Farther objectives, e.g., Glasgow, where the British are taking all their valuables for safekeeping, can be reached only on bright nights.

d.   *Operations:* Centralized: ObdL selects the targets for the following night and decides what has to be done the day after.

e.   *Strength:* At present three thousand to four thousand planes in operation, including eighteen hundred bombers; bombers can go out on missions every fourth night.

f.   *Appraisal:* Personnel show occasional signs of fatigue because no conclusive results have as yet been achieved. If operations are carried on consistently and with sufficient weight, our blows will one day pass the limits of human endurance. At present we have only a few positive indications of cracking morale. ''One day the bow will break.'' Fighter opposition is weakening already.

g.   Organization: No new units will be activated, but existing units will be reinforced to fifteen planes each.

. . .

8 December 1940

Afternoon, 1800. Keitel (OKW). I see him at his home.

a.   *Albania:* Last night Alfieri informed v. Rintelen, later the Fuehrer, of critical situation in Albania. The Italian army has again fallen back 30 km; Fuehrer holds that this time it is not a matter of poor leadership, but rather of bad troop morale.

    b. *Spain:* Caudillo told Canaris point-blank that entry into the war at the time proposed by us is impossible, since no preparations have been made. The reasons are mainly of an economic nature: food, etc. The transportation problem defies solution. —Canary Islands and Spanish overseas possessions would be lost (also the Portuguese islands would be occupied by the enemy). The islands would simply starve to death.

       Nevertheless, Spain will carry on with her preparations. Camouflage must be fully maintained. OKW has telegraphed Canaris, instructing him to find out the earliest possible date.

    c. Fuehrer is now examining the extreme consequences: if Caudillo refuses to cooperate, we could not get into Morocco; disaffection would spread in North Africa; Weygand would set up countergovernment. Conclusion: If anything happens in North Africa, we must at once occupy the remainder of France.

       Trip to see Il Duce planned for tomorrow noon.

    d. I outline a tentative operational plan (ATTILA) and stipulate a ten-day alert period.

2200 (Zossen). Keitel (OKW):

    a. Trip put off for several days. Il Duce does not view situation as particularly dangerous. Wants to await developments.

    b. Fuehrer approves my operational plan. Thinks that not many troops would be needed. SS and SS "Adolf Hitler" will be available for this purpose, as well as the units destined for FELIX.

       Preparations for MARITA will go on. The troops assigned to that operation must not be used for ATTILA. This conversation was preceded by conference with Op. Sec. (Pistorius) and Sec. Foreign Armies on capabilities for assembly of troops, and situation in Albania.

Midnight: Conference with Pistorius, v. Stauffenberg, etc., on ATTILA.

9 December 1940

1000. **Heusinger-Pistorius:** Draft of plan for Operation ATTILA. My estimate that ten days will be needed to get the troops ready to strike finds confirmation. If transportation is firmly planned and the divisions set up on organization which allows instant departure of all available forces, the interval between issuance of orders and start of operations can be cut to six days. Should this interval be too long for the political command, we must immediately start sending the troops to the jump-off areas. It is doubtful whether these movements could be successfully disguised.

At noon report to Fuehrer:

The Fuehrer approves the proposed plan of operation. The political command wants a shorter assembly period than six days. This will make it necessary to send the troops to the staging areas now.

Detailed review of the political situation:

Spain has finally declined. The Fuehrer is now weighing the possibility of regarding existing agreements voided by Spain's withdrawal; this would give him greater freedom of action in his dealings with the French, with a view to winning their support for his policy by promising to keep their African possessions intact. Italy need not be considered overmuch in all this.

I took the opportunity to draw the Fuehrer's attention to two points: (1) the necessity to continue the attack on the British Isles with every means; (2) the threat from British reinforcements in the eastern Mediterranean in view of existing Italian capabilities in Libya, and the possibility of a British front in the Balkans. Fuehrer concurs. He will advise the Italians not to advance beyond Sidi Barrâni, and to limit themselves to defensive operations in Libya. (Luncheon with the Fuehrer.)

1700.   *Heusinger* receives instructions based on conference with Fuehrer. Also current matters.

11 December 1940

. . .

1700–1830.   Conference with Schniewind (Naval Operations Staff):

    a.   Personnel difficulties make it impossible to meet our wishes for liaison officers.

    b.   Review of the entire war situation. Our views are largely in agreement.

    c.   War in the Atlantic very effective; SS *Scheer* in southern Atlantic, SS *Hipper* in northern Atlantic. Numerous auxiliary cruisers also in Asiatic waters and in the South Seas.

   d. Two new capital ships (*Bismarck*) will be commissioned in April and May.

      England has nothing to match them. In addition two heavy cruisers are going to be returned to achieve service; as a result, Britain's situation will become increasingly difficult beginning next May, at the latest.

   e. Plans for the submarines campaign call for construction of eighteen to twenty submarines each month next year, starting about June. It is still uncertain whether this goal can be reached.

   f. Constant improvement in mine warfare by new types. Acoustic mines.

. . .

13 December 1940

Conference with chiefs of staff of army groups and armies.

Morning. Conference on eastern operation held by Paulus.

Noon. Luncheon.

Afternoon. Military political situation. —Reports by Op. Sec., Org. Sec. Konrad, Loyke, Tng. Sec. Central Branch.

Notes by General Halder [for 13.12.40].

Military-political situation—based on our version of a discussion with the Fuehrer.

England:

   a. Land power—recovered and reorganized.
      Sea power—fundamentally intact.

   b. Major difficulties in the air force and in the naval leadership— better base, more effective weapons, details Konrad and Loyke.

   c. Success not easily measured (40 percent industrial capacity), but perceptible in uncertain efforts courting America and the propaganda throughout the world, which England cannot rationalize away (economic apprehension, gold).

   d. Production weaker, imports difficult (London, Southhampton, Bristol, Liverpool, Glasgow).

e. *Nationalistic movements, distribution problems.*

f. Internal political situation (Churchill, Bevan)—Labor Party—Conservative.

g. *Fuehrer's opinion* paper [not found]!

England's hopes:

a. *America's material help* perceptible, but not decisive—certainly not before 1941/42. War declaration improbable.
Imperial politics—England's overextended position (Greenland-Azores-Canaries, Gulf of Guinea).

Narrows of Natal-Dakar.

b. Africa–northwest–de Gaulle (Dakar) (Central Africa).
Influence on North Africa (Weygand).
East Africa–Egypt–Syria.
Military politics.

c. Russia, who hopes that there will be no German hegemony over the Continent. Until now no success. More later on Russia's role.

England's intentions:

Hold out in the homeland with American help.
Organization of supplies (Glasgow, etc.).

Draw *Ireland* in order to obtain special advantages against our convoy attacks.

"Free French" base in Africa and bring in the French fleet (France's fate will be decided in Africa).

East Mediterranean—perhaps North Africa as well as a base to hit the weakest part of the Axis (Italy) and, when possible, to attack our oil supplies in the Balkans.

The *Turks* may well have a role. If Russia could be drawn in, the ring would be closed.

We cannot, at the moment, destroy England on its island.
Prerequisite: Air superiority, which does not seem possible in the immediate future.

Therefore, SEA LION is set aside; must remain active and can be improved. Execute should a moment of weakness appear.

Against England's African plans the best counter-measure is an appearance in Morocco after settling Gibraltar.

Preparations:

Difficult:

a. Political game Spain-France dangerous for position of African colonies.

b. Inner situation of Spain.

Therefore, for the moment, endure. (Preparations remain in place.)

Against the east Mediterranean anticipation in the Balkans, Romania as the basis.

Currently under development.

In the area of these considerations are certain specific views:

France:

a. Pétain-Laval-accord. Huntziger.
Strong countercurrent, in officer corps as well.
Weygand–Noguès–North Africa.

b. Our position: We want to use France for ourselves. We must be prepared by certain signs of disloyalty to attack immediately. Preparations.

c. Raise Pétain's position piece by piece.

Italy:

a. Loss of Axis prestige (Albania-Cyrenaica-Libya).

b. Plays a smaller role in demands.

c. Fissure between army and Party.

Balkans:

Romania: Antonescu's situation.
Totally at our disposal.
Reorganization of the army twenty-nine divisions (ten with double cadres).

Yugoslavia has become more secure since Italy's defeat ("go with us rather than the Italians").
Still no accession to Three-Power Pact.
Economically tied to us.

Militarily hemmed in by us.
Not an enemy! A friend only without risk (Salonîki).

Greece: No hostilities. Ensure that there are no English bases against us.

Bulgaria is our natural line of departure. Its national goals and military camaraderie from the World War place it on our side. Racially: Slavic infusion which Russians use extensively. Fear of Turkey. Result: Passive; nonmilitaristic! When we must attack, it can take place only from Romanian soil.

Turkey wants peace. Agreement with Greece.

Hungary. An attack brings Russia into the game. An Axis partner— willing support—inner difficulties.

Russia. Despite all of Britain's efforts to disrupt the new structure of Europe by interruptions on the periphery, the structure will be carried out.

Fuehrer's thoughts:

Russian complications—Bulgarian example.
"Every weakening in the Axis position brings a Russian push. Russia cannot set the rules of exchange, but will use every opportunity to weaken our position." The Molotov discussions have clarified our view of the total situation, especially on Finland and the Balkans. No acute opposing views.

The decision over the hegemony over Europe will be made in war against Russia.

Therefore the preparations, when the political situation allows, for action against Russia. (The necessary offices will have directions!)

For us a one-front war requiring 130 to 140 divisions by spring; for the air force a two-front conflict, which allows on both fronts a defense of the homeland and army. (Curtailment of the day-bombing possibilities during the summer.)

For the navy a closure of the Baltic, which makes a two-front war possible.

We do not seek conflict with Russia, but must be prepared for this mission by spring 1941.

1. *Recognition of General Staff officers.*

   Improve the spirits! A clear word is necessary. One tells me:

   a. Hitler and the ObdH are unified. As a result recognition: Knight's Cross.

   b. When an army chief of staff assumes command of a division, he should receive the rank and pay.

   One threatens me with the idea that the youth no longer have the ambition to became General Staff officers when the only reward is honor.

   I grew up in a time when over the General Staff, in large letters, stood the phrase "Perform well, without being conspicuous." I had the good fortune to be near the great individuals in this area—Gallwitz, Kuhl, Ludendorff, von Hindenburg—and confirmed the validity of this motto.

   Why has the circle around Hans von Seeckt closed down? Egotism perhaps? Individuals who served as chiefs-of-staff during the war and never complained about doing clerical work; individuals who missed the best positions in order to serve their superiors.

   So long as I am the keeper of the grail, I shall not retreat one hair's width from this spirit of the German General Staff. I demand that the German General Staff be trained in this sense. When one's festive uniform and one's assignments mean no more than a star or a pay increase, one lives on another level than the one where the Prussian General Staff was planted and grew to greatness.

17 December 1940

Von Etzdorf:

a. The Laval affair is viewed by Foreign Office as a dangerous embarrassing incident.

b. Turkey-Bulgaria: Talks on issuance of declaration of nonaggression and withdrawal of troops from both sides of frontier.

c. Italy: Rumors about Ciano's resignation denied. "Il Duce is still strong enough to be able to afford Ciano." Rift between army and political command: The situation in Cyrenaica is really not the fault of the political command.

d. Friendship Pact Yugoslavia-Hungary.

e. Ill feeling as a result of tardy presentation of credentials by the new Russian ambassador.

. . .

18 December 1940

. . .

Von Stuelpnagel (on phone):

a. Confirms reports about Laval. The accusations against Labal evidently refer to attempts to squeeze out Pétain.

b. Von Ribbentrop not yet satisfied. He wants every means of pressure applied until Laval is again in the saddle; (no French minister is allowed to go to Paris).

c. At the moment Laval has taken over Laurencie's job in Paris (as liaison to Abetz). Final composition of French Cabinet still uncertain.

d. Fuehrer now has doubts whether he still needs France. He is always thinking of making peace with England at the expense of France.

e. In the Armistice Commission everything is at a standstill. No progress in the question of the Demarcation Line.

f. Darlan, straightforward, honest old tar, has much influence on Pétain. No politician.

g. Reich Marshal's demands to France (stock majority of the entire aircraft industry).

Gercke:

a. Communications problems in the east and road construction. Uniform regulation necessary. Report on conference in Posen.

b. MARITA. Maximum railroad schedule necessary when our shipments start. OKW has made no preparations for that. (Romanians to be informed through diplomatic channels.)

. . .

21 December 1940

. . .

A telegram is received from von Rintelen, stating that four Italian divisions are encircled at Bardia; this means that the Italian Tenth Army is virtually wiped out. Only two to three Italian divisions are left. Distress calls for German tanks!

In Albania there is greatest concern for the southern wing, in view of Greek regrouping from the right to the left wing.

. . .

23 December 1940

Communication from v. Etzdorf:

> At the moment Pétain does not see his way to receive Laval back into his Cabinet.

> The projected Directorate would accordingly consist of three persons only: Huntziger, Darlan, Flandin.

> The Foreign Minister claims to have learned from a secret source that Pétain had remarked he would hold out until he could be sure whether *Germany* was genuinely willing to continue the policy of cooperation.

Conference with Fromm (0930 to 1130):

> *Supply situation:* Horses are available in sufficient numbers; new age-class still unallocated.

> *Steel* quota for the army has been drastically reduced. Present production figures can be kept up till beginning or middle of March, then will drop.

> TNT is mainly used for the air force. A portion of artillery projectile production must be stocked as empty shells.

> *Nonferrous metals:* Stocks seized in occupied territories will carry us to about the end of 1941.

> *Rubber:* Difficult. New Buna factories. Absorbs steel!

> *Food:* Reasonably assured for 1941, but not beyond that. "We'll swindle ourselves through 1941."

Manpower situation: Fuehrer order: All personnel measures must be subordinated to the operational requirements of air force and navy. No drafting of armament workers before 30 June. Dates for recall of men on furlough, 1 February and 1 April; furlough divisions as of 1 February.

Men furloughed to industry must be left at their jobs until 31 March.

OKW must be notified four weeks in advance of any plans for earlier recall of men. *Org. Sec.*

The age group which normally would be called up in fall will already have been called up next spring.

. . .

Heusinger:

    a. Von Greiffenberg in Vienna.

    b. OKW apparently wants List to act in an entirely official capacity in Romania.

    c. Reconnaissance Team Bulgaria. Zeitzler will return to Vienna on 28 or 29 December.

    d. Two out of fifteen German steamers canceled; thirteen German steamers in Italy (Genoa).

Von Ziehlberg: Current General Staff personnel matters.

Von Thoma:

    a. Scanty information on Russian tanks. Inferior to ours in armor and speed. Maximum thickness of armor 30 mm. The 4.5-cm Ehrhard gun penetrates our tanks at range of 300 m; effective range 500 m; safe at over 800 m. Optical sights very bad; dim, limited range of vision. Radio control equipment bad.

    b. Total of captured enemy tanks: 4,930, including ammunition carriers. Twentieth Regiment will get captured enemy tanks (are now at Gin). The entire number will have been taken over by the end of January. French driving instructors. Driving classes in progress all the time. Another regiment will be activated in February.

. . .

25 December 1940 to 15 January 1941

Away on leave.

16 January 1941

OQu I: *Fuehrer conference 8 and 9 January at the Berghof:*

Appraisal of the situation based on industrial capacities. The British are trying unconvincingly to show a good industrial picture. Germany is the biggest industrial nation of the world.

European situation: *Norway is now safe.* English demonstration, however, not impossible.

West: *France:* Only danger from the air. Occupied zone peace-minded. — Some circles in the unoccupied zone are dreaming of a possible change. Definitely hostile elements in the colonies. There is a difference in the attitude toward us and toward Italy! Weygand is a German-hater. Laval's overthrow engineered by him! France as a whole observes a wait-and-see attitude. "We are no longer bound by any obligations toward France."

Spain must be written off as a potential ally.

Russia is making demands, which did not occur to them before: Finland— Balkans—Mariampol.

Balkans: *Romania* is on our side (Antonescu in Obersalzberg, 15 January 1941).

Hungary makes no difficulties.

Yugoslavia leaves everything open.

Bulgaria very cautious. King intelligent, but very cautious! Does not want to risk the dynasty.

Specific points: What is Britain's war aim? Britain wants to dominate the Continent. To achieve this she would have to defeat us on the Continent. This means that I must be so strong on the Continent that this aim will never be attained.

British hopes: U.S. —Russia.

We cannot knock out England with a landing operation (air force, navy). Accordingly our position on the Continent must be so consolidated by 1941 that we may with confidence face continued war with England (and U.S.).

(Eden is advocate of collaboration with Russia.)

Russia: Stalin: Intelligent and shrewd; his demands will become bigger and bigger. German victory incompatible with Russian ideology. Decision: Russia must be smashed as soon as possible. The British might easily have forty divisions within two years. This might induce Russia to side with Britain and U.S.

Japan: Ready for serious cooperation. By tackling the Russian problem, we give Japan free hand against Britain in the east.

Decision: Force a radical settlement of the continental issue as soon as possible.

Russian armaments: Obsolete materiel: what is new is copied from foreign nations. Command mechanical! Lack intellectual caliber.

Operations:

The war in Africa need not bother us very much. Even as it is, the military situation is still better than a year ago, but we must not risk the internal collapse of Italy. Italy must be saved from that. It will be necessary to send some help. Reverses are due to lack of modern materiel in Africa (AT guns).

Decision: A force must be sent with the lacking equipment. We must shake them out of their tank scare! Protection! (The force must combine mobility with a certain amount of offensive strength.)

Libya: Difficulties about armored reconnaissance cars. As soon as possible. (Will not be ready before 10 February.)

Albania: A corps for the left wing. Question still pending. First Mountain Division ready as of 20 January. Fourth Mountain Division ready as of 10 February.

MARITA: One armored division on the ground on 26 January. Then order will be given to cross over to *Bulgaria*.

.   .   .

18 January 1941

Von Altenstadt:

a.   Reorganization of Military Administration France. Elimination of intermediate level.

    b. Transfer of Jews and Poles in Poland (at least 569,000 as of 1 February 1941).

Von Etzdorf: Orientation on the political situation. Interesting points:

    1. Conversations on Spain and Gibraltar are coming up again. This means that Operation FELIX may one of these days become acute again.

    2. The Foreign Office is talking about the possibility that Russia may react to our march into Bulgaria by attacking Finland.

    3. Visit of the Japanese foreign minister: Apparently the question of Indochina and the Dutch East Indies is going to come up for discussion. If we want Japan to take an active part on our side, we must give up the Dutch East Indies to them. I consider such a decision justified, for we have no means of holding that territory and only would complicate our policy in Holland if we attempted to keep these possessions a part of the Dutch state.

    4. France: Cooperation at the moment improving and more promising for the future.

24 January 1941

1030. **Conference with ObdH:** MARITA. List's report on General Staff conference has arrived. Bulgaria willing, but timid. All of a sudden List will need only two days to construct bridges. AAA defense for bridges will be ready by 7 February. Bulgarians must reinforce their border guard through concealed mobilization.

We can then start off early in February, when we have the armored divisions in the Dobruja and some AAA in Sofia, etc. (which must yet be put across the Danube). At the same time we can start building the bridges, so that the forces which depend on them can follow up beginning 7 February.

Recommendation to this effect to the Fuehrer, emphasizing that early action in this theater would relieve pressure in North Africa.

Bulgarians want to join the Tripartite Pact only after we have marched in.

. . .

25 January 1941

. . .

Von Etzdorf: Conference Fuehrer/Il Duce. Il Duce just sat by "with a bland smile."

Spain: Fuehrer wanted to get Il Duce to make use of his "Latin" connections.

Russia: "Bulgaria and the Straits belong to Russia's security zone."

. . .

27 January 1941

1000.   (Tirpitzufer): Reception for the generals of the Japanese Study Mission.

1200.   Phone talk with ObdH on report by Funck/v. Rintelen.

We cannot send to Libya anything more than originally planned, both because time is short and because we cannot cut any further into resources for BARBAROSSA.

For the time being the initiated measures must suffice.

. . .

28 January 1941

. . .

1300.   Conference with ObdH:

    a.   MARITA: List's latest reports give a new picture. In view of the risk involved, the tendency to postpone the start of the operation is increasing noticeably. Sending of AAA by way of Yugoslavia is urged. Proposal to OKW: We should start operations on 15 February. We must accept the risk. Turkey can be given reassurances.

   b. BARBAROSSA: Purpose is not clear. We do not hit the British that way. Our economic potential will now be substantially improved. Risk in the west must not be underestimated. It is possible that Italy might collapse after the loss of her colonies, and we get a southern front in Spain, Italy, and Greece. If we are then tied up in Russia, a bad situation will be made worse.

   c. *Abetz's report:* (Saw ObdH yesterday.) Fuehrer has made up his mind that he does not want Laval in the French government. He is to stay in Paris for possible use as a rival for Pétain. The policy of *cooperation* is at the moment held in abeyance. Fuehrer wants to notify Pétain to this effect and fall back on the armistice terms. Also wants to keep Laval in reserve for a future French government in case Weygand goes over to the British and de Gaulle.

Darlan is the "Dauphin" now. He is certainly not pro-British and, moreover, is flattered by his present role. He must be supported. For this reason we won't raise too many objections about leaves to the occupied zone for French sailors returning from England. (It is interesting to note that out of eighteen thousand French sailors in England, only six hundred stayed.)

. . .

Meeting with the Commander of the Reserve Army and the Chief of Army Ordnance as well as other generals concerning the preparations for BARBAROSSA on 28 January 1941.

. . .

At conference proceed from: Operational mission. Space—no pause; that alone guarantees victory. Continuous movement is a supply issue. Everyone must help with resolution. Distances! Space relationships in north. Coordination of air force and army during the operation to utilize every possibility.

Complications through differing equipment types (troops, trucks, workshops). The railroads provide the only means to maintain the advance without additional transport.

Conference 28 January:

   1. Mission East (BARBAROSSA) must be assumed to be known.

   2. Around 110 infantry divisions, 20 armored divisions, 13 motorized divisions, 1 cavalry division; total 144 divisional units.

   3. Mission:

       a. Commit all available units.

b.   Crush Russia in a rapid campaign.

4.   Execution should evidence the following characteristics:

a.   Great space to the Dnieper = Luxembourg—mouth of Loire.

b.   *Speed*. No stop! No waiting for the railroad. Depend on motor transport.

c.   *Increased motorization* (as opposed to 1940): thirty-three mobile units, motorized artillery, engineer, signal, etc.

Since the railroad (destruction, water courses, gauge) cannot be counted on for the desired tempo, the continuous operation depends on motor transport.

Why is an interruption-free operation necessary? We must destroy the Russian army without pause over the Dnieper-Duna line (500 kilometers into north Russia and other goals another 500 kilometers, i.e., 1,000 kilometers).

Satisfaction is possible only when the point of main effort is prepared through the collaboration of all forces in order to solve the most significant supply issues concerning transportation, tires, fuel, and storage. The air force and army must use the available transportation through careful, coordinated effort.

On this theme there was a discussion on 20 January with the Gen Qu where the innumerable questions concerning the military leadership, the armament program, and the economy from the attending officers did not lead to any conclusive results.

That is the purpose of this meeting. You should, in the event that you cannot reach a satisfactory solution for the operational leadership, clarify the issues for a Fuehrer decision.

.   .   .

29 January 1941

.   .   .

Heusinger:

a.   Issue of orders for SUNFLOWER.

b. Fuehrer does not want to give SS "Leibstandarte" for MARITA; wants to leave motorized units in France as a means of pressure. If List needs additional forces for the march into Bulgaria, we must help ourselves by substituting 16th Armored Division for SS "Adolf Hitler." We must also turn to use the motor transport no longer needed for SS "Adolf Hitler," for supply and for air force.

5 February 1941

(At Hq. AGp.A, Saint Germain)

Discussion of operation in the Ukraine viewed as an operational study, with General von Sodenstern in charge. Very well thought out; good discussion. It shows the difficulty of accomplishing an enveloping operation west of the Dnieper, with the northern wing alone, particularly in view of the possibility that this wing might be threatened or at least slowed in its advance by enemy attacking from the Pripet area. The plan of the initial attack, which provided also for an eastward advance of a sizable group in the northern Carpathians, south of Lwów, eventually led to a bunching in the center (direction Tarnopol), which then had to be broken up again. A contributory factor was the fact that the forces coming from the Bucovina advanced hard to the north instead of east northeast.

Afternoon. Conference with Military Administration Paris on the local situation. Afterwards, conference with the chiefs of staff taking part in the operations of AGp. South, on operational plans and the truck situation. (Buhle)

10 February 1941

General von Mittelberger reports on:

a. Possibilities of a Turkish operation in the direction of Plovdiv. He holds that the Turks could attack on a ten-division front north of the Maritsa River, and on a five-division front south of the river. Their advance would have to be covered by a deep echelon on the right flank. The movements must follow mountain paths throughout. Since their supply service uses mainly pack animals, the Turkish divisions would find the terrain no obstacle. But both the higher and the intermediate command echelons probably would not measure up to the task. Moreover, supply would prove a major difficulty in any operations over larger distances.

b. Turkish defense capabilities in Thrace in the face of a German-Bulgarian attack:
The fortified camp of Kirk-Kilisse commands the road to Istanbul, which the main thrust would have to follow. It is supplemented by border fortifications in the north, and strong fortifications round Edirne, facing west. Farther to the rear the existence of a position has been established west of the Chataldsha position, the line Mydia-Ereğli. Then comes the Chataldsha position, which lies very close to the Bosporus. Landing possibilities on the Black Sea coast exist near Mydia, on the Aegean coast east of Enos.

c. An operation against Turkey in Thrace should be conducted with armored forces along the Istanbul road, and must aim at splitting the front in order to prevent a retreat of the Turkish forces to the Bosporus. An armored spearhead breaking through to Istanbul would find sufficient shipping to cross over to the eastern shore in the initial confusion. For a crossing of the Sea of Marmara to the Pandirma railhead, the few vessels in the small ports would be insufficient.

d. Operation through Anatolia:
Must follow two main roads and main railroads and accordingly would be very slow. Unless Turkish morale suffers a complete collapse, we must expect tough resistance also by isolated groups. Difficulties presented by the Taurus Mountains. South of them we must get across another important obstacle before we reach the better-developed communications network leading to Syria.

e. Ammunition is one of the main problems of the Turks.

OQu IV: Computation of British strength.

Von Rintelen reports: No crisis in Albania, but it will take a long time before everything is straightened out. A German High Command of the Italo-German forces must be established: Difficulties of such an arrangement. —Il Duce's directive on operations in Libya conforms with the Fuehrer's demands.

Japan and the possibilities of her joining in the war against England. Spain, Gibraltar.

Position of the attachés and other current questions.

. . .

Paulus (on phone): Bulgarian demand for full mobilization. Decision must be taken soon.

Schniewind (on phone): Protection of our convoys to Libya. We ask him to get arrangements under way through Liaison Officer Rome.

12 February 1941

. . .

Heusinger-Gehlen-Stieff:

    a. Gehlen reports on observations on tour in Romania. Important points: List wants deployment of his forces completed, before the start of operations, which, if possible, should not come off before 28 February.

    List would like the Bulgarians to mobilize before his jump-off.

    Romanian army cannot be looked upon as an army at all. Our troops have supply difficulties due to foreign currency restrictions.

    b. Hauffe must be informed as soon as possible of our stipulations to the Romanian army and on requirements for BARBAROSSA. At the moment nothing has to be done as regards List.

    c. Difficulties with Russian maps. Especially the tactical maps (1: 100,000) are very poor. Lower echelons must be warned on how staff work will be affected by such bad maps.

    Luncheon with v. Mittelberger.

Lieutenant General Dihm reports as Field Supply Chief.

OQu IV: a. Schildknecht reports on Koestring's study on Iran and Russian operational capabilities. Koestring holds that fourteen infantry divisions, seven cavalry divisions, and four motorized-mechanized brigades could be committed on that front, partly east of Caspian Sea.

    b. Miscellaneous: Materiel deliveries to Hungary, temporary assignments of Swiss officers, etc.

14 February 1941

Morning conference: Shipments are running normal. Intention: Begin bridge building and march into the Dobruja on 21 February; cross Danube on 24 February.

Von Altenstadt: Police requirements for BARBAROSSA; activation of new units and transfers from the west.

Wagner: OKW draft on executive power in BARBAROSSA. Organize Military Government Russia! —Current matters.

Heusinger:

    a. Aid for Finnish operations for seizure of Hangoe and closure of the White Sea Canal.

    The only thing we can do for the Finns is send heavy artillery (heavy howitzers). We would have to ship them at an early date, so that the Finnish crews could be trained. OKW will have to decide whether this is politically feasible. Support for the attack on Hangoe will be mainly an air force mission, i.e., keeping enemy planes away from the Finnish artillery (Heinrich's request). Air force would have to operate from bases on the Aaland Islands, which in turn calls for German occupation of these islands.

    b. The White Sea Canal is exclusively a requirement for the air force or Lahousen's organization.

15 February 1941

OQu IV: Franco-Caudillo.

    a. Convinced that the Axis will win the war.

    b. Demands: Economic and military aid, precise definition of "legitimate interests."

    c. Il Duce: The only possible course is to "keep Spain in the political lineup of the Axis."

Japanese foreign minister will be here middle of March.

Conference with ObdH on Operation MARITA. Interrelation between Greece and Turkey.

17 February 1941

. . .

Von Etzdorf:

    a. Conference with Yugoslavs at Obersalzberg. Fuehrer is pressing the Yugoslavs to join the Tripartite Pact, but they defer all decisions to the Prince Regent. They are not interested in annexation of Saloníki. Make a counterproposal: Yugoslav-Bulgarian-Turkish block against any foreign landing attempt. Are ready to act as mediators in the Italo-Greek conflict. Fuehrer refers them to Rome; thinks that the proposal might be accepted.

    b. Fuehrer's remark about *Russia:* He is stunned by the reports on the Russian air force. A conflict is inevitable. Once England is finished, he would not be able to rouse the German people to a fight against Russia; consequently Russia would have to be disposed of first.

Heusinger:

    a. MARITA will be delayed by weather difficulties of the air force. Buildup of supplies for air force operations from Bulgaria cannot be completed before 2 March.

    b. Bridge building can start within two days; preparations have been made.

    c. Suggestion: Highway not before 28 February, then Danube crossing on 2.

Konrad: Presents digest of his reports to the Reich Marshal: Future economic problems, structure of the army, assembly of the army, cooperation army/air force. Report on tanks and demonstration before the Reich Marshal.

. . .

19 February 1941

. . .

Prolonged talk with ObdH concerning operational capabilities against Turkey. British capabilities next spring and summer. —Current matters.

Noon luncheon with von Stuelpnagel (Army Hq. 17), von Thoma, Mueller, Radke.

Gercke: Necessary extensions of road network in Hungary, Slovakia. Progress of work in Poland satisfactory. —Coal supplies for the state railroads have reached the lowest level compatible with operation. —Passenger traffic will be curtailed.

Fifteen thousand trains needed for the entire buildup; in addition, ninety-six trains daily for current supplies. (Excluding Libya and MARITA); 160,000 railroad cars. Eight trains of empties required. Eight different types of trains.

Assembly plan, Transport Echelons III and IV.

Preparations for railroad extensions behind the BARBAROSSA front. One line in each army group! In all, six possible.

20 February 1941

Morning conference: Recapitulation of the individual points of ground forces cooperation with Abwehr, navy, and air force. "German Africa Corps." —Plans must be made for another full armored division.

Paulus, Heusinger, von Grolman, Gehlen: Discussion of the individual drafts for operations of the army groups in BARBAROSSA.

AGp. South: Sound. Our conference has produced excellent results.

General Jodl: Alarmist report on bridge construction on the Danube received from Bruckmann.

.   .   .

22 February 1941

Morning conference: No important new developments.

General Konrad: Russian air force.

    a. Air force is not an independent part of the armed forces (*organization*).

    b. *Ground facilities and strength:*
        Eleven hundred airfields, 200 serviceable. Equipment inferior to ours. Estimated strength 4,000 to 5,000 bomber and fighter aircraft.

North of Pripet: Reconnaissance and bombers 1,530, fighters 2,200.
South of Pripet: Reconnaissance and bombers 675, fighters 1,250.
Main concentration north of Pripet.

Our air force considers this the final Russian disposition for their concentration in the west. (New Russia pamphlet.) —Transport aircraft and parachutists: Based on Kiev.

By next summer, it is estimated, 60 percent of the above strength will be ready for commitment.

c.   *Types:* Reconnaissance craft obsolete, range around 300 km (a few new ones have range up to 640 km); speed 150 to 250 km.

Close-support craft: Majority old types; cooperate with armored troops. Between 100 and 200 are modern (speed: 380 km; range: up to 700 km). Armament: Only machine guns (4 fixed forward firing MG).

Fighters: Rata J 16 is good; 4 machine guns, or 2 machine guns and 2 cannon. Inferior to the German fighter (Spain); is slightly slower. Craft now under construction probably not ready for 1941.

Bombers: Two-thirds good; SB 1–3 and TB 3 make up two-thirds of total. SB 1–3, range 600 km, night and bad-weather craft.

Fair game for German fighters. { TB 3: range 1,000 km (bomb load 2,000 kg)
TB 3: range 1,500 km (bomb load 800 kg) }

Transport craft: Not much is expected.

Paratroops: Same.

d.   *Training, leadership, tactics:*
Fighters and bombers good while in formation; depend heavily on lead pilot. Blind and bad-weather flying deficient. Fighters are especially trained for action against ground targets, but their foremost mission is to fight enemy air force in the air and on the ground. Between fighter and bomber, teamwork poor.

Leadership: Hard and brutal, but without training in modern tactics; mechanical, lacking adaptability.

e.   *Ground organization, air force signal troops:* Air force signal troops, as we know them, are nonexistent. Only radio communications! Transmit in clear in emergencies. Ground organization scanty. Large parts attached to flying organizations. Supply stocks apparently low.

f. Probable dispositions: See b.

Deployment will take considerable time; is being watched. Fighters work in close support of their own and against enemy ground troops. Close-support craft against enemy armor. Bombers have targets in the enemy rear area. Clear nights essential. Targets: East Prussian supply base, Silesian industries, Romanian oil fields, Baltic ports, Berlin.

g. Own air strength: Our air force expects Russians to have 4,000 (probably more) plus 600 new craft.

Russian		Friendly
1,600 bombers ⎱ Ratio 1:2 ⎱ BARBAROSSA and ⎱ West		
4,050 fighters ⎰ ⎰ Homeland 2,500 ⎰ 900		

If we assume 60 percent operational: 1,100 to 1,700 [*sic*] bombers
2,650 to 4,050 fighters

BARBAROSSA: AGp. North 380 ⎫
Center 910 ⎬ Planned strength
South 510 ⎭

Russian AAA: 300 medium, 200 light and AAA MG batteries
Own total: 798 medium AAA batteries
827 light AAA batteries

Von Tresckow (Ia AGp.B):

Discussion of our broad viewpoints regarding conduct of Operation BARBAROSSA in theater of army group:

1. No battle at Białystok, but at Minsk.

2. Watch against gap between his army group and von Leeb!

3. Press with all means available behind southern wing, so as to obviate threat to flank. Technical details of buildup.

. . .

27 February 1941

. . .

Conference with General Jeschonnek (present Major Christ, Colonel Heusinger):

North: Reconnaisance off Murmansk (based on central Norway). Hangoe-Aaland: No facilities.

BARBAROSSA: Fighters 6:1 (3:1); training and material said to be considerably inferior.

Bombers 2:1 (1:1). Training inferior.

Fighters: Only 400 modern, total 3,000; for close-support effort.

Bombers 1,600 to 2,000, mostly older types.

Air force expects concentrated attacks against our spearheads, but thinks they will collapse owing to our superior technique and experience. Targets for long-range fighters.

Russian ground organizations, being organic to operational flying units, are clumsy and, once disrupted, cannot be readily restored. Distribution of forces: One air fleet for each army group. Further details later.

Mediterranean: Lemnos possible, but purpose must be clearly defined. Malta-Crete in preparation (airborne landing). I call attention to possibilities for airborne operations in Tangier and Ceuta. Corsica still being studied.

France: Relatively strong fighter and long-range fighter forces under Sperrle. In Holland, Belgium, and northern France, excluding Brittany. —Night fighters. Fight for control of air for reconnaissance over the sea. XI Airborne Corps probably to go to France (deception). ATTILA still on active list. AAA ample.

Homeland: Weise. —XI Corps. Either use right off the start or not at all. Discussion of possible airborne operations in the Mediterranean and in BARBAROSSA.

AAA: Fuehrer wants no serviceable piece to remain inactive. Personnel for thirty batteries. AAA Corps, of six battalions, for Sixth Army (Armored Group 1) and for Armored Group 2.

Norway: Unchanged, under Stumpff.

Liaison air force-ground forces: Konrad's position.

Buhle: Tanks for Norway. —Eight Hundredth Regiment as "fire brigade" against uprisings! Use of tanks in BARBAROSSA. Roechling projectile for armor in Libya.

1 March 1941

Morning Conference: Construction of bridges on the Danube makes good progress. (Last bridge finished 1000 hours. Tested for loads of 26 tons.)

Conference with Paulus and Heusinger:

1. Situation in Libya. Rommel's preparations for forthcoming attack.
2. SOUTH WIND: Expression of opinions on Hilpert's study; forestalling action.
3. Norway: Organization of command agencies for Operation SILVER FOX.

OQu IV (with Liss): Situation in England (homeland): Now forty divisions, including one new armored division.

Squabble between Hq. Second Army and 9th Armored Division as to who is to have credit for capturing the French war archives.

2 March 1941

Twelfth Army (List) marches into Bulgaria.

Crossing was effected at 0600 hours, as per schedule, on the two eastern bridges; 1000 hours on the western bridge. Delay was due to bridge damage sustained when opening for passage of oil barge train.

Reports from von Rintelen on alleged Italian plans for offensive in Albania. Attack is to start within a few days on the supposition that the Greeks will withdraw troops from the Albanian front in reaction to our advance into Bulgaria.

The mere fact that Italy believes it is able to launch such a drive on a few days' notice shows that no more than local attacks are to be expected. They do not in any way affect our plans.

3 March 1941

Conference with ObdH:

1. Military-political situation in the Balkans. Coordination with political leadership again very tenuous.

2.   Operational possibilities in Libya now and later, when additional troops could be released from BARBAROSSA.

3.   Continuous intrigues by various nonmilitary agencies against us, to undermine the position of the military.

Jodl OKW (on phone): Liaison with political command is too loose. We must have a clear knowledge of what is going on.

a.   Is the political command interested in having German advance elements appear at the Greek frontier to impress on the Greeks that we are faster than Mr. Eden's troops? He is just now in Athens?

b.   What are Turkey's reactions: Must we expect interference from that quarter?

c.   Are the Italians being made to understand that piecemeal attacks in Albania are only disrupting plans?

Reply:

Concerning a.: OKW welcomes everything calculated to further an early appearance of German troops on the Greek frontier. However, the question is still being discussed with the Fuehrer. Definite instructions soon.

Concerning b.: Turkish question "settled."

Concerning c.: Wholly in agreement with OKH.

Von Etzdorf:

a.   Effect of note informing the Russian government of our march into Bulgaria. General reaction: Obvious concern. Molotov replied to the German ambassador in writing, as follows:

1.   Events have not developed on the line recommended by Russia. It is a matter of regret that contrary to the Russian proposal of 25 November, the German government has deemed it desirable to take a course infringing on Russian security interests. The march into Bulgaria is in opposition to the Russian conception of security zones, which include that country.

2.   The Reich government cannot expect Russia to give any support of its action in Bulgaria. (This probably refers to diplomatic support.)

b.   Effect of the information on the Turkish government: Friendly in tone, no direct reference to the matter. Eden had shown understanding for Turkey's situation. Nothing tangible has come out of Eden's visit. Turkey has not been maneuvered into any new commitments, because Turkey is not yet sufficiently armed at the moment. Eden had pointed to the Italian collapse. Turkish foreign minister and Yugoslav envoy cooperate to keep Yugoslavia from tying herself to Germany.

c. A similar announcement of the German march into Bulgaria, by the Bulgarian government, met with an unfriendly reception, without any comments, in Yugoslavia.

d. Letter of the Fuehrer to the Turkish state president: "No further intentions."

. . .

General Jodl:

a. The question as to whether armor should soon be sent up to the Greek frontier will not be decided before tomorrow, since we must first clear up the situation with the Yugoslavs.

b. For the time being the Fuehrer will not use his influence with Il Duce in the question of the Italian attack in Albania. Let them scorch their noses! On the whole, the Fuehrer shares our view.

c. Great excitement on the "Mountain" caused by receipt of a picture of a British tank with 80-mm armor. What can we put up against it in Africa, and what else could we do?

. . .

5 March 1941

. . .

Wagner Gen Qu: Draft of an OKW directive on organization and administration of the occupied areas in the east. Behind the advancing troops. Government commissars will be established who will have armed forces commanders attached to them. The stipulations of the ObdH are to be observed, but otherwise the army must not be burdened with administrative tasks. Special missions of the chief of the SS.

ObdH-Keitel:

a. The Fuehrer will not advise Il Duce against an offensive in Albania; he will merely tell him that we shall come in later.

b.   Yugoslavia: Conference with Regent Paul produces no positive results. No intention to join the Tripartite Pact. No transportation facilities across Yugoslavia. It is hoped to settle the Greek question without the use of force. However, so far I can see no signs that such a solution has a chance.

c.   Great excitement over Lofoten raid.

8 March 1941

Morning conference: Yugoslavia apparently veering round to the Tripartite Pact. Three possibilities for the British. Report of British efforts to trade capital ships for destroyers.
Seventh convoy arrived in Libya; Eighth convoy Palermo; Ninth still in Naples on account of British cruisers.

. . .

Enemy intelligence from Turkey reveals that apart from air support England is preparing to support Greece with two to three divisions, now standing by on islands between Lemnos and Crete, so as to be moved into Greece via Vólos, or also into Turkey, if necessary.

Greek intentions: At start, defense of Struma or Vardar, as the case may be. In case of an attack on Vardar Valley, a defense is planned, with the right wing based on Mount Olympus, and the left wing extending over Mount Gramosi (on the Greek Albanian border) to the present left wing in Albania.

Paulus:

a.   Organization of road improvement work. —A new map of Russia showing road conditions (good work).

b.   Military-political data for von Grolman's study.

Report on Yugoslavia's reply. Regent Paul thinks he can induce his Cabinet to accept the Tripartite Pact, on three conditions:

a.   No transit for German troops. Discussion possible on transportation of materiel by rail and by Danube.

b.   No commitment to active participation in this war.

c. Access to the Aegean for Yugoslavia.

.   .   .

10 March 1941

.   .   .

OQu IV:

a. *Yugoslavia.* Belgrade Cabinet meets today. Yugoslavia's three conditions for joining the Tripartite Pact have been accepted by Germany and Italy.

b. Greece: Up to 4 March, only seven thousand British in Greece (air force), in Athens area. In the last few days additional five thousand arrived in Athens area (claimed missions: protection of airfields). Reports state that evacuation of Thrace is being prepared. Greece said to be getting ready for war. Change can be hoped for only if Yugoslavia changes her attitude.

c. Turkey's reply to Fuehrer's letter still outstanding.

d. Conference Goering-Antonescu: Increase in oil deliveries. German production aids accepted. Sparing of Iron Guard refused. Wants to form new Party from reliable elements.

e. *France:* Darlan announces convoy protection against England for French shipping; will use arms if necessary. Proposal to appoint Laval Minister-President.

f. *Spain:* Franco's letter stating reasons preventing his entry into the war now demands clear-cut statement on colonial promises.

g. Fuehrer's demands on Japan. Japanese capabilities.

11 March 1941

Morning conference: Report of Russian movements from Moscow Military District toward Smolensk and Minsk. Intelligence on new roads in Russia, which would indicate existence of better roadnet than heretofore assumed. Encroachment on command fraction of OKH by OKW, which orders that 4th Mountain Division must join MARITA in place of some other division.

. . .

14 March 1941

Morning conference:

1. Albania: The Greeks are attacking, instead of the Italians.
    Yugoslavia: Slovenia is being evacuated.
    First, 3rd, and 5th divisions are setting up rear services.
    Greece: Flight of population in Thrace; no Englishman in Saloníki
    up to 10 March.
    England: Britain requests 1 cruiser, 119 submarine chasers, 115
    patrol vessels, 2.5 million tons from U.S.

2. OKW: Movement of third wave (MARITA) must wait on order
    of OKW.

3. Libya: Graziani—difficulties.

4. BARBAROSSA: Twenty-five hundred trains of first echelon have
    been dispatched.

OQu I: Deception maneuvers in the west. —More friction with Konrad over
delivery of materiel.

Operations Sec: Heusinger, v. Grolman, Gehlen report on plans of the armies
in Operation BARBAROSSA:

Twelfth Army: Operation against Cernăuţi with only one division of
the left wing is wrong. Will have to use also Romanian mountain
brigade (4) on this wing.

Seventeenth Army: Hungarians and Slovaks must be mobilized about
two days before the operation starts and follow behind. Fake commotion
on the front between Tarnów and the mountains (Security Division,
etc.).

Sixth Army: On the whole, in agreement with the very heavy concentration of forces; should point left wing farther to north (Kowel)!

Fourth Army: Its southern portion still rather weak; its central portion
is getting too close to Białystok. Concur on all other points.

Ninth Army: Disposition with objective Łomża is waste of effort. On
the northern wing coordination between Armored Group 3 and army
not yet perfect. Feel for operational requirements lacking here. Army
Hq. evidently cannot assert itself over the CG of armored group and
is reluctant to place infantry units under the command of armored group.

Eighteenth Army: Our suggestions have not been paid much attention to. Teamwork Hoepner—infantry corps must still be brought into line with our ideas.

Sixteenth Army: Front still too wide. In any event striking power will be greater when reserves close up.

OQu IV with chiefs of subsections: Report on situation: *Libya* and Egypt:

Fifteen British divisions (including two of armor). In Libya itself between four and eight (including armored divisions).

England: Activation of five divisions has started. Total of forty-five divisions now in the homeland, including four armored divisions (two new). Of the forty-one infantry divisions, about twenty-one are ready for assignment. Flow of materiel permits fitting of one or two infantry divisions per month.

France: Must reduce her troops in North Africa to 120,000 by 1 April.

Russia: Reported mobilization of four age groups probably only replacements, as the specialists are already in the services. Intensified concentration on the borders of the Baltic provinces. Reported road movements from direction Moscow toward the frontier via Minsk.

Conference with ObdH: Situation and intentions Libya. —Situation in Bulgaria. —Personnel matters. —Heusinger reports on armies for Operation BARBAROSSA.

Wagner Gen Qu: Fuel situation (stocks for only three months). —Preparations in Romania: Fuel preparations adequate, ammunition varying. Definition of command powers of Gen Qu. Command posts. —"Administrative orders" for BARBAROSSA.

Noon. Demonstration of pyrotechnics and signal devices. Inspection of Zeppelin signal center.

General Brand: Questions regarding use of artillery on coasts of Norway, Denmark, Holland, western France. Railway artillery on the BARBAROSSA front. —ObdH reserves allocation for himself. Unfortunately ObdH emphasizes security of French west coast to such an extent that his specifications can be met only by sacrificing striking power in BARBAROSSA. Of course, when you ask the navy and everybody else whether they could carry out their missions 100 percent or whether they would need some aid from the army, everybody wants something from the army. The point, however, is not to be 100 percent sure everywhere, but rather to make sure of the necessary minimum of safety, and then put everything behind Operation BARBAROSSA.

Heusinger: Current business. —Preparations for report to Fuehrer.

Notes by General Halder for his report to Hitler on 17 March 1941.

MARITA:

1. *Beginning attack:* 1.4. can probably be achieved.

2. *Enemy:* Currently five divisions of limited combat value.

   Saloníki doubtful Greek opportunities. Our attack possibilities after breaking into Greek territory.

3. *Goals* of the Greek operation English view: Peloponnesus-Crete, Rhodes-Cyprus: as a basis for an operation against Egypt. Our strength requirements for an extended goal (six infantry and mountain divisions; six motorized divisions).
   Time requirements of the operation.
   When can we count on these units for BARBAROSSA?

4. *Coordination with the Italians.* Until now only vague reports concerning a reputed attack.

   For this operation only exhausted divisions are available. Cannot expect extensive operations. Greeks should be able to disengage without difficulty.

5. **a.** After completing the operational goals, how many units must remain in Greece? (Stance of Yugoslavia and Turkey.) Return over Yugoslavian railroads?

   b. Circumstances in Bulgaria? (Military mission approximately two divisions.)

6. *Links of MARITA-BARBAROSSA.* III Echelon belongs to the Pruth Army—4th Mountain Division for 15.5.
   BARBAROSSA; otherwise do not send to Bulgaria!

7. *Details:*

   a. Demarcation line on the Turkish border south of Edirne.

   b. Aegean islands: Thásos, Samothráke immediately.
   Lemnos—air-landing and then artillery.

    c. Smash Suez Canal!

    d. Demands on Greece in the event of unified purpose.

SUNFLOWER:

    1. a. Rommel's intention to use an advanced defense (an Italian division will be available to relieve 5th Light Division) agreeable.

    b. Coastal shipping (without Tunis!) in motion and can be improved.

    c. Unity of transport management.

    2. Rommel's intentions for an 8.5. attack—goal Tobruk.

Fifth Light Division plus 15th Armored Division as the base (two motored divisions desired). Italian occupation troops.

Demands: Three armored reconnaissance units, etc.

One must report:

    a. Demands cannot be realized.

    b. Italian divisions are not usable as occupation troops.

    c. Supplies must be moved along the coast; the attack requires leadership both in the desert and along the coast (Benghazi).

An operation directly through the desert against Tobruk requires an additional 1,500 tons = 4 battalions = $\frac{1}{12}$ BARBAROSSA. Four battalions from the Italians! The average is about $\frac{3}{5}$ of the above.

Disadvantage: Slower; a five-day stop between goals.

    3. *Egyptian attack:* One armored corps after release and reconstitution from BARBAROSSA (prepared). Time requirements three to four months; attack at end of winter.

BARBAROSSA:

    1. Time of 16.5. to be held by army when the III Echelon of MARITA can begin the march movement by 10.4.

    2. Enemy: Impact on the Baltic countries—Smolensk-Minsk.

Advance transport because of earlier German air force demands has alerted the Russians.

334 The Battle of Britain to Barbarossa

Countermeasures: Entrenchment as well in general government. —Populace in rear areas! Universal speech limitations!

3. Force relationships:

Additional: Romania three good divisions, one motorized, four cavalry brigades, four mountain brigades for Bukovina, an additional division for occupation.

Hungary: One mountain brigade on left front, another three brigades as reserves.

Shifting of forces without damaging BARBAROSSA is not possible.

Enemy	We
100 inf. divs.	101 inf. divs.
25 cav. divs.	1 cav. div.
30 mot. divs.	32 mot. divs.
155 divs.	134 divs.

4. *Army reserves:*

Total twenty-one divisions (includes two armored plus one motorized division); from which nine divisions for MARITA; certain, for the moment, twelve divisions very tight! Five divisions in west.

5. *Navy:*

    a. Transport area: Baltic with a fourteen-day warning. Black Sea has 100,000 available.

    b. Blockade Russian fleet—Hangoe-Aaland.

6. *Air force:*

    a. Landing on Odessa.

    b. Transport for supplies.

    c. AAA thin; sufficient only for rear areas.

    d. Hangoe.

7. *Von Falkenhorst* goals should be less! No colonial area. Division Norway/Falkenhorst. Time?

8. Political demands. Already in place.

Urgent: *Finland* (Hangoe, strength commitment) mobilization preparations. Training, replacements (otherwise must rely on us).

Romania (mobilization requires preparation) language rules.

9. *Question of Russian preventive measures.*

Finland-Romania?

Water-air.

By March 1941 Hitler's position had changed considerably. Spain's adamant refusal to enter the conflicts, America's expanding role as a supplier and ally to Great Britain, Italy's disastrous military campaigns, and Russia's uncertain neutrality cast doubt on Germany's military fortune. The lull in the struggle helped Britain more than it did Germany. In an effort to regain the initiative and hasten the final reckoning, Hitler pushed forward diplomatic efforts to expand his role in central Europe and to develop his military plans for the final denouement with the Soviet Union.

As part of this ordering process, Hitler, in marked contrast to his 1940 views, decided to help his Italian colleague, Mussolini, out of the latter's travails. This meant sending German troops to Africa and into the Balkans against Greece. He expanded the context of war from a singular theater of operations to theaters of limitless distance and difficulty. Only the sword could force Hitler's will and demands on an unwilling world. To be sure, he understood the gamble, but his overreaching confidence and disdain for the Russian people overwhelmed any good judgment. Given his record of successes, no one challenged his assumptions.

The issue was a quick settlement of Italy's problems with the Greeks (for which Hitler obtained diplomatic understandings with Hungary, Romania, Slovakia, Bulgaria, and Yugoslavia) and then the ultimate, decisive struggle with the Soviet Union.

17 March 1941

Wagner (no entries)

Conference on situation: Albania: Operation without conclusive results.

Greece: British troops 18,000 to 20,000 strong (including air force). No higher command staff. Attaché tour canceled.

Buschenhagen: Svolvaer. —Fuehrer requires Norway must be rendered absolutely safe against any surprise attack. British now are in position where they must take the offensive. West is impregnable, perhaps Syria; best chance Norway. Our air force largely centralized; navy weak, shipping lacking for large-scale land operations. If the British secure a lodgement, Russia will become possible. Construction of continuous defense system impractical and, moreover, unnecessary. Objective of defense. The English must not be allowed to gain a foothold, not even for two weeks. Safeguarding of our traffic along the coast, both by sea and by land. All centers of economic and military importance must be secured against surprise raids. (Air raid warning posts, etc.) To ensure accomplishment of this task set up 160 batteries (echelonned in depth, with infantry and AAA cover). —Transfer all replacement organizations of Norway units to Norway, as well as one or two of the occupation divisions earmarked for France. —Increase strength of construction troops.

BARBAROSSA: Fifty percent cannot be taken out of Norway. —Sweden is not likely to let us use their facilities. —Dietl will strike via Petsamo. Two divisions to Narvik to relieve Dietl.

Strengthening of defenses: Von Falkenhorst's proposal: For Murmansk only two mountain divisions. Third Mountain Division cannot be managed. One occupation division for Norway: one-third to northern Norway, two-thirds to southern Norway. Fifty-four batteries can arrive in northern Norway by sea on 15 April; five or six large steamers. Personnel will proceed to Narvik as "furlough personnel." This plus one-third of the occupation division and two MG battalions for northern Norway will make up for 2nd Mountain Division by 15 May.

Central Norway: Batteries by 25 April. Fifty batteries in ports (reinforced by infantry).

Southern Norway: Fifty batteries and two-thirds of one occupation division will sail from Stetten on May 1.

Operation SILVER FOX: Second Mountain Division will strike toward Polarnoje, one Finnish division (12th Brigade) and one German division from Kemijaervi in eastern direction. Seaborne movements: Allow six days for unloading at Kemijaervi and Uleåborg.

Fuehrer conference (with Colonel Heusinger): 1500–2030 hours.

1. MARITA: The operation must be carried to the objectives that will assure us a base for air domination of the eastern Mediterranean.

This requires control of Attica, perhaps even of the Peloponnesus. Operation must be carried out with maximum speed. Occupation of Thásos and Samothráke if possible should be simultaneous with occupation of the coast. To accomplish this we must try to obtain shipping from Romania and Bulgaria. —Lemnos will be seized by paratroops as soon as possible thereafter.

Turkey: Satisfactory letter from the Turkish chief of state would suggest that Turkey is desirous to keep out of a conflict with Germany. Forces assigned to watch Turkey may be withdrawn after we have reached the Aegean coast.

Conclusion: The forces allocated for MARITA must be written off from buildup for BARBAROSSA.

2. BARBAROSSA:

    a. We must score successes from the very start. There must be no reverses.

    b. It would be pointless to base our operational plans on forces which cannot be counted on with certainty. As far as actual fighting troops are concerned, we can depend only on German forces.

    The *Finnish* forces can only be counted on to attack Hangoe and prevent a Russian withdrawal into the Baltic area.

    On *Romania* we cannot rely at all. Their divisions have no offensive power.

    From *Sweden* we can expect nothing, for we have nothing to offer.

    Hungary is unreliable. Has no reason for turning on Russia. Her political aims lie in Yugoslavia, where they see something for themselves.

    Slovaks are Slavs. May perhaps be used for occupation purposes later.

    c. Rokitno marshes would not restrict movements.(!) It is a terrain in which armies could maneuver freely.(!)

    d. AGps. North and Center will push as far as the Dnieper, then, taking advantage of the protection afforded by the river, mass forces for a thrust to the north. Moscow is of no importance whatsoever.

e.   AGp. South: "It would be fundamentally wrong to attack every-where." Pruth and Dniester rivers, which will block any offensive. The Dniester is much more impregnable as a defense line than the Rhine. Hence, no attack across the Pruth. "Here we would only drive the Russian away from a spot where we should ask him to stay put."

f.   *Conclusion:*
In the Romanian sector, employ only the forces necessary for the protection of Romania. All other available forces will be used for frontal attack north of the Carpathians, with greatest weight on the northern wing, where additional armor will be brought to bear. Armored units must be pulled out of Romania at the earliest!

3.   *Finland-Sweden-Norway:*

a.   No plans can be based on the assumption that Swedes will tolerate transit of combat troops.

b.   Present security of Norway insufficient. The British will make diversionary attacks. Norway vulnerable: fjords, roads.

c.   No threat in the west: Air incursions impossible in daylight. Landings in the west out of the question. Some troops in the area can be released for Norway (two or three divisions).

d.   Proposal to Sweden: We want to relieve two mountain divisions in northern Norway, and request right of transit for two divisions (materiel by sea). If arrangements cannot be made, exchange must be made by sea.

e.   One mountain division is to be released in this manner. An attempt will have to be made to ship another division into the Gulf of Bothnia shortly before beginning of operations. These two divisions will have the double mission of keeping the British from establishing a foothold in Murmansk, and of closing the White Sea Canal.

4.   General Wagner presents the great picture of supply. No comments.

5.   *Rear areas:* No difficulties in northern Russia, which will be taken over by Finland. Baltic states will be taken over together with their administrative machinery. Ruthenians will welcome us with open arms (Frank). Ukraine uncertain, Don Cossacks uncertain.

We must create republics isolated against Stalin's influence. The intelligentsia put in by Stalin must be exterminated. The controlling machinery of the Russian Empire must be smashed.

In Great Russia force must be used in its most brutal form. The ideological ties holding together the Russian people are not yet strong enough, and the nation would break up once the functionaries are eliminated. Caucasia eventually will be ceded to Turkey, but first must be exploited by us.

6. *Libya:* Agrees to the forward shift of the defensive front. Current preparations must enable us to pass over to the offensive as soon as a favorable balance of strength is attained. Sending of additional troops now impractical. Landing operation in Tunisia is rejected; plan to purchase ships in Tunisia must be studied.

2230.   General Paulus is given outline of the results of Fuehrer conference.

20 March 1941

. . .

Heusinger: Current matters: Norway. —Romania. —Greece.

Enemy intelligence: Greece. Landing of British troops seems to have started. Movements, also motorized elements, from Attica northward.

General Rommel: Report on Libya. Overall impression: British passive and apparently thinking in terms of defense only. British armored units apparently being concentrated in direction of Benghazi. The area to the south, around Agedabia and Sollum, seems to be treated as a no-man's-land. This would indicate British intentions to defend the Djebel area, which offers favorable health and tactical conditions.

We shall not be able to attack on the baseline of the arc in the direction of Tobruk before the enemy in the Djebel is beaten. But the Africa Corps is not strong enough at the present to do this. Nevertheless, we could weigh the possibility of occupying the no-man's-land around Agedabia and making preparations for a drive in direction Tobruk next fall.

Afternoon. OQu I and Gen Qu confer on details with General Rommel, who then will present an estimate of what he could achieve with available forces before onset of the hot season.

. . .

25 March 1941

Situation:

    a. In Greece: One Australian division from Palestine, one New Zealand division from Tobruk. Troops from Palestine are being replaced, apparently from Mesopotamia. Concentration of British eastern Mediterranean fleet off Crete, purpose unknown. Possibly Crete staging area for movements.

        British are disembarking troops in Greece: Attica, Vólos.

        Scattered British detachments reported on Kateríni-Edessa line. Greek islands off Turkish coast said to be still free from British troops, as are Thásos, Mytilene, Kephalonia, and Lemnos.

    b. Roatta, Chief of Italian General Staff.

    c. Alleged trouble between Twelfth Army and Romanian authorities over supplies, on account of demands by Twelfth Army not previously discussed.

. . .

Heusinger:

    a. Change in the instructions on assembly of troops for BARBAROSSA in view of the new situation on the southern wing. Changes in the demands on air force.

    b. Comparison of Russian and German strength ready for commitment. We are extremely weak compared with the Russians up to 20 April. After that the divisions arrive in such numbers as to eliminate all danger. Meanwhile, of course, our supply base is under a threat, but I believe that we must avoid any unusual forward concentrations at this time.

    c. New instructions for AGp. South.
        Various possibilities of operational disposition in AGp. Center (Ninth Army).

    d. Mission of Army Hq. 11 in Romania. Also various minor current matters.

. . .

26 March 1941

Situation: No important news. British strength in Greece is hardly more than thirty thousand at the moment. This number, however, is reported to include air force and supply services, which means that they would not even have two complete divisions as yet.

1030. **Paulus:** British capabilities. For my part, I don't think it very likely, at least for the present, that the British would send to Kirkenes any of the twenty domestic divisions they may have gotten up by now. Such a move would be more likely later on, after getting in touch with Russia following the start of our attack. But even then the mutual distrust of the British and Russians in this area is so strong that we can expect more benefit than trouble from such a move. England's foremost concern is the eastern Mediterranean and the land route to India. Here they are building up strength, but only with defensive intentions for the time being.

. . .

27 March 1941

From 0930. Conference of ObdH with the CGs of the army groups, armies, and armored groups.

AGp. Center: No significantly new viewpoints. Only, Ninth Army and Hoth will need direct orders to get them to team up infantry divisions with armored group in the jump-off.

AGp. North: Plan to strike with one division (SS Division "Reich") in the direction of Kowno is criticized; is changed by army group. At Kowno we must do as well as we can with improvisation and keep armored group together. In this case, too, cooperation of infantry divisions in the attacking sector of the armored group is discussed and accepted by army group.

1200. Called to the Reich Chancellery on account of Yugoslav coup d'état.

1300–1430. Fuehrer demands earliest possible march into Yugoslavia. Four invasion thrusts:

   a. On List's right wing, reaching Axiós River via Novo Selo, to give quick support to advance of List's right wing.

b.   Detached from the right wing, but still under List's command: Strike from the area around Sofia towards Skoplje, to join up with the Italians and to prevent linking up with Greece.

c.   With a separate group from the Sofia area, in direction of Belgrade, to seize enemy capital and open up the Danube.

d.   From Germany, in the north, perhaps even from Hungary, with armor.

1600.   After return: ObdH continues conference with the CGs of the army groups, etc. (AGp. South). General discussion. Present: OQu I. I discuss with Operations Section the operational possibilities against Yugoslavia and their ultimate effects on BARBAROSSA. Subsequently, conferences with Operations Officer, Transportation Officer, Gen Qu, and ObdH on time needed for assembly and grouping of forces for Yugoslavia.

28 March 1941

. . .

1230.   **Reich Chancellery:** (myself, Paulus, Heusinger):
Fuehrer reviews the courses of operations open to us, thinks that group against Nish must be made as strong as possible, because strongest resistance may be expected in this sector (armament center, capital). Approval given for negotiations with Hungary. Accordingly, I instruct Paulus to proceed to Budapest immediately.

Negotiations with Bulgaria must refer only to preparative measures.

Italy: Fuehrer's letter to Il Duce. Speaks of situation which is serious but not disastrous, and of determination to crush Yugoslavia. Demands suspension of drive in Albania, covering of northern flank of Albanian front, and readiness for attack in Istria.

Il Duce's letter to the Fuehrer: Promises to call off drive in Albania, to cover three northern approaches to his wing, and to add six divisions to the seven divisions stationed in northeastern Italy (in addition to the fifteen thousand frontier guards). Also pledges support of Croat separatist movement.

Turkey: List must report immediately if Turks march into the Edirne corner; such a move is not very likely. The Fuehrer's appraisal of Turkish attitude is highly optimistic. He has told the Turkish ambassador that Russia did not join the Tripartite Pact because the Fuehrer would not agree to Russian bases in the Straits.

Other matters put before the Fuehrer:

a. List should not be confined to Mount Olympus line.

b. Timing: List is to strike at the earliest; the drive toward Skoplje should coincide with List's attack, if possible.

c. Air Defense Africa. Fuehrer thinks Rommel should make the decision.

d. Airborne operation: Fuehrer suggests an airborne landing at Kruševac (Yugoslavia's arsenal). Regiment Goering to von Vietinghoff.

.   .   .

29 March 1941

Kinzel (reports from Finland):

a. European Russia: Fifteen divisions more than previously estimated.

b. Russian Armored Corps Pskov with two armored divisions: two tank regiments.

c. Paratroops: Ten brigades of three battalions each.

Situation: *OQu IV:* Italian defense measures against Yugoslavia in the north, and preparations for attack in Albania (contrary to promise to Fuehrer).

Three divisions, including Armored Division Centaur to Libradz, Kukes, and Scutari.

Italian fleet: Motor torpedo boats to Suda Bay (Crete).

Three British divisions left Alexandria for Crete on 9 March (reported by Japanese General Staff).

.   .   .

Von Etzdorf: Conversation with Matsuoka apparently successful. Attack on Singapore seems to be contemplated. Noncommittal on dates. Matsuoka was informed that we are not interested in a Russo-Japanese nonaggression pact; agreement on fishing rights, etc., would be enough.

State secretary is being informed on dates for attack on Yugoslavia and for BARBAROSSA. Watch Belgrade diplomatic corps!

.   .   .

THE BALKANS
1941

30 March 1941

0830.   To Berlin. Phone talk with ObdH on List's proposal and my criticisms.

1100.   **Meeting of generals at Fuehrer office.** Address lasting almost 2½ hours. Situation since 30 June. Mistake of British not to take advantage of chances for peace. Account of subsequent events. Italy's conduct of war and policies sharply criticized. Advantages for England resulting from Italian reverses.

England put her hope in the U.S., and Russia. Detailed review of U.S. capabilities. Maximum output not before end of four years; problem of shipping. Russia's role and capabilities. Reasons for necessity to settle the Russian situation. Only the final and drastic solution of all land problems will enable us to accomplish within two years our tasks in the air and on the oceans, with the manpower and materiel resources at our disposal.

Our goals in Russia: Crush armed forces, break up state. —Comments on Russian tanks: Redoubtable; 4.7-cm gun (AT) a good medium weapon; bulk of tanks obsolete. Numerically Russia's tank strength is superior to that of any other nation, but they have only a small number of new giant types with long 10-cm guns (mammoth models, 42 to 45 tons). Air force very large in number, but mostly outmoded; only small number of modern models.

Problems of Russia's vastness: Enormous expanse requires concentration on critical points. Massed planes and tanks must be brought to bear on strategic points. Our air force cannot cover this entire huge area at one time; at the start of the campaign, it will be able to dominate only parts of the enormous front. Hence, air operations must be closely coordinated with ground operations. The Russians will crumple under the massive impact of our tanks and planes.

No illusions about our Allies! *Finns* will fight bravely, but they are small in number and have not yet recovered from their recent defeat. *Romanians* are no good at all. Perhaps they could be used as a security force in quiet sectors behind very strong natural obstacles (rivers). Antonescu has enlarged his army instead of reducing and improving it. The fortunes of large German units must not be tied to the uncertain staying power of the Romanian forces.

Mines! *Questions regarding Pripet marshes:* Flank protection, defenses, mines. Problems arising if Russians should make strategic withdrawal. Not likely, since they are anchored on both the Baltic and the Ukraine. If the Russians want to pull out, they must do so at an early stage; otherwise they cannot get away in good order.

Colonial tasks! With our goals in the east achieved, we shall need no more than fifty to sixty divisions (armor). One part of the ground forces will be discharged into armament production for air force and navy; the others will be required for other missions, e.g., Spain.

Clash of two ideologies. Crushing denunciation of Bolshevism, identified with a social criminality. Communism is an enormous danger for our future. We must forget the concept of comradeship between soldiers. A Communist is no comrade before or after the battle. This is a war of extermination. If we do not grasp this, we shall still beat the enemy, but thirty years later we shall again have to fight the Communist foe. We do not wage war to preserve the enemy.

Future political image Russia: Northern Russia goes to Finland. Protectorates: Baltic states, Ukraine, White Russia.

War against Russia: Extermination of the Bolshevist commissars and of the Communist intelligentsia. The new states must be Socialist, but without intellectual classes of their own. Formation of a new intellectual class must be prevented. A primitive Socialist intelligentsia is all that is needed. We must fight against the poison of disintegration. This is no job for military courts. The individual troop commanders must know the issues at stake. They must be leaders in this fight. The troops must fight back with the methods with which they are attacked. Commissars and GPU men are criminals and must be dealt with as such. This need not mean that the troops should get out of hand. Rather, the commander must give orders which express the common feelings of his men.

Embody in ObdH order. This war will be very different from the war in the west. In the east, harshness today means lenience in the future. Commanders must make the sacrifice of overcoming their personal scruples.

Noon. All invited to lunch.

Afternoon. Fuehrer conference:

  a. *Yugoslav question.* Decision in conformity with my ideas. List will attack with XXXX Corps and on his MARITA front on 5 April. SS "Adolf Hitler" attached to corps. Kleist will attack with three armored and two infantry divisions and one Bulgarian division on 8 April. Group Temesvar on 12 April. Von Weichs likewise on 12 April.

Italy is no help as a partner. In Albania they are paralyzed with fear. On the Ginlia frontier they claim they cannot attack before 22 April. No need to define a boundary for them against sector of Second Army since they will not attack anyway.

Details: Airborne landing Kruševac. —Assignment of Regiment Goering. —Location of GHq.

Op. Sec.: Ship 22d Division to Hungary.

    b. BARBAROSSA: Reports of army group leaders and of several subordinate commanders (Guderian). Nothing new, except a clever plea by von Rundstedt for assigning the Carpathian sector to the Hungarians and making the Pruth line an offensive front.

1 April 1941

. . .

ObdH: Discussion of offensive possibilities against southern Serbia. Von Brauchitsch plays with the idea of having 2d Armored Division strike toward Veles instead of against Greece, in order to be stronger in southern Serbia. I oppose this disposition, which would allow the entire Greek Second Army to get away from us. We must steel our nerves to believe in the devastating effect of the attack of 9th Armored Division and SS Division ''Adolf Hitler'' on Skoplje.

Must yet talk over missions of Army Hq. 2 in Operation 25 with von Witzleben.

. . .

2 April 1941

. . .

1300–1400. Fuehrer conference on overall situation in Yugoslavia (Heusinger with me). No new viewpoints. Emphasis again on Nish. Mission of Twelfth Army discussed. Plan regarding Croat autonomy. Strong language about Italians, who should use their air force on front of Twelfth Army, instead of on their Albanian front.

. . .

3 April 1941

Situation: Agedabia taken by German Africa Corps (apparently heavy British losses). Enemy in hasty retreat to the north.

Turkey estimates British strength in Greece at three divisions, as we do.

Heusinger:

a. Airborne division needs five trips to get to Nish. Air route via Bucharest. Total fifteen days (starting 7 April). Better to transfer parachute regiment to Bucharest, which is then available for missions anywhere (Yugoslavia, Greece).

b. Date for jump-off of Operation 25 will be set by OKW.

OQu IV:

a. Reports from Finland: Attempts to recruit men for SS Regiment "Nord" are viewed with disfavor; Finns would rather have revival of Jaeger Battalion 27 idea.

b. Italian-Portuguese arms deals are purely financial transactions; no raw materials involved.

c. Bircher, Danniker visit schools, etc., in Germany.

d. Material turned over to Oshima (situation maps) and Marras (secret regulations); other current matters.

. . .

Heusinger:

a. Control of Hungarian army by the Fuehrer, not by OKH, is due.

b. Twenty-second Division all of a sudden is supposed to go to Ploeşti, taking the place of Regiment Goering. Cannot be moved by rail.

c. Fuehrer order to Africa Corps. Recognition of accomplishments and reminder not to be reckless, as air force units are being withdrawn, and arrival of 15th Armored Division will be delayed; moreover, the Italians now need all their strength against Yugoslavia and so have nothing left for North Africa. Under these circumstances there is danger of English counterattacks on flanks. Further advance authorized only when sure that British armored elements have been taken out of area.

d. Army Hq. 12 wants to start operations on 6 April, at dawn. Air force first against Rupel Pass.

Paulus:

    a. Tartar reports from Hungary: Teleki has committed suicide; his death is supposed to have political reasons. Horthy will not mobilize the entire Hungarian army, but only border guard and one motorized corps. Reported resignation of Hungarian government.

    b. Study for SOUTH WIND.

.   .   .

Paulus: Reports of Teleki's suicide are confirmed. Apparently there have been serious disagreements in the Cabinet concerning participation in the campaign against Yugoslavia, which overtaxed the strength of the ailing prime minister. The current foreign minister is his probable successor. Mobilization will be limited to IV and V Corps, motorized. War Minister von Bartha is on his way with a letter from Horthy to the Fuehrer. Fuehrer's decision on start of Operation 25: 6 April, as was recommended by us after receipt of List's report.

4 April 1941

Situation: British reported to be evacuating Benghazi, setting fires. In northern Greece, the presence of three British divisions is confirmed. Now, after all, the Bulgarians make their 6th and 11th divisions available for Operation 25.

Paulus: Study for SOUTH WIND. —Paulus, too, has got the impression at conference in Vienna that supply officer, Twelfth Army, is not equal to his job.

.   .   .

Colonel Kinzel: Situation report on Yugoslavia: Reports on disposition of enemy forces show that border troops are being reinforced by divisions from the interior of the country. This will result in stronger initial resistance, but later on, when this has been broken, in a speedy collapse. No central reserves will be available after that. In the south of the country (mountains), the divisions of the Third Army are being split up into nine brigades strung out along the border. Against northern Albania, comparatively strong forces have been brought up; in Scutari area at least three brigades, on the northeastern border three brigades, and on the border north of Lake Ochrida three more brigades, making a total of a maximum of nine brigades. The direction in which they are pointed is a little awkward for us in view of the lack of Italian preparedness for defense in Albania. We must expect Serbian penetration into Albanian territory and some very costly fighting there. There is no evidence of a weakening of enemy defense measures in their northern border area.

Situation report Russia: Foreign Armies East now admits that strength of Russian army in European Russia must be higher than estimated originally. (The Finns and the Japanese stressed that all along.) The total figure is now put at 171 infantry divisions, 36 cavalry divisions, and 40 motor brigades. The newly activated armored corps of three divisions apparently is stationed around Leningrad.

. . .

Conference with ObdH: Gives me his account of tour to the Balkans. Conversation with King Boris and Antonescu, List and von Weichs. —No news from List. Apparently a good deal of friction between von Kleist and List, because List regards his drive as the main thing and wants to cut down on von Kleist.

Von Weichs does not want to give any infantry to Corps Vietinghoff, disregarding ObdH's suggestion.

Boris is mobilizing six Bulgarian divisions, but will not allow them to cross into Yugoslav territory, on account of Balkans Pact.

Antonescu knew nothing at all of our impending offensive against Yugoslavia. Requests that Hungarians should not operate east of the Tisza River. By 20 April, Romania will have fifteen divisions and two-thirds of one motorized division in the Russian border region. Of our German divisions one will go to the Bucovina border, one to the Pruth River knee; armored division to the approaches to Ploeşti.

Kinzel: New intelligence from Yugoslavia, which gives an entirely different picture: The forces stationed near and north of Nish have moved south and are being replaced by units from central Serbia. Report that two divisions in the Banat have been withdrawn behind the Danube. On the northern border no change.

Liss: a. Australian corps has disappeared from Cyrenaica. Still in area: 7th Armored Division, one Australian division, 6th British, 9th Indian. The bulk of the forces sent to Greece come from Cyrenaica. After the victory over the Italians, strong forces seem to have been transferred to Abyssinia.

b. Greece: No British on Serbian soil. Wilson in command?

c. French West Africa: No change. De Gaulle has not made any progress.

. . .

Paulus took my place at conference this afternoon with the Hungarian War Minister von Bartha.

Von Bartha told him that Teleki committed suicide because he felt he could not take the responsibility for this policy after having himself signed friendship pacts with Yugoslavia. Left letter to regent, urging on him a policy of loyal observance of pacts. This has made the regent waver in his original decision. He sends the minister to the Fuehrer, to appeal for sympathetic understanding and submit new proposals. Mobilized: Border guard, IV, V, motorized corps (so he says). Promised additional mobilization of I and VI. II and VII (and III) still outstanding from original commitment. Promises that all corps will be ready by 15 April (?), armored corps by 12 April.

Paulus had been instructed by the Fuehrer before the conference as to what arguments he wanted him to use against Horthy. Apparently von Bartha was extremely embarrassed by these views and after the reference to the agreements concluded in Budapest. We must wait and see what comes of this.

5 April 1941

Morning conference:

a. Reports are confirmed that Yugoslavia is shifting her main forces to the area south of Nish. The information—often grossly overdrawn—differs a good deal. One source places twelve infantry divisions and one cavalry division in southern Serbia along Bulgarian border; another reports ten infantry divisions, one cavalry division, eight infantry brigades. Reports on Greece generally portray an unchanged situation. Estimates of British strength in Greece vary between 45,000 (which may be correct) and 120,000. The report that the Yugoslav High Command, in case of war, would seek to join up with the British and Greek forces, probably is correct.

b. North Africa: Benghazi taken; equipment of one Italian medium artillery regiment and one armored battalion recaptured. Reconnaissance in direction of Derna in progress.

ObdH! Outcome of Fuehrer conference on the evening of 4 April.

a. Situation Hungary. The Fuehrer seems to be soft in his dealings with Horthy and appears to be impressed by the Teleki business. Hungary is not going to strike right away; she wants to wait until the Croats have declared their independence. With that, the state, with whom it concluded a friendship pact, will have ceased to exist.

b. Fuehrer is greatly concerned over the Italians, particularly in Albania, as also over the possibility that the Serbs might fall back before the Italians in southward direction into the Serbian mountains.

c. Lines of action:

1. Seize Agram quickly. Have von Vietinghoff, with one armored division (8th), move on Agram.

2. Provide against developments south of Sava River. Von Vietinghoff's tanks must push farther on toward Sarajevo.

3. Serbia is assembling very strong forces in southern part of country. This increases the likelihood that von Kleist would have to be shifted south from Nish.

4. Move Reinhardt and von Vietinghoff closer to border.

5. Airborne operations: Nish 22d (Airborne Division), Ueskueb (paratroops).

d. Overall picture: The conduct of the campaign once more comes under the dictate of political considerations and, what is more, considerations of purely transitory character. This precludes any planning with clear goals and harbors the danger of dissipating our strength in a series of isolated operations. Always the same story. Good nerves are the only antidote.

. . . .

Schuchard (Paris): Rivalry between embassy and military commander more sharply marked. Abetz in Berlin to see the foreign minister. Embassy is overstepping its jurisdiction in all fields and tries to squeeze out the military commander. Proof that embassy is working against us: De

Brinon said to be afraid that Abetz might leave his post, on the allegation that he could not work any longer with the generals and Wiesbaden. Commerce Adviser Lehrer has mentioned a similar remark, indicating Abetz's attitude toward us. Reasons: Pressure from von Ribbentrop. —Abetz making every effort to score successes against us before his minister. Arrest of Americans, which von Stuelpnagel refused, leads to dispute. "If higher authorities intervene, the fight might become unending."

.   .   .

6 April 1941

Morning reports: Operation IRON GATE successful. Against southern Serbia, surprise apparently complete. Resistance on Rupel Pass. Ninth Armored Division, 73d Infantry Division, and 2d Armored Division have crossed border. Second Army sector: Seizure of points of tactical importance on Yugoslav territory; demolitions in the interior.

Conference with ObdH: *Situation:* Corps Reinhardt: date fixed for start of operations. —Report from von Witzleben (Army Hq. 2), that a strong advance combat team of armored corps of von Vietinghoff will be ready to strike on 10 April. Preparations for bridge construction at Belgrade. Hungarians will help with bridging equipment; German engineer troops (underwater cutting and welding, and demolition detachments) stand by in Bucharest and Vienna.

Hungary: In addition to motorized corps and IV and V Corps, I and V from original commitment: III, II, VI Corps.

Disposition of Russian forces: Strong concentrations in the Ukraine are noteworthy. Would be right for an offensive against Hungary and the Bucovina, but I feel sure this possibility can be discounted.

.   .   .

Evening report: Air force has made three attacks on Belgrade (Palace Citadel, Ponton bridge).

Destroyed forty-four aircraft on the ground, twenty shot down; own losses two twin-engine fighters. AAA defense thin.

Sofia reports bombing attack by planes flying at high altitude.

Twelfth Army. Ninth Armored Division in action against retreating enemy west of Vetunica at 1400 hours.

The 73d Infantry Division Advance Combat Team reached Kočani in the evening.

Second Armored Division fighting at Strumica. Intends to drive southward.

Sixth Mountain Division reported on railroad line near Kalo Horjo.

Fifth Mountain Division and 125th Regiment in heavy fighting on Rupel Pass.

The 72d Division at Ohiron, pushing on toward Kate Vendru.

The 164th Division advancing on Xánthi.

The 50th Division still fighting in Nymphea area.

Enemy columns moving from Štip on Strumica.

. . .

7 April 1941

Morning reports. Progress over the evening situation only in 9th Armored Division sector. They have taken the mountain pass on their front. On the Greek border area fighting is rather heavy.

Libya: Reacting to the first surprise advances, the British seem to take energetic countermeasures to escape encirclement. Fuel difficulties.

Abyssinia: After abandoning Addis Ababa, the Italians concentrate resistance in some districts of the interior, in which they could hope to hold out until the rainy season.

Movements progressing satisfactorily. Twentieth Motorized Division, if ordered entrained now, would arrive from Auxerre area on 19 April, 2000 hours.

Disposition of the Russian forces gives food for thought. If one discounts the much-advertised idea that the Russians want peace and would not attack on their own account, one cannot help admitting that their troop dispositions are such as to enable them to pass to the offensive on shortest notice. This might become extremely unpleasant for us.

. . .

Jodl (OKW) on phone: Russia's uncertain attitude. Shall railroads be put on maximum schedule? On Fuehrer's decision, the reply is no, but defensive measures now can be taken openly.

Heusinger: Marching orders to 20th Motorized Division. Move SS troops to more central location in France for convenience of entraining.

Org. Sec.: *Requirements for future organization* of ground forces:

24 armd. divs., including 10 for tropical service ("light divs.").

12 mot. divs., including 5 lt. divs. for tropical service.

66 inf. divs., normal T/O, including 6 for airborne operations and 10 with tropical equipment.

10 mt. divs.

24 mobile divs., 8 with tropical equipment.

6 mt. regts. for operational assignments.

2 air transport squadrons, each with carrying capacity of 1 div.

Estimated Needs:

Theaters	Armd.	Mobile	MT	Inf.	MT Regt.
West	—	6	—	24	1
North	—	—	2	6	—
East	6	6	2	20	2
Southeast	—	—	—	6	—

Operational Groups					
Spain-Morocco	3	2	—	2	1
North Africa-Egypt	6	2	—	—	1
Anatolia	6	4	—	4	—
Afghanistan	3	4	6	4	1

.   .   .

THE BALKAN CAMPAIGN

8 April 1941

Von Kleist starts offensive in direction of *Nish*.

Situation conference: New advances. Skoplje taken. Second Armored Division on way to Saloníki. Overall picture shows complete disintegration of the enemy operating in southern Serbia.

Paulus: Discussion of instructions on deception maneuver on the western front (SHARK).

Von Ziehlberg: Current General Staff personnel matters. —With *Matzky* attaché matters.

Conference with ObdH: He is still concerned about Albania, and wants to urge List to move even closer to the Albanian border. Doing this would serve no good purpose, for we are no longer threatened from Albania. Any forces detached in this direction are a waste of troops which now are needed for building up swiftly the front facing south.

Airborne landing at Ueskueb desirable.

Afternoon. Leave on special train at 1500.

2130.   Breslau: List wants to get 5th Armored Division to the south as reinforcement for 9th Armored Division as quickly as possible, so as to be able to break through to Flórina. Can't have it.

Von Kleist has not yet pushed beyond Piret. The battle for Nish is still to come. Fifth Armored Division is needed there now, but after completion of its mission, it can be released for the south. The request to have 16th Armored Division brought up is justified.

In the evening, ObdH talks with the Fuehrer from his train. No decision on 16th Armored Division. Fuehrer suggests that, if road trouble impedes closing up of 5th Armored Division behind 11th Armored Division toward Piret, 5th Armored Division might strike toward Kumanovo. (No! In that event the division would be lost for the Nish operation.) It would be better to have 5th Armored Division attack Leskovac via Piret.

9 April 1941

0800.   (Train one hour late.) Arrival at Wiener Neustadt. Our office is in the Maria-Theresa Academy.

Situation conference: Our troops have entered Saloníki (2d Armored Division). Local army commander has offered capitulation. In southern Serbia, apparently only remnants of the enemy forces left. Italians report slackening of enemy pressure in Albania. At Skutari, too, nothing has happened. North of the Danube, enemy seems to be evacuating. No report yet as to when Reinhardt could start operations. In Second Army sector, troops on the border are approaching the Dráva. Maribor taken. Drava crossing near Bares in hands of 14th Armored Division.

Kuebler reports entry of 2d Armored Division into Saloníki at 0700 hours.

List protests against yesterday's Wehrmacht communiqué, which fails to do full justice to the achievements of the ground forces and the honor of the attacking troops.

1130. **OKW** disapproves release of 16th Armored Division.

By noon it is clear that the Nish front also is collapsing. Hence, 5th Armored Division is moved up via Nish in order to be brought to bear against Leskovac. The Greek army between Turkish border and the Vardar River has capitulated. So far 20,000 prisoners are reported (not counting the Greeks), including 5 generals and a complete divisional staff; 100 guns; 28 AAA guns, 25 AT guns; several hundred MG; 131 new Dernier aircraft engines (on two fields); aircraft spare parts depots; 4 bridge columns; 1.5 million liters, or 1,500 tons, of gasoline; several rations depots and rations trains and spare parts depots.

Skoplje radio transmitter intact in our hands.

Evidence of demoralization: Only the Serbians want to continue fighting; Macedonians and Croats throw their weapons away.

.   .   .

10 April 1941

(Second Army starts operations with XXXXVI Corps.)

Morning situation: Nothing substantially new. Fifth Armored Division apparently is still on the move to close on Piret and probably will take two to three days to join XXXX Corps because of the detour over Priština they had to take. Eleventh Armored Division is pursuing the enemy retreating toward Belgrade. In southern Serbia an advance combat team has broken through to Flórina via Bitolj, and has made contact with the enemy. Let's hope that the eagerly desired junction with the Italians in Albania will come off soon, with XXXX Corps having taken not only Bitolj, Kičevo, and Tetovo, but also to meet us by advancing to Bitolj via Struga, and to Kičevo and Tetovo via Debar (Alpinis).

Reports indicating disintegration of the Serbian army continue to come in. In northern Yugoslavia Croats seem to have refused to obey orders in some instances. Concerning the liquidation of Thrace, we have no detailed reports as yet.

The Greek government has resigned. Political situation obscure. Unrest in Turkey and apparently also in Romania. Hungarians (in response to the letter of the Fuehrer) have now promised to strike on 12 April, in the direction of Osijek, perhaps already on 11 April.

Reinhardt, who still thinks he has major forces in front of him, now wants to start out on 11 April. We think he will find only border guards and cavalry.

. . .

1730.   Conference ObdH with Fuehrer:

1.   New offensives against Greece. Boundary line against the Italian zone: from eastern bank of Lake Prespa to Pindus Mountains.

2.   Has agreed to continuation of drive on Larissa. Permission is obtained to transfer 60th Division.

3.   Italians: Second Army must start operations with parts of 14th Armored Division (from Zagreb) in the direction of Fiume at earliest date. The bulk of the army may move in general direction Sarajevo.

4.   Russia: No reasons for anxiety.

Turkey: Attitude not quite clear yet; it would seem that British money again has been greasing palms. The Fuehrer does not want to let the Bulgarians march into Thrace as long as the Turkish attitude is not clarified.

. . .

11 April 1941

Good Friday. (Operational Group XXXXI Corps starts operations.)

During the night the Fuehrer had us on the phone again, trying to make us change the plans for 14th Armored Division, which is poised to drive west, and for 8th Armored Division, which will push southeast. Apparently Heusinger was able to contain this outbreak of jitters. Eighth Armored Division will still drive toward Osijek; 14th Armored Division is already moving on Karlovac and will be pushed on toward Deinice.

Morning conference: Yesterday's picture confirmed: 14th Armored Division roaming the country almost without enemy opposition. Eighth Armored Division has come up against some resistance near Slatina and will attack again today. The remainder of Second Army finds little opposition in its southward advance, but has difficult terrain and poor roads.

Nothing substantially new from Twelfth Army. The Italians on the Albanian front have not really got going yet, and it looks as if we shall actually have to go up to the border to make the junction. In the south our troops are still in contact with the British southeast of Flórina. No positive measures which would indicate that British front is being taken back.

Talk with ObdH: I express resentment over interference with the conduct of operations. This timorousness, shying away from every risk while continuously clamoring for victories, may be acceptable politically, but from the military standpoint it is intolerable. We have our job cut out in the south, against Greece. Every unnecessary step in another direction is a sin against success.

Wagner:

  a. Labor pains in the setting up of a Military Government Serbia. Air force wants to furnish the general; and Consul-General Neubauer, in his capacity of representative of the Four-Year Plan, already seems to have a mission of blocking any constructive work.

  b. Constanza: One ship can sail. Await orders for further sailings. List needs nothing for Kavála.

  c. Rommel makes preposterous demands. His wishes can be satisfied only insofar as preparations for BARBAROSSA permit.

Himer reports that Hungarians are set to start off on both sides of the Danube today, at 1400. Dive-bombers of our Second Army will give ground support. Talk on future missions south of the Danube.

Von Greiffenberg reports, 1300: Saloníki harbor taken over empty. —SS "Adolf Hitler" is in action against the British southeast of Flórina, between the lakes (British still have artillery in area!). —Von Kleist: This morning's action still in progress. Rupel Pass open for vehicles since last night. —Seventy-second Division will reach Seres tonight.

Reports coming in the course of the day and evening show quickening disintegration of the northern Yugoslav front. Units are laying down arms or surrender to our planes flying overhead. One bicycle company captures an entire brigade, complete with staff. An enemy division commander radios to his higher Hq. that his men are throwing away their weapons and leaving for home. The only fighting still going on is south of Belgrade, in the sector of 11th Armored Division, but here, too, enemy resistance was broken by evening. XXXXVI Corps is with its right wing at Karlovac, where they are to wait for the Italians who have at last come out via Fiume, which has surrendered to them. With its left wing, XXXVI Corps is in the area south of Novi Sad. In southern Serbia a junction with the Italians has at least been effected on the northern shore of Lake Ochrida (Struga). On the Greek-British front, west and southeast of Flórina, no new progress. Here we must wait for our forces to close up, which should take another day or two. In the Saloníki area, XVIII Corps is advancing westward.

The Hungarians are reported to have started operations. Effect is not noticeable as yet. Reinhardt has started off, but his progress has been slowed by bottomless roads.

12 April 1941

(Bardia, North Africa, taken.)

The situation is developing according to plan. Yugoslav resistance in the north has completely collapsed. Croatia wants to declare her independence. North of the Danube, Reinhardt; south of the Danube, Cruewell; and from the southwest, 8th Armored Division are closing in on Belgrade. The fall of the city is imminent.

In northern Greece the British are making a stand and fight back at Vévi, supported by artillery, apparently rear guard units.

After conference with ObdH: New operational order directing assignment of 1st Armored Group (Kleist) to Second Army as of 13 April 1941, 0600. Divisions previously earmarked for GHq. Reserves have been stopped en route. We need no additional troops for Serbia.

. . .

13 April 1941

Belgrade taken.

Morning reports: *In Yugoslavia* things are developing according to plan. Second Army moves in general direction of Sarajevo; in Croatia a Croat National Government is being formed. No news from von Vietinghoff (XXXXVI). The orders to turn south reached him yesterday noon. Since then we have had no signals from him. This must be investigated.

Von Kleist entered Belgrade with 11th Armored Division this morning at 0632, after an officers' patrol of Regiment "Grossdeutschland" had crossed the Danube and occupied the Ministry of War during the night.

More signs of demoralization in the Yugoslav army are reported. The Croats have stopped fighting altogether. Only on the Adriatic coast, some energetic commanders still seem to be trying to keep their troops together.

Greece. The heights barring the approach to Vévi were taken after a concentration of medium artillery. Enemy situation shows the British with about one corps (three divisions) in the Kozáni area, whereas the Mount Olympus front (facing Saloníki), which previously seemed to have been held by the British, has been taken over by the Greeks (with British artillery). The plan of attack of Twelfth Army is to launch a double enveloping movement, with parts of its forces pushing on west of the Aliákmon River and with the XVIII Corps striking from Saloníki in the direction of Mount Olympus, and thereby to crack the British out of the Greek front. This plan is completely in line with our ideas. Casualty reports so far are gratifying: 400 killed, 1,900 wounded. Ammunition expenditure very small.

Morning conference with ObdH produces no new developments.

. . .

General von Beldy (Hungary):

    a.   Reports Hungarians have entered Novi Sad.

    b.   We reach an agreement with him to the effect that the motorized and bicycle units of the Hungarian army will cross the Danube and will be further employed in the sector of Armored Group 1. Hungary's consent to this measure will be secured.

    c.   I inform him of our decision regarding eventual transfer of the Trans-Mur area to Hungary, at a date yet to be set.

    d.   Hungary's wishes regarding Nagykikinda and Agaye areas.

Jodl calls up (for Keitel):

1. Belgrade. On 12 April, 1700, Captain Klingenberg of the SS Division "Reich" hoisted the German flag on our Belgrade legation. At 1845, the mayor of Belgrade handed over the city to the representative of the Foreign Office and to Klingenberg. Great excitement in Fuehrer Hq. over fact that this report did not reach top level through the OKH.

2. Protection of the Bor mining district.

3. SS "Reich" and Regiment "Grossdeutschland" should not, if possible, move southward across the Danube, but rather stand by for other missions.

4. Projected letter to Horthy on continued Hungarian participation. Parallel agreements between both army commands.

ObdH (from Engel): Fuehrer considers sending one motorized infantry regiment to North Africa. ObdH had previously refused on the following grounds:

a. Matter was under consideration for a long time here.

b. We don't see our way to spare troops for North Africa in view of the impending great tasks.

c. Shipping not available until 15th Armored Division has reached Africa.

d. Impracticable owing to lack of motor transport and fuel.

e. Without strongest air support it would certainly be unwise to enter upon operations with ambitious objectives.

f. As we approach Egypt, British resistance will stiffen.

.   .   .

14 April 1941

Morning reports: Continuing advance of Second Army toward Serbian mountain area from the northwest.

Resistance on the southern bank of the Sava against elements of the XXXXVI Corps which are wheeling northward. Resistance also in the area of Čačak, in the Morava Valley west of Kruševac.

On the Greek front: Advance of the 9th Armored Division, which has taken Ptolemais. SS "Adolf Hitler" pushes westward in order to reach the Aliákmon Valley south of Lake Kastoría, and XVIII Corps strikes out eastward along the coast, via Kastoría.

Orders are issued to stop movements of:
XXXXI Corps north of Danube (elements which have entered Belgrade will remain there).

Second Army
- 1st Mt. Div. and Corps
- 125th Div. and 79th Div. under LI Corps
- 101st Div., which will be shipped back by 602d Mt. Regt.

Twelfth Army
- 76th Div.
- 198th Div.

Rommel wants to drive toward Suez from Sollum via Mersa Matrûh. Reich Marshal willing to furnish air support.

Discussion with Jodl (OKW): This operation can be staged only as a raid. To hold Suez, we have neither the troops nor the supply facilities.

OKW directive on continuance of the Greek operation has nothing new, only some rather awkward formulations.

Fuehrer letter received here sharply declines out-of-turn promotions in the General Staff. This, too, will pass. If there is any place where achievement should be the standard for promotion, it is our organization.

Nonaggression Pact Russia-Japan for five years!

Albania: Since 13 April, the Greeks have been quite open about pulling back their northern wing. The Italians are following cautiously through Ochrida and Pogradec.

1400–1930. *By plane to Hq. Second Army at Zagreb.*

Review of the situation produces no significantly new information for OKH. The instructions issued by us have not yet reached army Hq. owing to bad signal communications. Future political setup discussed. —Stopping of rear divisions. —Flight back over Barcs, Lake Balaton, Lake Neustadt.

ObdH at Hq. Twelfth Army, Sofia, and Hq. Armored Group 1, Belgrade. Apart from reports indicating desirable development of situation, nothing of significance. Casualties low.

Armistice request by Yugoslav government is answered with demand for unconditional surrender of arms. Destructions of any kind must cease. German operations are continuing.

Fuehrer's decision on Rommel's requests: Our prime objective is building up a front of ample width in the Sollum area (including Shiwa Oasis). Apart from this, only raids.

Submission of OKW directive on Operation SILVER FOX.

Decision on organization of command in XI Air Corps (22d Airborne Division): Contrary to our demand, air force gets full control.

15 April 1941

Wagner (Gen Qu): Military government in Serbia is arranged so that we are only in charge of military safeguards and retain supervision of a general nature over the civil administration (Thurner). In all other respects, we'll let the police and the agencies of the Four-Year Plan fight it out between themselves!

Situation conference: Our final operations in Serbia continue, with our forces converging from west, north, and east.

In Greece, 9th Armored Division has secured a bridgehead across the Aliákmon River, south of Kozáni, but terrain south of the river is very difficult. The westward drive of SS "Adolf Hitler" and 73d Division through Kastoría still encounters strong resistance. XVIII Corps is advancing through the Olympus area (Mone Petras) and south of Kateríni.

Reconstruction of Croatia will be in hands of v. Glaise-Horstenau.

General Wimmer is slated to head military government for Serbia when it is established.

Conference with ObdH produces no new viewpoints. He is casting about for ways to speed the buildup of a base for Rommel, and wants submarines and the airborne division for this purpose. I think both methods are wrong. The airborne division is nonmotorized and therefore useless once it is landed in Africa. Furnishing submarines is the business of the Italian navy; it would be a mistake to withdraw any of our submarines stationed around England and in Freetown.

General Marras pays his professional call. A rather unproductive interview, during which I tried to rouse his interest in new tasks for the Italians in Bosnia, and to draw his attention to their lack of information on Greek withdrawals on the Albania front. I doubt that he understood what I told him. —The possibility of Italian help in transferring our troops from the Balkans is mentioned.

Colonel Toussaint (lately military attaché in Belgrade) gives a dramatic account of his experiences previous to entry of German troops in Belgrade. The city suffered heavy civilian casualties and much material damage; water and electric supply disruption. He shares my views concerning our further military action, which is no longer of the nature of a campaign, but rather a sort of liquidation in which there must be no letup for even a moment, until the entire country has been combed through. Anyone refusing to surrender should be left to starve.

Captain Loyke (navy): Review of naval warfare problems: He doubts the reported closing of the *Dardanelles* by British submarines. Coastal shipping route to Sollum can be only partly protected by submarines. In any event, using submarines that way offers fewer opportunities for hitting the British than does leaving them where they are now. Employment of Italian submarines would be desirable.

Information on submarine warfare which should reach its peak in August. Roosevelt's declaration including Greenland in the Western Hemisphere is an effort to help the British with their convoys. So far only Iceland was included in the blockade zone; now perhaps we shall have to extend it to include Greenland as well.

SS *Bismarck, Tirpitz,* and *Prinz Eugen* are to go into the Atlantic shortly. SS *Scharnhorst* and *Gneisenau* (the latter hit by an aerial torpedo and bombs) will not return before July.

General Fellgiebel reports on plan to install a senior signal officer in Belgrade, who will at first be under his command and later serve under military government. Discussion of the new signal communication lines needed for continuance of the campaign (Zagreb-Belgrade-Skoplje-Larissa and Sofia-Saloníki-Larissa-Athens).

Rommel reports meeting stubborn resistance at Tobruk, which blocks his advance; apparently a strong garrison, supported by naval units from the sea. He has to use the two Italian divisions to tighten the line of encirclement. Moreover, he is being attacked on the land side from Egypt. Now at last he is constrained to state that his forces are not sufficiently strong to allow him to take full advantage of the "unique opportunities" offered by the overall situation. That is the impression we have had for quite some time over here.

General Zorn (CG, 20th Motorized Division) reports out.

Heusinger: Reintegration into BARBAROSSA of units employed in Operation 25.

Von Altenstadt (Gen Qu):

    a. Collection and screening of prisoners of war. Collecting points at bridges. Classification by nationalities and by following categories: war economy and armaments workers; agricultural laborers from the rich farming districts of Serbia; auxiliary services for our troops; remainder will be shipped home.

        Order to this effect to Army Hq. 2 and 12 and letter to OKW.

    b. Croat Legion (Nonsense!) and von Glaise-Horstenau's position.

    c. Reorganization of the reinforced border guard at the Styrian and Carinthian border sectors, and activation of new regional defense battalions.

Evening reports: The Armistice Commission sent by the Yugoslavs consisted of some generals of the Fifth and Second armies who could not be recognized as plenipotentiaries and so were sent back. —Group Kleist, coming from the north, cannot make any headway against the countless hordes of prisoners entangling his columns in the narrow mountain valleys. A spearhead of 16th Mountain Division, led by the division commander and pushing its way through the masses of surrendering enemy units, has reached Sarajevo, where he has taken control of military and other authorities.

The Yugoslav government has issued a surrender proclamation.

The movements of 11th Armored Division and 60th Motorized Division continue, but are hampered by Serbs who want to surrender.

In Greece only slight progress against the coast and in the area of Mount Olympus are reported. The enemy is still holding the Aliákmon Valley. Little shipping traffic in the Aegean.

In Albania, the Greeks are falling back slowly.

16 April 1941

Morning reports show no significant developments since last night. No progress in Twelfth Army sector.

Progress of the surrender negotiations. Von Weichs's formulation of the conditions is good and leaves no loopholes. The negotiators are not empowered to sign. Formal conclusion of the negotiations therefore cannot be expected before tonight or tomorrow. In the meantime, fighting is practically over.

.   .   .

17 April 1941

(Capitulation)

Morning reports: Nothing of importance from Second Army sector. The movement toward the Dalmatian coast continues. In the sector of Twelfth Army, it is still an open question as to what has become of the Greek forces west of the Pindus Mountains. I am quite sure that the opposition south of Serbia is sustained only by weak forces taking advantage of the exceedingly favorable terrain. But what may be the enemy's operational intentions remains obscure. A drive by our forces west of the Aliákmon River is the only way to prevent the enemy from building up a front. But such a drive would end at Tríkala and take us in front of the high ground rising north of Lamía, which must be regarded as the probable next defense position in the line from Gulf of Vólos to Gulf of Árta. Other possibilities are afforded by the line Thermopylae-Lepanto—southern shore of Gulf of Patras. This position would require the transfer of Greek forces from the area west of the Pindus Mountains across the Gulf of Patras to the northwestern part of the Peloponnesus.

Conference with ObdH produces no new viewpoints. One upshot is a request to air force liaison officer to intensify reconnaissance and aerial action against the rear of the Greek front in Albania, and to order Hq. Twelfth Army along same lines.

The fact that communications between Hq. Second Army and XXXXVI Corps and their armored divisions are quite poor is blamed by ObdH on the General Staff Service (Ic). I shall have the matter investigated.

General von Glaise-Horstenau gives an account on his report to the Fuehrer. He emphasized the necessity to include Dalmatia in the Croat state now in process of formation, because without this territory, inhabited by Croats, the basic concept of the new state, namely unification of all Croats in one independent state, would lack vitality.

The impression gained by von Glaise-Horstenau at the conference is rather discouraging. Out of consideration for Mussolini, the Fuehrer does not want to risk curbing Italian claims. As a result, Serbs and Croats will again make common cause against the Germans.

Von Glaise-Horstenau has been assigned the mission by the Fuehrer to carry on the drive, initiated by von Weichs, to raise Croat troop units of battalion strength, which will be the nucleus of a police army to be organized with two to three divisions now, and eventually six divisions; it will receive, on the quiet, support from Germany; efforts should be made to keep out Italian instructors.

. . .

18 April 1941

Morning situation: Confirmation of report that large bodies of Greek troops have been captured in Grevená Valley (20,000), and that the way to Tríkala is now open for our armored units advancing in this region. It would appear that the road from Grevená to Tríkala can be used also by motor vehicles.

This and the advance of 2d Armored Division and XVIII Corps through the Tempo Valley and across the surrounding mountains precludes any further resistance north of Larissa. The enemy will not have any trouble escaping, for the forces committed on the Aliákmon River probably consist only of very weak rear guards, who can take advantage of extremely favorable terrain.

The Greeks, in conjunction with the British, probably first tried to build up a defense line running from Mount Olympus along the Aliákmon Valley and the Grammos Mountains to the southern border of Albania. It seems that elements from Thrace and the British between Mount Olympus and the Aliákmon River had this mission, while troops brought up via Kastoría were to take over the central portion of this line. With this portion now cracked out of the defense position, the enemy has to take back his line of resistance. To effect this movement, he appears to have sent back the Greek forces to build up defense positions in the rear, the first of which must be assumed to lie on the high ground north of Lamía, whereas the second, and probably the main, line may be expected along the line Thermopylae-Lepanto. The motorized British troops seem to be forming the rear guard east of the Pindus Mountains and will soon disappear under pressure from us.

West of the Pindus Mountains withdrawal will be more difficult for the enemy. Here the retreating enemy cannot help being crowded together and forced into a bottleneck where our massed air force will have opportunity for effective action.

Major General Foerster to the air force, designated as military commander for Serbia, calls. I briefly outline to him our interests: effective military policing, restoration and safeguarding of lines of communications, keeping industries and crop collection going, protecting the Danube shipping route.

Wagner–von Altenstadt–Heusinger: Future military setup in the southeast. The best way will be to create a Commander in Chief Southeast, similar to the one we have in the west. Under his control should be: the Military Commanders Greece and Serbia, Liaison Command Bulgaria and Military Mission Romania, along with some divisions (controlled by corps Hq.). This Commander in Chief Balkans would carry on all the business of the ObdH, and so free us for operations in the east.

Radke: Current business: Mail censorship. —Check patrols in the occupied Balkan territories. —Conferences with SS General Wolff on Poland incidents in 1939 and Tiedemann case. —Morale reports.

General Paulus: Current business. —Deception order. Agreement has now been reached with navy and air force.

Kinzel:

a. Details of enemy situation. The assumption that the Greeks started early to move troops from Albania to the Olympus area has been proved correct. The Italians saw nothing and reported nothing.

b. A radio broadcast of the Greek government has been reported, to the effect that war was lost and that population should keep calm. This report, which OKW wants passed on to all commanders in the field, is most certainly an OKW invention.

Planes have dropped leaflets with purported proclamation of departing British commander in chief.

Fellgiebel: Communication difficulties in Second Army. The reasons seem to lie partly in trouble with improvised equipment, partly in lack of initiative and skill of radio service in Second Army.

General Wagner: Organization of refugee control and materiel collection in the occupied Balkans territories.

Von Ziehlberg: Fuehrer's birthday. —Reassignments. —Organization of training in General Staff and question of out-of-turn seniority promotions. —Anger over tactless interference of ObdH in my command function.

19 April 1941

The morning conference produces nothing significant in news or viewpoints. Among the intentions of Twelfth Army there is a plan to push XVIII Corps or at least 6th Mountain Division from area east of Larissa across the Ordris Mountains to Lamía. That would be a mistake, for such a move gets the division into terrain on the Thermopylae front, where it could not make use of its special training and equipment (frontal attack across a plain).

PW interrogations are beginning to indicate a crumbling of the Greeks' will to resist on the front west of Pindus Mountains. —Larissa taken this morning.

. . .

20 April 1941

(Fuehrer's birthday)

. . .

Situation: The British seem to be pulling out. South of Larissa our advancing troops are nearing the northern outskirts of Lamía. In the Thermopylae Pass, no evidence of enemy resistance. Roads clear as far as Athens. West of the Pindus Mountains the Greek withdrawal movement after all appears to be slower than was assumed; the bulk of their forces seems to be still north of Yoannia.

Métsovon Pass reported taken by SS "Adolf Hitler."

Rumors of formation of new government and capitulation of Greece.

In the evening, talk with ObdH, who feels there is some tension between us. Well meant, but nothing will be changed by it.

21 April 1941

0800.   Leave with Heusinger, Mueller-Hillebrand, and senior aide in Heinkel plane of OKW squadron (because my personal plane had a crack-up in Belgrade).

1400.   **Visit to Hq. Twelfth Army.** Itinerary Belgrade-Sofia (stopover)-Saloníki. Plan to continue to Larissa was canceled when we learned in Saloníki that commander of Twelfth Army was already flying back to Saloníki, and his chief of staff had flown on to Yoannia to conclude the armistice negotiations with the Greek Epirus Army.

1600.   **Talk with Field Marshal List:** The CG of the Greek Epirus Army has surrendered to the *German* High Command with the explicit understanding that he was not surrendering to the Italians, whom he defeated.

Of German troops, SS ''Adolf Hitler'' has entered Yoannia after crossing the Métsovon Pass. Truce already in effect. It has turned out that the entire Greek Epirus Army is still north of Yoannia. List has given orders for SS ''Adolf Hitler'' to advance to the Greek frontier in Albania, and occupy the roads leading into Greece, and for the Greeks to evacuate Albanian territory, then lay down their arms and march to PW collecting points, in compliance with the instructions of Twelfth Army Hq. Details will be worked out by General Bieler, CG, 73d Division, as deputy for commander of Twelfth Army.

1800–2000. Flight round Mt. Olympus and tour of Saloníki.

Evening at Hq. Twelfth Army. New orders from the OKW are received. It would appear that at the time when the OKW gave the order to conclude the capitulation negotiations, the Fuehrer thought he might manage to confront Mussolini with the accomplished fact. That fell through. Mussolini telephoned directly to the Fuehrer and demanded Italy's participation. The Fuehrer ordered that the capitulation concluded by Twelfth Army should not become effective pending his approval. This was to give the Italians an opening for appearing as partners in conclusion of the capitulation. Such a political maneuver makes the German field marshal and commander of Twelfth Army look foolish in the eyes of the Greek army, and, furthermore, lays the foundation for a systematic falsification of history, designed to create the fiction that it was the Italians who forced the Greeks to capitulate.

I discuss with List the inaccuracies in von Richthofen's reports to the ObdH, which belittle the achievements of the ground forces.

Overnight (21/22) at Saloníki Hq. Twelfth Army.

22 April 1941

In the morning, talk with List. He again emphasizes that he concluded the capitulation negotiations on the direct order of and on the lines laid down by

OKW, and bitterly speaks out against the OKW's subsequent action in repudiating the completed surrender. On the whole, reiteration of last night's arguments.

0800.   Departure for Larissa. Impressive flight over the Tempo Valley. Larissa airfield gives the impression of a fairground. There is a constant coming and going of bomber formations and transports. Thousands of men are waiting, working, or resting. No enemy far and wide.

Side trip to 2d Armored Division. Talk with Veiel (CG) and von Quast (Ic). The Division is closing up toward Larissa. Materiel is in good shape, casualties gratifyingly low.

Back to the airfield: Talk with von Greiffenberg, Bieler (CG, 73d Division). The Italian Armistice Commission, for whom Jodl had been waiting and now will accompany to Yoannia, has arrived. Talk with Speth, liaison officer to the Italian army in Albania: He says that the Italians had lost contact with the Greeks yesterday, and that they probably started off tonight following reports of armistice negotiations. (Heavy Italian losses!)

1000.   Start of return flight: Larissa–Kozáni–Upper Aliákmon Valley–Lake Kastoría–Lake Ochrida–Debar–Skutari–Adriatic coast as far as mouth of Marenda River, then in clouds over Mostar–Sarajevo–Brod–Lake Balaton to Wiener Neustadt. Arrived 1430.

News that transfer of GHq. postponed because of the negotiations in Yoannia. So back to the old place.

1700.   Talk with ObdH, who describes the agonizing seesaw during my absence. My suspicion that the Fuehrer, against our warnings, tried to get around the Italians in the negotiations from the start is confirmed. Apparently he hoped to double-cross his "friend." When the scheme misfired, the confusion started. Incidentally, it is reported the Fuehrer informed Field Marshal List that he would have acted the same in List's place. Such appeasements do List no good, as long as he remains publicly disavowed.

The question of an airborne operation against Corinth to prevent destruction of the canal is once more raised by the OKW with fretful nervousness. Exchange of views on the Peloponnesus. I do not believe that the British are going to defend it. They would have no ports that are needed as bases.

1800.   Report stating that *OKW has ordered air force* to prepare VIII Air Corps for an immediate airborne operation against Corinth. Fuehrer will give word when to start. That, of course, implies the risk of missing the critical moment.

Quite interesting are the Hungarian demands for compensation of all war costs and their claims to the Yugoslav booty, which would be a credit to a Jew.

2000.   Telephone talk Keitel (OKW)/ObdH: The Fuehrer does not give up the idea of letting the Greeks and Italians settle their war between themselves west of the line Pindus Mountains–Acheloos Valley, and to seal this line by German troops. He will not make his decision contingent on Jodl's return. The SS "Adolf Hitler" must be taken back to the Métsovon Pass.

2100.   General von Grieffenberg Hq. Twelfth Army (*on phone*):

1.   Orientation on impending directive along lines of conversation with Keitel.

2.   Hq. Twelfth Army reports:

   a.   The Greeks agree to sending a *parlementaire* to the Italian front.

   b.   Greeks and Italians agree to a demarcation line running west along the Kálamos River from a point 5 km north of Janina.

   c.   SS "Adolf Hitler" has been ordered to withdraw behind this demarcation line.

   d.   Greek CG or a plenipotentiary will arrive for the final signing in army Hq., Saloníki, tomorrow noon. Gen. Jodl will remain in Saloníki until that time.

   e.   (In response to my question): Hostilities between Greeks and Italians have not yet ceased everywhere.

23 April 1941

Negotiations with the Italians and Greeks dragged on till noon. In the afternoon at last the capitulation was signed. Earlier, however, the Italian radio blared out reports of the capitulation as an accomplished fact, causing annoyance in the OKW.

Our troops push close to the Thermopylae Pass via Lamía, and strike at Euboea from the Vólos area. In the Thermopylae Pass, the enemy is still holding, but apparently only with weak rear-guard elements. Tanks abandoned in the Lamía area were burned out by the British.

Up to noontime, there is a continuous seesaw as to whether or not we should move GHq. A decision is finally reached when I declare that I would go.

The reason for my insistence is the North African situation. It is worrying me, and the pertinent information is available only at Zeppelin. Rommel has not sent us a single clear-cut report all these days, but I have a feeling that things are in a mess. Reports from officers coming from his theater, as well as a personal letter, show that Rommel is in no way up to his operational task. All day long he rushes about between the widely scattered units, and stages reconnaissance raids in which he fritters away his forces. No one has a clear picture of their disposition and striking power. Certain is only that his troops are widely dispersed and that their striking efficiency has considerably deteriorated. The piece-meal thrusts of weak armored forces have been costly. Apart from that, his motor vehicles are in poor condition from the action of desert sand. Many of his tank engines need replacing. Air transport cannot meet Rommel's senseless demands, primarily because of lack of fuel; aircraft landing in North Africa find no fuel there for the return flight. In view of all this, it is essential to have the situation in North Africa cleared up without delay. After giving thought to the matter, I decline flying down myself. It would not do for me to go there merely for fact-finding purposes. If I go, I want to have authority to give orders. ObdH has his private objections on that score and pretends difficulties with the Italian High Command. The real reasons, of course, are others, but perhaps it is better to dispatch Major General Paulus. He has good personal relations with Rommel from way back, when they served together, and he is perhaps the only man with enough personal influence to head off this soldier gone stark mad. Representatives of Op. Sec., Org. Sec., Gen Qu, as well as Captains Loyke and Soltmann of the navy, would accompany him.

.   .   .

25 April 1941

Thermopylae Pass has been taken. The British are fighting apparently with portions of two divisions of a total strength of about three regimental combat groups. Our mountain troops (5th and 6th Mountain divisions) play a decisive part in the advance. The Thermopylae road is demolished in several places. No reports available on previously claimed crossing to Euboea.

Putting into effect surrender of the Greek forces seems to have run into a snag north of the demarcation line. In that area there is still a full division, which seems to be disbanding itself to escape the Italians. South of the demarcation line, collecting and disarming of prisoners seems to be proceeding in good order. Now, of course, SS "Adolf Hitler" cannot strike south (Gulf of Patras) except with reconnaissance forces. Lemnos occupied.

The parachute operation against Corinth is scheduled for tomorrow.

At our request, OKW has released to us, as of today, two air transport groups, which will be ready in Naples tomorrow and can be used to ferry over the engineers of 15th Armored Division, to be followed by rifle units of the division. They will fly to Derna, via Tripoli.

.   .   .

26 April 1941

Morning situation: In North Africa situation seems somewhat eased by beating back of British tank attacks at Sollum. At Tobruk enemy continues sorties. Our air force seems to have scored successes. Italian submarines, capable of operating only during nighttime, however, cut into supplies for Tobruk.

In Greece, our advances continue. Thebes taken. Advance toward Corinth (5th Armored Division). Parachute operation in progress. Bridge blown up.

Offer of Greek commander in chief to form a new government.

Kinzel: *Russia:* Overall situation unchanged since 1 April. Since that date strength in the west has been increased by 10 divisions. Expanded peacetime army (about 170 divisions) may now be regarded as being up to war strength. It is doubtful whether supply units have been activated. Trains are constantly moving up additional materiel (e.g., 250 trains to the Vilna area), to all evidence to bring equipment up to war strength; up to now many divisions were still short, especially in artillery.

Krebs reports that many units still have very large shortages in equipment.

As to personnel, complaints are heard on lack of commanding officers. Regiments are being commanded by young majors, divisions by colonels. Strengthening of the western front (by arrival of ten new divisions) is noticeable above all round Białystok and Lwów. Behind the front, which is very close to the western border, are stationed four armored groups of varying strength:

> Bessarabia
> Near and to the west of Zhitomir
> Vilna
> Pskov

OQu IV: If U.S.A. entered the war now, we would have to reckon only with the peacetime army, i.e., at most five infantry divisions, two armored divisions, one paratroop battalion, one or two marine divisions, thirty bomber squadrons, ten reconnaissance squadrons, twenty fighter squadrons.

. . .

27 April 1941

Morning reports indicate new advances of 5th Armored Division against enemy rear guards on two roads leading to Athens.

Greece: Embarkation of enemy troops on the east coast of Attica, at Piraeus and on the Peloponnesus, continues. Highly effective attacks by our air force on enemy transports at sea. The parachute operation has been successful, and Corinth is taken. West of Pindus Mountains, SS "Adolf Hitler" is advancing southward through Árta. Consultations between Italy and Germany on the formation of a new government under Greek commander in chief.

. . .

28 April 1941

Morning situation: Capture of Athens, Corinth, Patras confirmed. OKW directives on occupation of Crete. Argument with OKW over transfer of 22d Airborne Division to Greece by trucks. Using our road transport for this purpose would rob us of 602d MT Regiment for BARBAROSSA, where it has been apportioned among the armored groups.

Operation MERCURY: ObdL will have operational control of airborne troops and air transport units operating already in the Mediterranean theater. Army only will have to hold in readiness reinforcements including a mixed tank battalion.

Navy makes all preparations for sea communications. Protection of communications, etc., jointly with Italian navy.

Libya: The first reinforcements ferried over in planes have arrived. A situation estimate by Rommel describes the situation as tense, but despite the alleged inefficiency of the Italian troops, he has decided to attack Tobruk. He will concentrate all German forces for this task, leaving defensive operations around Sollum to the Italians. In my opinion this is all wrong.

. . .

29 April 1941

Morning report: Trípolis-in-Peloponnesus taken. The Italians now hold the islands of Corfu and Préveza. In Cyrenaica, the situation seems to have been relieved by the German thrust at Sollum. Whether this has improved prospects for success of the attack on Tobruk remains to be seen. Airborne landing on Crete set for 17 May.

General Brennecke: Brief discussion on the mission of his army group. No lateral diversion! Push straight ahead into the country! Report on progress of General Staff work. Satisfactory.

Wagner (Gen Qu): Organization of southeast after the end of the Balkans Campaign. High Command in Balkans to be assumed by Army Hq. 12: Military Government Serbia for administrative tasks, a new corps headquarters (reduced) for control of troops (three divisions). Corps Hq. XVIII for control of troops (three divisions) in *Greece.* Civil administration of Greece by Italy. Plenipotentiary German general in Bulgaria to take care of German interests (transportation, transit of troops, quartermaster service).

Romania will be placed under commander of Balkans as soon as operations based on Romania have started.

Major Deyhle (OKW): Report on tour to Army Hq. 2 and 12. —Danube shipping lane will be reopened early in May. —Croatia wants to activate thirty-seven battalions. Eight hundred rifles and sixteen MG each, as a beginning.

. . .

30 April 1941

Morning situation: Libya reports lessened tension. Softening-up operation for assault of Tobruk will start tonight, with main forces to attack on 1 May. In Greece, evacuation of the Peloponnesus completed. Five thousand British captured. Mytilene planned for 4 May. Brief conference with *ObdH:* Question of switch von Salmuth/von Greiffenberg/Foertsch.

1500.   Report to Fuehrer:

1. *Timetable for* BARBAROSSA:

    Transport Echelon III, peacetime railroad schedule, 8 April–20 May: seventeen divisions, GHq. troops from Germany and west.

    Transport Echelon IV A, maximum railroad schedule, 23 May–2 June: nine divisions and GHq. troops from west.

    Transport Echelon IV B, maximum railroad schedule, 3 June–23 June: twelve armored divisions and twelve motorized divisions from interior, west and southeast.

    Greater speed impossible because of transportation difficulties and time needed for refitting of units. No possibility to shift in time: two armored divisions (2d and 5th), one motorized division (60th).

2. *GHq. Reserves:*

    Thirty divisions, including five divisions from west and a police division. Of this total, eleven divisions, which are at present still in the Balkans.

3. *Comparison of Russian and German strength:*

    Discussion of the expected border battles, especially in sector of AGp. South. Opportunities for Hungarian troops. Opportunities afforded by Pruth front, if we have enough troops.

Fuehrer:

a. Formula for talks with *Hungary, Finland,* and *Romania:* "Major developments possible in the west. Hence, protection of the east essential. Russia has treated us unfriendly on several occasions, and we had better provide against surprises." Talks may start probably around 23 May.

b. Need for safeguarding Ploeşti, Cernavodă.

c. Von Schobert will take over command six weeks before the start of operations, i.e., on 15 May at the latest.

4. *GHq. troops:* Review of need to have all forces on hand for BARBAROSSA. The 10-cm guns and siege guns sent to Libya will be badly missed. Only one 10-cm battery is to leave, while developments are watched.

In case Tobruk falls, remainder will not be needed. Temporary shift of railway batteries from west to east (out of seventeen batteries).

5. *Review of line-up on completion of movements:* Fuehrer informed of activation of fifteen replacement brigades. Recommendation to send to Holland only one division of the reserves of Commander in Chief West, as second occupation division (OKW order!) is approved. Replacement units must not be used for guard duty! (Holland). Improvement of 82d Division impossible (Keitel).

Fuehrer: Appraisal of British possibilities for landings in Portugal and Spain (northern coast and from Gibraltar), perhaps also Spanish Morocco.

6. *Miscellaneous:*

a. Final policy for occupation of Aegean islands. Italians will do the Cyclades. We do Mytilene, Chios, and Sámos.

b. Divisions to stay behind in Greece.
Fuehrer: Captured guns for coastal defenses (British 9 cm). Fuehrer hopes that fewer than three divisions will do. Mountain divisions must be freed for other missions.

c. Plans for reorganization of Balkans High Command. Military Government Serbia will be subordinate to it. (*Fuehrer*)

d. Outfit additional armored corps for Libya. Required materiel by BdE.

In the evening General Paulus reports from Libya:

1.   In the event that Tobruk falls, he will instruct Africa Corps: Secure Cyrenaica along general line Sîwa-Sollum-Bardia with echelonned south wing to guard against enveloping attempts. No advance beyond line Sîwa-Sollum, except for reconnaissance forays, even if the enemy withdraws farther eastward. Forces must be regrouped and filled up. Watch coast.

2.   In the event that Tobruk holds out, he wants to instruct Africa Corps to prepare a position along the eastern border of Cyrenaica, with left wing at Ain el Ghazâl and deep echelonning on right flank; line is to be manned with newly arriving reinforcements. Investment of Tobruk will be upheld until onset of hot season or until the tactical situation at Tobruk or Sollum makes necessary the planned withdrawal to Ain el Ghazâl position.

1 May 1941

. . .

Heusinger:

a.   Basic military-political data of an operation against Spain, Portugal.

b.   Movement of GHq. Reserves to be scheduled so that units in west will be drawn upon as late as possible.

c.   Wishes of AGp. North concerning shifting of divisions.

d.   Preparations in the west for SEA LION.

Order to Paulus:

1.   I concur with proposed lines Sîwa-Sollum, but possibilities of line Sîwa-Mersa Matrûh also should be studied. Under no circumstance should Rommel advance beyond Sîwa-Sollum line without order.

2.   Preparation of defense line on the eastern border of Cyrenaica is all right and, if necessary, could be held by skeleton garrison consisting of Italian forces moved up for that purpose. Newly arriving German forces should not be immobilized in this line as long as there is a chance of using them for a new attack on Tobruk, protected by a covering force at Sollum. Use only armor at Sollum.

2 May 1941

. . .

OQu IV: Situation in Spain: Former disinclination of the generals to Spain's entering the war seems to be waning. British pressure must have let up. Monarchist tendencies. —Attaché tour to Rupel Pass. Russians, Turks, and Danes will be included. Return of Japanese commission will not coincide with date of our attack.

Hansen: New disposition of Turkish forces. Large elements in Thrace are being taken back to the Chataldsha line. —Troops in the Straits reinforced. —Reinforcement of garrisons on the western coast not yet confirmed. —Some troop movements from the interior to the southern coast.

. . .

3 May 1941

Morning report indicates:

1. The mopping-up operation in Serbia near Propastica turns out to be a minor matter, which seems to be running itself.

2. Our troops operating from Attica have occupied the island of Skythos.

3. Paulus radios that the Tobruk operation must be regarded terminated, bringing only inconclusive local gains. Troops in bad shape. He has instructed Rommel not to resume the attack unless it offers chances of a quick success without major expenditure of forces, i.e., if the enemy leaves of his own accord. For the rest, pursuant to our directives, he has instructed Rommel to regard the holding of Cyrenaica his primary mission, regardless of whether or not he had Tobruk, Bardia, and Sollum. To this end he was to reinforce the line Gialo-Sollum with mobile forces forthwith, regroup and dispose his troops in depth around Tobruk, and prepare a defense line along the eastern edge of the Djebel (El Ghazâl and southward).

   Whether the arrival of 15th Armored Division will permit resumption of the attack on Tobruk is contingent on developments in the near future.

Talk with ObdH: He approves Paulus's instructions. Telegram is sent to Rommel, confirming Paulus's instructions as an official order of ObdH. Prepare for sending to Libya: Two heavy battalions requisitioned from OKW, five independent battalions, and replacements. —Speed up transfer of trucks from Tunis to Tripoli; send captured British motor vehicles from Greece to Libya.

Wagner (Gen Qu): Query regarding SHARK. Answer: Must be geared to what is available on the spot.

Bordeaux Supply Base for Spain and Portugal. —Projected administrative setup in Greece. —Advance supply bases probably will have to be established at Saloníki and Athens.

. . .

4 May 1941

Reichstag: Serbian Campaign. Tribute to work of General Staff.

OKW directives:

a. Occupy the islands of Chios and Melos before start of MERCURY.

b. Directive on preparations for a military operation on Iberian peninsula in the event of British moves against Portugal and Spain (or Spanish Morocco). Our implementation orders were ready (e.g., Bordeaux Supply Base).

c. Directive on conversations with Finland, Hungary, and Romania.

 For *Finland,* with whom conversations are to start very soon, a program has been drafted, providing for OKW to initiate the talks, which then are carried on by the several branches of the armed forces. OKH's responsibility for talks concerning Finnmarken and southeast Finland is still undefined.

 By the end of May, *Hungary* will be warned of the possibility of a Russian threat and told of our readiness for defense; this will be coupled with the request for getting set to step up her defense measures.

 Romania will be informed only at the last possible moment, and even then we must speak only of defensive warfare.

 It is apparent from various indications that both Horthy and Antonescu had hints of the plans directly from the Fuehrer, which these two gentlemen interpreted as pointing to an imminent German attack on Russia.

Paulus: Remains in Africa in compliance with my teletype message. I am glad he is there to act as a guardian of our ideas, which have also the blessing of the Fuehrer.

5 May 1941

. . .

Colonel Krebs returns from Moscow, where he substituted for Koestring. He found the Russians very conciliatory. Russia will do anything to avoid war and yield on every issue short of making territorial concessions. Russian higher officers' corps decidedly bad (depressing impression). Compared with 1933, picture is strikingly negative. It will take Russia twenty years to reach her old level. Rearmament is in progress. New fighter planes, new long-range bombers apparently concentrated close to German border. Shipments of construction material for fortification are kept rolling to the border. However, there is no evidence of troop concentration.

. . .

6 May 1941

Morning conference: No significant news:

Reports from North Africa indicate that the British fleet air arm has become remarkably active again. The story is that they were short of bombs for a few days.

Beginning 12 May, only X Air Corps, with fifty flights a week, will be available for ferrying troops to Libya. The value of these shipments is in any case problematic, for the troops arrive without any equipment.

Italians want to have the use of Tunis. Memorandum by Guzzoni. They maintain, with the shipping situation being what it is, that they could not hold Libya, let alone prepare an offensive, without that port. It becomes increasingly evident that without Malta we'll never have a safe supply route to North Africa. But the Italians hold that Malta cannot be attacked and so want us to mount a drive on Suez, via Turkey.

. . .

General Mueller, with Judge Advocate General.

    a. Order to troops along lines of last Fuehrer address to the generals. Troops must do their share in the ideological struggle of the Eastern Campaign.

    b. Questions of administration of justice in the army group rear areas.

    c. Easing of rules concerning channels for approving death sentences against army personnel during operations.

7 May 1941

Situation conference:

    a. *Greece:* Greek prisoners are now being discharged. (Difficulties can be expected when the Italians enter the country.) Corinth Canal will not be cleared for another twenty days.

    b. *Libya:*

        1. At last a decent situation map; it shows that Rommel has broken up his units in a wild pattern and conducts a campaign with very scanty forces on a widely extended front which cannot be measured by European standards.

        2. *Tripoli:* Air attack and explosions during the night of 3/4 May caused heavy damage and losses in the port. Unloading capacity of Benghazi considerably reduced, and unloading of ships will be delayed: 24th Convoy cannot be cleared before 9 May; 25th Convoy cannot follow before 10 or 11 May.

        3. Fourth Air Fleet (Greece) now takes over night operations against Tobruk.

    c. *Iraq:* Local clashes with occasional use of arms over wide area; not a war as we know it. May last a long time! Combat action apparently only near Ḥabbānīyah, where Iraq troops have been in the attack. German mission being formed (probably Felmy, von Niedermayer).

    d. *Russia:* Stalin becomes Chairman of Soviet People's Commissars, which means strengthening of his position.

9 May 1941

Situation report:

1. Africa Corps reports loss of 53 officers and 1,187 EM and NCOs in offensive operations at Tobruk. Very high!

2. *Rommel's* distress calls for supplies are getting more urgent.

3. *Abyssinia:* Italian resistance seems to be drawing to a close. British officially still reckon with thirty thousand men.

4. Situation in *Iraq* confused. It would seem even now that the attempted uprising against the British is about to break down.

.   .   .

11 May 1941

.   .   .

1700–1930. Paulus: Report on his 2½ weeks' stay in North Africa. Stopped in Rome and reported to Mussolini.

Situation in North Africa unpleasant. By overstepping his orders, Rommel has brought about a situation for which our present supply capabilities are insufficient. Rommel cannot cope with the situation.

12 May 1941

(The R. Hess affair breaks.)

Morning conference: *Libya:* Sollum reinforced by one armored battalion and one motorcycle rifle battalion. Italian submarine with 79 tons of ammunition en route to Derna, another one being readied.

Italy: Conference Guzzoni–von Rintelen. Transfer of X Air Corps to Greece possible under Italian convoy escort. On the return voyage, the convoy will ferry over 2d Armored Division to Taranto and then complete the transfer of the second half of X Air Corps. Loading of 2d Armored Division for Taranto starts 13 May.

OKW conference, Salzburg (today 1800):

a. Operation MERCURY and its repercussions on BARBAROSSA. We are asked to release for MERCURY: Two mixed and four

> light AAA battalions. We can release them only until 25 May, and at that only for the protection of the jump-off airfields.

b. VIII Air Corps (von Richthofen) has to be transported by rail to Oderberg; now air force wants rail shipment all the way to East Prussia in order to arrive in time for BARBAROSSA. This means that we would need seven more days to complete assembly of troops for BARBAROSSA.

c. Air force has demanded one hundred more materiel trains for the east. That would make another delay of two days. They will have to make up their minds whether or not they want to do MERCURY. The delay for BARBAROSSA resulting from this operation is very awkward. Since 23 May must remain the date for the start of the maximum railroad schedule, the time during which the Russians can react is stretched to six weeks. In that period they could effect drastic changes in the disposition of their forces.

Conference with ObdH: Situation in Libya. —Form a new Hq.: "Commander of German troops in North Africa." Question of head (Kirchheim, von dem Borne, Ehlert).

.   .   .

14 May 1941

.   .   .

Buschenhagen: Reports on operation SILVER FOX. Conversations with Finns have not yet started, because OKW wants to keep all strings in its own hands. Timing is so complex that coordination with the BARBAROSSA schedule appears impossible. The whole undertaking is an expedition, not an operation. —It is a shame to waste the men allocated for this purpose.

.   .   .

Conference with ObdH on results of conference with the Fuehrer:

1. Hess case. Attempted unification of the Germanic races.

2. Fuehrer concurs with OKH measures in Tripolitania.

3. Setup in North Africa is to be revamped by attaching a "German chief of staff" to Gariboldi's Hq.

4. General review of political situation produces nothing substantially new. (Spain, northwest Africa)

5. Continuance of operations in Libya next fall is believed to require four armored divisions and three motorized divisions.

Radke: Press report on Yugoslav Campaign.

Wagner (Gen Qu): Shipping situation in the Mediterranean can be eased by using tonnage available at Marseille.

15 May 1941

Morning conference: Number of strikers at Liège has decreased (only 35,000 as against 50,000). —Naples so crowded with German troops that further inflow must be stopped until outflow runs more smoothly. —One supply vessel for Lemnos torpedoed by the British. —Hq. of the Italian Army Group *Albania* will be deactivated 25 May. Army Hq. 9 takes over command.

OQu IV:

a. A shipment of German ammunition has arrived in Iraq on the Baghdad railroad (Rahn reports). Enthusiastic reception.

b. Two German squadrons in Rhodes ready to take off for Iraq. Advance parties in Syria.

c. Personnel changes in Romania (Chief of General Staff, War Minister).

. . .

Conference with all OKH Section Chiefs: Case *Hess!*

I. Fuehrer's account of events to the ObdH is in agreement with the second, more detailed press communique.

1. The Fuehrer was taken completely by surprise.

2. Facts previously known:

a. Hess's inner conflict growing out of his personal attitude toward England and his grief over the fratricidal struggle between the two Germanic nations.

b. Depression brought on because Fuehrer had barred him from active war service; repeated requests to be sent to the front had been denied.

      c.   Mystical tendencies ("visions," prophecies, etc.).

      d.   His daredevil flying, which had prompted the Fuehrer to bar Hess from any flying.

3.   New facts discovered:

      a.   Since August last year, Hess had a standing order for reports on weather over England.

      b.   Attempt to procure radio direction information through Terboven in Norway (radio traffic).

      c.   Systematic training by Messerschmitt, after Udet had refused.

      d.   Planning of technical preparations for flight (reserve fuel tanks).

4.   Chronology of events:

      a.   Saturday: Fuehrer received package containing documents and put aside, thinking it was some memorandum. Later opened it and found a letter informing him of the plan, and explaining the reasons. Glasgow was given as his destination. Wanted to visit Duke of Hamilton (president of the British Veterans' Association).

      b.   Consultation of Fuehrer with Reich Marshal and Udet to determine if Hess was likely to reach his destination. The result being affirmative, and with the British bound to exploit the incident, a brief communiqué was issued to the press. Von Ribbentrop sent to Rome to inform Il Duce (separate peace offer).

      c.   Meeting called of all government and district leaders and documents relative to the case read to them.

II.   All present are requested to pass on this information and deny all divergent versions.

. . .

17 May 1941

Situation conference: *Libya:* Sollum retaken by Africa Corps, also Sidi Suleiman. One hundred prisoners. On the Tobruk front successful engagements of assault detachments (some prisoners, tanks destroyed, etc.).

Greece: Fuehrer orders occupation of Antikythera. Army Hq. Ia thinks this would compromise surprise. MERCURY probably will be postponed to 20 May.

. . .

19 May 1941

. . .

1500–1730. Conference at ObdH, with von Rundstedt/von Sodenstern, later von Reichenau/Heim, then also von Kleist/Zeitzler, and, finally, von Schobert. Questions relating to assembly of AGp. South. No fundamental difficulties with High Command of army group. Lively arguments with von Reichenau, who at last decides to group the three center corps under von Kleist's command right from the jump-off. Only tentative discussion on dispositions with von Schobert, since we still have not received any political directives on the command setup. (Von Schobert will get his instructions at Obersalzberg on Thursday.) Afterwards short talk with Heim.

Paulus (on phone) about his conversation with Jodl on the command setup in North Africa. All the Fuehrer cares about is that Rommel should not be hampered by any superior Hq. put over him. Jodl will send us another plan.

20 May 1941

(Attack on Crete.)

Morning conference:

1. 0500–0713. Landing on Crete prepared by bombing attack. Subsequent unopposed drop of paratroops and landing of gliders on Chania, Réthimnon, and Iráklion airfields. The "airborne landing" of airborne troops will not come off before tomorrow.

2. First echelon of 2d Armored Division (three ships) has landed at Taranto.

3. Unconfirmed reports that British Second Chief of the General Staff, General Haining, has taken over command in Egypt.

4. Syria: The French on the border are getting set to fight the British.

5. In recognition of the French attitude in the Syrian question, Germany will return eighty thousand prisoners.

6. Maribor Tunnel reopened for traffic. Bridges at Maribor and Belgrade will be reopened by 15 June.

7. Difficulties in fuel supply during July. In August, oil will be delivered to theater of operation directly from Romania, across the Pruth

River. —Italy's needs are filled by OKW at the expense of our own quotas. Gasoline supply for civilian use is bogged down.

. . .

Von Etzdorf: *France:* Cooperation in Syria. —Cooperation in North Africa. —Supply line via Toulon (?!) —Cooperation in West Africa. —North Africa: Use of port of Bône. In return: New regulation of travel into restricted zone (officials, industrialists, farm managers). —Easing of traffic restrictions for demarcation line. —Furloughs for prisoners of war (up to 100,000 at a time). —Occupation costs (prompt negotiations, aiming at reduction from 15 to 12.5 billion francs). Coastal batteries in North Africa. —Improvements of the navy. —Specialists for North Africa.

Plan to tie Turkey closer to us by a pact. Transit to Syria (against Iraq). *Von Papen* protests against his mission.

Japan: Matsuoka warns he will have to take a "zigzag course." American offers to Japan. —Also, status quo for Philippines. Offer of mutual undertaking not to enter European conflict (defense only).

Rome: Visit of our foreign minister: Hess-Darlan-Japan.

Spain: Crisis apparently put off for the moment. Concession to the Falange (two new ministries).

Crete: Dropping of paratroops (two regiments) seems to have been successful, but strong enemy resistance seems to have developed soon afterwards at Chania. Airfields, on which airborne forces were to land, are reported to have been rendered unserviceable.

21 May 1941

Morning reports: In Crete the situation is satisfactory. More paratroops have been dropped. Stubborn British resistance in some places. Report of landing of mountain infantry has not been confirmed. No new information on disposition of British troops in the Middle East. Situation still strained and forces as widely dispersed as ever. Report of British in Iraq advancing on Baghdād (Al Fallūjah) are unfounded.

. . .

Heusinger: Crete: Four mountain battalions have landed in Crete. Two west of Chania, two near Iráklion.

Situation at Chania improved. Town encircled. Contact established between isolated paratroop groups. Attempted sorties repelled.

Air transport hampered in area west of Chania where landing field is unserviceable. The transport planes land on the beach where they cannot take off.

Réthimnon in our hands. No reports received on Iráklion.

British naval forces northeast of Crete have disappeared, west of Crete still on the spot (under attack by our planes).

Shipments by sea will start tonight.

Army Hq. 12 thinks that the show in Crete may drag out quite a while.

During the night a signal indicates that two transport vessels of 2d Armored Division have struck mines in the western end of the Gulf of Corinth.

22 May 1941

Morning conference: Second Armored Division (which sailed from Patras) reported to have lost in sinking: 122 tanks, 200 motor vehicles, 29 motorcycles, 1,328 men.

Crete: Troops landed: *Malenes:* One assault regiment (General Meindl), one paratroop battalion, one mountain infantry battalion.

Chania: Five battalions.
At Malenes and Chania our troops are opposed by six New Zealand battalions and one artillery regiment.

Réthimnon: Town apparently not yet taken; the battalion set down by us may be in trouble by now.

Iráklion: Three paratroop battalions; airfield and town apparently taken.

Libya: Rommel states he cannot take Tobruk with the forces now at his disposal.

France: Has 214,000 tons in the western Mediterranean.

Belgium: Strikes dying down.

Syria: Reported invasion of Syria by de Gaulle troops highly doubtful.

Iraq: Mosul attacked. No British at Al Fallūjah.

Egypt: Attempt to get chief of Egyptian General Staff, who is collaborating with Germany, out of the country. Attitude of Egypt on the whole not friendly to Britain.

. . .

Heusinger: Reports from Greece:

1. The announcement of loss of tanks off Patras has proved erroneous. The tanks of 2d Armored Division have already been landed at Taranto. The losses seem to be largely in light and medium artillery of the division. Very hard to replace because of shortage of prime movers. Personnel losses: Morning figures confirmed.

2. The transfer of the light AAA battalion to operation in Crete was ordered by Army Hq. List and cannot be reversed at the moment. Must try to get replacement for BARBAROSSA from air force.

3. Situation in Crete seems rather complex. The British are in undisputed command of the sea north of Crete and seem to have scattered or sunk a convoy of small craft attempting to make the crossing. Reinforcements for Crete can therefore be sent only by air. It now looks quite doubtful that the air forces committed in Crete would be available for BARBAROSSA at the appointed date. Perhaps it will be necessary to postpone start of BARBAROSSA.

. . .

26 May 1941

Arrive Zossen 0900. Discuss with OQu I and Op. Off. material for conference with the Finns.

0900–1000. General von Tippelskirch calls (30th Division). Bluemke reports (new Chief of Staff, XIV Corps). Meyer-Ricks reports out (off with Iraq Commission).

1130.   Conference with ObdH on Finland.

1230.   Welcome of Finns, headed by Chief of General Staff Heinrich.

Luncheon.

After luncheon, conference with Finnish General Staff:

Along lines of OKW conference: Operational possibilities are discussed. Attack west or east of Lake Ladoga. With appropriate disposition for assembly, they strike east of Lake Ladoga on a six-division front.

Mobilization near border camouflaged, in rest of the country only after passage of German troops for Operation SILVER FOX (16 June).

Hangoe: The Finns must do this by themselves.

Aaland: This is likewise a job for them; at least they must make all preparations on this assumption. (German help needed: Two regiments.)

. . .

27 May 1941

(SS *Bismarck* sunk.)

Situation conference: SS *Bismarck* under heavy attack by superior British naval forces in the Atlantic. Reported to be making only 7 knots (down from normal 30). At noon, British report that *Bismarck* has gone down.

Twenty-seventh Convoy sailed for Libya (coastal artillery).

Thásos and Samothráke turned over to the Bulgarians.

Situation on Crete improved. The western part of the island now cleaned up; eastward advance continues.

OKW insists that original date for BARBAROSSA must stand: no objections on the part of the army, except that AAA might not be ready; two mixed AAA battalions and three light AAA battalions still engaged in Crete. The two mixed battalions were taken out of Army Hq. 11; the three light battalions out of armored divisions.

Air force must make up deficiency!

Air force, however, will have a hard time keeping the date.

Italy will touch bottom of her oil supplies unless oil deliveries can start early in June. Total required: 260,000 tons.

> 100,000 are to be shipped by rail
> 75,000 through Canal of Corinth
> 25,000 from Germany
> 60,000 have yet to be found

. . .

OQu IV:

a. With Chief of Attaché Sec.: Various attaché questions. Hungary, Krappe.

b. French transitional army (memorandum).

c. Negotiations with Darlan: 75 percent of the French materiel frozen in Syria is to go to Iraq: vehicles, port facilities, railroads, roads.

Movement of supplies to Iraq to be handled by French in French ships from Cyprus waters. Training for Iraq under French in Syria. Exchange with us information on British in Middle East.

North Africa: We are getting 1,740 trucks now, 400 more later. French take our supplies to North Africa in their ships and forward them to Libyan border. Bizerte will be available for our use.

French medium guns, including ammunition, for us in North Africa. *West and equatorial Africa:* Dakar available for German naval operations, effective 15 July.

d. Spain: Mobilization requires eight days. March readiness needs twelve-hour warning. —Munition supplies good for one to three months (depends on weapons). Problem with ammunitions. Food sufficient for two months.

e. *Portugal:* Will fight better against the Spanish than against the British.

. . .

28 May 1941

. . .

VIII Air Corps must leave Romania on 7 June, in order to reach Suwałki by 20 June.

Lieutenant Colonel Stieff: Observations made on tour in Greece: Hq. Twelfth Army. —Crete development slower than anticipated by air force. Air force was quite off in assessment of enemy: they expected the British to bolt.

British are in undisputed command of the sea. We are in equally undisputed command of the air.

Mistakes of tactical planning: Troops were set down, in three equal forces, in three places. Lack of reconnaissance of the landing area (olive groves). Landing of planes very difficult (olive groves, mountains).

Sailing of first seaborne echelon was timed too late to begin with, and then postponed once. This robbed us of the element of surprise.

Critical stage was over on 25 May. General Ringel has situation under control. Most urgently needed: Heavy weapons.

British were expecting airborne landing since 26 April and made effective preparations for defense, especially against parachute attacks. This explains our very heavy losses. Combat strength of 7th Air Division down to 3½ battalions, from 9 battalions. Assault regiment lost 50 officers and 1,000 men killed.

Transport considerably depleted. Out of 600 transport planes, 170 unserviceable; mostly total loss.

Losses in Convoy 1 were 500 out of 2,300 (5th Mountain Division, light AAA).

Twelfth Army ventures no estimate of the duration of fighting, as that largely depends on what the British are going to do. During night of 24/25 May, they brought five freighters to Suda, and two freighters to Iráklion; it is not known whether with reinforcements or supplies, or for evacuation.

Twelfth Army thinks it will be necessary to keep elements of 5th Armored Division in Athens for time being. Atmosphere in the city critical. The Italians are not doing anything about it, nor have they started any arrangements for looking after the country.

Also says it must keep six GHq. bridge columns in Greece (for Crete). Wants to leave 164th Division in Saloníki, 6th Mountain Division in Athens, and 5th Mountain Division in Crete.

In order to hold Crete against any British attacks, it is essential to secure domination of the Aegean from the air.

. . .

29 May 1941

Situation conference: *Crete:* Suda Bay cleared. —First tanks landed at Kastelli. —Iráklion airfield not yet mopped up.

Von Rintelen reports: Italian Eleventh Army has twelve divisions ready for occupation of Greece, of which one division, for Attica, and one division, for Peloponnesus, are available at once. Italian crack guard regiment is also assigned to the Peloponnesus.

British attack on Sfax. British air attack on convoy.

Syria: Hansen reports: France is changing her plans from defense of the Lebanon Mountains to defense of the southern border, i.e., defense of the whole of Syria. Strength of French forces: 50,000, mostly colored troops, 40 fighter planes from the homeland, 3 destroyers, 3 submarines. British: 50,000 in Palestine and Trans-Jordan. British are anxious about Cyprus.

Iraq: According to Hansen's report, situation not unfavorable, but no decisive turn for the better yet. Lack of fuel.

. . .

30 May 1941

Morning conference: In *Crete* things are now starting to run smoothly. The British are trying to make a getaway from the south coast. The Greeks are offering capitulation. The Italians have landed in the eastern part of the island. Large take of prisoners and materiel, including a satisfying number of guns.

Twenty-second Division will revert to ground forces after all. Ruling of the Fuehrer.

Iraq: Owing to deficient preparation and the impossibility of sending effective support, the Iraq show, which is more in the nature of a political uprising than a conscious fight for liberation, must eventually die. Whatever the outcome, however, it did force the British to spread themselves critically thin, both during the Crete operation, and at a time when our situation in North Africa was rather precarious.

Transport movements for buildup are proceeding in gratifying manner.

Fuehrer's decision that 22 June date will stand.

. . .

3 June 1941

. . .

OQu IV:

    a. General political situation all over the world.

    b. Joint action by Axis powers against Roosevelt's speech.

   c. Turkey: Since we are no longer interested in arms transit to Iraq, it will probably be possible to conclude a nonaggression pact and a guarantee treaty.

   d. Greece: Pro-German public sentiment is cooling. Reasons: Arrival of Bulgarians and Italians; alleged harshness of German occupation troops; food problem. British agents.

   e. Ireland: German bombs on Dublin.

   f. Russia: Stalin had a conversation with the Finnish envoy, stressing good relations. Offers 20,000 tons of grain.

   g. Italy: After Starace, Sebastiani, Mussolini's party secretary for many years, has been fired also.

. . .

4 June 1941

. . .

Notes by General Halder for the conference with the chiefs of staff on the eastern front.

East:

  I. *General questions on BARBAROSSA.*

 II. Tactical questions: (army chiefs of staff). —ObdH.

   a. *Use of smoke* by water crossings. No organizational problem, but a supply issue. Advanced planning where necessary! Use smoke in open country!

   b. *Employment of gas.* I expect gas and local poisonings. We cannot permit the enemy time to employ gas on any scale. Troops should be psychologically prepared. The use of gas requires seven days with the use of special transport.

   c. Commitment of infantry divisions drawn from armored groups. No concern about war organization or personnel questions. Protection by armor plating.

   d. From *infantry divisions in rear areas*—artillery, engineer, signal troops can be committed!

   e. *Attack points* in wide areas. Fire concentration. Flank protection through echelonning! No surrender mentality! Security secured by depth; leadership issues. Leadership forward.

f. *Russian armor tactics:* Use of tanks in small (counterthrust and counterattack) and in major (new!) operations. AT (possibly also from the rear divisions) forward.

g. *Air defense:* Night march. Troop air defense.

h. *Attack and pursuit at night.* Experiences in Greece. Surprise!

i. Troops take too many vehicles on a battlefield. Strong attack measures. In forward areas echelonning unnecessary. Control of support lines (right-of-way) is the proper approach. Dampen personal considerations.

k. *Overloading the troop vehicles*—Panjes! Depots for deposited articles as in the west.

l. *Transport control.* Curtail countertraffic. Advance thinking—aircraft! No direction through negotiation.

m. *Transport requirements:* Engineers (mines, equipment for expedient bridging). Help from the supply reserves, but they cannot be used constantly.

n. *Field hospitals.* Should remain by their divisions. Request that corps chiefs of staff and divisional operations officers note these points.

Must succeed!

Divisional personnel officers very young. Must improve their self-confidence!

More in afternoon (experiences from southeast).

War games of the troops (corps-division!).

III. Questions for specific army groups for BARBAROSSA.

. . .

General situation review:

Success in southeast will be felt far beyond the Balkans. I use the opportunity to express my particular appreciation to all of the participants—both those in our staff and elsewhere. Fuehrer appreciation as well.

Impressive is the rapid recognition of the German leadership of the suddenly successful situation which exceeded all expectations of the troops, even in difficult terrain; which includes mobile units. The effect on England is clear in France, the Near East and North Africa, and Russia. France's desire for understanding, which is largely motivated by the impact of our success on the soldier Pétain. The representative of this feeling is Darlan (Laval in reserve). Proof of this search for understanding: Syria (weapons, airfields), vehicles, North Africa; after July Dakar. Opposed to small reciprocal understandings. Cooperative spirit has some opposition. Strong counterviews in the army, navy, bureaucracy, and, especially, among professional diplomats.

The struggle of an old Party, legalistic, and soldierly mentality against the reality. France's future position depends on its relationship to Europe's condition as interpreted through Germany. The outcome is not yet clear, but can be interpreted optimistically. A conflict with England is not impossible.

The Wehrmacht is an important political factor, which is capable of defending North Africa if desired by the leadership. The economic situation is difficult albeit better in North Africa (incapable Frenchmen).

In Near East

Iraq has not left us. A sign for unrest against Britain. More political than a military issue. The military issues seem at end (troops removed, commission will be ready soon). Political unrest (Ibn Saud) will remain. Tensions between Britain and France are possible in Syria. (France will be able to hold Syria.)

Turkey has grown weaker because of the decline in Britain's position. Nonaggression pact, guarantee, Edirne peak and island promises. No reason to expect any animosity. England under pressure in eastern Mediterranean. Authority is insufficient and divided. Acknowledge the Italian performance in Abyssinia. Relief for us.

Fragment divisional units in Crete, Tobruk, Egypt. Throw in: Situation of Africa Corps–Tobruk–Sollum–supply situation. —Italian performance and strength. Possibility of other attacks in fall. Crete-Malta! —British control of Mediterranean.

In general: Britain's situation becomes more difficult: impact of submarines and air force. —Battle of the Atlantic.

Industrial performance is not enough; America's help not yet decisive (perhaps 1941/42). Transportation issues. Enough manpower. Britain, other than Iraq (counterattack), is totally on the defensive. Subsequent attack possibilities: Syria doubtful. Cyrenaica provides no operational goal, but is possible should we be occupied elsewhere.

America: Roosevelt's speech. Practical impact of American help is limited. Troops include five infantry divisions, (motorized), two armored divisions, and two marine divisions. Where would they land? (West Africa, Iberian peninsula) Canaries, Cape Verdes, Azores? Fleet commitment in Atlantic because of Pacific risks.

Japan: Basically follows Afro politics. Direction of impact unclear. Inner tensions.

Europe: Norway-Denmark. Holland-Belgium. Italy (economically all right for disaster, morale poor, generally disliked everywhere and the weakest point of the Axis). New rules for the Balkans. Greece (morale!). Russia-Finland. Nothing to say about Hungary, Romania, Bulgaria. Spain and Portugal later.

Decision BARBAROSSA: Influential decision. Based on the need to remove Britain's last hope for continental support and to build a Europe finally without Britain. Once this mission is completed, we will have a free hand, especially with air and naval arms, to bring Britain down finally. Possibly a mission directly against the country (achieved by submarine and aerial campaign). Britain on the periphery as well.

If we remain united and do not achieve rapid, decisive success, it is possible that the tension current in occupied area may increase and allow Britain an intervention opportunity. We must be able to meet this challenge in the northwest, southeast, and in Africa. Norway and western Europe provide no concerns over an English initiative.

In Spain and Portugal an English initiative is possible, but would require extensive preparations. German forces are ready.

Northwest Africa remains a difficult question, especially if Darlan falls and should Japan attack Russia. The important issue is the sudden execution of the BARBAROSSA operation, leaving only the minimal force elsewhere for sudden needs. After BARBAROSSA: Malta-Egypt. Also a possibility from southeast Russia or via Spain–northwest Africa. The basic organizational principles for reorganizing the army for missions after BARBAROSSA are under study.

6 June 1941

Morning conference:

. . .

Navy: In sea battle resulting in the loss of the SS *Bismarck,* the ship was under simultaneous attack by fifty torpedo planes, twelve of which were shot down (great performance!). It appears likely that acoustic torpedoes were used. British apparently have a radar instrument with 35-km range (ours has only 20 km).

Navy: SS *Prinz Eugen* ready to go to sea in eight days. SS *Luetzow* will carry out feints from Norway. SS *Scharnhorst* now completed, will probably leave for the Atlantic through the Channel, under cover of diversionary maneuvers. SS *Hipper* will be ready in July, SS *Gneisenau* in October. *Tirpitz* now on shakedown cruise, will enter service in August.

Romania: Increasing Russian movements along the border. —Communist propaganda.

. . .

7 June 1941

Situation conference:

    a. At *Sollum,* the British seem to be building up a new concentration. Something seems to be up also in the direction of Sidi Suleiman.

    b. We shall not approach Slovakia before middle of June (same as Hungary).

    c. Maximum railroad schedule on net west of Elbe River will be canceled effective 16 June, 0000 hours. Likewise in occupied territory.

    d. One hundred and fifty-five thousand Croat workers will come to Germany (for war industries).

    e. Gen Qu reports supplementary requisitions for 190 trains for period between 17 and 23 June. That again!

. . .

Colonel Kinzel, Heusinger, Hoelter: Kinzel's report on tour to Finland. Conversations with Heinrich. The Finnish High Command has squared its plans with ours, and seems to be going at it with every ounce of energy.

V Corps (Finns), with two divisions, is assigned to the *Kandalaksha* operation. *Aaland* will be handled by one infantry regiment, which is not needed elsewhere. For *Hangoe* they have set out one division.

Assembly of troops:

On border facing Leningrad	4 divs.
North of Lake Ladoga	2 divs.
In central sector	5 to 6 divs.

(operational group for offensive east of Lake Ladoga)

Reserves: Helsinki	1 div.
Turku	1 div.

(would be available for follow-up)

Time requirements: Mobilization and assembly, twelve days, including five days' warning on contemplated direction of attack.

The following *target days* have been fixed:

10 June: Call-up of border guard and 3d battalions of army units.
15 June: Mobilization of V Corps.
20 June: Ready to cross over to Aaland and attack Hangoe.

Full mobilization only after we open hostilities. They can start operations when we have crossed the Dvina.

Finnish General Staff urges attack east of Lake Ladoga.

Colonel Baentsch: Report on inspection at AGp. South. Assignment of mountain regiment, disposition and employment in AGp. South. Points for briefing of Quartermaster staffs in impending tasks.

Keitel OKW (on phone):

    a. *Crete* cannot be made an exclusive air force domain. Question of executive power.

    b. In *Finland,* Army Hq. Norway can only look after its own, and cannot take care of the southeastern operation. An assignment for Erfurth.

    c. Fuehrer's talk with von dem Borne on North Africa. Tactical details.

    d. Keitel's talk with Cavallero. Italy's plans for shipping troops to Africa are too high. What the theater needs are not large masses of troops, but small contingents of crack troops with the best equipment. Africa is a problem of logistics and equipment, not of mass concentrations.

Importance of protecting unloading operations in Benghazi (coastal artillery, escort planes, fighters, AAA).

Increase in Africa Corps' artillery firepower. —Safeguarding of coastal shipping lane and cutting of British supplies to Tobruk.

General Bogatsch:

    a. Presents Rowehl's latest reconnaissance photos. Some gaps left around Kovno.

    b. Timing of long-range reconnaissance. Staffeln must be held back at first: probably will not start operations before second day, in AGp. Center.

. . .

9 June 1941

By air to front. Warsaw (von Hobe), Biała, Brest Litovsk, and Tilsit. Return via Frisches Haff–Danzig–Gdynia.

Conferences with chiefs of staff of XII Corps (von Waldenburg) and XXXXVII Corps (Bamler), and the division General Staff officers. All know their jobs and are in high spirits. Preparations for 22 June completed.

The imposing vastness of the spaces in which our troops are now assembling cannot fail but strike a deep impression. By its very nature it puts an end to the doctrine of defeatism. The division as a self-contained operational unit becomes a dominant factor. All the work of decades, which was undertaken to train the division commanders for independent leadership, must pay dividends here. Artillery support at the jump-off will not be spectacularly strong, but must do. Engineer work and signal communications seem to be well prepared.

10 June 1941

Situation conference: *North Africa:* The British have finished regrouping their forces at Sollum; not yet clear whether for defensive or offensive operations. (Radio intelligence has located one more division Hq. and one more regiment.)

Crete: Command setup still unsettled. On top of all the combat missions which air force must carry through from its Crete base, they insist on having administrative control. (On his own authority, the CG of XI Air Corps has styled himself "Governor.")

Balkans: Transfer of GHq. troops from Saloníki to Eleventh Army is slow. Russians report presence of seven German divisions in Moldavia.

Syria: Minor advances of British. The French view the situation optimistically.

Turkey: Conclusion of pact likely.

Croatia: Reported to be about to join Tripartite Pact (15 June, in Italy).

. . .

OQu IV:

a.   Preparations for intelligence service in BARBAROSSA. All intelligence sources must be cleared through Ic officers.

b.   Preparation for intelligence service in future operations in eastern Mediterranean.

c.   France: Exploit channels for exchange of information on Britain.

d.   Exchange of cables, von Boetticher/Foreign Office.

e.   Conversation Fuehrer-Il Duce. Apparently an exchange of general ideas, without binding commitments. (Switzerland disgusting.)

. . .

12 June 1941

Situation conference:

North Africa: Minor changes in enemy dispositions, furnishing no clues to offensive intentions. Still, an attack need not be ruled out. It may well develop in the coming moon bright nights.

Fifth Light Division, having now been taken out of line, is held in readiness for counterattacking southeast of Tobruk. Will work together with elements of 15th Division, which were also withdrawn.

Syria: Local British advances, mainly along coast; in this sector, Dentz has no means for striking back.

Turkey: Will not intervene in Syria. It looks to them that Dentz has little chance to hold out long. Britain has not to date approached Turkey to take positive action in the fighting in Syria.

. . .

13 June 1941

Situation conference:

Tobruk: Sollum unchanged. Pavia Division has taken over southern front at Tobruk. Fifth Light Division taken out of line.

Romania: Readying of ships for Bessarabia. Dismantling of tracks on railroad bridge. Radio communication with navy.

East: Movements on schedule.

Syria: French reports sound somewhat better now; apparently British advance along the coast and south of Damascus has been checked.

. . .

Conference with ObdH after his return from the east:

a. Overall impression satisfying. Troops in good shape. Operational planning generally well thought through. Open questions. Timing of attack. Some of the corps want dawn instead of 0330.

What to do in the event that enemy attacks before we strike. Proclamation to troops on attack on Russia. Must set forth reasons!

b. Review of the situation created on the Balkans by the new OKW order (with Gen Qu present).

c. Review of general situation.

. . .

14 June 1941

General conference in Fuehrer's Office.

Reports on BARBAROSSA by the commanders army groups, armies, and armored groups.

1100. Von Falkenhorst together with Stumpff (air force) report on SILVER FOX. Northern group, B plus 7; Southern group, plus 9.

1300–1400. Report of CGs armies and armored group of AGp. South. The question of control of *Romanian* army is clarified. Up to the start of offensive operations, Antonescu will formally exercise supreme control in Romania. Army Hq. 11 will be attached to him as his "working staff," and thus will be in actual control, but orders to the Romanian troops must be issued through Antonescu. —In this setup the "Army Mission" will act as liaison staff between Army Hq. 11 and Antonescu. *Hungary* will not be taken into confidence, but merely advised that Hungarian defense measures must take into consideration the mounting strength of Russian forces on her border.

Slovakia will not be informed for the time being. On start of hostilities, their army command will be requested to get their troops ready to move, in order to be able to repel a Russian advance into Slovak territory. (Employment desirable on the Russian border south of Seventeenth Army.)

After luncheon, the Fuehrer delivers a lengthy political address, in which he explains the reasons for his intention to attack Russia and evolves his calculation that Russia's collapse would induce England to give in.

1630–1830. Report on measures in the Baltic (Admiral Schmundt), afterwards AGps. North and Center.

Prolonged debate on the dangers which threaten GHq. from the Białystok salient. Mine fields!

It has now been decided to advance 0-hour from 0330 to 0300.

16 June 1941

Situation report:

a.   Superior British forces, striking far to the south and southwest, have been attacking Sollum since Sunday morning. British throw in 150 to 200 tanks. Enemy has air superiority. Sixty tanks knocked out, also eleven airplanes. Tank battle southwest of Capuzzo. All attacks have been repelled.

British are transferring airplanes to the eastern Mediterranean. Intensified British submarine activity in the Mediterranean (embracing Aegean).

b. Operations area of Russian navy. Russian patrol activity at Hangoe and on the western end of the Gulf of Finland.

c. U.S. navy shifts its main concentration to the Atlantic.

. . .

18 June 1941

Tour by plane and car along northern and eastern border of Romania. Defense positions. In the evening conference in Eleventh Army Hq. At dinner I meet the Romanian war minister.

19 June 1941

Rain during the night causes severe floods which complicate ride to Backau airfield in the morning. Take-off delayed. Flight above clouds (4,000 m) to Budapest, where we are received by General Werth: Luncheon and conference. —By air to Bratislava (conference with General Ott and Military Attaché Becker). —Return flight to Rangsdorf.

20 June 1941

Situation conference:

a. *North Africa:* Defensive success at Sollum. Two enemy tank brigades at least badly crippled (two hundred tanks). X Air Corps transfers the following new units to Africa: one long-range fighter squadron and two dive-bomber squadrons.

b. *East:* Assembly of troops proceeding according to plan. Weather favorable. Rivers partly below normal.

c. Replacement units in Military Districts II and III go to XX and XXI on 23 June, from Protectorate to Military District I on 15 July.

d. Molotov wanted to see the Fuehrer on 18 June.

Heusinger:

a. Fuehrer concerned about area west of Augustów, and about Romania. *Augustów:* use SS and 900th Brigade. Romania: Parts of 5th Armored Division are to be sent over (Fuehrer's wish). Actually only components available are: two-thirds of 13th Rifle Regiment and 2d Battalion/31st Armored Regiment. Movement from Athens to Romania will take eight to nine days. For now they can go to Saloníki (two-three days).

b. *East:* Squabble between AGps. North and Center about jump-off time. Protection of Vistula bridges (AAA). SS "Adolf Hitler" will not be ready in time. Tracked components leave on 22 June, others not before 25 June.

c. *Romania:* New command set-up. Hq. of Romanian Third Army disappears.

d. The 46th and 294th divisions in Belgrade area ready to be shipped. Move 294th Division to Saxony.

e. AGp. South wants 4th Mountain Division. No! May follow up as GHq. Reserve behind Seventeenth Army in its drive on Jarosław.

General Oehquist: Wishes of the Finnish commander.

1. Want to receive request of German High Command to start Ladoga operation at latest possible date.

2. Operation east of Lake Ladoga is the one they want.

3. Seven days' alert notice for start of operation (five days only in an emergency).

4. Finnish High Command wants to have V Corps freed as soon as possible for Operation LADOGA. Other items of information:

    a. Difficult food situation.

    b. Mobilization starts on 18 June. Completed 28 June.

General Bogatsch: AAA protection of Vistula bridges. First use troops available on the spot. Nothing must be taken from the weak AAA of ground forces, at least not in the first days.

Colonel von Ziehlberg: Transfer of GHq. Current General Staff questions.

Conference with ObdH on my travel impressions and on BARBAROSSA. No important new viewpoints.

Fuehrer: In the evening we receive the Fuehrer proclamation to the troops for BARBAROSSA. A long-winded manifesto, surprisingly in a predominant political tenor.

Late in the evening von Ziehlberg still has some reports on personnel matters (Ia, VI Corps).

21 June 1941

Situation conference:

    a. Codeword "Dortmund" has come through.

    b. Materiel position of SS "Adolf Hitler" has improved. Division may yet get ready in time.

    c. Losses at Sollum are on a reasonable scale: total 560 men, with proportion of killed considerably lower than at Tobruk. Number of missing large, but that is probably inevitable in such desert battles.

    d. Hungary has effected certain improvements in her border defenses (AT guns).

    e. The SS destined as security force on border north of the Białystok tip, will go to Arys.

    f. *Syria:* Situation not unfavorable. Attitude of French airmen is becoming increasingly pro-German.

General Brand; General Buhle:

    a. Artillery developments. General Staff comments on development program of Chief of Armament.

    b. Brand reports on his inspection tour: Artillery assembly in the east.

    c. Ratio of combined German and Romanian artillery to Russian is 2.2:2.9.

General Matzky:

    a. *Britain:* Forty-two combat-fit divisions and seven newly activated divisions in the homeland.

    b. Resources for moving British troops to Senegambia.

    c. Time required for shipping one British division by sea: Three weeks (assembly, loading, and unloading) plus voyage.

    d. Rohde team for collection of intelligence in the Middle East installed in Ankara.

    e. Individual army officers on special missions will be subordinate to the military attachés.

f.   Twenty-five Romanian high school graduates will enter the German army as officer candidates.

. . .

Finnish mobilization proclamations reported to have been posted.

THE CAMPAIGN IN RUSSIA

On the eve of the Russian Campaign, Hitler believed in prompt, if difficult, success. For him the assault was the end goal of his entire political life, the destruction of Soviet Russia and the establishment of total German control of the Euro-Asian landmass. His belief that the struggle would bring this long-desired ideological confrontation to its highest level provided an emotional commitment which precluded any other consideration. Victory was a certainty!

His control of minor activities, involvement in daily decisions, and belief in his own talents made Hitler the military leader. General Halder, who had organized the earlier successes, was no longer able to control the Wehrmacht. He had a struggle with his own military concepts, with his colleagues, and, above all, with his superior. While distant from the front lines, Halder had his own combat zone.

The planning for the assault against Russia was complete to the smallest detail, and the units, despite some equipment difficulties created by the Balkan campaigns, were in good condition. The troops believed in their cause and accepted much of the propaganda against the Communist Russians. While Hitler planned for future campaigns after consolidating the eastern victory, Halder and others soberly hoped that their preparations were adequate. No one truly knew the Soviet soldier, Russia's extraordinary distances, or the planning adjustments necessitated by combat action. The following weeks would dictate much of Germany's future.

22 June 1941

The morning reports indicate that all armies (except Eleventh) have started the offensive according to plan. Tactical *surprise* of the enemy has apparently been achieved along the entire line. All bridges across the Bug River, as on the entire river frontier, were undefended and are in our hands intact. That the enemy was taken by surprise is evident from the facts that troops were caught in their quarters, that planes on the airfields were covered up, and that enemy groups faced with the unexpected development at the front inquired at their Hq. in the rear what they should do. More effects of the surprise may be anticipated from the assaults of our armor, which have been ordered in all sectors. The navy reports that the enemy seems to have been taken by surprise also in their zone of action. His reactions to the measures of the last few days were of a purely passive nature, and he now is holding back his naval forces in ports, apparently in fear of mines.

Paulus at 1100: State Secretary von Weizsaecker's appraisal of the situation: Britain will at first feel relieved by the news of our attack on Russia and will rejoice at the "dispersal of our forces." But a rapid advance of German troops will soon bring disillusionment, for the defeat of Russia cannot but lead to a marked strengthening of our position in Europe.

As to Britain's readiness for an accord with us, he has this to say: The propertied classes will strive for a settlement, leaving us a free hand in the east, but it would involve renunciation of our claims to Holland and Belgium. If these tendencies are to prevail, Churchill has to be overthrown, as he relies on the support of the Labor Party, which is not interested in a peace concluded by the propertied classes. Such a peace would bring the propertied interests back into power, whereas the Labor Party wants power for itself. The Labor Party therefore will continue the war until the propertied class is entirely eliminated. Under what conditions it would eventually be willing to come to terms with Germany cannot be predicted. Probably vehement opposition to National Socialism, by reason of strong Jewish influence and Communist connections. For the time being, in any case, the Labor Party will not be disposed to put an end to the war.

In the Far East, an attack by Japan on Britain appears unlikely. Both Japan and the U.S. will endeavor to keep from being drawn into the war. It is in Germany's interest to keep both out of the conflict; otherwise the war, both in duration and resources, would be entirely out of control, and the making of an eventual peace would be infinitely complicated.

Kinzel, Matzky:

a. Russian operational motorized Reserve Group Pskow has been located south of the Dvina River(!), 300 km southwest of the area where it was originally believed to be. That's just right for us!

    b.   Identity of various Russian units confirmed. Russian radio signal: Staff Third Army wiped out, send long-range fighters.

    c.   Situation in Syria is becoming critical. Damascus fallen, British motorized forces advancing on Palmyra from the east.

1200. **Report** that Russians have resumed international radio communications, which were interrupted this morning. They have asked Japan to act as intermediary in the political and economic relations between Russia and Germany, and are in constant radio contact with the German Foreign Office.

Captain Loyke (navy): Reports on war situation at sea. Russians surprisingly passive.

1330. **Op. Sec.:**

    a.   Air force reports 800 enemy aircraft destroyed (First Air Fleet 100, Second Air Fleet 300, Fourth Air Fleet 400). Leningrad sea approaches mined without losses. Own losses so far, 10 aircraft.

    b.   AGp. Center reports wild flight on the Brest Litovsk–Minsk road. Russian command organization in complete confusion.

    c.   AGp. South reports that own patrols have crossed the Prut River between Galatz and Huşi and Jassy without encountering any resistance. Bridges are in our hands.

Afternoon. Reports on advances especially north of Brest Litovsk (Hoth and Armored Group 4—Hoepner).

Italy declares war against Russia.

The *overall picture* of the first day of the offensive is as follows:

The enemy was surprised by the German attack. His forces were not in tactical disposition for defense. The troops in the border zone were widely scattered in their quarters. The frontier itself was for the most part weakly guarded.

As a result of this tactical surprise, enemy resistance directly on the border was weak and disorganized, and we succeeded everywhere in seizing the bridges across the border rivers and in piercing the defense positions (field fortifications) near the frontier.

After the first shock, the enemy has turned to fight. There have been instances of tactical withdrawals and no doubt also disorderly retreats, but there are no indications of an attempted operational disengagement.

Such a possibility can moreover be discounted. Some enemy Hq. have been put out of action; e.g., Białystok and some sectors are deprived of high-echelon control. But quite apart from that, the impact of the shock is such that the Russian High Command could not be expected in the first few days to form a clear enough picture of the situation to make so far-reaching a decision. On top of everything, the command organization is too ponderous to effect swift operational regrouping in reaction to our attack, and so the Russians will have to accept battle in the disposition in which they were deployed.

Our divisions on the entire offensive front have forced back the enemy on an average of 10 to 12 km. This has opened the path for our armor.

In AGp. South, Group Kleist was able to get its northern and central corps moving in the midday hours. If, as seems likely, they reach the Styr River still today, they will have to fight it out with the enemy motorized group east of the Styr tomorrow and the day after. The outcome will be decisive for their operational freedom of movement.

In Agp. Center, the right wing of Armored Group Guderian (3d and 4th Armored divisions) was for a time held up in difficult wooded terrain (which, I believe, could have been avoided) and will start rolling on the Brest-Minsk motor highway toward evening, if all goes well. The northern wing (Lemelsen) has pierced the opposing enemy forces and has gained operational freedom of movement. The two coming days will show in what way Guderian can dispose of the enemy motorized forces round Minsk. Once they are beaten, the operational success of this armored group is assured.

North of Białystok, Armored Group Hoth scored quite a remarkable success. It has pushed through the forest and lake country to the Njemen River. The important crossings near Olita and Merkinė have fallen into our hands intact. Advance elements of eight divisions thrown against it have been scattered, and there is no organized enemy resistance in front of it. Full operational freedom of movement appears to have been achieved in this sector.

In the area of AGp. North, Armored Group Hoepner has battled its way to the Dubissa River and captured two crossings intact. Here the enemy will be able to throw fresh forces against us from his depth in the next few days.

The army groups are pursuing their original objectives. Nor is there any reason for a change. OKH has no occasion to issue any orders.

The time is not ripe yet for a decision on how to employ Eleventh Army. Our assault troops have crossed the Pruth River at various points and have seized the bridges. But there are no signs that the Russians are yielding the area between the Pruth and Dniester.

Slovakia has offered for immediate commitment an armored group in the strength of about a reinforced regiment, to be ready at Prešov by 23, evening. The offered group is accepted and assigned to Seventeenth Army. In addition, two divisions, to be brought up to war strength immediately, will be available by 25 June. They, too, will go to Seventeenth Army.

Hungary, which has stationed two brigades on her border and three armored brigades behind them under VIII Corps Hq., has closed her frontier. On the political side we make no request to Hungary. If the soldiers want to join us, let them prevail on their politicians to do so.

Air force reports 850 enemy airplanes shot down. This number includes entire bomber squadrons, committed without fighter escort, which were taken on and destroyed in the air by our fighters.

23 June 1941

The morning reports of 23 June and the concluding daily reports for 22 June, which came in during the night, indicate that an enemy attempt at disengagement must be expected. AGp. North even believes that the enemy may have made this decision as far back as four days ago.

The assumption that considerable portions of the enemy are farther in the rear than we assumed, and are partly being taken back even now, is corroborated by the fact that our troops, although they had to fight for it, did penetrate the border areas to a depth of as much as 20 km on the first day, and by the absence of any large take of prisoners and the singular absence of any major artillery activity; another indication would be the withdrawal of motorized corps in the direction of Minsk.

In front of AGp. South the enemy also appears to be falling back eastward from the Hungarian border, in order to get his forces out of the pocket. The fact that troops are moving frontward in some places does not argue against these inferences, for these are spots where a rapid advance of German troops would compromise the withdrawal, e.g., opposite Armored Groups Hoth's and Kleist's northern wing, and in the IV Corps sector of Seventeenth Army.

In view of all this, we must adhere to our plan for the operations north of the Pripet marshes, that is, to push the two armored wedges of Guderian and Hoth on Minsk and pinch off the Białystok pocket. Prospects of success are good. If we succeed, the storm into the entire Russian front will be so large and elimination of so many enemy divisions will have changed the balance of strength so greatly in our favor that we shall have full operational freedom.

The situation is more difficult in the sector of AGp. South, because in abandoning the original plan of operation, based on Romania, we have thrown away our best strategic opportunity. We shall have to confine ourselves to probing for the soft spot and then drive an armored wedge through it as hard as we can. At the moment this soft spot seems to present itself on the motor highway in von Kleist's central sector, north of Tarnopol.

1200. **Himer** (on phone): We gratefully accept every kind of Hungarian cooperation, provided it does not strain our road and rail communications with Romania.

1400.   By plane to Elbing, and then by car to new Hq.

Development of situation: In AGp. South, in *Romania,* the Russians are attacking our Pruth bridgeheads and are making reconnaissance forays against the Romanian cavalry from Cernăuți. That's good!

In *Seventeenth Army* sector enemy resistance seems to be slackening in the direction of Lwów. In Sixth Army sector, the faulty development of 13th Armored Division has had the result that 13th and 14th Armored divisions could not start off and are now waiting on the northward highway, until the infantry has cleared the way for them. The greatest advance has been made by 11th Armored Division, after battling it out with enemy tanks. Unfortunately 13th Division is not now behind it. Another division will be moved up, but what a loss of time!

In AGp. Center everything goes according to plan. Hoth has advanced farthest, whereas Guderian is being checked again and again. This occasions a discussion with AGp.B as to whether Hoth should continue his drive on Minsk, or had better strike at once farther north, for Polotsk. As a matter of fact, von Bock, from the start, had objections against a joint operation by the two armored groups in the direction of Smolensk, and wanted Hoth to strike farther north. That, however, would have put an almost impassable strip of water and marshland between Hoth and Guderian, enabling the enemy to beat the groups separately. Such a possibility merits consideration all the more as the Russians are the originators of the idea of quick mass concentration (Budjonny), and inasmuch as some reports of withdrawals would indicate that the Russians might be attempting to concentrate armor far in the rear.

The overall picture is best characterized by the report from Fourth Army: The enemy in the Białystok pocket is not fighting for his life, but to gain time.

I very much doubt that the enemy High Command really has unified and organized control of the situation. It rather looks as if the local withdrawal movements both of the ground forces and of the air force are being carried out under the pressure of our advances, and that it is impossible at this time to speak of a planned withdrawal.

The only exception is perhaps the enemy in front of AGp. North. Here a withdrawal, probably behind the Dvina River, seems in fact to have been prepared long ago. We cannot yet see through the reasons for that. Perhaps the Russians thought we might demand disputed Lithuania and so were preparing to abandon the country to us. In spite of these preparations, the enemy has remained in his positions near the border around Białystok; this can be explained only by the deficient and plodding working of the Russian command machinery.

At the evening situation conference, the question is discussed whether Hoth and Guderian should continue to drive on Vitebsk and Orsha. In any case Hoth's right wing must advance to the high ground around Minsk. If necessary, he must wait there for Guderian. ObdH discusses the situation in these terms with Field Marshal von Bock.

. . . .

24 June 1941

Situation: The final reports for 23 June and today's morning reports confirm the picture we gained so far.

The enemy is making a stand almost everywhere in the border area. Our troops do not fully grasp this because resistance was disorganized and relatively ineffective in consequence of the tactical surprise achieved.

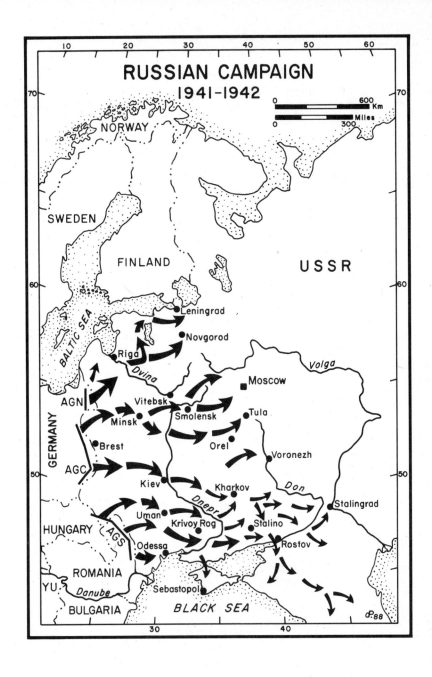

RUSSIAN CAMPAIGN
1941–1942

In the country traversed by our tanks there are still substantial active enemy forces broken up in smaller groups. The number of prisoners, which on the first day ran to about two thousand in every army sector (i.e., a total of about 10,000), will only increase in the next few days, when the drives of our armored wedges will have taken full operational effect. There are no signs of an operational withdrawal of the enemy. Only in the north an attempt is being noted to take back forces; this may be done with a view to building up a Russian Dvina front, which might compel us to move Hoepner's armored group nearer to Hoth, so as to cross the Dvina in its upper reaches.

The supply situation is taking a normal development. The first advance supply points are being moved forward. Fuel and oil consumption very high. Expenditure of ammunition low. Losses in wounded and killed are moderate. Remarkably high officer casualties.

.　.　.

Fellgiebel: Digest of radio intelligence: The operational reserve groups surmised north of Schaulen, around Minsk and around Shepetovka, far from moving eastward, are even shifting forces to the battlefront. Only isolated front corps opposite AGp. Center are being taken back in small bounds.

Gercke: Change of gauge of railroad track east of the frontier has been started, as planned.

1530.　ObdH returns from the Fuehrer:

　　a.　Fuehrer is worried that our ring around Białystok is not close enough.

　　b.　The Italians, who will send one corps to Romania, must in no case be allowed in the Crimea.

　　c.　Spaniards (Spanish Legion). Nothing definite yet about activation and arrival, but it will be best to equip them with arms ourselves.

Lieutenant Colonel Kahlden, Liaison Officer to Hoth's Corps, reports.

Noon. Vilna, Kovno, Kedainiai taken. Interesting historical coincidence that Napoleon also took Vilna on 24 June.

The picture in the course of the afternoon is as follows:

AGp. South is advancing against counterattacks, especially strong in IV Corps sector, north of Lwów. Very heavy enemy casualties. New heavy enemy tank! The right wing of Seventeenth Army has reached its objective, the high ground of Mosciska. Armored Group Kleist now has four armored divisions in line and has reached the Styr River. The enemy throws into the battle all reserves available in the rear, so that there is a chance that we might smash the entire enemy force in the Ukraine in the battles of the next few days. The stubborn resistance of individual Russian units is remarkable. Bunker crews have blown themselves up in their bunkers, rather than surrender.

In the sector of AGp. Center, closing of the ring east of Białystok, in the Minsk area, is nearing completion. Hoth, who against von Bock's opposition has been ordered by OKH to strike through Mołodeczno toward the high ground north of Minsk, is only 30 km from Minsk. He now stands in the rear of the last enemy reserve group which was thrown from Minsk toward Baranovichi against Guderian's advancing armored group. This force, supported by reinforcements brought westward through Slutsk, has engaged him in the Slonim area. If Guderian makes headway in the direction of Baranovichi, in the next few days the ring will be completely sealed. Air force must prevent any eastward retreat of the forces coming from Slutsk.

In the further development of the battle, Fourth Army must advance its left wing corps toward Volkovysk, and Ninth Army its right wing corps (XX) toward Lunno, in order to form an inner ring of infantry around Białystok; this ring must be made as tight as possible by moving up additional infantry from the west.

The time necessary to complete this will be utilized to allow the components of Guderian's and Hoth's armored groups to close up on the high ground around Minsk. Meanwhile strong advance combat teams can secure the crossings on the Upper Dnieper at Mogilev and Orsha, and on the Upper Dvina, at Vitebsk and Polotsk. Continuation of the offensive by the combined armored groups toward the high ground northwest of Smolensk only after consultation with OKH.

Army Group North has to fight off strong enemy tank attacks along almost its entire front; the only exception is the sector of 291st Division, which is advancing on Libau. These attacks are probably maintained by III Russian Armored Corps, originally in the area, and by several motorized-mechanized brigades. Nevertheless, the strong right wing of army group has forged ahead to Vilkovo. Here, too, the Russians are fighting stubbornly and doggedly.

Generally speaking, it is now clear that the Russians are not thinking of withdrawal, but are throwing in everything they have to stem the German invasion. Throughout this effort, the High Command seems to remain entirely in the background. The reasons are not clear, but the absence of any large-scale operational reserves probably precludes its effective intervention. That the Russians had adapted their plans to an all-out defensive near the border is also demonstrated by the large quantities of stores which were to be the logistical basis of the plan.

As to the previously known operational reserves, we have as yet no clear idea of the whereabouts of Armored Group Pskow, which is reported to have been moved forward to the area between Schaulen and the Dvina River, but apparently has not as yet been committed against AGp. North. Such a policy would be in keeping with Russian tactics, always to keep back some forces against the possibility of the breakdown of the enemy attack.

The course of the entire battle evolves gratifyingly according to plan. A new feature in the sectors of AGp. South and AGp. North is the new heavy Russian tanks, reported to be armed with 8-cm guns and, according to another, but untrustworthy, observation from AGp. North, even 15-cm guns.

The enemy air force is completely out of the picture after the very high initial losses (reports speak of two thousand).

After the evening conference with ObdH, the following orders are issued:

 a. Eleventh Army must get ready to attack (time needed: five days).

 b. The 900th Brigade is made available to AGp. Center to complete the ring circling Białystok.

 c. Liaison Staff North receives instructions that Finland must make all preparations for starting offensive east of Lake Ladoga. The operation must be on a front of at least six divisions, with main weight on left wing and objectives deep in enemy territory.

Prolonged discussion as to the most efficient command setup for continuance of operations by AGp. Center. Should Armored Groups 2 and 3, which probably can no longer be controlled by army group Hq., be placed under command of Fourth Army Hq.? Second Army Hq. then would take charge of the investment of Białystok. Or should Guderian assume command of all armored operations? —Talk with OQu I and Gen Qu.

I believe it would be impossible for Fourth Army Hq. to direct the offensive of Fourth Army and at the same time conduct the operations to reduce Białystok. Since von Bock cannot get through to Minsk on his signal communications, the best plan would be for von Kluge, as he once did in the west, to take over control (in addition to infantry, i.e., the two corps on the right wing of his army) of the two armored groups together with responsibility for their supply. It might be desirable to leave Supply Officer Fourth Army at Białystok, under control of Second Army Hq., which will be in charge there, and reassign Supply Officer Second Army to Fourth Army instead. I object to putting Guderian in command of the combined armored groups.

Sweden will raise no difficulties about transit of 163d Division through Swedish territory. Entraining at Oslo may start on 25 June, evening. Authorization will also be given for our planes to fly across Sweden. Russian planes will be fired at.

25 June 1941

Review of the situation in the morning generally confirms the impression that the Russians have accepted the great border battle and are taking back only those positions of the front which are being pushed back under the enormous impact of our attack.

This, for instance, is the case in the sector of *AGp. North*. It is hard to tell whether I Armored Corps (Pskov), which in the last few days was moved across the Dvina River to the area south of Riga, has been committed against von Leeb's northern flank, in its entirety or only in part. Certain is that III Armored Corps, which had been in this area from the start, has been beaten by Reinhardt's Armored Corps! and that von Manstein's armored corps has advanced so far to the east that the Russians have been compelled to take their forces behind the Dvina. They are trying to do this by striking at us with their armor, and meanwhile run a large transport movement from the north to the far bank of the Dvina, between Riga and Jakobstadt.

On the front of AGp. Center, inevitable critical situations develop, which are the normal accompaniment of any turning movement preparatory to a battle with inverted front. The Russians are making strong, if uncoordinated, attempts to gain elbow room by attacking in the direction of Grodno in the north, and on the front of Fourth Army in the south, and so check the sweep of our eastward drive. These attempts have failed everywhere, despite an occasional critical situation in VIII Corps, whose western wing is being attacked also by strong Russian cavalry. But it is necessary to supplement the pressure by Fourth Army, from the south toward Volkovysk, by corresponding counterpressure by Ninth Army, from the north, in order to form an inner encircling ring of infantry corps south of the confluence of Szczara-Njemen rivers, while Guderian's and Hoth's armored groups form an outer ring by linking up at Minsk. This will keep the enemy bottled up in the Białystok pocket and prevent repetition of what happened on the Bzura in the Polish Campaign, that is, his pressing eastward (toward Novogrudok), which would delay and hamper liquidation of the pocket.

The attempts of the encircled enemy to fight his way back to Minsk through Slonim have resulted in local crises at Slonim (17th Armored Division).

In the sector of AGp. South, the enemy is bringing new forces toward Kovel from the east by rail and toward Rovno, by motorized movements. West of Rovno, 13th and 14th Armored Divisions are still in aggressive action to force their way to the Styr River. On reserved roads in the central sector, 11th Armored Division, which is now followed by 16th, has got as far as Dubno across the Styr. Against this division, the enemy already yesterday brought infantry on a broad front from the south. It seems that he is moving new forces also from south and west against von Priesen's corps, and IV Corps, which now is slowly gaining ground toward the east after heavy fighting. The purpose apparently is to absorb the beaten elements and build up a new front— perhaps on the line Sambor-Lwów-Dubno. It is worth noticing that High Command of this front has moved Hq. up front, to Tarnopol.

Morning conference with ObdH shows full agreement of views. AGp. Center must be instructed to go out to meet right wing of Fourth Army (VIII Corps), so as to form an inner encircling ring.

Conference ObdH with Fuehrer: Fuehrer is now less worried about the eastern closing line of the Białystok pocket.

. . .

1800. General von Greiffenberg (Chief of Staff, AGp. Center) reports on the execution of my order given to von Tresckow. Twenty-eighth and 161st divisions will be turned southward in the direction ordered, to close the ring around Białystok. Correspondingly, V and VI Corps of Ninth Army will move to the right, against the line Lida-Vilna. In order to prevent a gap to AGp. North, 900th Brigade will move to the left wing near Vilna. This meets our specifications. It is characteristic that Field Marshal von Bock expressly demands a written order, and he does not agree with us. (He does not want to do anything about the pocket forming to the south, and would rather press on to the east.)

OQu IV reports on the Fuehrer's letter to Il Duce of 21 June, immediately before the start of BARBAROSSA. Noteworthy points in that string of disjointed ideas.

Attack on Russia explained on grounds of Russian troop dispositions. Lessons drawn from Crete operation: In attacking an island, air strength must be employed to the last plane.

War against Russia is aimed at England.

Syria will not be able to hold out long.

Attitude of France doubtful. Italy is requested rather bluntly to keep herself ready against France.

Egypt cannot be attacked before next fall. In that undertaking, Italy must be prepared to safeguard her western border in North Africa and if necessary also launch an attack in westward direction. Stepping up of submarine warfare in the Mediterranean is demanded.

Evening situation:

Russian strength on front of Eleventh Army is estimated at eleven or twelve divisions. —Eleventh Army can be ready to attack on 2 July. Air raids on Constanza are becoming heavier. —German fighter squadrons have been brought in for protection of the oil fields. —Brăila and Galatz also were attacked by Russian planes.

AGp. South: The battle has not yet reached full strength; it will be a few more days. Von Kleist has taken Dubno after hard fighting. Tank battle west of Łuck still going on. Troop movements from the east through Kovel and Rovno, also movements to the front at Tarnopol and points west. Slovak divisions (corps Hq. and two divisions) ready around Prešov on 28 and 29 June for assignment to AGp. South. Hungary's cooperation would be desirable, but Hungary wants us to extend an official request. That the Fuehrer does not want to do for political reasons.

AGp. Center: Situation at Slonim has been resolved. Action by 29th Division has freed 17th Armored Division at Slonim for operations toward Minsk. Third Armored Division has started drive on Slutsk. Eighteenth Armored Division, with parts of 3rd, has taken Baranovichi. Situation south of Grodno stabilized. Attack repulsed. Hoth has taken Volozhin and thus gained a foothold on the hill mass of Minsk.

AGp. North: In various sectors of the front, local encirclement of strong enemy elements reported. Orderly movement at good pace in the planned direction. Hoepner continues northeastward through Vilkovo.

In the evening an *order is issued to AGp. Center* on sealing the Białystok pocket and on preparations for the new command setup. By this order Hq. Second Army (with OQu IV) will take over command of the encircling forces. Von Kluge will assume control of the components of Fourth Army, which are not needed for this job, viz., Armored Groups 2 and 3 (together with OQu II, who is directly briefed by Gen Qu on building up an intermediate supply base around Minsk).

Later in the evening we receive a Fuehrer order on direction of operations of AGps. Center and South. It betrays concern that we are operating too far in depth. The old refrain!

But that is not going to change anything in our plans.

26 June 1941

The closing situation on 25 June and the morning reports of 26 June show:

AGp. South is advancing slowly, unfortunately with considerable losses. The enemy on this front has energetic leadership. He is continuously throwing new forces against the tank wedge, attacking frontally, as before, and now also the southern flank, and, on the railroad to Kovel, apparently also the northern flank. The latter attack will hardly develop to anything serious, but the southern flank at present is still vulnerable because we do not have sufficient forces available to give adequate infantry protection (the conveyor-belt system would be necessary here), and also because Armored Corps von Wietersheim, which is still far in the rear, cannot get to the front at the moment because the bad roads are crowded with vital supply traffic. It will be the overriding task of OKH to maintain a steady flow of reinforcements behind AGp. South.

AGp. Center: Development just as desired. Situation at Slonim cleared up. Guderian now is in a position to continue the attack with his right wing on Bobruysk, through Slutsk, and with the bulk of his forces through Baranovichi. Hoth, with three armored divisions in front, is making good progress toward Minsk, so that the ring in this area probably will soon be closed and concentration of a strong armored force for the thrust on Smolensk would appear assured.

The inner ring is closing according to plan. It seems that we might not be able to close it around Piaski, through Volkovysk, and would have to include the area around Novogrudok. For it is in that direction that enemy elements threatened with encirclement apparently are still trying to escape. Behind them, however, Hoth has already advanced toward Minsk, so that there is no danger of their escape. Nevertheless, it would be desirable to eliminate these forces with infantry divisions alone, without having to call on Hoth's armored group.

AGp. North is advancing eastward according to plan, encircling enemy elements in its path. The reported rail movement to Jakobstadt (through Riga) seems to be without any special significance.

A very large retrograde rail movement from Schaulen to Riga is new evidence that the Russians are swinging back their entire northern wing.

General Fellgiebel reports that signal communications to Minsk, through Kovno and through Baranovichi, could be set up in three days. This would make it possible for Hq. AGp. Center to follow the eastward-moving front.

General Bogatsch: Detailed air observations. Our reconnaissance organizations keep close to the front. Sporadic attacks on our airfields. —Distribution of AAA conforms with situation. —Reconnaissance missions for OKH squadron.

. . .

1415. **Report AGp. North:** Monitored radio signal from 8th Armored Division: Dvinsk taken after hard fighting.
From *Armored Group 3,* through liaison officer: Increasing enemy pressure on southern flank impedes advance.
Armored Group 2 has taken Slutsk.

1815. **Confirmed report passed on to Fuehrer:** Eighth Armored Division penetrated into Dvinsk at 0800, occupied town at 1250 after hard street fighting (railroad bridge and vehicular bridge).

The evening reports indicate no important new developments.

In the sector of *AGp. South,* the expected attack of strong tank forces against the southern flank of Armored Group 1 has started. Local enemy successes, but apparently no crisis. Armored Group 1 is under direct tactical control of army group. By moving 13th Armored Division behind 11th Armored Division, armored group has shifted its main concentration to the right shoulder. Moving armored divisions to the southern flank from the rear has been initiated.

In AGp. Center, the attempts of the enemy to escape from the Białystok pocket to the northeast or east are now becoming strongly felt, as are those in the direction of Armored Group Hoth's right flank. It will be necessary not only to push east with elements of Guderian's right wing (3rd Armored Division), which now has reached Slutsk, but also to send other elements (4th Armored Division) northward into the area between Baranovichi and Minsk in order to seal this last gap through which encircled enemy elements are escaping, and simultaneously to crack the Minsk barrier. Orders to this effect to AGp. Center.

In the sector of *AGp. Center,* extensive rail and road evacuations from Minsk and Vileyka toward the east and northeast. Evidently strong motorized elements are being taken back in order to build up a motorized group in the area west of Moscow.

In the sector of *AGp. North,* the enemy is falling back behind the Dvina River. Strong wedged-in enemy elements are causing our infantry divisions a lot of trouble, even far behind the front.

For the first time our radio intelligence picture shows Moscow functioning as the operational High Command.

Finland has been attacked by Russian air forces (ten ports and airdromes). She considers herself in a state of war with Russia.

Hungary has been attacked by the Russians from the air in the vicinity of the frontier. An official declaration of war is not intended, only retaliation for the air attack.

Croatia has made known her desire to participate with military forces in the war against Russia.

Romania: Russians have made a local thrust and started construction of a bridge across the northern arm of the Danube delta. Our fighters attack Odessa, inflicting heavy losses.

27 June 1941

Daily reports of 26 June and morning reports of 27 June present the following great picture:

In the sector of *AGp. South,* von Kleist has not only repelled all enemy thrusts against his southern flank, but his right wing has even gained ground toward the southeast. The front has moved a little eastward and, with its three armored divisions, is now strong enough to warrant expectation of major advances soon.

The Russian formations thrown against the southern flank have apparently been scraped together pell-mell. The Zhitomir Group probably has been committed against von Kleist's front, the Russian Armored Group Cernăuţi against his southern flank. The Russiam Armored Tiraspol, transferred from southern Bessarabia some days ago, is being moved northwest by rail and probably will soon turn up in front of von Kleist's right shoulder, to be thrown into the battle as a last resort. After that we shall have smashed everything that can be brought to bear against AGp. South by the Russian command in the Ukraine (which, one must admit, is doing a pretty good job), and we shall then be free to swing to the south in order to force the enemy still holding around Lwów and on the Hungarian border to a battle with inverted front. This probably will come about at the time when the Romanian assault army will just be ready to come out to meet us.

In the sector of *AGp. Center,* everything is going as anticipated. The Białystok enemy is moving more and more to the east. Our western front slowly follows him. Concentrations in the Novogrudok area, whose presence is now becoming more strongly felt, are pressing on Hoth's right flank and make it necessary for elements of V Corps (Ninth Army) to turn south, since enemy forces have also appeared north of the Njemen River. Fifth Division, thus detached from V Corps, will be replaced by 161st Division. VI Corps is being moved to the front well to the south of Vilna, and in its place 900th Brigade is thrown against Vilna in order to safeguard the gradually widening gap to AGp. North.

AGp. North is moving strong armor to Dvinsk and pushes Reinhardt's armored corps on Jakobstadt. The left wing of the infantry corps is advancing on Riga. Thus, everything is proceeding according to plan. The penetration at Dvinsk has set off heavy panic movements on the enemy side. The impression is that strong forces are streaming east away from the Dvina.

On the whole, therefore, the picture is satisfactory in AGp. South, as also in AGp. Center, though by now it is high time for 2d Armored Group to make headway on Minsk. In AGp. North the situation is very satisfactory.

At the morning conference, ObdH shows irritation because various movements in the army group sectors did not come off as agreed upon yesterday between ObdH and the commanders of South and Center. This is the natural consequence of interference in the command of army groups and armies. Back here we cannot have a clearly detailed picture and so should confine ourselves to assigning broad missions and not try to direct the movements of individual corps or even divisions. At the front, under the pressure of events, road conditions, etc., things take a different turn, and the result is the erroneous impression that OKH orders are being ignored.

OKH air reconnaissance effort is employed over the strategic triangle Orsha-Vitebsk-Smolensk in order to ascertain whether the enemy elements streaming back from Minsk and Polotsk are being formed into a new operational group between Minsk and Moscow. The plan may exist, but the capabilities for carrying it out appear to me slight.

Colonel Ochsner:

  a. Report on the effectiveness of the rocket launchers in the assault on Brest Litovsk. Apparently very satisfactory.

  b. Review of potentialities of bacteriological warfare against Britain (foot-and-mouth disease) and by Britain against us (cattle plague).

General Himer (on phone, 1245): Hungary has announced on the radio that she is in a state of war with Russia. The Hungarian General Staff knows nothing of a state of war.

Two days ago the political authorities inquired at the German Foreign Office whether Hungary's participation was required. The reply of the Foreign Office is still outstanding. It is not believed that the military authorities could readily comply with OKW and OKH's proposal that Hungary come in on her own accord. The Hungarian General Staff has assembled the Mobile Corps (two motorized brigades and one cavalry brigade) in the neighborhood of Marmoros-Szeged and is standing by for employment on the right wing of the Hungarian Carpathian front. I tell Himer that the Carpathian Mountains cannot be forced by armor alone. To accomplish this it would be necessary to attack along the entire front. We would welcome a Hungarian thrust toward Kolomea-Stanisławów. I tell him to discuss these possibilities with Laszlo.

. . .

1400. Keitel (OKW) on phone: Fuehrer wants to throw the whole weight of Armored Group Hoepner on Dvinsk. Possibilities of a crossing at Jakobstadt problematic.

As soon as there is a chance, Jakobstadt to be opened for the infantry corps from the rear by a raid on the northern bank.

Hoepner's armored troops, massing for thrust on Dvinsk, are at the earliest to push through to Ostrov from the east bank of the Dvina, safeguarding the flank toward Jakobstadt, in order to prevent escape of the Russian forces in the Baltic area to the country south of Lake Peipus.

1420. **Phone talk on this subject with ObdH** (who is at Hq. AGp. North): He tells me that only 36th Motorized Division is being sent against Jakobstadt, while the bulk of Hoepner's armored forces is striking for Dvinsk.

. . .

Evening reports indicate crumbling of enemy resistance in front of AGp. South and distinct withdrawal movements in front of the Seventeenth Army. Accordingly, at noon, commander of AGp. South ordered Seventeenth Army to attack forthwith in pursuit of the retreating enemy. Seventeenth Army has ordered main pursuit effort in direction Złoczew.
Armored Group 1 has ordered penetration beyond the Horyń River, without regard to flank and rear security.

In the sector of AGp. Center, the operation continues to develop according to plan. The enemy has abandoned Białystok. As a result, the western end of the pocket is getting narrower and the enemy is trying to fight his way out to the northeast and southeast in the Novogrudok and Roszna areas. Apart from creating local tensions, these attempts are fruitless.

AGp. North is reinforcing and expanding the Dvinsk bridgehead and continues to press on to the Dvina River with Sixteenth and Eighteenth armies.

28 June 1941

Daily reports of 27 June and morning reports of 28 June in the main only verify the reports received yesterday.

In the sector of *AGp. South,* the impression is gained that the strong local efforts of the enemy are only attempts at extricating himself, and not an operational or even strategic disengagement. A singular feature is a railroad movement from Zhitomir toward Kiev, for which we have no reasonable explanation.

In the sector of *AGp. Center,* the inner ring is now closing east of Białystok; in the Białystok forest, southeast of the town, there is violent fighting which quite unexpectedly has engaged the entire central portion and parts of the right wing of Fourth Army.

The outer ring, formed by the armored groups, is strained to breaking point north of Novogrodek (Hoth); between Minsk and Baranovichi it is still not closed. Fourth Armored Division is now advancing from the area of Slutzk on Minsk to close this gap.

The movements of *AGp. North* continue to develop according to plan. In front of the right wing of Busch's Sixteenth Army, an enemy group of several divisions is still fighting; let us hope it will be cut off soon, before it manages to get across the Dvina. With Armored Group Hoepner far in their rear, and newly arrived GHq. Reserves being moved up behind the left wing of Strauss's army, to the south, there is a chance that this enemy group, too, will be liquidated while still west of the Dvina.

1100.   Field Marshal von Leeb (on phone): AGp. North has arranged with AGp. Center that it, instead of Center, will move Hq. L Corps to the area north of Vilna, where it would remain at disposal of OKH. It also wants to place 206th and 86th, instead of 253d and 206th divisions, under this corps Hq. Such a change makes no difference to OKH, and proposal is approved.

. . .

Evening reports confirm the withdrawal of the enemy forces opposing *AGp. South.* For the past two days uncoordinated motorized movements have been running from southeast and east to the rear of the slowly crumbling front. Apparently the enemy is making an effort to organize resistance in the previously known fortified line Novograd Volynskiy–Proskurov–Dniester. But in taking back his forces to that line, he is consuming much of his strength in counterattacks.

Seventeenth Army is at the gates of Lwów.

Von Kleist has taken Rovno.

In the sector of *AGp. Center,* the desperate attempts of the enemy to break out from the Volkovysk and Novogrodek pockets cause many tight situations, which necessitate, e.g., in Fourth Army sector, a north-ward thrust of XII Corps, in Ninth Army, a southward thrust of V Corps. But these tensions will be overcome. The gap between Guderian's and Hoth's armored groups is still not entirely closed, but Guderian has arrived with his right wing at Bobruysk, and has perhaps still a chance to strike quickly across the Dnieper at Mogilev or Rogachev. That would be a decisive success.

AGp. North reports Dvinsk bridgehead expanded, and Jakobstadt taken by left wing of Armored Group Hoepner. The Dvina bridge at that town, however, has been blown up by the enemy. AGp. North has trouble with the many scattered enemy groups roaming the forests, some of them still with their tanks, which burn and loot villages. Application of effective countermeasures is frustrated by the expanse of the country and the limitation of our manpower resources. Libau has been taken. Motorized movements are reported from the Lower Dvina to Leningrad, the purpose of which is unclear.

What strikes one in all these battles is the singularly small number of prisoners compared with the large booty (including fuel), e.g., 35,000 prisoners along with 1,300 tanks.

29 June 1941

Summary of the daily reports for 28 June and the morning reports for 29 June:

Army Gp. South reports still heavy fighting. On the right shoulder of Armored Group 1, behind the sector of 11th Armored Division, a deep penetration by Russian Eighth Armored Corps in our lines apparently has caused a lot of confusion in the area between Brody and Dubno and temporarily threatens Dubno from the southwest. This would have been very undesirable in view of the large dumps at Dubno. Also in battle zone of Armored Group 1, enemy elements with tanks are still active behind the front, sometimes even covering large distances.

We must continually keep our minds on what must be done to arrive in time at a practical disposition for the operations of AGp. South. The present disposition is not particularly adapted to the impending tasks. In the next moves, the main objective of army group must be to break through the Russian rear position on the line Belokorovichi–Novograd Volynskiy–Mogilev Podolsk–mouth of the Dniester without engaging in major frontal attacks, and then swing south still west of the Dnieper. Two points are suitable for a breakthrough. One, in the north, where the main effort should be made, is between Novograd

Volynskiy and Zhitomir. The other, farther to the south, which can be tackled with a smaller force, though it must be strong enough to effect a breakthrough, is in direction of Starokonstantinov, where there seems to be a gap in the fortified line. If we succeed in punching through here, the northern assault wing can swing south on this pivot with cover against Kiev and the north.

AGp. South must now regroup its forces to break through the Russian rear position, which we must anticipate the Russians will be able to reach and man with the frontally retreating front armies as well as with reserves, which they can move up on a fairly undisturbed railroad network. For this breakthrough, Armored Group 1 must be furnished with infantry (which apparently was deliberately excluded when Armored Group 1 and Sixth Army were split off from each other). Also, Seventeenth Army will have to dispose its forces in greater depth and will transfer some of its divisions to Sixth Army and Armored Group 1 in order to give sufficient strength to the right wing, which will be open to attack from the north, i.e., for the eastern part of Polesia, after it has passed through the Rovno area. Additionally, artillery and engineer and signal troops must be placed suitably to fit into the new plan for the assault on the Russian rear position. Op. Sec. has been instructed to discuss these plans with army group.

In *AGp. Center,* the situation continues to develop as anticipated. The Fuehrer's worry that the armored forces would overreach themselves in the advance has unfortunately prompted ObdH at a conference with AGp. Center to refer to Bobruysk as nothing more important than the objective in a flank cover. Guderian, however, quite soundly from the operational point of view, is advancing on Bobruysk with two armored divisions and is reconnoitering in the direction of the Dnieper; he certainly does that not just to cover the flank, but indeed in order to cross the Dnieper as soon as there is an opportunity to do so. Were he not to do that, he would be making a grave mistake. I hope that he will take the Dnieper bridges at Rogachev and Mogilev still today, which would open for him the road to Smolensk and from there the country to Moscow. This is the only way right off to get around the dry gap between the Dnieper and the Dvina, now fortified by the Russians, and so block the way to Moscow for the enemy forces in the gap. Let us hope that CGs of corps and armies will do the right thing even without express orders, which we are not allowed to issue because of the Fuehrer's instruction to ObdH.

AGp. North by now should be strong enough at Dvinsk to push ahead on Ostrov, perhaps also facilitate construction of a bridge at Jakobstadt by a raid in that direction. The withdrawal movements by rail and road, which are reported to be rolling day and night from Riga toward Leningrad, are probably for the most part evacuations. It seems the Russian High Command is abandoning Lithuania, perhaps also the other Baltic states. Radio intelligence reports transfer of the high Hq. to the rear.

Bogatsch: Air reconnaissance furnishes no important new information, mainly because of bad weather. Trench digging at Orsha-Vitebsk.

Talk with Keitel (OKW) (on phone) again indicates that the Fuehrer is worried:

    a. About the tight situation of Armored Group 1 south of Dubno.

    b. About the threat from the Pripet marshes.

    c. About the possibility that AGp. Center might strike too early beyond the line Minsk-Bobruysk, before the "pocket" is completely liquidated. I give him reassurance on all these points.

Reports from all fronts confirm previous indications that the Russians are fighting to the last man. Sometimes treacherous methods are used, especially where Mongolians are among the troops (Sixth Army, Ninth Army). A singular note is that as a rule only very few soldiers are taken with captured batteries, etc. Some let themselves be killed, while others run away, get rid of their uniforms, and try to make their way back as "peasants." Morale of our troops everywhere is described as very good, also where they had to go through hard fighting. Horses very tired.

General Ott reports in particular on his impression on the battlefield of Grodno. Now, for once, our troops are compelled, by the stubborn Russian resistance, to fight according to their combat manuals. In Poland and in the west they could take liberties, but here they cannot get away with them. Enemy air effort against our troops appears to be on a very minor scale.

1700. Keitel (OKW) informs me that a group of long-range fighters will strike today in front of AGp. South.

Messages: Left wing of AGp. North has penetrated into Riga with the advance combat team of I Corps. Another advance combat team, of VIII Corps, is following up. Railroad bridge intact; road bridges destroyed.

Evening situation: In the sector of AGp. South, an unexpected battle has developed south of Dubno, in which 16th Armored Division joined from the south (after abandoning the high ground of Krzemieniec) 75th Division from the west, 16th Motorized Division from the northwest, 44th Division from the north, and 111th Division from the east. The enemy involved is Eighth Armored Corps. The situation at Dubno evidently is tight.

Also in the northern part of this sector, a lot is happening on the northern flank of Armored Group Kleist. All attacks by the (tentatively identified) Russian XVII Corps from the Pripet marshes were repelled. Behind 13th Armored Division, forming the spearhead at Rovno and advancing as far as the Horyń River, follows 25th Motorized Division. Fourteenth Armored Division covers the north flank, and is in turn followed by 298th Division; behind this division, XVII Corps is moving up from Kovel.

Near Lwów the enemy is taking back his front step by step to the east. Here for the first time many bridges are found destroyed.

In the central sector of *AGp. Center,* a wild medley of divisions is busy sealing the inner ring around the enemy, who is breaking out in all directions. The outer ring, formed by the armored divisions, is closed, but still fairly thin, of course. It will take several days before the disposition of our forces, which in its present form is the outcome of the developing of the situation, can be sufficiently reorganized to allow us to continue the attack toward Smolensk on the dry route Orsha-Vitebsk. (Not before 5 July.)

AGp. North: Everything is pressing in the ordered direction, toward the Dvina, as planned. All crossings have been occupied by our troops. At several other sites bridges have been struck by Armored Corps Reinhardt. Of the enemy forces which originally opposed AGp. North, a considerable body of infantry must still be south of the Dvina. Only a small proportion will succeed in escaping east through the lake country between Dvinsk and Minsk, in the direction of Polotsk.

Air reconnaissance has not been very productive today because of bad weather.

New plans. *AGp. South*—as has been discussed with them—will have to strike with a strong northern wing for the big Russian rear position north of the Dniester. This northern wing will be on a wide enough front to take advantage of any gaps and deep enough in order to cover the flank toward the north and, on wheeling southward later on, have sufficient strength to have forces to protect the wheeling wing toward the north (Gomel) and Kiev.

It is a question whether the tank spearheads of the northern wing will manage to break through by themselves; if not, and if they must wait for their infantry components, a decisive success cannot be expected before 10 to 15 July.

AGp. Center wants to place Armored Groups 2 and 3, which will certainly take at least until 5 July to re-form (for supply reasons alone), and von Kluge's Fourth Army Hq. and reinforce the army with two or three infantry corps. The divisions still tied down in the battle of the pocket in the rear will be moved up by Army Hq. 2 (instead of Army Hq. 4) and by Army Hq. 9.

AGp. North wants to advance with Armored Group 4 from Dvinsk on Ostrov and Opochka, 2 July, so as to cut off the area south of Lake Peipus. Perhaps this operation could be started even earlier, on 1 July. The infantry divisions will not be able to cross the Dvina in any strength before 3 July.

Enemy intelligence: In the south on the front of *AGp. South,* there are no reports of new frontward movements of the enemy. It must be assumed that all armored commands operating south of the Pripet marshes were committed in the attacks of the past days against the front of AGp. South. (Their designations are absolutely different from what we thought they were, e.g., cavalry divisions, motorized brigades, etc.) On the Romanian front the enemy is believed to be withdrawing behind the Dniester. On the front of AGp. Center, enemy road movements are reported south to Smolensk (formation of a defense group for Moscow); the railroad movement from Dvinsk to Pskow is still in progress; probably many evacuation trains. High Hq. shifted to the rear, from Dvinsk to Rostitten.

Hungary reports that the "Carpathian Corps" will be ready to start operations on 2 July. Command setup is still to be clarified. Control by AGp. South would seem the best arrangement.

Italy communicates order of battle of the corps of forty thousand men, slated for operations in Russia.

Slovakia participates with two infantry divisions and one motorized brigade; the latter is already committed on the right wing of Seventeenth Army.

Spain wants to send a "legion": fifteen thousand men. They will be assigned to Rembertów (Warsaw), where we shall equip them.

Norway, Dietl's corps has started out from Petsamo toward Murmansk. Air raid on Murmansk.

Finland presents a new plan of attack conforming to our wishes. It provides for an offensive on a front of at least six divisions east of Lake Ladoga. A German division recently brought over from Norway is to be moved behind this important wing, to strengthen it. It will be supplied by von Falkenhorst's army, but operated under direct control of Field Marshal Mannerheim.

In the afternoon, my three adjutants offer their congratulations on my birthday.

30 June 1941

The situation last night, rounded out by early reports in the morning, presents the following picture:

In *AGp. South,* the fight continues successfully despite local crises. The enemy allows himself to be pushed back step by step.

Lwów was taken by 1st Mountain Division this morning, at 0430.

XIV Corps is not yet in line, but its arrival can be counted on in the course of the day. The situation at Dubno is straightened out. Still, 16th Armored Division and 16th Motorized Division were not inconsiderably delayed by the episode, and 44th, 111th, and 299th divisions, which were brought up behind 3rd Armored Corps, will be stalled for some days; this greatly delays and hampers the follow-up of infantry behind III Corps. There is, however, an endeavor on all hands to make up for this dislocation in every possible way.

No arrivals of new enemy reinforcements from rear areas are reported on the army group front. Most likely, the enemy has already committed the greater part of the forces he was able to muster.

In *AGp. Center,* cleaning out of the pockets is tying down considerable forces. Army group must in particular see to it that infantry forces are brought up behind Guderian's and Hoth's armored groups around the pocket. Bringing together the forces, including infantry, for a strong northern wing in continuing the offensive past the line Mogilev-Orsha-Vitebsk-Polotsk will be the joint concern of AGp. Center and OKH.

AGp. North is sweeping ahead with its infantry corps to the Dvina. It has announced that its initial mission, viz., to beat the enemy this side of the Dvina, has been completed. Its next mission, viz., to push through to the high ground northeast of Opochka with a strong right wing, is well prepared by the disposition of army group.

Bogatsch brings no important new air observations. The rearward movements to Leningrad, behind the northern wing, continue. Between Vitebsk and Orsha, fortifications (antitank ditches) are being built in great haste. In the Pripet marshes, the situation is still somewhat obscure. Apparently the enemy is pulling out some of his strength, but we probably must still reckon with one infantry corps and some armor.

. . .

Afternoon (1630): Visit by the Fuehrer to the Hq. Report presented at ObdH's house. Afterwards tea.

Report by me on progress, with estimate of the situation and the resulting operational possibilities.

The Fuehrer stresses the following points:

a. Mastery of the Gulf of Finland must be secured quickly. For only elimination of the Russian navy will give us free communications through the Baltic (iron ore shipments from Luleå). After seizing the Russian seaports from the land side, we must allow three to four weeks for all enemy submarines to be positively out of action. Four weeks mean 2 million tons of iron ore.

b. *Ukraine:* Significance for food supply and industry.

He attaches great importance to reaching Leningrad as soon as possible with the infantry divisions of AGp. North, but armor need not wait for their advance. He does not see clear yet whether von Leeb's strength, especially his armor, is sufficient for the purpose. He expects that after reaching Smolensk in the middle of July, we would not be able to take Moscow by infantry assault before August; armor alone cannot do it. The time it takes for the infantry to get to Moscow, he believes, could be utilized by our armor to make a clean slate in the north. Then we could mass armor east of Moscow. Speeding of gasoline supply to Hoepner and Hoth is emphasized.

At tea the conversation turns mostly to purely political subjects: European unity as a result of common war against Russia. —Britain's domestic political scene: possibility of Churchill's overthrow by Conservatives with a view to forestalling a Socialist-Communist revolution in the country. Lloyd George, Hoare. —Possibilities of improving our relations with Turkey are viewed optimistically. Also, Afghanistan and other small nations will actively collaborate with us if they feel they need not be afraid of Russia any longer. Continental character of Germany's future mission is emphasized, without renouncing claims to a colonial empire, which might include Togo and the Cameroons, plus the Belgian Congo. East Africa desirable, but not essential.

Evening situation: Slow but steady developments in all army groups. In AGp. Center, however, enemy forces have broken through Guderian's armored group between Slonim and Minsk. This is awkward, but probably of no major importance. In AGp. North, the Riga railroad bridge appears to have been blasted by enemy elements, who penetrated into our lines in the confused fighting.

Hoepner thinks he will be ready to advance on 2 July. Coming behind him, AGp. North will be ready to cross the Dvina on 4 July. Hoth reports that he likewise will be ready to continue advance on 2 July. But Guderian is still lagging behind, south of Minsk, where his forces are partaking in the encirclement of the Novogrudok pocket. He will take several days longer than the others to get ready for new operations. Irrespective of these plans, Guderian's right wing could secure the Dnieper crossings at Mogilev and to the south.

Air force is being reinforced in the sector of AGp. South and on the Romanian front. In AGp. South, very effective action by our air force against enemy air force and enemy columns retreating before our troops (as many as three columns abreast are reported). A total of 200 aircraft shot down during this day. Enemy reported to be already reduced to sending very old four-engine models into the battle.

1 July 1941

Situation: In *AGp. South,* Seventeenth Army is having good going. On its left wing XIV Armored Corps is coming to the fore and is gaining freedom of movement toward the east. The Dubno episode seems to be over. The Russian VIII Corps is bottled up. Some of their tanks seem to have run out of fuel; they are being dug in and used as pillboxes. On the northern wing, 14th Armored Division and 25th Motorized Division are following behind. Moving of the infantry divisions, which will be needed both for attack at the front and for flank cover to the north and east in case of a turning movement to the south, is not proceeding at all well. AGp. South will need some vigorous prodding to get action.

Eleventh Army believes to have positive indications of a systematic withdrawal on its front. I don't believe it is so. I, too, am almost certain that the enemy will try to defend his rear position, but a planned withdrawal would have required a long-range decision, and we have no reason to believe that such a decision was ever taken. The enemy is just being pushed back by us.

Russian atrocities at Lwów.

In *AGp. Center* further progress has been made by Ninth Army and Armored Group Hoth in the buildup for the new attack. Progress is less in Fourth Army and Armored Group 2. In the case of the former, the reason is that it has to bear the burden of liquidating the Białystok pocket; in the case of the latter, the delay is due to the fact that Armored Group 2, in disregard of its orders, has neglected to attend to the mopping up of the territory traversed by it and now has its hands full with local enemy breakthrough. To our surprise, nothing is heard from the area around Bobruysk, which only yesterday was the focal point of Russian anxieties, with SOS signals to all forces in the vicinity and finally the hasty and extremely costly commitment of Russian planes. Either our troops are not getting anywhere, or they want to surprise us with big results. —A teletype order is necessary to make army group Hq. move one division toward Pinski, for protection of the right flank.

In *AGp. North* everything is going according to plan, except at Riga, where the advance combat teams of I and XXVI Corps seem to have had some trouble; the situation was saved by the timely arrival and crossing of a reinforced infantry regiment. The railroad bridge evidently is a total loss. The 291st Division has been detached to take Windau and clean up the country west of Riga. The new attack of Armored Group 4 from the line Dvinsk-Jakobstadt is set for 2 July.

The Hungarians will launch an offensive against the line Kolomea-Stanisławów on 2 July.

Eleventh Army has set 2 July as the date for its attack. It expects the Russians to withdraw behind the Dnieper.

Disturbances have broken out in Romania, involving also some localities in the assembly area. (Iron Legion?)

General Bogatsch: Air reconnaissance in the sector of AGp. South no longer shows any large-scale movements. Heavy concentrations of immobilized railroad cars have been observed everywhere. A possible explanation is that the trains, which are arriving in closest succession, are simply left standing on the tracks by the Russians, with only the locomotives going back to fetch more trains. A striking feature in the southern sector is a heavy concentration in the Proskurov "bastion," forward of the Russian rear position, and a certain loosening up around Cernăuţi.

In sector of AGp. Center, earlier reports of troop concentrations in the Orsha-Vitebsk-Smolensk triangle are confirmed. The enemy assembly area seems to extend as far as Mogilev in the south.

We still have no completely clear picture about what is going on in the Gomel area and the Pripet marshes.

In AGp. North, no new observations.

Transport movements from the east, perhaps also from the west into the Nevel area, apparently intended for the buildup of a defense line in the corner between the Dvina and the old Russo-Estonian border.

. . .

General von Waldau (Operations Chief, Air Force): We review the probable lines of development and the operational tasks resulting from them. OKL planning for the massing of air strength is again in an absolute muddle due to misconstrued talks of the Fuehrer with ObdL.

The air force has greatly underestimated the numerical strength of the enemy. It is quite evident that the Russians initially had far more than eight thousand planes. Half of this number probably has already been shot down or destroyed on the ground, so that numerically we now are about equal with the Russians. But Russian flying efficiency cannot nearly compare with ours, owing to the poor training of their pilots and crews; and that is why entire enemy squadrons, or large parts of them, get shot down so often in combat, as, for instance, happened yesterday over Dvinsk and Bobruysk.

At present, air force estimates Russian air strength opposite AGp. South, at 800 to 1,000 operational first-line craft; in AGp. Center, at 400 to 500; and in sector of AGp. North, at 400 to 500. In the battles of the last few days, the Russians have been using obsolete planes side by side with latest models.

General Oehquist (Finland): Orientation on our plans for the impending operations. —Discussion of Finnish operations. —Experiences with the Russians.

. . .

2 July 1941

Situation:

Eleventh Army launches offensive from Romania, Armored Group 4 from Dvinsk, in direction of Opochka-Ostrov. Also, the Hungarians start operations.

In *AGp. South,* the situation reports prove the correctness of my view concerning the northern wing of Armored Group 1. Only yesterday, on 1 July, Russian infantry from the Pripet marshes west of Rovno made quite a deep penetration into the flank of Armored Group 1, in the general direction of Dubno. I do not think this penetration imperils our operations, but the nearby infantry divisions, which I would like at last to move up behind the armored spearheads in an eastern direction, are again kept back to deal with this enemy thrust.

In *AGp. Center,* the Białystok pocket is in the final stages of liquidation.

ObdH now is worried about the Novogrudok pocket.

In *AGp. North,* I Corps should not move off to the east. Parts of it must first clean out the forests south of Riga. The 291st Division must comb out the northern part of the coast, west of Riga.

Bogatsch: Air reconnaissance shows something new: a movement, apparently from around Odessa, toward and east of Kiev, and then to the north. Air also confirms earlier reports of dense movements from the east in the direction of Orsha-Vitebsk and, farther north, in the direction of Nevel.

The resulting picture would indicate that in addition to the new group, assigned to the defense of the dry route Orsha-Vitebsk, whose sector extends perhaps to Mogilev in the south and to Polotsk in the north (Dvina bridges there are blown up), another new group is being built up northeast of the triangle formed by the old Russo-Estonian frontier and the Dvina.

. . . .

At noon ObdH is called to the Fuehrer:

Apprehensive about the Novogrudok pocket. The Fuehrer thinks the ring must be contracted and tightened, and wants it bolstered with reserves. It seems there was still some discussion about launching the new operations by Armored Groups 2 and 3, which have already been authorized by us. There they go worrying again.

ObdH makes various suggestions on how to compress and crack the pocket. He wants to use 18th Motorized Division and 10th Armored Division, which belong to the assault wave of Armored Groups 2 and 3, set to strike on 3 July. I object; I call up AGp. Center to discuss that with von Greiffenberg.

Field Marshal von Bock on phone: In reply to my talk with his chief of staff, he states: An enemy breakthrough from the forest pocket of Novogrudok to the northeast is highly unlikely. Behind 14th Motorized Division, 900th Brigade will be brought up from Vilna tonight. Pressure on the front of 14th Motorized Division is also eased by arrival of 161st Division on its right wing. Moreover, the northeastern edge of the forest area has been amply mined by Hoth.

Of V Corps, 35th and 5th divisions have reached the forest region. VIII Corps, south of the Njemen, has crossed the Baranovichi-Lida railroad.

The situation is more difficult for Fourth Army and Guderian. Armored Group 2 is under orders not to withdraw any units from the encircling ring, without orders.

Armored Groups 2 and 3 are ordered to push their inner wings ahead to the forest edge (eastern edge of the big forest), if the situation permits. The process is most difficult between the big forest and Slonim. This area would afford the enemy with the best operational opportunities; but there are no signs that he is trying to take advantage of them. This Novogrudok pocket cannot be compared with the Volkovysk pocket, where the enemy suffered very heavy losses. Any unit that escaped into the Novogrudok pocket is badly mauled, and the enemy has no ammunition or food. This accounts for his passivity. Nevertheless, it will be impossible to prevent some smaller enemy bodies seeping through to the southeast. IX Corps has already crossed the Szczara River and will reach Molczadz tomorrow.

XII Corps is one day's march, LIII Corps two days' march behind schedule. But advance elements of these corps are already committed next to Regiment ''Grossdeutschland'' to reinforce the ring encircling the Slonim area.

Fighting on the southern outskirts of Minsk. Von Kluge cannot move up his troops.

After this conversation, I *report briefly to ObdH* and talk with Jodl (OKW) to ease the Fuehrer's mind.

Major Golling (Liaison Officer, Armored Group 4) reports. Hoepner is nervous that infantry corps behind him might be moving across his lines of communication. It will be impossible to avoid that. There also seem to be certain differences in von Leeb's and Hoepner's views of what the next moves should be. That, however, depends on our directives, which have not yet been given, but are due now.

Armored Group 4 must proceed to block the gaps south and north of Lake Peipus and encircle Leningrad. Von Leeb's infantry corps must sweep Estonia clear of enemy forces and occupy the coast, meanwhile pushing all forces they can spare on Leningrad and the southeastern shore of Lake Ladoga, and guarding their right flank against Nevel.

Computation of enemy strength: My own computations and those of Foreign Armies East show:

On the fronts of von Leeb and von Bock, fifteen to twenty infantry divisions and about six armored divisions. To these must be added:

  3 withdrawn from the front
  1 (18th from Moscow)
  3 from Volga-Ural
  4 from Siberian railroad
  <u>1</u> from Crimea
12 armd. divs., plus divs. in Estonia and Leningrad.

Estimated total tank strength: 15,000, or thirty-five armored divisions, of which twenty-two have been identified. In the Far East are five divisions, which leaves eight divisions unaccounted for (3rd in the north, one from Moscow area, and 6th Division of II Corps). Excluding the three divisions in parentheses, five divisions would be left available as operational reserve.

Evening reports.

> *AGp. South:* A heavy enemy attack was repulsed with severe enemy losses west of Rovno; III Corps (northern wing of the armored group) temporarily stalled; central sector and southern wing advancing. In Romania, the Pruth River has been crossed and our forces have penetrated about 12 km into enemy territory. On the front of Seventeenth Army, the enemy is effecting a planned withdrawal, apparently under cover of strong armored forces. Our divisions are in close pursuit.
>
> In *AGp. Center* strong elements of Armored Groups 2 and 3 have started to move forward in order to be as close as possible to the Dnieper and Dvina line on jump-off day (3 July). Good progress. Stubborn enemy resistance on the Beresina is broken by Armored Group 2. The other components of army group after the close of the Białystok battle are regrouping for a new offensive against the line Mogilev-Polotsk. The ring encircling the forest pocket east of Novogrudok is now complete.
>
> In *AGp. North,* Armored Group 4 has started operations and advanced halfway to Pskov. The infantry divisions are following close behind.

At the *Fuehrer's Hq.* they now seem to be reassured about the situation in the Novogrudok pocket. Start of new offensive by armored groups is approved.

3 July 1941

Daily reports of 2 July and morning reports of 3 July indicate that the enemy fronting Eleventh Army has apparently withdrawn behind the Pruth River, but is still fighting strong rear-guard actions. Our advance is slowed by pouring rains, which turn roads into bogs.

The *Hungarians* are still fighting at the mouths of the mountain passes and have made no important advances. *Seventeenth Army,* where two Slovak divisions have been introduced on the right wing, is pressing on "in pursuit" behind the yielding enemy. This pursuit is repeatedly checked by counterthrusts of individual enemy groups, mostly against the flank and, as a rule, with tanks. Tarnopol is taken.

As a result of this advance, Seventeenth Army has developed greater depth, which is all to the good, and now has its main concentration on its left wing, in conformity with the basic operational dispositions of army group. Next to it, Sixth Army, with its main concentration on the right wing, has continued its southeastward movement in good formation. This puts its main weight between 9th Armored Division and 16th Armored Division on the right, and III Corps (11th, 13th, 14th Armored Divisions) on the left. Army group has developed a definite wedge pointing at Berdichev. To the north, armored group, that is, its left wing (III Corps), is still severely hampered in its movements by attacks from the Pripet area, which the enemy now is launching west of Rovno.

This threat to the northern flank from the Pripet area has been a matter of concern for days. Everybody is vying for the honor of telling the most hair-raising tale about the danger from the north. Foremost are the radio intelligence people, who claim to have located a large number of enemy troops, namely three armored corps and two infantry corps under the command of an army Hq. This assertion is baseless and therefore dangerous. The events over several days do show that there are enemy forces in this maze of swamps and forests, but they certainly are not stronger than two or three divisions; there cannot be any doubt that they include some motorized elements and tanks. The attacks are conducted in a manner which plainly shows that their command is completely confused. Also, the tactics employed in these attacks are singularly poor. Riflemen on trucks abreast with tanks drive against our firing line, and the inevitable results are very heavy losses to the enemy. Such desultory attacks cannot be regarded as a threat to our operations. Nevertheless, it would be intolerable to allow this factor of uncertainty to persist unchallenged on our flank. It must be removed by offensive action and systematic combing out of the marshes.

In *AGp. Center,* the Novogrudok pocket has been further contracted and sealed, as agreed upon yesterday. The moves of Second and Ninth armies are continuing according to plan, and with forced marches, in order to introduce infantry with greatest rapidity behind the armored groups, which are launching the offensive today. Both armored groups have already started off. Guderian forced the Beresina River this forenoon; Hoth's left wing reached the Dvina northwest of Polotsk by noon.

In *AGp. North,* Hoepner advanced, but slowly, owing to very bad weather, which gave him the worst road conditions. Still, his left wing is already midway between the Dvina and Pskov. He has been directed by teletype orders issued last night to occupy the areas between Velikiye Luki and Lake Ilmen and between Lake Ilmen and Lake Pskov, with a view to safeguarding them toward the east, and to advance northward beyond the line Lake Ilmen–Lake Pskov only on orders of OKH. The latter advance will have the twofold aim of closing the gap between the gulf of Finland and Lake Peipus, and of cutting off Leningrad between the Gulf of Finland and Lake Ladoga. Sixteenth and Eighteenth armies, by forced marches, are moving on in excellent formation, with a strong right wing behind armored group, toward the Dvina. On the army group boundary, close contact is maintained with the vigorously pushed left wing of Ninth Army.

Enemy intelligence (Kinzel and Bogatsch) brings no important findings. In front of our southern wing (*AGp. South*), the enemy has ceased reinforcing his front. In *Center* (triangle Orsha-Vitebsk-Smolensk) there is still some movement, but with the movement which apparently came from the Caucasus brought to a close yesterday, it is on a much smaller scale than in the past few days. In the "land bridge" trench, digging is in progress. Owing to bad weather, there are no new developments in the Nevel group.

The enemy situation in the Pripet marshes remains obscure. We must not overrate the strength of this enemy. On the whole, with no more signs of enemy activity in the Novogrudok pocket, we may be fairly sure that the enemy in the Białystok sector, who was estimated at fifteen to twenty divisions by a captured Russian corps CG, is annihilated except for some negligible remnants. On the front of AGp. North, we may also figure with twelve to fifteen divisions completely wiped out. On the front of AGp. South, the enemy's withdrawal and the crumbling of his front certainly cannot be interpreted as a disengaging movement planned by his command; it must be explained by the fact that his troops have been cut up and, for the most part, scattered by our unceasing, massive blows.

On the whole, then, it may be said even now that the objective to shatter the bulk of the Russian army this side of the Dvina and Dnieper has been accomplished. I do not doubt the statement of the captured Russian corps CG that east of the Dvina and Dnieper we would encounter nothing more than partial forces, not strong enough to hinder realization of German operational plans. It is thus probably no overstatement to say that the Russian Campaign has been won in the space of two weeks.

Of course, this does not yet mean that it is closed. The sheer geographical vastness of the country and the stubbornness of the resistance, which is carried on with all means, will claim our efforts for many more weeks to come.

Future plans:

    a. For the continuance of the Russian operations, it will be of primary importance to gain a new jump-off line between Smolensk and Moscow, and another base around Leningrad. From here we could proceed to the capture of northern Russia and the industrial region around Moscow, and, subsequently, in conjunction with AGp. South, of the Donets industrial region.

    Once we are across the Dvina and Dnieper, it will be less a question of smashing enemy armies than of denying the enemy possession of his production centers and so prevent his raising a new army with the aid of his gigantic industrial potential and his inexhaustible manpower resources.

    b. As soon as the battle in the east changes from an effort to annihilate the enemy armed forces to one of paralyzing the enemy economy, our next tasks in the war against Britain will come to the foreground and require preparation:

    Preparation must be made for the offensive against the land route between the Nile and Euphrates, both from Cyrenaica and through Anatolia, and perhaps also for an offensive from the Caucasus against Iran. The former theater, which will always remain dependent on the quantities of supplies we can bring across the sea, and so is subject to incalculable vicissitudes, will assume a secondary role and, for the most part, will be left to Italian forces. We will have to assign to it only two German armored divisions (5th Light and 15th), which will be brought up to full strength and reinforced by small additional complements. As an initial move for the operations through Anatolia against Syria, possibly supported by a secondary thrust from the Caucasus, we shall have to initiate concentration of the necessary forces in Bulgaria, which at the same time may serve as a means of political pressure to compel Turkey to grant transit for our forces.

Wagner (Gen Qu):

    a. Summary of casualty reports, booty reports, etc.

b.   Organization of rear areas and assignment of troops to these.

c.   Review of plans for moving forward our supply bases after the Dvina-Dnieper line has been gained.

d.   Spare parts for tanks and tank replacements.

1200.   **Through ObdH and Op. Sec.** we hear again the usual rumors from the Fuehrer's Hq. Now again the whole place is in a state of jitters, because the Fuehrer is afraid that the wedge of AGp. South now advancing eastward might be threatened by flank attacks from north and south. Tactically speaking, of course, this fear is not at all unwarranted, but that's what we have army corps CGs for. What is lacking on top level is that confidence in the executive commands which is one of the most essential features of our command organization, and that is so because it fails to grasp the coordinating force that comes from the common schooling and education of our Leader Corps.

I call up AGp. South (Lieutenant Colonel Winter, Ia) to make suggestions on how the threat to the northern flank could be removed once and for all by employing advance combat teams and moving the GHq. Reserves toward Rovno. Any threat to the southern flank, which will soon effect a linkup with the Hungarians, must be forestalled by Seventeenth Army with its own forces, by organizing advance combat teams amply equipped with AT units and obstacle-construction material.

.   .   .

4 July 1941

Situation: *South:* Eleventh Army is advancing slowly. Difficult road conditions, owing to recent rains. The mountain brigades of the Romanian northern front have started the attack against Cernâuţi.

The Hungarian right wing has reached the northern rim of the Carpathians.

In spite of difficult road conditions, Seventeenth and Sixth armies are getting on well. Main weight on the inner wings. On the northern wing of Sixth Army, our safeguarding measures against the Pripet marshes are beginning to show results. The enemy is withdrawing in the marshes to the east before our pressure from southwest and west, but at the same time is bringing reinforcements from the east. We must expect that von Reichenau will feel continued pressure on his left shoulder, at first from the area north of the line Rovno-Korets and later from the area between Korosten and Kiev.

Center: The right wing (3d Armored Division) of Guderian's armored group has crossed the Dnieper at Rogachev, establishing so far only a bridgehead. Farther north armored group has forced the Beresina at the destroyed crossings and is battling its way to the upper Dnieper.

The northern wing of Armored Group Hoth has reached the Dvina at Drissa, where it is encountering stiffer enemy resistance. Road conditions difficult. High tank casualties from bad roads. Hoth reports 50 percent combat strength.

Second and Ninth armies are pressing on behind armored group in rapid marches. But owing to the delay in the encirclement operations at Białystok, the distance between them and armored group has become so great, particularly behind Guderian, that special measures will be necessary to bridge the gap. Combined advance combat teams of the infantry corps must be moved ahead behind Guderian's armored group.

Von Bock has moved his Hq. to Baranovichi. Von Kluge, who on our orders and over their objections assumed command of the two armored groups, has moved his Hq. to Minsk.

North: Armored Group Hoepner is advancing rapidly, and is approaching Ostrov with its left wing. Right wing encountered stronger opposition shortly after crossing the Dvina, but, thanks to Field Marshal von Leeb's foresight, infantry forces were brought up here in time (on trucks), so that this enemy constitutes no threat; on the contrary, he is already being forced back by the troops originally on the scene. During this fighting, the commander of 121st Division, General von Lancelle, was killed. The bulk of the infantry corps is advancing briskly and has started crossing the Dvina. On the northern wing, almost an entire enemy division was captured in the forests north of Riga.

Enemy: On the front of AGp. South, local resistance, which leads to formation of pockets in some places; but on the whole we discern distinct withdrawal movements, covered by armored counterthrusts. Some troops are still arriving through Kiev from the east, but to all appearance they do not represent a large-scale coordinated movement. The large number of trains cramming the railroad stations and some eastward train movements probably must be interpreted as evacuation measures. Movements of fresh troops toward Korosten are observed, but apparently they are not on an operational scale.

On the front of Center, the situation is unchanged. Movements run from Smolensk to Orsha, but in the opposite direction. The large quantities of railroad cars around Bryansk seem less an indication that the Russians are forming an operational reserve—they would not have sufficient forces for that—than merely the accumulation of rolling stock used in the frontward movements of the last days, left on sidings for technical reasons.

In North, two movements are reported on the way from the area around Moscow. One is running into the area west of Velikiye Luki, i.e., between Hoth's and Hoepner's inner wings; the other one is swinging northward around Lake Ilmen, to the vicinity of Pskov.

Overall picture: The situation supports the assumption that the enemy does not have sufficient forces left for a sustained defense of the line running from the old Russo-Estonian frontier along Dvina and Dnieper to the south. This theory is borne out also by a Russian order, intercepted yesterday, to the effect that the Dvina River will be held only by groups concentrated at the crossings.

As our armies advance, any attempt at further resistance probably will soon collapse and we shall be confronted with the question of reducing Leningrad and Moscow. It remains to be seen whether Stalin's proclamation calling for a people's war of all workers against us will be successful. The result depends on the method by which we are going to sweep the enemy out of these extensive industrial areas. The main thing is to deny their use to the enemy at an early date.

As to the date when the Finns will strike, a decision will have to be made today (6, 7, or 8 July).

. . .

5 July 1941

Situation: The entire front is advancing in accordance with our intentions. In AGp. South, in the southern Ukraine, road conditions are very difficult as a result of cloudstorms, and rate of advance is slow. Apparently the enemy now is withdrawing eastward from the Pripet marshes opposite von Reichenau's left shoulder. In consequence, GHq. Reserves can be moved eastward beyond the line Dubno-Łuck.

In *AGp. Center,* Guderian's right wing (Model) has held its bridgeheads at Rogachev. But the central sector of the armored group, fighting all the way, is making little headway between the Beresina and the Dnieper. In addition to the Drissa bridgehead, Hoth now has gained another firm foothold at Ulla, on the northern bank of the Dvina, upstream from Polotsk. —The pocket west of Minsk is slowly burning out. Since yesterday morning 52,000 Russians have surrendered.

In AGp. North, Hoepner's armored group is sweeping the area assigned it clear of the enemy. The infantry corps are closing up at a satisfactory rate, especially on the right wing.

Report on enemy situation. Our troops have more or less lost contact with the enemy on the fronts of Seventeenth and Sixth armies. Air reconnaissance shows that the enemy is retreating in disorder before Seventeenth Army and the Hungarians, with several columns packed together on one road in some instances. We may assume that these movements are withdrawals, getting mixed up with refugee columns. Enemy AAA protection generally covers the rear position west of Kiev; enemy fighter protection covers the area around Kiev. Behind the northern part of the position, parallel troop movements and arrival of troops from the north.

On the front of AGp. Center, confirmation is obtained on unloading of troops around Orsha, from where they move westward to Guderian's front. AAA protection makes itself felt west of Orsha, fighter protection around Orsha and to the east. Strong fighter cover above Bryansk and Orel. The enormously large number of railway cars left standing on the sidings has again been observed. The purpose of these accumulations of rolling stock and of the movements into this area, apparently from the south, is not clearly understood. Operational reserves? Group for a flank thrust?

Air reconnaissance again confirms the existence of an enemy concentration round Velikiye Luki. No indications that it has been committed in the fighting. It might become effective against Hoepner's right flank, as well as against Hoth's left flank, especially if the latter should strike eastward from his crossing points at Drissa and Ulla. The enemy's fighter cover is above Velikiye Luki, his AAA protection is moved farther west in the direction of Dvinsk.

Enemy's command setup is as follows:

Russian AHq.   8 ⎫
                   27 ⎬ forming AGp. Northwest
                   11 ⎭

Russian AHq.   13 ⎫
Unidentified new AHq. — ⎬ forming AGp. West

Russian AHq.   5 ⎫
                    6 ⎬ forming southwestern front
                   12 |
                    2 ⎭

Odessa Army

Heusinger (1300):

  a. A teletype from Erfurth indicates that on orders of OKW (apparently
      the Fuehrer himself) the last regiment of 163d Division, now moving
      up behind Heinrich's assault group, was diverted for von Falken-
      horst's combat group at Salla. Apart from the fact that this regiment
      cannot be of any help in the Salla operation, the division as a
      result is disrupted and its striking power impaired where it was
      needed most. This clearly shows up the dubiousness of this entire
      Murmansk operation, which serves only political ends and is open
      to gravest censure from the operational point of view.

  b. In the episode with the Mongolian hordes (allegedly Stalin's body-
      guard) trapped behind the front of Sixth Army, 168th Division is
      reported to have broken down completely. Relief of COs is de-
      manded.

. . .

Situation in the evening: In *South,* advance slowed by terrain difficulties and
enemy opposition. The report that AGp. South has lost contact with
the enemy is not confirmed. Armored Group Kleist seems to have
punched through the enemy defense system. In *Center,* a victory of
Guderian's and Hoth's outer wings is in the making. Very bad roads.
In *North,* the attempt of the enemy to build up a front against Hoepner
with forces hurriedly thrown together does not seem to come off. The
"intentions" set forth in the army group reports are in line with the
ideas of OKH.

ObdH: Back from tour to AGp. Center, Army Hq. 4, and Armored Group 2:

Eighteenth Armored Division suffered heavy losses in the forest area. —PW problem is beginning to get troublesome. —Insecurity of rear areas. —Population movements on the roads.

OKW: Interferes in the moving of 163d Division to Finland with a direct order by the Fuehrer. The division was supposed to go to Heinrich's group east of Lake Ladoga and is now ordered to go "as a whole or in part" to the Salla front. Reason: SS Brigade "Nord," committed at Salla, has been a failure.

Chief of Staff, AGp. South sends an interesting situation estimate. It shows how widely AGp. South, which has decided to direct its main effort against Berdichev (nonexistent gap in the fortified line), diverges from our plan (main concentration on the northern wing).

6 July 1941

. . .

General Ott reports on visit to front (VII and XXXIX Corps). He describes pillbox fighting which he witnessed at VII Corps (heavy howitzers are very effective against them; also gasoline ventilator shafts). In sector of XXXIX Corps, heavy losses were sustained by 1st Mountain Division. Morale of troops very good; all are imbued with a sense of superiority over the enemy.

Infantry supply columns have proved very useful. —Everybody wants semiautomatic weapons and telescopic sights. —Close combat training has paid its way.

Russian attack method: Three-minute artillery barrage, then pause, then infantry attacking as much as twelve ranks deep, without heavy weapon support; the men start hurrahing from far off. Incredibly high Russian losses.

Casualties up to 3 July:

Wounded	38,809	(including 1,403 officers)
Killed	11,822	(including 724 officers)
Missing	3,961	(including 66 officers)

Total losses about 54,000 = 2.15 percent of 2.5 million

The large number of medical casualties (almost 54,000), practically equaling bloody casualties, is quite remarkable.

Larger proportion of officer casualties than in preceding campaigns.

Proportion officer casualties in the Russian Campaign to date: 3.8 percent wounded, 6.6 percent killed, 1.7 percent missing.

In the Western Campaign officer casualties were 3.1 percent wounded, 4.85 percent killed, 2 percent missing.

In the Polish Campaign officer casualties were 1.95 percent wounded, 4.6 percent killed, 1.35 percent missing.

In the afternoon, long talk with General Gause, OKH Liaison Officer to Italian High Command Libya, summoned from North Africa.

Summary:

a.   Personal relations are complicated by General Rommel's character and his inordinate ambition. The desired relationship of mutual confidence between Gause and Rommel has not been established. Rommel's character defects make him extremely hard to get along with, but no one cares to come out in open opposition because of his brutality and the backing he has on top level. The Italians at first met Gause with suspicion, but now are friendlier. Incidentally, Roatta's insincerity also was an aggravating factor in this connection.

This obviously brings a situation which might be rectified by modifying the mission of Gause's staff in the process of changing the command setup (formation of an Armored Group Rommel).

b.   The situation at Bardia and Sollum continues tight. The British have withdrawn after their last defeat, but it appears entirely possible that they might repeat their attack toward the end of July. The weather then is said to be no worse than it was at the time of the last attack, when the British used four hundred tanks and two infantry divisions. By the end of July, they may be in a position to put into the field six hundred tanks and three infantry divisions. It is a question whether the German forces then will be able to hold, for even at the last British attack it was touch and go. If there is another offensive, we shall have to reckon with attacks out of Tobruk too.

c.   The problem of transport now, as ever, is the dominating factor in the North African situation. Nothing has materially changed.

We now do use the direct route to Benghazi, but German-Italian shipping space is visibly diminishing. Strangely, Gause thinks it would be possible to substitute land transport for our dwindling shipping tonnage. I thoroughly disagree.

7 July 1941

Situation: *South:* Yesterday's optimism in Eleventh Army has vanished. XI Corps is again held back. The reasons are not apparent. Seventeenth Army is getting along well and is concentrating its advance combat teams against Proskurov. Von Wietersheim's corps, leading the army, has spread itself surprisingly far to the south (road conditions?). Sixth Army continues to advance, led on its left wing by Armored Group 1, of which only the southern wing appears to have made any sizable penetration into the enemy position west of Minsk, whereas its northern wing is still fighting in the pillbox line. The infantry wing of Sixth Army on the southern edge of the Pripet marshes is advancing nicely.

The enemy is trying with all means to extricate his forces from the pocket in the process of being formed by Eleventh and Seventeenth armies. It seems that he is retreating behind the Dnieper, but we have no conclusive evidence as yet. The numerous movements in the rear area between the Dnieper and the position to the west could well be shipments of materials and the concentration of large reserves, which would have to be assembled in the area south of Kiev, if he intends to hold the position.

Center: The enemy on our Dnieper front is still fighting hard and stubbornly against Armored Group 2 at Orsha and is shifting reinforcements from the south to the Dnieper line.

On the Dvina front, Hoth's left wing has gained elbow room on the northern bank of the river and, by swinging upriver, is endeavoring to move its entire front across the river. This situation offers the big chance for carrying forward our operation. Second and Ninth armies are following closely behind the armored groups.

North: Operations are proceeding according to plan, which means that a strong right infantry wing is taking over flank cover against Nevel, thus freeing armor for the regrouping against Leningrad.

Enemy: Apart from our uncertainty about enemy intentions in the south— is he or is he not retreating behind the Dnieper—there is still the open question of whether the observed larger enemy movements in the Bryansk-Orel-Kursk area are for the purpose of massing strength or are destined for the evacuation of industries. Radio intelligence indicates that there are still four enemy corps Hq. in the Pripet marshes in front of von Reichenau's left wing. However, we have no clear idea of the location of the combat troops, as XVII Corps, advancing through the marshland, has lost contact with the enemy.

Summary: At the moment the best chances of success are on the front of left wing of AGp. Center (Armored Group 3). To the north, the enemy group Velikiye Luki is less active than one would have expected after the large movements to that sector in the past few days. Since, moreover, the right wing of AGp. North is advancing well, and so holds this enemy group in check, Hoth may have a chance to roll up the Vitebsk positions from the north, and so open up a great operational opportunity.

If the enemy in the south falls back behind the Dnieper, such an opening might prove very valuable, since it could initiate a north-south operation east of the Dnieper.

. . .

8 July 1941

Situation: On the *Romanian front* our offensive is advancing slowly. Seventeenth Army is pressing on. Armored Group 1 wants to move XIV Corps to 11th Armored Division in order to use it for the encirclement of the enemy in front of Seventeenth Army. III Corps is fighting its way through the fortified line at Zvyagel and to the south. Sixth Army is pushing on close behind.

AGp. Center: Armored Group 2 is battering its way to the Beresina, partly against aggressive enemy resistance. It reports bitter enemy coun-terattacks, with tanks particularly against its northern wing from the direction of Orsha. Advance elements of Armored Group 3 have crossed the Dvina at several points and are fighting for maneuvering space in the direction of Vitebsk while repelling counterattacks from the north. The infantry armies are following, with strong forces on the outer wings and commendable depth in center.

AGp. North is fighting hard and soon will have gained freedom of movement to the north (Armored Group 4), and now is committing infantry arriving from the right wing to replace the forces of Armored Group 4 detached for covering the east flank.

The infantry armies are pressing on in rapid marches on a wide front and with great depth, with their advance combat teams following closely behind the armor. On the left wing of Eighteenth Army, it was possible to use sections of the railroad in moving infantry quickly to the north, into Estonian territory.

1100. Kinzel: Review of enemy situation:

Of 164 identified rifle divisions, 89 have been totally or largely eliminated.

Forty-six Russian combat divisions are on this front. Eighteen are tied down in other theaters (Finland fourteen; Caucasus four). Eleven are possibly still in reserve, in the rear.

Of twenty-nine identified armored divisions, twenty have been totally or largely eliminated; nine still have full fighting strength.

The enemy is no longer in a position to organize a continuous front, not even behind strong terrain features. At the moment the apparent plan of the Red Army High Command is to check the German advance as far to the west as possible by draining our strength with incessant counterattacking with all available reserves. In pursuing this policy they evidently have grossly overestimated German losses.

Meanwhile we must reckon with the attempt to activate new units with which they might eventually stage an offensive. The plan of a large-scale disengagement is nowhere discernible.

Activation of new units, certainly on any larger scale, will fail for lack of officers, specialists, and artillery materiel. This holds particularly for their armor, which even before the war was sadly lacking in officers, drivers, and radio operators, as well as signal equipment.

In the individual army groups, the situation works out as follows:

North, which at the start of the campaign was numerically equal to the enemy, definitely outnumbers him after annihilation of numerous enemy divisions on its front; this superiority applies to both infantry and armor.

Center, which was stronger from the start, now has a crushing superiority and can maintain it even if the enemy, as is expected, should bring new units to that front.

South, which in the beginning was noticeably weaker in numbers, now has equal strength, due to the heavy losses inflicted on the enemy, and soon will add numerical to tactical and operational superiority.

1230.   Report to the Fuehrer (at his Hq.):

ObdH first presents the latest tactical reports. I follow with an estimate of the enemy situation and an operational appraisal of our situation, and review the operational question on which a decision must now be made: continuance of the encircling operation in AGp. South. Start in AGp. Center of the battle of envelopment with strong outer wings against the Dnieper-Dvina line, calculated to crack the triangle Orsha-Smolensk-Vitebsk. Conduct of operations by AGp. North against Leningrad and start of operations by the Finns. A discussion follows.

Result:

1.   The Fuehrer has in mind the following "perfect solution," which should be aimed at:

AGp. North accomplishes with its own forces the missions assigned it in the original operational plan.

AGp. Center, by a pincer attack, will force the last organized resistance group north of the Pripet marshes out of the overextended Russian front and thus open the road to Moscow. Once the two armored groups have reached the areas assigned to them by the operational plan:

a.   *Hoth* can be halted (to assist von Leeb, if necessary) or else continue operating in an eastern direction, e.g., with a view to investing Moscow, but not proceeding to an assault of the city.

b.   *Guderian* can strike in a southern or southeastern direction, east of the Dnieper River, cooperating with AGp. South.

2.   It is the Fuehrer's firm decision to level Moscow and Leningrad, and make them uninhabitable, so as to relieve us of the necessity of having to feed the populations through the winter. The cities will be razed by air force. Tanks must not be used for the purpose. "A national catastrophe which will deprive not only Bolshevism, but also Muscovite nationalism, of their centers."

3. *Details:*

   a. The draft operational plans of the army groups are approved. An added feature is the stressed importance of cutting off the Leningrad area from the southeast and east with the strong right wing of Hoepner's armored group. This idea is sound.

   b. After destroying the Russian armies in a battle at Smolensk, we shall block the railroads across the Volga, occupy the country as far as that river, and, after that, proceed to destroy the remaining Russian industry centers by armored expeditions and air operations.

   c. Preparations must now be made for housing our troops during the winter. Our troops must not be quartered in villages and towns, because we want to be able to bomb them at any time in the event of uprisings.

   d. Reduction of the Italian contingent for the east is opposed (it was to be reduced in favor of Libya). A special point should be made of giving the Italian troops a big reception on arrival. With Italian troops at the German front, a visit by Mussolini to the Fuehrer's Hq. may be expected.

4. *Tanks:* The Fuehrer explains why he is keeping the new tanks coming off production concentrated in the homeland. He wants to make sure that we would have brand-new equipment for the missions still ahead, for these will again extend over thousands of kilometers. The tank losses suffered since the beginning of the campaign therefore necessitate reduction in the number of armored divisions. The personnel so freed will make up the crews for the new tanks in the interior. He envisages the following operations:

   a. Norway: Safeguarding of the "Norwegian flank." Required for this purpose: Two armored divisions. Could use captured tanks.

   b. *Anatolia:* Against the British land route in the Middle East. For this purpose we need at least four armored divisions. One of these (2d Armored Division?) should be sent as soon as possible to the Bulgarian-Turkish border as a warning to Turkey, which is again getting too frisky.

   c. Spain/Portugal: Against the potential British threat. To counter this threat, at least four armored divisions are required. One should go to France soon, to bolster our prestige there and show the world that Germany still has forces available over and above what is needed in the Russian theater.

d. In *North Africa* we shall confine ourselves to reinforcing the German divisions there, improving supply and establishing a supply base. (Raise number of tank battalions in armored division to three.)

After we plead the urgent requirements of the front, Fuehrer releases from the tanks stored in the homeland: Seventy tanks III, fifteen tanks IV, and the Czech tanks as materiel replacements for the Russian front.

. . .

9 July 1941

. . .

AGp. Center submits a final report on the twin battle Białystok-Minsk. Army group states its opponents were four Russian armies, comprising 32 rifle divisions, 8 armored divisions, 6 motorized-mechanized brigades and cavalry divisions. Out of this total it has destroyed 22 rifle divisions, 7 armored divisions, 6 motorized-mechanized brigades, and 3 cavalry divisions. The remaining divisions were severely crippled by very high, bloody losses. Figures counted up to 8 July: 289,874 prisoners (including several corps CGs and division commanders), 2,585 captured and destroyed tanks (including heaviest types), 1,449 guns, 246 airplanes. Also, large quantities of small arms, ammunition, and vehicles.

. . .

OQu IV: Military-political matters.

Japan's intentions still obscure. Having first tried to whet Japan's appetite for Singapore, we now are busy needling her against Russia. The new policy will take some time to show results.

In France, relations between Abetz and von Stuelpnagel are strained on the question of the volunteers.

Sweden still very reserved. Seems to be disposed toward a pact with Germany, but for the time being has no intention to join the Tripartite Pact.

From Farouk (Egypt) a report has been received that Britain is making preparations for a move from Iraq into Iran to seize the oil wells and advance to the north. This sounds quite plausible, for, besides giving Britain a better defensive position in the event of a German advance across the Caucasus, it enables her to build up, on Iran territory, air bases for attacks on the Caucasian oil fields. Moreover, Turkey would then be banded by British-held territory along her entire southern and eastern frontier and thus could be kept under pressure.

Elaboration of the necessity to capture Gibraltar soon and to begin preparations immediately. I don't think this is correct. Preparations cannot be made until directly before we march in, that is, when we positively know that we are going to do it. Otherwise, Britain simply lets the Spaniards starve to death.

U.S. has the following forces available for immediate action: Six infantry divisions, two armored divisions, two cavalry divisions.

.   .   .

Evening situation: In *AGp. South,* no reports have come in from Eleventh Army and the Hungarians. Seventeenth Army's advance is slow because the roads are rain soaked. Sixth Army is slowed down for the same reason; its northern wing is being moved around the southern edge of the Pripet forest area and will continue north when it reaches Korets. The forest area will be crossed directly only by mountain patrols. Reason: run-down condition of the horses.

The burning question now is the further employment of Armored Group 1. Army group states its intention to strike with its northern group (III Corps) for Kiev and with the bulk of the armored group for Belaya Tserkov, and then to push in southeastern direction.

In the meantime the Fuehrer has called up ObdH and told him that he wants armored group to swing the elements which have penetrated to Berdichev to the south, in the direction of Vinnitsa, in order to effect an early junction with Eleventh Army. At the evening situation conference with ObdH, this leads to an agitated exchange about the direction in which Armored Group 1 ought to be moved. My standpoint is as follows:

We must on no account ignore Kiev. There is so much evidence of enemy confusion that chances to take Kiev by some sort of surprise thrust look good; the enemy is building several pontoon bridges there,

462 The Campaign in Russia

which means that he is preparing a retreat precisely on Kiev. If this estimate, however, should prove wrong, then we must use no armor in the battle for Kiev. All divisions moving behind 13th Armored Division in the direction of Zhitomir could then be brought to bear advantageously against Belaya Tserkov and help block the roads and railroads leading to the Lower Dniester.

For the armored forces advancing south of III Corps (motorized), the immediate objective is Belaya Tserkov, in order to strike from there to the south (not to the southeast at first) in the direction of Uman, into the enemy's rear. In that case it will be indicated to direct the right wing of Eleventh Army toward Uman. Should it become necessary to advance from Berdichev toward Vinnitsa, i.e., on the inner ring, the armored divisions following behind 11th Armored Division could always do that on their commander's own initiative.

Thus the ring to be formed will run from Berdichev through Belaya Tserkov and to the sector of Eleventh Army. Sealing the ring is the primary objective. Kiev and the Dnieper crossing south of Kiev are secondary objectives.

ObdH outlines this scheme to the Fuehrer. He does not object, but apparently is not yet converted and emphasizes that he expects nothing from the Kiev operation.

AGp. Center: Armored Group 3 has broken through the enemy's Dvina position in the direction of Vitebsk. Enemy movements from Vitebsk in the direction of Velizh and slackening of enemy pressure around Senno suggest that the enemy might be trying to disengage. I don't see it. Nor, in my opinion, can the reported heavy movements of the enemy from Orsha to Smolensk be interpreted as a positive indication that the enemy is abandoning the dry route Orsha-Vitebsk. In order to exploit the success of Armored Group 3 to the fullest extent, XXIII Corps, with three divisions and the training brigade (900th), is being moved behind it.

Owing to the easing of enemy pressure around Senno, the attack of Armored Group 2 can be launched as planned, namely, on 10 July, with line of departure from Staryy Bykhov to the north. Second and Ninth armies are continuing their advance.

AGp. North: Armored Group 4 is approaching the line Porkhov-Pskov, but will not push beyond this line in the direction of Leningrad before LVI Corps has moved closer to XXXXI Corps by swinging northeast.

Eighteenth Army is to detach elements for a northward drive on Dorpat (airport). The right wing of Sixteenth Army will remain in the offensive in order to cover Armored Group 3 against enemy attacks from the direction of Nevel.

Conference with Heusinger and Paulus on direction of the battle of encirclement of AGp. South. Their ideas in substantial accord with mine.

Telephone conference with General von Sodenstern (Chief of Staff, AGp. South) on my ideas concerning direction of the battle of encirclement. I give explicit orders not to turn initially southeast from Belaya Tserkov, but do permit a strike toward Uman to effect encirclement.

They should make a try at Kiev, but if surprise is not achieved, must not risk armor against the city.

10 July 1941

Finns launch offensive.

0130.   **ObdH** calls. The Fuehrer has again telephoned him. He cannot put his mind at rest for fear that armor might be committed against Kiev and so needlessly sacrificed (Kiev has 35 percent Jews; we won't get the bridges in any case). The encircling ring is to run from Berdichev through Vinnitsa to Eleventh Army.

Accordingly, the following order goes out to AGp. South: The Fuehrer does not want armor beyond what is necessary for reconnaissance and security to be brought to bear against Kiev. Furthermore, he wants the immediately available forces of Armored Group 1 to strike from Berdichev on Vinnitsa in order to link up with Eleventh Army as soon as possible and encircle the enemy forces fronting Seventeenth and Eleventh armies. Only those forces of Armored Group 1 which are not needed or not adapted for this purpose will strike for Belaya Tserkov and then to the south.

1100.   **ObdH** calls up from Hq. AGp. South:

Early this morning, ObdH received the following teletype from the Fuehrer:

"I think it advisable and necessary, on reaching the line Zhitomir-Berdichev, to swing the loading elements of Armored Group 1 promptly to the south in order to prevent the enemy from retreating over the Bug River and to the south of Vinnitsa and, if possible, by thrusting across the Bug, effect a junction with Eleventh Army. —The rear elements of armored group must protect this movement against attacks from Kiev, but will not make any attack into the city. Should it become apparent that there are no large bodies of enemy troops left to cut off west of the Bug, Armored Group 1 will be massed for an advance on Kiev and the Dnieper line to the southeast. Investment must be executed in such a way as to bar enemy reinforcements from reaching the city from the northwest.''

Field Marshal von Rundstedt's analysis: Overtaking the enemy in pursuit means striking far ahead. If the ring runs through Vinnitsa, it becomes too close. Seventeenth Army has completely lost contact with the enemy, which means he has already withdrawn far to the rear. On the other hand, army group believes that there are substantial enemy forces in the area southwest and south of Belaya Tserkov, which seem to be moving on Kiev and to the area southeast of the city. In taking Belaya Tserkov, we should be astride the retreat routes to Kiev. Now von Rundstedt hopes to engage large enemy forces there, and then to be able to advance in a southwestern direction, to link up with Eleventh Army. —If this should prove inadvisable, we still would have two courses of action open to us: either advance in a southeastern and southern direction, west of the Dnieper, or across the Dnieper at Kiev and to the southeast and then drive on east.

This conception of army group, with which ObdH agrees, differs from the solutions envisaged by the Fuehrer. It is a compromise between the two alternatives outlined by the Fuehrer. ObdH will make no decision that would not have the Fuehrer's approval. It is now up to me to get the Fuehrer to agree.

1130.   Keitel: After unsuccessfully trying to get the sleeping Fuehrer to the phone, I have Field Marshal Keitel called and explain the plans to him emphasizing:

a.   That OKH has been directed by the Fuehrer to destroy the largest possible portions of the enemy west of the Dnieper, so as to prevent any possibility of a coordinated operation by large enemy forces east of the river.

b.   That the capabilities of Eleventh Army must be rated so low that no plans could be made which rest on Eleventh Army as a dependable partner in a paired attack.

1230.   **Phone call from OKW** (Christian): The Fuehrer approves the proposed plan, but wants us to make sure that nothing untoward happens on the north flank of armored group. The answer is transmitted to ObdH at 1300.

.   .   .

11 July 1941

Situation: *South:* Russian pressure on von Schobert's right flank and right wing has apparently resulted in a weakening of the Romanian contingent. Eleventh Army reports that it regards these elements disabled for attacking. A "new operation" against Kishinev is considered necessary. We shall have to watch that this "operation" is limited at most to LIV Corps, and does not result in dissipation of strength.

Center: Guderian's attack has started and come through. We have no reports on Hoth's planned attack at Vitebsk, but the overall enemy situation indicates that hastily gathered elements are all the enemy can put up against us. It has been learned that broken divisions withdrawing from the front are filled up with partly untrained replacements rushed to the front, and immediately committed to battle again. At Nevel the enemy has set up a big straggler-collecting point which is feeding to the front-line divisions totally disorganized masses of men, without officers and NCOs. Under these circumstances it is clear that the front, which also has no more reserves left, cannot hold much longer, despite the attempt to give that front apparently, at least, a backbone of energetic leadership by introducing a number of new tactical Hq. (AHq.). These new Hq. cannot make their presence felt and desperately radio to establish contact with their divisions. I do not share the opinion that the enemy in front of AGp. Center is falling back (this opinion evidently originates in the armored groups, not at army group Hq.). The foe is making an effort to hold, but he is cracking in the attempt.

But there is one question which this battle of Smolensk will not settle for us and that is the question of the enemy's armor. In every instance, large bodies, if not all, manage to escape encirclement, and in the end, their armor may well be the only fighting force left to the Russians for carrying on the war. The strategy of that war would have to be visualized on the basis of operations by two or three major and perhaps some subsidiary armored groups, supported by industrial centers and peacetime garrisons, and by the remnants of the Russian air force.

North: Enemy attacks against Hoepner have been beaten back, and preparations are made for continuing the drive to the area southeast of Leningrad, with a strong right wing. In the Estonian theater, more advances against merely local resistance. At last we have succeeded in arousing in AGp. North some interest also in Dorpat. On the right wing, there is more tough fighting against the enemy group apparently based on Nevel, but this does not seriously interfere with the movements of army groups for massing in a northward direction.

Enemy: Air force now seems to have succeeded in wrecking Russian railroads also far to the rear of the enemy communication zone. The number of lines with immobilized railroad transport is growing most satisfactorily, and the good work is being continued. A striking feature is heavy concentration of rolling stock in the area east of Gomel (Unecha), as well as to the west and southeast of that point. These concentrations seem to consist largely of trains loaded with vehicles and tanks. Either this is an attempt to supply new materiel to crippled armored units or an attempt to shift armor.

In the area south of Kiev, the large accumulations of railroad cars on the railroad lines probably must be interpreted as a blocked large-scale withdrawal movement, which I think is more of an industrial evacuation than a troop movement. The enemy is evidently trying to bypass the blocked lines by routing movements through Odessa and the north. But heavy traffic jams can already be seen on the lower reaches of the Dnieper also (e.g., thirty-four trains south of Cherkassy).

Field Marshal Keitel calls up at noon. Anxieties of the Fuehrer:

a. Ninth Armored Division and SS Division "Wiking" are closing up too slowly.

b. The frontal battles of II Corps on von Leeb's right wing, which he wants to have cut short by action from von Bock's left wing. (As a matter of fact, the two army groups do have perfect cooperation.)

c. Hoepner's operation (Armored Group 4). He is afraid that it is losing contact with its own infantry in its heedless push on Leningrad.

. . .

12 July 1941

. . .

1400. ObdH calls up: The Fuehrer is again nagging about the slow development of the attack on von Leeb's right wing, and demands that 19th Armored Division strike northward to encircle the enemy. In reply I explain: I am by no means advocating any eastward race of the two armored groups. It is quite clear to me that Hoth might have to swing northward with a considerable body of his group to get into the back of the new Russian Nineteenth Army and Group Nevel, and that Guderian might have to swing southward to encircle the new enemy appearing on his southern wing, perhaps even to push on down to the Kiev area in order finally to encircle and defeat the Red Fifth Army, which keeps popping up in the south. But the prerequisite for either move is that Hoth and Guderian break into the open to the east and so gain freedom of movement.

1800. Heusinger:

a. Planning on continuance of operations with the object of preventing frontal retreat of the enemy and ensuring liquidation of the largest possible enemy force. The operations are evolved from ideas outlined by me to ObdH, and crystallize first of all in plans for a new drive by Armored Group 3, aiming at liquidating the concentration of twelve to fourteen divisions now opposing von Leeb's right wing. By taking advantage of the marshland extending southward from Lake Ilmen, which is traversed by very few roads, we should be able to cut off the enemy facing von Leeb's forces. Accordingly, we should have to dispose Armored Group 3 in such a manner that, notwithstanding its original mission to reach the area northeast of Smolensk, it would be in a position, by advancing on Velikiye Luki and Kholm, to cut off the enemy elements falling back before von Leeb's right wing.

Applying his scheme of thought to the area south of the line Orsha-Smolensk, the northern wing of Armored Group 2 would have to strike for Yelnya, the southern wing for Roslavl. This southern part would have to be followed in echelon formation by the cavalry division, relieved by advance combat teams.

b. Report on intentions of AGp. South:

The recurrent threat to the northern flank from the direction of Korosten has prompted the decision to push this enemy in a northward direction, away from the advance and supply route Zvyagel-Zhitomir. Von Reichenau wanted the entire III Corps for this mission. Von Rundstedt decided that 25th Motorized Division and SS "Adolf Hitler" be placed under his command, while 13th and 14th Armored divisions remain in armored group to help carry out investment of Kiev from the south. This decision must be approved despite the consequent temporary disruption of the armored group.

. . .

13 July 1941

Situation: *AGp. South:* In Eleventh Army, pressure on the right flank is perceptibly slackening, as the Russians are falling back before the Romanian Fourth Army. Now only local Russian attacks.

Seventeenth Army is following in frontal advance; the Stalin line is said to be held only by weak forces. Contrariwise, reports coming in during the day indicate increasing artillery fire. According to prisoner statements, the troops in the positions are a jumble of ill-assorted units.

Sixth Army and Armored Group 1: Fighting at Berdichev continued and let up only toward the evening. It is not yet clear where the enemy, who attacked with strong armored forces, has disappeared to. The enemy penetration west of Berdichev has been wiped out. Our hopes, however, that 11th Armored Division might continue its swift advance in the direction of Belaya Tserkov have been disappointed. Farther northward, at and to the east of Zhitomir, repeated enemy attacks were repulsed at great cost to the enemy. Thirteenth Armored Division and, behind it, 14th Armored Division have reached the area west and south of Kiev.

In AGp. Center, Guderian's attack is developing surprisingly well. Misdirection of some units in initial deployment (3rd and 17th Armored divisions) is being straightened out. No clear picture yet on employment of the cavalry division, which should be on the right wing.

Hoth is making gratifying progress east of Vitebsk, gets on well farther northeast, but is almost at a standstill on his left wing (19th Armored Division).

AGp. North has made only slight advances, owing to condition of the roads. The right wing is still attacking, without making headway (II Corps). Some progress in Estonia, but resistance there is stiffening noticeably. More infantry is closing up in the direction of Lake Ilmen.

1230.   **Report to Fuehrer** (in his Hq.): After ObdH reviews the advances made by the armies, I report:

1.   In the enemy front, which is weakly held or manned by troops of dubious value in some sectors, but surely has no thought of giving ground, now that the new leaders have taken hold, we can make out the following grouping of forces:

   a.   *Leningrad:* Defense group consisting of forces hastily gathered up and strengthened by improvisations; showing no operational activity. As a first step, it will have to be cut off by a thrust into the Lake Ilmen and Lake Ladoga area.

   b.   *Nevel–Velikiye Luki.* This group is about seven divisions strong, including fresh troops, some of which arrived from the Ukraine and from the interior of Russia in the past few days. It has taken in also some battered units, veterans of the border battles, which were filled up at the straggler-collecting point at Nevel. This group is strong, and it would pay to mount a special operation to destroy it for good.

   c.   *Orsha-Vitebsk-Smolensk.* This group includes the enemy elements opposing Armored Groups 2 and 3; it has been reinforced on several occasions lately. Nineteenth Army, now in progress of formation east of Vitebsk, also belongs to this group; it is doubtful whether the enemy will be able to complete organization. The group will be attacked and destroyed by the offensive of the armored groups merged under Fourth Army Hq., which was planned as a pincer movement, but for the most part is taking effect as a frontal assault.

   d.   *Group Gomel.* Has not been attacked by us so far. Substantial portions seem to be moving against Armored Group 2. Calls for no major attention, save that Armored Group 2 must cover its right flank against it.

   e.   *Group Korosten* (about four divisions) comes from the Pripet marshes. It comprises elements which opposed our XVII Corps in the early border battles, and is reinforced by motorized forces. Its strength is occasionally put at as many as four corps Hq., but I have my doubts; the estimates are based on radio intelligence (deception?). This group as well as the one at Gomel can be cut off only in the course of the development of our movements, that is, with AGp. South also across the Dnieper, and Armored Group 2 cooperating from the north. For the present we must confine ourselves to containing it.

f. *Group Kiev.* It must be liquidated by the development operation started by AGp. South west of the Dnieper, or, if we see no prospects of success here, by envelopment east of the Dnieper.

2. *Next objects:* We shall temporarily halt the dash toward Moscow by AGps. 2 and 3, with the object of destroying a maximum of enemy strength on the present front. To this end Armored Groups 2 and 3 will be headed for the area northeast and southeast of Smolensk in such a way as to enable Armored Group 2, by striking for Velikiye Luki and Kholm, to cut off the enemy group mentioned under b., and Armored Group 3 to swing southward.

In AGp. South, Sixth Army will try with 25th Motorized Division and SS "Adolf Hitler" to destroy parts of Group Korosten, and, concurrently, with the bulk of Armored Group 1, by pushing the enveloping tank wing on Belaya Tserkov, to liquidate the enemy southwest of Kiev.

The *Fuehrer* approves the plans submitted. Particulars stressed by him:

a. A quick advance to the east is less important than smashing the enemy's military strength.

b. AGp. North must see its foremost object in breaking through north of Lake Ilmen, to close the gap to Lake Ladoga, and south of Lake Ilmen, to block the route at Staraya Russa.

c. The enemy group opposite the right wing of von Leeb's army group (referred to above under b.) must be attacked from the rear by motorized forces of Armored Group 3. Von Leeb must not be allowed to become too weak. Can we give him reinforcements?

d. Terror raid on Moscow is essential in order to prevent orderly evacuation of government agencies and to give the lie to enemy propaganda, which is speaking of exhaustion of German offensive capabilities.

e.   Transfer of 2d Armored Division will be stopped. Political reasons dictate its presence in the west.

General von Greiffenberg (on the phone): Commander of his army group holds that the chances are very good for our tank spearheads to smash through to Moscow. Their immediate objective would be the high ground northeast and southeast of Smolensk. He objects strongly to detaching forces in northeastern direction, sees no chance of cutting off any substantial bodies of enemy troops. All forces must be kept together to strengthen the thrust to the east.

A teletype received in the afternoon (addressed to ObdH, over von Bock's signature) develops the same ideas.

ObdH rings up shortly after noon: Since we left, the Fuehrer has been harping away on the following line:

There is a large gap between Zhitomir and 13th Armored Division, he thinks. Concentration of weight in the zone of action of 13th Armored Division is making no progress. Twenty-fifth Motorized Division and SS "Adolf Hitler" must be moved to 13th and 14th Armored divisions; they in turn would have to be relieved by advance combat teams, pushed into the area northeast of Zhitomir, which, for this purpose, must be temporarily combined into a force directed by army or army group.

This plan for solving the problems of army group, with which ObdH is not at all in sympathy, has prevailed because nobody around there is capable of standing up to von Reichenau's obstinate aggressiveness. Advance combat teams must, therefore, be combined, with a twofold purpose:

a.   Protecting the north flank of 13th and 14th Armored divisions.

b.   Relieving 25th Motorized Division and SS "Adolf Hitler."

The matter is discussed between Chief of Op. Sec. and army group, which must report what measures it will take.

These ideas are communicated to ObdH during the afternoon in a written order of the Fuehrer(!) (passed on verbatim to AGp. South).

. . .

14 July 1941

Situation: *South:* The attack into the northern flank at Zvyagel turns out to be an all-out offensive which has made local gains and even compelled us to commit 25th Motorized Division and SS "Adolf Hitler" to drive the enemy to the north, away from the Zvyagel-Zhitomir highway, which he had already crossed. This road is the only supply and communications line to III Corps sector. Its being temporarily under enemy pressure was the reason for the ammunition shortage in 13th Armored Division yesterday.

The battle around Berdichev, which at times was very bitter and turned into wholesale slaughter of the meaninglessly attacking enemy, is also now abating. Eleventh Armored Division has two thousand casualties(!). Army group thinks that the enemy was so severely beaten that 11th Armored Division could yet start its eastward thrust today. In conjunction with the latter, 16th Armored Division, next northward, is to strike against Belaya Tserkov.

Thirteenth Armored Division has destroyed the two railroad lines running into Kiev from west and south. Fourteenth Armored Division is following up closely. A reinforced batallion of 25th Motorized Division and a regiment of SS "Wiking" are following behind 14th Division. The rest of SS "Wiking" is following 9th Armored Division, which is striking for Belaya Tserkov from Zhitomir.

Center: Guderian's attack has made astonishing progress. Some of the enemy are running away in wild flight, some are making a stand. On the south flank, we have the first signs of a developing enemy counterattack, which will come from the previously reported Gomel group.

Hoth's central sector has made great strides with his right wing (12th Division) in heavy fighting. His left wing (19th Armored Division) is still immobilized.

North: The drive of the southern group now seems to be making progress. Hoepner has taken Reinhardt off the road to Leningrad, moving him to the west, into the area east of Lake Peipus. This creates a gap between him and von Manstein, who is striking at Novgorod (seat of Voroshilov's Hq.). The divisions of Eighteenth Army are following up at a good rate in the direction of Pskov.

Overall picture: The big battle in the south must be fought out by army group with its own resources. AGp. Center had better look after its right flank. On its left flank, the advance of the right wing of the Sixteenth Army offers the chance of achieving a partial success west of Nevel. To take advantage of this opportunity, the operations of the army groups must be closely integrated. In the central sector of Sixteenth

Army, another battle of encirclement is developing, which may lead to final destruction of the remnants of a Russian army (two divisions) fighting west of the big marsh area. AGp. North must do everything to keep its forces from dispersing and to mass them for the main thrust against Novgorod.

Talk with General von Greiffenberg (on phone): Coordination of AGp. Center and North in the battle of Nevel. Nineteenth Armored Division must be pushed on Nevel, but from there not any farther in the direction of Velikiye Luki before the battle of Nevel has been brought to a successful close.

South of the Nevel battlefield, another battle of encirclement is developing at Polotsk. Here it is important not to tie down the infantry of V and VI Corps, and to move them on as quickly as possible in a general eastern direction.

. . .

15 July 1941

Situation: *South:* Eleventh Army has gained elbow room on its right flank, but the enemy is still holding out south of the Dniester.

Seventeenth Army has made local penetrations in the Stalin line, but is under counterattack.

Sixth Army and Armored Group 1 have regrouped on their right wings, west of Berdichev.

The movement on Belaya Tserkov from Berdichev and Zhitomir has got under way and is already within a few kilometers of the objective. (Ninth Armored Division, behind it two-thirds of SS "Wiking.")

West and south of Kiev the situation of 13th and 14th Armored divisions, reinforced by motorized infantry, is unchanged. At Zvyagel and to the east, the enemy has been pressed back so that the Zvyagel-Zhitomir road is clear again. Second Armored Division has been ordered halted: the other GHq. Reserves are following behind center and northern wing of army group.

Center: In the territory passed through by Armored Groups 2 and 3, numerous local centers of resistance have become active and must now be liquidated. On the left wing, the situation at Polotsk is now gradually coming to a head. Here, and west of Nevel, the formation of pockets is becoming discernible. At Polotsk, a number of infantry divisions can now be freed to follow up behind Hoth.

North: Hoepner has been halted on the line reached today. The gap between his two groups is now being filled by an infantry division; he will have to wait for I Corps to come up behind von Manstein before he continues his drive on Novgorod.

Enemy situation: The overall impression is that the enemy, responding to the commanders and probably also to British efforts, is doing all he can to prevent being pushed back any farther to the east. The Russian troops now, as ever, are fighting with savage determination and with enormous human sacrifices. We can make out:

a.   A group at Leningrad, probably based on the marshlands southeast, south, and southwest of the city, which is attempting to throw a wide defense ring around the city and the industrial region.

b.   A new group in formation apparently between Kalinin and Rzhev which, securing its flank with the marsh and lake country, will have the mission to close, at Ostashkov, the gap between that area and the Moscow group. The defense positions at Rzhev are quite formidable.

c.   The Moscow group in the area Sychevka-Vyazma, west of Kaluga, which has the mission of blocking any advance on Moscow.

d.   A central reserve, which apparently is maintained in readiness on trains in the area Bryansk-Orel-Gorbachevo-Sukhinichi. It is probably the source of the forces fed into the counterattacks against Guderian's right shoulder.

e.   The small Gomel group.

f.   The Korosten group.

g.   The Kiev group, which embraces the entire region west of the Dnieper down to the Black Sea.

. . .

Heusinger (with OQu I): Operational disposition of enemy forces. My opinion (see today's entry under enemy situation) is shared by both. But it must always be remembered that this disposition is hypothetical rather than actual, for the enemy is short of troops. Paulus suggests that the mission of the Kalinin group may be not only to secure the gap between Moscow and Leningrad, but also to attack the flanks of the German forces advancing on Moscow, in conjunction with the Bryansk group kept mobile in trains.

.   .   .

16 July 1941

Situation: *South:* Enemy is evacuating Bessarabia. —Seventeenth Army has broken through the Stalin line on its entire front. —The breakthrough wedge, which points at Kiev, is being attacked from the north. —The Korosten enemy group has ceased attacking and has passed to the defensive. Artillery is still strong, but there are no more tanks. Railroad movements from this group to Kiev.

Center: From the Gomel area, a force of seven divisions is attacking the right shoulder of AGp. Center. This is the entire strength of the Gomel group, which thus is pinned down for the moment. In the area passed through by Guderian's and Hoth's breakthrough, there are still many enemy groups in fighting condition, which makes it necessary for our armor to attack in all directions. Even west of the Dnieper there are still some active enemy groups.

Hoth's right wing has reached the big concrete highway to Moscow, near Yartsevo, while Guderian's left wing has the sector of Smolensk. Here, then, the inner wings have linked up. Hoth's left wing apparently has pushed into an area only weakly held by the enemy. To check him the enemy may be forming a new enemy group in the Rzhev area.

On the northern wing of army group, 19th Armored Division has reached Nevel, but the planned junction with 12th Division has not been achieved, and so this pocket on the army group boundary has not yet been closed.

North: Regrouping continues in preparation for the drive, with main effort against and beyond Novgorod, but is still hampered by the local demands on Sixteenth Army, which is so very slow in releasing troops for the northward thrust.

Radio intelligence indicates presence at Dorpat of three enemy divisions opposing our advance unit, I Corps(!). This situation is intolerable. Army group will at least have to do something about this.

Enemy situation: Overall picture: On the front of AGp. South, the enemy is softening. His front is crumbling before Seventeenth Army; here, it seems, he has nothing left in the rear. I do not believe that here there is any coordinated plan for withdrawal behind the Dnieper. Possibly the Russian divisions falling back from southern Bessarabia will show up yet deep in the rear of the crumbling front. It remains to be seen whether the enemy will try to bring parts of his strong Korosten group to bear against our spearhead, through Kiev.

On the rest of the front the enemy no doubt intended to hold fast. I am entirely inclined to believe that the retreat movements from Smolensk to the east were momentary phenomena only. We have no clear picture yet of what is going on around Bologoye (southeast of Lake Ilmen), where unloading and movements of troops have been observed. Is an enemy group, gathered up in other places, forming in the Rzhev area? What about the Bryansk group? Does it really exist, and what is it doing?

.   .   .

17 July 1941

Situation: No important changes.

In *AGp. South,* the situation is developing along its logical lines. The enemy is attempting, with local forces, to counter the encircling moves against his northern wing at Belaya Tserkov and southeast of Berdichev, but, by and large, he appears to concentrate on extricating himself from the pocket developing between Eleventh and Seventeenth armies.

On the northern flank (Korosten-Kiev), the jumble of enemy units previously reported in the area between Korosten and Kiev has been reinforced by two new divisions, one coming from the Caucasus.

What I cannot understand is the inaction of 13th Armored Division, which seems to be doing nothing about the enemy reported to be retreating right past it from Korosten in the direction of Kiev.

AGp. Center: Formation of the pocket is proceeding consistently. Guderian's right wing seems to have obtained full freedom of movement in the direction of Roslavl. Quite far to the flank, the enemy is trying to turn the situation by launching attacks into Guderian's flank and, farther back, against Second Army, but without success.

AGp. North: Here, too, the formation of a pocket is developing. On the right wing, at Nevel, the junction with Hoth's left wing has not been accomplished quite yet. Also in this sector, enemy elements appear to have escaped to the east and are not moving in the direction of Velikiye Luki. The "eastern front" shows another promising pocket in the Opochka area; some enemy bodies initially got away to the east, toward Kholm, but appear to have returned to free their encircled comrades.

Situation of Hoepner's group unchanged. I Corps is closing up in rapid marches.

.   .   .

18 July 1941

Situation: *AGp. South's* operation is becoming increasingly shapeless. The front against Korosten still absorbs large forces. The appearance of new, strong enemy forces attacking from the north near Kiev compels us to move infantry divisions to that sector, to relieve and replace armor (III Corps). This pins down greater strength on the northern front than is desirable. The turning wing of Armored Group 1, too, does not seem to get started on its southward drive. It is still hanging back around Berdichev and Belaya Tserkov. Meanwhile, the breakthrough wedge of Seventeenth Army has advanced so far that right wing of Sixth Army (operating under Armored Group 1) might as well be switched from the encircling operation, for which it was slated, and sent on eastward to the area south of Kiev to be on hand for the Dnieper crossing.

The Fuehrer has now given orders to take Odessa. For that mission we have only Hansen's corps with two German and several Romanian divisions. This move, which, I agree, is necessary, would divert strength from the big envelopment now initiated.

In *AGp. Center,* the armored divisions are re-forming for the fronts to be established to the northeast and southeast. Infantry divisions are moving close behind. The organizations forming the rings around the pockets are continually changing, and it will be interesting to see how long this can go on without impairing the tightness of the encirclement. On the southern wing, east of Mogilev, the enemy keeps up his heavy attacks, which is precisely what we want him to do (Fifth Russian Army).

North of the line Smolensk-Orsha, on the northern wing of *army group,* the northernmost pocket seems to have been securely closed by 12th Infantry Division's moving down from the north and linking up with 19th Armored Division. Tension seems to be easing also in the process of forming the other pocket, but we cannot be quite sure yet.

In *AGp. North,* no important changes. At Opochka, the enemy is struggling to extricate his encircled units by attacking us from the outside; he is being repulsed.

At Gdov (eastern shore of Lake Peipus), a "special division" has been captured; it is composed of, respectively, a unit of women, convicts, and Communist youths.

. . .

Von Greiffenberg:

a. Overall mission: Smash all enemy forces that can be reached now. We must be sure to finish the job. On this account, and to ensure thorough mopping up, the area conquered must be safeguarded from incursions; further extensions only insofar as necessary to consolidate these gains.

b. Possible future talks: Form frontal group with Ninth Army and right wing of Second Army; on its northern wing, Armored Group 3. Another group for turning movement to the southeast, comprising the bulk of Second Army (inner ring) and Armored Group 1 (outer ring). Movements of reserves and bringing up of GHq. Reserves must conform with these ideas. What should be the command organization for this operation?

c. Direction of the mopping-up operations in newly conquered territory. Cover right flank.

d. Striking power of the armored divisions: 60 percent.

. . .

19 July 1941

Situation: In *AGp. South* all planning is dominated by the discovery of the imminent attack by the Russian Twenty-sixth Army; captured orders indicate that it consists of six infantry divisions and two divisions, under two corps Hq. Three of these divisions are supposed to come from the Lithuanian front, whereas the rest (VI Corps) are said to have fought in the Ukraine from the start. The weather continues bad, which will probably slow the movements of AGp. South to a considerable degree. If we add to this the effect of the impending enemy attack by quite a sizable force, it appears likely that the start of this large-scale armored-group offensive will be canceled or delayed again.

AGp. Center: Reports capture of a Russian order indicating that the Russian High Command is aiming at separating the German armor from supporting infantry units by driving attacks between them. In theory this is a very pretty scheme, but in practice it is something that can be carried out only by an opponent superior in number and generalship. Against our armies, and with the infantry corps never slackening in closing to the armor, I do not see a chance for applying such a policy. On the southern wing of the army group, enemy pressure continues.

AGp. North: No new trends discernible in the development. The appearance of a battalion of Moscow factory police demonstrates that communications between Moscow and Leningrad must still be open; it would be desirable from the operational standpoint if the enemy were not able to maintain communications between Lake Ilmen and Moscow. But I am beginning to wonder if we are not being confronted here with the incipient formation of a strong group between Bologoye and Rzhev, which eventually might make it necessary for von Leeb's right wing to advance beyond the northern edge of the Valdai Hills.

In Estonia, the situation is developing favorably due to the enemy's inaction. The possibility of a crisis is fading.

Navy thinks that the enemy is becoming increasingly aware of our weakness and passivity in the Baltic; we must therefore expect intensification of enemy activity and a mounting threat to the sea route to Libau and Windau. These ports are essential for our supplies.

.   .   .

20 July 1941

By plane to Hq. AGp. South.

0700. Situation report by Lieutenant Colonel von Grolman. No important change in the situation since yesterday.

0730. Leave by car; 0830 take-off at Loetzen; 1130 arrival at Stara Konstantinov.

Army Hq. is housed in a Russian military school. A characteristic feature is the tokens of "culture"; on the outside, colossal plaster columns with Corinthian capitals; on the inside, heroic-size plaster statuary (sitting group Lenin-Stalin, soldiers of army and air force).

Conference with Ia: Lieutenant Colonel Winter sketches the situation for me. The overall picture agrees with that we have at OKH. A new feature is the enormous difficulties besetting the movements of Armored Group Kleist. An example is 11th Armored Division, which is advancing on Uman in three distinct groups:

1. Tracked vehicles, with infantry on top.

2. Peasant carts carrying infantry, following behind the tracked vehicles.

3. Wheeled motor vehicles, which cannot keep up on the rain-soaked roads and so must be left behind in towns.

The main problem now is how to get von Kleist's group where we want it to go. Its main body, together with elements of III Corps, brought down from the north, where they were relieved by infantry, now is fighting the Russian Twenty-sixth Army, which is attacking with its northern wing just to the south of Kiev, and with its southern wing at Tarashcha; each wing has one fresh division, while the rest were hurt in earlier battles. The attacks have all been repelled, but they pin down the bulk of von Kleist's group so that actually only a weak armored force, 11th and 16th Armored divisions, remains available for tactical envelopment in the rear of the enemy now retreating before von Schwedler's drive. The operational envelopment in the direction of Kirovograd has not yet got under way and will probably hang fire for some time yet. The assumption that the Russian Twenty-sixth Army will soon be defeated looks to me too optimistic.

The next question, concerning von Reichenau's army, is answered to the effect that in consequence of the events at Zvyagel, his left wing has become comparatively strong. He is still confronted by a strong enemy, whose artillery is now less active. The right wing, which is a long way off to the east, is gaining ground, but it looks as if it will be impossible to give that wing the strong forces that would enable it effectively to interpose itself between the enemy's Korosten group and the Dnieper. Army group rather expects that the enemy will be pushed against the Dnieper, which will successively be crossed by von Reichenau north of Kiev. The city then would be taken from the east.

For forming the group which we would like to build up south of Kiev, army group has available only the GHq. Reserves standing far in the rear, now that LV Corps has been committed to relieve III Motorized Corps. We thus get the following picture, which is also presented in a sketch submitted by army group. The forces of army group fall into two groups moving in divergent directions: the big enveloping operation south of Kiev, in which von Kleist will push with his main concentration in the direction of Kirovograd, and von Reichenau's attacking operation. The link between them is a weak group, LV Corps, which will have to be satisfied if it accomplishes as much as blocking enemy action from Kiev against the two large offensive groups.

Von Reichenau's prospects of success are not too rosy, for his attack will back the enemy against the Dnieper, instead of pushing him away from it and so cut him off. The Russian Twenty-sixth Army, which von Kleist must shake off before he can strike southeastward with sufficient forces, will likewise be pressed back frontally behind the Dnieper. To cross to the other side, it has four military bridges available between Cherkassy and Kiev. It is altogether uncertain what von Kleist's offensive against Kirovograd, which is already behind schedule, would be able to catch. Undoubtedly there are still some strong enemy groups in the area west of Uman, but whether they can be cut off depends on how much time is lost in fighting the Russian Twenty-sixth Army.

I stress the following points:

a.   Von Reichenau's operation must be conducted in such a way that the enemy will be pushed away from the Dnieper. As of 25 or 26 July, it will be possible to have cooperation of XXXV Corps out of the Mozyr area.

b.   Everything must be done to form a strong group south of Kiev. In addition to the GHq. divisions earmarked by army group, it must be allotted also parts of von Reichenau's and von Schwedler's forces at the very earliest.

c.   Everything must be done to avoid pushing the Russian Twenty-sixth Army to the Dnieper in purely frontal fighting and to prevent its withdrawal to Kiev with elements still capable of giving battle.

d. We must soon be able to exert strong armored pressure in the direction of Kirovograd.

. . .

Development of the situation: In the meanwhile, the enemy on AGp. Center's front has succeeded in breaking out of the Nevel pocket. We cannot say as yet whether this is the result of 19th Armored Division's swinging toward Velikiye Luki too soon; in any case, this is a distressing development. The escaped elements will hurl themselves against Velikiye Luki and will make life miserable for the elements of 19th Armored Division in the area, which have very tough going even now. And there are many more sore spots on the front of AGp. Center. On the southern flank, for instance, the enemy has been able to penetrate at several points; and on the eastern front of von Kluge's army, which is forming north and south of Smolensk, several sectors are under heavy attack. Notwithstanding all this, we shall probably succeed in stabilizing our position east of Smolensk and so ensure an early liquidation of the big enemy pocket west of Smolensk.

The costly battles involving some groups of our armored forces, in which the infantry divisions arriving from the west can take a hand only slowly, together with loss of time due to bad roads which restrict movement and the weariness of the troops marching and fighting without a break, have put a damper on all higher Hq. Its most visible expression is the severe depression into which ObdH has been plunged. But in matter of fact there is really no reason for any such thing. We must let the great breakthrough battle take its course and judge its result later.

In AGp. South much ground has meanwhile been gained toward Uman, but the successes of our troops in the battle with the Russian Twenty-sixth Army are on the whole of a defensive character. AGp. North continues shifting its troops to the north as has been planned, without too much interference from the enemy now. AGp. Center reports a mounting bag of prisoners: nearly 100,000 since 10 July.

21 July 1941

. . .

General Oehquist reports on his journey to Finland. Erfurth's suspicion that Marshal Mannerheim is opposed to the operation east of Ladoga is unfounded. Talked with Mannerheim and Erfurth. The underlying cause of this storm in the teacup seems to be that Erfurth, having little to do and to say, suffered an attack of inferiority feelings.

The successes of the Finnish troops in the advance are very gratifying.

General Matzky reports on current business in his section.

Gehlen reports on the Fuehrer's visit to AGp. North. All seems to have gone well at the conference. Someone, apparently Keitel, is constantly pushing the Fuehrer that armor should be shifted from Center to AGp. North, that is, to the high ground east of Lake Ilmen. Doing that would be quite a mistake.

True, it might prove necessary to divert some of our steadily dwindling armor to the Bologoye area in order to eliminate this railroad center, but farther north von Leeb now has all he can use. The Bologoye mission would best be carried out as an AGp. Center operation (after shifting the boundary!).

.   .   .

22 July 1941

Situation: In *AGp. South,* heavy fighting is in progress at Uman, where 16th and 11th Armored divisions have clashed with strong forces of the enemy. Apparently the enemy is concentrating units taken out of his withdrawing front against our tank wedge in order to save as much as he can of the perhaps substantial force in the area, now threatened with encirclement. This policy may of course produce some tight situations for our armor in the Uman area, especially as the operation against the Red Twenty-sixth Army looks as if it might drag on awhile.

In von Reichenau's sector, adoption of our suggestion is showing results. He is now making his main effort on the right wing in order to push the Korosten enemy away from the Dnieper. Also, formation of the assault group south of Kiev has now been initiated.

In *AGp. Center,* the Smolensk pocket is actually not yet closed. Seventh Armored Division is apparently not on the great motor highway to Moscow, but north of it; fighting is continuing also in that area. Now with the Nevel pocket burst open and Velikiye Luki abandoned, the prospects of an overwhelming success in terms of enemy destroyed are dwindling. Also on the Dnieper, at Novi Bikhov, the enemy is still holding firm and fighting.

In *AGp. North,* the movements are developing according to plan.

. . .

In the afternoon, ObdH returns from the Fuehrer, who is again in a state over AGp. North. It is not concentrated anywhere and does everything wrong. As a matter of fact, things up there are not quite as good as in other places, and cooperation with us is a little less smooth.

In the afternoon, work on the directives for the coming operations of the army groups.

. . .

24 July 1941

Situation: In *AGp. South,* the situation in 11th and 17th Armored divisions is growing increasingly acute. The two divisions are much too weak to withstand the onrush of the enemy driven back by von Schwedler and Seventeenth Army, and it is difficult to get reinforcements to them from the main body of armored group, which is pinned down in fighting right now. Seventeenth and Eleventh armies are making good progress; but Eleventh Army is pointed very far to the southeast, instead of hard to the east! Sixth Army is still scattered all over the map. No concentration anywhere!

Center is closing up. Enemy pressure against the flanks is preparing or (in the north) already developing. Difficulties on the extreme right wing of Second Army.

North is regrouping for new advances. So far it is still impossible to make out at which point the main weight is going to be concentrated.

. . .

26 July 1941

Situation: *South:* The enemy is still finding means to escape the developing encirclement. Savage counterattacks against the advancing pursuit forces cover the effort of extricating troops from the threatened area, which is accomplished with exceeding skill, by both rail and motorized movements. The Red Twenty-sixth Army has been severely compressed; the Red Fifth Army is shifting its main weight to the east.

Center: On the front of von Bock's extreme right wing, the enemy is giving ground. The strong forces which recently were at Gomel apparently are being shifted northward, to the area of the Roslavl-Smolensk highway. At Yelnya, the enemy is continuing his attacks with new divisions and new tanks brought up from the east.

Attacks also from northeastern direction against Hoth's northern flank. Our infantry is closing up.

North: Enemy resistance by many small enemy bodies fighting stubbornly on the front of the southern wing and on both sides of Lake Ilmen. In von Manstein's sector, slow progress in very difficult terrain. West of Lake Peipus, the enemy forces are being pinched off at Dorpat.

Overall picture: Enemy defense is becoming more aggressive; more tanks, more planes. In addition to ten new divisions previously listed, fifteen more new divisions have been reported.

Morning conference with ObdH. I outline the proposal of the army groups for the next moves, adding my critical comments. I am surprised by his emphasis on the necessity of an early attack against the strong enemy group at Gomel. It soon becomes apparent that this is one of the Fuehrer's notions.

Such a plan implies a shift in our strategy from the operational to the tactical level. If striking at small local enemy concentrations becomes our sole objective, the campaign will resolve itself into a series of minor successes which will advance our front only by inches. Pursuing such a policy eliminates all tactical risks and enables us gradually to close the gaps between the front of the army groups, but the result will be that we feed all our strength into a front expanding in width at the sacrifice of depth and end up in position warfare!

ObdH calls up von Bock to talk over the possibilities for an offensive against the Gomel group. Von Bock vehemently opposes any attack with tanks from the east, holding that such a diversion of armor would sabotage the very operational conceptions underlying the plan for the new phase of the campaign.

Major von Below (Liaison Officer to Guderian) reports on enemy picture and situation. Combat strength of our own troops after five days of refitting will be an average of about 50 percent. —Memorandum in justification of himself.

Von Etzdorf: *Japan:* New Cabinet apparently continues pro-Axis orientation. Timing may be changed. —Indochina. —Vladivostok.

France has been put on ice. No reply to their notes before two or three weeks. Question of Bizerte is being worked on.

Turkey: Von Papen reports that things will follow their logical development if we make progress against Russia. German offers postponed until some later date. The Turks are thinking of the creation of buffer states in Caucasia and Turkostan.

Iran: Government virtually under British control (gold!).

U.S.A: Entry into the war unlikely at the moment. —Still, Roosevelt's "hectic policy" admits of surprises. —Efforts to give assistance by supplies are indicated by stepped-up shipments to Basra.

Finland fights shy of breaking diplomatic relations with England. Seizure of Finnish ships by England will perhaps speed up the matter.

Sweden has refused joining the Axis. We shall ignore her in the future.

Balkans: Bulgaro-Romanian conversations on frontier readjustment and resettlement of populations.

Italy: War unpopular. Strong voices against the policy of colonial and empire expansion. Fuehrer's letter to Il Duce, reminding him to keep watchful eye on France. (The motive probably is to dissipate Italian suspicions.)

General Konrad:

    a.   The Reich Marshal is critical of the army.

    b.   Air force wants army to clarify main effort.

    c.   Review of coming operations.

1800–2015. Report to the Fuehrer on plans of the army groups. Long-winded, at times warm, discussion on missed opportunities for encirclement. He wants:

    1.   AGp. South must abandon the plan of an operational envelopment west of the Dnieper if prospects of success are seen diminishing. All armored divisions must then be put across to eastern bank.

2. Disposition of Gomel by a purely tactical operation conducted by a new group to be formed under von Kluge. The operation must be launched at the earliest, regardless of the timing of other attacks, and if possible be developed into encirclement of the Korosten group.

3. Von Bock's group for the frontal offensive on Moscow should start pushing ahead slowly as soon as ready. No hurry.

4. Hoth should start his drive on the Valdai Hills as soon as possible, so that he would get there no later than the right wing of Sixteenth Army.

5. In AGp. North, main effort on Lake Ilmen.

The Fuehrer's analysis, which at many points is unjustly critical of the field commands, indicates a complete break with the strategy of large operational conceptions. You cannot beat the Russians with operational successes, he argues, because they simply do not know when they are defeated. On that account it will be necessary to destroy them bit by bit, in small encircling actions of a purely tactical character.

Of course, there is something in these ideas as regards the Russians. But following such a course implies letting the enemy dictate our policy, and reduces our operations to a tempo which will not permit us to reach our goal, the Volga. We must remember that the Russians have plenty of manpower, and it is very unlikely that we could pursue the new policy to the point where the enemy cracks and the way is clear again for operations on a big scale.

To me, these arguments mark the beginning of the decline of our initial strategy of imaginative operations, and a willingness to throw away the opportunities offered us by the impetus of our infantry and armor.

It remains to be seen whether this radical change in strategic conception, which at first certainly will come as a surprise also to the enemy, will bring the desired success. My representations stressing the importance of Moscow are brushed aside without any valid counterevidence.

General Paulus reports on his visit to AGp. North. Hoepner, von Manstein, and Reinhardt concur that the area between Lake Ilmen and Lake Peipus is unsuited to operations of armored units. All we can do at Lake Ilmen is to attack with infantry while keeping in readiness the armor not yet committed (von Manstein's corps), for a follow-up where infantry has cleared the path. As a consequence, development of the battle will be very slow.

The situation of Reinhardt's corps is very uncomfortable. Reinhardt vehemently demands to be given the go-ahead signal. But this is out of the question as long as the offensive from the direction of Luga has not become effective.

Greatly intensified enemy air activity is reported also in that area.

.   .   .

27 July 1941

Situation: In *AGp. South,* disastrous rainstorms have paralyzed all movements. All we can try to accomplish now is to push the tank wedge aimed at Uman sufficiently far to the south, so as to cut at least the railroad and roads going east through Uman.

In *AGp. Center* weak enemy attacks are reported on the Dnieper, at Gomel, heavier ones at Roslavl. All were repelled, at great cost to the enemy in prisoners and guns. At Yelnya, the front has quieted. In Hoth's sector, the enemy launched local attacks mostly in battalion or regiment strength, without success. Attacks were also repulsed on the left wing, south of Velikiye Luki. Enemy air activity is on the increase and in part quite uncomfortable.

AGp. North. Nothing new. Stiff enemy resistance on the front of our Lake Ilmen group; on the rest of this front, no major actions. West of Lake Peipus, part of the enemy force is encircled north of Dorpat. The other sectors are quiet.

.   .   .

30 July 1941

Situation: In *AGp. South,* the weeks of grinding at the Russian front in the Ukraine are beginning to tell. The enemy front is crumbling. Notwithstanding, we must expect that owing to the absence of any pressure from the Romanians and the existence of several well-preserved enemy divisions in the sector of the Front Group South, an attempt will be made to hold the coastal district around Odessa. Odessa may become a Russian Tobruk. There is only one way to prevent this: Armored Group 1 must strike due south through Pervomaysk.

Von Schwedler has re-formed a large portion of his group. It would be inadvisable at this time to send him off in northeastern direction for a crossing of the Dnieper south of Kiev; instead, it must be moved due east so that it remains available a few days longer for operations to the south.

Sixth Army has not completely detached its left wing. Von Reichenau, with his right wing, is probably pressing on to the Dnieper, north of Kiev. He has his orders to destroy the enemy group at Korosten, and must be kept from doing anything else.

Center: Attempts to withdraw the armored divisions from their sectors must be abandoned owing to the incessant enemy attacks. Fourth Armored Division had to be committed again at Krichev, "Grossdeutschland" at Roslavl.

South and southwest of Toropets, heavy fighting is reported. Here we have a chance to catch a large enemy force, and would need cooperation of AGp. Center, attacking with 14th Motorized Division from the south, and AGp. North, attacking with L Corps from the north, and with Schobert's group from Velikiye Luki. The order for such an operation must come from OKH.

North: It is becoming evident that OKH is revising its erstwhile notions and no longer insists on the impossible demand for AGp. North to cut off the eastward retreat route of the enemy around Leningrad. For the time being the commitment of VIII Air Corps in the sector of AGp. North has been canceled. —Eighth Armored Division has gone into action at Luga.

.   .   .

1600.   General Jodl calls up: The Fuehrer has arrived at a new conception of the next phase of the campaign:

AGp. North must defeat the enemy at Leningrad; is left discretion in choosing direction of main effort. Plan of thrust to cut the Moscow-Leningrad railroad is dropped.

Center: Here we must pass to the defensive. Only security measures on the line Lake Ilmen–Kholm–Toropets! Withdraw armored divisions for rehabilitation.

South: For the time being we must leave Gomel alone. Whether we shall do Roslavl is not yet decided at the moment.

Air force: Shift main strength to AGp. North, for close support in eliminating the enemy in Estonia. Will not be withdrawn before accomplishment of mission of AGp. North is assured.

. . .

2400. **Heusinger:** OKW has signed new "directive" which adopts our proposals! Limited objective: Rogachev. Not more than one armored division will be employed. At Roslavl, 263d Infantry Division will help. Toropets must be done. All necessary orders will be contained in the forthcoming Fuehrer order.

This decision frees every thinking soldier of the horrible vision obsessing us these last few days, since the Fuehrer's obstinacy made the final bogging down of the eastern campaign appear imminent. At long last we get a break!

Memorandum of the Naval Operations Staff on the battle of the Atlantic. Very gratifying, but also sober in its appraisal of the situation.

1 August 1941

Situation: *South: Seventeenth Army and Armored Group 1* are making good progress in their envelopment operation. Seventeenth Army is meeting fierce *frontal* opposition at some points. No change in the situation in the sector of the *Eleventh Army* to the south. LIV Corps is making slow progress, but so far the enemy still operating near the coast has brought to bear only partial elements against the flank of Eleventh Army. He is likely to cause more trouble in the coming days. *Sixth Army* has now reached the Dnieper, though as yet only with advance combat teams, and has taken enemy shipping under fire. The violent battle south of Kiev appears to have been decided in our favor. When it will be followed by our penetration into the city cannot yet be foreseen. The group fighting in the forest area west of Kiev (111th and 296th divisions) has not much chance to score any major successes. On the other hand, the concentric attack on Korosten is gradually developing.

Center: The attack on Roslavl (VII Corps and parts of 24th Motorized Division) has had a good start. As before, the Russians are launching local attacks against the rest of the front, always without any appreciable success. —The Smolensk pocket has been further compressed, but not substantially changed.

The situation invites comment on two important points:

1. The operation against the enemy in the Smolensk pocket is again being approached the wrong way. Four divisions are advancing eastward from the west, pushing the enemy against the eastern block formed by only four battalions of 7th Armored Division, which is also being attacked by the enemy from the east. We need hardly be surprised if 7th Armored Division eventually gets badly hurt.

2. The entire front of Hoth's armored group is uncomfortably thin. There is nothing behind it. This is due to the fact that Ninth Army has committed most of its infantry divisions against the Smolensk pocket, and needs what is left on its extreme left wing. Meanwhile army group cannot get up enough steam to make Guderian, fighting in the adjoining sector to the south, do anything to relieve the situation around Smolensk. But that would be the only way to free troops for the follow-up behind Hoth.

At Velikiye Luki the situation is unchanged. Here the enemy appears to have the initiative. South of Korosten we have with great effort pushed the enemy back northward.

North has enveloped Kholm from the south and east (12th Division) under hard fighting. The enemy apparently has brought up new forces from the east. It cannot be made out yet whether the three enemy divisions which were switched from the Leningrad front to this sector, according to the statement of the captured staff officer, have really arrived.

No change in the area of Lake Ilmen, apart from minor local gains. Eighth Armored Division has been taken out of the central group (Luga) and is kept in readiness behind the front. The disposition of this group shows nothing to indicate a tendency toward the Narva wing.

West of Lake Peipus: mopping up and moving of the Dorpat forces to the northwest, according to plan.

. . .

2 August 1941

Situation: The morning situation shows no new developments. In *AGp. South*, the pocket is forming according to plan. The confusion in the enemy movements is clearly appreciable. Here, too, the enemy is throwing into the battle whatever he can scrape together within a reasonable distance, but the time for a planned disengagement has passed. The southern flank of Eleventh Army bears close watching. Here we have no clear picture of the enemy situation, but as the main body of Eleventh Army is facing south, it is fair to assume that it is pinned down by enemy attacks. —It would not be advisable to launch the attack on Kiev directly from yesterday's positions. Troops must first close up and regroup. The fortification line of Kiev apparently is weakly held. In Sixth Army no important changes.

Center: Has made very good progress against Roslavl. In addition to VII Corps, IX Corps also will attack today. Nothing new from the rest of the front, apart from reports that the Russians are building a bridge across the Dnieper east of Smolensk. The extreme left wing of Ninth Army has started off on the attack on Velikiye Luki. The nearest rear divisions are closing up.

.   .   .

b.   *Clothing:*

Troops had been refitted; at beginning of the campaign they had a 5 percent clothing and 10 percent shoe reserve. Position now tight. Economies necessary in units in the west. Replacement units and newly activated units must now be equipped with lace boots and leggings instead of shaft boots. Winter clothing: Results of drive to return winter clothing issued last winter, which had to be turned in by May, were very disappointing. The west will have to shift for itself. For the east, sufficient stocks will arrive in depots of the Chief of Army Equipment before October. Problem of distribution. (Each man: Two woolen vests, toques, earmuffs, gloves, scarves, chest warmers.)

.   .   .

General Buhle reports on his tour to Guderian's group. A significant development is the clamor for loss replacements both by armored divisions and infantry divisions.

1.   Replacement situation:

AGp. South casualties: 63,000 repl. received: 10,000
AGp. Center casualties: 74,500 repl. received: 23,000
AGp. North casualties: 42,000 repl. received: 14,000

AGp. Center asks for additional 10,000 replacements within eight-
ten days. When they have been received, the situation will be as
follows:

Army Hq. 2: 30,000-man deficit
Army Hq. 9: 15,000-man deficit
Armd Gp. 2:   5,000-man deficit
Armd Gp. 3:   4,000-man deficit

Of the total Replacement Reserve of 300,000 in the homeland,
47,000 have to date been sent to the front.

2. *Report on road conditions.* Dust ruins the engines.

3. VII and IX Corps have apparently captured enough enemy vehicles
at Mogilev to fill all their requirements.

4. Situation is worst in 18th Armored Division. 30 percent are total
losses!

.   .   .

3 August 1941

Situation: *South:* Bad weather luck! The battle in the pocket which had such
a promising start is hampered by rainstorms restricting the mobility of
our armor. Nevertheless, prospects are good for a decisive success.
The encircled ten to twelve divisions will probably be destroyed. Whatever escapes to the southeast now or later on will be severely crippled
in its striking power. At Kirovograd the first of the newly activated
Russian units observed by our air reconnaissance (223d Division) has
shown up in a counterattack and was repulsed. —The intention expressed
by army group to drive ahead to Alyekandriya with III Armored Corps
should be reconsidered. Our first job is to win the battle at Pervomaysk
and to the south. To assure this, the infantry of Seventeenth Army
also must move up to support the armored divisions or else enemy

pressure will become too much for them. —On the bank of the Dnieper south of Kiev 132d Division is under attack from two sides.

At Kiev no new advances. In the northern sector of Sixth Army, the attacking wing is advancing at Malin. (LI Corps) *Center: Field Marshal von Bock* on phone: Von Bock accuses himself of foolhardiness, for making the attack on Roslavl at a time when he has practically no reserves to meet the enemy attack on his eastern front. Guderian has carried off his 137th Division for the drive on Roslavl. *Ammunition still a major problem,* because of failure of railroad deliveries. *Situation at Yelnya:* The troops are laughing off Russian attacks of armor and infantry, but feel very uncomfortable about the artillery fire, which they cannot return because of ammunition shortages.

. . .

4 August 1941

Situation: No unexpected developments along the entire front.

In *AGp. South* we must accept the fact that fairly large enemy forces could not be cut off by the closing ring and now are streaming toward the Lower Dnieper. Perhaps this movement promises evacuation; however, in striking contrast to former reports, the roads are clogged with columns on foot, at some points several abreast. Part of the movement is in the direction of Odessa and Nikolayev.

There are indications of a bridgehead at Cherkassy and AAA defense on the Dnieper. AGp. South seems to be rather reluctant to push armor farther south, beyond Pervomaysk, and would rather have the Hungarian mobile units do the mopping up west of the Bug. This is understandable, because army group is thinking of objectives farther east and the capture of the Dnieper crossings. Nevertheless, it will be necessary to employ strong armored forces in the southward pursuit, for the follow-through at least. In *Sixth Army,* nothing new.

Center. The Russian cavalry on the extreme southern wing is collapsing. Small Russian elements surrounded in the Roslavl area. Minor attacks on the rest of the front, directed chiefly against Hoth on the northern wing, are repelled.

North: Our attacks at Kholm and Staraya Russa, and also west of Lake Ilmen, are continuing. Preparations for the attack between Lake Ilmen and Narva planned for 6 August are in progress.

. . .

i. The Fuehrer explains:

1. Gives the reasons for his tight-handedness in allotting tanks to the divisions. Still, he releases 350 engines for Tank III (without being aware, however, that OKH has already released them). Will be shipped by air.

2. Reiterates the familiar points of view determining the pattern of the continuance of the campaign; as before, the emphasis is on Leningrad and control of the south (coal, iron, elimination of the enemy air base in the Crimea), with Moscow being brushed aside.

. . .

OQu IV:

1. *Bansai* stated that the army and the government are now determined to join in the war against Russia in spite of prevailing difficulties. He thinks it will be in September. By the end of August, sixteen divisions will be assembled in Manchuria (at present ten divisions). Capture of Vladivostok perhaps possible by November. The Chinese must be held in check during that period. Operations against Singapore have been prepared by establishing foothold in Indochina, but are being put aside for the time being.

2. *Attaché reports:* Finland cannot conceal a measure of disappointment at the performance of the German troops both on the northern front and in support of the Karelian army. The Romanians are in high dudgeon over a gratuitous telegram by Just on matters of military command.

3. *France:* General atmosphere of crisis. Tension between Darlan and Weygand intensified.

4. *Italy* holds herself ready for intervention in case of a British invasion of Corsica. (Alibi for Italian ambitions.)

Talk with Heusinger and Paulus, and along the same lines with ObdH in the evening:

Our command function is exhausted in details, which are really the responsibility of army group Hq., where we should be giving them clear-cut missions and the material means for independent action. In order to remedy this situation, it would be necessary for ourselves to have a clear idea of what the political command regards as the prime objectives in the campaign. What, in fact, is our chief object: to capture the Ukraine and the Caucasus as quickly as possible for economic ends, or else to defeat the enemy decisively? If it is the former, we should have full liberty in the use of our resources, without that constant interference from top level. OKH's objective for this year is the area around Moscow, leaving the gaining of more ground to the development of the situation. Under these circumstances, naturally we could not expect to reach the Caucasus before onset of this winter. For the former alternative, we would need strong forces for an invasion of the oil region, and then we would have to go all the way to Baku.

Evening situation: No substantial changes. AGp. Center is the only sector of the front where the enemy attacks in all directions, anticipated for today, have not materialized. Perhaps they will come tomorrow.

No other important news.

5 August 1941

Situation: *South:* The Pervomaysk pocket is being liquidated with the enemy still showing plenty of fight. He is still getting supplies, by air, and fights desperately, but developments have already bypassed this center of resistance. Accordingly, army group Hq. has already given the order for the next moves in the operation:

Eleventh Army is assigned the mission to destroy the enemy on its front by pushing armor to the Bug at Vesnesensk. Eventually it is to occupy the coast.

Armored Group 1 is ordered to strike with its main body for Alyekandriya on the axis Kirovograd and Smela and secure the bridges at Kremenchug and Cherkassy. Three armored divisions under Corps Hq. XII must stand by east of Pervomaysk in order, if needed, to work their way along and across the Bug and effect a junction with Eleventh Army.

Seventeenth Army is to proceed eastward beyond the line Krivoy Rog–Alyekandriya. The mission of *Sixth Army* remains unchanged.

Center: No major attacks except at Yelnya and on the northern flank of army group. Army group is endeavoring to straighten out the unsatisfactory situation on its right and left wings. Its central sector, i.e., the front facing east, is gradually developing some depth.

North: Eighth August has been set as date for resumption of the offensive.

ObdH is back from the Fuehrer conference.

He relates: The Fuehrer came out with the statement (i.e., we had it discreetly put into his system) that the present developments must lead to a solidification of the fronts, like that in World War I. To prevent this it is necessary to crack the front where it will hurt the enemy and cost us little, and so get out into the open and on the move again. We cannot do everything at once, and that not only in consideration of the army but also because of the air force.

He sees the following possibilities for the three army groups.

1. *Take the Valdai Hills with support from Hoth* (one to two armored divisions, one motorized division), thereby advancing von Bock's left wing; such a move would cover von Leeb's flank. No further advance in northward direction.

   The idea of providing cover for von Leeb's flank is completely wrong, but evidently he was not talked out of it because that was his starting point. What really matters to us is that with the Valdai Hills in our hands, Hoth has a jump-off base for the eastward drive along the Volga!

2. *Restore the situation at the southern wing of AGp. Center,* if possible in conjunction with liquidation of Korosten, followed by advance toward Moscow.

   Mogilev-Kiev! This idea dispels a nightmare. Still, this desire to liquidate Korosten is a dangerous idea. It will continually draw forces away from the main object, the drive toward the east. Let's wait and see!

3. *Liquidation of the enemy forces west of the Bug.* XIV Corps must swing toward LIV Corps while still west of the Bug, supported by the mechanized forces of the Hungarians and Romanians. Anything that becomes available must strike for the east, as originally planned by army group.

   In themselves, these decisions represent a cheering progress. But they still fall short of the clear-cut operational objectives essential to a sound basis for future developments. With these tactical reasonings as a starting point, the Fuehrer was deftly steered toward our viewpoint on operational objectives. For the moment this is a relief. A radical improvement in the future is not to be hoped for unless operations become so fluid that his tactical thinking cannot keep step with developments.

. . .

6 August 1941

Situation: *South:* Gratifying progress of the southern wing of army group. The Bug line is closed as far as Vesnesensk by the right wing of Armored Group 1. The left wing of armored group is advancing on Alyekandriya.

Sixth Army has almost reached the Dnieper with von Schwedler's group. Violent enemy counterattacks supported by tanks. At Kiev, some progress. Against our Korosten group (262d Division) enemy is putting on very strong counterattacks, with local successes.

Center: Enemy elements thought to be trapped at Roslavl have escaped. The Russians have an uncanny ability for moving on roads impassable for our troops and build concealed river crossings. At Yelnya we now have regular position warfare. Elsewhere, minor attacks.

North: At Staraya Russa, signs of enemy demoralization (tanks desert to us!). Otherwise no change.

Von Bock (Center) calls up: The drive on Rogachev, which Second Army wants to launch, has no chance of success. He wants to postpone the project and first arrive at a better grouping. A conference will be held today at noon. He wants me to come.

1200–2000. By plane to Borisov (Hq. AGp. Center).

Conference with commander of AGp. Center and CG Second Army.

The attack to straighten out the situation at Rogachev requires a strong right wing south of Rogachev. To have it that way we must await arrival of XXXXII Corps and parts of XXXV Corps (reduced).

On the northern wing we must form a strong task force with XII and XIII Corps; it will be given the necessary depth by addition of 162d Division, and will be reinforced by an armored division and the cavalry division. Then we have a chance that the attack, covered by the Dnieper in the south and by the South River in the east, will be carried as far as the Gomel area. XXXV Corps (reduced) will move concurrently with the attack on the southern flank, south of the Beresina. Preparations could be completed between 10 and 12 August.

On the return flight I fill the plane with wounded soldiers; the young men, some with severe limb injuries, carry themselves splendidly. Superb spirit!

Fuehrer conference at Hq. AGp. South (General Paulus taking my place):

Following my request, Commander of AGp. South raises also points of great strategy and emphasizes the importance of Moscow. The Fuehrer again showed himself absolutely death to these arguments. He still harps on his old themes:

1.   Leningrad, with Hoth brought into the picture.

2.   Eastern Ukraine. Here Guderian will be brought in; Gomel and Korosten must be liquidated.

3.   Moscow comes last.

The successful operations now being conducted by AGp. South were outlined and approved by the Fuehrer. In particular he is pleased with the drive of armored group on Krivoy Rog, because here he sees the promise of controlling the high-grade iron ore deposits and the large blast furnaces.

.   .   .

7 August 1941

Situation: *South:* Armored Group 1 has reinforced the elements blocking the Bug line by turning off 9th Armored Division. The other movements are proceeding according to plan against local opposition, such as in front of von Schwedler's group, in the Kiev fortifications line, in the sectors of the western front of Kiev, which have not yet been attacked, and, finally, on the northern flank of LI Corps.

The enemy elements encircled by Seventeenth Army are fighting desperately.

Center: Apart from local attacks, heaviest at Yelnya, nothing new on this front. Behind the enemy front, a group of five divisions has now taken up positions west of Vyazma; its mission apparently will be to defend this important railroad center at all costs.

North: Progress at Staraya Russa. —The whole front heavily mined. —We have penetrated into Rakvere.

.   .   .

1700.   Talk with General Jodl:

    a.   Strategic objectives: What do we want, defeat the enemy or pursue economic goals (Ukraine, Caucasus)?

    Jodl: The Fuehrer probably thinks that both could be achieved at the same time.

    b.   As regards individual objectives, I state that Leningrad can be taken with the allowed forces. We need not, nor must we, divert to the Leningrad front anything that we might need for Moscow. Von Leeb's flank is not in any way threatened from the Valdai Hills.

    The question whether we should try to get Moscow or the Ukraine, or whether it should be Moscow and the Ukraine, must be answered with the emphasis on the ''and.'' We must do it, or else we shall not be able to eliminate this source of the enemy's strength before fall. And we can indeed do it, with von Rundstedt's smashing victory in our favor and in view of the evident decline in the enemy's fighting efficiency. The Korosten group cannot be an operational objective. It must be left to die in its own rot.

    c.   We must not allow the enemy's strategy to dictate our operational conceptions. Reacting to his flank jabs with all-out efforts is rendering him the greatest service. We must aim at complete victory by keeping our forces together for distant, decisive objectives, and crippling blows, and must not fritter ourselves away on trivial objectives. Overall impression: Jodl is convinced of the soundness of these ideas and will pull with us in the same direction. We must come to see eye to eye on two ideas:

        1.   Von Bock must drive with all his forces on Moscow. (Ask the Fuehrer: Can he afford not to reduce Moscow before winter sets in?)

        2.   Minimize the importance of the Korosten group.

.   .   .

8 August 1941

Situation: *South:* Satisfactory development in the operations by *Eleventh Army, Seventeenth Army, and Armored Group 1*. In addition to the CG of the Russian Twelfth Army, we have now captured also the CG of the

Russian Sixth Army. All movements are hampered by the consequences of yesterday's torrential rains. On the *boundary between von Kleist and von Schwedler,* the enemy has broken through all the way to Boguslav. The thrust shows remarkable nerviness, very impressive in its daring and is bound to become embarrassing for our troops. Construction and replacement battalions, rapidly snatched together, are trying to check the enemy. There we now have the consequences of our wanting depth. However, these are the hazards which have to be taken in one's stride.

Sixth Army is making only very slow progress at Kiev.

Artillery fires from the eastern bank. River monitors in action.

At Korosten the enemy is now falling back. He will probably be able to get considerable elements to safety. The way he has delayed our advance is quite inconvenient, but we have only ourselves to blame.

Center: Nothing new.

North: The attack at Shimsk has been called off because of bad weather. Oddly, however, the left wing (Hoepner) is going to start the attack in the Narva area. The Shimsk attack is now set for tomorrow, weather permitting.

A Fuehrer order returns *2d Armored Division* to Germany. After releasing cadres for newly activated units the division will go to the west.

. . .

Bogatsch: Dnieper bridges, rear positions, movements during the day. Nothing new of any importance.

Personnel questions by AGp. Center.

Evening situation: In *AGp. South,* the enemy facing Seventeenth Army has been liquidated. With 100,000 enemy prisoners and 200,000 killed, we may estimate that about sixteen infantry divisions and six armored divisions were eliminated. Armored Group 1, with its main body in the Kremenchug area and near Krivoy Rog and considerable elements on the Bug, is so favorably situated that it will undoubtedly catch some more substantial enemy bodies trying to get away to the east across the Dnieper. It is therefore fairly safe to assume that as the result of this operation, with the enemy's southern wing west of the Dnieper completely destroyed, he now finds himself confronted with an entirely new operational situation.

Sixth Army is now doing everything to seal the enemy breakthrough to Boguslav on the boundary line between von Kleist and von Schwedler. Sixth Army is now also inside Kiev. Its left wing has thrown back the enemy beyond Korosten, thus gaining freedom of movement also in that sector.

Center believes it can discern a change in the situation on its southern flank. Over large stretches of the front, the enemy is distinctly drawing away from our line. South of Roslavl, VII Corps has started pursuit and gained ground in a half day's march, without any but negligible enemy opposition. North of *Gomel,* on the other hand, the enemy is holding, and his artillery is still active. Army group, in view of this situation, wants to launch with XXIV Armored Corps from the area west of Roslavl on a drive in the direction of Gomel tomorrow and have XII and XIII Corps, from the north, and the forces west of Rogachev, from the northwest, join the attack on 11 August, with the object of cracking the enemy block at Gomel.

On the western front of army group, the enemy has shown only local activity. On the northern flank, no change of the situation.

In *AGp. North,* the attack toward Novgorod and Luga has been postponed for another day, owing to bad weather. Reinhardt's corps has expanded its bridgehead. The enemy beaten at Rakvere is being pushed back eastward. The Fuehrer, in spite of his indisposition, has given ObdH most detailed instructions as to how he wants the air components (VIII Air Corps and First Air Fleet) employed; namely: they must first strike in the direction of Novgorod, with Reinhardt's attack starting later at a specified interval, to have the combined air components free for support of this wing. As things stand now, however, Reinhardt has already started operations and cannot stop without getting into trouble, and our air strength in Reinhardt's sector is not enough to allow exclusive commitment of these air components on the northern wing.

The evening conference with *ObdH* produces wasteful discussions. All of a sudden, Armored Group 1 cannot be raced off fast enough in the direction of Dnepropetrovsk, where all through the last few days the group could not be slowed down enough to please him. AGp. Center, too, where the emphasis was on refitting of the armored divisions, is suddenly supposed to forget all about that and start attacking in all directions. It would be better to give the army groups clear-worded, long-term missions and leave them a free hand in carrying them out.

The enemy situation, as suggested by various indications in recent days, has evidently changed, or is in the process of changing. Although there is as yet no evidence that the enemy is reducing or taking back the forces on our front, it is obvious that he is regrouping all he has and can use, for a defense along the line Lake Ilmen–Rzhev–Vyazma–Bryansk. His policy is similar to that pursued by the French in the second phase of the Western Campaign, that is, to form strong islands of resistance (several divisions under the command of an army Hq.), which would serve as the backbone of opposition in the new defense line.

Such tactics constitute a complete break with the former doctrine aiming solely at throwing back our front. The reasons for this change are possibly these:

a. British influence, which from the start sought to promote a policy of conservation of manpower, so that the Russians could count on sufficient forces for the coming year.

b. Recognition of the fact that the tactics pursued wasted away their strength.

c. The fact that with Smolensk eliminated, they had to give up hope of gaining important successes by continuing their frontal attacks.

d. The realization that with the southern wing completely smashed in the great battle in the Ukraine, they do not have enough forces to pursue an aggressive policy.

For further operations the enemy has only limited forces left. If we use the empirical yardstick that two divisions can be raised for every million of population, the number of enemy divisions which have appeared to date is the maximum that can be got up, and we need not anticipate any further large-scale activations.

The forces confronting each other:

In AGp. North	26 divs.	(including 6 of armor)
vs.	23 divs.	(including 2 of armor)
In AGp. Center	60 divs.	(including 17 of armor)
vs.	70 divs.	(including 8½ of armor)
In AGp. South	50½ divs.	(including 9½ of armor, plus numerous Allies)
vs.	50½ divs.	(including 6½ of armor)

This confirms my original view that *North* is strong enough alone to accomplish its mission, that *Center* must concentrate its forces to the last man to destroy the main body of the enemy's strength, whereas *South* is sufficiently strong to complete its mission; South may even be in a position to help out in Center.

10 August 1941

The situation is dominated by three developments:

North has started the offensive toward Novgorod and Luga against strong enemy opposition.

Center has scored good initial successes with XXIV Armored Corps and is readying the other corps selected to take part in the follow-up of the offensive so that they would be set to jump off at the appointed times.

South reports that the situation on the northern wing of army group (Sixth Army) had badly deteriorated. Next to the enemy group at Boguslav, which is estimated one armored division, two cavalry divisions, and three infantry divisions strong (our old friend, the Russian Twenty-sixty Army), the enemy is attempting to cross the Dnieper near Tripolye. Opposition against XXIX and LV Corps, which have penetrated into the Kiev fortifications belt, has stiffened considerably. Enemy artillery unpleasantly effective! Enemy railroad movements are reported running from Poltava to Kiev, and from Chernigov to Ovruch.

All this makes AGp. South think that the enemy wants to crush the northern wing of army group by attacks across the Dnieper, out of Kiev, and from the direction of Ovruch. Our exhausted infantry is in no position to counterattack when the Russians come. Accordingly, AGp. South for the present has called off the attack on Kiev and ordered Sixth Army to pass temporarily to the defensive between Tripolye, Kiev, and Korosten. Sixth Army will be regrouped and will await arrival of parts of armored group and Seventeenth Army before resuming the attack to destroy the enemy still holding west of the Dnieper. Army group requests release of 2d Armored Division and early support by AGp. Center from the Gomel area.

In our opinion the railroad movements interpreted as frontward troop shipments do not have the meaning attributed to them; on the contrary, it seems that troops are being evacuated from the direction of Korosten across the Dnieper, to the east and southeast. It cannot be denied that, in contrast to developments on the southern wing of army group, where the enemy is giving way and is only straining to escape to the east, a distressing situation has developed in the central sector, and that troops are being used up fast at the northern wing. The disposition of Sixth Army no doubt is awkward and lacks depth, but we cannot speak of any crisis present or developing.

1130. **Von Sodenstern (AGp. South) on phone:** Von Sodenstern admits that the sudden reversal in the estimate of the situation is not so much the consequence of a change in the enemy situation as a revised assessment of the capabilities of our own troops. The plain truth is that they are exhausted and have suffered heavy losses. The southeastern wing has at last gained operational freedom of movement, but the northern wing must yet get out of the tight spot it is in by regrouping and introducing new troops. I make it clear that half measures will not do here. An armored corps must be moved to and left at the northern wing; for once von Reichenau has regained freedom of movement; he will always have use for armor, to protect his wing and flank. If that is not done, it will be the same old story again: the infantry extended in enormous width to protect the flanks, and no punch left in the whole front. ObdH is now considering calling in Seventeenth Army to take care of the enemy penetration at Boguslav, in order to take some pressure off Sixth Army. In the south we must soon capture Odessa, in order to shake off restrictions on our freedom in that sector. Occupation would then be left to the Romanians. Nikolayev also must be finished and done with.

. . .

11 August 1941

Situation: By and large no change along the entire front since yesterday. Some advances are still being made on the right wing of AGp. South, where the beaten enemy is retreating across the Lower Bug.

Efforts have been stepped up on the attacking wing of Second Army, but developments are slow to materialize in XXIV Corps.

The results of the first day of the offensive in AGp. North were very significant. On the fronts not involved in the offensive movement reigns the quiet of exhaustion. What we are now doing is the last desperate attempt to prevent our front line from becoming frozen in position warfare. The High Command is greatly handicapped in its capability for modifying the situation, as the army groups are separated by natural obstacles (marshes). Our last reserves have been committed. Any regrouping now is merely a shifting of forces on the baseline within individual army group sectors. This takes time and consumes the energy of men and machines. The upshot is impatience and irritation on the part of the High Command and an increasing tendency to interfere in trivial details.

But this tendency to tinker with details, which, to be sure, we are careful to dress up in the form of requests or suggestions, avoiding any kind of an order, naturally harbors a great danger. We are ignorant of the conditions under which action must be taken. If the delay is more than we think it should be, we at once suspect lack of good faith or even willful disregard of our orders, especially in the case of armored commands, which, in the nature of the thing, are more liable to mechanical vicissitudes than are the other arms. My efforts to minimize this sort of meddling unfortunately have not always been successful.

The whole situation makes it increasingly plain that we have underestimated the Russian colossus, who consistently prepared for war with that utterly ruthless determination so characteristic of totalitarian states. This applies to organizational and economic resources, as well as the communications system and, most of all, to the strictly military potential. At the outset of the war, we reckoned with about 200 enemy divisions. Now we have already counted 360. These divisions indeed are not armed and equipped according to our standards, and their tactical leadership is often poor. But there they are, and if we smash a dozen of them, the Russians simply put up another dozen. The time factor favors them, as they are near their own resources, while we are moving farther and farther away from ours. And so our troops, sprawled over an immense front line, without any depth, are subjected to the incessant attacks of the enemy. Sometimes these are successful, because too many gaps must be left open in these enormous spaces.

. . .

Keitel (OKW) complains in ObdH's ears over our failure to advance on Nikolayev, on the capture of which the Fuehrer has set his goals. Concerning the situation and plans on the extreme southern wing, von Sodenstern has meanwhile given the following explanation to Heusinger:

a. As regards Odessa, army group has issued orders putting OKH's ideas into effect.

b. It is now acknowledged that the movement of Eleventh Army toward Nikolayev is producing the predicted congestion of troops. Army group will take action to restore the situation.

c. Nikolayev: Eleventh and 16th Armored divisions are reported already moving northward. Army group does not want to continue the southward movement toward Nikolayev beyond the line reached by 16th Motorized Division, because there are no enemy forces left to catch. The whole area between the Bug and the Ingul River line is said to be heavily mined.

d. Twenty-fifth Motorized Division and 14th Armored Division have been ordered to advance on Krivoy Rog.

Result: Direct order by teletype to army group to commit 16th Armored Division against Nikolayev, giving it fuel priority for this mission at the expense of any other mission.

. . .

12 August 1941

Situation: In *South*, the advance combat teams of Eleventh Army have reached the western outskirts of Nikolayev and cut off the landward approaches, while the armored combat groups, which were formed by calling off all operations and disrupting all units, are rushing down together with 16th Armored Division from the north, with the object of cutting off the enemy's lines of retreat at Nikolayev. We could have just as well saved ourselves this attack. The same old story again! In the other fighting sectors of AGp. South, no new developments.

In *Center*, XXIV Armored Corps is being halted to reduce encircled enemy elements, but soon will be free to continue to the southeast. XII and XIII Corps have had good initial successes. The southern wing operating south of Rogachev has reached the Dnieper. Local attacks in the other sectors have been repelled as usual. Several enemy penetrations have been wiped out.

North has continued its attack and gained ground, scoring a good success along the shore of Lake Ilmen. No advances in the central sector, some progress on the left wing. In Estonia, now small advances in the direction of Narva.

. . .

14 August 1941

. . .

Today's work is dominated by the following features:

1. "Supplement to Directive 34," which indeed follows our conceptions by ordering AGp. Center to strike on Moscow and by calling off departure of forces from this army group to AGp. South, but on the other hand makes launching of AGp. Center entirely dependent on completion of the missions of AGp. North.

2. The grave anxiety on top level over the enemy penetrations south of Staraya Russa. The incident is inconsequential even in the view of army group. Nevertheless, the Fuehrer had Jodl call up to order commitment of one armored corps (later reduced to one armored division) to contain the penetration. This reacting to all pinpricks frustrates any planning on an operational scale and prevents concentration of our forces.

Von Greiffenberg (on phone): I warn him against abandoning Yelnya. No matter how badly off our troops are, it is worse even for the enemy.

15 August 1941

Situation: *AGp. South:* It appears that army group at Nikolayev did come up against a larger enemy group than expected. The advance of 16th Armored Division on Kherson is held up as a result. Mopping up of the western Dnieper bend at Kanev is proceeding very slowly and takes the form of frontal compression instead of cutting off the enemy from the Dnieper. Otherwise no important changes in the situation. We must reckon with the possibility that the enemy will move troops from the north in the direction of Poltava. The object of these movements, the terminal of which has not yet been ascertained, probably is to assist in rebuilding the crushed southern wing.

Center: Army group has not yet reached any decision on whether the Yelnya salient should be held or abandoned. Enemy attacks continue. To the south, the enemy apparently is weak. The Rogachev attack is making good progress. It appears that the northern group (XII and XIII Corps) and the group coming from the west (XXXXII Corps) will shortly link up north of Gomel. We probably can expect large bags of booty and prisoners soon. XXIV Motorized Corps is making only slow headway. Fortunately the group is not essential for the final phase of the attack on Gomel. The northern part of the front of AGp. Center is relatively quiet.

North: Here we are paying again for our lack of courage to take risks. The Task Force Lake Ilmen–Narva has made very good progress in the direction of Novgorod. The enemy line has been breached, and there is nothing behind it. We shall need some extra reserves to cover the flank at Novgorod from the east. Army group is doing nothing about that. They want to take 3rd Motorized Division out and shift it to the northern wing, which, with 1st and 58th divisions and XXVI Corps, now coming over from Estonia, is strong enough as it is. But on the southern wing they have no reserves, a situation brought on mostly by developments south of Staraya Russa, which pin down the divisions in that area.

In the central sector, at Luga, they want to stop attacking at the moment, when we must contain the enemy to prevent his coming to the aid of his hard-pressed wings. Now OKW once again has put its finger in the pie. Everybody is in a terrible stew over the weak enemy elements which have broken into our lines south of Staraya Russa from the east, but meanwhile have already been stopped by units rushed in from all sides. The Fuehrer demands that mobile forces, a motorized division, at least, be dispatched by AGp. Center. Once again they are making that old mistake which has the result that a single Russian division, by an audacious thrust, ties up three to four German divisions. In view of our limited resources and the immense vastness of the territory in which we operate, such methods are not conducive to success.

. . .

1500.   **ObdH returns from the Fuehrer** with the order to send one armored division and two motorized divisions of Hoth's armored group to AGp. North at the earliest. We shall have to figure out how to manage the supply problem. If it gives trouble, transfer must be cut to one motorized division in addition to the armored division.

. . .

1800.   **Field Marshal von Bock telephones:**

   1.   Good progress at Rogachev. Cavalry division advancing on Gomel. Guderian now does not want to push XXIV Corps on Gomel, which at last has fought its way through the enemy, claiming that the armored divisions were not in any shape to make that long distance; if he were to do so, it would cripple the divisions. My reply is that, of course, we shall get Gomel also without XXIV Corps, but it would be a more complete success if XXIV Corps also were to get through and so smash everything that could still be caught on that enemy wing.

2. I discuss with him the order just written out, which instructs Hoth to give up an armored corps (one armored division, two motorized divisions) to AGp. North, and to do this at the earliest opportunity. Von Bock is furious: The divisions have stripped their tanks for overhauling, and only a few elements are ready to move. Von Bock had been playing an all-out gamble with the numerically superior enemy, but that calculated risk was justified in that it permitted him to pass to the offensive at any moment. Now army group is compelled to pass to the defensive, and all it accomplished to date is wasted.

After a short interruption (trouble on the line), he formulates his report to OKH: The order transmitted to him by phone, the execution of which cannot be vouched for except as regards 18th Motorized Division, previously pledged, destroys the basis for offensive operation by Ninth Army and therefore probably also for a front-wide offensive by army group. Moreover, it should be taken into consideration that changing to the defensive is quite impossible in the present position. The front of army group, with its forty divisions sprawled over a 130-km front, is exceedingly overextended, and a changeover to determined defense entails far-reaching planning, to the details of which no prior thought has been given. The present disposition and line are in no way suited for sustained defense.

1900. **Von Leeb reports to von Brauchitsch** that a strong enemy attack from the south against Staraya Russa is now in progress.

The 290th Division cannot hold any longer. The 30th and 290th divisions must be taken back, and a defense line facing south must be organized west of Staraya Russa. Army group must pull out LVI Corps with 3rd Motorized Division and SS "Deathhead" and send them on to Dno. The enemy is attacking with four infantry divisions and one cavalry division, which were previously fighting X Corps at Staraya Russa, plus six new divisions and two cavalry divisions of Thirty-fourth Army, which according to PW statements are to push through in the general direction of Dno.

So then there will be no way of getting around issuing that order for the transfer of a motorized corps to AGp. North. To my mind, it is a grave mistake for which we will have to pay heavily. Wild requests by AGp. North for engineer troops, artillery, AAA, AT units (on top of the three armored divisions) are turned down.

. . .

17 August 1941

Situation: *South:* Nikolayev in our hands. Assault on Odessa by Romanians not before 18 August. Seaborne movements from Odessa to Sevastopol. Kherson jammed with enemy retreat movements. Evacuation of the Crimea appears to be in progress. Armored group has started the attack to clear the Dnieper bend, and is mopping up the enemy still holding out on the Dnieper banks at Kanev and Rzhishchev.

. . .

18 August 1941

Situation: *South:* The Black Sea coast has been reached at Ochakov (50th Division). Von Kleist's front reports good going in the great Dnieper bend at Nikopol, near Dnepropetrovsk (here enemy bridgehead) and Zaparozhe. Heavy air action against our spearheads. At Cherkassy enemy still has a bridgehead. Western bank at Kanev has been cleared; at Rzhishchev not yet. No important developments elsewhere in Sixth Army, nor any retrograde movements.

Center: Suddenly, small enemy elements (battalion strength) have made their appearance in the Pripet marshes near Turov far behind the right wing of army group. They must be rounded up. Reports from XXXV Corps (reduced) are not clear. First they speak of enemy attacks from the south; then of own attacks on Mozyr. (Let's hope the latter is true.) The enemy pocket east of Zhlobin, where the enemy put up fierce resistance, appears to be burning out. The cavalry division, together with 17th and 131st divisions, has worked its way close to Gomel. Opposition is weakening on the front of XXIV Corps. Corps is swinging a little eastward before making the westward wheel. Guderian's group is regrouping behind the Yelnya salient. North of the highway to Moscow, in the sector of 161st Division, the enemy put on heavy attacks, with local successes, yesterday afternoon. Nothing new at Velikiye Luki. The enemy has evidently discovered the gap on the boundary with II Corps.

North: Sector of II Corps is more active. —In the bulge, our troops have repulsed a tank attack and an attack on Staraya Russa. —Third Motorized Division and SS "Deathhead" are standing about idle in the rear! —Strong enemy attack from the east on Novgorod. Apparently difficult tactical situation. Luga unchanged. Apparently no danger in that sector. On the northern wing, XXXXI Corps resumes movement toward the high ground south of Leningrad. Narva taken. This means that XX Corps can move up at last. —The 254th Division has returned to the Estonian front. Consequently, we can now expect progress in the direction of Tallinn.

.   .   .

1800.   **Field Marshal von Leeb calls up:** Very gloomy picture of the situation in X Corps. The last man has been thrown into the fighting; troops are exhausted. The enemy keeps on pushing north of Staraya Russa. Only the engineer companies are left for commitment. CG X Corps and commander of army group think they are lucky if this front holds another day. They expect relief from a counterattack initiated by von Manstein with SS "Deathhead" and 3rd Motorized. They will get ready for attack tonight.

Withdrawing one division would take until tomorrow night. We could anticipate 18th Motorized Division to arrive by that time from the south.

I Corps: Chudovo will fall tonight. To the east of I Corps is the Russian Fifty-first Army, which is known as the Volkhov Army. I Corps must get its front to face east. Then 1st and 21st divisions will each have a frontage of *40 km.* XXVIII Corps, west of the Luga River, is faced by four enemy divisions. This enemy cannot be bypassed. The 269th Division is too weak to attack. Police division is not in a position to attack. Therefore, XXVIII Corps must attack in western direction. Armored Group 4 must bring elements to bear against Luga from the north.

Purpose of the call was to inform us that army group cannot before tomorrow furnish the armored division which OKH ordered to be moved behind I Corps.

Reply: Army group is held answerable for taking Chudovo and containing the counterattacks from the direction of both Moscow and Leningrad.

Moreover, it must assume responsibility for securing its flank at Novgorod and on the Volkhov River line. The details of carrying out this directive are left to the judgment of army group. It also remains understood that the drive on Leningrad must be continued as soon as possible after capture of Chudovo.

. . .

20 August 1941

Situation: *South:* Odessa remains a sore spot. The Romanian border division did edge closer to the northwestern outskirts of the city, but it remains to be seen whether the Romanian command and its troops are equal to the task: our High Command wants no interference in the conduct of operations by the Romanians. So we shall have to wait and see how things run. Otherwise, developments run according to plan. Fighting is still continuing west of Dnepropetrovsk, as well as west of Cherkassy.

Center: Stubborn resistance on front of XXXV Corps, east of Gomel, and on the front of XII Corps. In the sector of XXIV Corps, the enemy is trying to break out to the east. Elsewhere on the front, minor attacks at Yelnya, heavier ones to the north, in sector of VIII Corps.

North: Corps Schmidt is arriving. Great gains by von Manstein's Corps south of Lake Ilmen. On the Volkhov River, no major enemy counterattack.

. . .

Keitel (OKW) on phone:

a. Fuehrer has made no decision yet on the next moves in the campaign. All he has said so far is that he insists on reaching the northern objective (Leningrad) and on liquidating the Russian Fifth Army.

b. Crimea—use mobile forces for a coup de main! Essential for our effort, deprives enemy of his air base. I reply: Without Odessa, no Crimea. Logistical reasons.

c. Recommends we let Antonescu settle the question of administration of the areas between Bug and Dniester and between Dnieper and Bug. I promise him to look into that.

d. Protest against arbitrary action by ObdL in shifting air force in AGp. Center.

. . .

22 August 1941

Fuehrer directive of 21 August (WFST L No. 441 412/41) is received. It is decisive for the outcome of this campaign:

> *The proposals of OKH for the continuance of the operation in the East, dated 18 August, do not conform with my intentions. I order herewith:*
>
> 1. *The principal object that must be achieved yet before the onset of winter is not the capture of Moscow, but rather, in the South, the occupation of the Crimea and the industrial and coal region of the Donets, together with isolation of the Russian oil regions in the Caucasus and, in the North, the encirclement of Leningrad and junction with the Finns.*
>
> 2. *The operational situation, uniquely favorable to us, which was brought about by our reaching the line Gomel-Pochep, must at once be exploited for a concentric operation by the inner wings of AGps. South and Center. The operation must be so conducted that the Soviet Fifth Army is not merely pushed behind the Dnieper by an attack of Sixth Army alone, but rather that this enemy is destroyed before he can break out to take shelter behind the line Desna River–Konotop–Sula River. This would make it safe for AGp. South to establish itself east of the middle Dnieper, and to continue the operation in the direction of Rostov-Kharkov with its central portion and left wing.*
>
> 3. *Regardless of subsequent operations, AGp. Center must employ forces on a scale sufficient to achieve the object of destroying the Russian Fifth Army, while retaining enough troops to be able to repel enemy attacks against the central sector of its front in a position that can be held with a minimum of losses. There is no change in the plan to advance the left wing of AGp. Center to the high ground around Toropets, where a linkup is to be effected with the right wing of AGp. North.*
>
> 4. *Capture of the Crimean peninsula is of paramount importance for safeguarding our oil supply from Romania. Therefore all available means—including armor—must be employed to cross the Dnieper quickly in the direction of the Crimea, before the enemy can bring up new forces.*
>
> 5. *Not until we have tightly encircled Leningrad, linked up with the Finns, and destroyed the Russian Fifth Army, shall we have set*

*the stage and can we free the forces for attacking and boating
the enemy Army Group Timoshenko with any prospect of success,
as specified in the supplement to Directive 34 of 12 Aug.*

. . .

Memorandum of the Fuehrer to ObdH. He reproaches ObdH for failure to
conduct operations on the lines desired by the Fuehrer and tries to
show that the shifting of the main weight to south and north is a prime
necessity, whereas *Moscow* is of secondary importance, both as an
objective and for the timetable of the campaign. The memorandum is
filled with contradictory statements and pointedly sets the Reich Marshal
above ObdH. ObdH is accused of lack of leadership in that he allows
himself to be swayed by the special interests of the individual army
groups.

**Afternoon and evening are spent in conferences with ObdH and Chief
Op. Sec.** Of the operational instructions that now should go to AGps.
South and Center, we must for the time being confine ourselves to
ordering AGp. Center to throw all forces available at Gomel against
Chernigov, with a view to cutting off the Red Fifth Army before it is
too late. Details of the operation and its implications for von Bock's
eastern front will be discussed tomorrow.

I regard the situation created by the Fuehrer's interference unendurable
for OKH. No other but the Fuehrer himself is to blame for the zigzag
course caused by his successive orders, nor can the present OKH,
which now is in its fourth victorious campaign, tarnish its good name
with these latest orders. Moreover, the way ObdH is being treated is
absolutely outrageous. I have proposed to ObdH to request his relief
together with mine. ObdH refuses on the grounds that the resignations
would not be accepted and so nothing would be changed.

The afternoon discussions are interrupted by telephone talks with Field
Marshal von Bock, who again emphasizes that he can maintain his
front against Moscow in the long run only by remaining in the offensive.

. . .

24 August 1941

Conference with General Guderian: Guderian had the interview with the
Fuehrer arranged for him by me last night.

At the conference at Hq. AGp. Center, Guderian stated it would be
impossible to strike with XXIV Corps southward through Starodub
(1) because supply of fuel could not be maintained on roads in their

present state, and (2) because his men were in no condition to attack before they had had a pause for rest and rehabilitation. Now, this morning, having been confronted with the categorical demand of the Fuehrer to strike at the earliest in support of the southern effort, he declares that XXIV Corps could very well launch a drive south through Starodub. He says he would have to put aside his original qualifications. My reply to him is that I had no sympathy for such a 100 percent change of mind. His retort was that what he told us yesterday was framed with a view to furnishing OKH with arguments against the ordered operation to the south. Now, having become convinced by his interview that the Fuehrer was firmly resolved to execute this drive to the south, it was his duty to make the impossible possible in order to put these ideas into effect.

This conversation shows with devastating clearness with what complete irresponsibility official reports are twisted to fit any specific purpose. ObdH, as a result, has issued very strict orders governing the drafting of reports. Not that they will do any good, for you cannot change men's characters with orders.

Situation: *South:* Very heavy fighting at Dnepropetrovsk. The enemy is throwing into the battle all newly activated units in the vicinity, so that our armored divisions, having to bear the brunt of the fighting alone, make very slow headway. Fighting is still going on at Rzhishchev, south of Kiev. The enemy is making counterthrusts across the river. The drive of Sixth Army is making rapid progress. Eleventh Armored Division has captured the Dnieper bridge at Gornostaipol and carried the thrust to the Desna crossing at Oster; its commander was seriously wounded in this action. The bridge at Oster has been set on fire by the Russians. The Gornostaipol bridge was subsequently set ablaze by Russian planes. The entire Sixth Army is pushing east.

Center: Good progress is made on the northern wing at Velikiye Luki. In the other sectors, isolated attacks on the eastern front and local advances at Gomel.

.   .   .

25 August 1941

.   .   .

1615–1830. Il Duce visits OKH as the Fuehrer's guest. Reception at the station. —Visit to the war room of Op. Sec. Outline of situation by

Transportation Chief and Signal Chief, and visit to the Signal Center. —Presentation of report by Gen Qu. Afterwards tea with ObdH.

The Russians and British have entered Iran.

. . .

26 August 1941

. . .

Replacements:

Received to date by:	Army Groups				
	South	**Center**	**North**	**Norway**	**Total**
From organic field replacement bns.	25,000	28,000	12,000	1,000	66,000
Until 25 Aug.	27,000	38,000	16,000	5,000	86,000
Scheduled to arrive before 31 Aug.	27,000	25,000	19,000	—	71,000
After 31 Aug. through field replacement divs.	40,000	40,000	20,000	—	100,000
Total	119,000	131,000	67,000	6,000	323,000

Enemy air strength: On 21 August 1941 we must estimate actual enemy strength at 750 fighters, 650 bombers, 300 other planes, and 700 planes from the Far East, giving a total of 2,400 planes, plus 1,100 trainers, plus 200 planes on factory airfields. We must therefore still reckon with possibly 3,700 planes operating in the area under observation. Of these we may assume 225 fighters and 195 bombers to be ready for action.

27 August 1941

Situation: No important news. The situation in the bridgeheads of Dnepropetrovsk and Oster (north of Kiev) is tense. The attack by Second Army and Guderian's group is making headway, though slowly. Supply difficulties (oil!).

Enemy: In the area of the Valdai Hills, around Voroshilov, the enemy is now attempting to regroup his forces beaten south of Lake Ilmen. The substitution of motorized for horse-drawn units and the siting of the position on Lake Valdai suggest that they are regrouping for defense in anticipation of a German attack from the direction of the Volkhov. But following Russian doctrine, this defense would be conducted aggressively by the elements in direct contact with the enemy. On the front facing AGp. Center, a major attack seems to be in the making against the area north of Smolensk. Southeast of Bryansk, the enemy is still very weak. Reacting to the southward advance of Guderian's group, he is trying to man the Desna position. (At Novgorod Severski we have already broken through!)

In the Desna bend he will try to block our crossing of the river with the typical Russian doggedness. But it is not impossible that he might postpone any sustained defensive effort until we are on the line Sula-Konotop. It is difficult to figure out the role assigned to Kiev in this setup.

Only weak forces on the Dnieper between Kiev and Zaparozhe. Also at our bridgehead at Dnepropetrovsk, the enemy has not yet sufficiently recovered from the heavy losses inflicted on him to put on any serious pressure.

On the Lower Dnieper (Russian Ninth and Eighteenth armies) a systematic river defense is being built up, though only with weak forces. Behind it the Crimea is being evacuated and prepared for defense.

. . .

28 August 1941

. . .

1030. **Field Marshal Von Bock** calls up, highly excited: Defenses of army group are near breaking point. Army group cannot hold its eastern front if the Russians continue attacking. Fresh divisions moving up from Gomel cannot arrive in the threatened sector of V Corps before 3 September. It is doubtful whether we can hold the sector that long. But if Ninth Army withdraws, Fourth Army must fall back too. The only chance to hold the front lies in committing armor. *AGp. North,* after continuously putting him off to some later date, has now again postponed the attack of II Corps. Operations cannot be based on the cooperation of so unreliable a partner. —I cannot approve a thrust by Stumme's armored corps to the northeast. It appears now fairly certain that it will be impossible to avoid taking back Ninth Army. If the Russians keep up the attack, the only solution is to push with the northern wing as far as the Upper Dvina and then attack southward with Stumme's armored group.

In reply to my question: The danger spot of the eastern front is between the boundary line 14th Motorized/28th Infantry divisions and the left wing of 129th Division. The combat strength of 161st Division is now only 25 percent. The 87th Division must replace 14th Motorized Division. That leaves only SS "Reich" in reserve. Abandoning the Yelnya salient is under consideration. Very hard decision, because it means losing a base for future operations. The final decision is up to Fourth Army.

General Buhle:

a. Strength reports as of middle of August: Infantry divisions all fit for operations. Combat strength about 66 percent. Between 20 and 27 August replacements totaling 63,000 men crossed the German frontier. This means that of 380,000 casualties, 175,000 will have been replaced (including replacements from field replacement battalions).

    Deficit of motor vehicles (16 August): 38,000; 50 percent in armored forces, and 25 percent each in GHq. troops and one-fourth of infantry divisions.

    Tank situation:

Armd. Gp. 1:	Average, 50 percent (16th Mot. Div. poorest)
Armd. Gp. 2:	10th Armd. Div., 83 percent
	18th Armd. Div., 57 percent
	All other armd. divs., average 45 percent
Armd. Gp. 3:	7th Armd. Div. has only 24 percent left
	All other divs., average 45 percent

Armd. Gp. 4:   Best (Czech materiel!), on an average between
50 and 75 percent

. . .

29 August 1941

Situation: *South:* Enemy situation on the lower Dnieper unchanged. We still have no clear idea what the enemy is up to. The puzzling withdrawal movements of tanks from Dnepropetrovsk to the east continue. On the rest of the Dnieper front, no important actions. Kiev, no change. West of the Desna, coming from the north, an enemy advance is reported against the bridgehead at Gornostaipol.

Center: Guderian's situation is not too pretty. He is being hard-pressed from the west by the enemy elements evading the thrust of Second Army, from the east by the newly arrived enemy forces, and on top of that has to cope with frontal opposition. And this front consists only of 3rd Armored Division and 10th Motorized Division, which are rather far apart at that. It is all Guderian's own fault. He devised this plan of attack, and even the most naive enemy could not be expected to stand by passively while an enemy flank is parading past his front. So the attacks from the east are only what he might have anticipated. Moreover, with Guderian straining away from Second Army instead of keeping close to it, a gap has developed through which the enemy is escaping to the east; that in turn accounts for the attacks against Guderian from the west. But in any case it is the enemy who is being thrown into the battle desperately and without a plan.

Relative quiet reigns on the eastern front of army group. On the northern wing, progress is reported in the direction of Toropets and in the sector of VI Corps.

North: No advances south of Lake Ilmen, apparently owing to bad weather and poor roads. Schmidt's corps is advancing both north of Chudovo and in the direction of Leningrad, where it is approaching the outer line of fortifications. Slow progress at Luga; in Hoepner's sector and in Eighteenth Army sector enemy opposition appears to be weakening. The Finns are making encouraging progress on Leningrad from the north. Port Baltic taken. Some fighting is still going on in the harbor district of Reval.

. . .

Casualties:

	Officers	NCOs and EM
Wounded	9,616	277,472
Killed	3,874	79,643
Missing	362	18,957
Total	13,852	376,072

Total casualties for period 22 June–13 August 1941:
389,924 = 11.4 percent of strength of eastern army.

30 August 1941

. . .

Conference with ObdH, who has had a long personal talk with the Fuehrer. He says they discussed also the issues which caused the grave dissonances of the past few days. It seems that the Fuehrer sidestepped the arguments, which probably were pressed with sufficient earnestness and emphasis, by explaining "he had not meant it that way." In any case, the result is bliss and harmony. Everything is just lovely again. Of course, nothing has changed, except that we are now supposed to wait upon not only the Fuehrer, but also the Reich Marshal with separate reports on the railroad situation. Supply, signal communications, and ground forces replacements. On the operational side, it is now advanced that the forces of AGp. Center driving against the Desna should not at all be used for continuance of the operation in the south, but instead should be made available as soon as possible for the operation against Timoshenko. Even if such an intention should exist, it would only serve to drive home the lesson that troops once they are committed against the enemy must stay committed. It is the enemy who determines when and how they can be shifted again.

31 August 1941

Situation: The morning picture is dominated by a decidedly uncomfortable development in Guderian's group. Carrying out his drive as a flank movement along the full length of the enemy front, he squarely invited heavy attacks into his eastern flank; then his advance, striking far to the east and leading him away from Second Army, produced a gap which was exploited by the enemy for attacks also from the west. These two developments have reduced his power to strike south to a point where his movements are paralyzed. Now he is blaming everyone in sight for his predicament and hurls accusations and recriminations in all directions.

He could be helped only by having infantry relieve his 18th Armored Division and subsequently also elements of 17th Armored Division, to the south of the former, and have forces of von Weichs's left wing close the gap to Armored Group 2. All this would take some days, and meanwhile Guderian would have to stay put, all as a result of his faulty planning.

But I think it would be all wrong to try to help him by this method; the original object of his operation, namely, to assist Sixth Army across the Dnieper, would be attained quickest by sharply speeding up the advance of Second Army on Chernigov.

The other sectors show no significant changes. Eleventh Army has established a bridgehead on the southern bank of the Dnieper.

Seventeenth Army is attempting a crossing south of Kremenchug.

In Sixth Army the situation is as tense as ever, but it is not critical.

Nineteenth and 20th Armored divisions are starting off from Toropets northeastward in the direction of Dubno. But their counterpart, von Manstein's corps, which strikes from the direction of Staraya Russa, has not made any headway, chiefly because of the weather. In the other sectors of AGp. North, some progress has been made. North of Luga, resistance of the remnants of the encircled enemy appears to be dying down.

Field Marshal von Bock, 1030 (on phone), on the situation of his army group. He is fully aware of Guderian's plight and wants to help him by pushing 45th and 112th Infantry divisions in a southeastern direction. While we are talking, I receive a message stating ObdH's wish that AGp. Center should place XXXV Corps (45th and 293d divisions) under Guderian's command to give him infantry reinforcement. The divisions are considered unnecessary in Second Army.

Von Bock justly protests against such interference in his command function and states that the measures initiated by him will produce the desired result quicker than would the eastward shifting of XXXV Corps. ObdH at last agrees that it must be left to the judgment of army group, by whatever methods it wants to straighten out the situation.

Von Greiffenberg on phone: OKH is most concerned that Guderian should be helped as quickly as possible and that steps should be taken to relieve him also by infantry reinforcements, from the north, to take over cover of his flanks. It is left to army group to decide how this should be done. Another important move is to drive Second Army sharply toward Chernigov, to effect a junction with Sixth Army and assist it across the Desna.

General Cruewell and Colonel Bayerlein (German Africa Corps) report in and are briefed on their missions.

1430.   Phone talk with Field Marshal von Bock: Personal relations between Hq. of army group and Guderian are increasingly deteriorating. Guderian is striking a tone which von Bock cannot tolerate on any account. He even appeals to the Fuehrer for a decision concerning the leadership. This is unparalleled cheek. First Cavalry Division is put under Guderian's command. Von Bock was thinking of sending him SS "Reich."

At noon lunch with Cruewell (new CG, Africa Corps) and Colonel Bayerlein (his chief of staff).

. . .

Conference with ObdH on prospects of operations of AGp. North against Timoshenko. We discuss the assault on Leningrad. This question is still open. The policy outlined in Keitel's letter to ObdH, viz., that, inasmuch as we are unable to feed the population and have to drive it from the city, the issue is wholly pointless.

3 September 1941

Situation: No significant changes in the morning. Good advances, if only of a tactical nature, on the Dnieper. No advances on the Desna, where the situation is completely messed up.

Colonel Toussaint called in to discuss the Hungarian demand for relief of their armored corps. This demand has no political motivations. Inasmuch as AGp. South finds that their equipment is not any worse off than that of our divisions, a letter is dispatched to Colonel General Werth requesting him not to insist on recalling the Hungarian armored corps for the time being. No decision at the moment as to whether his offer of a Hungarian "river guard" and Hungarian occupation forces to take

the place of German troops in Serbia should be taken under consideration.

.   .   .

4 September 1941

.   .   .

Situation: During my absence, there was again some great to-do. The Fuehrer
is very exasperated about Guderian, who stubbornly sticks to his notion
to push southward with XXXXVII Corps, east of the Desna. Order is
issued to direct Guderian to withdraw to the west bank of the Desna.
Strained relations between von Bock and Guderian. Von Bock requests
ObdH to relieve Guderian of his command.

The fighting in south is making satisfactory progress. Seventeenth Army
in particular has gained much ground on the northern bank of the Dnieper.
In Sixth Army sector, the attack along and across the Desna will be
continued tomorrow. Little progress reported by Second Army and Guderian. On the eastern front of AGp. Center, the enemy apparently is
taking time out from his attacks. In AGp. North, local gains.

5 September 1941

.   .   .

Afternoon, 1730. Fuehrer conference:

1. *Leningrad:* Our object has been achieved. Will now become a
    "subsidiary theater of operations." Chief target is Schluesselburg.
    Investment along the outer siege line (up to the Neva, six to seven
    divisions necessary). As much infantry as possible must be put
    across the Neva. Investment from the east, junction with the Finns.
    Armor (Reinhardt's corps) and air force units must be released.
    Mop up coast. Junction with the Finnish army must be sought
    through Lodejnoje Polje.

2. *Timoshenko offensive:* Must be a close envelopment. The operation
    should, if possible, be launched in eight to ten days. (Impossible!!)
    "Defeat and destroy by envelopment." One armored division and
    two motorized divisions must strike southward from Leningrad.
    Sixteenth Army, later on, must strike independently from the Valdai
    Hills. (Very obscure business!)

3. *Battle in the south:* Main feature: One division must strike against Chernigov, west of the Desna, so as to destroy the enemy elements still operating between Dnieper and Desna.

Seventeenth Army will attack on the axis Poltava-Kharkov (eight divisions). Armored Group 1 will drive northwestward and Armored Group 2 southward for a junction at the Sula River, and then jointly attack the enemy in the Dnieper-Desna area from the rear. Once this battle (''biggest battle in world history'') has been won, the forces no longer needed can be shifted northward to participate in the Timoshenko battle.

Second and 5th Armored divisions could be added to the buildup, provided new armored divisions are activated in the west.

4. *Turkey* will not be against us any longer. —*France* is no threat anymore. —Spain not before December-January.

Evening with Heusinger and Paulus. We discuss how these ideas can be carried out. It will be the end of September before the offensive against Timoshenko gets under way.

6 September 1941

. . .

Report to Fuehrer (with Heusinger): Operational dispositions based on yesterday's conference are approved. Tanks can be retained for continuance of assault on Leningrad, as desired by von Leeb.

Afterwards orders to this effect are sent to AGp. North.

Air situation: Air reports between 18 and 29 August indicate the following respective air strength:

		Friendly		Enemy	
North	Fighters	202		115	
	Bombers	604	886	15	133
	Rcn.	80		3	
	Cargo	—		10	
Center	Fighters	151		373	
	Bombers	281	457	158	549
	Rcn.	25		18	
	Cargo	—		136	

		Friendly		**Enemy**	
South	Fighters	213 ⎫		403 ⎫	
	Bombers	324 ⎬ 573		70 ⎬ 493	
	Rcn.	36 ⎭		20 ⎭	
	Cargo	—		263	
Total			1916		1175

(exclusive of cargo planes)

. . .

9 September 1941

. . .

Visit of the Hungarian regent, accompanied by the new chief of the General Staff. They are shown around GHq. Discussion of the question of continued participation of the Hungarian armored corps in the operations becomes heated at times. The new chief of the General Staff takes the self-centered position that withdrawal is essential to conserve Hungary's strength for her Balkan mission. This argument apart, the Hungarian armored corps seems to think that it is now the turn for other Hungarian units to do some fighting. Of course, there can be no denying that their losses in materiel are very hard to replace. We wind up with an agreement whereby armored corps will remain at the front until conclusion of current operation, and that replacements would be forthcoming if the corps should be withdrawn later on.

. . .

10 September 1941

Situation: *AGp. South:* Eleventh Army continues its advance. Seventeenth Army has captured the bridge site at Kremenchug. It will be able to build another 16-ton bridge, which will enable von Kleist's group to debouch rapidly tomorrow. Apparently the enemy is throwing in a new infantry division and armor through Kharkov, while evacuation and refugee movements are running in the direction of Kharkov. Sixth Army is crossing the Desna on a wide front.

AGp. Center: Second Army has made the crossing of the Desna, smashed several enemy units, and started moving in a southeastern direction.

Armored Group 2 had taken Romny and is clamoring for its opposite number, von Kleist; curiously, there are no attacks against its east flank. Perhaps this has something to do with the extensive railroad demolitions by our air effort. On the defensive front, the danger zones west of Bryansk and east of Smolensk stand out as before, but temporarily at least there is a lull in the attacks. Nevertheless, resumption of the attacks must be imminent in view of the railroad movements from Moscow or Tula to Bryansk, and of the very heavy motorized movement toward Smolensk. Preparations for such attacks appear to be in progress particularly in the Yelnya area. In the Toropets area, the enemy is bringing in more forces, probably with defensive intentions.

AGp. North: Several movements on two railroad lines toward the Volkhov River suggest the arrival of new divisions, on top of 286th Division, which was identified yesterday. It is not clear whether this is a last attempt to turn the fate of Leningrad or merely a defensive step.

Enemy air activity surprisingly is a little less intensive in South and Center, but this may be due to the weather. In Estonia, the island of Worms has been taken.

Captain Zimmermann (War Service Cross, First Class) and Lieutenant Colonel Lieckfeld of the Counter-Intelligence Service, who is joining Section Foreign Armies East, come in. L. has interesting things to tell about Russia, the country in which he was born and reared.

Von Etzdorf: *Japan:* Still undecided. The Fuehrer does not want to be pressing, so as to avoid the impression that we need the Japanese. The army has cold feet and will probably do nothing for the time being. The navy wants to pick off Thailand, Singapore, Borneo, and Manila, one after the other, and believe that the U.S. would be unable to do anything to stop them. There are also internal dissensions. Perhaps change of Cabinet; in any case, delay.

Il Duce's visit: Military questions are in the foreground. Il Duce wants "realization of the new order in Europe"; i.e., he wants to secure his loot. Claims that it is no longer in his power to steer Italian public sentiment as he would like to.

England: Churchill is forming a group of bitter-enders, and is governing against the moderates and also against Labor.

Turkey: The situation in that country is considered to be developing in our favor. "Wait and let things develop in our favor."

U.S.A.: Policy obscure. Unlikely to enter the war now.

Sweden: Sticks to the "Swedish line," i.e., keeps all possibilities open.

Iran: Germany is trying to get all German residents out of Iran.

. . .

12 September 1941

. . .

Evening situation: In *South,* Armored Group 1 has really got going. Linkup with Guderian may be expected tomorrow. AGp. South suspects that the enemy in the Desna-Dnieper area is beginning to break away to the east, and has ordered pursuit without, however, abandoning the idea of a large-scale encirclement on the Sula-Romen River line. The heavy withdrawal movements (at some points three vehicle columns abreast) eastward through Lochwiza must be regarded in part at least as evacuations and as movements of labor detachments (fortification construction) and refugees.

In the *east,* the enemy is maintaining the concentration opposite the sectors of the XX, IX, and VIII Corps. On this 120-km front, AGp. Center believes the enemy has twenty-seven rifle divisions, five of armor and seven in reserve in the rear, i.e., a total of twenty-nine divisions.

In *North,* very good progress in the drive on Leningrad. The enemy begins to soften on the front of Reinhardt's corps. It would appear that the population does not want to take a hand in the defense. The situation of Schmidt's corps has improved, but in 18th Division it is still somewhat tight.

Matters submitted for decision: Commander of AGp. North is insisting vehemently on keeping Reinhardt's corps and VIII Air Corps. Of course, we shall always give him the means to bring his operation to a successful close, but the buildup for the new operation in Center must have priority. Commander of AGp. Center presents a critical review of his operational instructions in which he tries to prove that the plan could not accomplish an envelopment on his northern wing. True, it will be a hard job for the northern wing, but the scheme underlying our directive nevertheless remains the only possible solution.

Enemy air strength, 11 September 1941:

$$\left.\begin{array}{l}\left.\begin{array}{l}\text{670 fighters}\\\text{600 bombers}\\\text{440 other craft}\end{array}\right\}\ 1{,}710\\\text{1,230 training craft}\end{array}\right\}\ 2{,}940$$

If 40 percent are operational, effective strength may be estimated at 270 fighters, 240 bombers.

Probable distribution of actual strength of 1,700 airplanes:

Southern theater: 850 (Crimea, Donbass, Voronezh, and east)
Central theater: 450 (Orel, Tula, Vyazma, Bryansk, Moscow)
Northern theater: 400 (east of Lake Ilmen, Rybinsk, some around Leningrad)

If training aircraft (1,250) and aircraft on factory airfields (350) are included, 3,300 is the total aircraft which our air reconnaissance has discovered.

Own operational airplanes on 6 September:

	Bombers	Dive-Bombers	Fighters	Long-range Fighters	Rcn.
Air Fleet 1:	203	60	166	39	13
Air Fleet 2:	141	55	44	—	11
Air Fleet 4:	96	71	85	—	21
Air Fleet 5:	25	29	11	7	7
Total (without 5):	440	186	295	39	45
Compared witn enemy:	−44 (7%)		−336 (100%)		

. . .

13 September 1941

Extract from an OKW memorandum on the strategic situation as of late summer 1941, approved by the Fuehrer.

1. It is too early to say how many of our troops in the east will become available at the onset of winter and what forces would be needed for continuance of the campaign next year.

2. Should the campaign in the east fall short of achieving total annihilation of the Soviet fighting forces in 1941—an eventuality which the Supreme Command now pretends was taken into account from the outset—the military and political effects on the overall situation might be the following:

   a. Delay in Japan's entry into the war against Russia. On the other hand, the U.S. might furnish Japan the immediate cause for entering the war. (Unlikely!)

   b. It will be impossible to prevent a linkup between Russia and Britain through Iran.

   c. Turkey will look at this development with great misgivings. Nevertheless, she will maintain her cautious attitude until she is thoroughly convinced of Russia's collapse.

   d. Military action *against* Turkey is out of the question for us. We must try to win her over by political means.

3. In the Mediterranean theater we see no signs of a material change in the situation. British drive against Sollum and breakout from Tobruk are doubtful. In the absence of a serious German threat from the direction of Syria and Iraq, the British position on the Suez Canal will become progressively stronger. Britain will be able to build up strong offensive forces in Libya undisturbed (American aid). The situation of the German-Italian forces in Libya will become increasingly difficult unless we succeed in greatly stepping up the sale of supply shipments across the Mediterranean, or take Tobruk yet before the British launch an offensive. (Impossible before October.)

4. Spain will not take any positive steps to enter the war until the German-Italian combination has achieved unchallenged mastery of the Mediterranean, or she is directly attacked.

5. France is watching developments and will in the meantime take advantage of any shift in the Axis position to better her own position.

6. Britain and the U.S. realize that Germany cannot be beaten on the Continent. Their strategy, therefore, is to aggravate our supply difficulties and so, with the added effect of air attack, gradually weaken the external and domestic position of the Axis powers. They know that the "invasion threat" can be safely discounted at the moment, while, at the same time, the erstwhile German air

superiority has been caught up with. The situation in the Mediterranean and, beyond that, the great strategic picture can be profoundly modified only if, by destroying German-French collaboration, the following objectives are achieved:

a. Elimination of the German-Italian bridgehead in North Africa.
Capture of the entire North African coast.
Sea and air domination of the Mediterranean.
Access to the African theater of war for the Americans in French Morocco (Casablanca) and French West Africa (Dakar).
Critical curtailment of the strategic capabilities of the Axis powers by the preceding means.
Tightening of the blockade of central Europe. Building up pressure on Italy until the country collapses.

b. In addition, direct contact with Russia must be established through Iran in order to sustain Russia's will to resist and to prevent Germany from gaining access to the Caucasian oil fields. (Probably the line of reasoning of our Anglo-Saxon enemies.)

7. *Own decisions:* Our goal, as before, is to defeat and force Britain to sue for peace. The air force alone cannot achieve this. Other means: Invasion and siege warfare.

Invasion: Surest means to finish the war quickly.
Prerequisites:

a. Air mastery.

b. Large-scale employment of all weapons that have so far been successful in sea warfare to eliminate effective British naval action against our transport fleet.

c. Mass production of first-class self-propelled vessels.

d. Creation of a powerful parachute and airborne force.

All this is possible only at the sacrifice of other armament projects. We would need time until late summer 1942. Our arms program now would have to be readjusted in accordance with the decision to attack Britain in her outlying positions or in her island. The means of attack in one and the other case are vastly different. A decision needs to be made now, but we are not yet in a position to do so. Our arms program, therefore, must be one that would leave both possibilities open.

Siege warfare requires sinking of enemy shipping at a rate of 1 million tons a month. Navy wants large sea reconnaissance units and an air squadron in the Atlantic for operations against supply convoys on coastal routes and the high seas, large-scale employment of the new aerial mines and torpedoes, and continuance of the systematic attacks on ports and shipyards. These plans cannot yet be fully realized in 1942.

Adequate air forces for a siege of Britain will not be available until the eastern campaign is substantially concluded and the air force is refitted and enlarged. In the judgment of the navy, it is therefore all the more important to acquire new cases in strategic locations in order to improve the prospects for a successful continuation of the battle of the Atlantic (Bizerte, El Ferrol, Cádiz, Gibraltar, Casablanca, Dakar). These bases can be obtained only with the political consent of Spain or France. Spain would perhaps accede to our pressure, but in the French Colonial Empire we lack any means for applying such pressure. Occupation of the whole of France would do us no good if the French African colonies and the French navy were to go over to the enemy.

"In view of the fact that the enemy has abundant military and political means to achieve the same end and that the possession of these French bases can be of crucial importance for the outcome of the war, it would be necessary as well as justified to risk high political stakes, provided the political gains could be explicated in the military field. Whether or not such political stakes can be played depends less on our own desires than on those of the French government." [This is an exact quote from Hitler's remarks.] Of equal importance with the battle of the Mediterranean is the battle of the Atlantic. Russia's defeat is the prerequisite of victory in either.

Britain's situation becomes hopeless immediately. The conflicting political interests of France, Spain, and Turkey, among themselves and in relation to Italy, can be reconciled to a point where the three states would join in the war against England. This ultimate objective will perhaps never be fully achieved.

If Turkey enters the war on our side, we shall have to support her with ammunition and war materiel. Also, Spain would be a heavy economic burden. In return she offers the naval bases at El Ferrol and Cádiz and elimination of the British naval base at Gibraltar. The political benefits would be very great, but the limiting condition is that there must be no change in the present attitude of the French Colonial Empire in Africa. The plan of controlling France's African possessions by force from the Spanish bridgehead would be difficult to realize. Spanish Morocco would probably be lost to a joint Anglo-French operation before German forces could be on the ground. And with North Africa in Anglo-French hands, possession of Gibraltar would lose its strategic importance for us.

France's entry into the war on our side would at once ease the situation in North Africa. Having the French navy at our disposal would be a very great asset. On the other hand, France's military resources in West Africa are limited, whereas a constantly growing British base is building up to the south. If, therefore, France were to enter the war on our side, she would first have to be given the possibility to strengthen her position in West Africa, and we would have to be in a position to back her up there. Our capabilities in that direction would be restricted.

Conclusion: *Turkey's* entry into the war any time at all is of great military advantage for us, but the sooner it happens, the better. Even without German aid, Turkey is strong enough to resist on land, on the sea, and in the air anything Britain and Russia could put up against her now; moreover, her assistance would be an important factor in controlling the Black Sea.

The situation is entirely different as regards France and Spain: unless we are able to furnish materiel aid, the entry of these countries into the war would be of problematic value. Even the convenience of using Spanish ports would not greatly alter the picture. The great advantage of having a broader basis for our supply movements to the Italian theater of operations would be offset by the very real danger of losing Dakar to the British, since the French forces at Dakar, and French air power in particular, are inadequate at this time.

8. *To sum up:* Britain's two major political and military aims are: (1) to sustain Russia's will to resist and so block Germany from the oil region by establishing a base to gain all of West and North Africa as an area of operations; and (2) Spain and Turkey are to be maintained at least in the status of nonbelligerents.

We must therefore draw the following conclusions for our own war strategy:

1. The collapse of Russia is our immediate and paramount objective. On achieving that goal, we must concentrate all forces that can be spared from other fronts. Insofar as this object is not fully attained in 1941, the continuance of the Eastern campaign in 1942 must be accorded first priority.

   Territorial gains on the southern wing would have far-reaching political and economic effects. We must persevere in our efforts to change Turkey's political attitude in our favor. Such a change would substantially improve our military situation in the southeast.

2. Not until Russia has been eliminated as a military factor can we bring all our forces to bear against Britain in the Atlantic and in the Mediterranean, possibly also from French and Spanish bases. Even if Russia should be substantially defeated already this year, neither the army nor the air force would be available for decisive operations in the Mediterranean, in the Atlantic, and on the Spanish mainland before spring 1942.

3. Between now and next spring it will be our business to keep the political and military relations with France and Spain not only from lapsing, but, on the contrary, to do everything to intensify them; to hold France under firm control and, finally, to bring further influence to bear to make her send military reinforcements to West Africa so as to be in a position to meet any Anglo-American attack. Our relations with France are complicated by the necessity to give due attention to the legitimate interests of our ally, Italy. But from the military point of view, France's contribution would be essential to an early defeat of Britain and so is something we cannot afford to neglect.

4. Having thus broadened our territorial situation, we would still have to wait for next spring before our increasing submarine effort could count on any large-scale air support to continue the siege of Britain with telling effect.

5. Operations in the eastern Mediterranean will be impracticable before Trans-Caucasia has been reached.

6. The invasion of England will again be the subject of serious consideration if, despite Russia's collapse, our efforts failed to secure Spain's and France's participation in the war on

the Axis side and as a result the battles of the Atlantic and Mediterranean did not achieve the successes that made it appear likely that Britain's defeat could be brought about by that campaign.

. . .

15 September 1941

. . .

Situation: *South:* South of the Dnieper, enemy positions between Yelisavetovka and the Utlyuf River indicate that the enemy will attempt to make a stand on that line. On the Dnieper northwest of Kremenchug, the river defenses are reported reinforced. Seventeenth Army is making good headway with its left wing, while its right wing evidently has trouble again on its flank. Armored Groups 1 and 2 have linked up; but the situation around the bridge at Sencha (south of Lochwiza) is still obscure.

Center: Enemy is digging trenches opposite IX and VII Corps. Rest of the front quiet.

North: The liquidation of the enemy on the extreme right wing of Sixteenth Army is taking unaccountably long. The enemy evidently has moved reinforcements into this area and is intent on holding up our advance. Continuing heavy attacks against 30th Division would point in the same direction. Corps Schmidt in hard fighting against attacking enemy (12th Armored Division). The attack against Leningrad is proceeding according to plan. Eighth Armored Division has been shifted eastward for commitment in Schmidt's sector.

Overall enemy situation: The enemy is probably hanging over to the defensive. The reasons for this change in policy are not clear. Perhaps high losses, perhaps the desire to get forces for a reserve now that the original reserves have all been committed. We have no indications that he is freeing forces for the buildup of a new southern wing.

In the Valdai lake district the enemy is expecting our attack; he is moving up forces for the defense and is digging trenches. At Leningrad he is throwing new forces into the battle. He may do this for prestige, or may be trying to hold Leningrad as long as possible so as to pin down large German forces.

. . .

16 September 1941

The situation conference produces nothing new of importance. In *South*, isolation of the Crimea may now be regarded as complete. The assault on the peninsula is being prepared. Seventeenth Army, which is advancing very cautiously because it must keep an eye on its eastern flank, has apparently broken the enemy's frontal resistance. The enemy is giving ground in the direction of Poltava, but at the same time he is evidently beginning to move reinforcements to Kharkov from the north; other movements farther south to Melitopol. In the light of the foregoing, it seems to be reasonable to expect that after the enemy at Kiev has been beaten, Eleventh Army would yet have to tackle a small battle group on the north shore of the Sea of Azov, and Seventeenth Army a possibly stronger group around Kharkov and northward before the route to the southeast is finally open.

The pocket east of Kiev is evolving according to plan. Army Hq. 2 has been taken out. The divisions of the Second Army, which will not be moved to the north, are to be attached to Sixth Army, with their supply continuing through Gomel.

In *Center*, all is quiet, as in the past few days.

In *North*, the assault of Leningrad is making good progress. South of Lake Ladoga, the tension has decidedly eased. The report that the enemy is falling back has, however, only local significance.

. . .

18 September 1941

Situation: Apart from the satisfactory progress of the converging movements east of Kiev, the most significant new developments are the increasingly noticeable enemy concentrations in the Belopolye area, fed from Kharkov, and in the area southwest of Kursk, moving in apparently from the north. (The latter movement has been going on through the past days on a small scale.) Neither the strength nor the striking power of these groups needs to be overrated. Yet their presence must be taken into account in launching Armored Group 2 northward, as well as in starting the offensives of the northern wing of Seventeenth Army, and perhaps also of von Kleist's group. It is interesting to note that AGp. South has captured Budënny's ranking engineer officer. He was on a personal reconnaissance to locate fuel dumps, especially of aviation fuel. This would indicate the degree of confusion on the enemy side and furnishes an explanation for the unaccountable inactivity of the enemy air force in the past few days. *Army Hq. 2* will probably be taken out today preliminary to its new assignment.

In AGp. *Center,* artillery activity is reviving. Withdrawal of three enemy divisions from this front has been confirmed. Their sectors were taken over by other divisions (PW statement). It has not yet been established whether these divisions are going south or what else they may be doing.

In AGp. *North,* clearly defined enemy movements into the Valdai Hills area and, to the north, into the lower Volkhov sector. The former movements may be composed of labor detachments for the construction of the Valdai positions, especially their northwestern part, together perhaps with some troops moved up in reaction to our attacks at Toropets and Kholm; the latter are perhaps less in the nature of reinforcements than of loss replacements. Either way, we must pay close attention to these movements, the more so as our forces in the north are stretched to breaking point. Clearance of the enemy from the Valdai lake country has been a sorry business. From the south (253d Division) we do not seem to be able to get into the area. For Germans it is a terrain in which troops can move about only with portable infantry weapons, while Russians are able to build positions in it. Perhaps it is the quality of 253d Infantry Division that is to blame. From the north, where 19th Armored Division was to strike, road conditions (cave-ins) confront our troops with backbreaking problems.

In view of the enemy attempt to reestablish communications with Leningrad (PW report), the presence of the enemy group on the Volkhov is as troublesome as ever. Presumably the group will become active soon. This is very distressing, as 8th Armored Division is scheduled to be withdrawn.

The ring around Leningrad has not yet been drawn as tightly as might be desired, and further progress after departure of 1st Armored Division and 36th Motorized Division from that front is doubtful. Considering the drain on our forces before Leningrad, where the enemy has concentrated large forces and great quantities of material, the situation will remain tight until such time when hunger takes effect as our ally.

1130. **General Brennecke** (chief of staff, AGp. North) on phone: I remind him of the necessity to turn over the armored divisions to AGp. Center on schedule.

General Jodl (on phone): Importance of a joint drive by Group Kleist and Eleventh Army into the area south of the Donets, with objective Rostov. Exchange of views on likely enemy strategy in the Konotop area and the countermeasures to be taken by Group Guderian.

Colonel Heusinger: We discuss the plan of AGp. Center for Operation TYPHOON. Examination of possibilities for establishing a Hq. OKH.

. . .

20 September 1941

Situation: The *enemy* is rallying in the direction of Krasnograd and Kharkov the troops beaten in the Poltava area, and trying to check any further eastward expansion of Guderian's group by attacks in the Romny area. The enemy must have been able to extricate from Kiev more troops than we thought he would, and he now seems to be fighting for elbow room in northeastern and eastern direction. We are now approaching the crisis stage of the encirclement.

Trains are still being unloaded (troops?) at Sumi and Belopolye. From the Kharkov area, northward and northeastward, shipments of materiel; the former apparently for work on the Moscow defense position, the latter evidently evacuations of industrial plants to the Ural.

Unloading of troops between Valdai and Volkhov, apparently destined for a reserve group to provide against any eventuality. Another enemy division has arrived on the Volkhov River.

River-crossing equipment!

Russian Army Hq. 28 has been withdrawn from the Bryansk area; is probably taken out to form a new front north of Belopolye.

In *AGp. Center* it is quite plain that the enemy is going over to the defensive; arrival of replacements; regrouping of artillery in depth.

. . .

23 September 1941

Situation: *Enemy:* Nothing new in *South*. On the front of Seventeenth Army and on its northern flank, weak and partly disorganized resistance. The pockets are making their last break-out attempts. The other enemy forces are retreating on Kharkov.

Evacuation movements northward from Kharkov in the direction of Moscow on several railroad lines through Yelets and Voronezh. On the front facing the southern wing of AGp. Center, the enemy is continuing his attempts to bolster the southern wing of AGp. Timoshenko. In the area west of Sumi, 100th Division has appeared from the area of Smolensk. In the sector south of Bryansk, there are added indications that the Russians are unloading more troops, to be committed against Glukhov. Large volume of traffic on the Sukhinichi-Yelnya line; cannot be interpreted.

In sector of *AGp. North,* Russian railroad movements from Ribinskto-Valdai continue. It is not clear whether they carry construction material, labor units, or fighting troops. Also, heavy railroad traffic between Tikhvin and Vologda. Newspaper reports talk about the great impression made by the battle of Kiev on Russia, as well as other countries. The British seem to be urging the Russians to abandon southern Russia and confine themselves to holding the Don and the Caucasus. It is possible that Stalin, perhaps much against his will, may have to take this advice. The implications for us would be that everything in AGp. South must be reoriented to pursuit, and more particularly that Armored Group 1 must be freed with a minimum of delay.

Friendly forces: *Southern wing,* no change. Romanian reverses before Odessa are inconvenient. East of Kiev everything is developing according to plan. Guderian starts regrouping for his new mission, but he still has some enemy forces sitting on his eastern flank between Akhtyrka and Sumi. In *Center,* Guderian is reinforcing the Glukhov sector, which is the right thing to do. For the rest, reinforcements are being moved to Second Army from the south. Second, the front is being re-formed according to our plan. Minor attacks have been repulsed. Air attack on Poltava.

In *North,* the situation is strained in the Valdai Hills, where the enemy is becoming more active, while the conditions for fighting are unfavorable for our own troops. Here Ninth Army will at last have to speed up regrouping in order, at the least, to consolidate the situation until Operation TYPHOON starts. Opening of the TYPHOON offensive will relieve the situation. —In the Lake Ladoga sector, only minor advances, apparently at considerable cost. Our forces here are sufficiently strong for the defense, but it seems not strong enough for a radical liquidation of the enemy. However, they are all we have. The advances in the direction of Peterhof gained by 1st and 291st divisions in hard fighting deserve the highest praise.

OKW "Directive"

    a. On new phase of the operation of AGp. South. It states belatedly what we have already ordered.

    b. On the next moves in Norway. The 163d Division is to be freed for the northern theater of operations. The attack by the Finnish III Corps is to be called off; the attack on Kandalaksha is to be continued. Dietl's operation must be restricted to capture of the western part of the Ribachi peninsula. The directive orders construction of a railroad from Rowanjemi to the north, and readying of transport, etc. There is concern about the British and Murmansk, and about a threat to the nickel mines. As soon as frost has set in, we must try a thrust on Murmansk through Kandalaksha.

    c. One of the Kiev divisions must be alerted for Serbia. Transfer will take three weeks.

. . .

25 September 1941

Back to Loetzen by plane via Smolensk, Minsk, Vilna. Arrive at noon.

Afternoon:

    1. Report on *occurrences in my absence*. On 24 September OKW was in the throes of a first-rate crisis. It was brought on when Sixteenth Army's attack in the Ladoga sector ran head-on into a strong enemy counterattack which threw back 8th Armored Division. As a result, we lost ground on the eastern bank of the Neva.

    To remedy the situation the Fuehrer gave the following orders in rapid succession:

    a. Twenty thousand mines by air transport to AGp. North.

    b. Hold off 36th Motorized Division.

    c. Ship paratroops (one regiment available at once, a second later) by air to AGp. North.

    d. Transfer one infantry regiment of AGp. Center by air to AGp. North. When it was discovered that air lift was not available, he ordered transfer of a whole division from Center to North by rail. The Spanish Division was picked for the job, and will be moved from Vitebsk at the rate of six trains a day. Will arrive at Don between 2 and 10 October.

e. The divisions scheduled for transfer from the west must be moved at a rate of seventy-two trains a day! The Seventy-second Division starts moving on 28 September and will be shipped on a 72-trains-a-day schedule as far as East Prussia. From there on it will be moved to AGp. North as the transport situation permits. First elements will arrive 2 October.

f. Replacement battalion of rehabilitation battalion is to go to AGp. North. (Impossible!)

With the enemy attacks at Ladoga not getting anywhere today, a certain serenity is spreading again over the scene.

2. The following divisions must be transferred from AGp. South: 99th Light Infantry Division for Serbia, where it will be reorganized as a mountain division. The 71st Division, for France, to replace the division transferred to AGp. North. Infantry will entrain in Berdichev; motorized elements in Rzeszow, beginning 5 October.

3. Ambassador Ritter called up regarding alleged indiscretions to Alfieri.

General Matzky: Current matters in his section. His tour to Sofia and Ankara.

. . .

26 September 1941

. . .

General Hauffe: (Army Mission Romania) reports on the situation at Odessa. Day before yesterday, Antonescu at last changed his mind about asking for German help. The Romanians cannot get Odessa by themselves. He wants: (a) troops, and (b) air support.

We discuss extent to which request ought to be granted. Hauffe estimates the necessary aid at two infantry divisions, three to four medium artillery battalions, one observation battalion, one corps artillery commander, one rocket projector battalion, one corps Hq. with accessories, in addition to air support.

The attack must be conducted on the following plan: The northeastern front is to be moved up to the lagoons on the northeast side of the city while preparations are being made for the attack from the northwest, and then the assault is executed with an overwhelming concentration of all forces. The attack on the northeastern front cannot be launched before the end of two weeks. German aid would take three weeks to arrive. Accordingly, in the event that this plan should be carried out, the decisive attack could not be launched before the end of four weeks. We examine our capabilities for meeting the demands. The suggestion is made to use the two Kiev divisions (99th Light Infantry and 71st Infantry divisions) slated to go to France before their transfer.

From OKW: The Fuehrer insists that (a) 16th Armored Division should help the right wing of Seventeenth Army along before starting to push through to the southeast, and is impatient to know (b) why Seventeenth Army's advance is so slow.

The day is dominated by our struggle to get 36th Motorized released for von Bock. The Fuehrer has stopped the transfer until such time when von Leeb would no longer need the division. When called up by ObdH, von Leeb replies after careful examination that he has to hold on to it because the other scheduled reinforcements would arrive too late. We then told OKW that in our opinion temporary help could be had from the Volkhov front pending commitment of the arriving reinforcements, and that withholding the transfer of 36th Motorized Division would be extremely detrimental to von Bock's offensive effort. The question was finally decided in our favor inasmuch as Sixteenth Army meanwhile saw the situation so greatly improved (the enemy did not attack today) that it even wants to take the offensive in Lake Ladoga sector (!).

. . .

1 October 1941

Situation: *South:* The attack against the western isthmus of the Crimea is making headway. Uncomfortable situation on the eastern front of Eleventh Army. Armored Group 1 is moving up 13th Armored Division and is advancing southward on the east bank of the Dnieper. The Italian mobile units have mopped up the north bank of the Dnieper.

Seventeenth Army is suffering from the effects of bad weather and reports no progress.

Sixth Army has started its drive, leading with advance combat teams.

Center: Armored Group 2 has had trouble in disengaging its right flank cover from the enemy. One regiment of 25th Motorized Division remained pinned down. Furthermore, 9th Armored Division had to be committed again, as a result of which closing up to the north will be delayed. On the whole, however, the break through the enemy, whose strength and disposition were accurately estimated, is making good progress. On the remainder of the front, no important development, apart from local enemy thrusts.

North: Only local thrusts in the Ladoga sector. Otherwise unaccountably quiet.

General Buhle:

a. Report on condition of tanks in all armored divisions. In Guderian's group about 50 percent; in the other armored groups about 70 to 80 percent; Hoepner's group is best off with four divisions with 100 percent.

b. Covering of replacement requirements. —Deactivation of divisions.

.   .   .

ObdH sees the Fuehrer: Outcome of discussion:

a. Odessa operation will be conducted in conformity with our recommendations. The Fuehrer wants to send a letter to Antonescu in this matter.

b. Worries that AGp. South is pushing Seventeenth and Sixth armies too far north. Seventeenth Army should stay south of the Donets. Kharkov also could be left to Sixth Army.

c. Concerned about the weakness of von Bock's northern wing.

d. Makes proposal to rectify the situation on the Ladoga front by an armored thrust on Tikhvin, which subsequently would swing around, across the Volkhov River, into the enemy's rear. (Fantasy!)

.   .   .

2 October 1941

TYPHOON

Second, Fourth, and Ninth armies start operations.

Situation: *South:* Counterattacks are in progress on the eastern front of Second Army. Von Kleist continues his southward attack while covering his eastern flank. Hq. AGp. South intervenes and regroups the front facing northeast: von Reichenau's two northern corps and von Stuelpnagel's two northern corps will advance on Kharkov as a new Sixth Army, while von Reichenau's southern corps will turn off to the east and, forming a new Seventeenth Army with von Stuelpnagel's two southern corps, will operate south of the Donets, driving southeast against the industrial region. This reorganization, which follows a suggestion from the OKH, is very desirable. Let us hope that the unfortunate persistence of bad weather will not unduly slow these movements.

Center: Favored by sparkling fall weather, army group opened the TYPHOON offensive today at 0530. Whereas Guderian has been gaining ground despite the handicap of his lagging right wing, the attacks of the other armies and armored groups by noon had carried the advances only between 6 to 12 km. In some sectors, the enemy is retreating in great disorder.

North: No change. The Spanish division and 227th Division transferred from France are arriving in AGp. North.

. . .

Evening Situation: *South:* In the Crimea, no change; troops for further attacks have yet to be brought up. —The crisis on the eastern front of Eleventh Army has been resolved. In Seventeenth Army, no important changes. Only minor advances in all sectors (left wing). —Sixth Army's advance combat teams have taken over from Guderian's southern wing.

Center: TYPHOON has started with smashing force and is making excellent progress. Guderian feels sure he has broken clean through the enemy line. His center is rolling against Orel.

Second Army had to do some hard fighting to get across the Desna. It has forced the crossing and thrown back the enemy about 5 km.

Armored Group 4 has broken through, scattered the enemy, and carried the advance about 15 km into enemy territory. Fourth Army is advancing irresistibly along its entire front, averaging about 6 to 12 km.

Hoth and Ninth Army have been getting on very well, advancing as much as 20 km in the day. Just as on 22 June, the opinion of the commanders is divided on the question as to whether or not the enemy had orders to hold the line. The former can be true only where rear positions were found, i.e., in the zones of attack of Fourth and Ninth armies. Elsewhere, we may presume, the enemy tried to make a stand, was quickly overrun by reason of his greatly reduced fighting effectiveness, and, while he is now running away in some sectors, certainly is not executing a planned withdrawal. The enemy elements which remained behind in the big forest areas between our attacking wedges will soon prove that the enemy has not taken back his front line.

North: Attack southeast of Lake Ilmen (30th Infantry Division). Otherwise fairly quiet day. PWs state that the enemy on the Ladoga front is regrouping and moving replacements into the line before resuming the attack.

3 October 1941

Situation: *South:* Nothing new. It might be a good thing if von Kleist were not to waste too much time on enemy elements still resisting on the eastern bank of the Dnieper, and instead widened his front a little, bringing up the Italians behind his right wing to mop up the eastern bank of the Dnieper. Regrouping of Sixth and Seventeenth armies has been initiated. The method chosen by army group, to order the two left-wing corps of Seventeenth Army to strike northeast, under its direct control for the time being, is an indication of tensions within army group.

On Hoth's northern wing there are complaints about the deficient mobility of 1st Armored Division. Small wonder, for the division comes straight from the battle of Leningrad, without a pause for rest and refitting. It will probably be the same story with 19th and 20th Armored divisions.

North: No new developments at the front. The arrival of the Spanish division and 227th Division is a little delayed by railroad disruption (partisans). The arrival of new forces makes army group uncertain again about its operational program. There is no reason whatever to make any changes in the program ordered.

Ambassador Ritter tries to explain his conversation with Alfieri and to prove that there could not have been any indiscretion on the part of the Foreign Office.

. . .

The TYPHOON front is making cheering progress. Guderian has reached Orel. Enemy resistance has been broken on the entire front, except in the sector of Second Army. The armored divisions have carried their penetrations as far as 50 km, the infantry divisions theirs as far as 40 km into enemy territory. The enemy is hanging on and defending himself as well as he can. Even reserves have been brought forward to the front. Nowhere are there any signs of deliberate disengagement. The southern assault group has broken through the enemy positions, while the northern group has overrun the advance positions and is now approaching the big continuous line of enemy positions.

North: The heavy attack against Eighth Armored Division on the Ladoga front, as well as the attacks from both east and west against our troops along the coast of the Gulf of Finland, was repelled.

4 October 1941

. . .

Operation TYPHOON is developing on a truly classic pattern. Guderian has reached Orel and is now pushing into completely empty space. Hoepner has broken through the enemy positions and has reached Mozhaysk. Hoth has pushed to Kholm (on the upper Dnieper) and has gained elbow room to the north as far as Byelyi. The enemy is holding all parts of the front not under direct attack, a policy that bodes well for the encirclement of pockets.

In AGp. North. An attack in the sector of Schmidt's corps has been repelled. Everywhere else, unusual quiet, most surprising in the Valdai/Rzhev area.

. . .

5 October 1941

. . .

The battle of AGp. Center continues along its truly classic course. Guderian is on the Orel-Bryansk highway. Enemy forces committed against his left wing have been beaten back and will eventually be encircled together with the rest. Second Army is advancing rapidly on its northern wing, meeting almost no resistance. Hoepner is driving on Vyazma, turning toward the big marshes to the west and east. His right wing, followed by the armored corps of the reserve, which has not been committed so far, has no enemy before it any longer. Fourth Army is swinging north. Enemy resistance varies according to locality and unit. It is quite evident that the enemy wants to make a stand, but cannot. Ninth Army has harder going. Armored Group 3, after being held up by lack of fuel, will not start moving again until this afternoon. The infantry is closing up with magnificent speed, so that we may expect that enemy resistance, which is partly stubborn and evidently skillfully directed, will soon be broken. From the front facing the northern wing of Ninth Army, which does not participate in the attack, the enemy is drawing all available forces to the south, against the northern wing of the offensive.

In AGp. North the attack against the Ladoga front planned for 6 October has been called off by OKH, and an order has been issued to take out the armored divisions, which would needlessly burn themselves out in that terrain. The attack will be launched with infantry as soon as sufficient strength has been built up with the newly arrived divisions. Meanwhile the armored divisions will rest and refit.

. . .

Egypt and North Africa: Apart from the forces in Tobruk, the following units are assumed to be stationed in Egypt: Eight infantry divisions, two armored divisions, and the occupation troops. In addition, GHq. troops and five GHq. armored battalions. This gives a possible strength of:
630 "cruiser"-type tanks
250 infantry tanks
775 light tanks and reconnaissance cars

That makes more than 1,650 tanks. Possibly more "GHq. armored battalions" will be added. The British garrisons at Giarabub and Shiva have been reinforced. Such strength, coupled with the preparations for an offensive by the British, constitutes a definite threat to Rommel.

General Oehquist:

    a.   Military situation on the Finnish front very satisfactory. Only weak Finnish forces left on the Karelian isthmus, but they could join in the attack when we shall have crossed the Neva.

    b.   Finnish assistance in our training program for winter warfare.

. . .

6 October 1941

Situation: The offensive is developing to our full satisfaction.

South: The breakthrough of von Kleist's Panzer Army in the direction of Mariupol has gained ground so quickly that we may expect sizable elements of that enemy to be cut off by tomorrow. On the other hand, the rear and the mobile elements of the enemy are fighting. Eleventh Army around Melitopol will by that time have been pulled back toward Rostov.

Seventeenth Army has launched its attack to the southeast with initial successes that afford the southern wing of the army a chance to overtake the pursued enemy.

Sixth Army is advancing on a wide front from the west against the lines Akhtyrka-Sumi. The enemy on this front appears to be capable of serious resistance in only a few places.

Center: Guderian's Panzer Army has come under heavy attack from the northeast on its way from Orel to Tula (4th Armored Division). Elsewhere on its right flank the enemy has remained curiously quiet, and so it was possible to bring up the lagging elements of the right wing and to move the infantry divisions to the right wing in the direction of Rylsk.

Seventeenth Armored Division has succeeded in isolating Bryansk from the east. Although the division has no contact yet with Second Army, converging toward it from the west, we can be sure that the capture of Bryansk will not only within a short time secure for Guderian the essential supply road Roslavl-Bryansk-Orel, but also use the enemy facing Second Army and 1st Cavalry Division, who is already crumbling at some points, to split in two and so make it all the easier for us to liquidate him in local pockets.

Fourth Army and Armored Group 4 are swinging northward unchecked. Signs of enemy demoralization. Hoepner's right wing and the left wing of Second Army have no major enemy forces in front of them and are advancing on and beyond Yukhnov.

Ninth Army and Armored Group 3 are now clean through the second line of enemy positions and have reached the motor highway also north of Vyazma (7th Armored Division). Ninth Army has gained elbow room also toward Byelyi. All in all, it can be said that the battle of encirclement conducted by AGp. Center is approaching its climax, i.e., the closing of the pocket.

North: In the *Valdai* Hills sector, only minor local attacks. The Ladoga front is quiet on the whole. On the coast between the Leningrad and Kronstadt fronts, another landing attempt was frustrated. Oesel now completely in our hands.

.   .   .

7 October 1941

ObdH and Heusinger visit Army Group Center to discuss further plans.

Situation: *South:* First Panzer Army has overtaken and cut off the enemy opposite the eastern front of Eleventh Army. Some of the enemy have escaped in the direction of Mariupol. Weak enemy forces standing between First Panzer Army and Seventeenth Army are falling back on Stalino. Seventeenth Army has continued its attack to the southeast with good success. The advance elements of Sixth Army are rapidly gaining ground in the direction of Kharkov. The left wing of the army apparently will also catch the enemy group Sumi, which is moving away in southeastward direction.

Center: Second Panzer Army is hampered in its movements by bad weather. On its southern wing it will have to push one infantry corps on Kursk (but not farther for the time being). With XXIV Corps it is now advancing on the Tula axis. Capture of Bryansk and encircling of the enemy elements opposite Second Army from the east may yet give them a good deal of trouble.

Second Army will assume control of all units committed for the encirclement of the enemy at Bryansk, with the exception of armor.

Fourth Army has no more major enemy forces before its right wing, which has been reinforced by the left wing of Second Army. This group, which will be strengthened by a strong armored combat team from the reserve corps of Hoepner's group, will move on Kaluga.

Hoepner linked up with Hoth at Vyazma this morning. A brilliant success after a five-day battle. Next thing to be done is to push the infantry of Fourth Army sharply on Vyazma to free Hoepner at the earliest for the drive against the southeastern front of Moscow.

Ninth Army has gained elbow room in the direction of Rzhev (Byelyi) and is already covering its wing swinging on Vyazma with infantry, both northeast and east. This is a magnificent feat of the troops and a demonstration of sure leadership.

North: No important events. Toward evening it becomes apparent that the enemy is falling back before the northern wing of Ninth Army and II Corps. Presumably he is retreating to the defense line Rzhev–Valdai lake district.

. . .

8 October 1941

Situation in the morning: No important changes since last night:

South has formed and sealed the pocket west of Mariupol. However, considerable elements have apparently escaped to the east. Seventeenth and Sixth armies are advancing slowly on bad roads.

Center: Still no pressure on Guderian's eastern flank. The western flank is under attack, but is covered. Advance beyond the Orel-Bryansk highway is delayed by bad weather, but is being prepared. North of the highway, enemy elements are retreating eastward and northeastward. Here, then, is the hole in the big encircling system.

Pocket at Vyazma is ringed and secured against attacks from the outside. Strong elements of the right wing of Fourth Army have already made great strides in the direction of Kaluga.

Ninth Army is covering itself with comfortably strong forces in the direction of Rzhev and to the east, so that the danger of any attack on the flanks and into the rear is now dispelled.

. . .

9 October 1941

Situation:

AGp. South: We must exploit the unexpectedly swift capture of Mariupol by SS "Adolf Hitler," by pushing through as quickly as possible to Rostov, and perhaps even crossing the Sea of Azov. The Italian divisions unfortunately are so ineffectual that they can be employed for nothing more than passive flank cover behind rivers, but not for broadening the attacking front of the Panzer Army. The attack by Seventeenth Army to the southeast is making good progress. The army should move rather more southeastward than to the east. Right wing must drive on Stalino! Sixth Army is making good headway in rapid marches. Only isolated enemy groups are offering resistance. Evidently the enemy is in no position to block us everywhere in the vast battle zone.

AGp. Center: Guderian is feeling the increasing pressure on his western flank. He will have to drop his objections for the time and use his tanks against this threat, even though it may delay the next move beyond Orel, against Tula. The eastern flank is free of enemy pressure! The encircling battle at Vyazma is proceeding in positively classic fashion. Outside that battle area the right wing of Fourth Army is pushing on to Kaluga, and the northern wing of Ninth Army is regrouping for the attack against Rzhev.

AGp. North: No important changes in the situation. Army group has not begun to feel anything yet of the anticipated introduction of enemy forces from the Ladoga sector.

.   .   .

10 October–3 November 1941

.   .   .

During that period operations proceeded according to plan. Details may be gathered from the estimates of the enemy situation, the daily intention reports of the army groups, and the operational orders. On 3 November overall situation is as follows:

> Apart from the gratifying successes of *Eleventh Army* in the Crimea and some, but very slow, advances of *Sixteenth Army* toward Tikhvin, the entire pursuit operation following the twin battle of Bryansk-Vyazma has been mired in bad fall weather.
>
> *Panzer Army Kleist* is approaching the lower Don and has gradually mastered its supply problems to a point where it can give attention to mopping up the north bank of the Don.
>
> The northern wing is slowly advancing through the Donets basin, which the enemy has evacuated; the scorched-earth policy has been widely applied here, and the population probably will soon be faced with a serious food problem.
>
> *Seventeenth Army:* The southern wing is painfully inching its way southeastward along the southern bank of the Donets. The northern wing is stuck.

Sixth Army has taken Kharkov and Belopolye, but beyond that line it can advance only with small detachments. Here the difficulties of supply and movement have so reduced the fighting spirit behind the drive that even Hq. AGp. South has caught that pessimism. Some energetic "persuading" would be in order to kick them.

In AGp. Center, Second Army (reinforced by armor and motorized units) is closing up toward Kursk with the object of continuing advance on Voronezh. That is pure theory. The grim reality is that the troops are stuck in the mud and will by lucky indeed if they can get enough prime movers through to get their food.

Guderian's Panzer Army has slowly and painfully worked its way loose to Tula (through Orel).

Fourth Army in conjunction with *Armored Group Hoepner* has breached the Moscow defense position all the way from the Oka River, near Kaluga, to Mozhaysk. But to the north, the planned thrust of *Armored Corps Reinhardt* on Klin had to be abandoned as a result of adverse ground conditions.

Ninth Army, after some days of critical fighting, has straightened out the situation around Kalinin and built up a sufficiently strong front facing north.

In AGp. North, Sixteenth Army by local attacks has pinned down the enemy in the Valdai Hills sector and is slowly pushing on Tikhvin. On the rest of the front, no important change.

The problem of supply dominates the situation. The supply position is positively bad in Sixth Army, but this is a sector where it is not quite so serious from the operational point of view if the advance is slowed down or even falls behind that of the other groups. The position is fair in Fourth Army and Armored Group Hoepner despite the unbelievable difficulties on the supply routes through Yukhnov and Vyazma. On the other hand, it is extremely difficult north of the Moscow motor highway, so that it appears doubtful that we could carry out the planned thrust south of the Volga reservoir on the axis Klin-Rybinsk.

The enemy, as was to be expected after the Kiev battle, was not able to defend the Ukraine with a continuous front. To gain time, he is conducting a retrograde defensive. For my part I believe that he is not in a position to hold more than the Moscow region (Vologda, Moscow, Tambov) and the Caucasus; he will have to abandon the intervening country, which, on the east, is bordered only by the steppes east of the Volga. Of course, he will not do this simply by marching off, the more so since he is just as much restricted in his movements as we are. However that may be, extensive evacuation movements from the Caucasus have been observed. It is hard to say as yet how he will react in the Leningrad area.

I believe that he is evacuating also that sector and withdrawing toward Rybinsk, in order to concentrate his entire strength in the Moscow bridgehead, which is the terminal point of all railroad lines from Asia. He will try to conserve these forces and so preserve the possibility to take the offensive again in 1942, or even later, with his strength regenerated through the resources of the Ural. Meanwhile, the Caucasus could be left to its natural defenses and the help of the British and Americans.

Organization: All preparations have been made for the conversion of 8th, 28th, and 5th divisions to mountain divisions, and of the cavalry division to an armored division. They will be taken back to Germany. Division Chevallerie (99th) goes to Norway; two divisions from France will go to AGp. North, in exchange for eastern divisions.

4 November 1941

.   .   .

Viewed as a whole, the situation is determined by railroad capacity and flow of supplies. There is no point in pushing operations outward before we have, step by step, established a solid foundation for them. Failing to do that inevitably would bring fatal reverses down upon us.

The northern wing of AGp. South and the southern wing of AGp. Center have lost contact with the enemy, so that we can base the present estimate of the enemy situation on only a few broad facts, i.e., that the enemy is hanging on to the Lower Don, that he is still in evidence also in the northern sector of the front. According to press and radio reports, the Russians seem to be having a bad time with their communications and their many withdrawals and evacuations. Also, the Russian government has gone from Moscow to Kazan on the Volga, a move that certainly is not going to further unity of Russian military command. In this light we may well expect enemy measures to be slow in reacting and at times even to be conflicting.

. . .

6 November 1941

Situation: Local gains in the Crimea. —The attack by First Panzer Army is severely hampered by adverse weather, and has gained only little ground north of Rostov. Some progress at Tikhvin and on the Volkhov River. On the rest of the front, only local fighting. There is evidence of stiffening of the enemy front west of Moscow and of efforts to bring reinforcements from east and south. Preparations for enemy attack on the anniversary of the revolution, 7 November.

. . .

7 November 1941

. . .

ObdH had a conference with the Fuehrer:

1. The Fuehrer sees three danger spots for future developments (apart from the Mediterranean, which is in the focus of interest):

   a. Murmansk (British). In spring another light division will be sent there.

   b. Activity of the Russians in the central sector. What we cannot accomplish this year must be finished next year. Seize country as far east as Volga. Expeditions.

   c. Oil region. Its capture will have to be postponed until next year. For the time, no plans going beyond the confines of Russia.

2. He concurs with our estimate of the military situation. Written reply forthcoming.

3. Reallocation of forces: light division goes to Finland. One armored division and one motorized division to Norway. No disbanding of divisions in excess of direct replacement requirements.

4. Interested in supply by air (but no practical possibility of an increase!).

5. Insists on improvement of armament of divisions in west. Materiel of disbanded divisions.

. . .

10 November 1941

In the morning I was notified that ObdH had a serious heart attack. Malignant cardiac disease, probably past cure!

Situation: Good progress has been made in the Crimea, but it will take a few more days before we have cleared out the last enemy. First Panzer Army reports very heavy air attacks. Opposite AGp. South, the railroad congestion around Liski is unchanged; apparently evacuation of rolling stock. New enemy forces have joined the attack against the flank of *Second Panzer Army*. The impression is that the enemy is trying to throw back this troublesome group threatening Tula, and to make a stand around Moscow. Farther to the south (on the front of *Second* and *Sixth armies*) he now maintains only light forces, whose obvious mission is merely to watch the vast area between the front on the Lower Don and the forces converging on Tula.

Unfortunately the restrictions of movement preclude making the most of our superiority afforded by Second and Sixth armies.

No important changes in the northern theater.

. . .

11 November 1941

. . .

Field Marshal von Bock on phone: Referring to my talk earlier with General von Greiffenberg:

Point A: Army group orders provide for a long-range and a short-range objective. Attaining even the latter appears doubtful to von Bock in view of the condition of his troops. He has given them as interim objective the line of the Moskva River through Moscow and the Volga Canal. Supplies stocked for the start of operations are gauged to assure maintenance to that line. The ammunition for the operation is still en route at this time. Owing to the "curtailment" of shipments to army group, it was impossible to build up stocks over and above daily requirements, and as a result army group could not be sure it would have the ammunition required; if flow of ammunition is maintained for the next few days, stocking would be completed. Von Bock argues that even if we were content to reach the interim objective ("the bird in hand"), we would have to commence the attack immediately, for every day was bringing us closer to the critical date for deep snowfall. If we were to wait until we had enough striking power for a more distant goal, we might well be overtaken by winter weather and then be immobilized for good.

The time for spectacular operational feats is past. Troops cannot be shifted around anymore. The only course lies in purposeful exploitation of tactical opportunities.

Point B: There can be no doubt that *Guderian* is under heavy attack. The situation is not fully understood. Second Panzer Army has drawn upon itself the enemy forces south of the Oka River, thereby relieving Fourth Army, which now would safely launch its operation. Even if Guderian is still moving freely, it is a question whether he would be able to shake off the enemy. In any event, the accomplishment of *von Kluge's mission* does not depend on that. Army group has moved XXXV Corps of Second Army sharply to the left.

. . .

16 November 1941

. . .

Field Marshal von Leeb (AGp. North) on phone: The situation between Lake Ilmen and Lake Ladoga has taken a bad turn. Very heavy pressure on Malaya Vishera and Vishera. No threat to Tikhvin last night. Today very large movements from the east again. Pressure from the south, from Kostrusa Plesso. Situation at Tikhvin not very acute, but may become so within next few days. Enemy also coming from the north.

Twenty-first Division thinks it can get as far as Volkhovstroi, but will not be able to advance farther unless it receives reinforcements.

The attack by 254th and 223d divisions has miscarried. The divisions had to be returned to their lines of departure; 223d is not yet equal to such a task; it was caught on its northern flank, and then also 254th Division had to fall back. The Volkhov front needs reinforcements. The only thing available is one-third of 61st Division, but it too will take a long time to move into line (initial elements day after tomorrow). Commander of army group wants to await today's developments. He has considered abandoning Tikhvin in favor of strengthening the "Volkhov front." I emphasize OKH's interest in holding Tikhvin at all costs. Two medium artillery battalions have been withdrawn from the Kronstadt front. Infantry line very thin. Enemy has three to four divisions and some MG battalions opposite Hangoe.

Evening situation: Advances by IV Corps on the southern wing of Seventeenth Army, and also by Guderian. The enemy everywhere is withdrawing eastward before Guderian and Second Army without offering much resistance. This confirms our view that he plans to fall back far to the rear. The country is quite empty. Much destruction. Only northwest of Yefremov, a rifle division is still putting up fierce opposition.

On the right wing of Fourth Army, heavy enemy attacks against XIII Corps. Situation tight. On the remainder of the front of Fourth Army, isolated enemy thrusts with artillery support.

The attack southeast of Kalinin has gained more ground. The enemy is falling back behind the Volga. Directly southward, the attack of LVI Corps has made headway against stubborn resistance by mountain division recently arrived from Iran. On the northern front of Ninth Army, the enemy has apparently passed over to the defensive.

In *AGp. North*, no further deterioration of the situation. On the Volkhov, the forces hold each other in balance. Otherwise, as outlined by commander of AGp. North on the phone.

19 November 1941

Situation: On the whole this has been a good day again. Von Kleist's attack on Rostov is making good headway. The enemy is trying to check von Kleist's southward drive by a flank attack from the east, but without success. In *Seventeenth Army,* also IV Corps has made progress. *Second Army* has started off with reconnaissance elements. Guderian is gaining ground to the northeast, and is freeing his flank at Yefremov.

In *Fourth Army* the hard-pressed right wing (XIII Corps) now has a quiet spell. Units are being relieved and re-formed.

The northern wing of army has attacked and gained its objectives against resistance of varying strength. *Armored Group* 3 has made good progress. Armored divisions on the Kalinin front are being relieved.

In AGp. North, a relatively quiet day. Situation on the Volkhov front stabilized. On the Leningrad front, the usual attack was repelled.

1100. **Talk with von Bock** over army group intentions. Strength of attack forces is weak. Impossible fuel use.

1300. **Fuehrer conference:**

    a.   Review of the situation.

        1.   Attach Italian forces to IV Corps. The 198th Division must strike northward!

        2.   Sixth Army must keep more to the southeast, to free the flank of Seventeenth Army. I point out that a gap between Sixth and Second armies would develop as a result.

        3.   Great importance is still attached to an operation in corps strength against Voronezh.

        4.   Operations around Moscow must be so conducted that each of the component drives of the offensive would conclusively eliminate a number of enemy divisions, not merely push them back farther. Yaroslavl-Rybinsk, if possible also Vologda, must be retained by long-range objectives, weather and supply permitting.

        5.   In *North*, enemy group Ladoga must be liquidated.

    b.   Objectives for next year. First, Caucasus: The goal is the Russian southern frontier; time: March to April. In the north, objectives will depend on the closing situation this year, either Vologda or Gorki; not before latter part of May in any case. The other objectives for the coming year must remain open; they will be determined by the effective capacity of our railroads. The question of an "East Wall" to be constructed later remains open.

Political part:

The success in Russia, which the Fuehrer regards as a prodigious achievement, is of great political value. He thinks that the Russian armament potential is seriously reduced by the loss of critical sources of raw material, especially coal, and that the Russian armament industry will need a long time to recover. As to Britain, he attaches great importance to the internal social strains. As regards *France,* he is greatly pleased that Weygand is gone.

His whole outlook is expressive of the belief that realization of the fact that the two groups of belligerents cannot annihilate each other, will bring about a negotiated peace.

General Thomas (OKW):

a.   Political situation.

b.   Fuel position. An operational reserve of 100,000 tons must be accumulated before end of December.

December:		
Eastern Army	88,000	tons
Southeast	2,000	tons
Africa	5,000	tons
Germany and occupied countries	12,000	tons
Total	107,000	tons

Armed forces quota for the first quarter of 1942 is only 75,000 tons, of which 55,000 are allotted for southeast, east, and Africa (instead of 95,000 in December).

c.   Metals program: Quotas of iron and nonferrous metals have been fixed. Fromm's office is at present working out allocations.

d.   Economic tasks of the occupied countries. Grain-threshing drive.

Food situation (painted in pessimistic colors!).

Colonel Heusinger: Review of the outcome of the Fuehrer conference.

20 November 1941

.   .   .

Situation: *Africa:* The big offensive of the British against Cyrenaica has started. Churchill's order of the day.

AGp. South: Successful continuation of attack against Rostov. On the northeastern front of First Panzer Army (XIV Corps), hard fighting and threat of an enemy breakthrough. Also the mountain corps, which is opposed by a strong enemy, was subjected to violent attacks; all were expelled. The Italians again have failed to make any headway. General von Briesen killed in action.

On the front of *Sixth Army,* the enemy has brought up reinforcements and, since the army does not advance itself, is pushing against it.

AGp. Center: Second Army is making heartening progress. Ninth Armored Division has taken Tim. Enemy resistance partly light, partly nonexistent. *Second Panzer Army* is fighting around Yefremov. No enemy between Yefremov and Yepifan. Stubborn enemy resistance between Yepifan and Tula. Heavy battles with enemy tanks.

Fourth Army: The enemy attacks on the right wing are letting up, but preparations foreshadow new attacks. All enemy attacks are conducted with mixed tank and infantry forces. Good progress by the left wing of the army and Armored Group 3, which now is under the direct control of army group. In the direction of Klin, the enemy is conducting a fighting withdrawal. Von Bock in advance command post behind Armored Group 3.

AGp. North: Valdai front quiet. Local attack on the Volkhov front. Against Tikhvin, attacks in regiment strength.

21 November 1941

Situation: Rostov has fallen to us. North of Rostov, heavy fighting against the numerically far superior and apparently well-led enemy, who is attacking in tightly integrated groups, each several divisions strong. It seems that there is no immediate danger, but both command and troops will deserve unqualified praise if they pull through and still reach the Donets bend. *Sixth Army* is forging ahead slowly but surely. Guderian had someone call up in the afternoon to report that his troops are on their last legs. It is true, they did have to fight hard and a very long way; and still they have come through victoriously and pushed back the enemy everywhere. So we may hope that they will be able to fight on, even against the repeatedly reinforced enemy (new Siberian divisions) until a favorable closing line is reached.

North of Tula there is an ominously quiet spot where the enemy now all of a sudden has intensified his reconnaissance effort across the frozen river. It is not impossible that, after being beaten back by Fourth Army, he is now trying his luck farther south under cover of the fog.

The situation in *Fourth Army* has not changed substantially. On the southern wing the enemy has ceased his attacks. On the northern wing we have made some progress. Still, Field Marshal von Bock has been profoundly affected by the severity of the fighting. My old 7th Infantry Division appears to have suffered heavy losses. Regiments with four hundred rifles are commanded by first lieutenants!

Armored Group 3 and the northern wing of Fourth Army have made good advances in the direction of Klin.

The rest of the front is quiet, except for the Volkhov front (local attacks), Tikhvin (attack from the southeast), Neva, and the usual attack out of Leningrad.

In *Africa* the big battle in Cyrenaica is in progress; we cannot obtain any clear picture as yet.

.   .   .

22 November 1941

Situation: Only three important points:

1. *Rostov* is in our hands. All bridges are reported destroyed except one that leads across an island south of the eastern part of the city. The Russians withdrew across the frozen river. On the southern bank, new Russian forces (two cavalry divisions).

    North of Rostov, First Panzer Army was forced into the defense by the Russian attack with superior forces, and will have a hard time seeing it through. The measures instituted are well taken and promise to be successful. However, after First Panzer Army has disposed of the attacker, it probably would be too much to expect it to clear the enemy out of the Donets bend with what is left of its forces. Despite all efforts of army group to get Sixth Army moving, there are no signs of an attack or of initiation of the transfer of the divisions destined for First Panzer Army. The consequence is that the enemy is withdrawing forces fronting the passive army to commit them against First Panzer Army.

2. In *Guderian's* group the tension seems to be letting up. Now he is again convinced he could continue the attack. The Russian army communiqué speaks about a dangerous situation at Tula.

3. Field Marshal *von Bock* himself has taken charge of the battle of Moscow from an advanced command post. With enormous energy he drives forward everything that can be brought to bear. Nevertheless it seems that nothing more can be gotten out of southern wing and center of Fourth Army for an attack. The troops here are finished (e.g., in my old 7th Division, one regiment is commanded by a first lieutenant; the battalions are commanded by second lieutenants). But northern wing of Fourth Army and Armored Group 3 still have a chance of success, and they are being driven relentlessly to achieve it. Von Bock compares the situation with the battle of the Marne, where the last battalion that could be thrown in turned

the balance. Here, too, the enemy has brought in new forces. Von Bock is moving up everything he can get hold of in the rear area, even 255th Division.

In *Africa* the course of the big battle cannot yet be clearly discerned. The various engagements to date seem to have resulted in considerable tank losses on both sides and to have forced Rommel to give up his plan of an attack from the northeast. Apparently he has formed a line south of Tobruk with the main body of his forces and for the time being leaves the Sollum front, which was prepared for that attack from the northeast, to its own devices.

. . .

23 November 1941

. . .

Notes by General Halder of a meeting which he conducted with the General Staff officers (for administration and supply) of the armies on the eastern front, 23 November 1941.

OQu.   Discussion 23.11.1941.

1. *Appreciation.* Dependence of the operation on supplies! The resolution despite the distances and tempo of this unusual operation. Excellent General Staff work. Appreciation also to railroads!

2. Finality of these operations which will continue. A break in the course of the war:

    a. *Military political:* England no longer possesses a continental dagger. She must shift her conduct of operations to the periphery (Russia, Near East, North Africa, French North and West Africa, America, and Iceland) in the hope of blockading the European continent. Whether England has sufficient power for this requirement or can continue the war on such a basis, since we can reorganize and properly harvest the occupied areas, remain questions of time.

    b. The means which are available to us for continuing the war are limited through use and the incredible strain imposed on our arms by the protected areas. Certainly the army, as it existed in June 1941, will not be available to us again.

        (a)   Manpower replacements.

(b)   Armaments (raw materials, copper, and fuel).

(c)   Workers.

(d)   Food.

(e)   Vehicle equipment and significance for the organization of the troops and supplies.

These issues will be discussed in more detail later. We must understand the possibility that belligerents may achieve either the destruction or decisive advantage over the foe. It is possible that the war will shift from the level of military success to the level of moral and economic endurance without removing the military possibility, using available materials to seriously damage the enemy. *The demand for frugality in the employment of our forces and arms and ammunition will increase markedly. The use of the militarily conquered territories will be more significant.*

3.   *The military situation:*

West: North Cap to Biscay.

Africa: Balkans.

East: Russia's military authority no longer a threat.

Europe: The enemy is decisively battered because of our operations—to which the resourceful performance of the supply efforts played a significant role—but not destroyed.

Despite our extraordinary performance, we shall not be able to totally destroy the enemy this year. Given the vastness of this country and the inexhaustibleness of the people, we cannot be totally certain of success. We knew that from the beginning. In this year we shall continue the attack until we reach the best lines for continuing the attack next year.
Moscow.
Oka area (Tula-Rjasen).
Don area (Jelez-Voronezh), occupy the Lower Maikop (from the Don and Kerch).

For major coordinated operations with the size of previous effort, the resources are no longer available (strength of the troops, supply situation). We must reach our goals, step by step and in various acts.

Given that, there will be no signal "Halt into the barracks," as had become the normal activity of previous years. We must sustain the pressure on the enemy, changing locations, always with a sense of next year's requirements. These demands (Caucasus, Volga, Vologda, and linking with Finland) require a renewed and, in some areas, restructured force with a sufficient supply base and a proper transportation network (rail, road, and communications net). The additional problem of a late fall and early winter, as well as other enemy damage, complicates the implementation of the refitting and reorganizing goals.

The basic rules are, insofar as they are leadership demands, that they should be achieved by setting the operational goals and through conferences with the armored group and army chiefs of staff.

However one addresses these problems in the various armored group area, the ultimate authority is the responsible authorities in the armored groups. The armies execute.

It is not acceptable that one army declares itself unable to operate until fully supplied while another army accepts the greatest risks while functioning within the operational guidelines. It is not acceptable that an army—as may be the case—dissipates its strength to prepare housing, even when it knows someone else will use it, or another army constructs no stables because it does not accept the possible mission of a forward movement.

For the execution of instructions, various documents were issued. These practical implementations demand the highest performance levels of the supply services. What is addressed here cannot provide useful answers to everyone. The discussions should explain the rationale for the continued support and refitting of the troops, who have richly earned it, and the preparation for next year's missions.

. . .

24 November 1941

. . .

General Fromm: Gives an overall picture of our arms production. Declining output! He thinks of the necessity to make peace! On 1 April we shall be 180,000 men short in the eastern army. At that time we shall still have available the trained age group 1922 (270,000) and then must draft age group 1923 (1 April).

General Paulus: Talk on tasks and disposition of forces during winter.

Reports from Africa convey the impression that the British armored forces have been pushed into a very bad corner. With this fighting engaging the German and Italian forces, the Sollum front appears to be temporarily in a difficult situation. At the moment it is still a mystery why the British forces committed in direction of the Sirte are wheeling south.

25 November 1941

Situation: At Rostov the enemy fortunately has not become active as yet. Also to the north, taking back our front appears to have had good results. In *Seventeenth Army* sector, intensive enemy activity, which compelled IV Corps to give ground in some places. *Sixth* and *Second armies* mainly unchanged. Guderian apparently now has freedom of movement in the direction of Kolomna.

Good advances by the northern wing of *Fourth Army* and *Armored Group 3*. The enemy is desperately throwing in what troops he has left (also from the Kalinin area).

In *AGp. North,* reconnaissance and artillery activity on the Volkhov River and at Tikhvin; no major attack as yet. The northward drive west of the Volkhov River has started today. First Division on the Neva again has beaten off heavy enemy attacks.

. . .

26 November 1941

Situation: Artillery duels at Sevastopol. It seems that the enemy is preparing for evacuation. North of Rostov the enemy is working himself closer to our new positions. He is readying forces for continuance of his attacks, and apparently is also bringing down more troops from the north. The situation will therefore remain tense, the more so as we cannot get any reinforcements to this front.

Sixth Army is still hanging around doing nothing. The enemy now appears to be moving forces from that front also northward, toward Tombov and Michurinsk, where road and railroad movements toward Ryazan are now reported in progress; we cannot make out as yet if they are destined for the buildup of a defensive front along the Oka

River, or if they go on into the Moscow area. Moreover, the enemy is moving his covering forces increasingly closer to the inactive Sixth Army.

Second Army reports stiffer opposition (three rehabilitated divisions have appeared on this front).

Guderian is making further progress, although some of his forces are pinned down around pockets. On the Moscow front, more advances from the north in spite of increasing enemy opposition.

In AGp. *North,* local attacks in the Valdai area and on the Volkhov front; at Tikhvin, only weak attacks. Heavier attack on the Neva. They are all repelled, unfortunately not without losses to our troops. The enemy is instituting truck-column traffic to the mouth of the Volkhov River, across frozen Lake Ladoga.

.   .   .

28 November 1941

Situation: At *Rostov* the enemy has apparently been withdrawing some more forces from his original attacking front north of the city in order to keep up his offensive. South of the city, large artillery concentrations. New heavy attacks seem to be coming.

Assault of Sevastopol scheduled for 8 December (estimated to take four to five days).

Both eastern and northern fronts of Seventeenth Army are relatively quiet.

On the front of *Sixth Army,* the enemy is not strong, but makes that up in aggressiveness. Sixth Army is unable to gain freedom of movement.

Opposite *Second Army* the enemy who in this sector is operating in small groups appears to have become stronger and more active. By and by, all the divisions of the old Thirteenth Army are turning up again. Toward Kursk and Yelets, minor enemy movements are in progress from the southwest. At Yefremov, the enemy has been reinforced. Also on the right flank of *Second Panzer Army* (18th Armored Division, 25th Motorized Division), the enemy appears to have been reinforced. Movements from Tula and a counterattack out of Kashira would indicate that the enemy has brought reinforcements against Second Panzer Army also from the north. He evidently intends to hold the Oka River west of Tula. Here our XXXXIII Corps reports only little headway in its attack, with substantial losses and heavy ammunition expenditure.

The attacking wing of AGp. *Center* has gained more ground. Second Armored Division, in particular, reports a considerable advance in the direction of Moscow. On the front of *Armored Group 3,* the enemy is withdrawing eastward while conducting delaying actions; intensive enemy air activity in the area. On the front of *Ninth Army,* the enemy has stepped up his activity (especially at and west of Kalinin), obviously to relieve the pressure on Moscow. The extreme western wing of the army for the first time reports heavy enemy artillery concentration.

On the front of *Sixteenth Army* southeast of Lake Ilmen, which beat off heavy enemy attacks yesterday, the enemy evidently has an unusually heavy artillery concentration. Possibly Stalin has ordered commitment of the last reserves along the entire front in order to save Moscow. At Tikhvin, enemy attacks in some strength, especially from the south, and on the Volkhov front, minor attacks; all abortive.

The attack of our I Corps in the direction of Shum has come up against enemy field fortifications south of the town. South of the Neva, attacks against 122d Division are in progress since early this morning.

The Russian radio commentator has stated that Leningrad is now no longer encircled. In fact, a road across Lake Ladoga is now open for traffic between Leningrad and the outside.

The situation in *Africa* is confused. After attacks of the Africa Corps to relieve the Sollum front, which appear to have succeeded in freeing our encircled strongpoints, the center of the battle has shifted again to the vicinity directly southeast of Tobruk, where the British assault force and the garrison of Tobruk apparently have made contact.

Our 5th and 21st Armored divisions now are rushing from Sollum to eliminate the strong enemy concentration there. We are threatened with a fuel shortage.

.   .   .

29 November 1941

Situation: The reports on Rostov confirm the picture obtained yesterday. The numerically weak forces of First Panzer Army had to give way before the concentric attack launched in very great strength from south (here apparently a main effort), west, and north. On the morning of 29 November, SS "Adolf Hitler" was taken back into the new defense position west of Rostov; the withdrawal of 16th Motorized Division is still in progress. Farther north, 1st Mountain Division is under attack.

In *Seventeenth Army* the main body of 111th Division has now at last arrived at the front. However, some time must elapse before it can become effective in IV Corps sector. The attack by 9th Division has secured us possession of the town of Izyum. The attack probably was inspired more by the desire for solid winter quarters than by any tactical necessity.

Behind the front facing *Sixth Army,* enemy railroad movements from Kupyansk northward. In view of this army's passivity, it would not be at all impossible if the enemy were shifting forces from this front to the north, where he needs them.

Second Army reports some local advances. The enemy opposing *Second Panzer Army* has reinforced his troops at Kashira; in this sector our spearhead (17th Armored Division) was taken back. Farther to the east, the enemy movements to Ryazan from the south are continuing.

On the front of *Fourth Army,* the enemy appears to be somewhat more active again. There is some talk that enemy is preparing for an attack (?). No news from northern wing of Fourth Army and from *Armored Group 3.* To counter the push of 7th Armored Division across the Volga Canal at Yakhroma, the enemy apparently is bringing up forces from the front of Ninth Army as well as from Yaroslavl.

Enemy attack, stronger than usual, against *Ninth Army* at Kalinin and to the west. The rest of the front quiet.

In Sixteenth Army sector the usual minor local attack on the Volkhov front. It is quite significant that the enemy south of Tikhvin has established as strong positions close to our main battle position. Also, northwest of the town he has for some days moved very close to our defense line. On the front facing *I Corps* there is now a division from Kronstadt, which the enemy seems to have brought across the ice of Lake Ladoga.

In the other sectors on left wing of Sixteenth Army and in Eighteenth Army, nothing of importance.

Reports from *Africa* still show a rapidly changing picture, with details blurred. Now, after the first assault south of Tobruk and the relief operation at Sollum, a climactic third act seems to be shaping up in the form of a battle southeast of Tobruk, in which both parties will keenly feel the losses of the preceding fighting. No prediction can be made of the outcome.

Phone talk with von Bock concerning the allegation that army group lacks DEFINITE OBJECTIVES (Goering's unconsidered opinion). Army group knows exactly what it is after. However, if the current attack on Moscow from the north is unsuccessful, he fears the operation will become another Verdun, i.e., a brutish, chest-to-chest struggle of attrition. It is still too early to throw Fourth Army (XX Corps) into the battle. The time for that will come when the advance from the north has overrun Svenigorod.

We discuss regrouping of von Kluge's and Guderian's armies for winter.

OQu I—Chief Op. Sec.: Brief review of the situation. Crisis in First Panzer Army unchanged. Early resumption of the attack cannot be expected. Transfer of divisions of Sixth Army to Seventeenth Army and First Panzer Army takes a long time. Now that First Panzer Army has been taken back from Rostov, the plan of a relief offensive by Seventeenth Army has become meaningless, and the crucial question now is whether possession of Voroshilovgrad and the anthracite coal district is considered important enough to warrant dissipating on that operation the striking power of IV Corps, which will be hard to replace before spring.

Sixth Army reports that for logistical reasons, it cannot move its right wing forward to the Oskol River at and south of Kupyansk before mid-December. These indications then give us a clear picture of the objectives which AGp. South may be expected to gain in the near future. Mobility and striking power are spent. We just have to resign ourselves to these facts.

In AGp. Center the position is not yet quite as clear as that. In any event, it can be stated even now that at most army group will be able to push the northern wing to the Moscow line, while Guderian may clear the enemy out of the Oka salient northwest of Tula to gain the area for winter quarters.

In AGp. *North* the given possibilities are obvious. Clearing of the Ladoga sector and linkup with the Finns.

We can therefore issue the orders for the changeover to the winter phase and need not wait for any further developments. These orders must be accompanied by basic directives on operations and supply. Accordingly, the offensive against the Maikop region must be called off for this year; it is the initial operation in 1942 and will be executed in one blow out of this year's final position.

Captain Weygold (navy) reports on developments in the naval theater. At the moment we have ten submarines in the western Mediterranean, fifteen in the eastern Mediterranean, and three off Lapland. Actual operations in the Atlantic, very restricted; fifty-six submarines in repair or en route to and from the areas of operations. The opinion is still upheld that submarine warfare has prospects of achieving a decisive success against England. —Surface operations: SS *Tirpitz* and *Hipper* are ready, at Trondheim, to put out to sea; will operate in northern Atlantic.

. . .

30 November 1941

. . .

Situation: In *AGp. North* it is becoming increasingly obvious that the attack on Shum has miscarried. The main effort, by von Boeckmann's group, must be shifted against Volkhovstroi. An order to this effect is issued. Otherwise the situation in AGp. North is the usual. Traffic across Lake Ladoga seems to continue.

AGp. Center: Further progress toward Moscow has been scored by the northern wing of the offensive against the enemy, who, throwing in reinforcements and using mines, opposes every possible resistance. The central sector of Fourth Army will join in the offensive on 1 December. In Guderian's sector, confirmation of the picture, with the enemy at Kashira introducing reinforcements in line with his general tendency on the Moscow front to shift forces from his center to the threatened wings. On Guderian's east flank (Yepifan), for instance, the enemy has disappeared entirely in some spots. In the Tula salient, he seems to be falling back.

This salient will have to be cleared before we can envisage further objectives. On the southern wing of the eastern flank and in Second Army sector, the enemy is apparently holding on, launching local attacks in all directions from his base at Voronezh.

Today's great worry is in *AGp. South*. This does not apply to Sixth and Seventeenth armies, which repelled the usual attacks. It refers to

First Panzer Army, against which the enemy has launched an enveloping attack in such overwhelming strength that army reserve (14th Armored Division) had to be committed on the very day that it reached its new position in the withdrawal. Even so, First Panzer Army could not prevent local penetrations; now it has to fall back once more.

The Fuehrer is in a state of extreme agitation over the situation. He forbids withdrawal of the army to the line Taganrog–Mius–mouth of the Bakhmut River, and demands that the retrograde move be halted farther east. Alongside this, there is even talk of an attack by Seventeenth Army on Voroshilovgrad. These people have no conception of the condition of our troops, and keep grinding out ideas in a vacuum.

ObdH was ordered to the Fuehrer at 1300. The interview appears to have been more than disagreeable, with the Fuehrer doing all the talking, pouring out reproaches and abuse, and shouting orders as fast as they came into his head. Regrettably, ObdH yielded to the Fuehrer's insistence and has issued the order not to fall back to the aforementioned line in one move. Field Marshal von Rundstedt's reply was that he could not comply with the order and asked that either the order be changed or he be relieved of his post. Inasmuch as the Fuehrer had reserved the decision for himself, the request was passed on to the Fuehrer in its exact wording. In tight situations such as these, only the commander on the spot can have a complete picture, and his decision must be trusted. Such confidence would certainly be in order in the case of von Rundstedt. The people at army group have done everything in their power. Let them have a free hand, and they will handle their end of the job.

Buhle:

a. The eastern army has a shortage of 340,000 men, i.e., 50 percent of the combat strength of its infantry. Company combat strength is 50 to 60 men.

b. Current losses and returning convalescents approximately offset each other at this time. Gaps can be filled only by disbanding some divisions.

In Germany we have only 33,000 men available. The bulk of the replacements are not yet broken in to the front-line routine and so have limited combat value.

c. Trucks: Serviceability, at most 60 percent.

    d.   Time needed for the rehabilitation of an armored division is six months. Units should therefore be returned to Germany for refitting as soon as possible.

    e.   We cannot replace even 50 percent of our motorcycle losses.

    f.   Truck replacements available are sufficient to:

Equip three divisions (22d, 23d, 24th)	100 percent
Equip two motor infantry divisions slated for conversion to armored divisions	50 percent
Rehabilitate four more infantry motorized divisions	50 percent
Rehabilitate two more armored divisions	75 percent

    We have completely new equipment for five armored divisions.

    We can convert one infantry division into a motorized division.

    (Olbricht's proposal.)

    g.   The first armored divisions can be ready beginning of February at the earliest; this applies also to the units for France. The other armored divisions could not depart from Germany before middle of May. We get at best four new armored divisions for one Panzer army by end of March.

    h.   I veto the proposal to deactivate one army Hq.

    i.   Readying of materiel replacements for Africa (including 20 5-cm AT guns, which will be shipped by air).

    k.   To be sent to AGp. Center, 6 December, for Moscow front:

          10   batteries 15-cm guns (11,300)
           2   batteries 15-cm guns (15,300)
           1   battery 19.4-cm gun (20,800)

    l.   Caucasian Legion.

    m.   Armored ammunition carriers: Twenty ready for issue.

    Starting December, 10 to 12 units each month; will first go to light divisions (seven for each infantry regiment).

General Konrad reports out on leaving GHq. (Stays for luncheon.)

Colonel Heusinger: Development of the situation in AGp. South. Several talks with OKW and army group. Von Rundstedt states that the order of the Fuehrer cannot be carried out.

1 December, 0200. The Fuehrer decides that von Rundstedt is to resign his command and appoints von Reichenau to carry out his orders.

General Wagner reports: Evacuation of Taganrog prepared so that it can be completed in two days.
Hospitals are already gone.

Stockpiling of sufficient ammunition and fuel in progress, will be based on Stalino.

1 December 1941

0400.   We receive three teletypes from the Fuehrer:

1.   Addressed to von Rundstedt: He is relieved of the command of army group.

2.   Addressed to von Reichenau, transferring to him the command of Army Group South with the mission to halt the retreat of First Panzer Army, take all necessary measures to bolster up the Panzer army, and strike as soon as possible for Voroshilovgrad from the sectors of 49th Mountain Corps and IV Corps.

3.   Addressed to BdE, directing him to move at once by rail and as far forward as possible, up to forty Tanks III and twelve Tanks IV each, for 13th, 14th, and 16th Armored divisions.

Situation: The picture is dominated by developments in AGp. *South,* where Field Marshal von Reichenau has taken over command. The withdrawal from the intermediate position to the Mius position was already in progress when Panzer army received the order to hold the intermediate position. The result was confusion, inasmuch as the shortage of operational trucks, which hampered withdrawal, now is a serious impediment for the return to the line.

1100.   Talk with von Sodenstern, in which von Reichenau cuts in. Von Reichenau is willing to accept responsibility. He upholds the order to defend the intermediate position despite von Kleist's report that he will be beaten on that line.

1200.   Talk with Colonel Zeitzler: He describes the condition and position of the individual divisions. They are all very much understrength. In 13th Armored Division the commander and one of the ablest regimental commanders have had complete nervous breakdowns. The "intermediate position" is no position at all, but a line selected for rearguard actions pending preparation of the Mius position for defense. This Mius position at least had infantry cover and battle positions from our earlier passage, whereas in the intermediate position the infantry lies without cover on the hard-frozen ground. A substantial portion of the artillery, which is only partly mobile, is set up way back in the Mius position. The bridgehead in front of Taganrog protects the airfield there so effectively that fighters can use its runway.

First Panzer Army is convinced that the intermediate position cannot be held. Its wings are being pushed by two strong motorized enemy groups, and its center is under pressure from exceedingly large infantry forces, which we will be able to withstand in this unfavorable position only temporarily, if at all. Panzer army cannot understand why our troops should stand here and have the enemy punch through their line when 9 km in back of them there is a much better position; accordingly, request is made for permission to move into the Mius position, which it believes it can hold.

1300. **Another talk with von Sodenstern** on the same subject. All this has been told to Field Marshal von Reichenau, but so far he has shown no inclination to endorse the arguments advanced.

1400. **Talk with Jodl, OKW.** I outline the situation. It is stark nonsense to expose the troops to a tactical defeat forward of the Mius position. Request him to present the facts to the Fuehrer.

1530. **While ObdH sees the Fuehrer, von Reichenau calls up.** Enemy motorized forces have broken through SS "Adolf Hitler" in the intermediate position. He asks permission to fall back to the Mius position tonight. Fuehrer concurs. Now we are where we could have been last night. It was a senseless waste of strength and time, and to top it, we lost von Rundstedt also.

ObdH's health, under the pressure of constant worrying, has again taken an alarming turn.

Afternoon conference with Paulus and Heusinger about the basic features of the disposition of our forces for the winter, which would allow refitting and a short rest.

Phone talk with Field Marshal von Bock regarding his report submitted to ObdH today on the situation and casualties. It is a tremendous feat of our numerically greatly weakened forces to break through well-developed enemy positions which must be taken on in frontal attacks, but full-scale operations cannot be conducted with such weak troops. All they can do is work themselves forward in small tactical units. The enemy positions can be assaulted only by frontal attacks.

XII and XIII Corps cannot attack before the enemy on its left and right has been dealt with.

I emphasize that we, too, are concerned about the human sacrifice. But an effort must be made to bring the enemy to his knees by applying the last ounce of strength. Once it is conclusively shown that this is impossible, we shall make new decisions.

Situation in the evening: First Panzer Army is being taken back behind the Mius. —We do not have the forces for the attack on Voroshilovgrad ordered by the Fuehrer. It seems that new enemy troops are moving to the front through Rostov and Stalingrad. The front facing Seventeenth and Sixth armies appears to have received Caucasian replacements. All quiet on Sixth Army front.

Second Army is advancing. North of Yefremov enemy resistance has stiffened, while to the south it has softened. Guderian is regrouping for tomorrow's attack on his front north of Tula.

Fourth Army has made good headway with its northern wing. Armored Groups 3 and 4 have again advanced a little in hard fighting.

On the rest of the front, there is but little fighting. Local successes toward Shum. The situation on both sides of the narrow sector held by us on the Neva at Schluesselburg seems to be deteriorating. Violent enemy attack across the Neva, which we were able to repel. Enemy concentration in the Ladoga sector for an attack toward the Neva River.

.   .   .

3 December 1941

Situation: In *AGp. South,* enemy pressure only against our combat outposts on the southern wing; on other portions of the front, the enemy is moving closer to the rear guards still forward of the new position. The enemy may still be preparing a major concentration of forces opposite the Italian corps. Railroad movements, possibly troops, from Stalingrad to Likhaya.

The movements of the forces to be shifted southward from Sixth Army are proceeding at a very slow rate.

Sixth Army is still doing nothing to move 299th Division to the front and to send 68th Division to the south.

AGp. Center: Stiffening enemy resistance south of Tim and in front of Yelets. Pressure from the direction of Kashira compels withdrawal of 17th Armored Division, with the enemy attacking from the east, north, and west. It remains to be seen whether we still have sufficient striking power north of Tula to effect local improvements in the situation in that sector. For more than that our forces certainly are not strong enough. In Fourth Army, the attack is nothing but a painful squeezing for local advances, against which the reacting enemy is scoring some tactical successes (encirclement of some German forces by enemy counterthrusts, e.g., 258th Division). We have yet to see how far the attacking wing north of Moscow will advance before its striking power is spent.

AGp. North: The situation created by yesterday's attack against Tikhvin from the south is not yet quite clear. The commander of 61st Division has taken over the defense of Tikhvin with his division. On the rest of the front nothing of importance. In several places preparations for attacks are surmised. Eighty Russian divisions east of the Neva.

. . .

Situation:

- **a.** Fuehrer has arrived at the conclusion that army group and Panzer army bear no blame for recent events in AGp. South. The troops fought gallantly. A number of directives issued pertaining to individual missions. Situation tight in the Italian corps. The 125th Division is to be moved to front. IV Corps gets permission to attack with 111th Division, as planned.

- **b.** In *South,* an enemy attack on First Panzer Army was repelled. In *Center,* Guderian has made good progress at Tula. Fourth Army is going back to the initial position. In AGp. *North,* no new signs of any forthcoming large-scale attack. A minor attack was repelled.

- **c.** Hangoe has been evacuated by the Russians.

- **d.** *North Africa. Armored group* reports heavy losses in tanks; requests various aids, including an infantry division, to be shipped by air.

Phone talk with von Bock: Spearhead of Fourth Army has again been taken back, because the neighboring units could not keep abreast of them.

Armored Group 3 has run into minefields and marshland. Nevertheless, he has not given up all hope yet and thinks that the attack might yet make some advances, but the moment can now be foreseen when the troops will be at the end of their strength. I point out what changing to the defensive would involve. The disadvantages of that policy were one of the reasons why we stuck to the offensive.

4 December 1941

. . .

1200.   Von Greiffenberg (on phone):

    a.   If Field Marshal von Bock thinks that the costly attacks northwest of Moscow promise no further success, he is free to stop them. Von Greiffenberg: They have already been stopped in Fourth Army sector. In Armored Groups 3 and 4, the attacks are scheduled to be continued on 6 December. In the sector of Guderian's Panzer army, there is no reason to call off the offensive.

    b.   I remind him to be cautious in pushing forward the widely separated groups on Guderian's eastern front. There is the double threat of sudden snowdrifts and of enemy thrusts from Voronezh.

    c.   The right wing of Second Army at Tim must not be pushed any farther, nor must it be further weakened by detaching elements to the north! Reasons: Threats from Voronezh and need of maintaining contact with Sixth Army.

    d.   He gives me his views on a possible position at the close of operations. It would involve only a local straightening of our line north of Moscow, and would still include the terrain north of Klin.

. . .

General Gercke:

Railroads:

    a.   Construction of additional lines in rear area will increase elasticity, but not capacity of system. The crux of the problem is in the railroad servicing installations (coal and water). Speed is dictated by bridges, strength of rails, railroad switching points, stations, signal network.

Centralized system (German) not as easily managed as Russian decentralized organization. The signal installations are geared to the Russian system. Locomotive repair shops were completely wrecked by the Russians. Are operating again, but only in a make-shift fashion. We cannot increase number of engines because we lack the requisite maintenance facilities. German engines are not built to withstand prevailing low temperatures. Transport of coal supply absorbs large volume of rolling stock.

Not enough personnel (instead of sixteen per km only ten, including one German); not accustomed to work under war conditions.

b.   Reconstruction program: Gradual elimination of the broad gauge.

5 December 1941

Situation: No important advances except by Seventeenth Army in a southeast-ward attack of IV Corps. Our line throughout has held against enemy attacks.

Guderian decides to fall back at Tula; 36 degrees below freezing. Scheduled attack by Armored Groups 3 and 4 must be called off. Enemy penetration east of Kalinin.

A series of Fuehrer orders on allocation of tanks to First Panzer Army and AGp. North causes some confusion.

1030.   Phone talk with Field Marshal von Reichenau. He wants mobile divisions. We haven't any. He gets tanks.

Von Leeb. 1800. With the shift of the boundary between Sixteenth and Eighteenth armies and the consequent changes in the ranking commanders, he now comes with an entirely new proposal regarding continuance of the Ladoga offensive, i.e., through 291st Division next to 223d Division. Must be turned down! First we must await arrival of the tanks, then we can perhaps strike from southwest and east.

Von Bock: They are at the end of their strength. Tomorrow's attack by Armored Group 4 is off. He will report tomorrow whether a withdrawal is necessary.

Conferences on current matters with Paulus and Heusinger. ObdH informs me of his decision to retire from the service.

6 December 1941

Situation: Stabilized in *South*. The heavy losses sustained in yesterday's unsuccessful attacks against First Panzer Army have had a sobering effect on the enemy. The successful attack by Seventeenth Army (IV Corps) to the southeast apparently draws away enemy forces from the south. Unusually large volume of shipping in Black Sea ports.

Center: Enemy attacks from Voronezh to the north, northwest, and northeast. Heavy traffic on the Dmitrov-Moscow line. Evacuation of Moscow continues.

North: Enemy before Tikhvin has been reinforced. Very severe cold (38 degrees below freezing); numerous cases of death from cold.

Africa: The situation no doubt is serious; Armored Group Africa has had heavy losses, which cannot be replaced owing to shipping difficulties, while the British are bringing in reinforcements. Considering alternatives for withdrawal on Ain el Ghazâl. Eastern investment of Tobruk is raised.

Visit of chief of Bulgarian General Staff.

Afternoon report to Fuehrer: He cannot be bothered with strength ratios. To him the PW figures are conclusive proof of our superiority.

Next objectives: He recognizes the need of rehabilitation for the troops, but securing the Donets bend in the south (as a jump-off base for Maikop), eliminating the Ladoga front, and linking up with the Finns in the north remain on the calendar as objectives which must be attained during the winter.

No disbanding of divisions in France to cover replacement requirements. Comb out Germany, Romania, etc.

Allotment of forces in Europe: No reduction of strength in the west (ATTILA, threat to the coast). Norway: One to two armored divisions (U.S.). We may even have to send more German soldiers to Croatia.

Notes of the Fuehrer conference on 6 December 1941.

The Fuehrer has read our proposals with care. He has the figures in his head. He expresses his specific views:

1. One cannot clarify the strength problem with numerical notions only. Our numerical losses amount to 500,000 men (under the number of replacements); i.e., 3,000 to 4,000 per division. Russians

have lost 8,000,000 to 10,000,000. Their numerical losses are minimally ten times more than ours. Seventy-eight thousand guns are lost. The enemy's artillery has landed at the zero point (Halder: Ours are no better because of immobility.).

If we have lost 25 percent of our fighting power, the Russians have lost far more, despite their 300 percent increase in newly activated units. When our divisions can hold 30 km, it proves the deficient strength of the enemy. Numbers prove nothing.

2.   a.   *North:* It is important that we lose nothing in the north and that we gain a linkup with the Finns. The enemy must not regain control of Leningrad as an industrial center, nor as the gate to the Baltic. Leningrad cannot hold out when it remains genuinely cut off. The ideal solution, as proposed from our maps, is approved. For the operation: 93d Division be withdrawn; both armored divisions be reconstituted; Volchow front be occupied through infantry units; Spaniards must remain (later the 5th Infantry Division on the Volchow). Hold Tikhvin. No attacks before experienced forces (replacement and arms) are available.

b.   *Middle:* The Russians have not abandoned any place voluntarily; we cannot do so either. In principle, no thoughts of shortening the line. It may be considered only when the new positions are sufficiently prepared (foxholes, heaters).

c.   *South:* We must gain the Maikop oil region (Halder: Thinking about Asia Minor). The bend in the Donets serves as the line of departure. It is very important to take the coal area. Should not write Rostov off for this winter. The enemy wears himself out in an area of 100 kilometers. The Russian attacks are no longer operational, but concern tactical issues.

Enemy losses by Rostov are very high. With decent weather one can mount counterattacks (concepts of von Kleist and von Reichenau). The front will be strengthened through continuous reinforcements (four thousand paratroops, etc.); the 125th Division belongs behind the Italians. Two armored divisions should be removed and refurbished with fifty tanks; then every division will have over one hundred tanks. Thereafter an attack from the northwest against Rostov with motorized units becomes possible.

3. Miscellaneous concerns: No divisions from the west without replacements! At home are many furloughed people; in Romania 65,000 (40,000 are air force); in the rear areas are young people, while the older ones are at the front. A demotorization would release maintenance personnel!

4. We have no problem with soldiers, but with support people. Russian PWs (high capabilities when healthy) must be used in the factories, mines, and steel works in order to free young workers for military service. The 1923 class is closed for industry.

5. *Europe:* In the west, no decline in strength. Should changes take place in Africa, we must do ATTILA. Norway needs one to two armored divisions. We cannot give up Croatia, despite Italy and Hungary. Therefore we do not seem able to free units in the Balkans.

6. *East-West* division exchange; for Maikop new, fresh western divisions; replace from other areas without weakening west.

7. *Air force:* Take combat units for Leningrad operation from the middle! Apparently no units can be taken from Moscow for this undertaking. Air force missions: Rybinsk, Moscow, Voronezh. The commitment of two air fleets does not change the three-part division or the independent corps for the middle.

8. Individual matters: Transportation chief: Locomotives for the east. No perfect ones, but the simplest ones which will last five years. *Gen Qu:* Use airplanes to bring viscous grease to endangered positions.

. . .

7 December 1941

Japan opens hostilities against U.S.

Situation: *South:* On the whole quiet. Success of Seventeenth Army (IV Corps) has been further extended.

Center: The withdrawal of 10th Motorized Division at Mikhaylov (Guderian) appears to have had very distressing consequences.

On the northern wing of the Fourth Army (Armored Group 4) and in Armored Group 3, the situation is very tense. Strong penetrations from the north toward Klin. East of Kalinin, serious enemy penetrations, which could be checked just in time.

North: Very tight situation at Tikhvin. Army group thinks it cannot hold the town and is preparing to take back its defense position to the baseline of the salient. In the Ladoga sector, enemy reinforcements have apparently arrived from across the lake. Violent attacks at Leningrad.

Air observation:

a. Enemy concentrations east of Kerch. Have gradually increased for the past few days.

b. For several days past, unusual loading activities at Rybinsk. Arrivals from Moscow, destination undetermined.

Numerous phone talks with von Leeb (situation at Tikhvin). *Von Bock* (situation of 3rd Armored Group), Jodl (OKW must leave local commanders freedom of decision). Finally von Bock is given a free hand; von Leeb must not withdraw farther than artillery range from Tikhvin.

The occurrences of the day have again been heartbreaking and humiliating. ObdH is now no more than a messenger boy, if that much. The Fuehrer, over the head of ObdH, gets in direct touch with the commanders of army groups. But, worst of all, the Supreme Command does not realize the condition our troops are in and indulges in paltry patchwork where only big decisions could help. One of the decisions that should be taken is the withdrawal of AGp. Center to the line Ruza-Ostashkov.

. . .

Von Etzdorf: Japan: A conflict with the U.S. possibly imminent. Thailand, Borneo.

France: Apparently the Fuehrer still hopes to come to terms with Britain at the expense of France. France is short of coal. (Paris: Question of the hot meal.)

England: Beaverbrook-Bevin-Hoare.

Italy: Populations fearful that Germany might swallow Italy.

. . .

8 December 1941

. . .

Friendly troops: AGp. *South* expects continuance of the offensive. The unusual movements along the east shore of the Sea of Azov, coupled with the freezing of that body of water, serve to warn us to be on our guard against surprises across the frozen sea, perhaps also against Kerch. Assault on Sevastopol will start on 10 December. Troop movements from Sixth Army to First Panzer Army are proceeding satisfactorily, but the troops are weakened and suffer severely from the cold. Ammunition supply to First Panzer Army is disrupted because the railroad must accommodate replacement transports.

Center: Satisfactory development in Second Army and Second Panzer Army. We may now think of changing over to the final winter position. Northwest of Moscow, Twentieth Russian Army has been in action since 6 December. In this sector we are anticipating increased enemy pressure which, so far, has not materialized. The Yakhroma front has fallen back without trouble, and so has freed small reserves for liquidation of the situation at Klin, which is now in progress. On the whole, the desired shortening of the front has been accomplished. Situation remains tight, however.

East of Kalinin the enemy attacks on a seven-division front. Here, too, the situation is serious. This pressure point looks to me the most dangerous of all, because we have nothing back of the line.

North: In the Valdai area, only local attacks. The front of the Spanish division has been under attack. Local withdrawals of our lines on the Volkhov front.

Evacuation of Tikhvin in progress. Attack against 254th Division repulsed. Over Lake Ladoga troops are moving eastward, supplies westward.

.   .   .

Africa: Rommel must call a halt and fall back to the Ain el Ghazâl position. In this process considerable elements will remain entangled in the Sollum front and at Bardia. The siege of Tobruk has been raised on the eastern side. The British are preparing to attack south of Tobruk on a one- or two-division front, in spite of severe losses. One to two divisions are in the Bardia-Sollum area, one in Tobruk. Another division is moving up from Egypt. The further course of the battle will depend on whether the British have armor in sufficient strength to envelop the southern flank of the Ain el Ghazâl position and then break through with sufficient forces south of the Djebel, toward the Sirte. This move alone is the crucial danger at the moment.

Japan: Appears to have opened hostilities against U.S. and Britain by air surprise raids and naval attacks against Honolulu, Shanghai, and Malaya.

. . .

Phone talk with Field Marshal von Bock: He outlines the situation. Result: "Army group is not anywhere in a position to check a concentrated attack." Grave concern about von Kluge's right wing and Guderian's left wing. XXXXIII Corps has only little defensive strength. Decision to withdraw involves loss of enormous quantities of materiel. If the enemy were to make a concentrated attack, the consequences would be incalculable. Unless we can form reserve, we face the danger of a serious defeat.

. . .

9 December 1941

. . .

Center: Increasing pressure on Second Army (where a cavalry division has broken through) and on the eastern front of Second Panzer Army. Forces comprising at least four divisions have evidently been moved to this sector on the Voronezh-Ryazan railroad; some are old units from Sixth Army sector; others are new activations.

Very tense situation on the northern wing of Fourth Army. Although some divisions located by our radio intelligence have not yet shown up on this front, it is safe to assume that these attacks have no depth and so are merely of tactical significance. The object of these very troublesome attacks southeast of Kalinin is probably the recapture of the city.

North: Attempts have failed to widen the Tikhvin corridor. Withdrawal will be necessary. Unfortunately, OKW interferes in this purely tactical matter with direct Fuehrer orders. The command of army group is vacillating, but this is in part due to interference from top level. Although the danger is not acute at the moment, it may well happen that the few available forces are wasted on tactical patchwork, leaving no troops to deal with the Ladoga business.

Constant radio communications between the Red General Staff and the armies at Tikhvin, Ladoga, and Leningrad suggest an attempt to coordinate the activities of these groups.

Phone talk with Field Marshal von Bock: Guderian reports that the condition of his troops is so critical that he does not know how to fend off the enemy. "Serious break of confidence" in the field commands. Reduced fighting strength of his infantry! He is scraping together in the rear whatever forces he can get hold of (in one armored division 1,600 rifles!); tank gunners and drivers, of course, are not used as infantry. Army group needs more men!

CG XXVII Corps is said to have completely failed.

. . .

General Paulus: Report on political plans. Conversation Darlan-Ciano. Further negotiations between France and Reich Marshal, to start conversations going with the French. Fuehrer expects France will come under pressure by reason of America's entry into the war. He wants to win France over to our side and use her in Africa and the Mediterranean in the struggle against Britain and U.S.

. . .

13 December 1941

. . .

AGp. South: The main body of 125th Division has joined III Corps. Seventeenth Army is relieving units within its sector, without serious enemy interference. Local fighting in Sixth Army sector.

AGp. Center:

a. All attacks against 9th Armored Division along the railroad line repelled. More attacks likely. German troops yesterday reported encircled at Yefremov are free again.

b. Two new enemy divisions between Tula and Yepifan. Attacks beaten back; heavy enemy losses. Enemy infiltration west of Tula.

c. Northwest of Moscow, four new rifle brigades and one new armored brigade.

d. Situation at Klin, which is still in our hands, apparently slightly improved. Second Armored Division has closed the gap south of 36th Motorized Division.

e. Successful disengagement southeast of Kalinin, but we hold Kalinin itself.

AGp. North: Patrol thrusts southeast of Lake Ilmen. Serious artillery losses in the retreat from Tikhvin (two light field howitzer battalions, one medium AAA battery). Severe weather complicates shifting of 291st Division. Opposite 122d Infantry Division, marked enemy movement. Attack is expected.

Africa: Ain el Ghazâl position reached. The southern wing, where the Italians fell back only slowly, had first to be freed in hard fighting. Two vessels, each carrying one armored company, sunk.

Phone talk with General Brennecke (North): Army group judges it impracticable to hold out for any length of time forward of the position now occupied east of the Volkhov River. There is even a slight intimation that withdrawal to the Volkhov River would be unavoidable. My objection is that the resulting pressure from the east would then make it impossible to launch an attack to restore the situation on the Ladoga front. Army group is convinced it still has a chance to carry off the Ladoga operation and so wants to move 254th Division across the Volkhov River into the position on the western edge of the big marshes. The 291st Division would replace the division south of Shum. Owing to the complication caused by the snowstorm and the strain of their long march, the striking power of the division must be expected to have fallen off severely.

. . .

14 December 1941

Situation: AGp. South: Motorized movement from Voroshilovgrad toward Seventeenth Army (IV Corps), apparently of tactical importance only. IV Corps is under attack; local penetrations. AAA and fighter protection north of the Donets is very conspicuous. Troops entraining at Kantemirovka. Railroad traffic from southeast and southwest to Liski. No confirmation could be obtained on reported enemy concentrations opposite Sixth Army.

AGp. Center: Nothing alarming on the southern wing of Second Army. In central sector and on northern wing, the situation seems to be improving a little. Guderian evidently has his Second Panzer Army firmly under control and is leading it back step by step. The gap southwest of Tula is rather awkward, but I can see no way of sealing it. In Fourth Army, no acute trouble, but some minor penetrations of merely tactical significance. At Klin the situation seems to be gradually stabilizing. At Kalinin, fluctuating battles with generally satisfactory results.

AGp. North: Enemy attack against 126th Division comes at a bad time. The withdrawal of XXXIX Corps apparently is proceeding according to plan. After a long time the enemy is again attacking I Corps at Volkhovstroi (as a result of Tikhvin!). Also, in XXVIII Corps sector, on the Ladoga front, enemy activity is reviving again. No important news from the Neva and Kronstadt fronts.

. . .

1830. **Field Marshal von Brauchitsch** on phone, after conference with von Bock, von Kluge, and Guderian:

Situation in Second Panzer Army: Gap between 45th and 134th divisions has not yet been closed. The troops dispatched to block the enemy are arriving very slowly. Farther north, Second Panzer Army is conducting a planned withdrawal in several bounds. The situation west of Tula is difficult. Open gap in this sector (137th Division is being moved into it from the north; present whereabouts unreported).

Fourth Army: The front holds, but is very thin. No reserves in back of it. The position from its southern wing all the way to VII Corps is good enough; in 267th Division sector the situation is obscure. Nothing big can be expected of commitment of 255th Division. Hoepner is sending down tanks.

Von Kluge: Will be able to decide tomorrow whether the situation can be maintained. Further enemy progress in 255th Division sector endangers our communications line between Mozhaysk and Volokolamsk. Very grave reports from Armored Group 3.

Intention: Kalinin must be evacuated. Gradual withdrawal to the protective defense line Staritsa—VII Corps.

Condition of the fighting: Second Army has little freedom of movement. Armored Group 3 reports heavy materiel losses. Fourth Army also will suffer materiel losses when it moves back its front. The troops will arrive in the new line greatly weakened, and it is doubtful that it can then be held against heavy attacks. In order to ensure orderly withdrawal, we must do everything to bring up fresh forces and, after that, artillery and explosives for engineers. Immediate decision required: Army group must be given discretion to fall back from the northern protective line, as the situation requires. Army group must be given freedom to order withdrawal to the Oka line if it judges that step necessary.

Talk with General Jodl: Portray seriousness of situation.

OQu I: Result of the Berlin conference on future organization of reconnaissance aviation. (Next spring we are going to get twenty squadrons of FW189, twenty squadrons HE126, the latter for reorganization.) —ATTILA. —ISABELLA. — Both still feasible even after withdrawal of forces from the west. —Need for more troops makes it necessary to cut down on Finland and the Balkans.

. . .

15 December 1941

AGp. Center: Weak spots: *Second Army:* On the southern wing the enemy is apparently attempting to widen the penetration by an attack on Livny, without success. However, we must still reckon with the possibility that he may be committing additional forces; *Second Panzer Army* is pulling out in good order. Critical weak point west of Tula; relief forces from the south cannot get through, and from the north we can send only weak elements which, moreover, will take long to get there.

Fourth Army: Heavy pressure against 255th Division where the enemy might be able to roll up the northern portion of the front or disrupt orderly withdrawal. B Corps also is under heavy pressure. Klin relatively free from pressure. Withdrawn from the Klin area: 14th Motorized Division and 7th Armored Division. —Attack beaten off north of Klin.

AGp. North: More active south of Lake Ilmen, but only patrol activity. In 126th Division, rather confused situation. Enemy elements which broke through our lines are now fighting in rear. All quiet on the Ladoga and Leningrad fronts.

North Africa: Rommel has fallen back to the Ain el Ghazâl position. The enemy is following only slowly. Heavy Italian losses in transport and tanks. The French help us with aviation fuel and food from Tunis.

1200.   Von Greiffenberg (Center):

    a. My talk with Jodl: Where front can be held, no withdrawal; where untenable, shorten line and then fall back; no retiring before all preparations are completed.

b. Situation in Reinhardt's corps tight (forests) and confused. The disengagement of Ninth Army seems to be proceeding orderly. Army group wants to hold on the Volga bend until 17 December evening, in order to safeguard planned withdrawal of Reinhardt and Ninth Army.

c. Situation at the Ruza position unsatisfactory; parts of 19th Armored Division and 3d Motorized Division have already been committed to relieve it. Rear elements are already in action in the Ruza position, but we are short of men. French regiment in Ruza.

.   .   .

16 December 1941

Situation: Air reconnaissance: Heavy railroad traffic Moscow-Bologoe-Tikhvin.

South: The enemy is bringing reinforcements, apparently also combat forces (artillery) to Sevastopol. The enemy is digging trenches opposite Sixth Army.

Center: The 134th Division has fought its way out; no report yet from 45th Division. The enemy is feeding new forces into the penetration between Yefremov and Yelets. Guderian is falling back. Heavy pressure on 3d Armored Division and on the front south of Aleksin.

North: Enemy pressure on Malaya Vishera compels us to take back the front. Shifting of enemy forces across Lake Ladoga has apparently resulted in a strengthening of Ladoga front. Attacks out of Leningrad have been stepped up in several sectors.

1200. **Von Bock** *calls up:* Situation report. Anxiety about Armored Group 3. XXXXIII Corps shaky.

General Fellgiebel reports on allocation of his raw materials. Army needs must have priority. Air force demands excessive.

General Gercke: Ordered to report to the Fuehrer. Troops will not be moved as divisions. Only infantry is to be sent to the front. The fighting lines need fighting men.

Field Marshal von Leeb: Report on Fuehrer conference: Fuehrer accepts army group's proposal to fall back to the Volkhov River.

Gen. Busch came in for report to Fuehrer. Drops in briefly.

Midnight. Ordered to the Fuehrer: ObdH, I, Chief Op. Sec.:

a. Order: General withdrawal is out of the question. Enemy has made substantial penetration only in a few places. The idea to prepare rear positions is just driveling nonsense. The only trouble at the front is that the enemy outnumbers us in soldiers. He does not have any more artillery. His soldiers are not nearly as good as ours.

b. Has directed added air support of four bomber long-range fighter groups, plus a long-range fighter group. This gives an increase of 120 planes, not counting the long-range fighters.

c. Withdrawal to shortened line only when fuel has arrived and fresh infantry is available to take up the units.

d. New divisions must be committed: At Dubna (2nd Armored Division) and in Armored Groups 3 and 4. Replacements necessary in Fourth Army. Also, Second Army must be reinforced.

e. Two hundred transport aircraft in addition to the air transport group of AGp. South will be available for air lift.

f. Railroads: Capacity limited. To the front first all of infantry with light weapons, AT units, and engineers, perhaps also an artillery battalion. Must take along canned food for eight to ten days, fuel tablets, chocolate.

g. Two thousand SS will be shipped from Cracow by air; can be driven to the front by SS brigade at Novosil.

h. Division from Denmark will go to Reval by ship.

17 December 1941

. . .

Evening reports:

a. At Sevastopol, stiff resistance after initial successes due to surprise. The assault will be continued tomorrow. Otherwise all quiet on the southern front; 168th Division is being shifted to the northern wing of Sixth Army.

b. In Center, the enemy appears to be regrouping for further attacks in the penetration area at Verkhovye. Our front has been fairly consolidated, but it is rather weak. Guderian has regrouped his Second Panzer Army in depth, but is not taking any serious measures to counteract the threats at Verkhovye and Dubna. In a phone talk with *von Greiffenberg,* army group is reminded that at least 29th Motorized Division must be brought up to Novosil. The situation at the Dubna danger spot is still confused. The enemy who breached our line here seems to be hampered by the difficult terrain. Up to now, at least, there has been no attempt to press home the attack. The situation west of Serpukhov is uncomfortable. Massed enemy attack. Seventeenth Division has been taken out of the line and is being shifted to South.

In Armored Group 4, the sore spot at Ruza is still very sensitive, but it looks as if the situation had slightly improved. This is certainly due in part to the firm stand by V Corps, whereas the command of IX Corps to all appearance was less determined and so is not without its share of blame in the resulting confusion. As to the situation in Armored Group 3, we are still unable to obtain any clear picture.

Monitored radio traffic sounds very listless. Ninth Army is doing its job with great calm and efficiency. The enemy is building up for an attack against its northern front.

c. *In North,* local fighting, which, however, does not interfere with the orderly execution of the scheduled withdrawal to the Volkhov line.

Initial forces arriving by air tomorrow: 1,600 replacements from East Prussia for Armored Group 4. Eight via Orsha. If possible, will be landed at Ruza.

The initial elements of the SS from Cracow will be a replacement battalion of AGp. South, consisting of three to four hundred men to be put down at Orel.

18 December 1941

. . .

Von Bock calls to say goodby. (Turns over the command to von Kluge on account of illness.)

Von Greiffenberg (several times on phone): Situation, arrival of replacements, and Second Panzer Army support for restoring the situation at Dubna.

Keitel informs me about the Fuehrer's talk with Guderian (support for Dubna breach).

Jodl: Situation estimate and orientation on Fuehrer's talk with Guderian.

19 December 1941

.   .   .

1300.   Summoned to the Fuehrer:

   a. The Fuehrer is going to take over the High Command of the army himself after departure of ObdH owing to ill health. I am to carry on the business functions, while Keitel will take over the administrative part. New routine: Daily conference, along with Transportation Chief, Signal Chief, and Gen Qu.

   b. Two mistakes have been made.

      1. The noting of "rear position" was installed into the lower echelon commands. Such positions do not exist and cannot be created.

      2. Provisions against extreme cold were inadequate. Army works too mechanically. Air force pointed out as model. Has been educated in entirely different spirit by the Reich Marshal.

   c. Orders to hold present positions. Not worried about any threats to the flanks.

   d. Concerned about Leningrad. New bomber groups are being committed, as are more fighters. Scheduled new forces must be transferred by sea, if possible, as far as Reval.

1700.   Talk with von Brauchitsch, who went to the Fuehrer to surrender his command. No essentially new viewpoints.

.   .   .

Field Marshal von Kluge reports: According to statements of local population, an enemy force, two thousand strong, is marching on Tikhvin. North of Khanino, forward elements of enemy cavalry are advancing on Kaluga. Heavy fighting in 31st Division sector. Holding at Titovka. Tanks have crossed the Oka River; cannot climb the steep banks. North of Aleksin the enemy has broken through in the direction of Shopina. South of Tarusa enemy ski battalions have broken through. Enemy in Lgov!

Blumentritt gives a sad picture of the situation. Troops are apathetic. Situation very unhealthy.

The Russians attack during night and turn up behind our positions at the break of daylight. No reinforcements can be expected for tomorrow.

. . .

Evening: Meeting of all officers in the General Staff: Reading of the order announcing assumption of the command of the army by the Fuehrer.

20 December 1941

Situation: Still very tense. In *South,* advances at Sevastopol. Otherwise quiet. In *Center,* the enemy attacked with local successes on the right wing of Second Army, and without success in the Verkhovye penetration area. Worst of all, he pushed into the gap west of Tula, and then thrust with ski troops and cavalry all the way to the area south of Kaluga. Against this it is heartening to see that the front of XXXXIII Corps withstands even heavy attacks. On the remainder of the front, several major attacks, which in part gained some local successes. In Ninth Army sector, intense fighting and local withdrawal. In *North,* local crisis. Only item to report is disengagement of I Corps, which apparently came off moderately well.

Situation conference: Fuehrer holds forth at great length on need of holding the line. Every man must fight back where he stands. No falling back when there are no prepared positions in the rear. Defends the encirclement of Leningrad. —Tanks to Africa.

. . .

21 December 1941

Situation: In South, no important new developments. The report that the enemy has broken through the northern wing of Sixth Army has not been confirmed. In the sector of Second Army, the enemy breaks through 16th Motorized Division and 9th Armored Division all the way to the Tim River. Local withdrawal necessary to prevent abandonment of the town of Tim. At Verkhovye, strong enemy attacks with local successes, but on the whole, the front stands. Guderian's front is holding the newly reached line.

The focal point of the crisis is south of Kaluga. The enemy has penetrated into the town from Odoev and was thrown back by elements of a security regiment which arrived at that moment; he is still sitting with tanks in the Kaluga Ghett. XXXXIII Corps (Heinrici), to the east of Kaluga, where the enemy effected a break through the east, must be taken back. In the remainder of Fourth Army sector, local attacks, some carried through with great violence and breaching the line. The commanding generals report that their troops are too exhausted to be able to cope with any further attacks. Order has been given to hold the front. Ninth Army was able to repulse violent attacks south of Kalinin. Here, too, our troops are overstrained.

In AGp. North, the withdrawals are on the whole going according to plan. Local enemy penetrations south of Gruzino. The situation on the left flank of I Corps is still obscure. Partly violent attacks out of Leningrad, which were repulsed west of the Neva. Also an attack across the Neva was beaten badly after hand-to-hand fighting.

Conference with the Fuehrer: He emphasizes the necessity for holding the front. Discussion on means for improving the supply situation by a fundamental reform of transport services. The jurisdictional division must be changed in such manner that specific individuals would be held responsible for operations on specified lines.

Several phone talks with Field Marshal von Kluge on situation at Kaluga and Tim. He is gradually yielding under the pressure of the demands by his subordinate commanders. We have to steel him against them. Guderian seems to have lost his nerve completely. I obtain a Fuehrer order making Guderian alone responsible for holding the Oka River line as far as the mouth of the Zhizdra River.

. . .

22 December 1941

Very heavy battles in Second Army sector on the Tim River and at Verkhovye, which, on the whole, came out well. In Second Panzer Army sector, overwhelming pressure from Tula against the northern wing, which has to be taken back. The southern wing of Fourth Army southeast of Kaluga is enveloped, and at the same time penetrated by a thrust from Tarusa. An exceedingly difficult situation has developed here, and it is beyond anyone's power to say how it will be restored. And yet it is impossible to prevail on the Fuehrer to order any long-range withdrawal. But at least he releases the hollow-charge projectiles.

Farther to the north, very heavy attack against Fourth Army front, especially in LVII and XX Corps sectors. No major developments in AGps. North and South.

. . .

29 December 1941

A very bad day! *In the Crimea,* the CG of XXXXII Corps (Count von Sponeck) withdraws 46th Division from the Kerch peninsula under the first shock of an enemy landing at Feodosiya. He has immediately been removed from his post, but the damage done can hardly be repaired. In First Panzer Army and Seventeenth and Sixth armies everything is in good shape.

In AGp. *Center,* however, the enemy's superiority on the fronts of Second Army and Second Panzer Army is beginning to tell. We did succeed in sealing the penetrations, but the situation on the overextended front, at which the enemy keeps hammering with ever new concentrations, is very difficult in view of the state of exhaustion of our troops. Strong penetration north of Mtsensk and on the northern wing of Second Panzer Army. In the Oka gap near Sukhinichi, a solid combat group is being formed, which has already been active with reconnaissance forces in combat strength (Stumme), but the bulk of the enemy is advancing unchecked in the direction of Yukhnov (paratroop landings!). Kaluga and the salient to the north must be abandoned in order to collect forces strong enough to stem the enemy breakthrough across the Oka. On the army front to the north, partly very heavy fighting resulting in enemy penetrations.

The situation in Ninth Army is becoming very difficult. Under pressure from the direction of Torzhok and after successive enemy breakthroughs, the army line had to be taken farther back again.

At Fuehrer Hq., dramatic telephone conversations with von Richthofen, who temporarily will take over command of VI Corps after its CG, Foerster, has been relieved.

In AGp. North, local enemy penetrations on the boundary of Sixteenth and Eighteenth armies.

OQu I: Training matters (instructional pamphlet). Preparations for a rear position on a big scale.

30 December 1941

Again a hard day! In the Crimea, the enemy landing at Feodosiya has created a very difficult operational situation. Nevertheless, army group has decided to continue the assault on Sevastopol. Behind the front facing Sixth Army, baffling rail movements. The flanks of the Oka salient are now slightly better lined by minor individual units and as a result of regrouping within XXXXIII Corps, but the gap is still far from being closed.

Crisis in 15th Division. Dramatic phone talk between the Fuehrer and von Kluge. The Fuehrer vetoes the proposal to take back the front of the northern portion of Fourth Army. Very serious crisis in Ninth Army, where the command must have lost its nerve for a time.

At noon von Kluge calls up excitedly to inform us that Ninth Army wants to fall back behind Rzhev. But in the end commander of army group appears to have asserted himself. By nightfall the front of Ninth Army is pressed back slightly, but the general atmosphere is clearer. Some small reinforcements have arrived. Fourth Armored Group must free reserves.

In North, a counterattack has been initiated against an enemy breakthrough on the Volkhov.

Also on the Ladoga front disagreeable attacks. Nervous tension!

.   .   .

31 December 1941

Again an arduous day! At Sevastopol, the attacks by 22d Armored Division have had no decisive success. We must now suspend the assault of free forces for Feodosiya, where the enemy has reinforced and expanded his beachhead. Second Army and Second Panzer Army have beaten off most attacks. Enemy pressure on the northern wing of Second Army at Byelyi. The enemy is moving infantry into the Oka salient. Pressure on XXXXIII Corps now also from the east. Penetrations in LVII Corps north of Maloyaroslavets. V Corps seems to have repulsed heavy attacks. In Ninth Army, very difficult situation following a breakthrough by strong enemy on both sides of VI Corps. In AGp. *North,* the front is generally quiet.

.   .   .

With the approach of a new year, Germany's position had changed completely. The victories of earlier years had soured in the Russian adjustments. America's entry heralded profound future difficulties, but, for Halder, the real issue was the Russian disaster. Earlier than most he had recognized the coming catastrophe, but found no way to prevent or mitigate it. The reality extended everyone's problems.

A frustrated, recalcitrant Fuehrer refused advice, divided his military advisers, and slowly slipped into his own dream world. Concurrently, the losses at the front could not be made good, nor could Germany's military commitments be kept in order. The new year would require renewed offensive action, but one of different dimensions and purposes than the failed efforts. With the Russian winter offensive still a major threat, Halder had to save the German army and prepare for such operations. The stress was great.

The previous six months had created disaster as Hitler had shifted his goals and lost too much time, men, and equipment. As a result, Germany entered 1942 with involvements on too many fronts. Africa remained both distant and uncertain; the Atlantic naval struggle was uncertain; Britain was stronger and had certain American help forthcoming.

In sum, Halder had to help the German troops survive the Russian onslaught, had to prepare for new campaigns, which could not achieve decisive results, and had to cope with an increasingly difficult Fuehrer. For Halder and Germany the new year would provide challenges.

2 January 1942

A day of wild fighting. In the Crimea a temporary check has been imposed on the enemy advance by our air effort. On the southern half of our front, the enemy is launching rather heavy drives against the northern wing of Sixth Army and the southern wing of Second Army, but there appears to be no threat of operational significance. In the Oka gap, into which the enemy is introducing sizable reinforcements, there are signs that the flanks of the penetration are being stabilized.

In Fourth and Ninth armies, however, the situation is taking a critical turn. The breakthrough north of Maloyaroslavets has split the front, and we cannot at the moment see any way of restoring it again. The front of Ninth Army has been broken through from the direction of Staritsa. As far as we can see, there was a mix-up in Hq., in which a nonexistent "Koenigsberg position," supposed to be in back of the front, appears to have played a disastrous role. The front was taken back, and now appears to be broken again.

In view of these situations, Field Marshal von Kluge demands withdrawal also of the adjoining sectors. Very stormy discussions with the Fuehrer, who persists in his own views. So the front will remain where it is, regardless of consequences.

The withdrawal of Ninth Army against the will of the Supreme Commander occasioned mad outbursts on his part at the morning conference. OKH is charged with having introduced parliamentary procedures in the army, and with lacking incisiveness of direction. These ravings interspersed with utterly baseless accusations waste our time and undermine any effective cooperation.

Subsequently, talk with the AGp. chiefs of staff to orient them on the pattern of views held on top level.

Repeated phone talks with von Kluge, who is at the end of his wits and talks of utter loss of confidence.

3 January 1942

The situation in AGp. Center has become very precarious in consequence of the deep penetration between Maloyaroslavets and Borovsk. Kuebler and von Kluge are deeply upset, and von Kluge demands authorization to move the front back northward.

Another dramatic scene with the Fuehrer, who calls in question the generals' courage to make hard decisions. The plain truth however is that with the temperature down to thirty below freezing our troops simply cannot hold out any longer.

The Fuehrer decides: First close the breach by attacking from the adjoining sectors, then we can talk about moving the front back. But in every individual instance he will have to give the word for withdrawal.

The other fronts are fairly quiet. Sixth Army has apparently eliminated the local penetrations. Second Army and Second Panzer Army seem to be holding. Some troops are being collected on the flanks of the Oka bulge, but the enemy, too, has gradually closed up in this sector and may yet give us a bad time in the days to come. In Ninth Army the situation is still rather confused in some sectors. Local penetrations into the newly withdrawn line.

In AGp. North all combat activity has died down in 42 degrees of frost.

5 January 1942

Casualties: 22 June–31 December 1941.

Wounded	19,016 Off.	602,292 NCOs and EM
Killed	7,120 Off.	166,602 NCOs and EM
Missing	619 Off.	35,254 NCOs and EM
Total	26,755 Off.	804,148 NCOs and EM

Total losses in the east 830,903, i.e., 25.96 percent of the eastern army (3.2 million).

Situation: *South:* Enemy landing at Yevpatoriya apparently is only a local effort. At Feodosiya, the enemy is building up his beachhead. Penetration on the northern wing of Sixth Army. Reinforcements coming up by rail.

Center: Increased tension in the Oka bulge! Danger of an expansion of the Maloyaroslavets salient. Heavy breakthrough west of Rzhev.

North: Continued enemy attacks, but nothing on a major scale; all quiet in the Lake Ilmen sector.

. . .

7 January 1942

Situation: Enemy has advanced against encircled Sukhinichi and to the north. The situation in this breakthrough salient is getting increasingly uncomfortable. AGp. Center must develop more determination in taking forces out of the stabilized front south of the breakthrough, to throw them against the breakthrough flank from the south. On the southern wing of Armored Group 4, our own attack drives head-on into an enemy attack. Outcome is not yet clear.

. . .

8 January 1942

Very grave day. The westward advance of the Sukhinichi breakthrough is becoming threatening for von Kluge. He urges taking back Fourth Army front to free forces for the protection of his supply line. —Von Kluge argues his point with me already in the morning! Put before the Fuehrer! The usual tug-of-war. No decision, but a great deal of energy is expended in thinking up piddling makeshifts to protect the supply road.

Finally the Fuehrer had a talk with von Kluge, which produced nothing conclusive. In the afternoon, von Kluge again urgently requests freedom of decision over the moves of Fourth Army, so as to enable him to disengage. I talk to the Fuehrer on this matter. He wants to talk to von Kluge himself. Result: Army group is authorized to disengage step by step in order to free forces for the protection of the supply line. At the conference von Kluge reports that Hoepner, on his own initiative, gave an order to withdraw without notifying army group. The Fuehrer at once orders his "expulsion from the army," with all legal consequences!

. . .

9 January 1942

The situation moves toward the grand decision: In the Sukhinichi breakthrough gap, the enemy is still pushing westward. We have only light forces to oppose him, but, somehow, with extreme effort, expansion of the gap southwest and northwest was checked.

West of Rzhev we have failed to contain the enemy breakthrough. It has widened, and there is every reason to anticipate a decisive battle here. We have no means available for countering this threat. South of Ostashkov, two enemy divisions threw back our weak holding forces and effected a penetration in this sector too.

In AGp. North, penetration at Staraya Russa. We probably shall be able to check it. The attack against the Volkhov front was repulsed. It seems that both here and on the Ladoga front, the main attack is yet to come.

Several phone talks with von Kluge and with Jodl. We have reached the point where a big decision on taking back the front is absolutely essential, but the Fuehrer cannot make up his mind yet and wants to talk to von Kluge directly. So, to our great distress, decision on this burning question is put off again, while we lose precious time.

11 January 1942

The whole day with Field Marshal von Kluge at Fuehrer Hq.

The Fuehrer upholds his order to defend every inch of ground. Very untoward developments in the Sukhinichi salient and west of Rzhev. The situation is now becoming really critical.

Return from the Fuehrer at 0100 in the morning. Subsequently, conference
with Op. Chief and OQu I.

12 January 1942

The southern wing of AGp. North came under heavy pressure today as the
result of an attack against 123d Division by elements of four divisions
across the frozen lakes. Von Leeb is at once thinking of withdrawing.
Fuehrer disapproves. Talk Fuehrer/von Leeb. Von Leeb is summoned
for a conference tomorrow.

.   .   .

13 January 1942

A particularly difficult day.

AGp. South is gradually eliminating the penetration on its northern
wing, but is expecting another enemy attack.

AGp. Center: Several desperate phone calls from commander of army
group. Whereas the breakthrough at Sukhinichi is gradually being contained at its southern head, Fourth Army apparently is still unable to
check the enemy pressing from the south against two points of its
supply road, which is already interrupted. Consequences for continued
supply of Fourth Army cannot yet be predicted. Fighting around Medyn
has reached such a pitch that von Kluge asks permission to abandon
the town. Reluctantly the Fuehrer agrees. The gap north of Medyn is
as perturbing as ever. Heavy penetrations in V Corps. At Rzhev a
southward push by strong enemy forces through the gap between VI
and XXIII Corps has resulted in pressure against the Rzhev-Sihevsk
railroad line. Fighting is in progress for the latter station. As a result,
the only railroad supplying Ninth Army and Third Panzer Army is
cut. The consequences cannot yet be estimated. In the afternoon, von
Kluge reports that Hq. Ninth Army has ordered XXIII Corps to withdraw.
This move further aggravates the situation in AGp. Center.

AGp. North: The conference of Field Marshal von Leeb with the Fuehrer
produced no agreement. The Fuehrer insisted on compliance with his
order that the front of the Valdai Hills must be held. Von Leeb stated
that, though he would try, he would not succeed, since the necessary
reinforcements were not to be had! (The earliest division due was 218th;

its first regiment was earmarked for the Volkhov front, and successive elements were scheduled to arrive at a very slow rate, starting 28 January.)

Evening report by Wagner and Baentsch on railroad matters (organization, dictatorial control) and supply situation of Fourth Army, as affected by the latest enemy successes.

Basis for formulating decisions [for presentation to Fuehrer] on 13 January 1942.

1. *Issued orders:*

   a. Hold the forward lines, which should be constructed as permanent positions.

   b. Attack from Rzhev to close the gap (Ninth Army).

   c. Attack from north to close the gap north of Medyn.

2. *Situation:*

   a. By Rzhev a strong enemy breakthrough (currently four divisions; four additional and one cavalry can follow). No counterpressure from XXIII Corps. We must be pleased if everything holds. Three to four divisions required to satisfy mission.

   b. By Ssytschewka there is danger of a stoppage on the road to Rzhev even after the current breakthrough succeeds. If this road link is lost, the Third Army can live and fight for only two to three days (munitions, fuel, foodstuffs!). As a result, the troops there must be used—including the 1st Armored Division—to resolve this danger permanently; i.e., they are not available for Rzhev.

   c. By Volokolamsk the enemy has a deep and serious breakthrough with tanks. The available segments of the 4th and 7th Armored divisions must be committed here because of the orders to hold the line. The expansion of the enemy attacks through the arrival of the 30th Russian Army probable.

3. *Conclusions:*

   To clean up Rzhev, the army group, when it must hold the front requires 1 to 1½ divisions, can expect no success. One has two possibilities:

   a. *Eastern front, as already ordered, hold under all circumstances.* Extraction of units for benefit of Rzhev; then only between Ruza and 11th

Armored Division is possible. Perhaps something can be withdrawn from 10th Armored Division (100-kilometer march on snow-covered roads needs ten days). Then Rzhev-Ssytschewka defense! The enemy will gradually attack to Vyazma. No means to hinder that (security Byelyi).

The enemy will require eight days to reach the Vyazma region. He will have supply difficulties. During these eight days a part of the 246th Division will arrive and, possibly, the advance elements of the 330th Division by truck, i.e., totally 1 division. With the front units and 10th Armored Division, some 2 to 2½ divisions are available to intercept the enemy. Passive solution! *Risk:* Holding XXIII Corps; danger Byelyi. Supplies, removal of wounded. *Advantage:* Material losses disappear. Troops can partially remain in position.

b. *Eastern front will be relieved of stand-fast orders.* Then the 5th Armored Division (perhaps the 7th Armored Division as well) and SS "Reich" and part of the XXVII Corps can be drawn out and, in eight to ten days, be reconstructed in an assault force Rzhev, which could attack in conjunction with the Ssytschewka forces the enemy troops by Vyazma. Active solution!

Risk:

(a) Ability of XXIII Corps to hold. Byelyi danger remains.
(b) Major difficulties in execution.
(c) Losses of material and munitions are unavoidable, even in a step-by-step execution.
(d) Troops in the new lines without emplacements.
(e) Counterplay against Schmidt given up.

Advantage:

(a) Intent to give enemy a blow. No security. Depends on the weather.
(b) Rail lines allow close approach, which means easier supply situation and more rapid development of the operation.
(c) Construction of emplacements in the Sukhinichi sack will be easier on the north front.

4. *Proposal:* Freedom of movement with Fourth Army to the proposed line. Execution by sectors. Purpose: In north, the assembly of a battle group to hit the enemy by Rzhev. Northern closure. Close the Medyn gap. Hurry! Cannot be done by snow.

14 January 1942

. . .

Situation: Situation southwest of Kursk is slowly improving. No major developments in the Sukhinichi bulge. The enemy apparently is moving in new forces. North of Medyn, contrary to expectations, enemy pressure has not yet been felt. Heavy, successful enemy attacks at Volokolamsk. The situation southwest of Rzhev is becoming increasingly dangerous. Three to four enemy divisions are already operating in our rear. XXIII Corps must be taken back. Situation in the Valdai area very uncomfortable. In these circumstances it is impossible to hold the front any longer. Von Kluge reports that he must move back if he wants to extricate himself from Rzhev. The Fuehrer appreciates the necessity for taking back the front, but will make no decision. This kind of leadership can lead only to the annihilation of the army.

. . .

15 January 1942

In AGp. South, the attack on Feodosiya has started. Good initial success. On the northern wing of Sixth Army the situation is being progressively restored. In the Sukhinichi bulge, the enemy is reinforcing. Main pressure to the north. The gap north of Medyn has not yet been closed. Enemy pressure against the southern wing of Fourth Panzer Army. Another attack at Volokolamsk. The enemy is moving more troops southward through the Rzhev gap. XXIII Corps under pressure, chiefly on its western wing. Penetration on the southern wing of Sixteenth Army. Slight advances at Staraya Russa. Relatively serious penetrations on the Volkhov front. Otherwise all quiet in AGp. North.

Von Leeb asks to be relieved of his post. —Strauss cannot carry on any longer. —Von Reichenau has had a stroke.

19 January 1942

Situation: The attack in the Crimea is making good progress. On the northern front of Seventeenth Army and in some sectors of Sixth Army, the enemy has now opened his full-scale offensive, which earlier indications linked with Kharkov. The most critical spot is the boundary of Seventeenth and Sixth armies. We shall go through trying days before this crisis is resolved. Another penetration has occurred in the southern part of Second Army front. We have no forces available to check it at the moment, but I see no threat to the broader operational situation.

Second Panzer Army has made further progress toward Sukhinichi. Meanwhile there has not been much change in the Sukhinichi bulge. Evidently the enemy here is experiencing major difficulties in collecting any sizable force.

Withdrawal of the eastern front of AGp. Center is continuing. We have not yet fully succeeded in closing the Medyn gap, but it looks as if good progress is being made in that direction. At Rzhev, the enemy is unaccountably inactive. In the direction of Toropets and Kholm, a rather embarrassing gap has appeared as a result of the rapid withdrawal of our troops in that sector. Approximately four enemy divisions are pushing on behind our retiring forces on this vast front. While this move does not constitute an operational threat, it does draw forces away from other sectors, and eventually the front will have to be straightened again by a large withdrawal.

Fighting continues at Staraya Russa. I suggest countermeasures from the east.

On the Volkhov River, very heavy battle in Sixteenth Army sector. We have succeeded in establishing an effective defensive barrier. Also farther north, in Eighteenth Army sector, major attacks seem to be getting under way. Ladoga front still quiet, but here, too, the enemy will soon come to life.

Von Etzdorf reports on his conferences with the State Secretary. We discuss the international situation: signs of beginning war weariness in Britain. Negotiations toward establishing a new relationship with France have not yet been definitely authorized by the Fuehrer. We have no binding French promise to join in the war with Britain. In Spain, Suñer's position is now weaker. As a result of the Río Conference, the Latin-American nations will probably sever diplomatic relations with us.

General Kuebler talks on situation at his front after conference with the Fuehrer. Nothing essentially new. He does not feel equal to the task.

21 January 1942 to 23 January 1942

Influenza.

24 January 1942

Situation: In *South,* the attacks on the Crimea have been suspended for the time being. Things are in bad mess in Seventeenth Army. In a three-day battle, the front was breached in two places (Izyum and boundary with Sixth Army). Later these two penetrations were merged into one large salient. The enemy is threatening railroad communications between First Panzer Army and Seventeenth Army. Sixth Army and First Panzer Army have come to the rescue, notwithstanding the gravest risks to their own safety. We are in for a stretch of difficult days before this threat will be eliminated. I think we shall make it.

The cavalry penetration at Kursk appears to have been contained. South of Sukhinichi an enemy attack from the west against LIII Corps creates an uncomfortable situation. Directly westward of this area, we mounted an attack and freed Sukhinichi.

South of Yukhnov, increasing enemy pressure. The breach northwest of Medyn has not been closed yet. We seem to be too weak there.

The corridor at Rzhev opened yesterday was widened today, but strong enemy forces are very active at Sihevsk.

In the gap between Center and North, we are faced with a full-stage offensive. Two enemy "assault groups" of about a dozen divisions have broken through in this sector and are advancing southward. That is, in any event, better than if they were going north, for now they are driving right toward our reinforcements that are moving up now; the other way the Leningrad front would become untenable.

In AGp. North, hard fighting. No important change.

. . . .

5 February 1942

Situation: In the south deep snowdrifts are impeding our counterattack. The 293d Division and 25th Motorized repelled unexpected enemy attacks (divisions) lacking depth. In Ninth Army sector, the enemy is falling back southwest of Rzhev. We gain some ground. —In *North,* continued stern fighting at Staraya Russa and on the Volkhov River.

General Dr. Handloser:

   a.   Report on medical casualties: Total in the armies of the east 60,000, plus 977 officers.

   b.   Typhus: 4,400 cases, 729 fatal.

   c.   Regular and improvised hospital trains.

   d.   Shifting of more medical corps units from the west (ambulance battalion, base hospital battalion, etc.).

   e.   Report on inspection of Sixteenth and Eighteenth armies.

. . .

21 February 1942

The development of the situation is dominated by the Russian offensive announced for 23 February.

South: In the Crimea, preparation for an attack at Sevastopol and at Kerch. In Seventeenth Army, heavy attack against IV Corps, which compels taking back of front. Grave situation on the western wing of Seventeenth Army, against which a strong infantry attack has been launched. In Sixth Army sector, unmistakable preparations for an attack against the "Kharkov front."

Center: Reinforcement and intensified activity of enemy behind front facing Fourth Army. Attack with new forces against central sector and western wing of XXIII Corps (Ninth Army).

It looks as if the enemy had no intention of launching any further heavy attacks against Velizh, and that, instead, he is trying with the fresh forces of his Fourth Assault Army to link up with 39th Army.

North: Three objectives of the enemy effort south of Lake Ilmen: Kholm, Staraya Russa, and isolating II Corps. On the Volkhov River and apparently also on the Ladoga front, no major developments are to be expected. The enemy broadly overlooks the relieving of police division on the Leningrad front.

. . .

28 February 1942

Situation: The entire front has become considerably more active.

Heavy attacks in the Crimea from both sides were repulsed. Heavy attacks against von Mackensen and on the Bakhmut River, weaker ones against XI Corps.

Intensified enemy activity at Mtsensk and Sukhinichi.

The usual attacks on the supply road to Yukhov and the eastern front of AGp. Center.

Sensation on the western wing of XXIII Corps! Enemy railheads reported to be operating right up to enemy front facing it. Also, roadways which did not exist before, carrying plenty of traffic, are now said to lead from Ostashkov and Toropets to the area.

In North, continued heavy pressure on Kholm from north and south. Situation in II Corps difficult and unchanged. Airborne supply barely sufficient. North of Lake Ilmen the enemy is collecting all his forces to bring greater pressure to bear on Lyuban in the bulge west of the Volkhov River, resulting in considerable slackening of pressure on XXXXIII Corps.

General Fuehrer conference with commander of AGp. Center and his army commanders, i.e., Second Panzer Army, Fourth Army, Fourth Panzer Army, Ninth Army, Third Panzer Army. Oak leaves are presented. Model is promoted to general. The conference confirms the situation pictures formed on the basis of army reports. The orders issued thus far remain in force.

2 March 1942

Fuehrer conference with commander in chief and CGs of AGp. North. Result: Start of operations on the Volkhov front: 7 March to last until 12 March. Concentration of air force in that sector is requested for period 7–14 March. Fuehrer specifies air preparation beginning several days before opening of offensive (heaviest bombs against camps in forests). After elimination of the Volkhov salient, no blood is to be wasted on reducing the enemy in the marshes; he can be left to starve to death.

Start of offensive at Kholm: 5 March. Infantry is yet to be moved to the front. Artillery and heavy weapons already on the ground. Reinforcement of II Corps by air force field battalions desirable. Replacements now ready at army group must be moved to front.

Start of offensive at Staraya Russa scheduled for 13 to 16 March. Plan of attack not yet decided. To my mind it must be divided into two phases: opening of corridor to II Corps and subsequent capture of the Staraya Russa–Demyansk road.

Inasmuch as the offensive of AGp. Center on Ostashkov will probably take place between 12 and 16 March, the air fleets of the two army groups can strike only for their respective army groups; this, however, does not preclude occasional help on special tasks.

The situation on the whole shows no important changes. The enemy attacks in the Crimea and against Seventeenth Army are beaten off. On the other fronts only minor fighting.

3 March 1942

Situation: In the Crimea, the enemy attacks are letting up as thaw is spreading. Von Kleist has had some heartening offensive successes, especially at the danger spot in 1st Mountain Division sector. No important developments on the rest of the front, only local attacks.

It remains to be seen whether the attacks aimed at Orel and against our Sukhinichi salient, which we have anticipated for some time now, will really materialize.

In AGp. North, south of Lake Ilmen, no important change; north of the lake, continued enemy regrouping to expand the northern head of the penetration.

.   .   .

11 March 1942

Situation: Despite bitter attacks against the eastern and northern front of von Kleist group, no serious enemy successes.

Fuehrer conference with Field Marshal von Kluge and General Model. Discussion of situation. (Von Kluge's mind reacts only to immediate impressions and never plans ahead, is swayed entirely by his strong-willed army commanders.) We discuss plans for the western front of Ninth Army (the Fuehrer again leaves altogether too much freedom of decision!) and for the Ostashkov offensive.

The presentation fails to convey any clear picture of the general idea underlying the plan of attack.

Several phone talks with *von Kuechler*. He is nervous about postponement of the Volkhov offensive, but the Fuehrer insists on putting it off until weather permits full employment of the air force.

We review the plan of attack for Staraya Russa; the main assault wedge looks too weak.

18 March 1942

Situation: The attacks on the fronts of AGps. South and Center continue, but are disjointed and have only local character. No sizable new units have been committed. At Kerch, the number of tanks committed is quite formidable, but the majority are worthless, obsolete types from training units, etc.

In AGp. *North,* the attacking wedge striking down from the north along the Volkhov River is slowly gaining ground west of the highway, but the southern attack does not make any headway, owing to very heavy enemy counterattacks in the sector. In the Volkhov bulge, the enemy's attacking power seems to be gradually weakening, but at Pogostye his continual small local gains are not adapted to alter our view of the seriousness of the situation.

Von Kuechler, worried by the steadily deteriorating situation in II Corps, wants to launch the attack at Staraya Russa on 20 March, but the Fuehrer intends to withhold the go-ahead signal until the Volkhov breach has been closed. We can only hope that the situation in Zorn's sector has not become untenable before then.

.   .   .

25 March 1942

.   .   .

Situation: Good defensive success on the *Kerch front*. Also von Kleist's group has scored a distinctive defensive success. Our troops are under great strain. Paulus launches a successful counterattack.

In *Center,* resurgence of attacks against Fourth Army (supply road). The main concern, however, is with the rear (enemy guards cavalry corps against Haase's group). In Ninth Army, new heavy attacks, in which the enemy commits one of his new armored brigades.

North: Good progress of the drive at Staraya Russa. Enemy attack at Pogostye resulted in fairly deep penetration, which seems to have been temporarily checked. Mountain infantry is moving up for counterattack.

At Fuehrer Hq.: Field Marshal List presents a long report on the result of his inspection tour in Lapland and Norway. Opposes an OKW theater command for the north as redundant inasmuch as the northern sector must always act on its own and the southern sector has good leadership.

28 March 1942

. . .

Fuehrer conference on the overall situation. Report on buildup for SIEGFRIED. Approved!

Notes to Hitler's explanation of the situation and intentions of 28 March 1942 (during the conference on summer operations).

a. General situation much improved. Anxieties have declined.

b. 1. Major concern is for a landing in northern Norway and impact on Sweden.

   2. A landing on the west coast of France and subsequent events (airborne unit, "Goering" Division to France). Captured batteries will be taken from the army for coastal defense.

c. Spanish-Portugal area less probable.

d. Northwest Africa is also less likely; North Africa remains uncertain. (Require total occupation of France.) In France three armored divisions required. The heaviest tanks in organized units should go first to France; to the east when troop levels prove insufficient (eventually North Africa as well).

e. North Africa supply problems. After putting Malta out of action, some aircraft should be used as domestic reserve.

f. Tonnage lost must be 600,000 to 650,000 tons per month. American production is 1,800,000 tons.

g. War will be decided in the east.

h. Ceylon-Australia-Japan will attack Russia when they have sufficient air power.

i. Air-armored heavy weapons. Must be combined in tandem. Operation must begin with success; new troops cannot suffer any setback. Reverses cannot be allowed. New troops require special support. Operation should be conducted in a way permitting new divisions. Opportunity to familiarize themselves with the enemy. Plan the operation after the arrival of units and dryout of ground. Must begin in the south: Crimea. The operation against Kerch as quickly as possible. Sevastopol a materiel attack using the heaviest artillery to protect the infantry. Fortress engineers report artillery to protect the infantry. Fortress engineers report of flame-throwing tanks.

[j.   and k. not in original.]

l. Before beginning the major operation cleanup Izyum, begin the Voronezh operation.

m. Along the Don, winter positions.

n. No great clinches.

o. There can be no lessening in the southern attack; Russians must meet this operation. The oil is essential to the Russians.

p. Remove divisions (not regiments) as soon as advance stops. Remove units!

q. **1.** Crimea: Kerch demands massive air power. Sevastopol through the experiences of the world war.

   2. Capture Izyum and expand east of the Don.

   3. Begin at Voronezh with goal of defeating enemy units. Construction Don.

   4. Middle: Activities depend on the southern successes. Goal: Black Sea, Caspian Sea, Batum-Baku.

   5. Leningrad cannot be considered today. Next Ingria.

r. Time: Beginning of September: North Caucasus

31 March 1942

Fuehrer conference with von Kluge and Model. Both state that the troops have been under too great a strain to sustain an offensive against Ostashkov at the present time. Decision: Ninth Army will limit its effort on the Rzhev front to creating favorable conditions for the start of Operation BRIDGE BLOW after the muddy season. In addition it will bar the lines of communication of the Russian Twenty-ninth Army with the greatest economy of forces. Apart from this, army group must restore order in its rear area and re-form its forces.

. . .

11 April 1942

Situation: New strong attacks on the Kerch peninsula were repulsed. A landing attempt on the west coast of the Crimea was thrown back. Russian fleet at sea. Striking movements of reinforcements to von Kleist's eastern front. Troop movements from the southwest into the Sukhinichi area. Heavy attacks against General Ruoff's southern wing. On Model's front, more movements in westward direction. Puzzling movements from Toropets to the southeast during the night. At Kholm, the situation is very tight. Von Seydlitz is scoring small advances. At Pogostye, tension is easing.

Fuehrer situation conference: He vetoes proposals of AGp. Center regarding attacks on Ostashkov and toward Toropets. For the time being, no attack at all. Ordered transfers of divisions to the west and to south must be carried out.

Work on the orders for Operation BLUE.

Keitel (Personnel Division): Personnel matters.

Heusinger: Operation South.

21 April 1942

. . .

Notes by General Halder for presentation to Hitler on 21 April 1942.

1. Effect of winter battles:

    a. Personnel: 1.11.1941–1.4.1942, including sick: 900,000 losses, 450,000 replacements. These numbers include the almost total use of the 1922 year and strong encroachment on the economy.

b. Material: 1.10.1941–15.3.1942: loss of 74,183 vehicles and 2,340 tracked vehicles; addition of 7,441 vehicles (10 percent) and 1,847 tracked vehicles (80 percent).
Weapons: shortages include 28,000 rifles, 14,000 machine guns, 7,000 AT guns, 1,900 guns.
Horses: 15.10.1941–15.3.1942: losses of 179,609, additions of 20,000.

2. Augmentations: 7 infantry divisions, later an additional 4; 3 armored divisions. Expansion of 2 motorized infantry regiments into divisions.

3. Vacancies 1.5.1942: In the east, short 625,000 men. *South:* Each infantry division short about 2,400; motorized units 1,000 to 2,000. Will probably be made good by start of operations. *Middle:* Infantry divisions 6,900; motorized divisions less *North:* Infantry divisions 4,800, motorized divisions similar. On 1.5. the southern units are 50 percent and in the north 35 percent of their original infantry combat strength.

4. Material replacements: *South:* By start of operations nearing assigned levels; *Center* and *North:* for six battalions enough light and heavy weapons; artillery has three guns per battery.

5. Tank status: *South:* Close to level; *Center* and *North:* one battalion for each armored division. AT equipment will in the course of the summer compare favorably.

6. Movements at the start of operations: *South:* Motorized units and army troops 85 percent mobile; infantry divisions at strength (although short reconnaissance battalion); *Center, North:* Insufficient mobility for extensive operations.

7. Loss of battle worthiness through losses of experienced officers and NCOs. Loss of experienced specialists. Fatigue of personnel, horses, and equipment. Irregularity of combat value.

8. Organization: Todt Organization I on 1.5.1941: 10,000; spring 1942: 25,000; II, end of 1941: 90,000; spring 1942: 195,000. Of these numbers, 45,000 are German and 150,000 are foreign nationals: 9,500 tons of transport capacity. RAD: 151 battalions; spring 1942: 200 battalions.

4 May 1942

Situation: Attack to free Kholm has opened with good results. Strong attacks against 290th Division were repelled; more attacks must be expected. At Group Winnenberg, acute tension again due to enemy penetration.

Fuehrer conference:

   a.   Von Kuechler, von Seydlitz. Report on situation in north. At times, very lively exchange of views. Von Kuechler's suggestion to abandon the offensive in south in order to maintain the operation in north is sharply disapproved.

   b.   Von Kleist gets briefing on mission.

Colonel Bamler reports en route. In the afternoon visit by Baroness Dueker.

12 May 1942

Situation: Good progress on the Kerch peninsula; 29,000 prisoners, 220 guns, 170 tanks, etc. Heavy enemy attacks at Volschansk and in VIII Corps sector against Sixth Army; objective Kharkov. The enemy used 100 tanks in each attack and has scored considerable initial successes. Air force units must be diverted from the Crimea to this battle area. Twenty-third Armored Division is released for commitment at the front.

. . .

13 May 1942

Situation: On the Kerch peninsula, the battle appears to have been decided in our favor (more than forty thousand prisoners). What resistance the enemy will be able to put up in the eastern part of the peninsula cannot yet be estimated. In Sixth Army sector heavy attacks south and northeast of Kharkov, supported by several hundred tanks. Serious penetrations. Counterattack by 23d Armored and 3d Armored divisions east of Kharkov. Grave crisis south of Kharkov (131st Division). No important developments on the rest of the front.

. . .

14 May 1942

Situation: *Crimea:* We are approaching the town of Kerch in pursuing the enemy. South and east of Kharkov heavy enemy attacks supported by large numbers of tanks. The southern attack has the following strength:

six or seven rifle divisions, three to five armored divisions, one cavalry division, and, behind them, four rifle divisions, one motorized brigade, three cavalry corps (eight cavalry divisions), and four to six armored brigades. The eastern attack comprises twelve rifle divisions, three armored brigades, and, behind them, one rifle division, two motorized brigades, one cavalry corps (three cavalry divisions). On the rest of the front, no important changes.

Fuehrer situation conference: Von Bock calls up and is taking three to four divisions out of von Kleist's group to patch up the front south of Kharkov. Proposal is disapproved. The situation can be restored only by an attack from the south, in connection with the preparations for operation FREDERICK. Von Kleist's eastern front must be covered by regrouping, with main concentration to the north.

Notes from the telephone discussion von Bock–Hitler on 14.5.1942 at 1330.

Von Bock: The enemy attacking again today. The situation on the right flank of Sixth Army is bad. The 454th Security Division gives way. Specifics unclear. To the north, situation improved, largely because of air force. The enemy makes strong attacks on the right side of Berecks; over fifty enemy tanks destroyed. Until midday, not threatening.

Bad situation by the 454th Security Division where the enemy breaks through. Intention is a northern counterattack. Von Mackensen with new forces and the 454th Security Division.

Volschansk: Tschernowaja still holds. Russians have very strong air power here. Our counterattack has begun; air force will participate in armored attack. The northern strong point Urow holds: one regiment from north. This evening on the western corner Volschansk tanks destroyed (forty?). Our tank losses acceptable.

Fuehrer: Penetration VIII: Penetration cannot be resolved in the current positions with von Mackensen's strength. Only a massive aerial commitment can help; more Stuka units. Then the enemy attack will be slowed. In the north one must hope that the committed units will stop the penetration. One must juggle the air force between the two penetrations. It is necessary to implement our attack; if possible, one day earlier. Suggests the possibility of an attack in the direction of Izyum. Not just on Izyum; from the left flank one can attack and cave in the enemy. Slawiansk diversionary attack. Two to three days of massive air force commitment will slow penetrations. Great opportunities through an attack on the enemy rear. Then air force in front of armored groups. (We have 180 to 200 tanks.) The major problem now is to stand by the southern attack against Izyum and the west.

. . .

15 May 1942

Situation: The Kerch offensive may be considered closed. Town and harbor are in our hands. Only the neck north of the town needs to be mopped up yet. South of Kharkov, the enemy penetration has been extended only slightly. Our front south of Kharkov was strong enough to throw back the enemy by a counterattack; high enemy losses. However, there is still a gap north of 454th Security Division which has been closed only precariously by the defense unit at Krasnograd. Here we may yet witness further enemy advances. On the whole, however, the impetus of the offensive seems to have been broken by our air efforts.

In the penetration area Volschansk, our counterattack has not had the expected success. Nevertheless the main thrust of the enemy offensive in the direction of Kharkov appears to be checked. A certain danger still exists north of Ternovaya, where we have only light forces.

On the other fronts, attacks are repulsed and troops can be exchanged; no major fighting.

At the situation conference at Fuehrer Hq., he exhibits extreme interest for the commitment of the M IV tanks with long-barreled guns and the medium AT guns on SPM now coming off the line. —Apparently the output in Germany of medium AT guns has been much larger than anticipated.

Accordingly, after my return from the Fuehrer conference, I call a meeting with Gen Qu and the chiefs of Organization, Operation, and Transportation sections to discuss the measures necessary to assure commitment of these weapons wherever needed by OKH.

Major von Wedekind goes as Liaison Officer to von Kleist (FREDERICK offensive).

Gen Qu and Lieutenant Colonel Toppe report on the supply buildup for BLUE.

17 May 1942

Situation: On the Kerch peninsula, the remnants of the enemy are still putting up fanatical resistance northeast of the town. The offensive of von Kleist's group (FREDERICK) has got off to a good start.

The enemy attacks south of Kharkov have made only minor advances. We cannot be too sure that we are past the crisis entirely, but it very much looks that way. East of Kharkov, there has been a big tank battle with the enemy attacking with large numbers of new tanks. While this battle was in progress, we were able to gain ground to the north, at Ternovaya, so that the crisis east of Kharkov may in the main be regarded as overcome. On the boundary between Second Army and Second Panzer Army, the enemy apparently has not yet completed his buildup. An attack is being anticipated. On the remainder of the front, no important changes.

. . .

18 May 1942

Situation: On the Kerch peninsula, the few small remnants left are still fighting fiercely. While the battle raged around Kharkov, von Kleist's offensive gained much ground in the direction of Izyum and to the southwest. The situation of VIII Corps south of Kharkov is difficult, even after corps has successfully beaten off the enemy's frontal attacks.

The number of tank brigades committed by the enemy is really astounding: von Bock's estimates eight or nine south of Kharkov, and seven or eight on the front of LI Corps. At Volschansk, the overall situation looks pretty good. Our tanks encircled at Ternovaya have not been freed, but it seems that they soon will be. Farther to the north, the situation is consolidated.

On the boundary Second Army/Second Panzer Army the possibility of an enemy attack must still be reckoned with. On the other fronts, no important developments.

. . .

19 May 1942

Situation: The Kerch offensive can be regarded as closed; 150,000 prisoners and large quantities of booty. The situation south of Kharkov has developed in gratifying manner. Von Kleist's offensive has made good progress. VIII Corps felt only little pressure today (whether or not as a result of von Kleist's offensive is too early to say) and was moreover able to adjust its line by a counterattack.

The situation east of Kharkov is no longer dangerous.

The final success of the counterattack will not be apparent before tomorrow.

The remainder of the front is strikingly quiet.

. . .

20 May 1942

Situation:

a. Counteroffensive FREDERICK south of Izyum is making good progress, even though the Romanians have gained only little ground. The enemy has reacted to the offensive from the south with great speed and vigor, opposing it chiefly with tanks and troops on trucks. The offensive substantially relieves VIII Corps, which now has been able to launch counterthrusts at some points of its front. Army group reports intention to shift main effort of FREDERICK to the north and, after regrouping VIII Corps, to converge toward it in the area southeast of Kharkov.

b. Baffling north-south railroad movements in the area north of Rostov.

c. In AGp. North, attacks against SS "Deathhead" at and east of Molovitsi and, from the south, against the corridor linking X and II Corps. The attacks were launched in bad weather to avoid our air force. Individual tanks succeeded in piercing our lines, but the massed infantry attacks were repulsed with considerable losses to the enemy.

d. On the remainder of the front, no major fighting.

. . .

21 May 1942

Situation: Kerch operation concluded. Regrouping at Sevastopol, where the enemy is evidently making preparations against our impending attack. The Izyum offensive is taking a gratifying course. Von Kleist's northward drive has gained ground. Along the entire front we are now recapturing the initiative.

The situation at Kharkov continues to develop to our satisfaction. We have established firm contact with our encircled forces at Ternovaya.

The front is closing. We can now take out forces from this sector and get them ready to meet von Kleist converging from the north. All quiet on the remainder of the front, except in II Corps, where the enemy continues his unsuccessful attacks.

. . .

22 May 1942

Situation: The Izyum pocket has been weakly sealed on its eastern periphery. The plan envisaged by AGp. South for strengthening the ring in this sector, which probably will be subjected to considerable pressure in the coming days, is not well conceived: it calls for an attack in that direction with parts of 3d and 23d Armored divisions from the constricted bridgehead at Andreyevka. To my mind this is a very ineffectual solution. The right thing to do would be to have the armor now becoming available east of Kharkov strike for Savintsi, on the north bank of the Donets. Von Bock had a talk with the Fuehrer and secured approval for army group's plan. I think it is wrong.

In the Kharkov sector, the enemy is pulling back his offensive front behind the Donets River.

From the other fronts we have reports only of continuation of the attacks against the southern and the northeastern sectors of II Corps, all unsuccessful.

. . .

24 May 1942

Fuehrer back at GHq.

Situation: In the pocket west of Izyum, which at last is solidly sealed, the enemy is making unsuccessful efforts to break out eastward. Attempts from the east, through Izyum and Savintsi, to crack the ring from without were repelled. East of Kharkov the enemy launched local attacks, apparently to keep us from withdrawing forces from this sector, and was thrown back. On the boundary of AGps. South and Center, the enemy appears to be massing for an attack (eight to twelve divisions); radio silence in his sector. The attacks by AGp. Center against Cavalry Corps Below, have made good progress (even without air and tank support, which apparently was precluded by the weather). Stubborn enemy resistance. Increased enemy artillery activity from the outside. The enemy seems to be concentrating forces for an attack against Byelyi.

In *AGp. North,* a generally quiet day. Attacks against II Corps have let up.

. . .

25 May 1942

. . .

Situation: The battle around the pocket west of Izyum continues to evolve satisfactorily. The enemy's desperate and resolutely directed attempts to break out eastward were repelled, as were the feeble attacks with tanks from the east through Savintsi.

East of Kharkov the enemy has resumed the attack and made some negligible local gains.

In *AGp. Center* the operations against the enemy in its rear (south of Vyazma) have made only slow progress due to bad weather and the resulting restrictions of movement.

All quiet on the other fronts (including North).

. . .

28 May 1942

Situation: The battle at Kharkov and on the Donets is brought to a close with a large take of prisoners and booty. AGp. South had issued the orders for the next phases of the offensive: "Volschansk" and "Izyum."

Fourth Army has closed the ring around the main body of Cavalry Corps Below.

No noteworthy developments on the remainder of the front. In *North,* the enemy seems to be pulling out slowly but steadily from his bulges on the Volkhov and at Pogostye.

. . .

10 June 1942

Situation: Notwithstanding heavy enemy counterattacks, good progress at *Sevastopol.* It appears that the enemy has moved artillery and infantry from the southern sector to the threatened northern sector; the attack tomorrow therefore is to be launched with maximum surprise.

Attack on Volschansk has started off well. The attack of the two assault wedges took the enemy lines by surprise.

In Center further progress of mopping-up operation behind the front.

The escaped Cavalry Corps Below is being pursued.

In Ninth Army sector, the enemy is evidently reducing his forces on the northern front. Reinforcements reported moving up in the Staritsa area.

All quiet on Sixteenth Army front.

Eighteenth Army repelled serious attacks against the "bridge" on the Volkhov. At Kirishi, only local attacks.

.   .   .

11 June 1942

Situation: Local gains at Sevastopol, in both northern and southern sectors. The enemy artillery, which for the largest part is still firing, remains quite troublesome.

The Volschansk attack is making very satisfactory progress. There is a danger that the enemy would slip the noose of our developing movement. —Fourth Army is making further progress in the mopping-up of its rear area. Unluckily, the main body of von Below's cavalry corps and of 4th Airborne Brigade has escaped south.

Situation in enemy line facing northern front of Ninth Army is unclear. (Railroad movements, concentration of armor.) Nor is there any clear picture of what the enemy facing the northeastern front is up to (increase in enemy artillery). South of the "corridor" to II Corps the enemy unaccountably has abandoned some ground. To the north he is attacking (a new brigade). Wandel's group has repelled severe attacks from the east.
Concentrations at Kirishi.

.   .   .

12 June 1942

Fuehrer at Obersalzberg.

Situation: Only minor gains at Sevastopol and Volschansk. On the other fronts, no important changes.

Reports: Colonel Schulz (Engineer Chief): Instruction to study road and bridge conditions on the Lovat River (communications line to II Corps). Major Hess, Gen Qu, Lapland, presents report on supply situation in his territory.

Vice Admiral Fricke (with Captain Assman, navy): Conference on situation. The Naval Operations Staff's picture of the war situation strays far from our sober view of facts. Those people are dreaming in terms of continents. Having watched the army's performance to date, they assume without another thought that it all just depends on what we like to do and when, to push through on the land routes to the Persian Gulf over the Caucasus, or from Cyrenaica to the Suez Canal via Egypt. They are glibly talking about land operations through Italian Africa to the East African coast and South Africa. The problems of the Atlantic are treated with offhanded superiority and those of the Black Sea with criminal unconcern.

.   .   .

17 June 1942

Situation: At *Sevastopol* the attack of LIV Corps has scored remarkable success in the northern sector and captured several key works. The attack on the southern sector has gained some ground and will be pushed again tomorrow.

Center is regrouping for Operation FREDERICK II, which probably cannot start before 20 June. Raining. Cavalry Corps Below is now floating around the area west of Kirov. Quite a man that we have to send no less than seven divisions after him.

In North we have neither positive nor negative evidence on the enemy's intention of giving up the Velizh pocket. In any event, North has freed the larger part of eight armored divisions for a southward drive through Demyansk.

On the Volkhov, attacks were again repelled and the sack further compressed. Otherwise, nothing of importance.

.   .   .

18 June 1942

Fuehrer back.

Situation: Substantial advances by LIV Corps at Sevastopol, lesser advances by XXX Corps. Regrouping in Sixth Army delayed by bad weather.

In Center, Cavalry Corps Below, both the groups, the one which broke out and the segment which remained behind and was encircled, has been split into several groups. We must reckon with the ability of some elements to fight their way through the forests toward Kirov. The enemy at Kirov will support these break-out attempts by launching an attack of his own.

In North, no major actions. The enemy troops in the Volkhov sack are running short of food.

. . .

19 June 1942

Fuehrer away.

Situation: In the northern sector of Sevastopol, coast and great bay have been reached. Only the Severnaya Kosa tip with its batteries is still in enemy hands. No change in the situation in XXX Corps.

The railroad line north of Volschansk has been captured. No changes on the rest of the front. Only on the Volkhov, very heavy enemy attacks with local successes against Wandel's group, made possible by poor air support, which was not possible because of adverse weather.

The discussion with the top command on the efficient conduct of the Kupyansk-Izyum offensive follows a familiar and unpleasant pattern. Whereas von Bock, because of the terrain, wants to launch his tank drive directly from the west, top command considers that a mistake, but feels no change ought to be ordered at this advanced stage of preparations, and approves von Bock's plan against its better judgment.

20 June 1942

Situation: At Sevastopol, local advances were made by LIV and XXX Corps. On the Lovat River, heavy attacks were repulsed.

Otherwise, no change.

General Wagner (Gen Qu) reports on rehabilitation situation (satisfactory) and on conferences in Berlin.

Plane carrying Major Reichel (Ia, 23d Armored Division), with orders of the highest importance for Operation BLUE, has apparently fallen into enemy hands.

Tobruk captured. Thus, the heavy battle in Cyrenaica has culminated on a victory that is of equally great value from the military and the political aspect.

AGp. South shows great nervousness in its situation estimate. The enemy is moving new troops from Rostov to the north and assembling a large force of armor opposite Sixth Army, which would indicate that heavy attacks are forthcoming.

Reports on impending attack (22 June) with heavy tank support out of Staraya Russa.

General situation review on 20.6.1942.

The regulating rules come from our side. The morale and performance of our troops are good.

BLUE I. Equipment of the attack units for the first act satisfactory. (The performance earns recognition in Germany, transport, and by the troops.) The personnel improvements for the first act proved successful. The noncommissioned officer issue remains difficult.

The weak points remain:

a.   The uncertainty concerning the effectiveness of renewed equipment.

b.   The horse issues.

c.   The fuel issue (planning only to September 1942).

BLUE II: Equipment support and supply are improving, as are personnel. Both should improve pleasantly since transportation situation is improved.

BLUE III: No current overview.

Elsewhere: The switching efforts in AGp. Center have made good progress. Divisions with six battalions and sufficient artillery are combat ready, albeit with limited mobility. The increase in the number of replacements over losses (narrowly) brings a good balance. Furloughs continue.

By AGp. North the strength issue remains difficult since replacements and losses tip the scales. Equipment situation, particularly AT, has improved.

Enemy situation: The enemy anticipated our attack. The reports in the enemy press reveal information about our strategic operational intentions for the entire front between the gulf of Finland and the Black Sea. They reveal the details concerning the shift from strategic goals to tactical aspirations.

The enemy has organized, basically, a defensive posture: a thin occupation of the front—often dangerously thin—supported by mobile forces.

The general structure:

270 divs.	217 committed	(80%)	53 reserve	(20%)
115 sec. divs.	181 committed	(70%)	34 reserve	(30%)
69 armd. brigs.	26 committed	(36%)	43 reserve	(64%)
2 armd. divs.	0 committed	(0%)	2 reserve	(100%)

. . .

21 June 1942

Fuehrer away.

Situation: At Sevastopol, the important peninsula is in our hands and consequently we are now controlling almost the entire north shore (LIV Corps). Good progress by XXX Corps. The enemy appears to be abandoning the front opposite the Romanian in order to concentrate his forces against XXX Corps. On the Volkhov, heavy attacks supported by tanks, which were repelled with difficulty. Otherwise, no change. Tobruk taken.

Major Reichel's plane has been found. He probably is dead. The documents, filled with vital information, must by now be in enemy hands.

. . .

22 June 1942

Start of second year of the war against the Soviets.

Situation: At Sevastopol, the northern part of the fortress area, north of the great harbor bay, is in our hands. Shifting of our main effort to the southern sector has been initiated.

Offensive FREDERICK II (Izyum-Kupyansk), as a result of surprise, made substantial initial ground gains, but later encountered stubborn resistance west of Kupyansk. Crossing of the Donets from the south has been executed without major difficulties.

At Olkhovatka, shifting of troops, but the concentration there apparently is still quite dense. Opposite Second Army the enemy seems to be regrouping in depth. At Yelets, confused troop movements cutting across one another.

The assembly movements for BLUE (scheduled for X-4 to X-3) will be carried out during the night 22/23 June. X-order still withheld.

On the remainder of the front, no significant developments apart from local reconnaissance thrusts, especially in the Sukhinichi salient. On the Volkhov front heavy fighting has flared up again. Enemy tanks have penetrated into our "bridge," but, on the other hand, it is believed this will prevent the enemy from getting his forces out of the sack. I have my doubts about that and feel sure that some of the troops in there will get away. Starvation among the penned-up enemy is beginning to take its toll.

Tobruk proves to be a great victory. Rommel has become a field marshal.

. . .

24 June 1942

Fuehrer back, but no conference.

Situation: At Sevastopol, local improvements preparatory to the next phase of the assault. Operation FREDERICK II has achieved its objective. No reports yet on figures. Northeast of Volschansk various improvements are gained for our jump-off position against feeble and disorganized enemy resistance.

No important changes on the remainder of the front. More advances in the Volkhov sack. The situation of the encircled enemy appears to be critical.

In OKW, which returned today, the campaign against the General Staff is in high gear again. The unfortunate Reichel affair (Ia, 23d Armored Division) seems to have crystallized ill feelings of apparently long standing. We only have to brace ourselves now for the explosion.

Several phone talks with AGp. *South* about the Reichel affair. Field Marshal von Bock will report to the Fuehrer in person tomorrow.

. . .

25 June 1942

. . .

Situation: More local gains at Sevastopol. Successes of the Romanians.
Operation FREDERICK concluded with eighteen thousand prisoners.
Deserters at Staraya Russa state an attack is forthcoming (early in July).
Volkhov sack is nearing its final liquidation.
Remainder of the front without important events.

Report to Fuehrer: Decision on BLUE II: We shall strike from the south; also current questions.

Afternoon. Field Marshal von Bock reports to the Fuehrer on the Reichel case. *Evening* with von Bock at Vorwerk [army guest house].

General Wagner (Gen Qu): Effects of curtailment of the fuel supply on our plans in Center and North.

26 June 1942

Situation: On the whole unchanged. AGp. South is regrouping (First Panzer Army) for BLUE II. Further progress in the liquidation of the Volkhov sack. Offensive BLUE I has to be postponed to 20 June because of thundershowers.

Von Kluge reports to the Fuehrer: Review of situation. Fuehrer will transfer approximately two armored divisions to Center, as the development of BLUE I permits. Operation SEYDLITZ approved. Will be followed by preparations for Sukhinichi, when von Kluge has forces of his own, and for Kaluga, as soon as he gets the two armored divisions from south. Will be launched in the last third of July. Then Ostashkov can be prepared, starting middle of August.

. . .

27 June 1942

Situation: At Sevastopol, also the central sector (Romanian corps) is now approaching the inner fortifications ring, against which the assault is now being initiated.

In South, no signs of any enemy reactions to the lost orders. The tank concentration east of Sixth Army is no longer in evidence. Where it got to is a mystery. Tank movements have been observed only in the direction of Korocha. Railroad movements through Penza to Ryazhsk continue (reinforcements for Tombov-Yelets-Tula group). In the Volkhov sack, now only local resistance. Attacks against the Kirishi bridgehead repelled.

Field Marshal von Mannerheim visits the Fuehrer. From 1215 to 1330, report on military situation. Luncheon. In the afternoon, at OKH.

. . .

28 June 1942

Situation: At Sevastopol, the inner fortifications ring is reached, and concurrently the initial moves are made to breach the central portion.

Offensive BLUE has started. The attack by von Weichs's group has achieved tactical surprise, but after the initial easy penetrations, our troops had to overwhelm partly stubborn enemy opposition. The offensive is making very satisfactory progress. The results of the attack have fully corroborated our picture of the enemy disposition. The front is weakly held, and there is some organization in depth. It remains to be seen whether substantial forces would be moved up from the enemy's hinterland. No indications to that effect can be made out on this first day of the attack.

. . .

29 June 1942

Situation: Very good progress at Sevastopol. The assault from north and east by way of Severnaya Bay and Chernaya has broken into the inner defense ring on both sides of the mouth of the Chernaya River, and has from the east gained a foothold on the commanding heights of the Sapun heights. This means that the assault has entered its final phase, which we hope will be concluded within a week. Army group will then have to decide how to employ the forces that become available for the next phase, that is, whether to advance through Kerch or through Taganrog.

The attack of the northern wing of BLUE during the night failed to improve on the very satisfactory results of the preceding day because all trucks were immobilized by a rainstrom. Still unfulfilled is one hope, i.e., that the Hungarians should make some advances in the southern wing.

In Center, evidence is accumulating that the enemy is reducing his forces in the rear of Ninth Army. Unfortunately, heavy rains in this area, too, made it necessary to postpone Operation SEYDLITZ.

In North, the enemy's Volkhov operation can now be regarded as finally liquidated. New strong attacks at Kirishi. It is uncertain if new attacks will come from the Ladoga front.

In Africa, Mersa Matrûh has fallen. Five thousand prisoners (mostly Indians).

.   .   .

30 June 1942

Von Kuechler promoted to field marshal! XXXX Corps starts off.

Situation: At Sevastopol our advances in the afternoon were so big that we may now expect the immediate fall of city and harbor.

Attack of XXXX Motorized Corps has started off well. Von Weichs's drive continues to gain ground. Resistance of enemy front groups is stiffening; also enemy pressure on the northern flank from Livny. All quiet on the other fronts.

Conference with von Kuechler and Fuehrer: Submits his plans. He envisages four offensives in his sector, which, as they supposedly could be carried out only one after the other, would take all of twenty weeks, i.e., six months. The individual projects are put up for discussion. The Fuehrer specifies:

1. The corridor to II Corps must be extended northward, as planned, and now also southward.

2. Pogostye must be disposed of at the earliest; no further waiting. Fuehrer will give him the first company of "Tiger" tanks for this job.

3. Preparedness for defensive action along the bottleneck. The liquidation of the Volkhov bridgehead is also discussed. The Fuehrer reiterates his plan to restore the situation on the eastern bank.

Von Kuechler estimates that four divisions would be needed for the job.

. . .

1 July 1942

Von Manstein promoted to field marshal.

Situation: Fall of Sevastopol. The drive of the northern wing of Sixth Army (XXXX Corps) is getting on well; its right wing reaches and crosses the Oskol River. The left wing of the drive makes a striking advance on Staryy Oskol; central part reports stiff fighting.

Von Weichs is making good strides on his right shoulder, whereas the Hungarians on the right wing of the breakthrough wedge are gaining ground only slowly. The central part is also making good progress against frontal resistance. Pressure from Livny against the northern flank is increasing and has compelled von Weichs's left wing to pass to the defensive.

Nothing to report from other fronts.

Today's *Fuehrer situation conference* was not attended by me.

. . .

3 July 1942

Situation: At Sevastopol, only mopping up.

South of the Donets, nothing new, apart from air attacks.

Also, in First Panzer Army, no new developments. The enemy is apparently shifting forces northward.

Sixth Army has beaten the enemy and broken through to Valuiki. Its armor has crossed the Oskol River and is advancing toward Korotoyak. VIII Corps, together with Weichs's inner wing, has closed the ring at Staryy Oskol and is advancing with its main body southeastward across the Oskol River.

Weichs is approaching the Don with the spearhead of his assault wedge (24th Armored Division and "Grossdeutschland"). In this sector the enemy is apparently being extended eastward toward Voronezh under continuous enemy pressure, which is likewise constantly extending farther eastward. On the whole developments are very satisfactory.

Center: Enemy appears to be withdrawing troops from Second Army front to strengthen the Voronezh sector. Operation SEYDLITZ is advancing only very slowly.

North: More deserter statements about an impending attack at Staraya Russa. The front is quiet.

0400.   **Left Angerburg with Fuehrer for conference** at Hq. AGp. South. Three points:

1.   Operation no longer contingent on capture of Voronezh.

2.   Enemy must be steadily weakened by secondary operations as the progress of the offensive permits.

3.   It has been decided to continue operation of Eleventh Army through Kerch.

(Arrive Poltava 0700–0900. Take-off 0900. Back at Angerburg 1240.)

Notes to Hitler's remarks on 3.7.1942, 0700 to 0900.

The enemy knows our operational plans. Clear from our approval. Reinforced through loss of orders. Danger that the Russians can avoid destruction.

Washington provides empty promises. No genuine second front. May take place in 1943. Churchill proves it.

Diversionary movement in west? Doubtful; probably no serious promises to Russia. Intimidation rather than risking defeat. Reasons for Russian surrender: oil areas, Leningrad, Moscow, economic catastrophe. The old stubbornness disappears in siege.

Two thoughts: The northern pressure and the shift to the east.

1.   Not necessary to take Voronezh. Should the enemy attack in superior strength, reaching the Don south of Voronezh will suffice (Voronezh still has its industrial segments).

2.   Limited efforts in support of operation should isolate enemy units.

. . .

4 July 1942

Situation: All of Sevastopol mopped up and finished.

The beaten enemy on the attacking front of AGp. South is retreating behind the Valu-Tikhvin-Sosna River line and the Don. Some of the enemy elements are cut off. Other elements are still offering stubborn resistance west of the Don. Enemy pressure on von Weichs's northern front is increasing and probably will become heavier yet, but a crisis is not to be feared. Operation SEYDLITZ made better progress today. The relative weakness of the group and the difficult terrain are hampering the advance. Determined enemy counteraction from west and east, chiefly in the Byelyi area.

.   .   .

5 July 1942

.   .   .

Situation: The offensive of *AGp. Center* is making good progress. The Don has been reached on a wide front west and south of Voronezh, but any attempt now to rush fortified Voronezh might result in total dissipation of the striking power of the 24th Armored Division and "Grossdeutschland" Division. Von Weichs's front facing northward has repelled enemy attacks partly supported by tanks, but lacking coordination. The enemy is bringing up reinforcements to the northern front and to Voronezh.

Turning southward, Sixth Army has crossed the Tikhvin-Sosna and established a bridgehead.

At the Fuehrer situation conferences, a warm debate developed over the conduct of the operation. The Fuehrer questions that von Bock is applying sufficient vigor in pushing toward the lower reaches of the Tikhvin-Sosna and specifically takes exception to directing 23d Armored Division (XXXX Corps) northeastward, and 16th Motorized Division eastward instead of southeastward.

As a result of my phone talk with von Sodenstern, von Bock calls me up to explain that these movements were conditioned by the threat to Hoth's southern flank (Fourth Panzer Army). Neither von Sodenstern nor I can see any such threat. There are just some isolated armored units of the enemy, which, in their desperation, attack in every direction, but do not constitute any operational threat to the southern flank of Fourth Panzer Army.

To me the situation looks this way: Hoth had the mission to strike for Voronezh, but did not relish the idea and so approached the operation with reluctance. Being directed to keep together all his forces in that direction, he asked von Bock to look to the protection of this southern flank. Von Bock has become completely dependent on Hoth's initiative and so has oriented the offensive toward Voronezh, to a greater degree than he could answer for. Following my telephone call, he shifted the advance of Sixth Army more toward the Tikhvin-Sosna, but in the main did so only as regards the infantry, which in fact has reached the river. Meanwhile, the bulk of his armor, which was to be concentrated on Svoboda, subsequently to thrust southeastward along the Don, is still roaming about in isolated groups.

Although the Fuehrer himself, at the conference on 3 July, made it emphatically clear that he did not attach any particular importance to Voronezh and left it to the judgment of army group to let that objective go if it could be taken only at great cost, von Bock tolerated Hoth's senseless rush for Voronezh, and even encouraged it.

Upon receipt of the evening report, stating his intention to strike across the Tikhvin-Sosna between Valuiki and the Don River mainly with infantry, while continuing the assault of Voronezh with "Grossdeutschland" and 24th Armored divisions, he is given explicit orders to (a) stop the assault and prepare to hold the bridgeheads, and (b) take out the two divisions. Immediate relief can be provided, then push with concentrated strong armored forces down the far back of the lower Tikhvin-Sosna, below Nikolayevka, to the confluence of Sosna and Don, while keeping the infantry close to the inner wing of the Panzer Army. First step toward carrying out this plan is the expansion of the bridgeheads. This is to prevent the enemy's being pushed back frontally. The plan is to envelop him from the north by forcing his wing leaning on the Don and swinging forward our pivoting wing on the Don, and then in a combined operation with First Panzer Army. This would clear the way to the Don bend. The order is issued instituting the new command over First Panzer Army, Seventeenth Army, and Group Wietersheim as of 7 July 0000 hours.

. . .

6 July 1942

Situation: The offensive of AGp. South has taken an unexpected turn. Whereas yesterday von Bock still was concerned over Hoth's southern wing and reported heavy opposition at Voronezh (fortifications, workers' battalions, etc.), in addition to several attacks and reinforcements against the northern flank (von Weichs), we are informed this afternoon that

(a) Voronezh has been evacuated, (b) the enemy on the northern flank is running away in headlong flight, and (c) Sixth Army, after crossing the Tikhvin-Sosna on a broad front, is advancing southward.

The reason for this surprising development seems to lie in the fact that Hoth, who approached his mission against Voronezh with serious mental reservations, was prone to take a pessimistic view of the situation. Von Sodenstern refers to "slanted reports." Von Bock, as usual, allowed his decisions to be swayed by his army commanders. The net result was that von Weichs was ordered to keep his forces together toward his own north wing, and Hoth, in his anxiety, drew forces away from XXXX Corps, while Paulus, irrepressible as ever, went right ahead and overran the enemy. Army group command, assigned a task plainly pointing southward, fell sadly short of wielding any effective influence in bringing these divergent spirits into line with the basic intention of the offensive.

At the Fuehrer situation conference, there is again a big scene over the conduct of the offensive by army groups; loud insistence on holding all forces together in conformity with the southward objectives; prohibition to strike on Voronezh and, finally, orders to stop Ninth and Eleventh Armored divisions and speed freeing of all armored divisions and moving them behind XXXX Corps across the Tikhvin-Sosna.

The actual picture of the enemy situation is not yet clear to me. There are two possibilities: either we have overestimated the enemy's strength and the offensive has completely smashed him, or the enemy is conducting a planned disengagement or at least is trying to do so in order to forestall being irretrievably beaten in 1942. The Fuehrer, on the strength of foreign reports, inclines to the view that Timoshenko has adopted a strategy of "elastic" defense. As the situation stands now, I would doubt that. He cannot, without decisively harming his cause, abandon the country about the Don bend and the industrial district, nor can such a strongly held front as he has built up opposite AGp.A be taken back "elastically" without serious disruptions. So we'll have to wait and see. In any event, Sixth Army must keep pushing on, and First Panzer Army must get ready at maximum speed. The necessary orders have been issued.

The Fuehrer does not want to release SS "Adolf Hitler," which could have an essential part in the offensive of First Panzer Army, out of concern for the west. Let us hope we won't have to pay heavily for that.

In the course of the day, phone talks with *von Bock* (this one highly disagreeable), with the *Fuehrer,* with *Keitel* (OKW), and with *von Sodenstern,* always about the same questions. This telephoning back and forth about matters which should be thought out quietly and then be incorporated in clear orders is very distressing. The hardest to endure is Keitel with his undigested spoutings.

Notes of the Fuehrer discussion (1850) and the discussion of Keitel-Halder on 6.7.1942.

Fuehrer: When Voronezh is free, it should be occupied. Rostov. Contradicts the reports! Rail links cut. Everything depends on hours. Timoshenko leaves. Motorized support.

Keitel: Fuehrer agreed to a northern demarcation line limiting any further advance. Voronezh will be cleaned up and occupied by infantry. Keep motorized division out! One must involve the "Grossdeutschland" and 24th Armored divisions as quickly as possible behind XXXX Corps. The 11th and 9th Armored divisions will follow. Fuel supplies!

List is prepared to use all improvisations!

. . .

7 July 1942

Great success against convoy in the Polar Sea!

Situation: Azov will be ready for the offensive as of 9 July. Also had orders to prepare the speedy occupation of the industrial district.

In *South,* very satisfactory progress. The Kalitva River has been reached by our armor and infantry. The enemy apparently is in a complete rout.

Twenty-third Armored Division is following up; 24th Armored Division and "Grossdeutschland" are relieved and moved southward. No advances at Svoboda and Korotoyak.

The follow-up of units behind the big wheel is running satisfactorily. Von Weichs is building up his defensive front facing north and keeps pushing east. The enemy has resumed his attacks against this defensive front, mainly in its easternmost sector.

Center: On the northern front of Second Panzer Army, violent attacks, south of Byelyi with 180 tanks, and in the sector of 18th Armored

Division with 120 tanks. Assistance needed in form of AT defenses. Nineteenth Armored Division and 52d Division are moving to this sector. The attacks, though very violent in some places, have no operational significance. Operation SEYDLITZ is developing very satisfactorily. The enemy seems to have been caught just as he was falling back. Complete success is imminent.

North: No important events.

8 July 1942

Situation: Opposite armored group and southern wing of Sixth Army the enemy now is soft. He is still holding against right wing of First Panzer Army (von Wietersheim) and left wing of Sixth Army (XXXX Corps), where he is committing three armored brigades and an AT brigade. It is not yet clear to what extent he is disengaging.

At Svoboda and Korotoyak the enemy is again more active. Voronezh is evacuated.

Von Weichs has completed the buildup of his northern front and is repelling the enemy, who is again probing with tanks. Moving up of divisions from the rear is in full progress.

Center: The enemy attack against the northern front of Second Panzer Army has died down. It was, after all, an attack in which between 25 and 30 units were committed against 6½ German divisions. Out of 600 enemy tanks, 289 were knocked out. Operation SEYDLITZ continues to develop desirably. The encircled enemy apparently had not thought of falling back.

Attacks against the corridor from within and without were repelled.

North: Attacks against our corridor from the south and from the north; attacks against Kirishi beaten off.

.   .   .

9 July 1942

Situation: The attack south of the Don continues. Overall impression: The enemy is resisting at Lisichansk and south of Rossosh, and is pulling back in the east. West of the Aidar River there remain apparently only rear guards offering stubborn resistance. It is doubtful whether the enemy wants or is able to make a stand on the Aidar River, since we have already crossed the Boguchar River at Tali. Order to XXXX Corps to thrust along the railroad line Rossosh-Rostov. Elements of the armored units arriving now will drive southeast, down the Don. No new units reported on the enemy side.

Von Weichs's northern front is again under serious enemy attacks. Several new units from the Tula area.

In *Center,* very heavy attacks against the northern front of Second Panzer Army. Again a number of new units with tanks. British tanks out of 1942 production.

We have heavy losses at Byelyi. Gratifying progress in compressing the pocket. No major break-out attempts.

In *North,* only minor fighting.

.   .   .

12 July 1942

Situation: The *southern offensive* develops consistently. The southernmost enemy wing is still holding. West of Voroshilovgrad the enemy is falling back to prepared positions south of the Donets. North of the Donets, 16th, 22d, and 14th Armored divisions have pushed eastward across the Aidar, while farther north the infantry divisions of the southern wing of Sixth Army are continuing their smashing advance.

In Fourth Panzer Army, 3d and 23d Armored divisions have gained further ground to the south; fuel shortage unfortunately has so far held up the arrival of "Grossdeutschland" Division and 24th Armored Division. However, it looks as if Fourth Panzer Army will be sufficiently strong when the time comes to interpose itself on the southeastward line of withdrawal of the enemy's northern wing. Closing to the Don to establish a line for defending the territory gained against the attacks from the north has been mainly completed.

Von Weichs's northern front, in sometimes very bitter fighting, has beaten off the enemy attacking with large masses of armor.

In *Center,* the attacks against the northern front of Second Panzer Army were much weaker today. On the remainder of its front, army group repelled a larger number of local attacks. Operation SEYDLITZ is drawing to its close with impressive figures of prisoners.

In *North,* attacks were repelled at Gruzino and Kirishi.

The Fuehrer situation conference dealt largely with the advance of the assault wing (Fourth Panzer Army).

Subsequently *luncheon at Fuehrer Hq. with General Muños-Grande,* commander of the Spanish division.

.   .   .

13 July 1942

Situation: The southern operation has now really got going. While the enemy is still holding the Taganrog front, he is being compressed by the converging attacks from west and north of von Kleist's Panzer Army and Sixth Army. Fourth Panzer Army is striking in his rear. Its leading column (3rd Armored Division) has already reached Kamensk, while armored and motorized divisions, which now at last can move freely, are closing up.

In von Weichs's sector, intense tank battles northwest of Voronezh in which the enemy was beaten.

In *Center,* the attacks at Below were not resumed today. The enemy is believed to be disengaging in this sector(?). On the other hand, the attacks against XXXXVII Corps went on, and were repelled. Third and Fourth Panzer armies beat off local enemy thrusts. In Ninth Army sector, Operation SEYDLITZ is drawing to an early close.

In *North,* only minor fighting.

Situation conference started with the Fuehrer's expressing his utmost displeasure over the delay in the move to the front of 23d Armored Division (pinned down by an attack from the west), 24th Armored Division, and "Grossdeutschland," as well as of the two other motorized divisions of Fourth Panzer Army. He blames this failure on the fact that 24th Armored Division and "Grossdeutschland," against the Fuehrer's order, were sent into Voronezh, causing a delay that could have been avoided.

The Fuehrer accordingly ruled to relieve commander of AGp.B, and he also wanted to relieve the chief of staff. Only the reminder to the Fuehrer that commander South exclusively was responsible for the ill-conceived proposal for the frontal attack instead of the prepared rear attack on Izyum, and that the former plan had been opposed by his chief of staff, averted a simultaneous change of commander and chief of staff, with all its consequences.

Fourth Panzer Army is placed under the command of AGp.A, with the mission to prevent the enemy's escape to the east, by attacking him in the rear. AGp.B will cover the rear and flank of AGp.A. Orders to this effect have been issued. (Personal evening report to the Fuehrer.)

. . .

15 July 1942

Situation: The battle in the *south* continues, though hampered by thunderstorms. From the west (Ruoff), where the enemy is still holding, progress is slight, but this is of no matter since we want to avoid any unnecessary bloody losses in this sector. The enveloping movement by First and Fourth Panzer armies from the north has reached the Donets at Kamensk. The enemy to the north has been broken into several groups which are being ground up between our armored divisions and infantry divisions sweeping down from the north, in individual and, in some instances, very furious battles.

The buildup of the Don front is completed. New attacks at Voronezh, of less intensity than those preceding, were repelled!

Against the front northwest of Voronezh, only attacks in regiment or battalion strength, which were repelled.

. . .

16 July 1942

Removal of GHq. to Vinnitsa.

Departure from Camp Fritz at 0700. Arrive at Vinnitsa at 1115 (3¼ hours by air from Angerburg). Quarters very well prepared. Good office space for all sections. Good billets. Dispersed layout impairs supervision.

Situation: The enemy is beginning to soften also in the Voroshilovgrad area. In this sector Ruoff is pushing on behind him, while north of the Donets, von Kleist, close on his heels, is driving on Kamensk with armor and infantry, while moving 13th Armored Division and 60th Motorized

Division to Millerovo, as scheduled. North of Kamensk all the way to the Millerovo area, a zone of confused battles in which the enemy elements, squeezed between First Panzer Army from the west and Fourth Panzer Army from the north, are trying to break out in several groups and in all directions. Meanwhile, east of this seething mass, "Grossdeutschland" and 24th Armored Division are racing to the Don without serious check by the enemy.

According to reliable intelligence, we must expect that the enemy will use every available means to hold Stalingrad.

At Korotoyak and Voronezh enemy attacks supported by tanks were repelled. The fighting at Voronezh is very costly for us. In the sector adjoining to the northeast, only weak attacks. But his front, which is formed by unseasoned divisions, will need bolstering by reserves.

In *Center,* the prisoner haul of Operation SEYDLITZ is mounting.

All quiet in *North.* At Gruzino the enemy is even disengaging.

Conference with Gehlen and Heusinger: Preliminary planning for the forthcoming battle of Stalingrad. We shall have to prepare for, perhaps even embark upon, the battle of Stalingrad while we are still fighting the battle of Rostov north and south of the Don. Compute time and strength requirements.

With Wagner (Gen Qu): Same subject. Fuel by air to the lower Don! AT ammunition to the Voronezh front!

17 July 1942

Situation: *South:* Enemy has evacuated Voroshilovgrad. Ruoff's army is pushing on behind the enemy retreating southeast and south. First Panzer Army is encountering enemy resistance at Kamensk, but has formed a bridgehead to the southeast and expanded it to such an extent that the attack in the direction of Shakhty will be launched tomorrow. Infantry is following up closely.

Fourth Panzer Army has reached the Don east of the mouth of the Donets with "Grossdeutschland" and 29th Motorized Division. No bridges. Far bank held by enemy.

Movement of Sixth Army down the Don is proceeding smoothly without enemy opposition.

At Korotoyak enemy attack supported by tanks, air force, and artillery. At Voronezh, attacks from the east and north were repelled. Minor attacks against northern front of Second Army. Tank concentrations.

Center: Confused reports from the Mtsensk area and from left wing of XXXV Corps. Only feeble attacks against the northern front of the army, but apparently major tank concentrations. Elsewhere, little fighting.

North: Against the corridor to II Corps, full-staged attack from north and south, prepared by heavy artillery bombardment and supported by tanks and air force. Notwithstanding some local enemy gains, the attack was repulsed. On the remainder of the front, no major fighting.

. . .

18 July 1942

Situation: In *South,* the encircling operation north of Rostov is proceeding according to plan. The Don east of Rostov is held by the enemy. As a result of heavy thundershowers during the night, troop movements and fuel supply were severely hampered today. On the Don and on the northern front of AGp.B, no major fighting apart from isolated attacks northwest of Voronezh. The enemy continues to move reinforcements from the north and northeast in the direction of Voronezh. According to agent reports, Stalin is doing everything in his power to hold Stalingrad, and to get his troops safely across the Don, which he wants to hold.

In *Center,* no new developments. Something seems to be brewing on the supply road in Fourth Army sector.

In *North,* the attacks against the corridor were resumed with stronger forces. We regained the main line of resistance in a counterattack.

At the situation conference the Fuehrer surprises me by approving my very recommendation which yesterday he rejected in a less-than-gracious manner in favor of a plan which would produce a meaningless concentration on the north bank of the Don at Rostov. And, immediately, his most lordly order is issued, directing a crossing of the Don on a wide front and the initiation of the battle of Stalingrad.

The Fuehrer has also suddenly changed his mind about having Eleventh Army strike across the Kerch Strait. Now it is only the mountain divisions which will be put across there, and that, moreover, only after our pressure on the Rostov front has opened the way to the Taman peninsula.

.   .   .

19 July 1942

Situation: The heavy downpours effectively strangle all movement in the south, and special credit must be given to the infantry, which, leaving its vehicles behind, continued the pursuit of the enemy in many places (Voroshilovgrad, north of Kamensk). On the Taganrog front, the enemy is still holding. On the northern wing of this front, at Voroshilovgrad, he is retreating after thoroughly wrecking all road and rail communications. He has failed in his attempt to form a front on the Donets bend southeast of Kamensk, calculated to protect the retreat from attacks from the northeast. It is here that 22d Armored Division has formed a bridgehead and broken through the enemy, followed by 97th Jaeger Division and 14th Armored Division.

On the Don east of the mouth of the Donets, with Division "Grossdeutschland" turned off, only a smaller bridgehead has been established, at Tsimlyanskaya, opposite a division brought up from the Caucasus. Our 24th Armored Division is still lagging behind; 3d and 23d Armored divisions have linked up and are refueling.

In AGp.B, the southeastern movement south of the Don is making rapid strides in forced infantry marches. Sixteenth Armored Division, 60th Motorized Division, and 3d Motorized Division are following up and eventually will form the spearhead.

At *Voronezh* and to the north, attacks on a reduced scale, but heavy railroad traffic indicates forthcoming serious assaults.

Overall enemy situation: Planned disengagement behind the Don in the Rostov area; feeble attempts to defend the Don east of Rostov; efforts to form a grouping of forces for the protection of Stalingrad. North of the Don, a big gap in which only isolated broken remnants are still hanging on to bridge sites, until we come and drive them away.

With Svoboda as its anchor, the enemy is attempting to build up a front east of the Don. At Voronezh and on the "dry front," concentration of large forces which will be used to breach our line so as to compel us to change the disposition of our forces.

In Center, only weak attack against XXXXVII Corps. Concentrations opposite the Yukhnov salient, which foreshadow attacks. Increased railroad traffic east of the Sukhinichi salient, the purpose of which is not clearly understood. Operation SEYDLITZ is continuing satisfactorily with the new mission to mop up forest area north of the Smolensk-Vyazma road. The enemy is now using minefields. Minefields observed at Velizh and Velikiye Luki on the enemy retreat line would suggest that the enemy is already in the process of regrouping.

North: More attacks from north and south against our "corridor." On the Volkhov, only minor attacks at Kirishi.

Fuehrer situation conference: Greatly upset about the supposedly slow progress in forming the stipulated assault group Taganrog.

The realization of the necessity for pushing Fourth Panzer Army across the Don on a wide front is at last becoming a concrete factor. In view of the dwindling chances for striking an annihilating blow yet at Rostov, such a plan offers the only opportunity indeed for smashing south of the Don all of the enemy forces now in disorderly retreat across the Don. Transfer of 11th Armored Division from AGp.B to Center is authorized.

Lengthy discussion on the objective of Operation BLUECHER (Taman) produces no conclusive results. There is the desire on the one hand to free all but two of the German divisions in the area for Leningrad, while on the other hand BLUECHER should be kept open as an alternative until a clearer picture is had of the development of the situation south of Rostov.

.   .   .

21 July 1942

Situation: Attack against the Lower Don is proceeding well. Our attack from Taganrog and the area to the north is making good progress against enemy rear guards. Our pressure from the north and northeast (Shakhty) is cutting into a totally demoralized enemy ("butchery"). "Grossdeutschland" has been ordered to form a bridgehead. Fourth Panzer Army has established bridgeheads at Tsimlyanskaya and to the west. *Paulus (Sixth Army)* is advancing at a promising rate in the direction of Stalingrad, where the enemy is trying to form a concentration with troops now being moved in from the northwest by rail and on trucks. Exchange of troops on the Don front and follow-up of divisions is proceeding well. At Voronezh, attack repelled at great cost to the enemy. Northwest of Voronezh, sizable enemy attacks breach our line on a 10-km front (3 km deep).

Center: No important developments, only local attacks. At Velizh, the enemy is falling back and evacuating the "southeast tip."

. . .

22 July 1942

Situation: Gratifying progress of the battle for Rostov, with our troops already within the inner defense ring. The Don east of the city has been crossed at four points. The advance of Sixth Army and the buildup of the Don defense front are progressing satisfactorily. At Voronezh, attacks on a minor scale. Northwest of Voronezh, new heavy attacks in the gap opened yesterday, which are still going at this hour.

. . .

23 July 1942

Situation: In *South,* satisfactory progress of the assault on Rostov. East of Rostov only 3d Armored Division could report substantial gains on the southern bank. The enemy facing 29th Motorized Division has been reinforced. The situation, as a result, became so tight for a time that Fourth Panzer Army was considering abandoning the bridgehead. Railroad demolition attempted by the enemy was prevented.

Sixth Army made very satisfactory progress on the Don bend against reinforced enemy attacks (with tanks), lacking coordination. At Voronezh, no major attack, but apparently preparations for a full-scale attack from south and north. Northwest of Voronezh, heavy battles with attacking massed enemy. Our line was breached on a wide front. Counterattacks by 9th Armored Division.

Center: Nothing noteworthy. Enemy regrouping makes attacks appear imminent in several sectors, including northern front of Ninth Army. At Dyemidov, the enemy continues his retreat.

North: Heavy attack at Kirishi, resulting in local penetration. Local attacks by enemy debouching from western part of Leningrad against Jaeckeln's group and Kolpino. Also thrusts against 58th Division on the Ingermanland front.

Fuehrer situation conference: In consequence of the concentration of army ordered by the Fuehrer on 17 July over my opposition, and the diversion of 24th Armored Division to Sixth Army, directed by him on 21 July, it is becoming obvious even to the layman that the Rostov area is crammed with armor which has nothing to do, while the critical outer wing at Tsimlyanskaya is starving for it. I warned emphatically against both these developments.

Now that the result is so palpable, he explodes in a fit of insane rage and hurls the gravest reproaches against the General Staff.

This chronic tendency to underrate enemy capabilities is gradually assuming grotesque proportions and develops into a positive danger. The situation is getting more and more intolerable. There is no room for any serious work. This so-called leadership is characterized by a pathological reacting to the impressions of the moment and a total lack of any understanding of the command machinery and its possibilities.

. . .

24 July 1942

Situation: *Rostov,* for the most part, in our hands; there is only some fighting going on in the eastern quarter. Crossing to the southern bank, where there seems to be no organized opposition, is now in progress. East of Rostov, new successes of "Grossdeutschland" and 3d Armored Division, with only minor gains by 29th Motorized Division.

Sixth Army is in continuous advance toward the Don bend west of Stalingrad. The enemy, still putting up stiff opposition in some places, is being enveloped.

At Voronezh and on the "dry front": Heavy fighting with substantial defensive successes; striking number of tanks knocked out.

Center and North: No major fighting.

. . .

25 July 1942

. . .

Situation: On the lower Don, gratifying advances by AGp.A. In this sector we may discount now any coordinated defense of the Don. What conclusions, however, the enemy will draw from this situation, are not yet apparent. The first phase of the *battle of Stalingrad* consisted in the scattering of enemy elements thrown against our forces; in this process our troops, with tremendous punch, but badly disrupted into groups, battered their way through a bitterly resisting enemy as far as the Don. It remains to be seen whether we shall yet succeed in capturing the Kalach bridge. In any event, it will be necessary after a while for the widely extended components of Sixth Army to close up again. Lack of fuel caused sizable elements of the armored and motorized divisions to lag behind.

At Serafimovich, the outlines of a northern defense group are becoming discernible; it will play its part in the third phase of this big battle, after the fight for Stalingrad is over.

The attacks at Voronezh are not as violent as on the preceding days. At Zemlyansk, very violent attacks against the enemy, who now is apparently putting up a much stiffer fight.

In *Center* and *North,* nothing of importance. The attack in North is postponed once more (to 27 July).

26 July 1942

Situation: On the Don front the enemy apparently intends to make a stand south of Rostov, but our drive is gaining despite heavy counterattacks. Between the Manich and Sal rivers the enemy seems to be softening. North of the Sal he has put two new divisions into line, but is not moving up any more troops from the southwest; as a result, this defensive front will collapse soon. Not enough fuel!

Hard battles west of *Stalingrad.* The enemy, split into four groups, is fighting doggedly and throwing new forces, including much armor, across the Don. There must still be a strong force in Stalingrad itself. Lack of fuel and ammunition!

Attacks at Voronezh repulsed; evidently new concentrations, including many tanks south, east, and north of the city.

27 July 1942

Situation: At Rostov, the enemy is softening under our frontal pressure, but it seems that he is bringing up new forces. Manich crossing captured; dam and bridge blown up. On the eastern wing of AGp.A, the enemy has not been bringing up any new forces, but resistance is still stubborn.

At Stalingrad, the battle of Sixth Army west of the Don is still raging with unabated fury. Apparently the central part of the enemy line, heavily supported by armor, is holding while our wings continue to gain.

All quiet on the Don front. Also at Voronezh and Zemlyansk all is quiet following our defensive battles, but the enemy is massing again.

. . .

28 July 1942

Situation: Battle of Rostov: South of Rostov the enemy is soft. It is not yet clear whether he is falling back south or in a more southeastern direction, with the object of organizing a line of resistance on the Manich River. But this intention has already been foiled by the push of First Panzer Army across the Manich.

Unfortunately, Fourth Panzer Army is still lagging behind with its left wing at Tsimlyanskaya, which has enabled the enemy to the south to build up a front facing west, where he is now attacking even with tanks.

Battle of Stalingrad: Due to lack of fuel and ammunition, Sixth Army was unable to attack. After suffering a defeat in his violent attacks (nine new armored brigades), the enemy appears to be retreating behind the Don.

Relative quiet at Voronezh and Zemlyansk.

On the front of Second Panzer Army, certain indications suggest the formation of a substantial armored group in the Chern area.

. . .

30 July 1942

Situation: The situation continues to develop well for *AGp.A*. Before Seventeenth Army, the enemy is falling back along the entire line; on the eastern wing he is in wild rout (First Panzer Army). Fourth Panzer Army has reached Proletarskaya and pushed ahead to the Manich bridge farther south. The attack on Tsimlyanskaya will get under way tomorrow.

In AGp.B, a wild battle is raging in Sixth Army sector inside the Don bend west of Stalingrad; we do not have yet an accurate picture of its development. Sixth Army's striking power is paralyzed by ammunition and fuel supply difficulties. Apparently the northern front (hill has bastion) is gaining in importance (enemy is constructing eight bridges in area). At Voronezh and Zemlyansk, only minor local attacks.

In AGp. *Center,* heavy attacks with partly fresh forces at Rzhev; enemy penetration is carried 6 km. We lost several medium and light batteries. On the northeastern corner of Sixth Army, a diversionary attack with some tanks seems to have been repelled. All quiet on the rest of the front. In Second Army sector, the situation at Chern is still obscure. The enemy Panzer Army observed in that sector may be intended as a new assault group, but may as likely be a feint.

In AGp. *North,* only minor attacks from the north at Kirishi, and local attacks at Leningrad.

At the situation conference, Jodl is given the word: He announces pompously that the fate of the Caucasus will be decided at Stalingrad and that, in view of the importance of the battle, it would be necessary to divert forces from AGp.A to AGp.B, if possible, south of the Don. This is a dressed-up version of my own proposal, which I submitted to the Fuehrer six days ago when Fourth Panzer Army struck across the Don. At that time, though, no one in the illustrious company of the OKW seemed to be able to grasp its significance. He goes on to explain that First Panzer Army must at once wheel south and southwest to cut off the enemy now being pushed back step by step from the Don by Seventeenth Army, before he reaches the Caucasus.

That is rankest nonsense. This enemy is running for dear life and will be in the northern foothills of the Caucasus a good piece ahead of our armor, and then we are going to have another unhealthy congestion of forces before the enemy front.

First Panzer Army must strike southeast for the Kuban knee north of Armavir. The development of the situation in the course of the day strikingly corroborates my view.

Phone talks with commanders of AGps. A (List) and B (von Weichs). The former wants "Grossdeutschland" to remain on his left flank, which requires no order since it follows automatically from the transportation situation; the latter is sharply complaining about failure of supply.

. . .

1 August 1942

Situation: South of the Don, resistance to Ruoff's advance by enemy rear guards is slightly stiffening; whereas it is weak on the front of von Kleist, who is making good headway. Hoth, transferred to AGp.B, is making satisfactory gains against enemy resistance. No important change in the great picture of the battle west of Stalingrad. Counterattacks weaker. Our troops cannot attack for lack of fuel and ammunition. All quiet at Voronezh and Zemlyansk.

In AGp. Center, attacks against Ninth Army (eastern front and Rzhev), which cause local difficulties; the enemy is also launching a local containing attack against the western front.

. . .

2 August 1942

Situation: South of the Don resistance is stiffening in some places before Ruoff's center and right wings. Before his left wing and before von Kleist, all opposition has ceased and the enemy is streaming to the south and southeast.

Hoth has made good strides. His spearhead has driven into an infantry division just detrained from the Far East. Fuel situation in AGp.A continues tight.

In AGp.B, Sixth Army is on the defensive due to failure of supply. The enemy is reinforcing here as also on the northern front. At Voronezh and Zemlyansk, concentrations and movements.

. . .

3 August 1942

Situation: The day is marked by the thrusts of First Panzer Army to and across the Kuban north of Armavir, and to Voroshylovsk, as well as by the attacks of Fourth Panzer Army on and beyond Kotelnikovski. On the other fronts, only unimportant local engagements.

At the Fuehrer situation conference, sharp issue is taken over the volunteer problem. He vetoes any increase in the numbers of army volunteers from the age groups 1924 and 1925. He gives as grounds for his refusal that these young men, coming from the genuinely national Socialist elements of the population, failed to find in the army what they were looking for and so preferred the air force (conservatism of large portions of the Army Officers' Corps, e.g., church matters, "standards of honor," etc.).

Lieutenant Colonel Mueller-Hillebrand on current questions of organization.

New Russian Units—Winter 1941/1942, 3.8.1942
In winter 1941/1942 (1 October–1 March) newly created:

	Rifle Divs.	Rifle Brigs.	Cav. Divs.	Armd. Brigs.
October	15	12	2	2
November	9	13	—	—
December	11	9	—	3
January	20	6	—	8
February	5	6	—	4
Total	60	46	2	17

Since February, no new units (officer shortage).

New Russian units from May 1942 and enemy intelligence from 3 August 1942. *Rifle divisions:* From our estimates of early May and from information from foreign sources, we believed that the enemy could organize 60 divisions before the muddy period. In reality came: May 27, June 5, July 54 = 86 rifle divisions, of these 8 in the Caucasus were known; 9 from Izyum and Kerch, which were only partially beaten. As a result, 69 *new units* remain. The expected number is, therefore, exceeded by 9.

Sources: Higher use of women (Russia 60 percent, Germany 41 percent); use of the 1924 group. Any new units can come only from these resources. The 1924 group brings 1,400,000. If one takes 50 percent for troop duty, one can create 34 new rifle divisions. (One can probably expect 30 divisions.) Equipment issue!

The 1925 group is partially called up. Doubtful that sufficient equipment on hand. Tanks: Certain to have 56 new armored brigades in July; losses, 3,900 tanks. Reported to Fuehrer on 3.8.1942.

Enemy intelligence:

30.7.:

1. In Tiflis, English tanks, AT, and clothing (via Basra).

2. Voroshilov is in command of the Caucasus from Krasnodar.

30/31.7.: Reputed reinforcement for Taman peninsula; movement from Anapa toward northeast.

29.7.: Japanese military attaché (via Stockholm): West of Stalingrad, three armies. Divisional numbers very weak.
Unified army leadership no longer certain. Army groups operate independently without coherence.

26.7.: Agent radios: Troop transports via Saratow toward the west: Industrial evacuation to the east.

28.7.: From Near East, three divisions to the west (terminated on 18.7.). Some segments have arrived already.

Annexes:

a. Stalin order: "Attrition!"

b. Organization of an air-landing brigade for commitment in rear area. (Question of the winter landing quality of our aircraft!)

Russian tank production, 3.8.1942:

1. OKW reports, based on the newest information: Total tank production:

	June	**July**	**August**
KW	120 (cut 50 percent because of Stalingrad evacuation)	170 (increased at cost of T34)	220
T34	520	400	280
T60	350	350	350
Monthly production	990	920	850

2. *Foreign deliveries,* January–July: 2,800; i.e., monthly average, 400.

3. *Results:* In July alone, 3,900 tanks lost. The surplus of the months January to July is not enough to cover these losses. The same will be true in August. By continuing this same production, the Russians can either resupply the battered units or, not doing that, organize thirty brigades or do some of both.

4 August 1942

Situation: In AGp.A, it looks as if the enemy is going to fall back now also on Ruoff's front. To what extent this move is deliberate, in order to reach the Caucasus line, is still a question. Movements to Novocherkassk and Tulpa. *Von Kleist* has secured a bridgehead across the Kuban, but his troops must close up before he can push ahead on Maikop.

In AGp.B, Hoth has made the most of his opportunities and is advancing at great speed overrunning local opposition in his path. Only minor fighting on the front west of the Don. On the northern front of XIV and VIII Corps, the enemy is reinforcing. Heavy column movements and railroad traffic northwest of Stalingrad. All quiet at Voronezh.

Center: All quiet on the southern wing; opposite Schmidt's group, the enemy is obviously reducing his forces. Very heavy penetration on the eastern front of Ninth Army in direction of Zubstov (the enemy apparently is attacking with seven infantry divisions and one armored brigade, supported by ample artillery). Fifth, 2nd, and 1st Armored divisions and 102d Infantry Division under XXXIX Corps Hq. are being committed against this thrust. The northern front of Ninth Army at Rzhev has beaten off new heavy attacks. Behind the front facing Ninth Army in the east, unusual activity, heavy railroad movements on Toropets.

North: Only local attacks, but there is great unrest in several enemy sectors, which indicates that the corridor between X and II Corps will be attacked again.

. . .

5 August 1942

. . .

Situation: *AGp. A:* Ruoff finds weakening resistance and keeps pushing on. Von Kleist, in rapid advance, has pushed far to the southeast. Bridgehead across the Kuban River. *AGp.B:* Ruoff has made good headway against newly arrived enemy forces. Situation is somewhat confused on his eastern flank. Paulus: Heavy attacks against XIV Corps from the south. On the northern front of XIV and VIII Corps, the enemy is apparently concentrating forces for major attacks. On the rest of the front, only minor local fighting.

Center: The attack against the eastern front of Ninth Army seems to have resulted in a very wide and deep penetration. Countermeasures have been undertaken. The attacks against the northern front of Ninth Army were on the whole beaten off.

North: No important developments.

6 August 1942

Situation: *AGp.A:* The enemy continues to fall back to the Caucasus before Ruoff's advance. Many bridges captured are intact. Resistance continues on the Kuban knee. But south of the knee, von Kleist is already on the west bank of the Kuban and advancing on Maikop.

AGp.B: Hoth is in heavy fighting on the railroad line south of Stalingrad. Paulus is fighting stern defensive battles on the northern front. The Hungarians let the Russians recross the Don! In Second Army sector, mainly quiet.

Center: The enemy seems to be falling back on the northern front of Second Panzer Army. Very difficult situation on the eastern front of Ninth Army, where the enemy has penetrated to Zubstov, and his drive for Sihevsk is checked only with great effort. All his attacks at Rzhev have been repulsed. On the western front of Ninth Army and at Dyemidov, local but costly battles.

North: Local fighting flares up at Kirishi and Leningrad, but for the time being there are no signs of another major Russian attack.

7 August 1942

Situation: *AGp.A* reports good gains. Deep penetration into the Caucasus on the right flank.

In *AGp.B,* heavy fighting in Hoth's group. The attack on the pocket in Paulus's sector achieved full success in the afternoon: eight infantry divisions and ten armored brigades are said to be wiped out. Elsewhere, enemy activity has fallen off. All quiet at Voronezh.

Center: In the deep penetration in Ninth Army sector, the crisis seems to be over. Attack against 342d Division repelled.

. . .

9 August 1942

Situation: *South:* Krasnodar and Maikop taken. The impression is increasingly gaining that the Russian forces south of the Don are rapidly disintegrating and that only the units compressed in the northwest Caucasus are making an organized effort to escape yet to the coast. Fourth Panzer Army has passed to the defensive in the face of intense enemy pressure. The defense line has been taken back in some places.

The attack of *Sixth Army* is progressively squeezing the enemy pocket. On the northeastern front, small-scale enemy attack. In the Hungarian sector, the situation is not yet restored, especially south of Voronezh. *Second Army* has improved the defensive position on the northern edge of Voronezh; apart from that, no major engagements.

Center: Operation WHIRLWIND postponed one day because of bad weather.

On the front of Third Panzer Army, increasing signs of an early enemy attack. The heavy penetration into the front of Ninth Army was not widened to any considerable extent today, despite the enemy's efforts. At Rzhev no important combat actions.

. . .

11 August 1942

Situation: *AGp.A:* Enemy resistance is stiffening. Our troops are closing up. *AGp.B:* Sixth Army has liquidated the pocket and started regrouping for continuance of the offensive. Hoth is closing up. Local battles. Second Army relatively quiet. Only on the northern front is attack supported by many tanks. The situation on the Hungarian front, which gives ground in every enemy attack, is getting increasingly unhealthy.

Center: WHIRLWIND launched with good initial success. Opposite the southern wing of Third Panzer Army, enemy attack appears to be in preparation. Fierce fighting in the salient in Ninth Army and at Rzhev. Severe strain on our troops.

.   .   .

12 August 1942

Situation: In *AGp.A,* enemy resistance is increasing further on the northern edge of the Caucasus (Krasnodar, etc.).

AGp.B. Regrouping for the next moves in the offensive proceeds without major enemy interference. Enemy reinforcements on Hoth's front. Intelligence reports suggest that the enemy is concentrating on holding the eastern part of the Caucasus, Astrakhan, and Stalingrad.

Heavy attacks at Voronezh and on the northern front were beaten off.

In *Center,* the first difficulties have arisen in Operation WHIRLWIND and must be mastered before the way will be open for 11th and 9th Armored divisions. Apparently, the enemy in this sector, while still at his former strength, was in the process of regrouping. Agent reports speak of a strong armored group around Tula, which is scheduled to attack on the front Mtsensk-Orel. In *Third Panzer Army,* the enemy seems to be ready to attack on the front of XX Corps. In the big salient the situation continues fortunately! It is quite obvious that the enemy is making every effort to crack the two prongs of the eastward offensive. The attacks have let up in the direction of the Rzhev rail-road.

.   .   .

13 August 1942

Situation: No important change in *South,* only local gains. It is becoming increasingly evident that the enemy intends to hold the northern Caucasus and is forming a group at and to the south of the Terek River to defend the southern Caucasus. At Voronezh and to the northwest, a stern, but successful defensive battle. Operation WHIRLWIND is slowly gaining ground, but enemy opposition is not yet broken. The possibility is still strong that the enemy might attack either at Mtsensk or around Yukhnov. In the sector of 3d Armored Division, the attack started today, as expected. Local penetration.

In the big salient the situation has become a little easier, but there is still a possibility of new and more severe crises. It seems that the enemy is not bringing up any sizable reinforcements. He is diverting to this front merely some units from the adjoining sectors. Our own losses, notably in tanks, are highly unpleasant.

.   .   .

14 August 1942

Situation: *AGp.A* makes good strides despite violent resistance by enemy rear guards. In *AGp.B,* preparations for the next moves of the offensive. At Voronezh and to the northwest, successful defensive battle against several hundred tanks.

In *Center,* very serious situation. Operation WHIRLWIND has made gains, but is approaching its objective only slowly in very difficult, fortified terrain and against very strong opposition.

In Third Panzer Army, deep penetration on a wide front.

On Ninth Army front, the enemy is shifting his main weight to the western sector of the salient and to Rzhev. Here, 14th Motorized Division and 256th Infantry had to be taken back.

In *North,* fighting as in the preceding days.

2015. **Von Kluge** gives a very grave picture of the situation. Talk with OKW. Result: Two groups (one from south, one from the west) and two groups (from the west) are transferred to Center. Also 72d Division, operating against Leningrad, is diverted to Center, in addition to ''Grossdeutschland.'' Fifth Mountain Division remains in north.

.   .   .

15 August 1942

Situation: Attacks in *AGp.A* are making satisfactory progress. In *AGp.B,* Paulus has had a good offensive success. Defensive success at Voronezh.

Center: Slow and struggling advance in Operation WHIRLWIND. In Third Panzer Army, an enemy penetration compels us to take back parts of the front. In Ninth Army, on the whole satisfactory defensive success. Situation eased by enemy regrouping. Difficulties have apparently developed directly east of Rzhev.

. . .

16 August 1942

. . .

Situation: South of the Don, slow but steady advances against rearguard opposition in the mountains. The enemy in the northern Caucasus evidently is retreating to the Black Sea. At Ordzhonikidze we must expect heavier resistance.

New forces apparently moving from the direction of Baku on Makhachkala.

At Stalingrad Paulus's attack is continuing successfully.

At and north of Voronezh, the front is fairly quiet. Local attacks beaten back. Own counterattack on the northern front.

Center: In Second Panzer Army, only very slight advances, with high casualties. Third Panzer Army in difficult situation due to enemy penetration. Operational danger unlikely. Ninth Army: Very tight situation at Rzhev. Hard to say what the outcome will be.

North: Attacks against Sixteenth Army, as in the past days. In Eighteenth Army sector, rather quiet.

. . .

17 August 1942

Situation: *Caucasus:* Slow advances in the west; highest part of the mountains has been reached in center; enemy opposition apparently is stiffening in the east.

Stalingrad: Hoth's and Paulus's attacks are making good strides. Front against Paulus has been reinforced with good troops.

Von Salmuth: Only local attacks. Apparently preparations for repetition of attacks west and south of Voronezh.

Schmidt: Attack brought to a standstill, but is apparently pinning down large enemy forces of good quality.

Reinhardt: Chief threat over for the moment, but more attacks must be expected. Bad weather.

Model: Quieter day. Enemy apparently exhausted. Is attacking in uncoordinated local groups. New forces moving up from the adjoining sectors.

North: Only local fighting on the usual scale.

Fuehrer report: Discussion of the projected formation of a Romanian army group on both sides of Stalingrad. No decision yet about Ostashkov. Cord present. Recalled to his division (''Grossdeutschland'').

18 August 1942

Situation: In South, slow advances both in the Caucasus and at Stalingrad against growing enemy resistance. All quiet on the Don and at Voronezh.

In *Center,* Operation WHIRLWIND has not yet been able to get really going. Very stiff opposition, difficult terrain. In Third Panzer Army and Ninth Army, enemy attacks have temporarily let up a little.

In *North,* decision to call off ''creeper.''

Local attack against Sixteenth and Eighteenth armies, as in the past days.

General Hauffe (Bucharest): We dismiss the planned formation of a Romanian army group on Don and Volga.

. . .

19 August 1942

Situation: In the *Caucasus,* only local advances. At Stalingrad, Hoth has successfully opened his attack; Paulus is regrouping and expanding his bridgehead. Difficult situation on the left wing. On the rest of the Don front, all quiet.

In *Center,* no important advances by Second Panzer Army.

Situation in Third Panzer Army slightly easier. —In Ninth Army sector, the enemy appears to be very exhausted.

North: Local attacks as usual, this time also on the Neva, where fast, small boats were used.

. . .

20 August 1942

Situation: On the whole, no change along the entire front. AGp. Center reports that Second Panzer Army cannot attack unless reinforced by two or three divisions.

. . .

22 August 1942

Situation: The general picture is unchanged. Details: AGp.A reports small local ground gains. Our flag has been hoisted on Mount Elbrus. Closing up of von Kleist's forces is a slow process in these vast spaces. Hoth's Panzer Army scores good tactical successes, but also begins to show signs of fatigue. On the attacking wing of Paulus's army, preparations for the tank assault (bridges, etc.) are progressing despite violent enemy counterattacks; on the northern wing, the enemy attacking in great force was beaten off. In the Italian sector, a penetration on the right wing was contained; otherwise, no major fighting in this and in the Hungarian sector. The same applies to Second Army.

In Second Panzer Army, very heavy enemy counterattacks with a large number of tanks against the right wing. Deep penetrations. Still all quiet in Third Panzer Army, but we must expect heavy attacks with newly arrived reinforcements. In Ninth Army, the enemy attacking our weakened lines at Zubstov and Rzhev with very strong forces scored substantial ground gains.

. . .

At the Fuehrer Hq.: First a personal talk with *Field Marshal von Kluge* (commander of Center) on the plan of attack for Second Panzer Army.

At the situation conference following, Operation WHIRLWIND is being diluted from a full-stage offensive to a containing action.

The realization has been driven home that nothing could be gained in that sector anymore, yet the notion persists that we cannot afford to let our grip go from the strong enemy forces assembled here.

23 August 1942

Situation: No significant change in the Caucasus. At Stalingrad, Paulus has made a surprise thrust across the Don with XIV Corps and reached the Volga north of the city. The battles on the left wing of the army are going back and forth. All is relatively quiet on the Don front all the way to Voronezh. In Second Army, violent attacks against the eastern flank have resulted in local penetrations. In Reinhardt's sector (Third Panzer Army) the air force has very effectively smashed enemy troop concentrations. The situation at Rzhev, where the enemy has been attacking heavily, is still most grave.

In North, the situation at the front is unchanged, and there are more signs of an impending enemy attack.

Fuehrer situation conferences: Order to direct 16th Motorized Division of First Panzer Army against Elista.

.   .   .

24 August 1942

Situation: No important change in Seventeenth Army; local advances at Novo-cherkassk. No major change in First Panzer Army.

Fourth Panzer Army has beaten the enemy on its front and is regrouping for further attacks to the north. Fuel difficulties. *Sixth Army:* XIV Corps, which had broken through to the Volga, was for a time driven into a bad corner by enemy attacks from the north. The situation eased after the arrival of reinforcements. Left wing of army is kept under pressure by enemy attacks.

Don front, no change apart from local attacks.

In *Center,* heavy attacks against Second Panzer Army (eastern flank), Third Panzer Army (penetrations), and Ninth Army, where enemy made local gains. The situation remains difficult despite arrival of 72d Infantry Division. On the eastern front, an attack on Byelyi was beaten off.

In *North,* the picture is the same as in the past few days, also as regards railroad traffic.

Fuehrer situation conference: Sharp clash over interpretation of the situation at Rzhev, where I perceive a distinct danger of attrition for our forces. The newly arrived elements of Division "Grossdeutschland" are released as reserves for the Byelyi sector.

.   .   .

25 August 1942

.   .   .

Situation: No change in the Caucasus. At Stalingrad, Hoth has come up against well-fortified positions. Enemy harassing his deep eastern flank. Paulus is slowly exploiting his offensive success. Attacks against his western wing are repelled. Deep penetration in the Italian sector. Rest of AGp.B front, on the whole, quiet.

In *Center,* very heavy attacks against Second and Third Panzer armies and Ninth Army continue without distinct gains by the enemy.

In *North,* situation unchanged. Very heavy railroad movements toward our front. The enemy is moving his Hq. forward toward the Volkhov front.

. . .

26 August 1942

Situation: *Caucasus* unchanged. At Stalingrad, the situation is grave due to counterattacks by numerically superior enemy. Our divisions are all below strength. Severe nervous strain on the responsible commanders. Von Wietersheim wanted to withdraw his advanced outpost on the Volga, but was prevented by Paulus.

Everything went wrong in the Italian sector on the right wing. Counter-measures have been instituted.

Center surprises us in the morning report with the announcement that Schmidt has taken back the front. It is quite upsetting that we should have another case of voluntary abandonment of a position without advance notice clearly stating such an intention. Army group states in its defense that mention had been made of the matter. That's true enough, but the intention as such was not reported. Moreover, such a step is tactically wrong because it removes the pressure maintained on the enemy.

In Reinhardt's sector, successful counterattacks have improved the situation. A somewhat quieter day in Model's sector until evening, when another major enemy attack is launched south of Zubstov.

In *North,* signs are increasing that the Russians will soon strike south of Lake Ladoga.

27 August 1942

Situation: No important change in south. Situation at Stalingrad consolidated.

The penetration in the Italian sector turns out to be not so serious. Nevertheless, 298th Division has been diverted to it and Alpini troops are being rapidly moved there.

663 29 August 1942

The Voronezh front seems to be quiet. Elements of the enemy assault forces on this front have appeared at Stalingrad.

Center: In Second Panzer Army enemy attacks were weaker than yesterday. All quiet in Third Panzer Army. In Ninth Army sector, enemy is regrouping in the area south of Rzhev, where more attacks are expected.

North: The anticipated attack south of Lake Ladoga has started. The attacks on the whole were repelled; only minor local penetrations. On the rest of the front, no change in the normal picture.

. . .

28 August 1942

Situation: In *AGp.A,* local advances into the northern Caucasus.

AGp.B: Situation easier in Sixth Army; regrouping in Fourth Panzer Army. Something is brewing on the left wing of Sixth Army. All quiet on the rest of the front of B. Second Army is withdrawing an increasing number of frontline divisions into reserve.

Center: Heavy attacks against Second Panzer Army and the northern flank of the penetration in Ninth Army were beaten off.

In *North,* a very distressing penetration south of Lake Ladoga. Also, preparations for an attack on the Volkhov front.

. . .

29 August 1942

Situation: Local improvements in the Caucasus, especially north of Novocherkassk.

Fourth Panzer Army has opened the attack with very good success. An attack by Sixth Army strengthened the link with XIV Corps. Trouble is beginning to develop on its left wing. In the Italian sector, the situation has not been aggravated, but it has not been set right either.

All quiet on the Hungarian and the Second Army front.

Center: Second Panzer Army has again succeeded in repelling strong attacks. The enemy suffers heavy tank losses again. No important enemy attacks against Third Panzer Army. Also, Ninth Army has had an easier day. Apparently enemy is regrouping for an attack to the west. Enemy air activity has fallen off.

North: The counterattack to liquidate the enemy penetration has started off well. No report yet of the result. Tiger tanks could not be committed; are held up at bridges which cannot support such loads.

General Ochsner: Reports on his tour to AGp.A.

Fuehrer situation conference: Very peevish about the conduct of operations by AGp.A. —Talk with Field Marshal List by phone to find out what could be done to get the offensive going again.

Phone talk with Field Marshal von Kluge on antipartisan measures and moves to close the gap. Deny request for commitment of "Grossdeutschland" for time being, but authorize alerting of division.

30 August 1942

Situation: On the northern wing of AGp.A, advances toward Novocherkassk. In B, good progress by Fourth Panzer Army. —A quieter day today for Sixth Army, but a strong attack against its northern wing seems to be preparing. Rest of the front of B rather quiet.

In *Center,* Second and Third Panzer armies repulsed attacks. In Ninth Army, trouble again at Zubstov and north of Rzhev. "Grossdeutschland" released for commitment.

In *North,* the enemy continued his attacks south of Lake Ladoga without making significant gains, but neither did our attack achieve any important advances. The forces set aside for the Leningrad offensive are increasingly diverted to this sector to repel the enemy drive.

Today's conferences with Fuehrer were again the occasion of abusive reproaches against the military leadership abilities of the highest commands. He charges them with intellectual conceit, mental nonadaptability, and utter failure to grasp essentials.

. . .

31 August 1942

Situation: *In A,* substantial progress at Anapa and Novocherkassk. On remainder of the mountain front, no change. In First Panzer Army, hard fighting for the Terek crossing.

In B, very gratifying progress by Fourth Panzer Army. Sixth Army has relatively quiet day in spite of local enemy counterattacks. No important events in the other sectors of the Don front.

In *Center,* reports actions only in Ninth Army, where violent attacks continued west of Zubstov and at Rzhev.

In *North*, the enemy penetration in the bottleneck seems for the most part to have been checked. Counterattack is under preparation.

Conference with Field Marshal List at Fuehrer Hq.:

Decision: Transfer and earliest commitment of the Romanian 3d Mountain Division with the mission to advance on the coastal road from Novocherkassk.

All possible means must be used to reach the coast around Tulpa with maximum speed. Concentration in that sector of all mountain battalions still available. All forces of mountain corps, apart from small detachments guarding passes, will be concentrated in 4th Mountain Division sector, in the High Caucasus.

Chief mission of First Panzer Army will be to destroy the enemy in the Terek bend.

Use Turkish battalions and 2d Romanian Mountain Division to liquidate the enemy remnants on the mountain slopes.

All available forces, especially armor, will strike for Groznyy, to seize the oil fields.

1 September 1942

Situation: *In A*, progress at Novocherkassk. Otherwise, no change. *In B*, good advances at Stalingrad; the situation on the Italian right wing is improved by a German attack. Otherwise, all quiet.

In Center, curious quiet along the entire front.

The enemy has regrouped his forces in great depth.

In *North*, the enemy is pressing northward against the Ladoga penetration. No change in the situation on the rest of the front.

At Fuehrer Hq.: *Field Marshal von Kluge.* Discussion of the situation in his army group. He is promised transfer of 95th Division. Straightening of the front for winter is rejected. Presentation of decorations.

Notes of the von Kluge discussion with Hitler at 1300 on 1.9.1942.

Von Kluge:

Situation: The attack on Schmidt resolved by our attack; will pull 9th Armored Division out in next few days; subsequently 11th (only after pulling back to winter positions on the heights, 2 to 3 km in the rear). —

Fuehrer agrees with understanding that this will take place when position is properly prepared.

Fuehrer:

    a. *Enemy's relative strength:* Between 160,000,000 and 175,000,000. Lost 55,000,000 last year, 45,000 this year. In sum, 100,000,000 lost. Stalin order.

       Military strength: We: 1,400,000 total losses. Enemy: 3,000,000 prisoners in previous year, 1,000,000 this year, totaling 4,000,000. Dead: 4 to 5 million (admitted by Stalin); low estimate 3,000,000. Wounded (we have 60 percent recoveries): two or three times as many as we (we have 1,000,000), which means 2 to 3 million. Total enemy losses: 8 to 10 million. In the east the enemy has 35 divisions [?]. Ten Hungarian divisions, 11 Italian divisions, 24 Romanian, 24 Finnish brigades equals 60.

       Russian divisions of differing value: Division with infantry regiments of 600 to 800 men has normally 7,000.

       Army Group Center has suffered approximately 100,000 men, more than 100,000 prisoners. One can see how the enemy makes sacrifices. Essential to train troops in holding on; nothing can be given up without a struggle.

    b. *Ninth and 11th Armored divisions must be pulled back* in the area of the road! Four to six Porsche tanks for patrolling that road.

    c. *Army Group Center* should receive twelve rifle battalions. For partisan actions? First the partisans, then as assault troops. Each battalion should have an assault gun battery. Four French battalions can be evacuated.

Von Kluge reports: On the road a division without a regiment equals four battalions.

Fuehrer: Porsche tanks, 60 tons, capable of moving through snow (up to 50 cm of snow).

Von Kluge: Front on the road is too thin.

Fuehrer: Will undertake the Kirov affair with 9th and 11th Armored divisions.

Von Kluge: By 3d Armored Division, no great concern; with the 9th Armored Division and its currently available units, one can do nothing. Harsh wear and tear.

Fuehrer: Problem of toughness! The enemy will need his strength sooner than we do. —"Grossdeutschland," "Adolf Hitler," and "Wiking" are guard units which are used for brief crises. So long as the enemy suffers losses in his approach, let him run; someone will collapse; not us. By Petersburg [Leningrad] six to eight divisions are free.

Von Kluge: Forty-eight thousand men lost.

Fuehrer: World War I circumstances. Heavy barrages. Two points of view: Into the west a second front cannot be permitted; in Norway nothing will happen. Submarine war. Ostashkov should take place in winter. Ninety-fifth Division to Rzhev. Tanks for von Kluge.

. . .

4 September 1942

. . .

Situation: Advances on the Taman peninsula, at Novocherkassk and on the Terek River; also gratifying progress at Stalingrad. Stern defensive battles in Second and Third Panzer armies and Ninth Army.

Less reassuring picture in the XVI Corps salient.

Now 24th Division also is being thrown away into that defensive effort.

. . .

6 September 1942

Situation: Novorcherkassk taken. Otherwise, no change. At Stalingrad, very heavy attacks were beaten off. General situation on the entire front relatively quiet and without major changes.

. . .

7 September 1942

Situation: The attacking wing reports slight advances on the Terek River, and good progress at Stalingrad, where enemy attacks against the northern flank have become weaker. Nothing special on the remainder of the front. Enemy rather quiet.

.   .   .

8 September 1942

Situation: Opposition near Novocherkassk, and advances at Stalingrad: There are no changes.

Lack of progress in AGp.A is a bitter disappointment for the Fuehrer. Cuttingly reproaches the army group command and the generals as a whole. Jodl, on the return from his visit to List, proposes not only not to advance mountain corps any farther, but, on the contrary, to take it back. The effect is annoyance of the highest degree.

.   .   .

Notes of a telephone report by von Greiffenberg on 8.9.1942.

Fuehrer has refused to issue an order:

When the Supreme commander—who is incomprehensible and also may understand later—is convinced that he cannot organize a strong thrust by the 4th Mountain Division along the coast, he should leave it alone.

He should observe how the mountain corps brings everything together and realize the sense of the assigned mission on the briefest time frame.

The required strength and acceleration demanded for continuing the attack on Tulpa cannot be made dependent on increasing the corps' strength.

A directive telegram will follow.

9 September 1942

Situation: At Stalingrad slow advances again. Rest of the front quiet, except in Ninth Army sector, where the enemy has achieved penetration, west of Zubstov, and on the Neva front, where heavy attacks were beaten off.

Division "Grossdeutschland" has been released for a counterattack at Zubstov.

Talk with Minister Speer on collaboration before we go into Fuehrer situation conference.

1630.   Field Marshal Keitel comes to see me. List must resign. Hints of more changes in high posts, including mine.

. . .

15 September 1942

Casualties: 22 June 1941–10 September 1942 in the east:

Killed	336,349	including	12,385 officers
Wounded	1,226,941	including	34,525 officers
Missing	75,990	including	1,056 officers
Total	1,637,280 [*sic*]	including	47,966 officers

Situation: No progress in *AGp.A.* von Kleist must take back his assault wing, but relieves his eastern flank.

In *AGp.B*, gratifying advances inside Stalingrad. Heavy attack against Voronezh from north and west. Penetration from the west.

Center: Enemy attacks getting weaker at Zubstov and Rzhev. Otherwise, all quiet.

. . .

18 September 1942

Situation: In the Caucasus, on the whole no change. On the Terek River we score defensive successes; also on the eastern wing. New gains inside Stalingrad. Big defensive success north of the city against major enemy attack (150 tanks).

All quiet on the rest of the Don front. Voronezh continues to be under heavy attack from north and east.

Rest of the front quiet because of bad weather.

. . .

19 September 1942

Situation: Local advances in von Kleist's sector and inside Stalingrad. Otherwise, no fighting along the entire front, which is immobilized by bad weather in its northern two-thirds.

. . .

20 September 1942

Situation: Good progress in von Kleist's sector on the Terek River. In Stalingrad we are beginning to feel the approaching exhaustion of our assault troops.

At Voronezh dive-bomber sweeps have greatly relieved the situation. Attacks against the northern front were beaten off.

The remainder of the front is quiet in consequence of bad weather and waterlogged roads. Something is brewing at Nelidovo.

. . .

21 September 1942

Situation: Advances in von Kleist's sector and inside Stalingrad. Von Manstein has launched the main attack with some initial successes. All quiet on the rest of the front.

. . .

22 September 1942

Situation: Only minor changes at Stalingrad. Some progress in von Manstein's attack. Otherwise, no change.

No presentation of reports. Animated phone conversation with Field Marshal von Kluge, who all of a sudden does not believe in the Nelidovo project and wants to use 96th Division and Ninth Armored Division for the attack on Osuga.

24 September 1942

After situation conference, farewell by the Fuehrer. (My nerves are worn out; also his nerves are no longer fresh. We must part. Necessity for educating the General Staff in fanatical faith in The Idea. He is determined to enforce his will also into the army.)

After 1700. My farewell to the several groups: General Staff. —OQu. —Arms chiefs. —Individual callers.

General Halder left his office a tired, dispirited man. In many ways he represented a generation of soldiers who had served an earlier time while struggling in a different era. He had grown to maturity, in both peace and war, as a monarchist who found order, integrity, character, responsibility, patriotism, and many other traits as life directive. The early years of the Nazi adventure provided an exhilarating prospect, which he quickly discarded under the press of events. After a difficult moment of doubt and resistance, he accepted national duty and obedience as his personal guideposts.

Halder's departure marked the watershed between his generation, imprisoned by the experience of the past, and the new individuals, misdirected by the Nazis. Halder understood that struggle better than most of his contemporaries. He likened many of his soldierly associates to the ancient Egyptian scarab (dung beetle) which survived through dedication to singular purpose.

With Halder's dismissal the entire direction of the conflict adjusted course. His professional, traditional sense of both history and military need foundered in the debris of National Socialism. As well the orderly structure of conducting the conflict shifted to the whims, dreams, and fantasies of a crazed demagog.

This transfer from an orderly, understandable situation became an emotional, chaotic organization. Hitler desired none of Halder's experience, understanding, or character. He wanted unquestioning obedience. As a result he jump-promoted the recently promoted Brigadier General Kurt Zeitzler, an officer known for his ambition and dedication. Zeitzler had a reputation for brutality toward subordinates and subservience to superiors. He was a useful representative of the new order.

Clearly General Franz Halder served his country, his profession, and his family to the best of his abilities. Unfortunately his patriotic efforts also made him a "fellow traveler" of the Third Reich. His sincere professionalism was clear but his judgment was faulty. He participated in the activities of the totalitarian system and must share responsibility. Certainly he understood that paradox. One may not agree with his decisions, but one should acknowledge and recognize his soldierly endeavors while not neglecting his errors. He was a distinguished soldier.

APPENDIX

CHRONOLOGY

1939

August	23	Signing of Soviet-German Nonaggression Pact.
	25	Mussolini's note to Hitler that Italy will not fight; Hitler cancels invasion of Poland.
September	1	German attack on Poland opens Second World War.
	3	France and Great Britain enter war.
	4	Polish officials begin departing Warsaw; German forces successful everywhere.
	5	German troops cross the Vistula and occupy Cracow.
	8	German armored units reach Warsaw and surround 60,000 Polish troops near Radom.
	14	After heavy fighting, German forces in East Prussia smash Polish defenses and sweep around Warsaw.
	17	Russian units invade Poland.
	25	Major German aerial bombardment of Warsaw.
	27	Polish surrender of Warsaw.
	29	Soviet-German treaty dividing Poland.
October	6	Hitler's speech proposing peace discussions.
	9	Fuehrer's Directive No. 6 to prepare western offensive.
	19	First conceptual plan for attack in west.
	25	Establishment of general government in Poland.
	27	Renewed Hitler command for western offensive.
November	5	Efforts by Halder and von Brauchitsch to postpone offensive fail. Hitler sets November 12 for attack.
	7	Hitler delays operational start; the first of twenty-nine such postponements.
	8	Attempt on Hitler's life fails.
	23	Hitler's speech to commanding generals concerning decision for western attack.
	29	Spain signs friendship pact with Germany, promising special treatment.
	30	Russia invades Finland.
December	6	Memorandum by Major General von Manstein concerning the western campaign.
	11	Reception by Admiral Raeder for Vidkun Quisling from Norway.

| December | 13–17 | *Graf Spee* battle and scuttling. |
| | 18 | Hitler promises financial support to Quisling. |

1940

January	10	Emergency landing at Mechelen by two air force majors reveals German offensive plans.
	13	Belgium mobilizes; Holland cancels all leaves.
	16	Hitler cancels attack dates until spring. Allies begin military preparations for Scandinavia.
	27	Start of German WESERUEBUNG plans.

February	10	Expanded Soviet-German trade treaty.
	12	Finland decides on negotiations to end Russian war.
	16	British forces free naval prisoners of war on *Altmark* in Norwegian territorial waters.
	17	Exchange between Hitler and von Manstein on western offensive.
	21	Creation of working staff for WESERUEBUNG.

March	1	Hitler signs first operational directive against Denmark and Norway.
	2	Allied request to Norway and Sweden for transit of troops to Finland.
	5	Major exchange over WESERUEBUNG between Hitler and responsible officers.
	12	Russo-Finnish war terminates in agreement.
	18	Mussolini-Hitler meeting at the Brenner Pass. Il Duce agrees to enter the war.
	26	Hitler decides, following a conference with Admiral Raeder, that WESERUEBUNG would precede the western offensive.

April	9	Beginning of the German occupation of Denmark and Norway.
	14	Landing of English troops in Norway.
	17	German decision to hold in Narvik despite difficult situation.
	18	German forces move inland in Norway. English troops land there.
	24	King Haakon of Norway refuses peace negotiations, and Germans assume control of the country.
	26	Allied units in Norway begin retreating under German pressure.

May	1	Allies evacuate Namsos in Norway.
	3	Evacuation of British troops in Norway, except for a small force at Narvik.
	10	German invasion of Low Countries and France.
	11	Start of British strategic bombing offensive against Germany. Fall of Fort Eben Emael in Belgium, allowing progress of German offense.
	13	German armored units establish bridgeheads at Dinant and Sedan, and infantry groups outflank Dutch fortification.
	15	Dutch surrender.
	18	German forces capture Antwerp in Belgium while reaching Amiens in France.
	19	Tanks of Armored Group von Kleist reach Abbeville and isolate Allied forces to the north.
	21	Admiral Raeder raises issue of cross-Channel attack.
	23	Germans occupy Amiens, Arras, and Boulogne.
	24	Order halting German armored units, allowing Allies to develop Dunkirk evacuation.
	27	Beginning of Dunkirk evacuation.
	28	Allied troops occupy Narvik.
June	3	German aircraft bomb Paris environs.
	4	Completion of Allied evacuation of Dunkirk.
	5	German forces open second phase of French operation.
	6	Allied troops leave Narvik.
	10	Italy enters the war. Capitulation by Norwegian troops.
	14	German troops enter Paris. Army Group C starts offensive against Maginot Line.
	17	General Heinz Guderian's tanks reach Swiss frontier. France requests peace. Russia assumes control of Baltic states.
	18	Hitler and Mussolini discuss armistice terms.
	22	Signing of German-French Armistice at Compiègne.
	25	End of fighting in France.
	27	England declares blockade of Europe from Norway to Spain.
July	2	Hitler orders preparations for invasion of British Isles (SEA LION).
	3	British naval attack on French fleet units in Mers el Kebir.
	10	Beginning of German aerial attack on England.

July	16	Fuehrer Directive No. 16 for invasion of British Isles.
	19	Hitler's speech offering vague peace.
	21	Russia absorbs Baltic states. Hitler asks for preparation of attack on the Soviet Union.
	31	Hitler commits himself to Russian campaign in 1941.
August	5	First draft of German operational plan for Russia (Marck's Plan).
	13	Start of EAGLE DAY, the major aerial attack against England.
	20	First draft of plan for seizure of Gibraltar (FELIX).
	23–24	German aircraft bomb London in error.
	25–26	English bombers retaliate against Berlin.
September	2	Transfer of fifty old American destroyers to Great Britain in exchange for use of British bases.
	7	Beginning of "revenge" night attacks on London, which carried on for sixty-five nights.
	13	Italian troops cross into Egypt from Libya.
	15	German air force launches major assault on British fighter defenses and suffers serious losses.
	17	Hitler indefinitely postpones SEA LION.
	18	Italian offensive in Africa comes to a standstill.
	19	Fuehrer orders German "instructional" units to Romania to protect oil and to improve Romanian effectiveness.
	23–25	Abortive attempt by Charles de Gaulle's "Free French" forces to occupy Dakar.
	27	Conclusion of Three-Power Pact (Germany, Italy, Japan) in Berlin.
October	4	Meeting of Hitler and Mussolini at the Brenner Pass to discuss strategies for France, Spain, and the future.
	12	Hitler puts SEA LION off until early 1941.
	23	Meeting of Hitler and Francisco Franco at Hendaye.
	24	Hitler confers with Henri Pétain at Montoire.
	28	Italian assault against Greece; Mussolini and Hitler meet in Florence.
November	3	British units begin landing in Greece.
	11	British aerial attack on Taranto cripples Italian fleet.
	12	Hitler orders preparation for possible German undertaking against Greece from Bulgaria.
	12–14	Visit by Soviet Foreign Minister Molotov in Berlin.

November	14	Bombing of Coventry. Greek troops drive Italians back into Albania.
	20	Hungary joins Axis in Tripartite Pact.
	23	Romania also becomes member of Axis.
	29	Initial war game for the Russian campaign.
December	5	Major discussion of Hitler with senior army planners over Greek and Russian undertakings.
	7	Admiral Wilhelm Canaris talks with Franco, who declines entry into the war. Effectively terminates FELIX.
	8	Italy requests German intervention in Greece.
	9	British launch flanking offensive in North Africa.
	13	Fuehrer Order No. 20 for operation against Greece (MARITA).
	18	Fuehrer Order No. 18 for Russian attack (BARBAROSSA).
	19	Italians request German armored division for North Africa.

1941

January	9	Hitler decision to transfer an armored unit to Africa.
	10	German and Russian accord on increased trade.
	19–20	Meeting of Hitler and Mussolini in Berchtesgaden over Libya and Greece.
	22	Fall of Tobruk to British units.
	30	Chief of the Finnish General Staff, Erik Heinricks, visits Berlin concerning participation in the eastern campaign.
	31	Orders completed for BARBAROSSA.
February	3	General Franz Halder presents his proposals for BARBAROSSA to Hitler.
	6	Orders for German commitment in Africa (SUNFLOWER). General Erwin Rommel receives command.
	8	First convoy with German troops for North Africa. Arrival on 11 February.
	22	Rommel pushes reconnaissance units forward against British in Africa.
March	1	Bulgaria joins the Axis.
	2	Units of German Twelfth Army advance into Bulgaria.
	7	British troops begin disembarking in Greek ports.
	24	Reconnaissance in force by Rommel's troops leads to major success.

March	25	Yugoslavia joins Tripartite Pact.
	27	Yugoslavian officers overthrow government in favor of King Peter II. Hitler orders immediate creation of Operation 25 against the country; forces delay of Greek and Russian campaign.
	30	Hitler directions to meeting of senior military commanders in Berlin over BARBAROSSA.
April	2	German troops cross into Hungary for future operations.
	6	Start of German operations against Yugoslavia and Greece.
	9	Rommel's troops take Bardia.
	12	Belgrade falls to German armored units.
	14	Yugoslavia seeks peace.
	20	Capitulation of Greek army begins.
	24	British begin evacuation.
	25	Hitler's decision for parachute operation against Crete (MERCURY).
	30	German troops complete occupation of Greece.
May	15	British counterattack in Egypt slows Rommel's advance.
	20	German parachute drop on Crete.
	31	Evacuation of British troops from Crete.
June	5	Hitler approves final preparations for Russian campaign.
	11	Fuehrer's instruction for strategies after completing BARBAROSSA.
	15	British forces attack in North Africa.
	22	Opening of German operation against the Soviet Union.
	28	German units capture Minsk, 200 miles inside Russia.
	30	Guderian's armored units cross the Berezina River while other units take Riga in the north.
July	3	Stalin orders a "scorched earth" policy against invading Germans.
	4	Yugoslavian leader Tito announces a general resistance movement.
	9	Closure of Minsk and Vitebsk pocket. Russians lose more than 300,000 men and 3,300 tanks.
	10	Josef Stalin assumes supreme command of Red army. Finnish offensive begins.
	16	Smolensk captured by Germans who trap some 600,000 Russians.

July	21	First German aerial bombing of Moscow.
	30	Hitler orders Army Group Center to stop drive toward Moscow.
August	2	American and Soviet agreement on aid program from the former power.
	5	Final destruction of the Smolensk pocket.
	8	Completion of the Uman encirclement with more than 100,000 prisoners and 300 tanks.
	9–12	Franklin Roosevelt and Winston Churchill meet in the Atlantic.
	21	Against army recommendations, Hitler orders continuance of offensive in north and south Russia.
	26	Hitler accepts idea that German troops cannot finish the Russian campaign in 1941.
September	8	German tanks complete encirclement of Leningrad.
	12	First snowfall on eastern front.
	16	Surrender of Russians in Kiev pocket. Germans enclose some 600,000 men.
	21	German forces reach Azov and cut off Crimea.
	26	Hitler orders preparations for attack on Moscow (TYPHOON).
October	7–20	Germans trap large numbers of Russians by Vyazma and Bryansk.
	16	Russian officials leave Moscow; Stalin remains.
	19	Serbian troops begin arriving at the front.
	20	Germans take Stalino while Russians declare state of siege in Moscow.
	25	German advance on Moscow slowed by weather.
November	1	Start of southern German operation against the Caucasus.
	3	Germans capture Kursk.
	15	Start of final offensive effort against Moscow.
	18	Beginning of major British counterattack in North Africa.
	23	German troops capture Rostov.
	26	Tanks reach lines twenty miles from Moscow.
	28	Russians recapture Rostov.
December	5	End of German offensive against Moscow.
	6	Start of Russian winter counteroffensive.
	7	Japanese attack on Pearl Harbor.

December	11	Germany and Italy declare war against the United States.
	17	Powerful Russian offensive along a broad front.
	19	Field Marshal von Brauchitsch dismissed, and Hitler assumes personal command of the German army.
	23	Rommel's troops evacuate Benghazi.
	28	Hitler's order to stand fast in the east.

1942

January	2	Russian breakthrough north of Rzhev.
	6	British offensive in Libya slows.
	8	General Eric Hoepner orders his units into winter positions; Hitler relieves him.
	11	Soviet forces break rail line between Rzhev and Bryansk.
	14	"Arcadia" meeting of Winston Churchill and Franklin Roosevelt ends. Commitment to fighting in Europe first.
	15	After extensive effort, Hitler permits withdrawal of Army Group Center to winter positions.
	21	Rommel initiates counterattack in North Africa.
	25	Major Soviet advances in south Russia.

February	3	Germans counterattack near Vyazma and isolate a Russian army.
	5	Rommel's offensive halted west of Tobruk.
	12	Preparatory thoughts for German offensive after winter period.
	13	Russians reenter Byelorussia.

March	1	General stagnation along eastern front.
	5	Fuehrer Directive No. 41 for renewed eastern operations.
	15	Hitler decision to combine Allied troops (Italian, Hungarian, and Romanian) into independent armies.
	18	Mud period reduces mobility of eastern campaign.
	29–30	Hitler and Mussolini meet at Berchtesgaden to discuss problems of Allies and of North African offensive, to include seizure of Malta (HERKULES).

May	4	Orders for conquest of Malta.
	8	Germans begin southern offensive in Crimea (Kerch).
	9	Russians launch offensive against Kharkov.
	17	German counteraction blunts Kharkov effort and former push forward.
	21	Hitler postpones Malta operation.
	26	Rommel opens major attack.

May	28	Germans complete encirclement south of Kharkov (240,000 prisoners, 1,200 tanks).
June	7	Start of German investment of Sevastopol.
	12	Rommel, after fierce fighting, continues advance.
	13	Germans in North Africa destroy 230 British tanks.
	21	In surprise assault Rommel's troops capture Tobruk.
	28	Germans open summer offensive in Russia.
	30	Axis troops reach El Alamein.
July	1	German conquest of Sevastopol.
	2	Major German operation in eastern front.
	3	Germans turn south along the Don.
	4	Germans complete occupation of Crimea (100,000 prisoners).
	9	Start of German drive on Rostov and into the Caucasus.
	13	Russian retreat to Stalingrad, the Volga, and the Caucasus.
	28	Russian orders at Stalingrad, "no retreat."
August	1	Germans reach Kuban River.
	9	German units capture Krasnodar and Maikop.
	15	German forces make extensive territorial gains without capturing many prisoners in Caucasus. Start of major offensive against Stalingrad.
	23	Army Group B reaches Volga River.
	30	Rommel initiates fierce assault on El Alamein.
September	9	Hitler removes General List as commander of Army Group A and assumes command.
	15	Soviet attack toward Voronezh.
	20	Savage house-to-house combat in Stalingrad.
	24	General Halder leaves his position and is replaced by General Kurt Zeitzler.

INDEX

Note: All military units are sorted in ascending numerical order.